Debt Advice Handbook

10th edition

Mike Wolfe

Updated by Peter Madge

with Nicola Connop, Edward Graham, John Kruse, David Malcolm and Katherine Rock

CPAG promotes action for the prevention and relief of poverty among children and families with children. To achieve this, CPAG aims to raise awareness of the causes, extent, nature and impact of poverty, and strategies for its eradication and prevention; bring about positive policy changes for families with children in poverty; and enable those eligible for income maintenance to have access to their full entitlement. If you are not already supporting us, please consider making a donation, or ask for details of our membership schemes, training courses and publications.

Published by Child Poverty Action Group
94 White Lion Street, London N1 9PF
Tel: 020 7837 7979
staff@cpag.org.uk
www.cpag.org.uk

A CIP record for this book is available from the British Library

ISBN: 978 1 906076 66 5

Child Poverty Action Group is a charity registered in England and Wales (registration number 294841) and in Scotland (registration number SC039339), and is a company limited by guarantee, registered in England (registration number 1993854). VAT number: 690 808117

Cover design by Devious Designs
Typeset by David Lewis XML Associates Ltd
Printed in the UK by CPI Group, (UK) Ltd, Croydon CR0 4YY
Cover photo by Paul Box/Reportdigital

The authors

Peter Madge is a money adviser and has worked for Citizens Advice since 1991. He is a consultant for the Money Advice Specialist Support Consultancy Service, and writes and delivers training and presentations on money advice issues. A former editor of the *Adviser* magazine, he still contributes articles to various money advice publications. In 2010, he was elected an Honorary Fellow of the Institute of Money Advisers.

Nicola Connop is Team Manager at Business Debtline and has worked for the Money Advice Trust for six years. Nicola is one of the subject matter experts for Wiseradviser on business debts.

Edward Graham is CPAG's Advice and Rights Manager.

John Kruse has worked as a debt adviser, trainer and consultant for the last 30 years. He has had a specialised interest in enforcement law for the last 25 years and founded the *Bailiff Studies Centre* in September 2010. John is the author of a number of books on enforcement law, including *Sources of Bailiff Law, Law of Seizure of Goods, Powers of Distress* and a two-volume history of the subject, *Bailiffs' Law.* He has also written texts on court procedures and the rights of users of common land, as well as numerous articles in the professional and academic press.

David Malcolm is the Head of Social Policy at the National Union of Students, responsible for its work on student finance, student welfare and equalities. He is author of CPAG's *Student Support and Benefits Handbook*.

Katherine Rock is Team Manager at Business Debtline and has worked for the Money Advice Trust for seven years. Katherine is one of the subject matter experts for Wiseradviser on business debts.

Acknowledgements

The production of this tenth edition has been made possible by a number of other authors who have contributed their specialist expertise.

Nicola Connop and Katherine Rock from Business Debtline have updated the chapter on business debts, Edward Graham from CPAG has rewritten the chapter on maximising income, David Malcolm from the NUS has updated the chapter on student debts and John Kruse has revised the bailiffs chapter.

Thanks are also due to Carolyn George, Mark Brough and Keith Houghton for their valuable contribution.

I would also like to acknowledge the efforts of the authors of previous editions of this book, most notably Mike Wolfe.

Thank you to all my colleagues at Citizens Advice Specialist Support, particularly Marina Gallagher, and also Jan Channing of Caerphilly County CAB for checking and making useful comments on the text.

I am grateful to Alison Key at CPAG for producing this edition. Thanks also to Anne Ketley for producing the index, and to Kathleen Armstrong for proofreading the text.

Peter Madge
Citizens Advice Specialist Support

The law covered in this book was correct on 1 September 2012 and includes regulations laid up to this date.

Foreword

When I wrote the foreword for the previous edition of this *Handbook* two years ago, personal debt problems were at an all time high – caused by years of access to easy credit. Although, at the time of writing, debt problems still form a very high proportion of the work undertaken by advice agencies, there has been a change in the nature and causes of the debt problems seen by advice agencies over the last two years.

While it continues to be true that most people consulting a debt adviser still owe money to a variety of high street credit providers, like banks and credit card companies, we are seeing an increase in the number of people who are in debt with high-cost credit products, particularly short-term payday loans. Rising unemployment and higher prices for essentials like fuel, petrol and food has meant that more people are struggling to make ends meet, particularly with household bills and priority debts such as rent arrears, telephone, water and fuel bills and council tax arrears.

Changes and cuts to the welfare benefits system mean that the number of people in financial difficulties is growing and will continue to grow. We are now seeing the impact of those cuts that have already been implemented. Advice agencies are already seeing private tenants who are facing eviction for rent arrears because their housing benefit has been cut and people with chronic illnesses experiencing hardship and debt because their entitlement to contributory employment and support allowance is now limited to 12 months.

Further cuts in welfare spending and other government policy initiatives mean that this trend is likely to continue. Although the new universal credit system will bring some much needed simplification to the means-tested benefits system and provide better incentives to work, changes to the method and frequency of payment of this benefit will result in more people needing help to budget or deal with debts. For example, universal credit will contain help with rent for all types of tenants and this will usually be paid directly to them rather than to their landlord as is already the case for tenants of social landlords. Without support, advice and the right current account to help them budget better, many will fall behind with their rent and prioritise paying credit debts. The move to a single monthly payment of universal credit per household will also cause financial difficulties for some families who are used to budgeting their income over shorter periods.

From April 2013, localisation of council tax support combined with a cut in funding for this help is likely to result in advisers seeing more people with council tax arrears, because most people of working age will receive less help. Many of these debts are likely to be enforced by unregulated private bailiffs, who, in our experience, often intimidate vulnerable people in debt, abuse their powers and charge fees not allowed by law. Although the government has stated that it intends to take action to curb 'aggressive bailiffs', these plans do not appear at present to include independent regulation of the enforcement industry, but allow bailiffs to increase their fees. Many families in severe financial difficulties could see their council tax debts grow by £300 in bailiff fees.

Other government initiatives in the pipeline will have a positive impact on the debt problems that we see. The Financial Services Bill currently going through Parliament should result in a strong, well-resourced conduct regulator, with the right powers and determination to root out unfair practices and intervene in the design of all financial services products, including consumer credit.

The provision of well-funded, high-quality, free debt advice will therefore continue to be vital to allow people to manage their debts before they spiral out of control and to cope with debt crises. Since the last *Handbook* was published, the free advice sector has maintained high-quality services in a time of uncertainty, cuts and increased targets. The Money Advice Service now distributes funding for debt advice raised from a levy on the financial services industry. We sincerely hope that with the advent of a secure, long-term source of funding and an enhanced remit to co-ordinate debt advice, the Money Advice Service will add significant value, helping the sector develop systems that support high quality face-to-face, telephone and online debt advice services.

This *Handbook* continues to be an essential resource for all those working in debt advice and will help advisers meet the challenges ahead. I congratulate the authors on another excellent publication.

Gillian Guy
Chief Executive, Citizens Advice

Contents

How to use this *Handbook*

This *Handbook* is produced:
- as a guide and training aid for the new debt adviser;
- as a reference work for those who undertake debt advice alongside other sorts of advice work or other professional disciplines – eg, social workers and housing officers;
- for the specialist debt adviser as a first step in accessing primary legislation and regulations;
- for the manager or purchaser of debt advice services to help understand and evaluate debt advice.

The subjects covered within debt advice are vast and could fill many volumes. In this *Handbook*, much detail has been deliberately excluded in order to make it accessible to the reader and to make clear the structure of debt work.

Most relevant legislation and court forms are now available online from www.legislation.gov.uk and www.hmcourts-service.gov.uk respectively and so are not therefore included in the Appendices. The Civil Procedure Rules are available online at www.justice.gov.uk/courts/procedure-rules/civil and many judgments of the higher courts are available in the legal/professional section of www.justice.gov.uk. Most debt packages used in advice agencies include standard letters and forms, and so these are also not included in the Appendices. The common financial statement is increasingly the standard form of financial statement sent to creditors and this is available online at www.moneyadvicetrust.org together with supporting documentation.

The *Handbook* can best be used as follows.

Training aid

The **Introduction** and **Chapters 1 to 3** are written to assist those who are interested in debt advice and outline the processes and skills involved. These should be read by new debt advisers and those who have done some of this work and would like to think more about the structure behind their practical experience. The chapters can also be used by those who commission or manage debt advice as a means of clarifying the product with which they are dealing.

The new adviser should ensure that s/he is familiar with the Consumer Credit Act 1974 (this is explained in **Chapter 4**) and is able to identify each type of debt (explained in **Chapter 6**) because this is fundamental to using the rest of the *Handbook*. Maximising income is a key part of the debt advice process and this is summarised in **Chapter 7**. The new adviser will also need to be familiar with the criteria to be used in prioritising debts (**Chapter 8**). S/he will find it useful to skim through the different strategies for priority and non-priority debts (**Chapters 8 and 9**). These can be examined in detail as they arise in the course of advising.

The debt adviser

Readers already familiar with the processes of debt advice may wish to use **Chapter 5** (minimising debts) and the strategy selection (**Chapters 8 and 9**) to help them think about the best strategy for a particular debt. This might include bankruptcy or an individual voluntary arrangement (these are discussed in **Chapter 15**). Court procedures are covered in **Chapter 10** (county court), **Chapter 11** (money only claims), **Chapter 12** (claims for possession of goods or land) and **Chapter 13** (magistrates' court). If the client is threatened with bailiff action, the adviser should refer to **Chapter 14**. Specific debts are dealt with in **Chapter 16** (business debts) and **Chapter 17** (student debts). The index will enable you to find detailed information on a particular strategy, type of debt or court process. References can be accessed via the endnotes contained at the end of each chapter for those readers who want more in-depth information about a particular topic. Details of other useful reference material and organisations are in the Appendices.

Abbreviations

AA	attendance allowance	IS	income support
AO	administration order	IVA	individual voluntary arrangement
APR	annual percentage rate	JSA	jobseeker's allowance
BRO	bankruptcy restriction order	MA	maternity allowance
BRU	bankruptcy restriction undertaking	MCOB	Mortgages and Home Finance: conduct of business sourcebook
CA	carer's allowance		
CAB	Citizens Advice Bureau		
CFS	common financial statement	MIG	mortgage indemnity guarantee
CIVEA	Civil Enforcement Association		
CMEC	Child Maintenance and Enforcement Commission	MP	Member of Parliament
		NHS	National Health Service
CSA	Child Support Agency	NI	national insurance
CTB	council tax benefit	NSEA	National Standards for Enforcement Agents
CTC	child tax credit		
DLA	disability living allowance	NUS	National Union of Students
DRO	debt relief order	OFT	Office of Fair Trading
DRRO	debt relief restrictions order	PAYE	Pay As You Earn
DRRU	debt relief restrictions undertaking	PC	pension credit
DVLA	Driver and Vehicle Licensing Agency	PGCE	Postgraduate Certificate in Education
DWP	Department for Work and Pensions	PIN	personal identification number
		PIP	personal independence payment
EEA	European Economic Area		
ESA	employment and support allowance	RPI	Retail Prices Index
		SAP	statutory adoption pay
EU	European Union	SDA	severe disablement allowance
FOS	Financial Ombudsman Service	SERPS	state earnings-related pension scheme
FSA	Financial Services Authority		
FTVA	fast-track, post-bankruptcy voluntary arrangement	SFE	Student Finance England
		SLC	Student Loans Company
GA	guardian's allowance	SMP	statutory maternity pay
GAP	guaranteed asset protection	SPP	statutory paternity pay
HB	housing benefit	SSP	statutory sick pay
HE	higher education	UC	universal credit
HMCTS	HM Courts and Tribunals Service	UCAS	Universities and College Admissions Service
HMRC	HM Revenue and Customs		
HP	hire purchase	VAT	value added tax
IB	incapacity benefit	WTC	working tax credit
IMA	Institute of Money Advisers		

Introduction

Debt has always been an inevitable consequence of borrowing and is recognised by the credit industry as a necessary corollary of its lending. Lenders will always make provision in their accounts for debts that are to be written off. This *Handbook* is based on the assumption that debt is caused by lenders who predict it, but lend nonetheless.

While the causes of debt may not be individual, the effects are: bailiffs, disconnections, repossessions and imprisonment. Money worries are a significant cause of relationship problems, depression, anxiety and stress, with many of those in debt receiving treatment from their GP.

Mental health problems are both a cause and effect of debt and so it is good to see that the money advice sector and the credit industry are continuing to work together under the auspices of the Money Advice Liaison Group to produce good practice guidelines for dealing with this particular situation.

Although the number of personal insolvencies has fallen substantially from its 2010 peak of just over 135,000 and unemployment is falling, increasing numbers of people are seeking debt advice. The number of debt relief orders continues to rise year on year (and, according to the Insolvency Service) are now comparable to the number of bankruptcies for the first time). Most people have seen a drop in their real disposable incomes due to a combination of factors and many more people are having to work part time in order to stay in employment.

The number of people struggling with unmanageable debt seems likely to remain high for the foreseeable future and may even increase further, given that we have yet to feel the full impact of the government's welfare 'reforms'.

What is debt advice

Debt advice may be defined by the Financial Inclusion Taskforce as 'problem-solving advice relating to debts that individuals are unable to afford to repay. This can take the form of general advice on debt problems, including the provision of self-help materials, or can involve detailed and individualised assistance, including casework support for clients with complex debt problems.'

Debt advice is one component of what is now called money advice. Money advice also comprises financial literacy (the ability to understand finance), financial capability (the skills, knowledge and understanding to manage money) and money guidance (helping someone manage her/his money better). Virtually everyone has debts. But, when debt becomes unmanageable, the need for debt advice arises.

Debt advice should be distinguished from 'money management' and 'financial capability'. On the other hand, debt advice should not reinforce financial exclusion; it should seek to promote financial inclusion. Debt advice does include a comprehensive check of a person's entitlement to state benefits, but it goes much further than welfare rights. Debt advice is, essentially, crisis management, and the other components can hopefully prevent the need for debt advice recurring or even occurring in the first place. An ideal money advice model integrates all the various components.

In the past, the words 'debt counselling' and 'money advice' have been used almost interchangeably to describe what we shall call 'debt advice'. We prefer this term to 'money advice' because of the issues discussed above. 'Debt counselling', on the other hand, can appear to suggest that debt is a problem about which individuals merely need counselling. Counselling may sometimes be important in the early stages of debt advice, but is not a substitute for the work of the debt adviser. Debt advice is not just about making offers (token or otherwise) to the client's creditors. The processes described in this *Handbook* are not set in stone and advisers should not be afraid to step outside them in order to help their clients. Advisers should not assume that creditors and courts always get it right, but should examine their practices and their paperwork to protect their clients from inappropriate enforcement action.

Chapter 1

Debt advice: an outline

This chapter covers:
1. The adviser as a professional (below)
2. The debt advice system (p4)
3. Administration (p11)

1. The adviser as a professional

Debt advice is a series of tools and professional strategies that can be used to help clients with financial difficulties. Debt advice provides help to clients by:

- enabling them to maximise their income;
- explaining the implications of non-payment of each of their debts and, on this basis, deciding which are priorities;
- establishing whether or not they are liable for their debts and assisting them to challenge their creditors if appropriate;
- assisting them to plan their budgets;
- helping them choose a strategy (usually to reduce or stop payments) that will minimise the effects of their debt on their financial, social or medical wellbeing by giving them impartial, independent and confidential advice to enable them to make an informed choice about the options available;
- preserving their home, fuel supplies and liberty;
- assisting by advice or representation with the implementation of whatever strategy is chosen.

Debt advice is a professional activity. There is a package of attitudes, skills and strategies that are part of any debt advice service. This guarantees consistency and quality assurance. Users of such services are misled if anything less than this package is offered.

Debt advice can be provided by specialists or by professionals whose job primarily involves other activities – eg, housing officers and social workers. It can be provided by paid or voluntary workers. Recent years have seen the growth of debt management companies. These charge clients a fee for setting up and handling debt repayment programmes.

A professional debt adviser needs a mixture of skills, knowledge and attitudes, which together form the basis of good practice. For many years there was no qualification that recognised the profession of money advice or acknowledged the wide range of skills and knowledge that money advisers have. However, the Institute of Money Advisers (IMA) (the professional association for full-time, part-time or volunteer/trainee debt advisers in England, Wales and Northern Ireland who deliver or promote free, confidential, impartial and independent debt advice services) in partnership with Staffordshire University has introduced a Certificate in Money Advice Practice. Worth 15 higher education credits and broadly equivalent to an NVQ level 4, this award is offered to IMA members with at least 12 months' full-time (or part-time equivalent) experience in debt advice casework or a related activity. The award is gained by studying a combination of skills and knowledge based on the national occupational standards for legal advice. The course is delivered online and involves a number of modules, each ending with a formative assessment, and finally an examination, which is sat online.

The award is supported by a 'continuing professional development' requirement to ensure advisers keep their skills and knowledge up to date.

The provision of debt advice as discussed in this *Handbook* generally requires the adviser (or her/his employer) to have a consumer credit licence from the Office of Fair Trading (OFT) (see p60), unless s/he is in an organisation with a group licence, such as Citizens Advice or Advice UK. In December 2001, the OFT issued guidance on the minimum standards of service that debt management companies should provide, but made it clear that its principles applied equally to the free advice sector. In March 2012, the OFT issued revised and updated guidance, *Debt Management (and Credit Repair Services) Guidance*.[1] This mainly underlines what should be good practice and will be referred to in this *Handbook* where relevant.

An unambiguous role

In any situation where money is owed, there are two parties whose interests may conflict. Both have a range of legal remedies and defences, and well-established professionals know that they cannot advise both parties in such a situation. A debt adviser, similarly, needs to be clear that s/he is working only for the interests of the client. This is true even if the adviser's employment is funded by the finance industry or other creditors, such as a local authority, or if s/he works for an organisation that seeks to be impartial.

The OFT guidance makes it clear that all advice given and any action taken must have regard to the best interests of the client and be accurate, sufficiently clear and appropriate to her/his individual circumstances taking into account:
- the client's financial position;
- her/his personal circumstances, including the reasons for her/his financial difficulty and whether they are temporary or long term; *and*

- any other relevant factors, which should include the powers of the creditor and whether interest or other charges have been frozen.

A professional attitude

A debt adviser should be aware of experiences in her/his own past which may give her/him judgemental attitudes towards clients and/or creditors. Debt advisers must consciously rid themselves of any personal bias and adopt a professional approach to the work.

A professional adviser must also offer a high quality, accessible service to all groups in society and should work towards understanding that debt can affect clients from different social groups in different ways.

A commitment to social policy

A professional debt adviser should not allow the same problem to affect adversely the lives of countless users, but will make known the lessons which can be learnt from her/his work to as wide an audience of policy makers as possible.

A sound knowledge of law and procedures

A professional debt adviser should be knowledgeable and imaginative about the ways in which the law can be applied to mitigate the effects of debt. S/he should be able to offer and explain each of these to any user.

A commitment to developing the service

A professional debt adviser should take regular opportunities to enhance her/his own skills through training, research and education, and should participate in offering this to others, so that the practice of debt advice continues to be refined and developed.

Advisers should subscribe to periodicals such as the *Adviser* and *Quarterly Account* (see Appendix 2) to keep up to date with developments in debt advice law and practice. Advisers should also subscribe to free newsletters such as *Arian*, not only to keep up to date but also to be aware of creditors' contact details and their latest policies on arrears management and collection. Advisers should try to attend their local money advice group (details can be found in *Arian*), which will usually have updating and information exchange sessions, as well as presentations by creditors or representatives from other relevant organisations.

A systematic approach

A professional debt adviser should apply a single systematic approach to each individual client. However, the adviser also has a duty to ensure that any advice given is:

- in the best interests of that particular client;

- appropriate to her/his individual circumstances;
- realistic; *and*
- where an offer of payment is made, sustainable and based on a true and accurate assessment of the client's circumstances.

An ability to involve the client in informed choices

A professional adviser should always try to involve the client, ensuring that s/he understands the implications of her/his situation and the steps the adviser proposes be taken. The adviser assists the client to make informed choices by giving her/him all her/his options and explaining their consequences before anything is done. An adviser should never assume that a client is seeking a particular outcome, but should establish what s/he wants while recognising that it may not necessarily be realistic or achievable in the particular circumstances. The adviser should also manage the client's expectations of the adviser and agency.

Many advisers tend to put pressure on themselves to solve their clients' problems, and client expectations can add to this. While advisers should always do the best they can for their clients, there will be times when the options are limited because matters have simply gone too far and the adviser cannot make the problem go away. Advisers should not feel that they have somehow 'failed' the client as they are likely to need supporting through the situation.

Also, many debt cases involve very distressing facts, and advisers need to feel that they can share and discuss these sorts of issues with colleagues and supervisors/managers.

2. **The debt advice system**

The debt advice system is a structured set of procedures and activities that must be worked through if a debt adviser is to provide the best possible service to someone with a multiple debt problem. It is designed to:
- maintain the client's home, liberty and essential goods and services;
- advise the client about her/his rights and responsibilities and also the rights of her/his creditors;
- give the client the information s/he needs to make informed choices in dealing with the debt situation;
- treat all creditors equally;
- empower the client, where possible.

A systematic approach is essential because of:
- the large amount of information and paperwork generated by most debt enquiries;

- the need to avoid overlooking a particular strategy;
- the need to keep detailed records of the agency's work – both to ensure effective advice and to enable case material to be used for evaluating the service, quality of advice assessments, and for social policy development;
- the need to train new workers in a clearly defined set of skills and knowledge;
- the need to guarantee consistency in spite of the diversity of clients using the service;
- the need to protect the adviser from the strain of having continually to 'reinvent the wheel'.

There is more to debt advice than mere administration. A system should not be seen as a straitjacket, and it does not prevent the need for individuals to operate in a creative and flexible way in the best interests of the individual client. Different agencies will need to develop their own systems based on demand and resources, and any reporting requirements of funders.

A debt adviser needs to perform a wide range of tasks in order to provide effective help to clients. This section provides a list of these tasks, in the order in which they should be performed. In practice, a number of these tasks can be performed alongside each other – eg, maximising income while waiting for information needed to check the client's liability for her/his debts. If the adviser is going to contact third parties on the client's behalf, the client will need to provide a signed authority for this to happen (most agencies have a standard form of client authority).

Essentially, there are three stages to the debt advice process:
- exploration;
- options;
- action.

These can, in turn, be broken down into the following steps.
- **Step one: explore the debt problem**. This involves establishing the extent of the client's debts, and the reason(s) for her/his financial difficulties and whether these are temporary or long term. This includes finding out who the client's creditors are, how much is owed to each one and the action each creditor has taken to collect its debt (which may have involved passing the debt to a firm of debt collectors or even selling the debt to a debt purchaser, in which case it is necessary to see what action the collector/purchaser has taken[2]). In this *Handbook*, the word 'creditor' includes not only the original creditor but also, if the debt has been sold, the debt purchaser (unless stated otherwise).
- **Step two: deal with emergencies**. Emergencies, such as bailiffs' warrants, threats of disconnection of fuel supply or loss of the client's home or liberty, are dealt with first. Where court action is involved, the adviser can help the client to complete court forms.

- **Step three: check that a client is liable for each of her/his debts**. This may require further information from the client, the creditor or a third party before this can be established. Specialist advice may also be required.
- **Step four: explore all possible ways of increasing a client's income**, particularly by checking that s/he is receiving all the benefits to which s/he is entitled. Some clients may be receiving benefits to which they are not entitled. The implications of this need to be discussed in full, along with the effect this may have on the client's financial statement.
- **Step five: draw up a financial statement** showing what income a client is receiving, her/his essential expenditure and whether there is any income available to make payments to creditors. The financial statement is an essential tool, not only in negotiations with creditors but also in determining which options are appropriate for the client – eg, her/his eligibility for a debt relief order (see p472) or a debt management plan. There may be instances in which a client's expenditure needs to be challenged. Should this be the case, the adviser must discuss the reasons for this – eg, that it is unlikely to be accepted by a court or creditor.
- **Step six: explore and discuss all available options** that are suitable in the client's individual circumstances for resolving the debt problem. A strategy (or strategies) should then be agreed with her/him and an action plan drawn up. For each option, the adviser must clearly explain:
  - the advantages/disadvantages;
  - any eligibility criteria;
  - the debts included in that option;
  - any costs involved;
  - the risks associated with that option.
  The adviser should also explain why these options are considered suitable and why other options are not considered suitable or viable. Options fall into two categories:
  - arrangements made directly with the client's creditors; *and*
  - formal insolvency options.
- **Step seven: negotiate with priority creditors** – ie, creditors whose sanctions for non-payment include imprisonment, disconnection of essential services or loss of essential goods or the home. Usually, some form of payment will be required to deal with such debts, unless a formal insolvency option is the agreed strategy and the debt can be included in that option.
- **Step eight: negotiate with the remaining creditors** (known as non-priority creditors) with a view to persuading them to accept the agreed strategy. Some clients can and want to negotiate with their creditors directly. This approach enables clients to regain control of their finances and allows the advice agency to offer greater support to those clients who cannot deal with these matters themselves.[3] Such self-help clients are likely to benefit from the CASHflow process discussed on p18.

- **Step nine: implement the action plan**. This may involve representing the client at a court hearing, periodic reviews of the client's options/strategy, referral to another agency (eg, for a debt management plan) or arranging for the client to have a session with a money adviser (previously known as money guidance) or financial capability session. Sometimes the adviser may have to challenge creditors on whether they are entitled to recover what they are claiming from clients – eg, if clients are not liable for their debts.

Information to clients

It is not necessary for an agency to have any written agreement with the client, but the adviser should provide:
- adequate written information about the nature of the service being offered in plain language;
- warnings:
  - that creditors need not accept offers or stop interest or other charges;
  - that creditors may still continue to try to collect their debt and such action could incur additional costs, which will be added to the debt;
  - that the client's credit rating could be adversely affected;
  - about the importance of meeting priority commitments;
  - that correspondence from creditors should not be ignored;
  - about the implication of court action;
  - about the possible consequences of missing prearranged appointments with her/his adviser.

If the agency uses a form of written agreement, it should:[4]
- be clear and written in plain, intelligible language;
- set out the nature of the service to be provided by the agency, together with the amount to be repaid or an estimate (ie, the total amount the client is to pay under the strategy chosen to deal with her/his debts), although it may not be possible to provide this information to the client until later in the process, if at all;
- make clear that:
  - clients are not prohibited from corresponding or communicating with creditors;
  - the agency will deal appropriately and promptly with any correspondence it receives;
  - the agency will keep the client informed of the progress of her/his case, including sending her/him copies of correspondence sent to, and received from, creditors.

It is good practice for the adviser at the first interview to point out also:
- the agency's commitment to confidentiality;

- the steps the agency will take and the steps the client has agreed to, or is expected to, take her/himself;
- that the client should not incur any further credit commitments without prior discussion with the adviser;
- that the client should inform the agency of any change in her/his financial circumstances;
- that a successful outcome cannot be guaranteed.

Monitoring creditor practices

The effectiveness of pressure for change often depends on the ability of an agency to produce evidence in support of its recommendations. For this reason, case recording must not just be accurate and detailed, but must also be stored in a form that allows details of particular practices and the hardship they cause to be retrieved and patterns detected. In July 2003, the Office of Fair Trading (OFT) issued guidance to the credit industry on what it regards as unfair debt collection practices (see p30). An updated version was issued in October 2011. Debt advisers should, therefore, keep a record of the collection techniques and tactics favoured by individual creditors. This will be useful in the future choice of strategy. In addition, they should note practices or situations that continually cause hardship to clients and should monitor which creditors are responsible for such situations for use in their social policy work.

There are frequent changes in the law and procedures that affect debt and agencies are often in a very good position to look closely at how these are working in practice. Agencies often carry out such exercises as part of a network of local and national debt services.

Credit reference agencies

There is no right to credit and most lenders decide credit applications on the basis of 'credit scoring' – ie, a system used to assess the probability of applicants meeting their financial commitments, using information supplied on the credit application form, the lender's own records (where available) and data from credit reference agencies. Different lenders use different systems, which should not only establish the likelihood of the applicant repaying but also whether s/he can afford to do so.

Credit reference agencies provide factual information about clients and their credit records. They do not:

- make the decision or express any opinion about whether clients should be granted credit and are unable to tell clients why they have been refused credit; or
- keep 'blacklists' or details of clients' credit scores.

Credit reference agencies usually keep details of:

- electoral roll entries;

- county court judgments (these are held for six years from the date of judgment unless paid within one month, when any record is removed);
- bankruptcy orders, administration orders, debt relief orders and individual voluntary arrangements (these are held for six years from the date of the order/ arrangement);
- credit accounts (a record is held until the account is paid off and then for a further six years);
- whether the client has defaulted on the credit agreement (a record is held for six years from the date the default was registered, normally when the account is three to six months in arrears);
- mortgage repossessions, including voluntary repossessions (these are held for six years);
- aliases, associations and linked addresses – ie, any other names the client has been known by, previous addresses or correspondence addresses, and whether the client shares financial responsibility for an account with another person;
- a warning from the Fraud Prevention Service (known as CIFAS). This is a fraud avoidance system developed to protect people whose names, addresses or other details have been used fraudulently by other people in order to apply for or obtain credit. It does not mean that the client is being accused of fraud, but any credit applications may be checked out to ensure s/he is, in fact, the applicant;
- information from the Gone Away Information Network (known as GAIN) – ie, on clients who have 'gone away' without informing their lenders of a forwarding address (this information is held for six years);
- previous credit searches by lenders in the past two years. Several searches within a short period of time may indicate attempted fraud or over-commitment.

From October 2004, a client's credit file should only hold information about her/ him and any other person with whom s/he has a 'financial association' – ie, joint account holders or applicants, or people who inform the agency they have financial ties. Associations allow lenders to take account of information about anyone 'linked' to the client. Although the client can 'opt out' (ie, ask a lender only to take account of information about her/him), this does not prevent the lender carrying out checks to make sure that this is not merely intended to hide a partner's poor credit rating. If there is no financial association, the client should inform the agency so the link can be removed.

Guidelines from the Information Commissioner state that an account should not be recorded as in default unless the relationship between the creditor and the client has 'broken down' (ie, the client has been in arrears for at least three consecutive months on the contractual instalments or under an agreement to reschedule repayments), but should be recorded as in default if such payments have not been made in full for six months. Accounts which are subject to repayment arrangements or debt management plans should only be recorded as 'defaults' if the client:

- is only making token payments (see below); *or*
- defaults on the arrangement and the arrears are equivalent to three months' payments under the original contract; *or*
- is making reduced payments, but no agreed arrangement is in place.

A client who is making token or reduced payments can file a 'notice of correction' to record this fact if an arrangement to pay has not been recorded by the lender.

A zero balance on a credit reference report marked 'balance satisfied' (with or without the flag 'partially satisfied') indicates that there has been a default, but that:

- the account has been paid in full; *or*
- the account was included in an individual voluntary arrangement which has been satisfactorily completed or in a bankruptcy from which the client has been discharged (see Chapter 15); *or*
- the creditor has agreed to accept less than the full amount due in full and final settlement of the account.

A client who has been refused credit should be informed whether or not the lender used a credit reference agency and details of the agency should be provided on request. Since 1 February 2011, when a creditor informs a client that it is rejecting a credit application and that rejection is based on information obtained from a credit reference agency, the creditor must inform the client of this fact and provide details of the credit reference agency, including the name, address and telephone number. Failure to do so is a criminal offence. **Note:** this requirement does not apply to agreements secured on land.[5]

A client has the right to obtain a copy of her/his file at any time by sending details of her/his full name and address (including any previous addresses in the past six years), together with a fee of £2 to the credit reference agency concerned.[6] Advice agencies can obtain free reports for their clients. A client can also obtain a copy of her/his report online (for £2).

If the client considers that any of the information on the file is wrong and that s/he is likely to be prejudiced as a result, s/he can write either to the lender or the credit reference agency. However, as the credit reference agency would have to contact the lender to ask it to investigate the complaint, it might be quicker to write to the lender and send a copy to the credit reference agency. The client should write to the lender and credit reference agency stating why the information is wrong and submitting any supporting evidence – eg, that a debt has been paid. In the case of credit reference agencies, the agency must respond in writing within 28 days, stating either that it has corrected or removed the information, or done nothing.[7] In the meantime, the information is marked 'account query' while the agency checks its accuracy. If the agency fails to remove the information or the client does not agree with the proposed amendment, s/he can ask the agency to add her/his own 'notice of correction' to the file – eg, an explanation of how the debt arose. This must be no more than 200 words long and must be sent to the agency within a further 28 days. The agency must inform the client within 28 days if it accepts the notice. If it does not, the agency must refer the case to the Information Commissioner for a ruling.

If, after writing to the lender and/or the credit reference agency, the client receives no response, s/he can complain to the Information Commissioner. A client can also complain to the Information Commissioner if s/he believes inaccurate information is being held but a 'notice of correction' is not appropriate – eg, it needs to be completely removed. If the information about the client's credit history is factually correct, however, it will not be removed just because s/he does not want it made public. Credit repair companies who claim to be able to 'clean up' people's credit reference files (in return for a fee) should be avoided, as the information they give may be misleading or worse.[8]

The Information Commissioner can be contacted at Wycliffe House, Water Lane, Wilmslow, Cheshire SK9 5AF or at www.ico.gov.uk. The Information Commissioner's Office produces a useful leaflet, *Credit Explained*, available at www.ico.gov.uk/for_the_public/topic_specific_guides/credit.aspx.

3. **Administration**

Good administrative systems and time management are essential in order to manage the debt advice process in an efficient way and to meet the client's needs appropriately.

Triage interview

Many agencies use preliminary or diagnostic interviews that do not involve the provision of advice but are time-limited, fact-finding interviews designed to identify:
- what service the client needs;
- any action that needs to be taken straight away; *and*
- the next steps, which might be:
  - the provision of information; *or*
  - signposting or referring the client to another agency; *or*
  - arranging for the client to receive further advice, either immediately or by appointment.

A triage interview uses specific set questions to ensure that all relevant details have been collected. Triage is often the client's first contact with the agency. It is therefore important that it is accurate so that s/he can be dealt with appropriately.

Clients who are assessed as able to help themselves can be provided with the information to enable them to do so. A client can also be referred to other agencies if these are better placed to meet her/his needs.

Appropriate referrals

It is important to establish whether a case should be referred to a specialist or more experienced adviser, and if there is a mechanism in place for referring cases, if appropriate, to other organisations.

Key dates (eg, court hearings) and time limits should be recorded so they are not missed and adequate preparation can be made. It may be appropriate to keep a record of referrals to track the outcome.

Once a case is opened, a record should be made of the case and the client's name and address to ensure the file can be accessed in the future should the client return after the case is closed.

In some situations, the adviser may do no work for the client but instead signpost her/him to a more appropriate organisation.

Files and cases

All documents relating to a case must be kept in an adequate file. All the papers should be kept in date order. Incoming letters could be stored on one side of the file and outgoing on the other. There could also be dividers to separate each different creditor, so it is easy to access each debt and monitor its progress. Alternatively, papers relating to each creditor could be kept together with a separate sheet on file to indicate the action on each debt.

Correspondence

The client should be kept informed of each stage of the case and given copies of correspondence from the creditor. Telephone conversations should be recorded on the file and names kept of the person spoken to and the date. It is good practice to follow up the call with a letter from either the adviser or creditor, as appropriate, to confirm information discussed if it is relevant to the case. A financial statement should be prepared to give a clearer picture of the client's circumstances and whether s/he is in a position to present offers and at what rate (see p50).

Reviews

Each case should be regularly reviewed to check that replies have been received, that preparation for any court hearings has been carried out, and what the next step in the case should be. The use of a brought-forward diary system may be useful to ensure that important dates are noted and follow-ups are done regularly. There is no point keeping a file open if there is no further work to be carried out, or if the client has ceased contact and the adviser is carrying out work for the client without any confirmation that s/he is maintaining payments as agreed.

By managing the caseload, advisers will also have a clearer idea of how many additional cases, if any, they can take on.

Cases should also be reviewed, if possible, by other workers to check that the advice given is appropriate and correct.

Closure

At the outset, the adviser should give the client an indication of how long the case will remain open. This gives the adviser an idea of how many cases s/he is dealing with and when s/he will be able to take on additional ones. As the adviser is trying to empower the client, the aim should be that, once the work is done on the case, clients can continue with the work themselves, but possibly with the option of returning in the future should they feel unable to deal with matters themselves or if there is a change of circumstance.

A case can be closed if:
- the strategy for the client is up and running successfully; *or*
- the adviser has lost contact with the client; *or*
- the client no longer wants help from the agency or is changing adviser; *or*
- the agency is no longer able to provide a service to the client.

The Institute of Money Advisers' *Money Advice Statement of Good Practice* says that a creditor should only be informed that a case has been closed if:
- the adviser has been unable to obtain instructions from the client; *or*
- the client has informed the adviser that s/he is now dealing with the creditor in person.

This is to address the problem of a case being closed because a payment arrangement has been set up and the creditor then contacts the client directly to try to persuade her/him to increase payments. If a creditor contacts an agency again in those circumstances, it should be informed the case has been closed and be referred directly to the client.

If clients return for help when creditors are asking for a review of the finances, it may be advisable to assist them with a new financial statement and then advise how to prepare an offer letter, with the intention that they act for themselves.

Clients should be warned that some funders have time limits on when cases can be reopened on the same issue. This can be problematic if a client fails to keep in contact, the case is closed and the client then returns.

Client contact

As much information as possible on all the debts should be gained at the first interview and this should be recorded in a clear and concise manner. In practice, many clients do not bring all the information required to the adviser at the outset and so much of it may have to be obtained later, possibly from other sources – eg, from a client's creditors for outstanding balances or credit reference agencies for details of the client's creditors. If the first interview is being conducted by telephone, information will have to be brought or sent to the advice agency subsequently (and a signed authority to act obtained before creditors can be contacted).

It is vital to obtain sufficient information at the earliest opportunity, as otherwise:

- income/expenditure details and, consequently, the financial statement may be inaccurate and payment offers unsustainable, leading to the client failing to maintain the arrangement;
- incorrect advice may be given, leading the client to choose one option when another option might have been more appropriate;
- opportunities to maximise income may be lost.

A pro forma could be used to record the information, which could also remind the adviser what to ask the client in order to establish the full facts of the case. Debt clients are known to reveal only debts that they are worried about. It is therefore important that the adviser goes through all the priority commitments, whether or not they are in arrears, and then moves on to the non-priority commitments. Advice could be given in each area on the consequences should the client default. The adviser should be realistic about the outcome and be honest with the client at all times.

The adviser should check that agreements have been drawn up correctly and consider any applicable time limits.

It is a good idea to have standard letters held electronically to cut and paste the relevant facts of each individual case. The first letter after the interview should confirm all the advice given, setting out the creditors' powers and the client's options and consequences. The agreed action and the expected time scale should also be outlined.

The adviser should keep clients informed and involved at each stage, with the intention that they will be able to deal with the case themselves once the case is closed. The client should also keep the adviser informed of any change in circumstances throughout the life of the case.

Once all the work is completed on the case, the adviser should send a closure letter, detailing the work carried out and the outcome, and giving general advice on how to deal with the various creditors in the future.

Notes

1. The adviser as a professional
1 OFT, *Debt Management (and Credit Repair Services) Guidance*, March 2012, available at www.oft.gov.uk/shared_oft/business_leaflets/credit_licences/oft366rev.pdf

2. The debt advice system
2 The sale of a debt is known in law as an 'assignment' and the purchaser is known as an 'assignee'.
3 In one case, the FOS found that a bank had not treated a customer who had approached it for advice and assistance about her debts 'sympathetically and positively' by insisting that the income/expenditure form she had completed had to be checked by an advice agency. See *Ombudsman News* 83, 2010 (*Adviser* 140 abstracts)
4 paras 6-10 and 20-21 DMG
5 ss157 and 157A CCA 1974
6 s158 CCA 1974
7 s159 CCA 1974
8 OFT, *Credit Repair Promises Fall Short*, May 2000

Chapter 2

Key skills

This chapter covers:

1. Interviewing

The following is not a general guide to interviewing, but there are some features of an interview with a person in debt that are important to note.

- The debt adviser must immediately make it clear to the client that s/he will not be judged.
- The debt adviser must be aware of the ways in which preconceptions or personal attitudes affect the interview process. S/he must work to recognise any negative images s/he may have of borrowing, debt or debtors and eradicate them.
- Reassure the client that s/he has done the right thing in seeking advice. Being in debt can be stressful and clients may feel embarrassed at having to talk about their financial problems. It is important to build the client's trust (see p40) and to emphasise that s/he will not be judged in this process.
- It is important that the client is enabled to express her/his emotions in order to get these out of the way and concentrate on remembering, thinking and decision making as the interview progresses. For example, many people in debt fear imprisonment. For the vast majority of debts this is not a possibility, but this fear must be voiced if progress is to be made. The client may also have problems which initially do not appear to be debt-related – eg, relationship issues. Clients need to be able to express whatever is important to them and their concerns so that they can concentrate on sorting out their debts.

- Because of the numerous threats from individual creditors, many clients feel hopeless about their situation. Advisers cannot afford to raise false expectations by dismissing these threats, but they should be positive and explain that it is possible to do something.
- The debt adviser must anticipate problems the client may face. It is important that the client does not depart from decisions made as part of a strategy, but the adviser is unlikely to be there when these decisions are tested. For example, an adviser and client may agree that, because the client has been paying creditors who call at the door and not paying her/his priority creditors, the best course of action is to withhold all payments to unsecured creditors until the arrears on the client's priority debts have been cleared. This decision will not be tested until an unsecured creditor calls, perhaps late at night, making threats. The client may find it difficult to stick to her/his earlier decision unless this possibility has already been explored with the adviser.
- Partners, or other people with whom the client lives, will usually need to be consulted if a good decision (ie, one which is likely to be adhered to) is to be made. Many of the decisions taken involve third parties who may not be at the interview. Even if the debt adviser considers that urgent action is required, this can generally be delayed long enough for the client to consult these people. Occasionally, there will be compelling reasons for not consulting – eg, if there is a fear of violence.
- Tell the client abut the service s/he can expect from the adviser/agency. A clear explanation should be given of what is expected of the client and what the adviser will do. This must be must be written down and a copy given to the client and one kept by the agency (see p7).
- Performing realistic tasks can reduce the sense of hopelessness and empower the client. Modest tasks, such as asking a particular creditor about arrears, can help the client feel involved in the processes that are being carried out on her/his behalf. While it is important for the adviser to offer expertise and services, s/he should not take over the client's life and should avoid creating dependency.
- The debt adviser must always be impartial and not assume s/he knows what is best for the client. All options open to the client must be considered before any course of action is agreed.

2. Negotiation

Negotiation is a process of communication between the adviser or client and creditor. It takes place over a period of time, after which an agreement is made that both sides find acceptable. A decision must be made about whether it is appropriate for negotiation to be carried out by the client or the adviser. Sometimes, it is more empowering for the debt adviser to support a client by providing, for example, a financial statement and some standard letters, rather than negotiating her/himself. In the past, creditors would routinely reject offers made by clients themselves unless and until they were made by the advice agency itself, even though it was the same offer and based on identical information.

Some creditors have a policy of refusing to deal with advice agencies. If the client has authorised the debt adviser to negotiate with a creditor on her/his behalf, the Office of Fair Trading regards it as an unfair and improper business practice for a creditor to refuse to do so. Similarly, creditors should not refuse to deal with clients who are attempting to negotiate their own repayment arrangements. A creditor who refuses to negotiate with an adviser or a client without an objectively valid reason should be challenged.[1]

A debt adviser must only represent the interests of the client and should ensure that s/he does not offer more than s/he can afford. Advisers should do their best to enable the client regain control of her/his financial situation as quickly as possible, as opposed to being tied into a repayment programme, which may take many years to complete (if ever).

A debt adviser is often in a powerful position in relation to creditors because no one in the credit industry wants to be accused (particularly publicly) of acting illegally or oppressively. If a debt adviser from a well-respected local or national agency contacts a creditor to negotiate on a client's behalf, it is likely that the creditor will want to reach a settlement. In some cases, the adviser's power is increased because debt advice is likely to lead to payment and, in others, because the creditor realises that a debt cannot profitably be pursued. This does not mean that creditors should routinely be expected to agree to each and every proposal that a debt adviser puts forward. On the other hand, if the debt adviser thinks that the creditor is being unreasonable and/or unrealistic, s/he should consider referring the matter to a more senior person in the creditor organisation with a view to using the creditor's complaints procedure, if necessary.

Arguments should be supported by referring to any relevant code of practice. All negotiations should be conducted with the aim of resolving the debt problem and bearing in mind that the client's best interests are paramount.

Informal arrangements with creditors (eg, for reduced payments) are generally not long term and clients should be warned that creditors will invariably require a review at some stage.

CASHflow

Following publication of *With a Little Help From My Friends* by Citizens Advice in 2008, which recommended better design, co-ordination and delivery of assisted self-help debt advice services to support clients to negotiate directly with their creditors, the CASHflow pilot project was launched in 2009. It has now been rolled out nationally. Agencies are able to access a CASHflow self-help toolkit badged with a logo to reassure creditors that the client has gone through an approved money advice process. *With a Little Help From My Friends* contains guidance on the factors advisers should take into account when assessing clients for self-help.

A money adviser assists the client to draw up a financial statement which is 'locked' and so cannot be changed. The tool kit includes a suite of letters which the client can use to make offers to her/his creditors and deal with any follow up and requests for reviews.

The financial statement is drawn up using common financial statement principles (see p51) and creditors have agreed to deal with offers from CASHflow-assisted self-help clients in the same way as they would deal with offers from the agency itself. The client should be warned that debts may be sold on and, even though the debt purchaser should be informed of any existing payment arrangements, the client may have to come to a new arrangement with the debt purchaser.

3. Letter writing

Much negotiation begins with a letter. While emergency applications, particularly concerning priority debts (see p227), may have to be initiated on the telephone and confirmed in writing later, it is more effective to send a letter in the first instance so that full details can be enclosed. Important changes to agreements reached through negotiation should always be confirmed in writing.

It is sometimes more appropriate for the adviser to help the client prepare a financial statement using the standard CASHflow forms and letters, which are sent from the client her/himself (see p18). The client will receive the replies and must be encouraged to seek further advice, as required. In this way, the client regains control over her/his own affairs and, in the long term, may be more able to cope. In addition, the workload of the adviser may be reduced.

It is essential that letters are sent to the right place. In many cases, local branches are no longer able to deal with their customers' financial difficulties. Instead, most creditors now have dedicated departments. Wherever possible, advisers should use the address(es) provided by the creditor for dealing with communications. Both *Arian* and *IMA News* have up-to-date creditor contact details.

Format of a letter

Letter writing needs to follow a basic format, explained below.

Use simple language

Write letters in simple, clear language. 'Thank you for your letter of 11 June' is just as meaningful as 'Your communication of 11 June is gratefully acknowledged'.

Assume nothing

Letters, particularly initial ones, will generally be read by a person who knows little or nothing about the situation in question. A letter should, therefore, contain all the background information needed to make a decision.

Holding letters

It will often be necessary to write an initial letter requesting information which the adviser needs in order to advise the client and identify the available options. Such information includes:

- copies of any agreement and of any default notice (see p281) or termination letter where relevant;
- a statement of account, showing full details of the outstanding balance and how this is calculated;
- details of any court orders or other enforcement action.

The letter should also ask the creditor to put a hold on any further collection activity until the information requested has been supplied and the client has had an opportunity to put forward her/his proposals for resolving the matter. Any breaches of Office of Fair Trading (OFT) guidance (see p30) by the creditor or debt collector should also be addressed in this letter.

Use a framework

As well as standard letters or phrases, new or unusual situations require individual letters. These are easier to write with a framework to follow.

- **Address.** The letter should begin with the address to which it is sent, which must appear on the adviser's copy as well as the top copy.
- **Client and references.** Next comes the full name and address, including postcode, of the client and all references or other identifying numbers. Major creditors may have borrowers of the same name and thus detailed identification is essential to avoid confusion.
- **Standard opening phrase.** This can usefully explain the agency's status. For example, 'The above has contacted us for advice about her/his financial affairs and we are now helping her/him to look at these as a whole.'
- **Outline the background.** Next, tell the story so far (although not necessarily in the holding letter as the adviser may not have all the details at this stage). It is essential to give all the necessary background and details. Go through the story in chronological order. Keep sentences short and factual. Avoid long explanations. Do not include demands or excuses.
  The statement of facts must include those on which the adviser is basing the strategy, in particular any unusual expenditure or special circumstances of the client or the members of her/his household. Thus, if asking for a temporary suspension of payments and interest charges, the adviser should ensure that

s/he has explained there is at present no available income or capital, and has set out the client's future prospects.

- **Make the request.** The next stage of the letter should be the request. This needs to be clearly and simply phrased. Do not be apologetic or circumspect – link the request to the facts outlined and make it appear to be an inevitable consequence of them.

  The letter should continue by stating in what period it is proposed to review this strategy. This may be expressed either:
  - as a fixed period; *or*
  - with reference to other factors – eg, 'We will be happy to review this when Mr Parkinson gets a job.'

- **Add any special reasons.** After outlining the request, add the special reasons why this should be accepted. These may be obvious from the facts you have listed and it is not worth repeating them. If arrangements have broken down in the past or it is believed a creditor will be resistant to the suggestion, however, it is useful to list whatever special reasons you can.

- **Details of any offer.** If an offer of payment is being made, this should be clearly described – eg, 'The first payment of £... will be made on 27 August and following payments will be made on the 27th of each month.' The client should be advised to begin making the payments in accordance with the offer without waiting for confirmation from the creditor, as some creditors are prepared to accept offers but do not notify that acceptance and then complain that the client has not kept to the payment arrangement.

- **Response expected.** Your letter could then suggest the kind of reply that you expect – eg, 'We would be grateful if you could confirm, in writing, that this will be possible and send a paying-in book.'

- **To whom should the creditor reply?** It is worth considering whether or not it is desirable for creditors to reply to the agency or to clients directly. If the volume of debt advice is great, it may be advisable to ask creditors to reply directly to their customer. It may be worth explaining why this is necessary.

  The adviser should also include her/his contact details and availability (or alternative contacts where appropriate) so that creditors can contact her/him where necessary. On the other hand, some creditors and collectors contact the client directly even when asked to reply to the agency, usually in an attempt to persuade the client to increase their repayment offer. This is a breach of the OFT's *Debt Collection Guidance* (see p30).

- **Ending.** The letter can end with a conventional politeness, such as 'We are very grateful for your help in this matter', followed by 'yours sincerely/ faithfully' (by convention the former is used when the letter is addressed to a named individual and the latter when it is addressed 'Dear Sir/Madam').

4. **Court representation**

Many debt advisers regularly represent clients at court hearings, but if the court has not had experience of representation by lay advisers, the advice agency will need to talk to its local courts to arrange this. For more details about the courts, see Chapters 10, 11, 12 and 13.

Type of hearing

Chambers

The majority of hearings at which advisers represent clients are in chambers.[2] This means that the hearing is usually held in private in the district judge's office, with only the client and her/his representative, the solicitor or representative acting for the creditor, and the district judge present. The district judge does not wear a wig or gown, and everyone remains seated throughout the hearing. Before a hearing the debt adviser is obliged to make known to the court and creditor all information and documents to be used at the hearing.[3] There is also a duty to reveal any application which will be made at a hearing as soon as this is known.[4]

The claimant or her/his solicitor presents her/his case to the district judge. The claimant is normally the creditor, except if the client has applied for something like a time order (see p340) or the suspension of a warrant (see p229 and p355). After this, the other side gets the opportunity to speak. The client's representative has an opportunity to explain briefly the client's circumstances and make a proposal. A financial statement (see p50) is essential if making an offer of payment. The solicitor or agent is able to comment on the proposal and the district judge will make an order.

It is always worth introducing yourself to the creditor's representative at the court while waiting to be called and finding out what s/he has been instructed to ask the court for. The hearing will normally take five to 10 minutes, but this can be reduced if the adviser has successfully negotiated with the creditor or solicitor before the hearing.

The court always needs to know what powers it has to make a decision, and if the district judge is unsure (or sceptical), s/he may ask an adviser to point out where in the Civil Procedure Rules 1998 or elsewhere the proposed order is sanctioned (see Chapter 10).

Open court

Some hearings (such as appeals to judges) occur in open court and an adviser may wish to represent the client. At present, there is no right of audience for lay advisers (except in the small claims procedure), but most courts welcome the assistance of a debt adviser. It is important to ask an usher or clerk to find out the views of the judge or magistrate in advance, if possible.

As the name suggests, hearings are held in public, and are more formal than hearings in chambers. A circuit judge, a district judge or magistrate hears the case. The court may be full of people waiting to have their cases heard, and solicitors or barristers waiting to represent. The creditor or a solicitor presents the case and may bring witnesses to cross-examine.

The client may be asked to speak on oath, but the adviser may be able to present the case without the client needing to speak. It is customary to stand when addressing the judge.

Many courts do not allow lay representation, but the adviser may be able to be a 'McKenzie Friend'- ie, a person who accompanies the client to the hearing, advises her/him, suggests what s/he should say and makes notes of the proceedings. Advisers considering attending court as McKenzie Friends should read the practice guidelines issued in July 2010 (see www.judiciary.gov.uk). The court clerk is likely to be a useful contact at the magistrates' court.

Techniques of representation

Planning

Plan everything to be said in advance. Make sure it is logical and clear. Use notes where necessary. Rehearse presentations if possible, particularly if you are a new representative. You should inform the court if you have not had time to obtain full instructions – eg, in the case of emergency hearings or court/duty desks. It may then be in the best interests of the client to request an adjournment, even if this involves the client in increased liability for the creditor's costs.

Be brief

Local courts operate to very tight timescales (hearings are often listed for five or 10 minutes) and judges expect representations to be short and to the point. Avoid any repetition.

Summarise

The court wants to know what order it is being asked to make and the reasons why it is appropriate to make that order. A written summary of the case briefly setting out the issues, the facts and any relevant law is often helpful and can be handed out at the beginning if it has not been possible to circulate it in advance (take copies for the judge and creditor's representative). This can then be expanded on at presentation.

Prepare clear documents

Financial statements or other documents used to support a case should be clearly presented and photocopied for the judge and creditor's representative.

Tell the story

Explain the background to the case clearly and concisely in chronological order. Do not assume that the judge has read the papers.

Quote precedents and powers

Give clear references and explanations of any past cases cited in support of your case if it is unusual and the legal powers upon which it depends. Have references to the Civil Procedure Rules (see p265) and any caselaw on which you intend to rely. Take copies for the judge and creditor's representative.

Admit ignorance

If stuck, it is better to admit this and ask for help rather than pretend otherwise. Provided your case appears reasonable, many judges will be helpful if they are asked. However, this should never be used as an alternative to thorough preparation of the case. The debt adviser should never pretend to be a solicitor or allow others to assume wrongly that s/he is one.

Use court staff

It is helpful before the hearing to tell the usher you wish to speak on the client's behalf. S/he will then inform the court clerk or the judge and tell you if there is anyone to represent the creditor.

Address

Address a district judge or magistrate as 'sir' or 'madam' and a judge as 'your honour'.

Look smart, be polite, speak clearly

Wear smart clothes (or apologise for your inability to do so – eg, if it is an emergency application). It is usually acceptable for lay representatives to dress less formally, but the dress prejudice of the judiciary should not be underestimated. Use standard English where possible; slang may not be understood and will almost certainly not further your case. Appear as confident as possible without being 'cocky'. Be respectful, but pleasant. Use eye contact and smiles to retain the attention of the judge.

Know your own limits

Do not attempt to represent in court without being aware of all the possible outcomes. Complex representation may require lay advisers or lawyers who are not specialists to refer to lay advocates, solicitors or barristers who are.[5]

5. **Changing social policy**

If a particular law, practice, structure or policy adversely affects many clients or affects vulnerable groups of clients, the adviser should work to change the policy.

When contacting individual creditors, the adviser should stress that this is a general social policy approach and not an attempt to reopen a case that has already been discussed.

Other organisations can be helpful. The ways in which creditors deal with debt may be controlled or overseen by one of a number of organisations.

Advisers should also pass on details to umbrella organisations, such as Citizens Advice, AdviceUK or the Institute of Money Advisers.

The Office of Fair Trading and trading standards departments

The Office of Fair Trading (OFT) is a central government body, which regulates trading or company practices and which has statutory responsibility for licensing those who require a licence under the Consumer Credit Act 1974 (see p60).

Trading standards (or consumer protection) departments are part of a local authority. They have certain statutory functions for weights and measures and consumer safety. They also have a responsibility to investigate breaches of the Consumer Credit Act and to report to the OFT on problems encountered in their geographical area.

It is best to seek the help, first of all, of a local trading standards department with both gathering information about a trader's practices and putting these to the OFT. Building a good relationship with the local trading standards department is worthwhile for obtaining local information about creditors. In addition, if the adviser is having problems with a creditor in a different area, some departments will contact their colleagues to see if they are aware of similar issues in that area.

The OFT can issue a number of different types of notice to traders before it actually revokes their consumer credit licence (without which they cannot operate in that field). Since 6 April 2008, the OFT has had new powers (see p60). These include a power to impose requirements or conditions on a licence holder, which the OFT has done on a number of occasions. In addition, the OFT and trading standards departments can use Part 8 of the Enterprise Act 2002 to require creditors to cease engaging in conduct which breaches consumer protection legislation and harms the interests of consumers generally. If the matter cannot be resolved informally, the court can be asked to make an order to prohibit the conduct concerned. A breach of the order is punishable as a contempt of court by imprisonment or a fine. If a local trading standards department is not helpful in pursuing a particular company, it can be reported directly to the OFT. It is important that even relatively minor infringements or bad practice are routinely reported because it is generally the volume of reported cases on a particular issue or individual that gives rise to investigation by the OFT.

Advisers should remember that trading standards departments may also be able to assist in resolving individual cases. As the regulator, the OFT is not able to provide redress in individual cases.

Ofgem, Ofcom and Ofwat

The suppliers of fuel, telecommunications and water all have regulatory bodies (see Appendix 1), which have varying powers to investigate and comment on their activities. The fuel regulatory bodies have a responsibility to prevent unlawful price increases or disconnections. They can also be very useful in exercising pressure in other areas.

Trade associations

Many industries have trade associations. These are bodies that are regulated by their members, but impose certain agreed standards as a membership condition. A list of trade associations is in Appendix 1. Many have a code of practice or conduct, and all have some kind of complaints procedure, which can be used to resolve individual cases.

Trade associations exist primarily to protect their members. However, they can be a vital tool in changing the behaviour of an individual company. Trade associations do not want the good name of their other members affected by the poor behaviour of one company. The peer-group pressure they can exert, either through a complaints procedure or less formally, is probably much greater than the pressure an advice agency acting on its own could create.

Local councillors and MPs

Much debt is payable to local or national government. This includes council tax, income tax, VAT and rent. The statutory powers which the state has given itself in order to enforce these debts are considerable and thus they all become priority debts. However, as government debts, they are subject to scrutiny by elected members – ie, councillors or MPs. This can provide a powerful method of ensuring that the state's powers are not used in too draconian a fashion.

Elected members are often not aware of the measures being used by their officers to collect debts. For instance, many local councillors are unaware of the extent to which their authority uses private bailiffs and, once briefed by an advice agency, can make it a live political issue and change the way these debts are collected. For example, under a protocol drawn up between the national bodies representing advice agencies and local government, regular liaison is encouraged at a local level on practices and policies on the collection of council tax arrears.

Ombudsmen

If the administration of debt collection by the state is poor and results in individuals experiencing hardship, complaints can be made to an Ombudsman (see Appendix 1).

The **Parliamentary and Health Service Ombudsman** investigates complaints of maladministration by any central government department. Complaints must be made via an MP. A simple statement, with dates and supporting evidence, should, if possible, be sent to the MP with a request that it be forwarded to the Ombudsman.

Complaints about local government matters are probably best made through a local councillor, but can also be made directly by a member of the public. Complaining to the Local Government Ombudsman (or the Public Services Ombudsman for Wales) is important, even where the maladministration has been corrected in an individual case. Negative adjudications by the Ombudsman are disliked by local government officers and will usually lead to procedural changes to prevent a recurrence of the event complained about.

The **Local Government Ombudsman/Public Services Ombudsman for Wales** often investigates a particular department or function of an authority – eg, council tax collection. The debt adviser should collect a few cases of maladministration and then discuss with staff at one of the Ombudsman offices whether it will investigate. A report on the workings of a department is much more powerful than a single case.

The **Adjudicator's Office** deals with complaints about the way things have been handled by Her Majesty's Revenue and Customs (but not about the amount of tax or VAT the client has been asked to pay). See Appendix 1 for address.

The **Financial Ombudsman Service** is the body that handles complaints between clients and finance firms (including banks and building societies) and, since 6 April 2007, firms with a consumer credit licence (including debt collectors and sub-prime lenders). See Appendix 1 for the address and also p268.

Since 1 July 2006 (1 September 2007 in the case of mis-selling), complaints about gas and electricity suppliers can be referred to the **Ombudsman Services: Energy**. A complaint must first be made to the supplier and it should be asked to put the account on hold while it deals with it. If, after 10 days, there has been either no response or an unsatisfactory response, the complaint should be escalated through the supplier's complaints procedure (refer to its code of practice for details). The case can be referred to the Ombudsman Services either eight weeks after the complaint was made or after the supplier has issued a 'deadlock letter' – ie, negotiations have broken down and neither party will reconsider their position. The complaint must be referred to the Ombudsman Services within either six months of the deadlock letter being issued or nine months of the complaint first being made.

Since 6 October 2010, the **Legal Ombudsman** has considered complaints about legal services provided by lawyers (including solicitors, barristers and employees of businesses and partnerships). The complaint must relate to services provided by the lawyer to the client and, unless there are exceptional circumstances, the client must first have used the lawyer's/firm's complaints procedure. If the complaint is not resolved within eight weeks, it can be referred to the Ombudsman. The Ombudsman can consider the complaint earlier if s/he decides that delay would harm the client or if the lawyer has refused to consider the complaint. The complaint must be made to the Ombudsman within six months of the lawyer's response and within 12 months of the matter complained of. The Ombudsman need not consider a complaint about an issue that is being dealt with by a court, unless the case is 'stayed' either with the consent of all the parties or a court order to enable the Ombudsman to deal with it.

Ombudsmen are not regulators and their primary role is to assist in the resolution of individual cases. They expect the client to give the creditor the opportunity to investigate her/his complaint and resolve the matter before referring the case to them.

Monitoring local courts

Court procedures should be monitored on a local basis by debt advisers. Having collected information about the way in which a particular court operates, it is important to decide whether pressure for change needs to be exerted upon the court staff, the judiciary, or both.

Neither judges nor magistrates are open to being lobbied by groups about individual decisions or types of decisions that they are required to take. However, particularly when an adviser works for a charitable organisation with a good reputation locally, it may be possible to arrange meetings with the chair of the bench (ie, the senior magistrate, or representatives of the judges in a county court) to discuss ways in which the advice centre can assist the courts in their work or other issues of mutual concern. In practice, this means it is generally possible to discuss procedures and engage the decision makers in an analysis of the effects of their judgments.

In a magistrates' court, the chief executive will generally discuss procedural matters and policy issues (eg, when and how the court uses its discretion to allow the payment of fines by instalment), and any such matter should be discussed with her/him if its operation causes problems.

Local liaison groups

Some public services have liaison groups. These include local court users' groups and are set up, for example, by the Department for Work and Pensions and local authorities. The debt adviser should investigate groups that exist (and perhaps advocate their creation where they do not). S/he should use membership of these groups as a means of gaining credibility through networking, and changing policies and procedures that are unhelpful or oppressive. Some groups (for instance, court users' groups) may have existed for a long time with a fixed membership (perhaps solicitors, probation service and police). The debt adviser may have to invest time to secure membership, but this may be rewarded with a direct line of communication to powerful local decision makers.

Using the media

Discussion with the various bodies outlined above can often bring about useful changes that prevent continued injustice. However, it is often only when something becomes a live, public, political issue that real change can occur. It is important, therefore, to cultivate links with local and national media so that publicity can be gained for particular injustices.

When considering using the media, general advice work issues, such as confidentiality, will need bearing in mind. However, even if an individual client does not wish to have her/his case publicised, it may be acceptable for an anonymous description of the issues involved in it to be part of a media campaign. There is an almost endless demand from media organisations for examples of individuals who have suffered by being in debt. Many people do not wish to have their private affairs so publicly paraded, but for others this can be an important way of regaining a sense of power after the experiences they have faced at the hands of creditors. It is certainly the way to bring an issue to public debate.

6. **Dealing with harassment**

What is harassment

Many creditors harass debtors. Much of this goes unreported and unchallenged, and is expected by many clients. Section 40 of the Administration of Justice Act 1970 defines harassment as trying to coerce a person to pay a contract debt by making demands for payment that are calculated to subject a person to 'alarm, distress or humiliation, because of their frequency or publicity or manner'. In addition, any false representation that a type of non-payment is criminal or that the person is a court official or other publicly sanctioned debt collector is also regarded as harassment.

Harassment can take place in writing or orally. It can include using obviously marked vehicles, calling repeatedly at anti-social hours, or visiting neighbours or places of work. Harassment occurs if a debt collector purports to be enquiring about a person but explains to neighbours why the enquiries are necessary. Harassment might also include posting lists of debtors in public. It includes abusive or threatening behaviour and all acts of violence.

Since 26 May 2008, a breach of section 40 is no longer a criminal offence. However, it is likely to involve a breach of the Office of Fair Trading's (OFT) *Debt Collection Guidance* (see below).

Debt collection guidance

The OFT's *Debt Collection Guidance* (OFT664) was first published in July 2003 and was revised and updated in October 2011.[6] This document, along with Part 7 of the OFT's *Irresponsible Lending Guidance* (published in February 2011) is indispensable for debt advisers, as it sets out practices which the OFT considers to be unfair, and provides advisers with the basis for challenging unacceptable behaviour. Copies of both can be downloaded from www.oft.gov.uk. The guidance covers anyone who has a consumer credit licence – ie, lenders (both secured and unsecured), debt purchasers, utilities and telephone companies, solicitors and bailiffs, and in-house as well as external debt collectors engaged in the recovery or enforcement of regulated consumer credit debts. Advisers can find out if a creditor has a consumer credit licence at: www2.crw.gov.uk/pr.

The guidelines state that creditors who employ external debt collectors must take responsibility for their conduct and the OFT expects creditors to investigate any complaints about such debt collectors and take appropriate action. If this does not happen, advisers should consider complaining not only about the debt collectors but also about the creditor.

Creditors and debt collectors are expected to abide by the spirit as well as the letter of the guidelines. They cover the following areas.

- It is unfair to communicate with clients or their representatives, in whatever form, in an unclear, inaccurate or misleading manner – eg, if those contacting clients do not make clear who they are, who they work for, what their role is and the purpose of the contact.[7]
- Those who contact clients must not be deceitful by misrepresenting their authority and/or the correct legal position – eg, by pursuing third parties for payment when they are not liable.
- It is considered to be oppressive to put physical or psychological pressure on clients or third parties – eg, by pressurising clients to pay in full, in unreasonably large instalments, or to increase payments when they are unable to do so.
- Dealings with clients must not be deceitful and/or unfair – eg, by contacting clients directly and bypassing their appointed representatives.
- Charges for debt collection should not be levied unfairly – eg, by claiming collection costs from the client in the absence of express contractual or other legal provision.
- Those making debt collection visits must not act in an unclear or threatening manner – eg, by entering a property uninvited or not leaving a property when asked to do so.

- In the case of 'statute-barred' debt (see p275), although the debt still legally exists:
  - it is unfair to pursue it if the client has heard nothing from the creditor during the relevant limitation period (but not if the creditor has been in regular contact with the client before the debt became statute-barred);
  - it is unfair to mislead clients about their rights and obligations – eg, by falsely claiming that the debt is still recoverable through the courts;
  - it is unfair to continue to press for payment after a client has stated that s/he will not be paying a debt because it is statute-barred.
- Businesses should ensure that customer data is accurate and take reasonable steps to ensure that accurate and adequate data is passed on to third parties, such as debt collectors, debt purchasers and credit reference agencies, to avoid cases of 'mistaken identity' (where the wrong person is pursued for payment of a debt) and to ensure that clients are pursued for the correct amount of any debt.

Specifically, the guidelines state that it is an unfair practice to:
- if a creditor informs a client that it has decided not to pursue the debt, fail to make the client aware that the debt may still be sold by the creditor and the debt purchaser might decide to pursue the debt. **Note:** if the creditor has accepted a payment in full and final settlement of a debt, the creditor should formally and clearly confirm this;
- fail to investigate, and/or provide details as appropriate, when a debt is queried or disputed (eg, if the client is not the actual debtor, the debt does not exist or the amount being pursued is incorrect), and fail to provide information on the result of such investigations;
- require an individual to supply information to prove s/he is not the client in question – eg, a driving licence or passport;
- continue with debt collection activity while investigating a reasonably queried or disputed debt;
- make undue, excessive or otherwise inappropriate use of statutory demands when a borrower falls into arrears;
- pressurise clients to pay more than they can reasonably afford and fail to allow for alternative, affordable repayment amounts where a reasonable offer is made;
- fail to suspend recovery of a debt from a client in default or arrears difficulties for a reasonable period where a debt adviser is assisting her/him to agree a repayment plan;
- fail to suspend recovery of a debt from a client where notification has been given and it is reasonably believed that s/he lacks the mental capacity to make decisions about her/his debt problems unless or until a reasonable period has been allowed for relevant evidence to be provided.

Paragraph 3.9(m) of the *Debt Collection Guidance* deals with the misuse of continuous payment authorities by creditors – eg, making repeated attempts to collect a single amount. A proposed amendment will deal with cancelling continuous payment authorities and debiting an account without the express consent of the account holder. For further information of continuous payment authorities, see p123.

Breaches of the guidelines should first be raised with the creditor and debt collector concerned. If the matter is not resolved, the client should use the complaints procedure to escalate the matter to the Financial Ombudsman Service.[8] The issue should also be raised with the appropriate trade body (eg, the Finance and Leasing Association (FLA)) or the regulator (eg, the OFT). Complaints can be made online to the OFT's debt collection team at http://tinyurl.com/2ko7zz or www.oft.gov.uk/about-the-oft/legal-powers/legal/cca/debt-collection.

Codes of practice

Many creditors have their own codes of practice. For example, all gas and electricity suppliers are required to have a code of practice on dealing with customers in financial difficulty. Other creditors subscribe to trade associations, which have codes of practice with which members should comply – eg, *The Lending Code, the FLA Lending Code* and the *Credit Services Association Code of Practice*. Some regulators (eg, the OFT, Ofwat and Ofgem) issue guidelines on how customers in debt should be dealt with. There is also guidance for bailiffs (*National Standards for Enforcement Agents*). This is produced by the Ministry of Justice and was updated in January 2012.

All these codes set high standards, which creditors and collectors are expected to meet in their dealings with clients. *The Lending Code* even requires subscribers to ensure that when they sell a debt, the purchaser agrees to comply with its guidance on handling financial difficulties. However, creditors and collectors often fall short of the standards set in the relevant code of practice. Unfortunately, codes of practice are invariably voluntary in the sense that they cannot be directly enforced in the event of non-compliance. The only remedy is a complaint, which in some cases can be referred to an independent Ombudsman.

This *Handbook* refers to codes of practice where relevant. It will often be in a client's best interests to point out to a creditor or collector where there is non-compliance with a code of practice and request that it is complied with. In the case of collectors (and private bailiffs) it is also worth copying in the creditor. This does not mean that a complaint should be made in every case. The aim of a complaint should be to achieve a better outcome for the client than currently appears likely and so, if a complaint is likely to impede, rather than promote, negotiation, the adviser should discuss this with the client and consider deferring it.

Dealing with harassment

Much debt collection activity takes place verbally over the telephone, at the client's home and sometimes at her/his place of work. Debt advisers, therefore, should always ask how demands were made and, in the case of verbal demands, exactly what was said, and check all written communications for evidence of inappropriate behaviour. It is important to take urgent action to protect the client from further contact. As with breaches of the OFT's *Debt Collection Guidance*, a letter of complaint should be sent immediately, outlining the facts as understood and warning the collector and creditor that, if not resolved to the client's satisfaction, the complaint will be taken to the next level. In cases of violence or extreme harassment, the police and the local trading standards department should be informed as soon as possible. Feedback from creditors suggests that many advisers are not acting professionally when making complaints on behalf of clients – eg, by using rude, abrupt and sarcastic language. In addition, hearsay evidence is often reported as fact instead of, for instance, 'our client informs us that …'. The complaint letter should be objective and factual, and not personalised (unless the complaint is about the actions of an identified individual).

The client should then be advised to have no further contact with the collector/creditor until the matter has been clarified. This may involve politely, but firmly, refusing her/him entry to property or not answering the telephone. The client should be advised to keep a diary recording details of any further attempted collection action. If possible, practical steps should be taken to ensure that friends, neighbours or relatives know about serious harassment and are able to provide a safe haven or support to the client. Some agencies give clients a sheet of their letterhead, and advise them to show this to any collectors/creditors who visit and tell them to contact the agency.

7. **Budgeting advice**

Although advice on budgeting is not debt advice, a debt adviser must use the procedures and skills described in other parts of this *Handbook* to assist clients deal with their debts. Budgeting advice is fraught with difficulties, but it can play a useful part in the debt advice process. Discussing a person's finances can be a sensitive subject and so a good interview technique is required. An adviser should be careful not to impose her/his own values on a client.

It can sometimes speed up the debt advice process if the client has a session with a money adviser. The money adviser will go through the client's budget in detail and look at ways in which s/he could cut back on expenditure. The budget can then be brought to the debt appointment.

There are particular problems when budgeting on a low income. Often, people on a low income only have access to the more expensive forms of credit. In the absence of credit, goods available are generally more expensive because it is impossible to buy enough to benefit from the lower unit prices charged for larger quantities. Similarly, access to the cheapest sources of goods may be denied if transport is not readily available to the large out-of-town stores. Budgeting on a low income often requires purchasing inferior goods because money is not available to buy more expensive ones which would last longer and thus be much cheaper in the long run.

If poverty exists alongside other factors, such as disability, parenthood or the breakdown of a relationship, it is likely that budgeting is constrained by the time available, which in turn is constrained by the practical and emotional demands of these other situations.

The financial statement

Very often, the process of producing a financial statement (see p50) will enable people to see the sources of their financial problems. It will often be clear, when all items of expenditure have been listed, that these cannot be met from available income. Ideally, if there is a need to cut expenditure, it will occur to the client her/himself. If this does not happen, the debt adviser may wish to suggest ways of budgeting and put to the client the likely results of such strategies. The adviser must be aware of vocabulary, body language and tone of voice, to avoid giving the impression that s/he is judging the client. Issues such as drinking, gambling and smoking will need to addressed, and the adviser should explain to the client that these are matters which creditors are likely to raise and so have to be tackled.

On the other hand, this exercise may establish that the client is able to meet all her/his contractual liabilities together with any accruing charges as well as maintaining her/his essential expenditure, and consequently does not need debt advice or any of the strategies discussed in this *Handbook*.

'Luxury items'

There are some items of expenditure which may, in comparison to the possible loss of other goods or services, be less essential.

- Cars are generally more expensive than is realised to purchase, run, maintain, tax and insure. If a car is not necessary for personal and family mobility or work requirements, the client may need to consider either selling it and acquiring a cheaper one, or doing without.
- In the past, telephones, particularly mobiles, have been considered a luxury. This is not always the case, and would certainly not be so if someone's health might require her/him to summon assistance in an emergency or, for instance, if someone has been subjected to racial abuse or marital violence and this could happen again. The telephone may also be an important social lifeline or a means of making emergency help available to another person outside the client's home. However, where no such factors exist, particularly if phone bills

are large, the possibility of doing without or changing to incoming calls only could be considered. If a mobile phone is used, the cost (which may be less than that for a landline on some tariffs and usage patterns) and appropriateness of this should be explained. Clients who are in receipt of income support, income-based jobseeker's allowance, income-related employment and support allowance or the guarantee credit of pension credit may be able to benefit from a low-cost phone package available from BT. Known as BT Basic, the line rental of £14.40 every three months includes £4.50 worth of free calls. Clients can have broadband from a provider of their choice. For more details, visit www.bt.com/btbasic.

- DVD players were often considered an extravagance and a cause of debt. In fact, the cost of a DVD player would never cause serious debt and its value as very cheap entertainment (particularly where people are housebound or have children) is very high. The sale of a DVD player will generally have a negligible effect on a client's current debt and ending a hire agreement is unlikely to do very much more.

- Cable or satellite television is more expensive than DVD. If a client has an agreement that has already run for its minimum period, the adviser could discuss whether satellite TV is more important than other items on which the money could be spent. On the other hand, it may well be part of a package, including the telephone, where the overall cost can be justified.

Non-dependants living with the client

A particular problem for a client can be the contribution made by non-dependants living in her/his household. The complexity of family budgeting is well demonstrated by a parent's wish to charge an adult son or daughter only a nominal amount for board. This may also be generated by a desire to keep the family together and can save money – eg, by reducing childminding costs. In some cases, challenging the amount being paid by a non-dependant could lead to family disruption.

Faced with this difficult situation, a client will need information and support in order to make decisions. For example, if housing benefit or housing costs in means-tested benefits are being claimed, s/he will need to know by how much this is reduced by the non-dependant living with her/him. From the financial statement (see p50), a client can judge what might be a fair share of the total household expenditure to be attributed to the non-dependant.

Financial exclusion

Over-indebtedness and poverty often go hand in hand, particularly in deprived communities where many people are on a low income and financially excluded – ie, lack access to basic financial products such as bank accounts, ways of saving and affordable credit. In addition, financially excluded people can find themselves paying more for essential services, such as fuel, insurance and essential goods because they only have access to high-cost credit, provided by sub-prime lenders or, even worse, loan sharks.

Financial exclusion is the opposite of financial inclusion, which has been defined as:

> ... a state in which all people have access to appropriate, desired financial products and services in order to manage their money effectively. It is achieved by financial literacy and financial capability on the part of the consumer and access on the part of the financial product, services, and advice suppliers.[9]

An important factor in financial inclusion is 'financial capability', defined by the Treasury in 2007 as:

> ... a broad concept encompassing people's knowledge and skills to understand their own financial circumstances, along with the motivation to take action. Financially capable consumers plan ahead, find and use information, know when to seek advice, and can understand and act on this advice, leading to greater participation in the financial services market. [10]

Without financial capability, the risk is that clients will not get value for money and the products they obtain will not meet their needs. Several products have been introduced that are aimed at meeting the needs of low-income clients – eg:

- basic bank accounts;
- child trust funds;
- stakeholder pensions.

Advice on buying a specific financial product from a particular provider is a 'regulated' activity that requires the adviser to be approved by the Financial Services Authority (FSA).

However, successive governments have recognised that there is a need for more general advice to help clients understand their financial affairs and the options available to them. Generic financial advice is provided in England and Wales by the Money Advice Service, which is free, independent of both government and the financial services industry and which aims to help people manage their money better by giving clear, unbiased 'money advice' to help people make informed choices. The service is available face-to-face, by phone or online at www.moneyadviceservice.org.uk. The service provides free and impartial advice on budgeting, saving and borrowing, retirement planning, tax and benefits, but does not recommend specific courses of action, products or providers. It is available for everyone, but is particularly targeted at people who are financially vulnerable and those at key life stages – eg, women who are pregnant. The Money Advice Service website contains online tools and planners, including calculators, comparison tables and a financial health check.

Advisers may find CPAG's *Personal Finance Handbook* useful for more information on financial exclusion and financial literacy.

Credit unions

A credit union is one way of extending low-cost financial services to local communities. Credit unions are financial co-operatives owned and controlled by their members. Each credit union has a 'common bond' which determines who can become a member – eg, people living or working in a particular area. They offer savings facilities and affordable loans sourced from their members' savings. By law, a credit union cannot charge more than 2 per cent a month on the reducing balance of a loan (26.8 per cent APR), although the average is 1 per cent a month (12.7 per cent APR). Many now provide current accounts, bill-paying services through budgeting accounts, payment of benefits directly to the claimant's credit union account, and savings accounts. Credit unions with access to the Growth Fund (supported by the government's Financial Inclusion Fund) may be able to offer loans to people who are not yet savers with the credit union.

The government's stated aim is to encourage credit unions to make loans which might otherwise be judged 'risky'.

Credit unions, together with advice agencies, offer a range of potentially complementary services which can assist in tackling financial exclusion and over-indebtedness. For example, a credit union can help clients gain access to financial services and manage their finances effectively, help and encourage them to save and budget, and may even be able to provide a loan to pay off debts. However, a loan – even at a much lower rate – is not always in a client's best interests and more effective assistance can be provided by money advice. Some credit unions have an arrangement with their local authority for the local housing allowance for private-rented properties to be paid directly to the credit union, which in turn forwards the money to the landlord. This ensures the client's rent is paid and avoids arrears.

Advisers should ensure that the debt advice process does not reinforce financial exclusion by cutting clients off from mainstream products. There are, however, a number of issues for money advisers in referring clients to a particular credit union. In order to preserve independence, the adviser must make it clear that s/he is not an agent of the credit union and must not give clients unrealistic expectations of the assistance they can expect from a credit union. The adviser should also make it clear that a referral does not guarantee immediate access to financial services, such as a loan. Credit unions are not charities and should only lend to people who have the capacity to repay. Provided the referral is in the best interests of the client, the fact that s/he may be borrowing to pay off other debts should not be ruled out in all circumstances. Advisers should also bear in mind that affordable credit is not the only financial service offered by a credit union, and that access to current and savings accounts also promote financial inclusion.

If the client defaults on a loan, the credit union not only becomes one of the client's creditors but also a non-priority creditor. Most credit unions will negotiate debt repayments terms if a client has fallen into financial difficulties, but some tend to refuse low loan repayments (such as token offers) and may decide to impose membership restrictions on other products and services. If not treated as a priority, the client is likely to lose the benefits of membership. Citizens Advice has adopted the following policy:[11]

> Most credit union debts are considered to be non-priority credit debts and should therefore be offered pro rata repayments from disposable income in the normal way. An adviser can discuss the option of prioritising any creditor outside of accepted money advice practices if there is a good reason, such as high interest rates or another unintended consequence detrimental to the client. In these special circumstances, the client must be fully advised of potential challenges from other creditors to any offers they put forward and the implications of potentially preferring a creditor should also be considered (see p467 and p474). Citizens Advice considers that membership restrictions resulting from a credit union's refusal of a reasonable and affordable repayment offer can constitute an unacceptable barrier to valuable member savings products and therefore impinges on the financial inclusion ethos that a credit union represents.

Credit unions can, in certain circumstances, apply to the Department for Work and Pensions (DWP) to have loans repaid to them through deductions from certain benefits.[12] In order to do this, the credit union must agree that no interest or other charges will be added to the debt following the application. In addition, the client must:

- have failed to make payments as agreed for a period of 13 weeks and not have resumed making those payments;
- have given written permission for the credit union to provide her/his personal data to the DWP;
- not already be having deductions made to pay another eligible lender (another credit union or certain other third-sector lenders);
- not already be having deductions made to repay an overpayment of benefit or a social fund loan.

DWP guidance states that lenders must apply to the DWP to join the scheme and prove they have responsible lending criteria and practice.[13] They must also have taken other reasonable steps to collect the repayments (including writing to the client on three occasions, with the final letter notifying her/him that deductions from benefit will be sought).

Notes

2. Negotiation

1 paras 3.48 – 3.49 DMG; para 3.9(c)
DCG

4. Court representation

2 r39.2 CPR and Part 39 para 1 PD CPR
3 Part 1 CPR; Part 23 para 9 PD CPR
4 Part 23 paras 2.7 and 2.10 PD CPR
5 For further information, see P Madge,
'Advocacy for Money Advisers', *Adviser*
44

6. Dealing with harassment

6 See S Edwards, 'Debtors' Shield', *Adviser*
100
7 Guidance on the use, form and content
of standard debt collection letters can
be found on the OFT website at http://
tinyurl.com/6dwzso2 or
www.oft.gov.uk/shared_oft/
business_leaflets/consumer_credit/
debt-letters.pdf
8 *Ombudsman News* 99, 2012 contains a
number of case studies involving debt
collection which are covered in *Arian* 35
caselaw update and *Adviser* 150
abstracts.

7. Budgeting advice

9 Resolution Foundation/Transact,
*Financial Inclusion and Financial
Capability Explained*, 2009
10 HM Treasury, *Financial Capability: the
government's long-term approach*, 2007
11 *CAB Money* 35, June 2010, pp15-16
12 Sch 9 para 7C SS(C&P) Regs
13 Available at www.dwp.gov.uk/other-
specialists/eligible-loan-deductions

Chapter 3

Stages of debt advice

This chapter summarises the eight stages essential to debt advice and shows how the individual stages link together as a single process. It covers:

1. Creating trust (below)
2. Listing creditors and minimising debts (p41)
3. Listing and maximising income (p43)
4. Listing expenditure (p46)
5. Dealing with priority debts (p49)
6. Drawing up a financial statement (p50)
7. Choosing a strategy for non-priority debts (p53)
8. Implementing the chosen strategies (p57)

1. Creating trust

The adviser must create a trusting and safe environment in which the client can talk about her/his personal and financial affairs. This may take some time to develop but should start at the beginning of the process, when the adviser makes it clear that s/he will not judge and is on the client's side.

The adviser must explain what s/he will do and why. S/he should obtain as much detail as possible about the client, other members of the household, the debts and the financial situation. It is important to make the client feel as comfortable as possible so that s/he feels able to provide the detailed information needed to advise her/him properly. When collecting information, the adviser is not intruding unnecessarily into people's affairs but needs information to help the client decide a strategy and/or negotiate with creditors. It is, therefore, important to tell the client that such information is confidential and explain how the agency's confidentiality principles operate. Often, people seek advice about a specific debt and are reluctant to discuss other debts they are managing to pay or if they feel the creditor has been particularly helpful. However, it is often impossible to deal with a particular debt in isolation. This stage can include a discussion of the whole position.

2. **Listing creditors and minimising debts**

The first facts to gather are details of the debts and the creditors, including those with no arrears or ones with whom the client has already negotiated lower payments.

A client may not have all the necessary information with her/him on the first visit to enable the adviser to complete the creditor list. It is, therefore, important to agree how the missing information will be collected, by whom and when. The client's credit reference file may be a useful information-gathering tool if the client has no, or incomplete, paperwork.

The creditors

Advisers should record the following.

- **The name, address and telephone number of each creditor.** Exact company names are important, as the proliferation of credit has led to a surprising number of creditors with very similar names.
- **Account/reference numbers.** Most creditors access their computers with a reference number and this must be included.
- **Letter references.** If the client has received correspondence from the company, any letter reference should be noted together with any contact details.
- **Agents' details.** Solicitors or commercial debt collectors are often used. Record details of these (and their references) separately. Record details of the one who has made most recent contact with the client. Check whether the collector has actually bought the debt (in which case s/he will now be the creditor) or whether the agent is acting on behalf of the original creditor (in which case s/he will be accountable to that creditor). Creditors should inform clients when debts are either passed on to collectors or sold to third parties.

The debts

The following details must be noted.

- **Age of debt.** Find out when any credit was first granted. The length of time for which the agreement has run or a bill has been unpaid can be a factor in negotiation (and might even provide grounds for challenging the debt). For instance, a creditor is more likely to be sympathetic if payments have been made for some time than if a new agreement is breached. The legal position on some agreements depends on when they were made – eg, see p67 for credit agreements made before 6 April 2007. An old debt may also be 'statute-barred' – ie, unenforceable through the courts (see p275).
- **Reason for debt.** It is important to ask the reason for the debt. This is necessary – eg, to refute suggestions that the debt was unreasonably incurred.
- **Status of the debt.** Note the status of the debt. This should either be a priority or non-priority. Chapter 8 explains the criteria for making such decisions. If

possible, check any documents or agreements to confirm this information, as clients can be unsure or may describe debts incorrectly – eg, 'hire purchase' is often used to mean 'credit sale agreement', but has very different legal consequences (see pp115–16).

- **The written agreement.** Check whether the debt is based on a written agreement and, if so, whether or not it has been seen and photocopied for future reference. Ensure agreements are checked for defects which may affect their enforceability. Obtain a copy from the creditor if necessary. Note the absence of a written agreement, which can render some agreements unenforceable. See Chapter 5.

- **Liability.** This means checking that the client is actually responsible for the debt. Note in whose name(s) agreements were made and/or whose name(s) is/are on the bill (although this is not necessarily conclusive). This may either be the client alone, the client and a partner, or a friend or relative who acted as a guarantor. This will ensure that all debts listed are challenged where appropriate. See Chapter 5.

- **Payments.** Note the amount currently owing. State whether the figure is approximate or exact. Note contractual payments under any original agreement and any subsequent amendment to them. Note the existence of arrears in payments, although initially these need only be approximate. Note the payment method. Advice may be needed about coping with doorstep collectors, changing or cancelling standing orders or direct debit arrangements, or opening a new bank or building society account if the current bank or building society is one of the client's creditors (see p49). However, clients should not be advised to stop or reduce contractual payments to creditors before a repayment arrangement is agreed with creditors unless it is clearly in their best interests to do so – eg, if the client has insufficient available income as a result of the need to meet essential expenditure and/or to make payments to priority creditors (see Chapter 8). The date and amount of the last payment made are needed, especially for priority debts, to assess the urgency of any action.

- **Insurance cover.** Many people take out insurance (known as payment protection insurance) with a mortgage or credit agreement against, for instance, sickness, death and redundancy. Sometimes, such insurance is given by the creditor as part of the contract. Always check whether a particular debt is insured and that the insurance has been correctly sold, so this important way of minimising the debt is not overlooked (see p102).

The threats

The adviser needs to know what the creditor has already done to obtain repayment of the debt and what threat is posed to the client by the recovery action.

- **Warnings.** The first stage of recovery action is normally a reminder letter. The date of this should be recorded. Exact details of further action should be noted. For instance, regulated consumer credit agreements (see p65) may require a default notice to be served before any further action is taken. Other creditors must issue different warnings – eg, notice of proposed disconnection of fuel or notice of intention to seek possession of the client's home.
- **Court action.** If court action has begun, a claim form will have been issued. The date and type of claim should always be recorded. Courts work on a system of case numbers and it is essential to record these. Refer to the claim form to note whether solicitors are now acting for the creditor. If they are, the adviser will need to deal with them rather than the creditor until further notice. If a date for a hearing has been set, this should be noted. In many cases, a court will already have made an order and details of the judgment, including its date, the payment or action ordered, and the time or amounts required, should be recorded. See Chapters 10, 11 and 12 for further information, including what action should be taken if a judgment has been made.
- **Enforcement action.** After judgment, enforcement can mean bailiffs' action (see Chapter 14), a third-party debt (formerly garnishee) order (see p312), an attachment of earnings order (see p309), or a charging order (see p301). Note whether any of these have actually begun, with dates and full details.

Action to be taken

- **By the client.** Any action required of a client relating to a particular debt should be noted on the list – eg, 'get exact balance'. This section will normally be completed once the strategy has been decided.
- **By the adviser.** Record the action required on each debt. This can be crossed through when it has been carried out. If the case is a complex one and likely to involve a lot of work, the adviser should prepare a case plan, summarising the action to be taken, who is responsible for any action and the timetable.

3. **Listing and maximising income**

After identifying and dealing with any emergencies (ie, eviction, repossession, imprisonment, disconnection or bailiffs (see Chapters 8 and 14), the next stage is to list all possible income for the client (and her/his family where applicable).

Whose income to include

Creditors are likely to expect the income and debts of a couple (particularly if they are married or civil partners) to be dealt with together. There is no basis in law for this expectation (unless they are jointly and severally liable for the debt), and the client and adviser will be able to decide later how to present things. The overriding consideration must be the best interests of the client. As always, the final decision lies with the client.

A decision must eventually be made about whether to include the income of a partner or spouse or, rarely, someone else living as part of the same household as the client (although any contribution s/he makes to the household expenditure shown in the financial statement will have to be taken into account). This depends on several factors.

- If all the debts are in the name of one person only (or are in the joint names of the client and a previous partner) and s/he has little or no income or property against which action could be taken, the other person may be unwilling to contribute out of her/his income.
- If one person has a number of debts and a partner also has a number of debts, it might be more convenient to deal with both partners' debts in one set of strategies.
- If only one person has sought advice without the knowledge of her/his partner, the adviser should find out why and encourage both partners to be involved. The person who seeks advice may not know details of her/his partner's income or may not want her/his partner to know about the debts – eg, if s/he fears violence if her/his partner finds out about the debts. If there is a jointly owned property, it is important to stress the possibility of creditors applying for charging orders and, as the court will contact the client's partner, the likelihood of her/him finding out.
- The type of debt. Many partners will wish to pool their income and help with each other's debts, irrespective of legal liability, if they themselves could face dire consequences (eg, eviction) if they failed to do so or if, for example, all members of the household have benefited from the debt being incurred. At this stage it is, therefore, important to note the income of all household members (if possible) so that a decision can be made later as to which will be used to implement any strategy.

Types of income to include

- All benefits (remember to include child benefit and tax credits). Note, however, that clients may decide not to use disability benefits (such as disability living allowance and attendance allowance) to make payments to creditors. This view is supported by the revised *Determination of Means Guidelines*[1] and the Money Advice Liaison Group's (www.malg.org.uk) *Good Practice Awareness Guidelines* on dealing with clients with mental health problems.[2] It is based on the fact that disability benefits are designed to meet only the additional costs of disability, but they must still be included in any court forms. They should be included in the list of income even if they do not appear on the financial statement. Usually, however, they will be balanced by an identical item of expenditure, or mobility or care costs.

If it is decided to exclude disability benefits from the financial statement, do not forget to exclude also any additional expenditure incurred from those benefits. The fact that the client is in receipt of disability benefits should always be disclosed to creditors, as the fact that s/he is a disabled person is likely to be a relevant factor. The decision whether or not to include/use disability benefits is ultimately for the client, not the adviser.[3]

- Earnings – ie, net pay from full-time and part-time work.
- Self-employed earnings, net of estimated tax and national insurance contributions.
- Regular maintenance/child support payments received. Include what and who it is paid for.
- Investment income – eg, from savings (if any).
- Contributions from other household members – eg, non-dependent children living with the client.
- Occupational pensions.

If income has recently been unusually high or low, this should be noted and the basis on which it is assessed should be clear – eg, the average of five weeks' wage slips. Only include regular sources of income, as any offer of payment must be realistic and sustainable.

The Office of Fair Trading expects advisers to take reasonable steps and use appropriate means to verify the client's income (eg, wage slips) while recognising that what is 'reasonable' and 'appropriate' will depend on the nature of the service being provided – eg, advisers working at court duty desks or providing telephone/email advice will, in practice, be unable to do so.[4]

Note any impending changes/additions to income and circumstances, such as benefits recently claimed but not yet awarded, or if a member of the household is about to start or end paid employment.

Capital

The client may have capital or potential capital in the form of realisable property or other assets which it would be reasonable for her/him to use. The adviser should discuss this issue with the client and make a separate note of any such items. Unless the circumstances are exceptional, creditors are unlikely to accept that a client is unable to pay her/his debts if s/he has capital and may even refuse to accept nil or token offers of payment if they believe it would be reasonable to expect the client to dispose of an asset.

Maximising income

Follow the advice in Chapter 7 to maximise the client's income. Income from benefits that have been claimed but not yet paid should be listed only where this is in the best interests of the client. The adviser should explain that a claim is pending if it is included. Also check whether the client is eligible for a social tariff for her/his fuel and water (and, in the case of fuel, whether s/he would benefit from switching suppliers. Check whether the client is eligible for a grant from local or national charities or an energy efficiency grant.

4. Listing expenditure

The next stage of the debt advice process is to list everything on which the client is currently spending her/his income. The budget sheet used with the common financial statement is comprehensive and useful as a checklist to ensure nothing is missed. Most people spend money on different items in different periods of time, and it is important to standardise everything to a particular period – generally weekly or monthly. Predictable events such as Christmas, birthdays, holidays or school trips are not unreasonable items of expenditure, but they must be budgeted for. Expenditure should include the following.

Items of expenditure

Housing

Costs include:
- rent/mortgage repayments;
- other secured loan repayments (there may be several);
- council tax;
- water charges;
- ground rent;
- service charges;
- an amount for household repairs and maintenance based on a full year's expenditure if possible;
- household insurance for both buildings and contents;
- any insurance linked to a mortgage, if not already included in mortgage expenses;
- the housing costs of any boarders, which can simply be the amount they pay for their board and lodging.

Fuel

Fuel costs include charges for electricity, gas and other fuels. Take an annual cost and divide it into weekly or monthly figures.

If payments to fuel suppliers include an amount for items other than fuel (eg, payment for a cooker), these need to be deducted and only the fuel expenditure listed here.

Furniture and bedding

Costs should be separately itemised. This item may require research by the client or discussion with others with whom s/he lives.

Laundry

Costs should be averaged out over the previous couple of months.

Telephone, television and licence

These costs should be converted into weekly/monthly figures.

Other household items, toiletries and food

The adviser should ensure that the individual circumstances of the client dictate the amount allowed for these items. Other household items, toiletries and food include:

- housekeeping;
- cleaning materials;
- meals taken outside the home, such as school lunches or canteen meals;
- expenses incurred in children going to school or being given pocket money.

Clothing and shoes

These are often bought seasonally and so costs will have to be estimated annually and divided. It is important to include all small items in this category.

Health costs

Costs include:

- prescriptions;
- dentistry;
- optical charges.

These are often high and advisers should check entitlement to reduced or free treatment, or free prescriptions.

Religious and cultural activities

Costs include:

- donations that are an essential part of a person's membership of a religious community;
- classes for children in religious institutions (particularly mosques).

This is potentially a very sensitive area. If a person is committed to such payments, they should be protected to ensure that debt does not further exclude individuals or families from community life and support.

Transport

Costs include:

- public transport;
- the cost of owning a car or motorbike. In this case, the amount spent on tax, insurance, repairs, MOT and petrol should be included. If a car is essential (eg,

for travel to work), the cost of its hire purchase (but not any credit sale) agreement should be included with a note to explain why the item is essential.

Hire purchase

The hire purchase or conditional sale (see p114 and p116) costs of any items that are essential for the individual family to own, the loss of which would cause serious problems (eg, a washing machine) should be included.

Fines

Instalments payable on fines (see Chapter 13 for ways of reducing these) should be included.

Other costs

Other costs include:
- maintenance/child support payments;
- childminding costs;
- self-employment costs not taken into account when calculating the client's net income;
- spending for exceptional circumstances – eg, special diets or extra heating because of illness. Apparent 'luxury' items need to be explained. For example, a telephone (landline and/or mobile) is an absolute necessity for some people (eg, for health or safety reasons) and therefore counts as essential expenditure.

The Office of Fair Trading (OFT) expects reasonable steps to be taken to verify the client's expenditure, but says that estimates or industry recognised standard expenditure guidelines (eg, the common financial statement 'trigger figures' (see p52) or the Consumer Credit Counselling Service's budgeting guidelines) can be used as an indicator of the client's outgoings if more precise figures are unavailable, provided they are appropriate. Although standard figures should not be used if actual figures or accurate estimates are available, they are useful as a 'benchmark' against which to test the client's level of expenditure and as a tool with which to challenge creditors who claim that the client's expenditure is too high. The OFT warns that it is not appropriate to use industry figures/guidelines to manipulate a client's income and/or expenditure in order to meet the eligibility criteria for a particular debt remedy or to encourage clients to mislead creditors about their financial position.[5]

At this stage, the adviser can discuss overall income and spending with the client. Use Chapter 7 to increase income wherever possible, and discuss which, if any, items of spending could be reduced, either permanently or temporarily. See Chapter 5 for information on how to minimise debts. This should be done in a sensitive and non-judgemental way, and any items of high or unusual expenditure should be explained to creditors in a covering letter. Clients are not required, and should not be expected, to live on the breadline and are entitled to a reasonable

standard of living. However, although it is not part of the advise
to clients how to spend their money, clients should be warne
expenditure is likely to be challenged by creditors. If the adv
creditors are likely to challenge an item of expenditure and it cannot be justified, it is not judgemental to point this out to the client and explain that, as a consequence, creditors or the court are unlikely to accept the client's offer based on it.

Opening a new bank account

It may be necessary to advise the client to change the bank account into which wages are paid to prevent the bank (a non-priority creditor) taking control over her/his income. If a client finds it difficult to open another account (eg, because of her/his credit reference details), s/he may find the Money Advice Service's list of basic bank accounts useful.

First right of appropriation

If it is not possible to open a new bank account immediately, the client may have to consider exercising the 'first right of appropriation'. This gives an account holder the right to earmark funds paid into the account to be used for specific purposes. This process can also be useful as a temporary measure on overdrawn accounts. In order to exercise this right, the client should inform the bank in writing (before funds are paid in) specifically where they should be applied – ie, how much and to whom. The bank must honour such instructions, but it will continue to charge interest on the overdraft and may refuse to undertake further transactions.[6]

By this stage, it should be clear why the debts have arisen, and how the client's circumstances have led to financial difficulties. This information will be essential when negotiating with creditors.

5. **Dealing with priority debts**

The next stage of the debt advice process is to deal with those debts that are described as priorities (see Chapter 8). This will ensure that the threat of homelessness, the loss of goods or services or the threat of imprisonment is lifted. It is essential that arrangements for dealing with these debts are negotiated at this stage so that any extra payments for priority debts can be included in the expenditure details before they become part of a financial statement (see next stage).

However, a financial statement may be needed when negotiating priority debts, and this stage of the process can therefore overlap with Stage six.

Each possible strategy, along with its advantages or disadvantages, must be explained to the client. It may be necessary for the client to consult with a partner or other family member, and strategy information may need to be written down. Once agreed, the adviser implements the strategy by negotiation or court application and the client must then carry out her/his own agreed course of action – eg, start paying rent or set up direct debits. An orally agreed strategy must always be confirmed in writing with the creditor, and an acknowledgement confirming this must be requested. The client should be advised to start making any agreed payments immediately and not wait for confirmation from the creditor.

6. **Drawing up a financial statement**

A financial statement is a document, which can be presented to creditors and courts, that presents a sufficiently clear and complete picture of the individual (or family), her/his income and expenditure, details of her/his creditors and whether there is any surplus income with which to pay those creditors. It must be based on a true and accurate assessment of the client's circumstances, and any offers made must be realistic and sustainable. It can also be a useful budgeting tool for the client as, in many cases, it will be the first time s/he has reviewed her/his income and expenditure. Advisers must be aware of what a court may consider reasonable for the client to spend on a particular item if it is being asked to agree to the client paying the debt at a particular rate, especially, for example, in possession proceedings where the client's home is at risk (see Chapter 12).

A financial statement based on either the income and expenditure of a single person or the joint income and expenditure of the client and her/his partner should be fairly straightforward to prepare. A financial statement based on the income and expenditure of only a client who is a member of a couple needs more care. It is usually better to look at the household budget as a whole in order to get a clear picture of how things are arranged between the members of the household, rather than just splitting figures 50:50, or apportioning them on some other basis as a matter of course. The financial statement should always reflect what actually happens in practice – eg, if the client actually pays all the household bills from her/his own income and contributions from other members of the household, the financial statement should be drawn up on this basis. On the other hand, in many cases it is not possible to identify who actually pays what because all income is pooled. In such cases, expenditure should be apportioned proportionately to income.

A financial statement is a vital document because it summarises information in a standard form and allows the adviser to present this to the other side in a structured way. A carefully drawn up financial statement is probably the adviser's most important negotiating tool, as it forms the justification for any repayment proposal as well as for any request for non-payment.

Many agencies now use either the common financial statement (see below) or computer software which includes a financial statement as part of the package. For agencies that do not use either of these, it is useful to devise a standard format and to prepare blank statements. The statement must be clearly and neatly presented, and must include all relevant information. Advisers should use all the facts discovered in the previous stages in this chapter when preparing the statement. Provided it is stored electronically, it is easy to amend the statement as circumstances change.

The statement should include:

- the basis on which it was prepared. For example, 'This financial statement has been prepared on the basis of information submitted by:
Mr A Client
123 High Street
London SW1 1ZZ';
- the members of the household whose income and outgoings are being considered together;
- a breakdown of all the income for the individual or household;
- a list of expenditure under the headings used in Stage 4 plus expenditure to deal with priority debts. Certain types of expenditure may best be combined – eg, cigarettes are probably most persuasively included in 'other household items, toiletries and food' rather than on their own. No expenditure is shown for debts other than those that have been defined as priorities;
- comparison of income and expenditure. In some cases, the financial statement will show there is more income than expenditure. Such excess of income over expenditure should be calculated in the financial statement and described as available income. If expenditure already equals or exceeds income, the available income should be stated as none. In many cases, expenditure will exceed income. This may be because amounts have been included that are not actually spent, but are what should be spent if the client was able to do so. Whatever the reason, the adviser should be prepared to explain if challenged by creditors.

It is good practice to ask the client to check and sign the financial statement to confirm that it is accurate to the best of her/his knowledge.

A covering letter should explain any unusual items of expenditure and any special circumstances or needs – eg, whether any member of the household has a disability.

Common financial statement

The common financial statement is an initiative of the Money Advice Trust and British Bankers' Association. It was launched in November 2002 following a two-year pilot, and is incorporated into a number of software programmes and case management systems.

The common financial statement consists of:

- a budget form for completion by the adviser with the client. This contains a detailed checklist of income and expenditure as an *aide-memoire* for advisers and clients, so that income and expenditure items are less likely to be overlooked;
- a financial statement to which the summarised figures on the budget sheet are transferred and which is then sent to the creditor with the client's offer of payment (if any);
- **'trigger figures'**. This is a set of expenditure levels considered 'reasonable' for sample types of household. There are four trigger figure headings – telephone, travel, housekeeping and other – with a 'child multiplier' to take account of the actual number of children in a household;
- best practice checklists for advisers and creditors;
- a specific car expenditure allowance;
- a licence agreement covering the use of the trigger figures to ensure that the common financial statement is only used in accordance with the published forms and guidance.

Subscribers to *The Lending Code* and members of the Finance and Leasing Association have agreed that, if the common financial statement is used:[7]

- they will not query expenditure items falling within the trigger figure levels unless they have reasonable cause to believe that the client's income and expenditure figures may be incomplete or inaccurate (advisers are expected to provide an explanation if expenditure is above these levels);
- they will accept the common financial statement as the basis for negotiations with the client for a debt management plan and should then be prepared to accept offers made on a pro rata basis, as long as the guidelines have been followed;
- accounts transferred or sold to third parties for collection will remain subject to these principles.

The trigger figures are not 'budget' or 'standard' figures and, in many cases, the common financial statement will contain figures that exceed the trigger figure level. In such cases, the adviser should explain in the 'additional information' section on the common financial statement why the needs of the client are above the trigger figure level.

The budget forms and guidance documents can be viewed on the Money Advice Trust website at www.moneyadvicetrust.org. However, the trigger figures are now protected and not shown unless the adviser ticks a box accepting the licence terms. The Money Advice Trust then issues a 'licence key' enabling the adviser to view the trigger figures via the website. A licence number is also issued which appears on the common financial statement so that creditors know that the adviser is operating within the terms of the licence.

The advantage for advisers and agencies of using the common financial statement is that it is intended to be recognised and understood by all parties. It therefore provides a fast-track route to proposing repayment arrangements and means advisers can save time in securing acceptance of offers from creditors. However, feedback from advisers suggests that:

- not all collection departments are familiar with the common financial statement and reject financial statements prepared in line with the trigger figures;
- explanations for exceeding the trigger figures are not always accepted.

If a creditor who is signed up to the common financial statement does not accept the financial statement or offer, the adviser should draw the creditor's attention to its commitment and to the fact that the adviser has followed the guidelines. Many creditors will not accept offers which are lower than their minimum payment and may inform the adviser that the offer is 'declined' or 'not accepted'. This does not mean that the offer has been rejected and the client should continue making the payments as offered, as the creditor will accept them. When not accepting an offer a creditor may also say that 'further recovery action will follow'. Usually this does not refer to court action, but to passing the debt on to debt collectors or selling the debt. The client should continue to make payments until s/he is contacted by the collector or debt purchaser, who will ask for an(other) offer, but may well accept the one made previously to the original creditor.

The commitment to accepting offers does not extend to freezing or reducing interest or other charges. This will have to be requested and justified when using the common financial statement as with any other financial statement. A payment arrangement that is not accompanied by a concession on interest or charges is not usually in the client's best interests (see p247).[8] *The Lending Code* says that creditors should consider reducing or freezing interest/charges if the client shows that s/he is in financial difficulties and is unable to meet the contractual repayment terms. If clients are only able to make token payments, their debt should not increase as a result of interest/charges.

7. **Choosing a strategy for non-priority debts**

From the financial statement, the adviser knows whether or not there is any available income or capital and any likely changes in circumstances. This stage involves using these factors to decide a strategy for all non-priority debts (see Chapter 9). The starting point should be what the client wants, but s/he must be given the full range of available options so that s/he can make an informed choice of action. All advice given should be realistic and in the best interests of that particular client. If the chosen strategy is to offer payments to creditors, the client should be advised to start making any payments offered immediately and not wait for confirmation from the creditor. If the creditor does not confirm that interest/charges have been frozen, the creditor should be pressed for a decision. If the creditor refuses to freeze interest/charges, the adviser should ask for specific reasons and either urge the creditor to reconsider its decision or review the strategy with the client. If the adviser thinks the creditor is not treating the client 'sympathetically and positively' in line with a relevant code of practice, s/he should discuss with the client whether or not to complain.

By the end of this stage, the client will have made an informed choice of the strategy that is most likely to resolve the debt problem.

Clients with mental health problems

It has been estimated that people with mental health problems are three times more likely to experience financial difficulties than other people and research suggests that one in four people will experience a mental health problem during their life. This does not mean that taking on borrowing will necessarily lead to debt problems, but there is a need to strike a balance between allowing access to financial services on the one hand, and treating people fairly on the other. When people with mental health problems do experience financial difficulties, it may be because:
- benefits provide their only source of income;
- their income fluctuates, possibly because of irregular work;
- they lack financial management skills;
- of communication difficulties, including a reluctance to discuss their condition;
- of relationship breakdown.

There is a clear link between debt and mental health issues. Being in debt can negatively affect a person's mental health, while living with a mental health problem increases the likelihood of falling into debt. Financial problems can, in turn, trigger fresh mental health issues or exacerbate existing ones. Many conditions have no physical signs, and fluctuations in the severity and effects of an illness are common. In many cases, creditors will not even be aware that there is a mental health issue until payments have been missed and the collections process has reached an advanced stage. Even then, it may not be apparent whether a question of the client's capacity to conduct transactions arises (see p89). Money advisers and creditors are not trained to diagnose mental health problems and often do not understand the implications. However, once a creditor is aware of the issue, it should have processes and systems in place to take account of the situation, and should respond fairly and appropriately. There is also a need to bring health professionals involved in treating clients into the process to try and ensure a joined-up approach.

Existing codes of practice in the credit industry tend to set out an approach to dealing with clients with mental health problems, rather than guidance on dealing with the debts themselves. However, in September 2011, the Office of Fair Trading (OFT) issued its *Mental Capacity Guidance* (available at http://tinyurl.com/6d3v864) together with a leaflet, *Mental Capacity Guidance for Creditors: quick reference guide* (available at http://tinyurl.com/6zt24co). Both are available also at www.oft.gov.uk/about-the-oft/legal-powers/legal/cca/mental-capacity-guidance. The guidance points out that a person with mental health issues does not necessarily lack mental capacity to make financial decisions so that creditors need to employ practices and procedures designed to maximise the likelihood that s/he will be enabled to make that decision. In many respects, the guidance reflects the pre-contract requirements imposed by the European Commission Consumer Credit Directive on credit agreements made on or after 1 February 2011 (see p68). The guidance recognises that, if there is no face-to-face interaction between the creditor and the client, the creditor is less likely to be in a position to 'observe' any indicators that might suggest that the client may have some form of limited mental capacity. Similarly, the use of remote channels, such as the internet, limit the creditor's ability to assess the client's level of understanding of any explanations provided. However, other than recommending that local rate telephone contact details are provided so that clients can ask for further information and explanations, the guidance does not specifically address this issue or suggest any other steps that creditors could take.

Recognising that improvements need to be made in the way both money advisers and creditors deal with this issue, the Money Advice Liaison Group set up a working party consisting of representatives of stakeholders to propose good practice in this area. Its *Good Practice Awareness Guidelines* were first published in November 2007 and re-issued in 2010. The guidelines are endorsed by the latest versions of the OFT *Debt Management (and Credit Repair Services) Guidance* and *The Lending Code*. Its supporting guidance includes the following.

- Creditors should have procedures in place to ensure that people with mental health problems are treated fairly and appropriately.
- If creditors sell debts once a mental health issue has been advised, they should ensure that the debt purchaser agrees to comply with the guidelines and any relevant codes of practice.
- If a debtor has a serious mental health problem, creditors should only start court action or enforce debts through the courts as a last resort and only when it is appropriate and fair for lenders to do so.
- The OFT considers that, if a debtor lacks the capacity to make financial decisions, it would be appropriate to delay pursuing a debt until s/he regains capacity (or else to deal with someone appointed to deal with the client's financial affairs – eg, under a power of attorney).
- Creditors should consider writing off unsecured debts when mental health problems are long term and unlikely to improve, and if it is highly unlikely

that the client will be able to pay outstanding debts, or if the client lacked the capacity to make financial decisions at the time the agreement was made (even though the agreement is valid because the creditor was unaware of this (see p89).[9]

- Disability benefits (eg, disability living allowance and attendance allowance) should be recognised as being specifically awarded for meeting mobility and care needs. Creditors should not expect these benefits to be included as disposable income in any financial statement. The decision whether or not to do so is the client's.

Note: these guidelines only apply to the management of debt problems and not to the stage when the debt was incurred. However, the guidelines suggest that creditors may wish to 'flag' the files of clients who have notified relevant mental health information – ie, information that explains the effect of a given mental health problem on money management and debt issues. In addition, a client and someone holding a power of attorney for her/him might decide voluntarily to add information about her/his mental health problems to her/his credit reference file so that creditors who carry out a search as part of an application for credit are aware of the position. This can be done by a 'notice of correction'.[10]

Much of the guidelines deals with obtaining evidence to demonstrate the effect of a client's mental health on her/his ability to deal with her/his debt problems. The Money Advice Liaison Group has produced a debt and mental health evidence form to assist advisers in this process. The form (together with guidance notes, which should be read before using it) can be downloaded from the Money Advice Trust's website at www.moneyadvicetrust.org.

The form can be used to request information from health and/or social care professionals who may be in the best position to provide evidence about the client's capacity to deal with money and debt issues. Its use is not compulsory. There are, however, a number of issues.

- The form does not specifically address the question of whether or not the client was able to understand the contract s/he originally entered into. This is relevant to the enforceability of the contract and, therefore, the client's liability for the debt. This is a matter that advisers should consider first of all (see p89).
- The client is required to give her/his written consent to the form being used to obtain information about her/him and may, of course, lack the mental capacity to provide that consent, an issue which the guidance recognises but does not resolve.
- The form is long, but there does not appear to be any agreement that it will be completed without requiring payment of a fee. This is always an issue when requesting any report from a professional, particularly if the report required is long and detailed. The Money Advice Liaison Group is aware of this issue and is seeking to address it.

8. **Implementing the chosen strategies**

Although some emergency work may have been done to prevent catastrophes, it is only when all the information is available and decisions have been made that the major work of implementing a debt advice strategy will begin. Implementation is by means of communication with creditors by letter, telephone, email or sometimes in person or via the courts. The strategy to be implemented may require different letters to a number of creditors or groups of creditors. This requires communication skills, both written and oral, as well as representational skills.

The implementation of debt advice strategies involves more than mere individual casework. In addition, the effectiveness of strategies used should be continually monitored and work should be done to change policies that are found to be oppressive.

If a strategy is rejected for no apparent reason, the adviser should contact the creditor(s) and specifically request the reason(s) for rejection. Creditors reject clients' proposals mainly because of the following.

- Insufficient information has been provided. Provide additional information/ evidence to enable the creditor to understand the client's financial situation.
- The creditor has conflicting or different information. Clarify the real position and either explain or point out that the creditor is incorrect – eg, the client's circumstances may have changed since the creditor obtained its information.
- The chosen strategy is inappropriate – eg, it is based on incorrect information. Consider the alternatives.
- The creditor's collection policies do not permit the proposal to be accepted. Either try to persuade the creditor to treat the client's situation 'sympathetically and positively' on an individual basis or consider whether it might be in the client's best interests to comply.[11]
- The creditor's collection system cannot deal with the proposal – eg, the case cannot be transferred to the creditor's debt recovery section until there are at least three months' arrears. Deal with a more senior person who is authorised either to handle the proposal or to transfer the case to someone who can.
- The client has a poor payment record or history of broken payment arrangements. Point out that previous payment arrangements were unrealistic and that the current proposals are not only realistic but sustainable.
- Items on the financial statement are disputed. Either explain or justify, and use supporting evidence where available.
- The creditor wants more money. Ask the creditor where the additional money is to be found, given that other creditors are likely to object to having their payments reduced.
- The creditor is determined to take court action. Point out that parties are expected to act reasonably and to avoid unnecessary court proceedings. If the

matter goes to court, it is the judge not the creditor who will decide the rate of payment (see Chapter 11).

- The creditor will not deal with the agency. Point out that this is a breach of both the Office of Fair Trading's (OFT's) *Debt Management (and Credit Repair Services) Guidance* and the *Debt Collection Guidance* (see p30), and so could be the subject of a complaint.

Some reasons for rejection could amount to a breach of a code of practice. If appropriate, advisers should find out what trade association a creditor belongs to (see p26) and check with the relevant code of practice – eg, *The Lending Code*. Advisers should also familiarise themselves with the various OFT guidance documents discussed elsewhere in this *Handbook*. Complaints under a code or guidance can be made the subject of a complaint to the Financial Services Ombudsman (see p27) or the OFT. See Appendix 1 for details of these.

If a creditor rejects a client's proposal for repayment, the client should usually make the payments regardless. If the client decides not to pay, the adviser should be able to demonstrate there was a good reason for this and that it was in the client's best interests.

The remainder of this *Handbook* explains the practical knowledge and skills necessary to put into effect the strategy agreed by the client and debt adviser.

Notes

3. Listing and maximising income
1 HMCTS, *Determination of Means Guidelines*, April 2006, para 5.4.2
2 MALG, *Good Practice Awareness Guidelines: for consumers with mental health problems and debt*, November 2009, guideline 11
3 See D Shields and M van Rooyen, 'In or Out?', *Adviser* 93
4 para 3.26(a) DMG

4. Listing expenditure
5 para 2.26(a), (d) and (i) DMG
6 See J Wilson, 'First Right of Appropriation', *Adviser* 98

6. Drawing up a financial statement
7 Members of the Finance and Leasing Association have not agreed to adopt the common financial statement in the case of secured loans or loans that relates to the purchase of an asset, such as a vehicle.
8 For more information (including details of the current trigger figures), see the elearning and library section at www.wiseadviser.org and see articles in *Adviser* 103.

7. Choosing a strategy for non-priority debts

9   OFT, *Irresponsible Lending Guidance*, commentary to para 7.13

10 A recommended form of words agreed by the credit reference agencies is at para 4.16 of the guidelines.

8. Implementing the chosen strategies

11 The phrase 'sympathetically and positively' is much used but never defined. In its *Irresponsible Lending Guidance* , the OFT says that creditors should treat clients in default or with arrears difficulties with 'understanding and due consideration' and should treat such clients 'with forbearance'.

Chapter 4

. . . .

The Consumer Credit Act

This chapter covers:
1. Introduction (below)
2. Licensing traders (below)
3. Regulated agreements (p65)

1. Introduction

Most clients dealt with by a debt adviser are likely to have at least some credit debts. Many clients will only have credit debts and the majority (if not all) of these are likely to be 'regulated' by the Consumer Credit Act. It is, therefore, essential for a debt adviser to be familiar with this legislation.

The Consumer Credit Act 1974 is a wide-ranging piece of legislation that regulates almost all aspects of personal credit. It provides definitions of every type of credit agreement and is framed to cover every imaginable type of agreement.

Substantial reforms of the Act have been made by the Consumer Credit Act 2006 (see p66) and as a result of the European Commission Consumer Credit Directive 2008. However, many of these changes are not retrospective and do not affect agreements entered into or judgments made before the relevant provisions were implemented.

The Consumer Credit Act provides protection by:
- licensing traders (see below);
- regulating agreements (see p65);
- providing sanctions for non-compliance with its provisions (see p71–74).

2. Licensing traders

The Consumer Credit Act requires most businesses that offer credit or lend money to consumers to be licensed by the Office of Fair Trading (OFT). This includes if credit is arranged to finance the purchase of goods or services. Debt collectors, debt advisers and businesses that offer goods for hire or to lease may also need a licence. Since 1 October 2008, businesses that administer agreements for creditors or debt purchasers (known as 'debt administration'), or help clients locate and correct records about their financial standing (known as 'credit information services') have also been required to have a licence.

A licence must cover all categories of credit activities that the business carries out. Trading without a licence is a criminal offence and can result in a fine and/or imprisonment.

All professions or trades are 'businesses' for licensing purposes, even if they are non-profit making, make no charge for their services, or the credit-related activities only comprise part of the overall activities of the business. However, businesses that only 'occasionally' carry out a licensed activity are not treated as carrying out that type of business and do not require a licence. What is 'occasional' depends on the facts of the case.

The OFT keeps a register of applications for, and holders of, consumer credit licences. The register can be found at www2.crw.gov.uk/pr. This provides basic information on licence holders, including:
- the start date of a licence;
- the type of activities covered;
- the authorised trading names and main business address of the licence holder; *and*
- details of any undertakings given, requirements imposed and any subsequent financial penalties.

Note: unlicensed creditors cannot pursue their claims for debt through the county court without first applying to the OFT for an order to validate the agreement[1] but, in practice, this rarely happens. See p97 for more information.

The OFT has published various guidance, referred to elsewhere in this *Handbook*, particularly on debt management (see p2), irresponsible and second charge lending (see p63), mental capacity (see p89) and debt collection (see p30), which identify activities that the OFT regards as unacceptable (see p63). Advisers should advise clients to complain to the creditor/debt collector about any examples of bad practice, refer them to the Financial Ombudsman Service where appropriate, and report them to the OFT.

However, the OFT is restricted in the information it can reveal about its ongoing licensing work. This, coupled with the fact that it cannot act on behalf of individual clients, can lead to frustration on the part of advisers and doubt as to whether passing information about a business to the OFT is worthwhile. Without information on which to build up a file of its business practices, however, the OFT is unable to act against the business.

For more information on licensing, see *Consumer Credit Licensing: general guidance for licensees and applicants on fitness and requirements* (OFT969), which can be found at www.oft.gov.uk/publications.

Credit intermediaries

From 30 April 2010, businesses which operate as 'credit intermediaries' do not need to be licensed. A 'credit intermediary' is someone who carries out the following activities for clients in return for a fee (including commission from a creditor) and who is not a creditor or the creditor's agent:

- recommending or making available prospective credit agreements to clients. Just providing information (eg, displaying leaflets) does not count;
- helping borrowers by undertaking preparatory work connected with a prospective agreement; *or*
- entering into credit agreements on behalf of creditors.

Most credit brokers (who do have to be licensed) are also credit intermediaries, but a credit intermediary is not necessarily a credit broker. For example, a business that only provides advice to clients or assists them fill in forms and charges a fee is not a credit broker. However, a business which introduce clients to creditors or other credit brokers is a credit broker.

Credit intermediaries are required to disclose to the client:

- the extent to which they operate independently, particularly whether they work exclusively with one or more creditors; *and*
- the amount of any fee payable by the client, what it covers and how and when it is payable. The client must agree to pay this fee in writing.

The amount of any fee must also be disclosed to the creditor but, unlike for credit brokers, there is no requirement for intermediaries to disclose to clients any fees or commission they have or will receive from creditors.[2]

What the Office of Fair Trading considers before issuing a licence

When considering whether or not to issue a licence, the OFT can take into account any circumstances that appear relevant, including evidence of:[3]

- any past misconduct, such as criminal offences, particularly involving fraud, violence or dishonesty;
- the skills, knowledge and any relevant experience the people operating the business have in relation to the licensed activity;
- the practices and procedures the business proposes to operate; *and*
- evidence of business practices that appear to be deceitful or oppressive, or otherwise unfair or improper. These do not have to be unlawful. The OFT considers, in particular, any breaches of OFT guidance. This could include evidence of irresponsible lending (see p63).

The OFT takes a targeted and 'risk-based' approach to consumer credit licensing and has identified a number of debt-related activities that it considers to be of higher potential risk to clients. These include:

- businesses offering debt adjusting or debt counselling on a commercial basis;
- credit repair (see p11); *and*
- debt collecting.

Businesses that apply for a licence to undertake any of these high-risk activities are required to provide a 'credit competence plan'. They are also likely to have an on-site inspection by the OFT and/or local authority trading standards officer.

The OFT has also identified the following types of credit activity as being of higher potential risk and consequently requiring greater levels of scrutiny:

- secured lending, brokering and debt administration to sub-prime clients;
- lending and brokering which takes place in the home; *and*
- credit reference agencies.

Businesses intending to carry out any of these activities are required to give further details to the OFT on a 'credit risk profile'. The OFT uses this information to consider the business's competence. The business may also have an on-site inspection by the OFT and/or local authority trading standards officer.

The OFT checks the information in the application with a number of different sources, including local authority trading standards officers. The OFT assesses fitness and competence in relation to each individual activity, and licences are only issued to cover those activities for which this assessment has proved satisfactory.

If the OFT receives evidence that raises sufficient doubts about an applicant's fitness to hold a consumer credit licence, the application is passed to an independent OFT adjudicator. The adjudicator decides whether to issue a notice informing the applicant that the OFT is considering refusing the licence application.

If there are insufficient grounds to consider refusing the application, but the OFT is nevertheless dissatisfied with certain aspects of the business's conduct, it may require the business to do (or stop doing) something to remedy the matter. Over the past few years, the OFT has imposed requirements on a number of creditors about various matters, including the collection of statute-barred debts (see p275) and the use of statutory demands (see p444). The OFT has powers to impose a financial penalty of up to £50,000 if the business subsequently fails to comply with the requirement.

Responsible lending

'**Irresponsible lending**' is now a specific business practice that the OFT can consider when deciding whether or not a business is fit to hold a consumer credit licence. From 1 February 2011, a creditor or broker must assess the clients' credit worthiness before entering into a contract (except agreements secured on land or pawnbroking agreements) – see p68.

In July 2009, the OFT published guidance to lenders and brokers on agreements secured on land ('second-charge secured lending'). The basic principles are that there should be:

- transparency in all dealings with borrowers with early disclosure of all key contract terms (including interest rates and charges);
- fair and clear contract terms and conditions, written in plain and intelligible language which can easily be understood by borrowers;
- no high-pressure selling, with the borrower being given sufficient time to reflect on the proposed transaction and encouraged to obtain independent advice before entering into the transaction;
- no irresponsible lending, with all decisions being subject to a proper assessment of the borrower's ability to repay the loan without undue hardship and without resorting to the security, taking account of all relevant circumstances, including any reasonably foreseeable future circumstances;
- forbearance towards borrowers who are experiencing financial difficulties, with proportionate action on default and arrears with all options being considered;
- possession only to be used as a last resort (unless in the best interests of the borrower).

In March 2010, the OFT published *Irresponsible Lending: OFT guidance for creditors* (OFT1107) on what it considers may constitute irresponsible lending practices. The guidance was updated in February 2011 in readiness for the implementation of the European Commission Consumer Credit Directive 2008. It covers each stage of the lending process from the pre-contract stage of advertising credit to handling default and arrears under agreements. In general, creditors should:

- not use misleading or oppressive behaviour when advertising, selling or seeking to enforce a credit agreement;
- make a reasonable assessment of whether a borrower can afford to meet the repayments in a sustainable manner without incurring further financial difficulties and/or experiencing adverse consequences;
- explain the key features of the agreement to enable the borrower to make an informed choice;
- monitor the borrower's repayment record during the course of the agreement, offering assistance if s/he appears to be experiencing difficulty;
- treat borrowers fairly and with forbearance if they are experiencing difficulties.

More specifically, there should be:

- transparency in dealings between creditors and borrowers;
- disclosure of key contract terms and conditions, which should be fair, clear and intelligible;
- fair treatment of borrowers;

- forbearance and consideration towards borrowers experiencing financial difficulty. Creditors should suspend active recovery for a reasonable period where an adviser is assisting a client to draw up a repayment plan and allow for alternative, affordable payment amounts if a reasonable proposal is made, and not unreasonably require that all arrears are paid either in a single payment or in unduly large amounts and/or within an unreasonably short period;
- proportionality in dealings with creditors and borrowers, with proper consideration being given to available options for dealing with default and arrears, and repossession of a borrower's home only being used as a last resort.

After a licence is issued

New licences last indefinitely. During the life of the licence, as well as asking for information from licence holders from time to time, the OFT receives information from other sources including:
- local authority trading standards officers;
- the Financial Services Authority;
- consumer bodies, such as Citizens Advice and AdviceUK;
- individual advisers;
- consumers;
- complaints data from the Financial Ombudsman Service.

Information from these and other relevant sources can raise doubts about a business's activities and trigger fitness investigations. If this occurs, the OFT may consider suspending, limiting or revoking the licence, or imposing a requirement. If concerns about conduct are serious, or there are concerns about the integrity of the business, the OFT may conclude it is not fit to hold a licence and will take action to revoke it. However, if the OFT considers it sufficient to ensure the business changes its conduct and does not have concerns about its integrity, it may take a different approach in the first instance and use one of the other enforcement tools.

3. **Regulated agreements**

Most credit agreements that a debt adviser comes across will be regulated by the Consumer Credit Act 1974, although there are some important exceptions (see p66). A regulated agreement is an agreement which:
- provides credit of £25,000 (if made before 6 April 2008) or £15,000 (if made before 1 May 1998) or less; *and*
- is made by the creditor with one or more individuals or clients.

The credit must be given in the course of the creditor's business. If a client borrows money for a business, provided s/he is not a limited company, this will still be classed as lending to an individual. However, if the agreement was made on or after 6 April 2007, an 'individual' does not include partnerships comprising more than three people and may also be covered by the 'business-related' exemption (see p67).

From 6 April 2008, the Consumer Credit Act 2006 removed the financial limit for regulation of consumer credit and consumer hire agreements. From this date, all such agreements are regulated by the Consumer Credit Act 1974 (unless specifically exempted), regardless of the amount of credit provided or the hire payments. However, if the borrowing or hire is wholly or predominantly taken out for the purposes of the borrower's or hirer's business, the £25,000 limit remains. Such agreements are not regulated if the amount of credit provided or the hire payments exceed this figure (see p67).

Unregulated agreements

Agreements that are not regulated include:
- agreements providing credit of more than £25,000 (if made before 6 April 2008) or £15,000 (if made before 1 May 1998);
- 'small agreements' not exceeding £50 – eg, vouchers;
- 'non-commercial agreements' not made in the course of business – eg, agreements between friends;
- some low-interest rate credit, including loans to employees from their employers;
- agreements involving goods or services repayable in no more than four instalments in 12 months – ie, normal trade credit, for example payable in 30 days. For agreements made on or after 1 February 2011, the credit must be provided without interest or other charges, otherwise the agreement will be regulated;
- mortgages taken out to buy land or property;
- secured loans for home improvements where the mortgage for the purchase of the property was provided by the same lender;
- accounts involving goods or services repayable in one instalment – eg, charge cards. For agreements made on or after 1 February 2011, there must either be no, or only 'insignificant', charges payable for the credit (see p70). 'Insignificant' is not defined;
- regulated mortgage contracts (see p147) made on or after 31 October 2004, even if the amount borrowed is within the consumer credit limit;
- agreements made on or after 6 April 2008 to a 'high net worth' individual (see p67);
- agreements made on or after 6 April 2008 for more than £25,000 entered into 'wholly or predominantly' for the purpose of the client's business (see p67).

High net worth borrowers

The 'high net worth' exemption allows individuals to opt out of Consumer Credit Act regulation. It applies if the individual's net income is at least £150,000 a year or her/his assets (excluding her/his home and pension) are at least £500,000. Since 1 February 2011, the exemption only applies to agreements that provide credit of more than £60,260 and to agreements secured on land.

The individual must sign a declaration of high net worth, supported by a statement from an accountant. The rationale for this exemption (asked for by the credit industry) is that such people have the resources to seek their own financial and legal advice and, if such exemption were not available, might seek finance involving less formality from outside the UK.

Loans for business purposes

The business-related exemption applies if someone has been granted credit of more than £25,000 'wholly or predominantly' for the purpose of her/his business. If the agreement contains a declaration by the borrower that it has been entered into wholly or predominantly for business purposes, it will be presumed that this is the case. However, if the agreement either contains no declaration or contains a declaration but the creditor either knows or reasonably suspects it is not true, the presumption will not apply and the issue will depend on the circumstances of the case.

Note: an agreement granting credit of £25,000 or less *wholly* for the purpose of the client's business is not a regulated agreement if it is a 'green deal' plan' for energy efficiency improvements to her/his property under the Energy Act 2011.

The form of the agreement

The form of a regulated agreement is very important. If an agreement is not made in accordance with the Consumer Credit Act, it can only be enforced with special permission of the courts. In the case of some agreements made before 6 April 2007, it will be irredeemably (ie, completely) unenforceable.

Pre-contract information

If the agreement was 'executed' (ie, signed by both parties) on or after 31 May 2005 (but see p68 if the agreement was made on or after 1 February 2011), the creditor is required to provide specified information to the client before the agreement is made,[4] except in the case of:
- secured loans (see p125); *and*
- 'distance contracts' (see p76).

The specified information includes:
- the appropriate consumer credit heading describing the nature of the agreement;
- the names and addresses of the creditor and the client(s);

- financial and related information, such as details of any goods or services, the amount of credit, total charge for credit, rate of interest and repayment details;
- statements of consumer protection rights and remedies.

There is no prescribed format, except that the information must be headed 'pre-contract information', handed to the client before the agreement is made and must be capable of being taken away to be studied. As there is no prescribed period for providing the information, the creditor can give the pre-contract information document to the client and then immediately invite her/him to sign the actual agreement.

If the creditor does not comply with the pre-contract information requirements, the agreement will be improperly executed and the creditor will need the permission of the court to enforce it.

Agreements made on or after 1 February 2011

Following the implementation of the European Commission Consumer Credit Directive 2008, additional rules on pre-contract information apply to all regulated agreements made on or after 1 February 2011,[5] except those:

- secured on land;
- for credit of more than £60,260;
- for business lending.

The provisions outlined above continue to apply in the case of these agreements.

The information must be provided 'in good time' before the agreement is made, except if it has already been provided by a credit intermediary (see p62). It is the creditor's responsibility to ensure that this has been done. The information must be disclosed using a standard European consumer credit information form,[6] which must be in writing and in a format which the client can take away to consider.

The creditor (or credit intermediary) must also inform the client:

- that it will tell her/him if a decision not to proceed is based on credit reference agency information;[7]
- of her/his right to request a copy of the draft agreement;[8]
- of the period of time for which the pre-contract information remains valid (where applicable).

Separate rules apply to:

- certain telephone contracts;
- non-telephone distance contracts;
- excluded pawnbroking agreements (see p121);
- overdraft agreements.

If the creditor does not disclose the required information or it does not use the proper form and format, the agreement is improperly executed and is enforceable only with the permission of the court.

These provisions are very complex and prescriptive. For more information, see the Department for Business, Innovation and Skills website (www.bis.gov.uk/policies/consumer-issues/consumer-credit-and-debt/consumer-credit-regulation), which include links to all the regulations implementing the Directive and guidance on the regulations.

An adequate explanation

If the agreement was made on or after 1 February 2011, the creditor must provide the client with an explanation and advice.[9] This applies to all regulated agreements except:

- those secured on land;
- pawnbroking agreements (but see p121);
- overdrafts;
- those for credit of more than £60,260.

Before making the agreement, the creditor (or the credit intermediary) must provide the client with an 'adequate explanation' of:

- any features that may make the agreement unsuitable for particular types of use;
- how much the client will have to pay, periodically and in total;
- any features that could have a significant adverse effect in ways the client is unlikely to foresee;
- the main consequences if the client fails to make the payments due under the agreement;
- the effects of withdrawing from the agreement, and when and how to exercise this right.

The client must be advised to consider the pre-contract information and given the opportunity to ask questions. S/he must be advised on how to ask for further information and explanations.

Explanations can be verbal, in writing, or both, and must be given in sufficient detail to enable the client to assess whether the agreement is suitable for her/his needs and financial situation. For further information, see section 3 of the OFT's *Irresponsible Lending Guidance* at www.oft.gov.uk/about-the-oft/legal-powers/legal/cca/irresponsible.

There are no sanctions for non-compliance in the legislation, but it could be the basis for an unfair relationship allegation (see p98) or lead to a complaint to the Financial Ombudsman Service (FOS – see p268).

Assessment of creditworthiness

If the agreement was made on or after 1 February 2011, the creditor must assess the client's creditworthiness – ie, her/his likely ability to repay the credit.[10] This applies to all regulated agreements except:

- those secured on land;
- pawnbroking agreements.

The creditor must carry out an assessment before:

- making a regulated agreement;
- significantly increasing the amount of credit under the agreement; *or*
- significantly increasing the credit limit under the agreement.

'Significantly' is not defined.

The legislation does not specify how creditors should assess a client's creditworthiness, what information they need or where that information should come from, except to say that the assessment must be based on sufficient information obtained from the client, where appropriate, and, where necessary, a credit reference agency. The Office of Fair Trading has provided detailed guidance in section 4 of its *Irresponsible Lending Guidance*, available at www.oft.gov.uk/about-the-oft/legal-powers/legal/cca/irresponsible. See also p63.

There are no sanctions for non-compliance in the legislation, but it could be the basis for an unfair relationship allegation (see p98) or lead to a complaint to the FOS (see p268).

A copy of the draft agreement

If the agreement was made on or after 1 February 2011, the creditor must provide the client with a copy of the prospective agreement on request and 'without delay'.[11] This applies to all regulated agreements except:

- those secured on land;
- pawnbroking agreements;
- those for credit of more than £60,260;
- those for business lending.

The creditor does not have to comply with the request if it has decided not to proceed with the transaction. If the creditor does not comply, it breaches its statutory duty. However, there is no action the client could take to remedy this.

Once the agreement becomes an executed agreement, the creditor must provide a copy of this to the client 'without delay',[12] except if the client has been provided with a copy of the draft agreement and the executed agreement is identical. If this is the case, the creditor must inform the client that:

- the agreement has been executed and the date of the agreement; *and*
- s/he can request a copy before the end of the 14-day withdrawal period (see p77).

In the case of authorised overdraft agreements, instead of a copy of the executed agreement, the client must be given a document containing the terms of the agreement.[13] With certain exceptions, this must be done before or at the time the agreement is made.

If the creditor does not comply, the agreement will be improperly executed and enforceable only with the permission of the court.

Information that must be in the agreement

All regulated agreements (except current account overdrafts before 1 February 2011)[14] must be made in writing, must be signed by all the borrowers and must contain the following information. The agreement should also contain further terms, depending on when it was made (see pp72–74).

- The amount of credit (or the credit limit). Some creditors confuse the 'amount of credit' with the total amount of the loan. The **'amount of credit'** is a technical term and is the amount borrowed less all the 'charges for credit'. An item forming part of the charges must not be treated as credit even if time is allowed for its payment. Some creditors get this wrong, with serious consequences. For example, in the case *London North Securities v Meadows*, the clients borrowed £5,750 under a secured loan, including £750 for a premium for payment protection insurance, described in the agreement as 'optional'.[15] The county court judge found that the insurance was not optional but required by the lender and so was a 'charges for credit' item. The amount of credit was, therefore, £5,000 and the agreement was completely unenforceable. The Court of Appeal upheld this decision, with the result that the lender was unable to enforce payment of the outstanding balance of the agreement and had to remove its legal charge from the Land Registry.[16] Arguably, the agreement does not need to use the phrase 'amount of credit', but this may not be the case where the agreement is ambiguous about which figure is the amount of credit.[17]
- The rate of interest and whether it can vary (if the amount of interest is not fixed at the start).
- A notice of cancellation in the prescribed form (if the agreement is cancellable).
- A term stating how the client is to discharge her/his obligations to make repayments – ie, details of payments, how many, how much and how often. Many secured loans provide for the client to pay the creditor's legal fees in connection with drawing up documents and provide for payment of these to be made immediately or deferred to the end of the loan period. Interest usually accrues on this amount and is compounded monthly, so by the end of the loan a substantial sum is likely to be due. Many agreements do not make the client's obligations in relation to such deferred fees clear and, as a result, the whole agreement could be irredeemably unenforceable.[18]

The terms listed on p71 are 'prescribed terms' in the Consumer Credit Act. If the agreement was made before 6 April 2007 and any prescribed term is missing or stated incorrectly, or if the agreement has not been signed by all the borrowers, it is irredeemably unenforceable. So too is any security – eg, on a secured loan.[19]

The prescribed terms must be 'contained in' the document signed by the client. Whether 'application form' agreements (eg, for credit cards and store cards, which the client signs and returns and which then becomes the agreement[20]) comply with these requirements has recently been considered by the High Court.[21] It is not sufficient for a piece of paper signed by the client merely to cross refer to the prescribed terms without a copy of those terms being supplied to the client at the point when s/he signs. However, a document can comprise more than one piece of paper, and whether several pieces of paper together constitute a single document involves looking at practical considerations rather than their form. In this particular case, the document signed by the client referred to 'the terms and conditions attached', which were fixed by a staple and were held to be one document.

Agreements made before 31 May 2005

In addition to the prescribed information described on p71, agreements made before 31 May 2005 must also contain (but see also p104):

- the appropriate consumer credit heading that describes the nature of the agreement;
- the names and addresses of the client and creditor, and a signature box;
- details of any security to be provided as part of the agreement;
- a brief description of any goods supplied under the agreement;
- the cash price(s) of any goods or services;
- the amount of any deposit or part-payment;
- the total charge for credit if the amount of interest is fixed at the start. This includes not only the total interest (if any), but also other charges payable under the transaction – eg, brokers' fees and compulsory payment protection insurance. If it is a condition of the loan that any arrears owed under a different credit agreement are paid from the advance, payment of those arrears may be a 'charge for credit' item if the client was unaware that the lender was going to pay them. The arrears, however, are not a 'charge for credit' item if payment of them was part of the purpose of the loan in question, or the client agreed that they could be paid out of the loan;
- the annual percentage rate (APR);
- a statement about the rights of the client – eg, termination rights and paying off the account early.

If one of the above non-prescribed terms is missing or incorrectly stated, the creditor can only enforce the agreement with the permission of the court.

Note: if the agreement was provided to the client before 31 May 2005, but was not executed before this date and became an executed agreement no later than 31 August 2005, it is covered by the rules on pre-31 May 2005 agreements. However, the creditor must have been required to provide pre-contract information to the client in the new format before the agreement was made. An agreement is 'executed' or 'made' when the last person who must sign it has done so.

Agreements made on or after 31 May 2005

In addition to the prescribed information described on p71, agreements made on or after 31 May 2005 must also contain the 'non-prescribed terms' listed below and should also set them out in a particular format in the following order:[22]

- the appropriate consumer credit heading that describes the nature of the agreement;
- the names and addresses of the creditor and the client(s);
- key financial information:
  - amount of credit or credit limit;
  - total amount payable (but only in the case of fixed interest rate agreements);
  - repayment details;
  - the APR;
- other financial information:
  - description of any goods or services;
  - cash price(s) of any goods or services;
  - advance payments (where appropriate);
  - total charge for credit;
  - details of interest rates and whether these are fixed or variable;
- key information:
  - description of any security provided;
  - list of default charges;
  - where applicable, a statement that the agreement is not cancellable;
  - examples of the amount required to settle the agreement early;
  - statements of consumer protection and remedies;
- a signature box;
- a cancellation box (where appropriate);
- if the client is purchasing optional insurance on credit under the agreement, a form of consent to taking out the insurance(s) to be signed by the client(s).

If any of the above provisions is not complied with, the creditor can only enforce the agreement with the permission of the court (but see p104).

Note: if the agreement was provided to the client before 31 May 2005, but was not executed before this date and became an executed agreement no later than 31 August 2005, it is covered by the rules on pre-31 May 2005 agreements. However, the creditor must have been required to provide pre-contract information to the client in the new format before the agreement was made. An agreement is 'executed' or 'made' when the last person who must sign it has done so.

Agreements made on or after 1 February 2011

The Consumer Credit (Agreements) Regulations 2010 apply to all regulated agreements (except for unauthorised overdrafts) made on or after 1 February 2011 except those:

- secured on land;
- for credit exceeding £60,260; *and*
- for business lending.

The rules outlined on p73 continue to apply in the case of these agreements, unless the creditor 'opts in' to the 2010 Regulations by providing pre-contract information as outlined on p68. Creditors are likely to take advantage of these provisions so that they can use the same documentation for all their regulated agreements.

Under these regulations, which are less prescriptive that the provisions outlined on p73, agreements must contain specified information, but this does not need to be provided in any particular order or sub-divided under particular headings. Information must be provided in a clear and concise manner, and be easily legible and readily distinguishable from the background. There is no box in which the client signs the agreement: the client now signs in the space provided.

If the creditor or broker does not comply, the agreement is improperly executed and enforceable only with the permission of the court.

Agreements made on or after 6 April 2007

From 6 April 2007, the court has discretion to allow agreements made on or after this date to be enforced even if:

- there is no agreement signed by all the borrowers; *or*
- the agreement does not contain a prescribed term or it is incorrect; *or*
- in the case of a cancellable agreement, the creditor has failed to comply with the provisions on cancellation notices.

Note: these changes are not retrospective, therefore improperly executed agreements made before 6 April 2007 can still be irredeemably unenforceable.[23]

The court must decide whether or not to allow the agreement to be enforced and, if so, on what terms. The court can refuse to make an enforcement order only if it considers it 'just' to do so, having regard to:

- prejudice caused to any person;
- the degree of culpability;
- the court's powers in relation to the agreement – ie, to reduce or discharge any sum payable by the client and/or to make a time order.

The court could allow the agreement to be enforced unconditionally (eg, if the client has 'suffered no prejudice' as a result of the creditor's failure to comply with the Act), allow it to be enforced subject to conditions, or refuse to allow it to be enforced at all – eg, if, had the agreement not been improperly executed, the client would not have entered into it.

Electronic communication

Since 31 December 2004 electronic communications can be used to conclude regulated agreements, and send notices and other documents. Documents may only be transmitted electronically if the client has agreed to this. Creditors can also make provision for clients to sign agreements electronically.[24]

The right to cancel: cooling-off period

A regulated credit agreement made before 1 February 2011 or made on or after that date which is for credit exceeding £60,260 can be cancelled if it was signed somewhere other than the trade premises of the creditor or supplier of goods and following face-to-face negotiations with the creditor or supplier (including their agents or employees). Telephone calls do not count as face-to-face. If the agreement is for credit not exceeding £60,260 and was made on or after 1 February 2011, see p77. **Note:** there is no right to cancel an agreement secured on land.

A copy of the agreement must be given to the client immediately s/he signs it (whether or not it is cancellable). Unless the creditor has already signed it or signs at the same time, another copy must be sent within seven days,[25] with a notice of cancellation rights, where applicable. Otherwise, a separate notice of cancellation rights must be sent within seven days of the agreement being signed. The cooling-off period begins with the receipt of this second copy of the document/separate notice of cancellation rights, which will also have a notice of cancellation to be used if desired.

Any such agreement must be cancelled within five days.

Cancellation must be in writing and, if posted, is effective immediately even if it is not received by the creditor. The client should, therefore, obtain proof of posting or send it by 'recorded signed for'. Cancellation is probably best made initially by telephone, but must be followed up immediately by a letter, fax or email. A letter can simply state: 'I hereby give you notice that I wish to cancel the regulated credit agreement signed by me on… [date]'.[26] It should be sent to the company providing the credit, with a copy to the company supplying the goods, if appropriate. Any goods already supplied under the agreement should be returned or await collection by the trader. Any deposit or advance payment for the goods must be refunded to the client.

The client can also withdraw from an agreement if, when s/he signs, it has not yet been signed by the creditor and it is not signed by the creditor on the same occasion so that it becomes an executed agreement. The client must communicate to the creditor that s/he wishes to withdraw before the creditor signs it. Withdrawal has the same effect as a cancellation.[27] Withdrawal can be verbal (if time is short) or (preferably) in writing, including email. If the agreement was made on or after 1 February 2011, there are further rights to withdraw (see p77).

Distance contracts

In the case of unsecured credit agreements made on or after 1 October 2004 without face-to-face contact between the client and the creditor/intermediary, such as online, by post or on the telephone, the creditor must supply certain information to the client about her/his cancellation rights in good time before the agreement is entered into.

The creditor must also supply the same prescribed information to the client in writing in good time before the agreement is entered into. The client can waive this requirement in certain circumstances, but the prescribed information must then be supplied immediately after the agreement is made.

The client can cancel the distance agreement within 14 days:
* from the day after the agreement was made, if the written information referred to above was supplied on or before the date the agreement was made; or
* from the day after all the written information referred to above was supplied to the client, if this was not supplied before the agreement was made.

The client may give notice of cancellation:
* verbally, if the creditor has informed the client that notice may be given orally; or
* by leaving the notice at the creditor's address. Notice is given on the day it is left; or
* by posting, faxing or emailing the creditor. Notice is given on the day it is posted or sent; or
* by sending it to an internet address or website which the creditor has indicated can be used to give notice of cancellation. Notice is given when it is sent.

Secondary contracts

If the credit agreement is a debtor-creditor-supplier agreement, cancellation of the credit agreement automatically cancels any secondary contract to be financed by the credit agreement, except if the secondary contract has been carried out at the client's express request before s/he gave notice of cancellation – eg, if the client asked the supplier to fit double glazing, which was being financed by the credit agreement, and then gave notice of cancellation after the double glazing had been fitted.

Following cancellation, the supplier must refund any sum paid by the client in relation to the contract, less a proportionate charge for any services already supplied within 30 days. No charge may be made if the supplier began to carry out the contract before the expiry of the cancellation period without the client's consent. The client must repay any money received, and return any property acquired, in relation to the contract within 30 days.[28]

Agreements made on or after 1 February 2011

If an agreement was made on or after 1 February 2011, the client has the right to withdraw from it without giving any reason within 14 days.[29] This applies to all regulated agreements except those:

- for credit of more than £60,260;
- secured on land.

This right to withdraw after a contract has been made replaces the cancellation rights described on p75.

Notice of withdrawal must be given before the end of the 14-day period starting with the day after the 'relevant day', which is the latest of:

- the date the agreement was made; *or*
- the date the client was informed of her/his credit limit under the agreement; *or*
- the date the client either receives her/his copy of the executed agreement or is informed that it has been executed.

Notice of withdrawal may be given either verbally or in writing using the contact details provided in the agreement.

The client must repay any credit advanced together with interest accrued up to the date of repayment, but is not liable for any other fees or charges under the agreement. The client must repay the credit and any interest without 'undue delay' and, in any event, within 30 days. If repayment has not been made within this time, the creditor can take action to recover the money, recover possession of any goods or enforce any security.

Although a client can withdraw from credit agreements, these do not affect contracts for the supply of goods and s/he remains liable to pay for the goods. Ownership of goods bought with a hire purchase or conditional sale agreement (see p114 and p116) passes to the client on repayment of the credit and accrued interest.[30] The client is not entitled to return the goods to the supplier so that, in effect, withdrawal operates as a forced cash purchase.

It is the OFT's view that the creditor retains the right to repossess the goods if the credit and accrued interest is not paid within the 30-day period. It is unlikely that the client is entitled to have her/his deposit or part-exchanged goods returned or to have their amount/value set off against the amount owed. This should be explained to the client as part of the required 'adequate explanation' (see p69).

Note: regardless of when the agreement was made, the client can also withdraw from an agreement if, when s/he signs, it has not yet been signed by the creditor and it is not signed by the creditor on the same occasion so that it becomes an executed agreement.

Post-contract information

Annual statements

From 1 October 2008, creditors of fixed-sum credit agreements with a term exceeding 12 months must provide annual statements to borrowers. If a creditor does not comply with this requirement, it will not be entitled to enforce the agreement during the period of non-compliance, and the client will not be liable to pay either any interest or any default sum (see p79) accruing during the period of non-compliance.

There is no corresponding sanction in the event of non-compliance for running-account credit agreements (where there is already a statutory duty to provide annual statements), but statements must contain warnings about the consequences of failing to make repayments or of only making the minimum repayments (which many statements already include). This applies to existing fixed-sum and running-account credit agreements, as well as new agreements.

Arrears notices

To avoid the situation where the client is making either reduced or contractual payments plus a payment towards the arrears and is unaware that the debt is escalating because the creditor is adding interest or charges, creditors must inform clients when their arrears reach a certain level and that interest/charges may be accruing. This applies to arrears arising after 1 October 2008 on both new and existing agreements. There are different provisions for fixed-sum and running-account agreements.

Once at least two payments have fallen due under a fixed-sum credit agreement and the account has gone into arrears by the equivalent of at least two repayments, the creditor is required to give the client notice of the sum(s) in arrears in a specified form within 14 days ('arrears notice'), and thereafter at six-monthly intervals until the client has cleared the arrears, any interest on the arrears and any default sum (see p79).

For running-account agreements, the notice must be given once at least two payments have fallen due and the last two payments have not been paid in full. The notice must be given no later than the end of the period when the next periodic statement is due. A further arrears notice is only triggered once the client has again failed to pay two consecutive months' payments in full.

The arrears notice must be accompanied by an information sheet about arrears produced by the OFT. The duty to send an arrears notice ends once the creditor has obtained a judgment for the sums payable under the agreement. If a creditor does not comply with this requirement, it is not entitled to enforce the agreement during the period of non-compliance and the client is not liable to pay any interest or any default sum accruing during the period of non-compliance.

For both new and existing agreements, once an arrears notice is served, the client can apply for a time order (see p340), provided s/he has given 14 days' notice to the creditor of her/his intention to do so. The client's notice must be in writing, but not in any prescribed form and must state that s/he intends to apply for a time order and s/he wants to make a repayment proposal to the creditor. S/he must give details of that proposal. The client can still apply for a time order following a default notice having been served or during proceedings for enforcement of the agreement or any security, or to repossess any goods or land. In these situations, however, the client is not required to serve the 14-day notice. See p340 for more information on time orders.

Default sum notices

If the client incurs a 'default sum' (ie, any sum, other than interest, which becomes payable under either a new or existing agreement as a result of a breach of the agreement) payable after 1 October 2008, the creditor is required to give the client a notice in a specified form. Costs ordered by a court are not payable 'under the agreement' and so do not fall within the definition of default sum. If a creditor does not comply with this requirement, it cannot enforce the agreement during the period of non-compliance. The creditor cannot charge any interest on the default sum until the 29th day after the notice is given. After that date, it can only charge simple interest on the default sum (although the arrears themselves continue to accrue interest at the contractual rate, provided the creditor has given the appropriate statutory notices). If a creditor does not comply with this requirement, it cannot enforce the agreement during the period of non-compliance.

Default notices

Before the creditor can terminate the agreement, demand early payment, recover possession of goods or land, or enforce any security, it must serve a 'default notice' on the client (see p281). From 1 October 2008, in addition to the information and wording previously required, the creditor must provide information on the client's right to terminate a hire purchase or credit sale agreement and the procedure involved (see p117). Where applicable, the notice must also contain a statement of the creditor's right to charge interest under the credit agreement after judgment. The creditor is also required to attach a copy of the information sheet about arrears produced by the OFT (see p80). Since 1 October 2006, default notices must give the client 14 days in which to comply, instead of the seven days previously required, regardless of whether the breach occurred before or after this date.

Interest after judgment

From 1 October 2008, a creditor who wants to recover post-judgment contractual interest from the client is required to give her/him notice of its intention to do so in the prescribed form. The notice must be given after the judgment is made and further notices must be given at six-monthly intervals. The client is not liable to pay post-judgment interest for any period for which the creditor has not served the required notice(s).

It is not enough that the creditor 'wants' to claim interest after judgment. The agreement must specifically allow it to be claimed (see p293).[31] The intention appears to be that if the client either refuses to pay or cannot come to an agreement with the creditor, the creditor will have to sue for it separately. The client can then defend the proceedings if s/he challenges the creditor's right to claim post-judgment interest under the contract or the amount claimed, or s/he can make an offer of payment through the court, if appropriate.

Until the judgment is made, the client only has a potential liability for post-judgment contractual interest and, even after the judgment is made, that liability is conditional on the creditor serving the appropriate notice(s). Therefore, once these provisions apply to a judgment, arguments that such interest should have been provided for in the judgment, if the creditor wants to be able to recover it, will no longer be available. If the client receives notice(s) of the creditor's intention to claim post-judgment contractual interest, s/he should consider applying for a time order (see p340) and asking the court either to freeze, or reduce the rate of, the interest or charges.

In the past, some creditors have successfully argued that time order applications cannot be made once there is a judgment, as there is no longer any 'sum owed' under the agreement. However, the prescribed wording of the notices invites the client to apply, in effect, for a time order and so such arguments from creditors should not apply.

Note: the above provisions do not apply to post-judgment statutory interest (although this can never be claimed if the judgment arises out of an agreement regulated by Consumer Credit Act, regardless of the amount). They apply to agreements made before 1 October 2008, but only in relation to judgments made after that date.

Information sheets

The Consumer Credit Act 2006 requires the OFT to prepare information sheets to accompany arrears notices and default notices. From 1 October 2008, lenders are required to include a copy of the current information sheet with each relevant notice. The legislation says that the information sheet must be 'included' in the notice, so it is arguable that, if a notice is sent out without an information sheet, the notice is invalid.

The OFT has produced an information sheet for each notice regardless of the type of agreement involved. These are two sides of A4 in length and are available in Welsh as well as English, and can be made available in large print, audio tape and Braille. They set out some of the client's key rights, such as the right to terminate the agreement, apply for a time order or complain to the FOS. They also set out the effect of failure to pay, such as the effect on credit rating, additional interest and court action by the creditor. They include a list of sources of help, such as Citizens Advice Bureaux and National Debtline.

Notes

2. **Licensing traders**
   1   s40 CCA 1974
   2   s160A CCA 1974
   3   s25(2A)(e) and (2B) CCA 1974, as amended by s29 CCA 2006

3. **Regulated agreements**
   4   s55(1) CCA 1974
   5   Consumer Credit (Disclosure of Information) Regulations 2010, No.1013
   6   Sch 1 Consumer Credit (Disclosure of Information) Regulations 2010, No.1013
   7   s157A CCA 1974
   8   s55C CCA 1974
   9   s55A CCA 1974
   10 s55B CCA 1974
   11 s55C CCA 1974
   12 s61A CCA 1974
   13 s61B CCA 1974
   14 Authorised overdraft agreements made on or after 1 February 2011 must comply with reg 8(1) Consumer Credit (Agreements) Regulations 2010, No.1014. Current account agreements which allow for overdrawing without prior arrangement must contain the information specified in s74A CCA 1974 and the creditor must supply the information specified in s74B if there is 'significant' overdrawing on such an account. There are no requirements for unauthorised overdraft agreements.
   15 *London North Securities v Meadows* [2005] EWCA Civ 956 (*Adviser* 107 and 108 abstracts)
   16 *London North Securities v Meadows* [2005] EWCA Civ 956 (*Adviser* 107 and 108 abstracts)
   17 See *Ocwen v Hughes and Hughes* [2004] CCLR 4 and *Central Trust v Spurway* [2005] CCLR 1
   18 See *McGinn v Grangewood Securities* [2002] EWCA Civ 522 (*Adviser* 92 abstracts); *London North Securities v Williams*, Reading County Court, 16 May 2005, unreported (*Adviser* 112 abstracts). Even if the prescribed term is present, it is unlikely that the agreement will contain the more detailed non-prescribed repayment obligations which will make the agreement improperly executed and enforceable with leave of the court only on such terms as it thinks fit; see *Hurstanger Ltd v Wilson* [2007] EWCA Civ 299 (*Adviser* 122 consumer abstracts)
   19 ss113 and 127(3) CCA 1974 and Sch 6 Consumer Credit (Agreements) Regulations 1983, No.1553
   20 *HSBC Bank v Brophy* [2011] EWCA Civ 67, CA (*Adviser* 145 abstracts)
   21 *Carey and others v HSBC and others* [2009] EWHC 3417 (QB) (*Adviser* 139 money advice abstracts)
   22 The Consumer Credit (Agreements) (Amendment) Regulations 2004, No.1482
   23 For a summary of pre-6 April 2007 unenforceability arguments, see A Leakey and B Say, 'Unenforceable Agreements', *Adviser* 117 and for a discussion of the position post-6 April 2007, see G Skipwith, 'Consultancy Corner 1', *Adviser* 124
   24 The Consumer Credit Act 1974 (Electronic Communications) Order 2004, No.3236
   25 s63 CCA 1974
   26 s69(7) CCA 1974

27 s57 CCA 1974
28 Regs 7-13 and 29 and Schs 1 para 13
    and 2 para 5 Financial Services (Distance
    Marketing) Regulations 2004, No.2095.
    These only apply if the client is a
    'consumer' – ie, the transaction must
    not be for the purposes of the client's
    business.
29 s66A CCA 1974
30 s66A(11) CCA 1974
31 Regs 34 and 35 and Sch 5 CC(IR) Regs
    2007; see P Madge 'Interesting After
    Judgment', *Adviser* 131

Chapter 5

· ·

Minimising debts

This chapter covers:
1. Introduction (below)
2. Using contract law to challenge or reduce liability (p84)
3. Using the Consumer Credit Act to challenge or reduce liability (p93)

---

1. Introduction

This chapter looks at the two main ways of minimising debts – ie, using contract law and/or the Consumer Credit Act to check, for example, whether or not the creditor is legally able to enforce the debt.

It is essential to identify accurately each debt before attempting to deal with it. Chapters 8 and 9 cover the most common types of credit or debt that advisers are likely to encounter. Debts fall into two groups – those covered by the Consumer Credit Act (regulated debts) and those that do not.

Advisers must first check that the client is legally liable to pay the debts claimed by her/his creditors. In general, a debt will be owed only if:
- there is a valid contract between the client and creditor (see p84); *or*
- money is owed because of particular legislation – eg, council tax; *or*
- the client has been ordered by a court to make payments to someone, or to the court itself, and there are no grounds to challenge the court order.

In addition, if the contract is regulated by the Consumer Credit Act 1974, the creditor must comply with the Act's provisions (see Chapter 4).

Inaccurate calculations

The adviser must check that the amount of any debt is correct and should not assume that the amount owed by a client has been accurately calculated.

The adviser should check the client's own records of payments and make sure that all payments have been credited to the account, and, if in doubt, request a full statement to confirm this.

The adviser should also request that any recovery action be suspended while the matter is being investigated. It may be necessary to contact a regional or head office if negotiations with the local branch are unsuccessful. If the creditor is not being co-operative in supplying information and the debt is regulated by the Consumer Credit Act (see p65), the adviser should write to the creditor asking for a full statement of account under ss77 and 78 of the Consumer Credit Act 1974 and enclose a payment of £1. If the creditor fails to comply with the request within 12 working days, the debt is unenforceable until the information is supplied.[1] See p93 for more information.

2. **Using contract law to challenge or reduce liability**

This section looks at the possible ways in which the law of contract can be used to minimise a client's debts.

A contract is an agreement between two parties that becomes binding (ie, legally enforceable) because it specifies that goods or services are to be exchanged by one party in return for a 'consideration', usually money, from the other.

The most common situation in which an amount of money claimed under a contract may not be due, or may be reduced, is when one party has not kept to her/his side of the agreement – eg, the supplier has sold defective goods. Sometimes, nothing is payable because a contract has not been made in the correct way or the rules on the way in which public bodies can demand money have not been complied with. In other cases, it may be possible to reduce the amount owed because the law says that a term of the contract is 'unfair' or, in the case of credit agreements, there is an 'unfair relationship' (see p98) or there has been irresponsible lending (see p63).

Even if the adviser has established that a debt does exist, the client may not be liable to pay it, either because someone else is liable or because the contract is not enforceable – eg, if the creditor is outside the time limit for taking court action to recover the debt (see p274).

Joint and several liability

If more than one person enters into a credit agreement, they are each liable for the whole of the debt. This is known as **'joint and several liability'**. If it is a regulated agreement (see p65), it must be signed by all parties in the form required by the Consumer Credit Act (see p67). If they have all not signed such an agreement and it was made on or before 6 April 2007, none are liable because the agreement is 'irredeemably unenforceable' (see p96).

Joint and several liability can also apply to rent arrears on joint tenancies, arrears on joint mortgages, water and sewerage charges, and to council tax on properties which are jointly owned/occupied by heterosexual and same-sex couples.

Guarantors

A creditor will sometimes ask for a guarantee before agreeing to lend money or provide services. The guarantor agrees to make the necessary payments should the actual customer or borrower fail to do so, and is bound by the terms of the guarantee s/he has given. If these terms are part of a regulated consumer credit agreement, they are governed by the Consumer Credit Act, so if the loan agreement is unenforceable, so is the guarantee. A guarantee must be in writing and signed by the guarantor. Sometimes, creditors ask for people to act as second purchasers. They are asked to sign the original agreement as purchasers and become jointly and severally liable for the debt. Guarantors should be given copies of the original agreement and also any notices required to be sent to the client on default.

If the creditor has not properly explained to a guarantor that s/he is equally liable for the total debt, there may be a way of challenging liability if it can be shown that the guarantor has been either misled or coerced. In any case, if there is a non-commercial relationship between the debtor and the guarantor (eg, they are cohabitees), the creditor is required to take reasonable steps to satisfy itself that the guarantor understands the transaction and the risks s/he is taking by entering into it. The creditor can either do this itself or require the guarantor to see a solicitor. If the creditor fails to take either of these steps, but the guarantor has seen a solicitor anyway, the creditor cannot assume the solicitor has advised the guarantor appropriately when no such advice was in fact given.

If the creditor fails to take these steps and the guarantor's consent to the transaction has been improperly obtained, the creditor may be unable to enforce the guarantee.[2] The client should seek specialist help.[3]

Agents

An agent sells goods or collects money on behalf of someone else – eg, s/he may show or distribute mail order catalogues to her/his friends and neighbours, take orders and pass them on to the supplying company. S/he collects money from the customers over a number of weeks, and is liable to pay any money collected, regardless of whether or not the creditor can enforce the agreement against the customer – eg, because s/he has not signed a contract. An agent is obliged to create a separate account for each customer. If s/he does not do this, s/he can become liable for money not paid by customers for whom s/he has failed to create an account. If there is a separate account, the agent will not be liable for money that customers do not pay.

An agent may lose commission with which s/he has already been credited (and thus her/his own personal account may go into arrears) if someone does not keep up the payments on items bought and supplied. However, an agent is not liable for the customer's default, except in the situation discussed above.

When advising an agent about liability, it is important to check whether the amount owed includes other customers' debts. If so, provide the creditor with a clear breakdown of the accounts, and the names and addresses of customers in arrears and ask the creditor to invoice them separately. If a client has not obtained signed agreements from her/his customers or has received payments but not accounted for these to the creditor, s/he may be personally liable for any debt. Specialist advice should be obtained.

The wrong person

An account may be sent to the wrong person or to the wrong address, and the person who receives the request for payment is not liable. If there is any doubt about this, check any documents relating to the debt and ask the creditor to produce original invoices, agreements and details of goods or services supplied. Full initials and addresses are obviously important in this process, as are reference numbers.

Using the wrong name, however, does not invalidate a debt and, if a name is shown incorrectly – particularly if it has always been inaccurate but both parties know who is intended – the debt can still be valid.

Forged signatures

If a signature on an agreement has been forged, the person whose name has been forged is not liable for any debt arising from that agreement. A signature may have been forged with that person's knowledge. For example, a person who wants a loan but has reached her/his credit limit with a particular creditor may use a relative's name to obtain the loan, receive the money and make repayments. The relative knows and agrees to this. In such cases, the adviser should proceed as though the signature was valid and the beneficiary of the loan should continue to maintain repayments.[4]

A partner or close relative's signature may be used without her/his consent – eg, if a person obtains credit by using her/his parent's name and signature without the knowledge of the credit company or the parent. If there is any accusation of fraud, the client should obtain legal advice. Fraud is a serious criminal offence and a solicitor specialising in criminal law may be required.

In some cases, the use of a more creditworthy relative's name may have been sanctioned by the credit company. If a representative of a creditor has allowed a false name to be given knowingly, that representative may be either conniving with a fraud or, if the signing occurred on her/his advice, creating a situation in which the creditor accepts that the borrower is allowed to use another name. A broker is not usually regarded as a representative of the credit company for this purpose.

The debt adviser should advise the person whose name has been used that s/he does not owe the money because s/he has not signed the agreement. The adviser should be aware of the possible repercussions for the actual signatory and should explain these to the client, as s/he may prefer to accept liability for the debt rather than risk, for instance, a prosecution of the actual signatory and/or a breakdown in family relationships.

Liability after a death

An individual's debts usually die with her/him, although creditors may be entitled to make a claim against her/his estate – ie, money, personal possessions and property. It is possible, however, that creditors will attempt to hold partners or close relatives responsible for an individual's debts, particularly if they lived with the deceased, although this could involve a breach of the Office of Fair Trading's (OFT's) *Debt Collection Guidance.*[5]

If someone is dealing with an estate of someone who has died, s/he has no personal liability for any debts that cannot be paid from the deceased's own property. Debts which may still have to be paid include:

- those for which someone had joint and several liability with the deceased (see p84). The co-debtor remains liable for the full outstanding balance owed;
- any debts if the estate has been passed to beneficiaries (including if the person handling the estate is the only beneficiary) without first paying creditors. If a client in this situation is being held personally liable by the deceased's creditors, s/he should seek specialist advice;
- a mortgage remaining on a property, even if this passes to a new owner by inheritance;
- rent arrears if someone has taken over a tenancy from the deceased by succession, if these cannot be paid by the estate. A tenant by succession can lose her/his home if s/he does not pay the arrears owed;[6]
- council tax by heterosexual and same-sex couples with joint liability. Although a person's liability ceases at the date of death, the estate and the surviving partner remain liable for any arrears.

Note: some debts are paid off on death by insurance policies. Many mortgages and some consumer credit agreements are covered, and advisers should check these.

If any claim by a potential creditor was 'statute-barred' (see p275) at the date of death, the estate can be distributed without taking that creditor's claim into account. However, if the claim has become statute-barred since the date of death, the question of whether the debt must be paid should be referred to a solicitor as it depends on trust law.

When a person has died and someone continues to live in her/his home and use services (eg, fuel and water) for which the deceased previously paid, the survivor should open a new account in her/his own name as soon as possible after the death. In this way, s/he is stating a willingness to pay for future goods or services used and also demonstrating that s/he was not previously liable. It is important to ensure s/he does not agree to take responsibility for the deceased person's debt when s/he opens the new account (although the deceased person's estate, of which the house may be part, will be liable).

Jointly owned property

The deceased's share in a jointly owned property is not part of her/his estate and passes directly to the other co-owner, regardless of whether s/he made a will or died intestate. It is, therefore, not available to creditors unless, for example, a creditor has obtained a charging order on the beneficial interest of one of the owners (see p308), one of the joint owners was made bankrupt, or the ownership of the property was originally set up in unequal shares because, for instance, one party contributed a lump sum to the purchase.

Joint owners in this situation are known as 'tenants in common' as opposed to 'joint tenants'. The effect of this is that each has a potential estate against which her/his creditors (including unsecured creditors) can make a claim on her/his death. Joint owners should be advised to seek financial advice on the most appropriate method of protecting themselves against potential claims on the estate by a co-owner's creditors, which could result in the loss of their home.

Even if the co-owners were not tenants in common, if a creditor presents a bankruptcy petition against the deceased and an order is made, a court can require the surviving owner(s) to pay the value of the deceased's share on the date of death to the trustee. The petition must be presented within five years of the death. It is advisable for a client faced with this possibility to make a payment arrangement with the creditor if s/he does not want the property sold. Advice should be sought from a specialist.[7]

Under-18-year-olds

If a client was under 18 (a 'minor') at the time a contract was made, check whether it was for 'necessaries'. If not, a court may decide the contract is not enforceable.

'**Necessaries**' are defined as 'goods suitable to the condition in life of a minor and her/his actual requirements at the time of sale and delivery'. Examples include fuel, clothes and possibly mobile phones. The client is expected to have paid no more than was 'reasonable' for such goods. Young people under 18 are often asked to provide a guarantor who is liable to pay if they cannot (see p85). If there was no guarantor and the goods were not 'necessaries', the client need not pay and the creditor is unable to use the courts to claim repayments. However, a court could order any goods to be returned if the supplier has experienced a loss.

Note: if the client specifically informed the creditor that s/he was 18 or over on the date of the contract, although s/he may not be liable for the debt, s/he could be prosecuted for fraud if s/he attempts to challenge liability.

Note also: a creditor who has given a loan to a minor to purchase 'necessaries' can recover the amount actually spent on those necessaries.[8]

Contracts made under 'undue influence'

If a contract has been made under 'undue influence' (ie, if a person has taken unfair advantage of her/his influence over another person), it may not be enforceable. Undue influence may be actual – eg, a person has been subjected to oppression. It may also be presumed – eg, if a person is persuaded to enter into a contract by someone on whom s/he relies for advice and guidance and the transaction is explainable only on the basis that undue influence was used, because it puts the person at a substantial disadvantage.[9] This issue can often arise with guarantees (see p85).

This situation commonly arises where one partner in a couple applies for a loan for her/his own purposes (eg, to pay off debts or fund a business), which the creditor requires to be in joint names so that it can be secured on jointly owned property or so that the income of the other partner can be taken into account as part of the creditor's lending process. If it appears that the agreement was only given to a joint loan because the first borrower used 'undue influence' (eg, by saying, 'we'll lose our home if you do not sign', or by misrepresenting the effect of the transaction – see below), the second borrower may be able to escape liability. S/he should always seek specialist help.

Misrepresentation of the terms of the contract

If one party misrepresents the terms of a contract to another (ie, does not explains the transaction accurately), the latter party may be able to avoid the transaction. For example, if a creditor persuades a client to sign a legal charge by stating that a secured loan does not put her/his home at risk, the loan may not be enforceable as the client would have the right to cancel the legal charge.

The client can seek compensation for any loss suffered as a consequence of a misrepresentation. As it is difficult to prove oral misrepresentation, it is important that the adviser obtains copies of all relevant correspondence. Alternatively, if the misrepresentation can be established, the creditor may decide not to pursue the debt to avoid bad publicity.

In the case of agreements regulated by the Consumer Credit Act (see p65), if the finance is arranged through the supplier or dealer, the lender is jointly and severally liable with the supplier/dealer for any misrepresentations made by the supplier/dealer about both the goods or services supplied and the credit agreement.

Capacity to make a contract

A contract is only valid if someone has the 'capacity' to make it. The Mental Capacity Act 2005 (fully in force since 1 October 2007) contains the following principles.

- A person lacks capacity if, at the time the contract is entered into, s/he is unable to make a decision for her/himself about it because of an impairment of, or a disturbance in the functioning of, her mind or brain. The impairment or disturbance may be permanent or temporary.

- A person is assumed to have capacity unless it is established that s/he does not.
- A person should not be treated as unable to make a decision merely because s/he makes an unwise decision.
- A person is unable to make a decision for her/himself if s/he is unable to:
  – understand the information relevant to the decision, including information about the reasonably foreseeable consequences of deciding one way or another; *or*
  – retain that information, although the fact that s/he is only able to retain the information for a short period does not prevent her/him from being able to make the decision; *or*
  – use or weigh up that information as part of the process of making the decision; *or*
  – communicate her/his decision, either in speech, sign language or some other means.

This means that if someone is unable to understand the nature and effect of the transaction, particularly the responsibilities involved, because of, for example, the influence of alcohol or drugs, mental ill health or a learning disability, the contract may not be enforceable provided the creditor either knew, or ought to have known, of the person's incapacity.

Advisers sometimes assume that, because a client has mental health or learning difficulties, any agreement s/he has entered into is automatically unenforceable. This cannot just be assumed and medical evidence will usually be necessary to establish the client's inability to understand the transaction in question at the time it was entered into. In many cases, the client's lack of capacity can be established, but not the creditor's knowledge or presumed knowledge. However, it will often be possible to ask the creditor to write off the debt, either because there is evidence of inappropriate lending and/or the client's situation is such that setting up a debt repayment programme is not a realistic strategy.[10]

The OFT has said that creditors should operate suitable business practices for identifying and dealing with clients who either have, or who may have, mental capacity issues. It has produced a leaflet for creditors, available at www.tinyurl.com/6zt24co.[11]

Specialist advice should be sought if the enforceability of a contract on the grounds of incapacity is being considered or if someone who appears to lack capacity is involved in court proceedings.[12]

For further information on dealing with clients with mental health issues, see p54.

Housing disrepair

In many cases where there are rent arrears, landlords have not always fulfilled their obligations in connection with repairs. The amount of rent arrears claimed by the landlord can then be reduced by either a 'set-off' or a 'counterclaim' by the tenant. A 'set-off' is money spent by the tenant to carry out repairs required by law and is, therefore, owed to the tenant by the landlord. A 'counterclaim' is money claimed by the tenant as compensation for a failure to repair and the resultant loss.[13] Specialist housing advice should be sought if this applies.

Faulty goods and services

If a client owes money on faulty goods or unsatisfactory services, s/he may be able to avoid paying all or part of the bill. A client may be able to obtain a refund on goods that are not of satisfactory quality or not as described.[14] The goods must be rejected immediately or very soon after purchase. Similarly, services should be carried out with reasonable care and skill and within a reasonable time.[15] In addition, faulty goods or services may entitle the client to claim for whatever expenses s/he has incurred as a result of the fault. Dangerous goods should be reported to the local trading standards department.

Mistaken payments

A client's bank account may be mistakenly credited with money to which the client is not entitled. Although the creditor or bank has made a mistake, generally, a client is legally required to repay money which does not belong to her/him. However, a client does not have to repay money if s/he has 'changed position' through believing in good faith that the money was hers/his. Spending the money on ordinary day-to-day living expenses or repaying a debt is not a change of position, but buying something that s/he would not otherwise have bought is.

It must be unfair for the client to have to repay the money. It is *not* unfair if:
- s/he has acted in bad faith – eg, s/he was aware of the mistake; *and/or*
- full or partial repayment is possible because all or some of the money is still in her/his possession.

The bank should not pay the money back to the party that made the mistaken payment into the account without the client's permission.[16]

Default charges

Many credit agreements (as well as mortgages and secured loans) allow the creditor to add charges to the client's account in certain circumstances. These are sometimes referred to as 'arrears charges' or 'penalty charges'. Usually, the amount of the charge is fixed. Often, such charges accrue interest while they remain unpaid. Examples of situations in which charges are imposed include:

- late or missed payments;
- exceeding a credit limit;
- dishonoured cheques or direct debit payments; *and*
- unauthorised overdrafts.

All these situations involve a breach of contract by the client and the charges are supposed to reflect the damages or financial loss for the creditor from this. The courts will only enforce them if they are seen as a genuine attempt to estimate in advance the loss the creditor will face for the additional administration involved as a result of the client's breach of contract. The provisions are then enforceable as what is known as 'liquidated damages'.

It may be possible to challenge the charges, arguing that they are either:

- a 'penalty' at common law (see below); *or*
- an unfair term under the Unfair Terms in Consumer Contracts Regulations 1994 (see below).

What is a penalty

In the case *Dunlop Pneumatic Tyre Co Ltd v New Garage and Motor Co,* the House of Lords gave the following guidance to help establish whether a charge is 'liquidated damages' (enforceable) or a 'penalty' (unenforceable).[17]

- It will be a penalty if the sum stipulated is 'extravagant and unreasonable' compared with the greatest loss which could conceivably be proved to have followed from the breach – ie, the sum claimed is disproportionately higher than the costs and expenses reasonably incurred by the creditor.
- It will be a penalty if the breach consists of not paying a sum of money only and the amount of the charge exceeds the amount of the unpaid sum.
- It may be a penalty when a single lump sum is payable as compensation on the occurrence of one or more of several events, some of which may occasion serious and others but trifling damage – ie, the same charge is payable regardless of the seriousness of the breach.

Although the case is nearly 100 years old and the language is archaic, the above still represents the law on penalties today.

What is an unfair term

A term is unfair if: 'contrary to the requirements of good faith, it causes a significant imbalance in the parties' rights and obligations arising under the contract to the detriment of the consumer',[18] provided:

- the client is a 'consumer' – ie, did not make the contract in the course of business; *and*
- the agreement was made on or after 1 July 1995; *and*
- the contract is in the creditor's standard form – ie, it has not been individually negotiated.

An unfair term is not binding on the client and so cannot be enforced against her/ him by the creditor. The remainder of the agreement is unaffected, provided it is capable of continuing without the unfair term.[19] Examples of unfair terms include those:[20]

- requiring clients who fail to fulfil their obligations to pay a disproportionately high sum in compensation;[21]
- that irrevocably bind clients to terms with which they had no real opportunity of becoming acquainted before the conclusion of the contract.[22]

What action to take

If an adviser believes that a default charge is either a penalty or an unfair term, s/he should first check the relevant terms of the agreement and, if the agreement allows the creditor to make the charge(s) in question, write to the creditor:

- pointing out that the default charges do not reflect the creditor's actual or anticipated loss in the particular circumstances of the client's breach of contract and are, therefore, a penalty and not recoverable;
- stating that the default charges are also an unfair term contrary to Schedule 1, paragraph 1(e) of the Unfair Terms in Consumer Contracts Regulations 1994/ 1999 because they require the client to pay a disproportionately high sum in compensation for her/his failure to perform the obligations under the contract;
- requiring the creditor either to refund these charges to the client's account or else justify the level of default charges.

If the client is not satisfied with the creditor's response, s/he could take the matter through the creditor's complaints procedure to the Financial Ombudsman Service (see p268) or part-defend any court action taken by the creditor (see p295).[23]

3. **Using the Consumer Credit Act to challenge or reduce liability**

The Consumer Credit Act (see p60) regulates the way in which most credit agreements can be set up. It gives the borrower certain rights and, if these are denied, a court may decide that the agreement is unenforceable and, therefore, the creditor will not be able to require repayment.

The courts also have powers that can assist clients, specifically when the relationship between the client and the creditor is unfair to the client (see p98) and via time orders (see p340).

Requests for information

In order to check whether or not an agreement actually exists and, if so, its terms and conditions and/or whether or not the amount the creditor is claiming to be due is correct, advisers often need to contact the creditor for information. Creditors are required to provide certain information within 12 'working days' – ie, excluding weekends and bank holidays. If they fail to do so within this time limit, the agreement becomes unenforceable unless and until they do provide it.[24]

The client is entitled to request that the creditor provides:

- a copy of the executed agreement;
- a copy of any other document referred to in the agreement – eg, a bill of sale, but not a default notice;
- a statement of account containing the prescribed information (see p71), not just the amount of arrears.

The request must be in writing and must include the prescribed fee of £1 per credit agreement. It is recommended that advisers keep a record of postage.

When to make a request

A request for information can be made to:

- obtain information which the adviser has been unable to get voluntarily and which is required to deal with the client's case;
- prevent enforcement action from being started while the adviser is investigating liability (but see below);
- halt enforcement action already taking place to enable the adviser to investigate liability (but see below).

Meaning of 'enforcement'

In a number of test cases, the High Court has adopted a narrow interpretation of 'enforcement'. In the context of an information request, enforcement means:

- repossession of any goods or land;
- termination of the agreement;
- enforcement of any security – eg, a bill of sale;
- demanding early payment;
- treating any right given to the client under the agreement as terminated, restricted or deferred;
- entering and enforcing a judgment.

Even though a creditor has failed to comply with an information request, it can still take the following steps, which are not treated as enforcement:[25]

- report the client's default to a credit reference agency;
- demand payment, but not early payment;
- pass the case to debt collectors;
- threaten legal action;
- issue court proceedings.

As a result of concerns that some consumers were being misled by claims management companies into thinking that these provisions could be used as a loophole to get their debts written off and that some creditors did not seem to understand their statutory obligations, the Office of Fair Trading (OFT) issued guidance on information requests (OFT1272) in October 2010. This guidance takes account of the court decisions, but disagrees with them in a number of respects, particularly on issuing court proceedings. The OFT says that it is an unfair or improper business practice for a creditor to mislead clients about the enforceability of the agreement (eg, by threatening court proceedings) when it is aware that a judgment could not be obtained because the information request cannot be complied with. Communication or requests for payment should not threaten court action in these circumstances and the creditor should, in fact, make it clear that the agreement is unenforceable.

Possible responses from the creditor

- No reply. Send a reminder after 14 days, pointing out that the agreement is now unenforceable unless and until the creditor complies with the request.
- The creditor says the request must come from client personally. People can usually act through agents and the Consumer Credit Act does not require a debtor to act in person in this situation. In the OFT's view, provided a proper authority is provided to the creditor, the request is still 'from the debtor' and should, therefore, be complied with.
- The debt has been sold and the new creditor ('debt purchaser') says it does not have the information and does not have to provide it because it is not the 'creditor'. The definition of 'creditor' in s189 of the Consumer Credit Act 1974 includes someone to whom the original creditor's rights and duties under the agreement have passed – eg, by assignment. Some debt purchasers argue that they only purchase the rights, not the duties, and so do not fit within the definition. They also argue (correctly) that, provided the client has had notice of the assignment, the debt purchaser is entitled to enforce the agreement, including by court proceedings. However, the 'right' to enforce the agreement carries with it the 'duty' to comply with the Consumer Credit Act (which is not a liability under the agreement). In addition, the right to enforce is not an absolute right because, if the client had a defence to any claim brought by the original creditor (eg, that the agreement is unenforceable), s/he also has that defence to any claim brought by the debt purchaser. The OFT's view is that any debt purchaser is a 'creditor' and so must comply with an information request and that, in any event, failure to make proper arrangements in a debt sale to enable information requests to be complied with does not excuse non-compliance.
- The creditor says it does not have to comply with the request because, for example, the loan repayment period is over or the account has been terminated. However, s77(3) of the Consumer Credit Act 1974 says that the

duty to comply with a request does not apply where no sum is, or will be or may become, payable by the client. So, by implication, it does apply if a sum is, will be or may become payable by the client, which is the case if the creditor is demanding payment. This view is supported by the OFT in its guidance.

- The creditor does not provide a photocopy but only a pro forma agreement with no client signature. The rules say that the creditor must supply a 'true copy', which can omit any signature and so this *does* comply with the Act.[26] The fact that the creditor says it cannot locate a copy does not mean that it cannot comply with an information request. The High Court has said that the creditor can supply a reconstituted copy from any source, not just from the original agreement. However, if a creditor does this, it must state this when the copy is supplied. However, if the creditor is aware that there never was a signed agreement, it cannot hide this fact by claiming that it cannot find it or by creating an untrue copy.

- No reply and the creditor contacts the client for payment. Seeking payment is not enforcement, but the adviser could point out that the agreement is unenforceable until a statement/copy of the agreement is provided and this means it cannot take any of the above action (which should be listed), but can comply by providing a 'true' copy which can be reconstituted from any source, provided it is indicated that it is reconstituted. If the agreement has been varied, the creditor must provide the original as well as the current terms and conditions. Consider complaining about any breaches of the OFT's guidance on information requests or the *Debt Collection Guidance*.[27]

- The creditor complies with the request. Note that, in order to comply, the client's address at the time of the agreement must be included and, if the agreement has been varied, the original terms and conditions must be supplied as well as the current version. Check the agreement to see whether any other documents are referred to in it, which could help the client's case (eg, a bill of sale), and ask for copies. The adviser should now be in a position to deal with the client's case.

If the creditor fails to comply

The courts have coined the phrase **'irredeemably unenforceable'** to describe the status of agreements when the creditor has failed to comply with an information request. This puts the client in a dilemma about whether to pay or not. If the client does not pay (or come to a payment arrangement), s/he runs the risk of the creditor either locating the original agreement or having sufficient information to provide a reconstituted copy as well as some evidence that originally there was a properly executed agreement signed by the client. In the meantime, the debt may well have escalated because of the addition of default interest and charges and the client will remain liable for these. The High Court has recognised this dilemma, but has said that neither the failure to comply nor the fact that there was not a properly executed agreement give rise, of themselves, to an unfair relationship.[28] However, if an agreement was made before 6 April 2007 which was not properly executed, it may be irredeemably unenforceable (see p67).

There are other arguments that can be put to creditors or debt purchasers who do not supply copies of agreements. Both the OFT's *Debt Collection Guidance*[29] and the *Credit Services Association Code of Practice*[30] place obligations on creditors, debt collectors and debt purchasers to provide information, and any failure to comply could be a breach of the Consumer Protection from Unfair Trading Regulations (see p98). If court action is threatened, the pre-action conduct protocols (see p266) require the parties to act reasonably in exchanging information and, if a claim is defended, the creditor (whether the original creditor or a debt purchaser) will have to produce any 'relevant documents'.[31]

Advisers should note that the real issue here is not whether the creditor/debt purchaser is able to produce a copy of the agreement, but whether a properly executed agreement complying with the Consumer Credit Act 1974 has ever existed. The fact that the original agreement cannot be produced or a reconstituted copy (or no copy at all) is provided does not mean that, if proceedings are issued, the client could defend the case on the grounds that the agreement is irredeemably unenforceable. An agreement is only irredeemably unenforceable if it was made before 6 April 2007 and either was not signed by the client(s) or did not contain the necessary prescribed terms (including cancellation notices where required). If the client wants to defend the case on the grounds that the agreement is irredeemably unenforceable, s/he will have to put forward a positive case about the circumstances of the making of the agreement and cannot just rely on the creditor's failure to produce a photocopy of the original. This does not mean that a properly executed agreement never existed.

The client may only have a temporary defence to any county court claim by the creditor if the creditor has failed to comply with a request for information as described on p93. This is because the creditor can always comply by producing a 'true copy' and, in the meantime, the court is likely to 'stay' the case – ie, stop the case from proceeding further until the creditor complies. If a client does not dispute the existence of a properly executed agreement, but the adviser is considering defending a claim on the grounds that the original creditor/debt purchaser/collector failed to produce a copy of the agreement, the adviser should seek specialist advice.

Unlicensed creditors

If a creditor enters into a regulated agreement (see p65), but does not hold a current consumer credit licence, s/he cannot enforce that agreement without permission from the OFT. S/he also commits a criminal offence.[32] If a creditor appears to be unlicensed (eg, because the company is clearly new, badly organised and unprofessional, its documentation is of a poor standard, or the adviser has not heard of it before), the adviser can check whether it has a licence by searching the Consumer Credit Register online at www2.crw.gov.uk/pr. Creditors who are not licensed will sometimes withdraw at this point when the need for a licence is pointed out to them. In the meantime, the client should be advised that s/he need not pay and be informed of her/his rights concerning harassment (see p29) and under the OFT's *Debt Collection Guidance* (see p30). If the creditor is a 'loan shark', see p241.

Early settlement of a credit agreement

If a regulated agreement is ended early by the client, s/he should pay less than the total amount that would have been payable if the agreement had run to its full term.[33]

One or more partial early repayments may be made at any time during the life of the agreement.

A formula (known as the 'Rule of 78') was contained in the Consumer Credit (Rebate on Early Settlement) Regulations 1983 as a means of ensuring that creditors can recoup costs associated with setting up an agreement and, therefore, a lower percentage rebate is given for settlement during the earliest parts of a credit agreement.

Note: the Rule of 78 has been replaced with a formula for agreements made on or after 31 May 2005.[34]

Unfair relationships

The Consumer Credit Act 2006 introduced the concept of an 'unfair relationship'.[35] This enables a borrower to challenge a credit agreement on the grounds that the relationship between the creditor and the borrower in connection with the agreement (or a related agreement) is unfair to the borrower. These provisions are in addition to the Financial Ombudsman Service's (FOS) new 'consumer credit jurisdiction' (see p268).

These provisions attempt to address situations where the creditor has taken 'unfair advantage' of the borrower or there has been 'oppressive' or 'exploitative' conduct, but not where the borrower has simply made a 'bad bargain'. They replace previous extortionate credit provisions and have applied since 6 April 2007. See p104 if the agreement was made before this date. The provisions apply to regulated and non-regulated agreements, including exempt agreements, and regardless of the amount of credit involved, except if the agreement is exempt because it is a regulated mortgage contract (see p147) and so regulated by the Financial Services Authority (FSA).

If an agreement has been paid off by a later, consolidating agreement (see p101), the earlier agreement can still be challenged, since an application can be made even though the relationship has ended. Under the old extortionate credit provisions for agreements made before 6 April 2007, only the transaction in question could be challenged and the agreement could only be considered at the time it was made. The unfair relationships provisions are much wider.

The provisions also apply to completed agreements (ie, where there is no longer any sum which is or may become payable) and also where a judgment has been made.

An order may be made by a court if the client applies either as a stand-alone application or as part of court proceedings relating to the credit agreement or a related agreement. If the client alleges that the credit relationship is unfair, the onus of proof is on the creditor to show that the relationship is not unfair. It is not sufficient merely to assert that the relationship is unfair: the facts in support of the allegation must be set out.

Relevant dates

The unfair relationships provisions have applied since 6 April 2007 to credit agreements entered into on or after this date.

From 6 April 2008, the new rules have applied to agreements made before this date, unless the agreement was paid off in full by then. Agreements made before 6 April 2007 consolidated by an agreement made before 6 April 2008 cannot be challenged as 'related agreements' because they have ceased to have any effect. Such paid-off or consolidated agreements remain subject to the extortionate credit bargain provisions in the Consumer Credit Act 1974. Advisers who are considering arguing that there is a case of extortionate credit should seek specialist advice.

The court's powers to make an order under the unfair relationship provisions are not limited to matters arising after 6 April 2007. The court can also take into account matters arising before this date. In considering a current agreement (whenever it was made), the court can take into account a related agreement made before 6 April 2007, but cannot make an order for repayment of any sum paid under a related agreement if that agreement ceased to be in operation before 6 April 2007.[36]

What is an unfair relationship

The Consumer Credit Act 2006 does not define an unfair relationship. However, it does set out, in general terms, factors that may give rise to an unfair relationship. These are:

- the terms of the credit agreement or a related agreement (see p100);
- the way in which the creditor has exercised or enforced its rights under the agreement (or a related agreement);
- anything done (or not done) by or on behalf of the creditor either before or after making the agreement (or a related agreement).

In some cases, unfair contract terms may be sufficient in themselves to give rise to an unfair relationship, but the court can also look at:

- the way agreements are introduced and negotiated;

- the way in which agreements are administered; *and*
- any other aspect of the relationship it considers relevant.

Both actions and omissions can be unfair (eg, if a creditor fails to take certain steps which, in the interests of fairness, it might reasonably be expected to take), including those on behalf of the creditor – ie, by employees, associates and agents, such as brokers and debt collectors. These include:

- pre-contract business practices such as misleading advertisements, mis-selling products, high-pressure selling techniques, 'churning' (see p101) and irresponsible lending;
- post-contract actions, such as demanding money the borrower has not agreed to pay and aggressive debt collection practices;
- failing to provide key information in a clear and timely manner or to disclose material facts.

The factors that are being relied on must make the relationship unfair 'as a whole'. The OFT's *Unfair Relationship Guidance* (issued in May 2008 and updated in August 2011, available at http://tinyurl.com/3u689ut or www.oft.gov.uk/shared_oft/business_leaflets/enterprise_act/oft854Rev.pdf) has an indicative list of potential unfair relationship situations. Although the guidance does not define an 'unfair relationship', it outlines what it means for the purpose of exercising the OFT's regulatory powers and should be the starting point for advising clients. The OFT also has summaries of the unfair relationships cases which have reached the courts, available at www.oft.gov.uk/about-the-oft/legal-powers/legal/cca/CCA2006/unfair/unfair-rel-full.

Instead of the list of specific factors in the extortionate credit provisions (eg, prevailing interest rates, the debtor's age, experience, business capacity, state of health and degree of financial pressure and the creditor's degree of risk), the court must now take into account all matters it thinks relevant, including those relating to the individual client and creditor. This means that a term or practice may not be unfair in a particular case because of the client's knowledge or experience, but may be unfair in another client's case if s/he is more vulnerable or susceptible to exploitation. There is also an expectation that clients will act honestly in providing accurate and full information to enable the creditor to assess risk.

Definitions

A **'related agreement'** is:

– a credit agreement consolidated by the main agreement; *or*

– a linked transaction in relation to the main agreement (or a consolidated agreement); *or*

– a security provided in relation to the main agreement (or a consolidated agreement or a linked transaction). For example, payment protection insurance is likely to be a linked transaction.

An agreement is *not* a related agreement if the later agreement is with a different creditor, unless the new creditor is an 'associate' or 'former associate' of the original creditor.

An agreement is **'consolidated'** by a later agreement if:
- the later agreement is entered into, in whole or in part, for purposes connected with debts owed under the earlier agreement; *and*
- at any time before the later agreement is entered into, the parties to the earlier agreement included the client under the later agreement and either the creditor or an associate or former associate.

This addresses the practice (known as **'churning'**) of creditors entering into successive agreements with a client (often before the earlier agreement has been paid off) and which usually involves not only refinancing the earlier agreement, but also providing extra finance, charging additional fees and selling further payment protection insurance, and which may, in itself, give rise to an unfair relationship.

Identifying potential unfair relationship situations

Possible examples of unfairness include:
- compounding default interest and charges, resulting in a very large debt;
- mis-selling subsidiary insurance products, such as payment protection insurance, including selling inappropriate products, aggressive selling and misleading borrowers into believing that a product is compulsory, or in a client's interests, when it is not;
- misleading clients about their legal rights – eg, misrepresenting a client's right to terminate voluntarily a conditional sale or hire purchase agreement or dishonestly obtaining a client's consent for protected hire purchase goods to be repossessed without a court order;
- draconian and/or unreasonable use of enforcement rights or powers – eg, the use of orders for sale to enforce debts which were originally unsecured;
- breaching the OFT's licensing provisions and guidance – eg, the *Second Charge Lending Guidance*, the *Irresponsible Lending Guidance* and the *Debt Collection Guidance*, or the FSA rules and guidance;
- breaching trade associations' codes of practice – eg, *The Lending Code*, the *FLA Lending* and the *Consumer Credit Trade Association Code of Practice*;
- failing to comply with the European Union Consumer Credit Directive by not providing adequate explanations or a copy of the draft agreement, or giving false, partial or misleading information to clients;
- applying unreasonable pressure on clients to sign agreements, particularly in face-to-face situations, and not giving clients sufficient time to read and consider the terms of an agreement or to take independent advice where appropriate;

- failing to assess a client's creditworthiness and irresponsible lending, including irresponsible consolidation of debts ('churning');
- replacing irredeemably unenforceable agreements with new agreements after 6 April 2007.

Payment protection insurance

Many loans are covered by insurance against sickness and unemployment, known as payment protection insurance. If the terms of the insurance policy are met, it will make repayments towards contractual instalments. Advisers should always check to see if repayments of a credit debt (secured or unsecured) are covered by insurance. Some policies only provide cover for a set period of time and, in the case of joint agreements, for only one of the parties, often the first person named in the agreement.

Payment protection insurance was often paid for with a single premium, which was then funded as part of the credit agreement and so interest was charged on it. If the client defaulted, s/he could still claim under the policy because the premium had already been paid. Alternatively, the insurance may be paid for through the monthly repayments under the credit agreement, but is not part of the credit provided under the agreement. If the client defaults, the policy often provides for it to lapse after, say, three missed payments.

In some cases, insurance companies refuse to pay – eg, if the client has an illness that started before the insurance policy began (a 'pre-existing condition') or was not actually employed when the policy was taken out. Some policies only provide cover for people under 65 or exclude certain situations altogether – eg, voluntary redundancy. In other cases, delays in processing claims result in creditors applying default interest/charges and/or threatening enforcement action.

Single premium payment protection insurance was invariably purchased at the same time as the credit agreement was entered into. The FSA *Conduct of Business Sourcebook* states that the business must take reasonable steps to ensure that its recommendation to buy, and the cost of, insurance is suitable to the customer's demand and needs. Before agreeing to take out the insurance, a client must receive a policy summary containing its 'main characteristics' – ie, its duration, price, benefits and 'significant' exclusions and limitations. In this context, something is significant if it would affect the client's decision whether or not to take out the policy.

There is considerable evidence of payment protection insurance being mis-sold. Following a super-complaint by Citizens Advice, a market investigation was carried out by the Competition Commission. As a result, the FSA proposed:

- a ban on payment protection insurance at the point of sale;
- the abolition of single premium policies.

The selling of single premium payment protection policies on unsecured loans was stopped in February 2009.

Many of the unfair relationships cases that have come before the courts relate to allegations of mis-sold payment protection insurance. If the client can establish that s/he was told that the finance was conditional on the insurance being taken out, the court is likely to find that the relationship is unfair. Whether or not the creditor told the client this is a question of fact in each case. Otherwise, provided the creditor can demonstrate that it complied with the *Conduct of Business Sourcebook*, the court is unlikely to find the relationship to be unfair. The court will not take into account the relative high cost of single premium payment protection insurance unless the client raised this as an issue at the time of the sale. Sellers of payment protection insurance are usually paid a high rate of commission. The court will not take into account the seller's failure to disclose this commission to the client as this is not a requirement in the *Conduct of Business Sourcebook*.[37]

If a client suggests that taking out a single premium insurance policy was a condition of being given the finance, the whole agreement may be unenforceable if it was taken out before 6 April 2007 and was regulated by the Consumer Credit Act 1974 (see p67).

Note: clients who complain that they were mis-sold payment protection insurance may be better advised to take advantage of the wider jurisdiction of the Financial Ombudsman Service (FOS – see p268)

The adviser must check the terms of the policy and the client's circumstances carefully, investigate any evidence of mis-selling and negotiate with the creditor and/or the insurance company as appropriate. If the client's complaint is about the way the claim has been handled, s/he must first use the insurance company's complaints procedure and can then complain to the FOS (see p268). If the policy has been mis-sold, the adviser should seek either a refund of the payments made or a reduction of the debt plus interest/charges together with a recalculation of the loan with the premium removed. Again, any complaint must first of all be made to the creditor before being taken to the Ombudsman.

Remedies

If the court determines that the relationship is unfair to the borrower, it can:
- require the creditor, or any associate or former associate, to repay (in whole or part) any sum paid by the client by virtue of the credit agreement or any related agreement; *and/or*
- require the creditor, or an associate or former associate, to do, not to do, or to cease anything specified in the order in connection with the agreement or a related agreement; *and/or*
- reduce or discharge any sum payable by the client by virtue of the agreement or a related agreement; *and/or*

- set aside (in whole or part) any duty imposed on the client by virtue of the agreement or a related agreement; *and/or*
- alter the terms of the agreement or any related agreement.

If security is provided in connection with a credit agreement or linked transaction, any surety can also apply to the court under the unfair relationships provisions. In addition to the above orders, the court can order the return to a surety of any property provided by her/him for the purposes of security.

In practice, the OFT anticipates that most consumers are likely to seek out-of-court resolution of disputes rather than initiate court proceedings, which may be costly and time consuming. Nevertheless, the unfair relationship provisions are an important additional protection for clients, and may be especially useful for people facing court proceedings for enforcement or repossession, or where the restrictions on the Ombudsman granting a remedy for conduct before 6 April 2007 mean that the client has no option but to resort to the unfair relationship provisions and their retrospective effect in order to challenge the creditor or defend the claim. However, it should be viewed very much as a remedy of last resort – at least until the Supreme Court clarifies the law. Advisers who are considering taking advantage of these provisions should seek specialist advice.

Procedural irregularities

The Consumer Credit Act 1974 specifies procedures that must be followed for a regulated agreement to be properly executed.[38] Further provisions are contained in regulations (see p67).

An improperly executed regulated agreement is enforceable only by court order.[39] An order can only be made if the court has considered both the creditor's culpability for the improper execution and its effect on the client.[40]

If a creditor has an unenforceable agreement with a client, it should apply to the court for permission to enforce it. The court can allow enforcement on such terms as it thinks fit – eg, reduce the amount owed by the borrower, make a time order (see p340) and reduce or freeze interest/charges.[41]

The court has no power to order enforcement if the agreement was made before 6 April 2007, and:[42]
- it has not been signed by the client(s); *or*
- it has been signed, but does not contain certain prescribed information (see p71);
- in the case of a cancellable agreement, the client was not given a copy before the creditor took court action, or told of her/his cancellation rights.

If a creditor has an unenforceable agreement with a client, it should apply to the court for permission to enforce it. The court can allow enforcement on such terms as it thinks fit – eg, reduce the amount owed by the borrower, make a time order (see p340) and reduce or freeze interest/charges.[43]

If a loan is secured, the creditor cannot enforce the security in order to recover more than it could under the agreement. This means that if the agreement is unenforceable, then so is any security.[44]

A creditor may sue a client for payment of a debt without informing the court that the agreement is unenforceable. If this happens and judgment is entered against the client, s/he may be able to get the judgment 'set aside' (see p314). Specialist advice should be sought.

Notes

1. Introduction
1 ss77-79 CCA 1974

2. Using contract law to challenge or reduce liability
2 *RBS v Etridge (No.2)* [2002] HLR 37; see also G Skipwith, 'Banks, Solicitors, Husbands and Wives', *Adviser* 95
3 See L Groves, 'Guarantors and Rent Arrears', *Adviser* 140; G Skipwith, 'Guarantees, Indemnities and CCA 1974', *Adviser* 149
4 Ombudsman's complaint 47/1, *Adviser* 113
5 para 3.5(g) states that it is an unfair practice to pursue third parties for a debt when they are not liable.
6 *Sherrin v Brand* [1956] 1 QB 403
7 Clients should be referred to the *Land Registry Public Guide* 18, which can be downloaded from www.landregistry.gov.uk/public/guide/public-guide-18
8 See 'Q & A', *Quarterly Account* 24, IMA, Spring 2012
9 *RBS v Etridge (No.2)* [2002] HLR 37; see also G Skipwith, 'Banks, Solicitors, Husbands and Wives', *Adviser* 95
10 See *Ombudsman News* 50, 2005, for details of some complaints which illustrate the FOS approach (*Adviser* 114 abstracts).

11 See also OFT, *Mental Capacity: OFT guidance for creditors* 1373, September 2011, available at www.oft.gov.uk/shared_oft/consultations/oft1373.pdf
12 For a more detailed discussion, see C Wilkinson, 'Mental Incapacity and Debt in England and Wales', *Adviser* 138
13 J Luba and others, *Defending Possession Proceedings*, Legal Action Group, 2010
14 s14 SGA 1979
15 s13 SGSA 1982
16 *Crantrave Ltd v Lloyds Bank* (*Adviser* 87 abstracts); see also P Madge, 'Consultancy Corner', *Adviser* 101. Also, for the FOS view of this issue, see *Ombudsman News* 87 (*Adviser* 142 abstracts)
17 *Dunlop Pneumatic Tyre Co Ltd v New Garage and Motor Co* [1915] AC 79 (HL)
18 Reg 5(1) UTCC Regs 1999
19 Reg 8 UTCC Regs 1999
20 Sch 2 UTCC Regs 1999
21 Sch 2 para 1(e) UTCC Regs 1999
22 Sch 2 para 1(i) UTCC Regs 1999
23 See 'Penalty Charges on Credit Cards and Current Accounts', *Quarterly Account* 78, IMA, Winter 2005/06; G Skipwith, 'Penalty Shoot-out', *Adviser* 113

3. Using the Consumer Credit Act to challenge or reduce liability

24 ss77 and 78 CCA 1974
25 *McGuffick v RBS* [2009] EWHC 2386 (Comm) (*Adviser* 136 abstracts); *Carey and others v HSBC and others* [2009] EWHC 3471 (QB) (*Adviser* 139 abstracts)
26 Reg 3 Consumer Credit (Cancellation Notices and Copies of Documents) Regulations 1983, No.1557
27 For example, para 2.8(k) (not ceasing collection activity whilst investigating a reasonably queried or disputed debt)
28 *Carey and others v HSBC and others* [2009] EWHC 3471 (QB) (*Adviser* 139 abstracts)
29 OFT, *Debt Collection Guidance*, para 2.8(i)
30 OFT, *Debt Collection Guidance*, para 4(r)
31 r31.8 CPR
32 ss39 and 40 CCA 1974
33 ss94 and 95 CCA 1974
34 Consumer Credit (Early Settlement) Regulations 2004, No.1483
35 ss19-22 and Sch 3 paras14-17 CCA 2006
36 *Barnes and Barnes v Black Horse* [2011] EWHC 1416 (QB), HC (*Adviser* 147 abstracts)
37 See *Harrison v Black Horse* [2011] EWCA Civ 1128, CA (*Adviser* 148 abstracts). For a fuller review of the history of this case, see *Arian* caselaw updates 26, 29 and 33. See also R Gardner, 'Payment Protection Litigation after the Harrison Settlement', *Solicitors Journal* 156/36, 2012, p10
38 ss60-64 CCA 1974
39 s65 CCA 1974
40 s127(1) CCA 1974
41 *National Mortgage Corporation v Wilkes*, *Legal Action*, October 1991
42 s127(3) and (4) CCA 1974
43 *National Mortgage Corporation v Wilkes*, *Legal Action*, October 1991
44 s113 CCA 1974

Chapter 6

Types of debt

This chapter covers:
1. Regulated debts (below)
2. Other debts (p127)

This chapter looks at the particular debts that advisers commonly encounter, the issues they are likely to raise and the action advisers and clients should consider taking to deal with them.

1. **Regulated debts**

Bank overdraft

A bank overdraft is a type of revolving credit (see p125). The bank allows a customer with a current account to overdraw on the account up to a certain amount. Repayment of the overdraft is made as money is paid into the account.

The legal position

Bank overdrafts are regulated under the Consumer Credit Act, provided the credit is for no more than £25,000 (if granted before 6 April 2008) or £15,000 (if granted before 1 May 1998). It does not matter whether the overdraft is authorised or unauthorised. If the agreement was made before 1 February 2011, no written agreement is required. If the credit is granted on or after 6 April 2008, the agreement is regulated regardless of the amount, unless it is exempt (see p66). An overdraft may be either secured or unsecured.

Special features

Interest is charged, usually on a daily basis, and repayment in full can be requested at any time. When the agreed overdraft limit is reached, cheques drawn against the account will usually be stopped.

If the overdraft is not approved by the bank or the limit is exceeded, a higher rate of interest is usually charged and additional service charges may be made at the bank's discretion.

When a customer has both a current account with overdraft facilities and a loan account with the same bank, it is common for banks to require payments to the personal loan account to be made from the current account. This may be done even if there are no funds in the current account, so that the higher overdraft rate of interest will apply to the payments made to the personal loan account.

Similarly, if someone has her/his wages paid directly into a current account, they will always be applied initially to reduce any overdraft on that account, even if debts such as mortgage arrears ought to be given a higher priority for repayment.

Emergency action may, therefore, be needed to ensure income is not swallowed up as it becomes available. It may be necessary to open a current account with another bank so that wages can be paid into the new account or, if this is not possible, exercise the 'first right of appropriation' (see p49).

Note: banks cannot transfer money from a joint account to a sole account in order to pay a sole debt.[1] In multiple debt cases, the bank should recognise the pro rata principle when considering a payment arrangement and that priority debts should take precedence over non-priority debts, which the bank's debt is likely to be unless it is secured on the client's home.

It may be possible to challenge any charges added to the account as a penalty (see p91).

Right of set-off

Although the bank has the right to offset any credits received against any debt owed to it (known as the bank's right of set-off), *The Lending Code* says that the client should be left 'with sufficient money for reasonable day-to-day expenses taking into account individual circumstances'. In other words, banks should not use standard figures to assess a client's needs. A bank should explain the circumstances in which set-off can be used at the time when it is considering using set-off for the first time. Clients should be notified promptly each time set-off was used.

The Financial Services Authority's (FSA's) *Conduct of Business Sourcebook* (which has applied to retail banking since 1 November 2009) say that banks must pay due regard to the interests of their customers and must treat customers who are in financial difficulty fairly. The FSA says that if a bank is considering using set-off on a client's account it should:

- consider each case and assess how much money needs to be left in the account to meet priority debts and essential living expenses;
- usually provide a refund if it becomes apparent that money taken in set-off was intended for priority debts or essential living expenses;
- not use set-off on money that it knows, or should know, is intended for certain purposes (eg, for healthcare) or if a third party is entitled to the money.

In addition, the Office of Fair Trading's (OFT's) *Irresponsible Lending Guidance* and *Debt Collection Guidance* says that banks should not exercise their right of set-off if, having carried out an assessment of the client's financial situation, it is clear that the client is already experiencing an unsustainable level of indebtedness or would do if set-off were to be used.

The Financial Ombudsman Service (FOS) also expects banks to have given their customers a fair and sufficient opportunity to discuss the situation and repay the outstanding debt before resorting to their right of set-off.[2]

Checklist for action

Advisers should take the following action.

- Consider whether emergency action is necessary (see Chapter 8).
- Check liability, including the enforceability of the agreement under the Consumer Credit Act.
- If the bank has resorted to set-off, check that it has complied with the guidance and codes of practice.
- Assist the client to choose a strategy from Chapter 9 as, if the debt is unsecured, it is a non-priority debt. **If is secured, it is a priority debt**. See Chapter 8.

Bill of sale

A bill of sale is also known as a 'chattel mortgage' and is a way of raising money by offering an item of personal property (commonly a motor vehicle) as security for a loan. The essential feature of a bill of sale is that the mortgaged goods remain in the possession and use of the client but ownership is transferred to the creditor, so the goods can be repossessed and sold if the debt is not repaid. Similar arrangements containing some, but not all, of these features are not bills of sale (eg, pawnbroking – see p121), where the goods are deposited with the creditor as security, but remain the property of the client.

However, bills of sale are increasingly used to finance the actual purchase of motor vehicles. With hire purchase (HP)/conditional sale, the dealer sells the vehicle to the creditor who then lets (HP) or sells (conditional sale) it to the client. With a bill of sale, the dealer sells the car to the client who then enters into a credit agreement with the creditor (likely to be regulated by the Consumer Credit Act) secured by a bill of sale. A bill of sale gives the creditor all the advantages of HP/conditional sale agreements – ie:

- security for the debt;
- the right to repossess the vehicle if the client defaults;
- provided there is a term in the bill of sale, the right to forcibly enter the client's property to repossess the goods without a court order.

From the creditor's point of view, a bill of sale also removes some of the disadvantages of an HP/conditional sale – ie:

- the client has no right to terminate the agreement and limit her/his lia~~bility to~~ one-half of the total price;
- the vehicle is not protected from repossession without a cou~~rt order once the~~ client has paid one-third of the total price;

- a private individual (ie, someone who is not a motor dealer) who purchases the vehicle from the client without knowing it is subject to a bill of sale does not obtain ownership. S/he is, therefore, not protected from having the vehicle repossessed by the creditor, as would be the case if the vehicle were subject to a HP/conditional sale agreement.

The legal position

Bills of sale are regulated by two pieces of nineteenth century legislation which still represent the law: the Bills of Sale Acts 1878 and 1882. The formal agreement, known as the bill of sale, must be set out in the way specified by the Schedule to the Bills of Sale Act (1878) Amendment Act 1882. If the bill of sale secures an agreement regulated by the Consumer Credit Act, there must be a separate agreement, which should itself comply with the Consumer Credit Act and the regulations. This includes the requirement for the agreement to refer to the bill of sale. If the agreement is improperly executed, the creditor will either need the leave of the court to enforce its security under the bill of sale or, if the agreement is irredeemably unenforceable, the creditor will be unable to enforce its security.

There are a number of formalities associated with bills of sale and, if the creditor fails to comply with them, the creditor risks it being void and so unenforceable (although this will not necessarily affect the underlying credit agreement, which will remain enforceable but as an unsecured debt).

Special features

In order to be valid and enforceable, a bill of sale must be:
- 'in accordance with' the statutory form set out in the Schedule to the Bills of Sale Act (1878) Amendment Act 1882. This means it must be to the same effect, but not necessarily word for word the same, as the Act (see below);
- registered at the High Court in London within seven days of being made and then re-registered every five years. A copy of the registered document is forwarded to the local county court. Anyone can search, inspect, make extracts from and obtain copies of the register on payment of the prescribed fee (currently £45). This can be done by personal visit to the court office.

To be 'in accordance with the statutory form' and, therefore, valid and enforceable, a bill of sale must contain:
- the date of the bill of sale;
- the names and addresses of the parties;
- a statement of the 'consideration'. This is the amount paid by the creditor to, or on behalf of, the client and does not include any item forming part of the total charge for credit in a regulated agreement secured by the bill;
- an acknowledgment of receipt of the consideration by the client. This is obligatory, even though the money is not paid to the client but to a third party – eg, the supplier of the goods;

- an assignment by way of security of the goods;
- no description of the goods in the body of the bill; this must be in a schedule to the bill;
- a monetary obligation. This can include an obligation to insure the goods or maintain the security;
- a statement of the sum secured, the rate of interest and the instalments by which repayment is to be made. Interest is an essential part of a bill and must be stated as a rate, even if it is also expressed as a lump sum. This is an area where creditors have frequently gone wrong, as it is not just a question of importing figures direct from the credit agreement. If the interest rate under a regulated agreement is not variable, there was no requirement before 31 May 2005 to include it in the agreement, as opposed to the annual percentage rate (APR). In the case of these agreements, if the bill of sale quotes the APR instead of the interest rate, the bill will not be in accordance with the statutory form. Nor will the bill be in accordance with the statutory form if the sum stated to be secured includes the interest charged under the credit agreement, because this would involve double charging of interest. Arguably, a bill of sale which refers to the credit agreement for the statement of these terms (or any of them) is not in accordance with the statutory form;[3]
- any terms that are agreed for the 'maintenance' or 'defeasance' of the security. A 'defeasance' is a provision in a document which nullifies it if specified acts are performed. For example, on payment of all sums due under the bill, the security will be void – ie, in this context, discharged. 'Maintenance of the security' means the preservation of the whole security given by the bill of sale in as good a condition as when it was made. The following terms are included:
  – to insure the goods and produce receipts for premiums;
  – to repair the goods and replace worn-out goods;
  – to allow entry to inspect the goods;
  – to allow the creditor to enter the premises in which the goods are situated in order to seize them (the bill of sale may even permit forcible entry);[4]
- a proviso limiting the grounds of seizure. The bill of sale will be void if it contains a power to seize in events other than in the case of:[5]
  – default in repayments or in performance of any terms in the bill of sale necessary for maintenance of the security;
  – bankruptcy of the client;
  – fraudulent removal of the goods, or allowing them to be removed, from premises. In the case of a vehicle, this might include a sale without the lender's consent;
  – unreasonably refusing to produce the last receipt for rent, rates or taxes;
  – the levy of execution on the goods or distress for rent or taxes. See Chapter 14 for more information on this;
- signature of the bill of sale by the client. A bill need not be sealed;[6]

- an attestation clause. This is essential and must be meticulously completed. The security will be unenforceable unless the client's signature is witnessed by at least one person who is not a party to the bill;[7]
- the name, address and description of the witness. The name alone without an address (which may be the business address and not necessarily a private address) and description (ie, the profession, trade or vocation of the witness) is insufficient;
- a schedule, referring to the goods comprised in the bill of sale. If the bill does not have a schedule, it is void.

Clients often present themselves to an adviser with either an HP/conditional sale agreement or an unsecured loan. In these circumstances, if the creditor is threatening to repossess the subject of the agreement (eg, the motor vehicle), the adviser should establish whether the debt is, in fact, secured by a bill of sale. If so, the adviser should check that the credit agreement is properly executed and that the bill of sale is validly drawn up and registered. The creditor could be asked to supply a copy of the bill of sale showing the court stamp.

If the agreement secured by the bill of sale is regulated by the Consumer Credit Act, the creditor must serve a default notice before being entitled to repossess the goods on the grounds that the client has defaulted. In cases where the agreement is irredeemably unenforceable, the bill of sale cannot be enforced either. In cases where the agreement can only be enforced with the permission of the court, the bill of sale cannot be enforced until the creditor has obtained an enforcement order.[8]

Seized goods should not be removed from the premises where they were seized until five clear days have expired.[9] During this period, the client could apply for a time order if appropriate (see p340).

If a bill of sale is believed to be invalid and unenforceable, but the creditor will not accept this and threatens to go ahead with repossessing the goods, a rarely used procedure, known as applying to 'expunge' (ie, remove) the registration of the bill of sale must be used. This is, in effect, a declaration of unenforceability. As bills of sale are registered in the High Court, the application has to be made to the High Court under Part 8 of the Civil Procedure Rules, even though the bill of sale may be securing a regulated consumer credit agreement. Specialist advice is needed.

If the creditor has already repossessed the goods under an invalid or unregistered bill of sale, the creditor should be challenged and, while the client may still owe the balance outstanding under the loan agreement, it may be possible to persuade the creditor to write off the debt. Specialist advice may be needed.

Following concerns about the use of bills of sale secured against vehicles, from 1 February 2011, the industry now operates under a code of practice.[10] This includes the following.

- Clients in arrears will be able to hand over the vehicle in full settlement of the debt and will not be liable for any shortfall between the outstanding debt and the value of the vehicle.
- Consumer loans will no longer provide for 'balloon payments' – ie, small, initial interest-only payments, with the capital being repaid in a single, final payment.
- Charges imposed on clients in arrears must be disclosed at the pre-contract stage and must only cover the creditor's costs.
- If a client gets into difficulty, creditors must consider proposals for alternative payment arrangements and will repossess the vehicle only if attempts to arrange alternative ways of repayment fail.
- Creditors will take all reasonable steps to ensure that repossessed vehicles are sold for the highest obtainable market price.

Checklist for action

Advisers should take the following action.
- Consider whether emergency action is necessary. If repossession of goods is threatened, **this is likely to be a priority debt**. See Chapter 8.
- Check liability, including not only the validity of the bill of sale but also the enforceability of the agreement under the Consumer Credit Act.
- If the goods have already been repossessed, this is a non-priority debt. Assist the client to choose a strategy from Chapter 9.

Budget account

A budget account is a type of revolving credit (see p125) provided by shops. The client can spend up to an agreed credit limit and makes regular repayments.

The legal position

This type of account is regulated under the Consumer Credit Act, provided the credit is for no more than £25,000 (if the agreement was made before 6 April 2008) or £15,000 (if made before 1 May 1998).[11] If the agreement was made on or after 6 April 2008, the agreement is regulated regardless of the amount, unless it is exempt (see p65).

Special features

Many large stores offer budget account facilities which, by requiring clients to pay a monthly amount even when they have not recently purchased anything, can be a powerful incentive to continue shopping at that store. Instant credit is often available, including interest-free credit (see p119) on larger purchases.

These debts are non-priority debts (see Chapter 9).

Checklist for action

Advisers should take the following action.

- Check liability, including the enforceability of the agreement under the Consumer Credit Act.
- Assist the client to choose a strategy from Chapter 9 as this is a non-priority debt.

Conditional sale agreement

A conditional sale agreement is a sale made on credit subject to conditions that give the client possession of the goods during the repayment period, but the goods only become the client's property when the last payment has been made. Conditional sale agreements are mostly used for motor vehicles (and are very similar to HP agreements – see p116).

The legal position

Agreements are regulated under the Consumer Credit Act, provided the credit is for no more than £25,000 (if the agreement was made before 6 April 2008) or £15,000 (if made before 1 May 1998).[12] If the agreement was made on or after 6 April 2008, the agreement is regulated regardless of the amount, unless it is exempt (see p65).

Special features

Conditional sale has a number of special features. These are the same as those for HP (see p116) and the two types of credit operate in the same way.

Checklist for action

Advisers should take the following action.

- Consider whether emergency action is necessary to prevent repossession of goods. See Chapter 8.
- Check liability, including the enforceability of the agreement under the Consumer Credit Act.
- Check that the goods purchased were as described and of satisfactory quality (see p91).
- Assist the client to choose a strategy from Chapter 8, if **this is a priority debt** or Chapter 9 if the goods are not essential.

Credit card

A credit card (eg, Mastercard, Visa) is a form of revolving credit (see p125) and allows the client to buy goods or services from a trader by use of a four-digit personal identification number (PIN). The trader invoices the credit card company and the client receives a monthly account showing all transactions made during that period. A minimum monthly repayment is required – often covering at least interest, fees and charges plus 1 per cent of the capital outstanding. Interest is added to balances outstanding after a specified payment date, or immediately for cash withdrawals using a credit card.

The legal position

Transactions made by credit card are linked agreements under the Consumer Credit Act. Consequently, credit card companies can be held responsible for misrepresentation and for defective goods or services costing between £100 and £30,000 if the trader is unwilling to remedy the situation. This could include a claim for damages due as a consequence of the misrepresentation or other breach. The House of Lords has confirmed that overseas transactions are covered.[13]

If an additional credit card is issued to another person (usually a member of the client's family) to enable her/him to use the client's account, the client is liable for all transactions incurred by the additional cardholder, including if the client has not specifically authorised the transaction in question.

Unless the credit card agreement is a joint agreement (signed by both the client and the additional cardholder), the additional cardholder has no liability under the agreement if the client fails to pay.

If the client withdraws the additional cardholder's permission to use the credit card, the client remains liable for any transactions incurred by the additional cardholder until the client informs the creditor that the second cardholder's permission has been withdrawn in accordance with the terms and conditions of the credit card agreement. Once that has been done, the additional credit cardholder is no longer an 'authorised person' and the client has no further liability for transactions incurred by the additional cardholder.

Special features

The use of a credit card is the cheapest way to obtain short-term credit (up to about six weeks) for specific items. This is because on most cards no interest is charged if the account is cleared at the first due date after a purchase is added to it. However, interest is charged immediately for cash withdrawals and there is often an annual charge for cardholders.

Checklist for action

Advisers should take the following action.
* Check liability and that the goods purchased were as described and of satisfactory quality (see p91).
* Assist the client to choose a strategy from Chapter 9, as this is not a priority debt.

Credit sale agreement

Goods bought on credit sale are owned immediately by the client. Regular payments are due in accordance with a regulated agreement. The creditor is often the supplier of the goods and this type of credit is used extensively to sell furniture and cars.

The legal position

The agreement is regulated by the Consumer Credit Act provided the credit is for less than £25,000 (if made before 6 April 2008) or £15,000 (if made before 1 May 1998). If the agreement was made on or after 6 April 2008, the agreement is regulated regardless of the amount, unless it is exempt (see p65).

Special features

The creditor has no rights over the goods. The client simply takes the goods, signs the agreement, and starts to make payments. Sometimes interest-free credit (see p119) is given in the form of a credit sale agreement.

Some credit sale agreements (particularly for cars) provide that:
- the client must not sell the goods during the lifetime of the agreement; *and*
- if the client does sell the goods, s/he must pay the proceeds to the creditor.

The OFT regards the restriction on the sale of the goods as an unfair contract term, which means a client will probably not be in breach of it if s/he does sell the goods. However, the OFT does not regard it as unfair for the creditor to require payment of the proceeds, although the creditor would need to serve the client with a notice under s76 of the Consumer Credit Act before being entitled to take action to enforce such a term.[14] If the client is unable to comply with such a notice, the OFT's view is that the client would then be in default. For a fuller discussion of unfair contract terms, see p92.

Checklist for action

Advisers should take the following action.
- Check liability, including the enforceability of the agreement under the Consumer Credit Act.
- Check that the goods purchased were as described and of satisfactory quality (see p91).
- Assist the client to choose a strategy from Chapter 9, as this is not a priority debt.

Hire purchase agreement

An HP agreement hires goods to the client for an agreed period. At the end of this period the client has the option to buy them (usually for a nominal amount). HP is predominantly used for motor vehicles. The creditor (who is the hirer) owns the goods, generally having bought them from the supplier who introduced the client to the hirer.

The legal position

HP agreements for up to £25,000 (if made before 6 April 2008) or £15,000 (if made before 1 May 1998) are regulated under the Consumer Credit Act. If the agreement was made on or after 6 April 2008, the agreement is regulated regardless of the amount, unless it is exempt (see p65).

The contract is between the client and the hirer of the goods, rather than the supplier – ie, in the case of a car, between the client and the finance company, rather than with the garage. Therefore the hirer (ie, the finance company) is liable for compensation for misrepresentation (see p89) and faulty goods. The Consumer Credit Act treats HP and conditional sale in the same way and so what follows also applies to conditional sale agreements.

Special features

The goods belong to the hirer until the end of the agreement. The client must not sell them during this period without obtaining the hirer's permission. The client can choose to return the goods to the hirer at any time during the lifetime of the agreement. The client must first give written notice to the hirer of her/his wish to terminate the agreement. In order that there should be no doubt as to what the client is doing (particularly if the hirer is threatening to repossess the goods), the letter should refer to the client exercising her/his right to terminate the agreement and request instructions from the hirer on the return of the goods.[15]

The amount payable on return depends on the amount already paid.

- If less than half the total purchase price (as stated on the agreement) has been paid, the client must pay either half the total purchase price minus the payments already made or any arrears of payments which have become due by the termination date, whichever is greater.
- If more than half the total purchase price has already been paid, the client may return the goods and will owe nothing further except any arrears on payments due.
- If the client has not taken reasonable care of the goods, s/he is liable to compensate the hirer.

When clients inform hirers that they can no longer afford the repayments and wish to end the agreement, they are often advised to surrender the vehicle voluntarily. A 'voluntary surrender' is not the same thing as a termination. A voluntary surrender has the same legal consequences as if the hirer had terminated the agreement and repossessed the goods (see p118). While hirers are under no duty to inform clients of their rights, they must not mislead them.

Hirers often put obstacles in the way of clients attempting to end their agreements – eg, by claiming that the client cannot end the agreement if it is in arrears or that the sum due on ending the agreement must be paid as a pre-condition of ending the agreement. This is not correct; the right to end the agreement is unconditional. Default notices issued since 1 October 2008 must contain the following statement: 'You will need to pay X if you wish to end this agreement' (where X is the amount calculated as above). The OFT has agreed that this sum is the amount the hirer is liable to pay if s/he exercises the right to terminate and is not a condition of termination. However, the regulations have not yet been amended to reflect this.

If the hirer challenges the client's right to end the agreement, specialist advice should be sought. It is not the creditor's responsibility to arrange collection of the goods if a client terminates the agreement and, if the creditor has to collect the goods because the client refuses to return them, the client is liable for any charges incurred. On the other hand, if the creditor insists on collecting the goods, the client should challenge any collection charges the creditor seeks to impose.[16]

If the client claims to have terminated the agreement, specialist advice should be sought if the creditor is nevertheless seeking to recover the total balance due under the agreement. The client will lose the right to terminate the agreement if the hirer has already done so or called in the balance due under the agreement.

If the client defaults on payments, the hirer can repossess the goods. It must obtain a court order, unless:

- the client gives permission. This must be free and informed – ie, the client has not been misled about her/his rights; *or*
- less than one-third of the total purchase price has been paid and the goods are not on private premises.

If the hirer repossesses the goods (including 'voluntary surrender' cases where the client returns the goods without terminating the agreement in writing), the client is liable for the outstanding balance due under the agreement, less the sale proceeds of the goods.[17]

Insurance

Many HP/conditional sale agreements also incorporate credit agreements for insurance sold as part of the same transaction – eg:

- payment protection insurance to cover the repayments in the event of the client's unemployment, sickness, disability or death;
- mechanical breakdown insurance;
- vehicle recovery insurance;
- accident assistance insurance;
- extended warranties or guarantees; *and*
- guaranteed asset protection (GAP), also known as shortfall insurance, which covers any shortfall if, following an accident, the write-off value of the goods is less than the balance owed to the creditor.

A credit agreement for such insurance (known as the 'subsidiary agreement') is a different type of agreement to the HP/conditional sale (known as the 'principal agreement') and is treated as a separate agreement. It is, however, permissible to include a subsidiary agreement for such insurance (but not for any other insurance or products) in the same document as the principal agreement containing only the consumer credit heading and signature box for the principal agreement. Agreements made before 31 May 2005 should not have included credit for GAP in the subsidiary agreement and any such credit agreement is improperly executed and unenforceable without permission of the court.[18] Permission will usually be granted on condition that the cost of GAP and its associated credit charges are removed.

The consequences of this practice are as follows.

- There is no right for the client to terminate the subsidiary agreement and so termination of the principal agreement does not affect the client's liability under the subsidiary agreement. The client must deal with this separately – eg, settle the agreement early, complain about any mis-selling of the insurance or raise any unenforceability issues.

- In calculating whether the client has paid one-third or one-half of the total price in connection with protected goods and termination rights, only the payments due or made in relation to the principal agreement should be taken into account. Advisers should check the one-third and one-half figures in the agreement.

- If the client was required to take out payment protection insurance as a condition of making the principal agreement, it may be that both agreements are irredeemably unenforceable and specialist advice should be sought.

Checklist for action

Advisers should take the following action.

- Consider whether emergency action is necessary to prevent repossession of goods. See Chapter 8.
- Check liability, including the enforceability of the agreement under the Consumer Credit Act.
- Check that the goods purchased were as described and of satisfactory quality (see p91).
- Assist the client to choose a strategy from Chapter 8, if **this is a priority debt** or Chapter 9 if the goods are not essential.

Interest-free credit

This is a type of credit sale agreement in which money is loaned to buy goods without any interest being charged. It is usually offered by larger stores. Some agreements offer interest-free credit provided the total balance is paid off within a specified period and, thereafter, become ordinary credit sale agreements.

The legal position

These agreements are regulated by the Consumer Credit Act, provided the credit is for no more than £25,000 (if made before 6 April 2008) or £15,000 (if made before 1 May 1998), even though there is no charge for credit. If the agreement was made on or after 6 April 2008, the agreement is regulated regardless of the amount, unless it is exempt (see p65).

An agreement is exempt if it requires the credit to be repaid in no more than four instalments within 12 months of making the agreement, provided in the case of agreements made on or after 1 February 2011, the credit is provided without interest or other charges. However, if it is not exempt, it must contain all the details required by a regulated agreement (see p67) and details of the circumstances in which interest could become chargeable. Interest can be charged on late payments if the agreement contains a clause allowing it. This type of credit can be expensive if it is not repaid during the interest-free period.

Special features

Interest-free credit is offered as an inducement to buy particular goods in a particular place and, therefore, is a linked agreement (see p100).

Checklist for action

Advisers should take the following action.
- Check liability, including enforceability under the Consumer Credit Act.
- Check that the goods purchased were as described and of satisfactory quality (see p91).
- Assist the client to choose a strategy from Chapter 9, as this is a non-priority debt.

Mail order catalogue

Mail order catalogues offer a way of buying goods by post and usually spread payment over a period of weeks by instalments. Payments are sometimes collected by an agent – often a friend or neighbour of the client. The arrangement is usually an ongoing one.

The legal position

Catalogue debts are covered by the Consumer Credit Act whether or not there is a charge for credit, provided the credit is for no more than £25,000 (if the arrangement began before 6 April 2008) or £15,000 (if before 1 May 1998). If the arrangement began on or after 6 April 2008, the agreement is regulated regardless of the amount, unless it is exempt (see p65).

Some mail order companies provide goods on the basis that they are paid for in full on receipt. These agreements are not regulated by the Consumer Credit Act. If in doubt about whether a catalogue debt is regulated, specialist advice should be sought.

Special features

Often clients do not receive an agreement to sign. This means that the client's liability for the debt is irredeemably unenforceable if the arrangement began before 6 April 2007 and enforceable only with the permission of the court if the arrangement began on or after this date.[19] In these circumstances, the client is not legally obliged to settle the debt if the arrangement began before 6 April 2007, although s/he may choose to do so.

Mail order purchases can be cancelled by returning the goods within seven days of receipt.

Catalogues are often particularly important to people on low incomes as the only way of affording essential items such as bedding or clothing.

Checklist for action

Advisers should take the following action.
- Check liability by asking the creditor to supply a copy of the agreement signed by the client.
- Check that the goods were of satisfactory quality and as described (see p91).
- If the client decides not to challenge liability, assist her/him to choose a strategy from Chapter 9, as this is a non-priority debt unless the use of mail order catalogues is the only way in which the s/he can buy essential goods (see p240).

Pawnbroker

Money is lent against an article(s) (pawn) left with the pawnbroker as security – a pledge. The goods can only be reclaimed (redeemed) if the loan is repaid with interest. If the loan is not repaid, the pawnbroker can sell the goods.

The legal position

Pawnbrokers must be licensed and lending is covered by the Consumer Credit Act, provided the credit is for no more than £25,000 (if the agreement was made before 6 April 2008) or £15,000 (if made before 1 May 1998). If the agreement was made on or after 6 April 2008, the agreement is regulated regardless of the amount, unless it is exempt (see p65).

Special features

There are certain exceptions that apply to pawnbrokers' duty to comply with the pre-contract information requirements outlined on p67.
- Unless the client is a 'new customer' (ie, s/he has not done business with the pawnbroker in the previous three years), the pawnbroker only has to inform her/him of her/his right to receive the pre-contract information free of charge on request (see p69).
- The pawnbroker's duty to provide the client with 'adequate explanations' (see p69) only applies to:

– the main consequences of her/his failure to make the payments due under the agreement. **Note:** the requirement to explain any features of the agreement which may make it unsuitable for particular types of use does not apply to pawnbroking agreements and so there is no requirement to explain to the client that they are a short-term product, and an expensive and unsuitable method of longer term borrowing;

– the effects of withdrawing from the agreement, and when and how to exercise this right. **Note:** if the client fails to repay the loan and interest within 30 days of exercising her/his right to withdraw, the pawnbroker can retain and sell the pawned goods.

- The pawnbroker does not have to assess the client's creditworthiness – ie, her/his ability to repay the loan (see p70).
- The pawnbroker does not have to supply the client with a copy of the draft consumer credit agreement.

The pawnbroker must give the client a receipt for the goods ('pawn receipt') and must keep the goods for at least six months, during which time interest is charged on the money borrowed. The client retains ownership of the goods in the meantime. If the goods are not redeemed after six months:

- if the loan was for £75 or less and the goods were not subject to an earlier pledge which was renewed, ownership of the goods passes to the pawnbroker;
- in all other cases, the pawnbroker has the right to sell the goods.

Unless the loan was for £100 or less, the pawnbroker must give the client at least 14 days' notice of her/his intention to sell the goods. The client can redeem the goods at any time before the goods are sold (except if ownership has passed to the pawnbroker) by handing in the pawn receipt, and paying off the loan and accrued interest.

It is a criminal offence for a pawnbroker to refuse to redeem a pawn unless it has reasonable cause to believe that the person handing in the pawn receipt is neither the owner of the goods nor authorised to redeem them. If the client is unable to redeem the goods, s/he must renew the pledge to prevent the goods being sold. If the goods are sold, the pawnbroker must inform the client of their sale price and provide details of the costs of sale. If the client challenges the amount for which the goods were sold and/or the costs of sale, the onus is on the pawnbroker to justify the figures.

Checklist for action

Advisers should take the following action.
- Check liability, including enforceability of the agreement under the Consumer Credit Act.
- Assist the client to choose a strategy from Chapter 9 as this is a non-priority debt (or Chapter 8 if the pawned item is essential).

Payday loan

These are small (generally between £100 and £1,000) loans intended to cover short-term financial difficulties such as an unexpected bill or an emergency. They are repayable in full on the client's next pay day.

The legal position

These are fixed-sum credit agreements and are likely to be regulated by the Consumer Credit Act as they will be within the financial limits for regulation and outside the various rules for exemption (see p65).

Special features

Clients with payday loans are typically paying back £25 for each £100 borrowed, which translates into an APR of 1,286 per cent (although APRs of 2,356 per cent are advertised).

They are, therefore, not appropriate for clients who are already in financial difficulties. In fact, they are likely to exacerbate any pre-existing financial difficulties because in such circumstances it is extremely unlikely that the client will be able to repay the loan on the due date (typically within 31 days).

Two of the requirements to provide the client with adequate pre-contract explanations (see p69) are of particular relevance to payday loans.

- Features of the agreement which may make it unsuitable: payday loans are a short-term product and are unsuitable for supporting borrowing over longer periods.
- Features of the agreement which may operate in an adverse manner: the effect of 'rolling over' such loans could accumulate an unmanageable level of debt. The Finance and Leasing Association's code of practice limits the number of times a payday loan can be rolled over to three, but it only has one payday lender among its members. The codes of practice of the four trade associations issued on 24 May 2012 (available at www.cfa-uk.co.uk/codeofpractice.asp) state that creditors should:
  – not pressurise clients to roll over loans;
  – only consider rolling over a loan if a client asks; *and*
  – tell clients if there is a limit on the number of times a loan can be rolled over. If a client is in financial difficulties and informs the creditor, the creditor should explore new arrangements for paying the debt with her/him.

Continuous payment authorities

The most common method of repayment is by debit card. Unlike standing orders and direct debits, there is confusion about whether clients can cancel a debit (or credit) card payment authority (known as a 'continuous payment authority' if it is for ongoing payment arrangements). In addition, unlike direct debits, they are not covered by the direct debit guarantee in the event of a payment being wrongly made.

The FOS has upheld a complaint and required the client's bank to refund payments made on a debit card where it was clear that the client had never authorised the payments.[20]

In the commentary in paragraph 3.9 of its *Debt Collection Guidance,* the OFT says that, in order to cancel a continuous payment authority, a client must approach the creditor who has the authority rather than the bank from which the money is to be paid, as there is no automatic right to cancel. In the past, this is what many banks have advised their customers.

However, this advice appears to conflict with the provisions of the Payment Services Regulations 2009 and the FSA says that a client has the right to cancel a continuous payment authority directly with her/his bank or card issuer by informing it that s/he has withdrawn her/his permission for the payments. The payments must then be stopped and the bank cannot insist that the client contacts the payee to agree to this first. The FSA has produced a leaflet, *Bank Accounts: know your rights,* available at www.fsa.gov.uk/consumerinformation/product_news/banking/know_y our_rights.[21] The FOS also agrees with this view.[22]

Unless a continuous payment authority is cancelled as described above so that a client is not pressurised into rolling over loans and can instead try to agree an affordable payment arrangement with the lender, s/he could find her/himself with an unauthorised overdraft, subject to interest and charges, and without money to meet essential expenditure. The client may have to extend the loan, for which a fee may be charged. This means that the outstanding balance will rapidly escalate due to the high interest rate and will further exacerbate the client's existing financial difficulties.

Checklist for action

Advisers should take the following action.

- Consider whether emergency action is necessary – eg, cancel any continuous payment authority.
- Check liability, including the enforceability under the Consumer Credit Act (although clients with payday loans made before 6 April 2007 are likely to be rare).
- If the client is in financial difficulties and the time for payment has not yet arrived, either ask the creditor not to take the payment from the debit card, or arrange to cancel the continuous payment authority if time is short or the creditor refuses to comply with the request.
- Consider whether the loan was inappropriate to the client's situation and, if there is evidence of irresponsible lending (including in dealing with the client's default and arrears), use the FOS complaints procedure (see p268). If the case has already gone to court, seek specialist support for a possible unfair relationship challenge (see p98).
- In other cases, assist the client to choose a strategy from Chapter 9 as this is a non-priority debt.

Personal loan

A personal loan is a loan offered at a fixed or variable rate of interest over a set period.

The legal position

Personal loans are regulated under the Consumer Credit Act, provided the credit is for no more than £25,000 (if the agreement was made before 6 April 2008) or £15,000 (if made before 1 May 1998). If the agreement was made on or after 6 April 2008, the agreement is regulated regardless of the amount, unless it is exempt (see p65).

Special features

Personal loans are widely available from banks, building societies and other financial institutions, including small moneylenders. Some personal loans have fixed interest rates and the total interest charged is set at the beginning of the period of the loan. Repayments are then made in equal instalments. Sometimes, a personal loan is part of a linked transaction (see p100). The amount to be loaned may be paid directly to the supplier rather than the borrower. With smaller moneylenders, repayments are often collected at the door by a representative.

Checklist for action

Advisers should take the following action.
- Check liability, including enforceability of the agreement, under the Consumer Credit Act (see Chapter 5).
- Assist the client to choose a strategy from Chapter 9, as personal loans are generally a non-priority debt.

Revolving credit

Revolving credit is a type of personal borrowing in which the creditor agrees to a credit limit and the client can borrow up to that limit, provided s/he maintains certain previously agreed minimum payments. Revolving credit takes a number of different forms – eg, credit cards (see p114), budget accounts (see p113) and bank overdrafts (see p107).

Second mortgage (secured loan)

A second (or subsequent) mortgage allows a homeowner to take out a (further) loan, using the property as security. The lender takes a legal charge on the property giving rights of repossession similar to those of a building society or bank holding the first charge on the property (in some cases, the creditor may also hold the first charge). If a property is repossessed and sold, the proceeds will be distributed to meet claims of secured lenders in the order in which loans were given.

The legal position

Second mortgages for £25,000 or less (if taken out before 6 April 2008) or £15,000 (if taken out before 1 May 1998) are regulated agreements under the Consumer Credit Act, unless they are exempt. The most common reason for exemption is if the secured loan is taken out for the purpose of improving/repairing the home and the creditor is the same lender which granted the mortgage to buy the home. If the agreement was made on or after 6 April 2008, the agreement is regulated regardless of the amount, unless it is exempt (see p65).

The changes introduced by the European Commission Consumer Credit Directive, outlined on p68 do not apply to secured loans.

Special features

Interest rates on second mortgages with finance companies are much higher than those charged by building societies or banks for first mortgages. Loans are often repayable over a much shorter term than for first mortgages and this, together with higher interest rates, means it is an expensive form of borrowing.

There are special rules for entering into secured loans under the Consumer Credit Act. The borrower must be given a copy of the agreement, which is not to be signed for seven days. S/he must then be sent a copy for signing and left for a further seven days. If the borrower does not sign, there is no agreement. The lender should not contact the prospective borrower during either of the seven-day 'thinking' periods unless asked to do so. If these rules have not been followed, the loan is not enforceable without a court order.

Checklist for action

Advisers should take the following action.
- Consider whether emergency action is necessary (see Chapter 8).
- Check whether the agreement is enforceable under the Consumer Credit Act.
- Assist the client to choose a strategy from Chapter 8, as **this is a priority debt**.

Trading cheque or voucher

Finance companies may supply a voucher or cheque to the client to be used at specified shops in exchange for goods. Repayments, which include a charge for the credit, are then made by instalments to the finance company. The shop is paid by the credit company.

The legal position

Agreements are regulated under the Consumer Credit Act, provided the credit is for no more than £25,000 (if the agreement was made before 6 April 2008) or £15,000 (if made before 1 May 1998). If the agreement was made on or after 6 April 2008, the agreement is regulated regardless of the amount, unless it is exempt (see p65). If the voucher is for £50 or less, the creditor is not obliged to comply with the rules on p67.[23]

Special features

This is normally an expensive way of borrowing and limits the client to shopping in a limited number of outlets where prices may be high. This will not usually be a priority debt – see Chapter 9 for details of how to deal with it. If this is the only way in which the client can buy essential goods, see p241.

Checklist for action

Advisers should take the following action.
- Check liability, including the enforceability of the agreement under the Consumer Credit Act.
- Assist the client to choose a strategy from Chapter 9 as this is usually a non-priority debt. If this is the only way the client can buy essential goods, see p241.

2. Other debts

Business debts

It will often be necessary to advise people with business debts (see Chapter 16). If a business is still trading but is facing financial difficulties, specialist advice should be sought from, for instance, an accountant, insolvency practitioner, local business centre or small firms advisory service on the viability of the business.

The legal position

If the business has already ceased trading, debts should be dealt with like any other case of multiple debt, using the same criteria to decide whether they should be treated as a priority or not (see Chapter 8).

Liability for the debts must be established and the adviser should check whether the client was a sole trader, in a partnership or a limited company. A sole trader is personally liable for all the debts; in a partnership, all partners are jointly and severally liable. In limited companies, only the directors can be held liable for any debts, and then only if they have personally guaranteed a loan or, under company law, if there has been wrongful trading or neglect of their duties as directors.

Checklist for action

Advisers should take the following action.
- Consider whether emergency action is necessary (see Chapter 8).
- Consider whether the client should be referred to a specialist agency – eg, Business Debtline.
- Otherwise, assist the client to choose a strategy from Chapter 8 for any priority debts and/or from Chapter 9 for any non-priority debts.

Charge card

A charge card (eg, Diners Club) is not a credit card. Purchases are made and the amount is charged to the account, but the balance must be cleared in full at the end of each charging period (usually monthly).

The legal position

Agreements for charge cards made before 1 February 2011 are exempt from the Consumer Credit Act because there is no extended credit. Agreements for charge cards made on or after 1 February 2011 are not exempt unless there are only 'insignificant' charges of the credit. There is no guidance in the legislation or in the Department for Business, Innovation and Skills guidance on what is 'significant' in this context.

Special features

In order to obtain a charge card, it is necessary to pay an annual fee and show proof of a high income. This will not usually be a priority debt (see Chapter 9).

Checklist for action

Advisers should take the following action.
- Check liability, including whether the Consumer Credit Act applies and, if so, the enforceability of the agreement.
- Assist the client to choose a strategy from Chapter 9 as this is a non-priority debt.

Child support payments

If a non-resident parent is liable to pay maintenance to a person with care under the statutory child support schemes, payments can be made directly between the parties (known as 'maintenance direct'). Alternatively, if any party to the case requests it, the Child Support Agency (CSA) may collect the payments and pass them to the person with care. If the non-resident parent is on certain benefits, the CSA can make direct deductions from benefit. For more information about deductions from benefit, see p223 and CPAG's *Welfare Benefits and Tax Credits Handbook*.

Parents with care on benefits are no longer required to use the CSA and have a choice about whether or not to seek maintenance from the other parent and, if so, how this should be done. Non-resident parents can also apply to the CSA for a child support maintenance calculation to be made.

The legal position

Child support payments are governed by the Child Support Acts 1991 and 1995, the Child Support, Pensions and Social Security Act 2000, the Child Maintenance and Other Payments Act 2008 and subsequent regulations and amendments.

The statutory child support scheme was established in 1993 and reformed in March 2003. The main changes in 2003 related to how maintenance is worked out and internal case administration. From October 2012, a new simplified calculation method will be introduced and, over time, all existing cases will close.

From July 2008, the CSA was run by the Child Maintenance and Enforcement Commission (CMEC). CMEC was abolished on 1 August 2012 and the CSA is now part of the Department for Work and Pensions (DWP).

Special features

Child support payments are worked out according to set rules. Advisers should be aware that the CSA's view is that payment of maintenance debt should be the top priority for non-resident parents who are liable to pay maintenance for their children. There are no set rules on how quickly arrears of child support maintenance should be paid. The CSA aims to clear arrears within a maximum of two years, at a rate of up to 40 per cent of the non-resident parent's income. However, enforcement officers have the discretion to extend this period in appropriate cases.

The non-resident parent should contact the CSA as soon as a payment is missed to explain why and to make arrangements to pay, if s/he wishes to avoid enforcement action. The CSA can take action as soon as it knows that a payment has been missed. The first step in enforcement is usually to make either a deduction from earnings order or, if this is not appropriate (eg, if the non-resident parent is not employed), an order to take money from a bank account. These orders are made, in practice, by a member of the CSA staff. The CSA does not need to apply to court to make either type of order.

Other enforcement action by the CSA currently requires a liability order from the magistrates' court. The court must accept that the payments specified are due by the non-resident parent and have not been made, but cannot question the child support maintenance calculation itself. An appeal to the First-tier Tribunal should be used if anything relating to the child support calculation is disputed. Specialist advice should be sought.

From 12 July 2006, the six-year limitation period on the CSA applying for a liability order was abolished. For debts already over six years old on 12 July 2006, the CSA may attempt other enforcement action which does not require a liability order or which does not recover money – eg, committal to prison or disqualification from driving. In cases where the limitation period is still relevant, time begins to run on the date the maintenance assessment in question was notified to the non-resident parent. [24]

If a liability order is made, it can be enforced by distress (see Chapter 14) or the powers of the county court can be used to make a charging order (see p301) or third-party debt order (see p312).

If all other methods of recovering arrears have failed, the CSA can apply to the court to commit a person to prison (for a maximum of six weeks) or disqualify the person from driving (for a maximum of two years). In order to do so, the court must decide that the parent has 'wilfully refused or culpably neglected' to pay (see p383).

Planned changes in the CSA's enforcement powers include: the introduction of 'administrative' liability orders which do not require court applications; the ability to apply to the court for an order to disqualify a non-resident parent from holding or obtaining a passport; and the ability to apply to the court to impose a curfew on a non-resident parent.

For more information about the child support scheme, see CPAG's *Child Support Handbook* (see Appendix 2).

Checklist for action

Advisers should take the following action.
- Consider whether emergency action is necessary (see Chapter 8).
- Check liability.
- Assist the client to choose a strategy from Chapter 9 as this is a non-priority debt.

Civil recovery

Over the past few years, many people have been threatened with county court action by civil recovery agents for the recovery of losses allegedly incurred by retailers following allegations either of theft by employees or shoplifting by customers, in many cases involving goods of relatively low value. Although in some cases the person has been charged and prosecuted for a criminal offence, in many cases there has been no police involvement and, in most shoplifting cases, the goods have been recovered undamaged and able to be resold by the retailer.

The legal position

As well as being a criminal offence, shoplifting is a 'tort' (civil wrong). The relevant torts put forward by civil recovery agents on behalf of retailers are trespass to goods and conversion.

It is a basic principle of the law of tort that a creditor only has a cause of action if it can prove that the client's wrongful conduct caused the damage for which compensation is claimed.

Special features

Civil recovery agents typically put forward demands for damages for 'wrongful actions' and threaten to issue proceedings to recover:
- the value of goods stolen but not recovered; *and/or*
- staff and/or management time investigating and/or dealing with the alleged tort; *and/or*
- administration costs resulting from the tort; *and/or*
- apportioned amounts for general security and surveillance costs.

Claims for time, administration and a proportion of security costs are often based on a sliding scale of fixed costs with the amount claimed rising in direct proportion to the value of the goods involved.

In a recent case in Oxford County Court, a circuit judge decided that there are recoverable amounts in certain circumstances:[25]

- loss of value and/or profit of items not recovered from shoplifters;
- specific, direct costs incurred in apprehending shoplifters;
- physical damage caused by shoplifters in the course of the theft or their apprehension;
- personal injury caused by a shoplifter to a security person;
- diversion of a member of staff, such as a cashier, from her/his usual duties in order to chase and capture shoplifters.

The judge said that in order to succeed in a claim for time, the retailer must establish either that the staff in question were 'significantly diverted from their usual activities' or that there was 'significant disruption to its business', or that there was loss of revenue generation. However, when observing, apprehending and dealing with shoplifters, security staff are, in fact, not diverted from their usual activities, but actively engaged in them and doing exactly what the retailer paid them to do. In these circumstances, no claim for time can be made.

The judge also said that claims for administration and apportioned security costs cannot be made unless the retailer can show that they were attributable to the activities of the shoplifter in question. If the amount spent by the retailer would have been the same regardless of whether the shoplifter in question had stayed at home or shoplifted at another retailer's premises, no claim can be made.

Checklist for action

Advisers should take the following action.

- Check liability, including the 'heads of damage' claimed by the retailer.
- If the retailer has taken county court action, see Chapter 11. Although these are 'small claims', representation at any hearing is advisable (see p361).
- If the client chooses not to challenge liability, assist her/him to choose a strategy from Chapter 9 as this is a non-priority debt.

Council tax

This is a tax administered by local authorities, composed of two equal elements – a 'property' element and a 'people' element.

Property element

All domestic properties have been valued and placed in one of eight valuation bands in England and nine in Wales.

In England, the valuation is based on what the property would have sold for on the open market in April 1991. In Wales, properties were re-valued on 1 April

2003 and the new valuations took effect from 1 April 2005. It is assumed that the property was sold freehold (99 years' leasehold for flats), with vacant possession and in a reasonable state of repair. Under some circumstances, an appeal against this valuation can be made. Certain properties are exempt, and advisers should check to make sure that exemption has been applied for, if appropriate.

Assuming the property is not exempt, the level of council tax is set annually by the local authority. Occupants of Band H properties in England pay three times as much as those in Band A. In Wales, properties in Band I pay four times as much as those in Band A.

People element

The tax assumes that two adults aged 18 or over live in each household. Nothing extra is payable if there are more than two adults. One adult living on her/his own receives a 25 per cent discount. If there are no adults, there is a 50 per cent discount. If the latter applies, it may be that the property is exempt and advisers should check whether this is the case.

When counting the number of adults in the household, certain people can be disregarded. Once again, this should be checked. Additionally, in certain cases, there are reductions for people with disabilities whose homes have been modified.

Liability

A council tax bill is sent to each domestic property. The person(s) nearest the top of this list will be liable for payment of the council tax:
- resident freeholder (owner);
- resident leaseholder;
- resident statutory/secure tenant (including a council tenant);
- other resident(s);
- non-resident owner.

If there is more than one person resident in the house who has the same interest in the property (ie, joint owners or joint tenants), they are jointly and severally liable. This means that all the people concerned can be asked to pay the full charge, together or as individuals.

Married couples and both heterosexual and same-sex couples who live together are jointly and severally liable. A single bill is sent, either in the name of one of the persons concerned, or in both names.

Bills should be issued less any discounts, deductions and council tax benefit, and must arrive at least 14 days before the first instalment falls due. The local authority must offer the option of paying by monthly instalments. As discount is not a benefit, provided a claim is made, the appropriate discount(s) can be backdated indefinitely.

Students and people who are 'severely mentally impaired' are disregarded and usually exempt. They cannot be jointly and severally liable either as members of a couple or with someone who is not exempt.

There is a right to appeal to a valuation tribunal against certain decisions, including those on liability, valuations, discounts and exemptions.

Since 18 November 2003, local authorities have had the power to reduce or remit sums of council tax, including arrears, in cases of hardship.[26]

Special features

For more detailed information, see CPAG's *Council Tax Handbook*.

Checklist for action

Advisers should take the following action.
- Consider whether emergency action is necessary (see Chapter 8).
- Check liability for the debt, including any associated bailiff's charges. Consider whether there are any grounds for a complaint.
- Assist the client to choose a strategy from Chapter 8 as **this is a priority debt**.

Fines

Fines are the most common form of punishment imposed by the magistrates' or crown courts for criminal offences.

The legal position

Magistrates' courts can impose fines for criminal offences by a wide variety of legislation. They are bound to consider the means of the defendant 'as far as they are known to the court'.[27] Maximum amounts are laid down for each offence.

Special features

Fines should be distinguished from costs or compensation, which are often also awarded against defendants in criminal actions.

Advisers should consider emergency action if payment of fines is difficult for a client. **This is a priority debt** (see Chapter 8). Court procedures and enforcement are explained in Chapter 13.

Checklist for action

Advisers should take the following action.
- Consider whether emergency action is necessary (see Chapter 8).
- Check liability including for any associated bailiff's charges.
- Assist the client to choose a strategy from Chapter 8 as **this is a priority debt**.

Gas and electricity charges

Gas and electricity suppliers charge for their fuel in a number of ways. Pre-payment meters, quarterly accounts, direct debit and online schemes are common payment methods. Clients have a choice of supplier, although a supplier to whom arrears are owed can object to a transfer in certain circumstances. The industry is regulated by Ofgem. Suppliers are required to operate codes of practice on the payment of bills and disconnection, including guidance for customers who may have difficulty in paying. Advisers should obtain copies of the codes of practice of their clients' suppliers.

Ofgem has published *Preventing Debt and Disconnection*. See p228 for more information.

The legal position

Electricity

A person is liable to pay an electricity bill if:

- s/he has signed a contract for the supply of electricity; *or*
- no one else was liable for the bill or their liability has come to an end (see below) and s/he is the owner/occupier of premises which have been supplied with electricity (known as a 'deemed contract').

A person is not liable to pay an electricity bill if:

- s/he has not a made a contract with a supplier; *and*
- someone else is liable to pay the bill and their liability has not come to an end (see below).

A person is no longer liable to pay an electricity bill under an actual or deemed contract if:

- s/he has terminated any contract in accordance with its terms (but s/he is still liable if s/he continues to be supplied with electricity); *or*
- s/he ceases to be the owner/occupier of the property, starting from the day s/he leaves the property, provided s/he has given at least two days' notice of leaving; *or*
- notice was not given prior to her/him leaving the property, on the earliest of:
  - two working days after s/he actually gave notice of ceasing to be an owner/occupier; *or*
  - when someone else begins to own/occupy the property and takes a supply of electricity to those premises.

This means that if the fuel supply is in the sole name as the client's partner who has subsequently left the home, the client has no liability for any arrears up to that date. However, s/he could be liable for the cost of any fuel supplied after this date, regardless of whether her/his partner has terminated the contract.

Clients should be advised to arrange for a final reading of the meter before leaving the property, if possible, and should, at least, read the meter themselves in order to be able to check their final bill.

Gas

A person is liable to pay a gas bill if:

- s/he has signed a contract for the supply of gas; *or*
- no one else was liable for the bill or their liability has come to an end, but s/he has continued to be supplied with gas (known as a 'deemed contract').

A person currently liable under an actual or deemed contract will remain liable until:

- s/he terminates the contract in accordance with the terms of the contract (but if s/he still occupies the premises and continues to be supplied with gas, s/he will still be liable to pay for the gas supplied); *or*
- s/he ceases to occupy the premises, provided s/he has given at least two working days' notice that s/he intended to leave; *or*
- if notice was not given before s/he left the premises, the earliest of:
  - 28 days after s/he informed the supplier that s/he has left the premises; *or*
  - the date when another person requires a supply of gas.

Clients should be advised to arrange for a final reading of the meter before leaving the property, if possible, and should, at least, read the meter themselves in order to be able to check their final bill.

Estimated bills

Arrears of gas or electricity payments may arise as a result of high bills. While high bills may be caused by high consumption, price increases or previous underpayments, they may also be caused by estimated bills based on wrong assumptions about the amount of fuel used.

Note: it may be possible to reduce charges by changing supplier. If there are arrears more than 28 days old, the old supplier can object to the transfer unless the arrears are paid. This does not apply to clients with pre-payment meters, provided the debt does not exceed £200 (£500 from 1 November 2012) and the client agrees that the new supplier can collect the arrears through the meter. If the transfer goes ahead without objection, the arrears cannot be transferred to the new supplier.

Many bills are based on estimated meter readings. Under their licence conditions, suppliers are only required to obtain actual meter readings once every two years. If the estimated reading is different to the actual reading, the client should read the meter her/himself and ask for this reading to be used in order to avoid either an overpayment or an underpayment which could lead to arrears. The name and address of the client, as well as the address to which fuel was supplied, should be noted from the bill. The prioritisation of the debt will depend on the client's continued need for that fuel at her/his present address.

If the bill is estimated and the estimated reading is higher than the actual reading, it is possible to reduce the amount owing. The bill will explain (often by means of an 'E' next to a reading) whether an estimated reading has been given.

Clients can read their own meters and provide the supplier with their reading and so should never be disconnected on the basis of an estimated bill. The adviser should ask the client to read the meter and request an amended bill.

Special features

Fuel supplies may be disconnected if there are arrears, and this is likely therefore to be a priority debt (see Chapter 8). **Note:** a supplier cannot transfer a debt from a previous property to a new account and then disconnect that fuel supply for the previous debt. A supply can only be disconnected at the address to which the bill relates. A pre-payment meter can only be fitted at the address to which the bill relates (unless the client requests otherwise).[28]

'Backbilling'

From July 2007, suppliers cannot recover fuel charges more than 12 months old if the supplier has:

- billed on estimated readings and has failed to use the readings provided by either the client or an official meter reader;
- billed incorrectly by mixing up meter readings;
- failed to bill the client when bills have been requested;
- failed to act on a query raised by the client about her/his bill or the meter and subsequently allowed a debt to build up.

If the client pays by direct debit, in addition to being unable to recover arrears that have arisen in the above situations, the supplier cannot recover any fuel charges more than 12 months old unless:

- the account has been correctly set up, payments taken and statements issued; *and*
- the supplier has reassessed the client's direct debits within the previous 15 months to ensure that her/his fuel consumption is covered (unless the client has failed to respond to a request from the supplier for a meter reading in order to carry out the reassessment); *and*
- it has been made clear on the statements that fuel consumption has been based on estimates.

Suppliers can recover charges more than 12 months old if the client has:

- used the fuel supply but made no attempt to contact the supplier to arrange payment; *or*
- not co-operated with attempts to obtain meter readings; *or*
- 'wilfully avoided repayment'.

An updated guide to the backbilling code of practice is available from www.energy-uk.org.uk/customers/energy-industry-codes/code-of-practice-for-accurate-bills.htm.

Social tariffs

A 'social tariff' is a reduction on the standard tariff, which most suppliers offer to vulnerable or disadvantaged clients. Each supplier's scheme is different and, if the client does not qualify for a social tariff from her/his current supplier but would qualify with a different supplier, it will usually be in the client's best interests to switch suppliers.

Social tariffs are not advertised and must be applied for.

Advisers should check the websites of their local suppliers to see what social tariffs are available, so they can identify clients who could take advantage of them.

Non-fuel items

Fuel bills may include payments for items other than fuel, such as repairs or goods sold by the supplier – eg, cookers and freezers. These non-fuel debts will generally be credit sale agreements (see p115). A client cannot have her/his fuel supply disconnected for arrears on a credit sale agreement.

The adviser should reduce repayments by arranging to pay for fuel costs only and treating non-fuel items alongside other non-priority debts.

Meter faults

If a gas or electricity meter is registering fuel consumption at too high a rate, the client will receive a bill that is higher than it should be. According to the industry, meter faults are rare but, if the client believes a meter is faulty, the fuel supplier will check the accuracy of the meter if requested to do so.

See CPAG's *Fuel Rights Handbook* for more details (see Appendix 2).

Meter tampering

Tampering with a meter in order to prevent it registering or to reduce the amount it is registering is a criminal offence. Accusations of tampering usually follow a visit to the client's home by a meter reader who has noticed and reported something unusual about the meter. The supplier should write to the client informing her/him of an investigation into suspected tampering. If the meter is considered to be in a dangerous condition, it may be unusable pending the investigation. The investigation should be carried out in accordance with the code of practice and advisers should obtain a copy of this from the supplier.

If a client is threatened with prosecution, s/he should be referred to a solicitor.

Other assistance

Clients may be able to obtain a grant to pay off fuel debts. The only suppliers who have energy trust fund schemes at the moment are British Gas, EDF Energy and npower, and only clients who are customers of one of these suppliers can apply. Grants are available for electricity and gas bills and may also be available to pay other essential household bills. Auriga publishes a leaflet summarising the schemes, and energy and water companies can provide to help customers, available at www.aurigaservices.co.uk/consumers.html.

Clients can also take steps to help save energy and reduce fuel bills. The Energy Saving Trust offers free advice on ways to reduce fuel consumption and should be aware of grants that are available locally to help cover the cost of energy efficiency measures. See www.energysavingtrust.org.uk or telephone 0300 123 1234/0845 602 1425.

All suppliers are required to provide a range of free services (including quarterly meter readings) to clients who are on their priority services register. This is available to clients who:

- have a disability; *or*
- are over pension age; *or*
- are chronically sick; *or*
- are visually impaired or have hearing difficulties.

See CPAG's *Fuel Rights Handbook* for more details (see Appendix 2).

Checklist for action

Advisers should take the following action.
- Consider whether emergency action is necessary (see Chapter 8).
- Check liability and whether the client is eligible for any assistance with the charges.
- Assist the client to choose a strategy from Chapter 8 as **this is a priority debt**.

Income tax arrears

Most income above certain fixed limits is taxable. Employees are taxed by direct deduction from their income by their employer (the Pay As You Earn (PAYE) scheme). PAYE taxpayers will rarely owe tax on their earned income unless mistakes have been made in the amounts deducted. Self-employed people receive their earnings before tax is deducted and are responsible for paying their own tax directly to HM Revenue and Customs (HMRC). Arrears are, therefore, more likely to occur with self-employment. See Chapter 16 for more information.

The legal position

Income tax is payable under the Taxes Management Act 1970 and the Income and Corporation Taxes Act 1988 and subsequent Finance Acts and regulations.

HMRC can levy distress for unpaid income tax without a court order and is not subject to any limitation period for taking court action to recover the debt. The client could even be imprisoned for non-payment. Tax debts of up to £3,000 owed by formerly self-employed clients can now be recovered through the PAYE system.

Special features

There are many ways of reducing liability for tax, unless it is deducted under PAYE. Self-employed people, in particular, will require detailed advice on how to complete their tax returns since the introduction of self-assessment in April 1997. They also need detailed advice on any arrears that HMRC may be claiming. Self-employed people should seek specialist help either from an accountant, Business Debtline or TaxAid if they wish to challenge the amount of any arrears claimed (see Appendix 1).

It may be possible to negotiate remission (write-off) of a tax debt if the client's circumstances are highly unlikely to improve – eg, if s/he is permanently unable to work because of ill health or if s/he is elderly with no hope of increasing her/his income.

If the business is continuing to trade, however, it is vital that the client pays any ongoing tax on time and makes arrangements to repay any tax debt, otherwise HMRC can seize essential goods without a court order and so close down the business.

Checklist for action

Advisers should take the following action.
- Consider whether emergency action is necessary (see Chapter 8).
- Consider whether the client should be referred to a specialist agency – eg, TaxAid.
- Otherwise, assist the client to choose a strategy from Chapter 8 as **this is usually treated as a priority debt**.

Maintenance payments

Before April 1993, either the magistrates' court or county court made orders to require a parent or ex-spouse to make maintenance payments to the other partner for her/himself and/or any children.

From April 1993, child maintenance payment powers passed to the CSA (see p128), although arrears due under court orders made before this date may still exist. The only new court orders are applications not covered by child support regulations (eg, applications for additional maintenance over and above the maximum awarded on CSA assessment) and for spousal maintenance.

The legal position

Magistrates' courts not only make maintenance orders but also collect and review maintenance orders made by the county court, divorce registry or High Court.[29]

Special features

If a maintenance order is unpaid, the magistrates' court has powers similar to those used where fines are unpaid (see Chapter 13). Maintenance payable under a court order should be distinguished from voluntary maintenance payments, even those written as a legal agreement.

Checklist for action

Advisers should take the following action.

- Consider whether emergency action is necessary (see Chapter 8).
- Check liability.
- Assist the client to choose a strategy from Chapter 9 as this is a non-priority debt.

Mortgage

Usually, the term 'mortgage' is used to describe a loan for the purchase of a house. If repayments are not kept up, the lender has the right to recover the money lent by repossessing the property and selling it. A 'charge' is registered on the property to safeguard the rights of the lender.

The legal position

First mortgages from building societies and the major banks are exempt from regulation by the Consumer Credit Act (see p66). Most will be regulated by the Financial Services Authority (FSA) from 31 October 2004 (see p147).

Special features

There are a variety of different mortgages.

- **Capital repayment mortgage.** The amount borrowed ('capital') is repaid gradually over the term of the mortgage. At the beginning, repayments consist of virtually all interest, but towards the end of the term of the mortgage they are virtually all capital.
- **Endowment mortgage.** Repayments cover the interest on the capital borrowed and separate payments are made to an insurance company for the endowment premium. The capital is repaid at the end of the term of the mortgage in one lump sum from the proceeds of the insurance policy. Endowment policies aim to pay off the mortgage capital when they mature and produce extra capital for the borrower to use as s/he wishes. However, there is no guarantee that the policy will pay off even the capital, let alone provide extra money. Any client with an endowment mortgage should contact the policy provider and enquire how much the policy is expected to produce on maturity and seek independent financial advice if a shortfall is predicted.
- **Pension mortgage.** The borrower pays interest only to the lender and a separate pension premium which attracts tax relief. When it matures, the cash available from this pension pays off the capital on the mortgage and the rest funds a personal pension plan.
- **Low-start/deferred-interest mortgage.** Reduced interest is charged for the first two to three years. In some schemes, interest accrues during the first few

years, but payment is spread over the remaining term of the mortgage. They are only helpful for people who expect their income to increase in order for them to afford the rise in repayments after the first few years. These are sometimes known as 'discount-rate mortgages'.

- **Fixed-rate mortgage.** The interest rate is fixed for a number of years, either at the outset or during the life of the loan. They are obviously more attractive during a period when interest rates are rising.
- **Tracker mortgage.** These mortgages guarantee always to follow the Bank of England's base rate or some other rate up or down, maintaining the same differential between the rate charged and that set by the Bank of England.
- **Other types of mortgage.** These include 'capped rates' (where repayments do not exceed a set level (the 'cap') or 'collared rates' (where payments do not fall below a set level – the 'collar').

See below for mortgage shortfalls after repossession of a property.

Checklist for action

Advisers should take the following action.
- Consider whether emergency action is necessary (see Chapter 8).
- Check liability. If possession proceedings have started, see Chapter 12.
- Assist the client to choose a strategy from Chapter 8 as **this is a priority debt** if the mortgage is on the client's current home. Otherwise, the arrears are a non-priority debt. Assist the client to choose a strategy from Chapter 9.

Mortgage shortfall

If a property has been repossessed by the lender and the outstanding balance due under the mortgage is more than the proceeds of sale, this is known as a 'mortgage shortfall'. A client who hands in her/his keys to the lender remains liable for any subsequent shortfall as her/his contractual liability remains.

Mortgage indemnity guarantee

Most mortgage lenders have a normal lending limit of 70–80 per cent of the property's value. Before the 2008 'credit crunch', if someone wanted to borrow a higher proportion (eg, 95–100 per cent), the lender would ask the borrower to buy an insurance policy to protect it against a mortgage shortfall. This is the mortgage indemnity guarantee (or indemnity insurance or building society indemnity). The insurance premium was usually, but not always, paid as a lump sum of several hundred pounds at the time of purchase. Advisers should note that it was to protect the lender, not the borrower. The only value to the borrower was that s/he was not given the amount of mortgage s/he required without agreeing to pay the insurance premium.

The mortgage indemnity guarantee will not pay the full shortfall. The amount paid will be a proportion of the shortfall relative to the lending risk. There will, therefore, still be a shortfall owing to the lender.

However, the insurance company can pursue the client for the money paid towards the mortgage shortfall under a process known as 'subrogation'. In some cases, the client may receive a demand for money from the insurer, even though the lender has agreed not to pursue the shortfall. Alternatively, some insurers appoint the lender to collect a client's liability on their behalf. In this case, the lender will contact the client to ask for payment of the entire shortfall. Commonly, the client can expect to receive a demand from the insurer and the lender for their respective proportions of the shortfall. Claims cannot be ignored and must be dealt with.

The legal position

Provided the loan remains secured, the lender has 12 years in which to take action to recover the principal amount (ie, the capital sum borrowed) and six years to recover arrears of interest. This limitation period (see p274) starts again every time the client or her/his representative acknowledges the debt (see p275). The limitation period for the principal (but not the interest) also starts again every time the borrower, a joint borrower or agent makes a payment into the account (including payments of mortgage interest by the DWP[30]). Once the limitation period has expired, it cannot be started again by further payments or acknowledgements.

In 1997, a judge in the Court of Appeal suggested that it was 'seriously arguable' that the six-year limit applied to the principal as well as to the interest.[31] After a period of considerable uncertainty, the Court of Appeal and House of Lords resolved the issue.

- The limitation period for the principal sum borrowed is 12 years from the date when the sum became payable under the terms of the mortgage deed, usually after the client has failed to pay two or three monthly instalments.[32]
- The limitation period for the interest is six years from the date when the lender had the right to receive that interest.[33]
- The fact that a mortgage deed contains an express provision under which the borrower agrees to pay any shortfall to the lender does not give the lender a fresh right of action starting on the date of sale.[34]
- The position is the same if the loan is regulated by the Consumer Credit Act 1974[35] or if the mortgage deed contains no covenant allowing the lender to call in the mortgage on default but it has, nevertheless, repossessed and sold the property.[36]
- The proceeds of sale will be treated as appropriated first to arrears of interest and then to capital.[37]

In the majority of cases, the shortfall will be made up of capital only because the interest will have been paid from the proceeds of the sale and the whole debt will be subject to a 12-year time limit. This should, however, be checked with the lender.

As a concession, lenders and insurers have agreed not to pursue the debt unless the client is contacted within six years of the date of sale of the property if:

- the lender is a member of the Council of Mortgage Lenders or was a subscriber to the old Mortgage Code (in practice, all the major high street banks and building societies), or the mortgage indemnity guarantee (see p141) insurer is a member of the Association of British Insurers; *and*
- no contact about the shortfall was made by the lender/insurer with the client before 11 February 2000 (see below).

'Contact' includes letters or telephone calls received but ignored by the client, but should not include letters sent to a previous address, unless these have been forwarded, and does not include failed attempts to trace the client. This concession does not apply if the client was contacted before 11 February 2000 or had entered into a payment arrangement with the lender/insurer before this date, even if the contact was made more than six years after the property was sold.

If there is a regulated mortgage contract (see p147), the lender must notify the client of its intention to recover the shortfall within six years of the date of sale of the property under Part 13.6.4 of the *Mortgages and Home Finance: conduct of business sourcebook* (*MCOB* – see p148).

Special features

A mortgage shortfall debt is, in many ways, no different from any other unsecured debt, since once the property has been sold, it is no longer a priority debt. The strategies, tactics and principles of good money advice described throughout this *Handbook* still apply. However, the debt is often disproportionately high compared with the client's normal income and expenditure and any other debts s/he owes. It can be very distressing for clients to be faced with such a huge debt.

Some lenders will already have a county court judgment for money. This does not prevent the client from using any of the strategies detailed, but in addition the adviser may need to protect the client's interest by applying to vary or suspend the judgment. This will be essential if the lender is attempting to enforce it (eg, by an attachment of earnings order) as the Limitation Act does not apply to enforcement action. Clients who have acquired assets, particularly another property, may be especially vulnerable. If possible, the client should try to resolve the shortfall debt before acquiring further assets such as a house or flat.

It is not unusual for clients to fail to give the lender details of their new address. Some may hope they will not be found. The Council of Mortgage Lenders has indicated that its members will vigorously pursue people with shortfall debts, using tracing agents if necessary.

Before entering into negotiations, always check whether the Council of Mortgage Lenders/Association of British Insurers concession (known as 'the CML Agreement') applies. See 'Debt Following Mortgage Possession' at www.cml.org.uk/cml/consumers/guides/debt, and then use the preceding paragraphs to check the account and, if appropriate, note any points which may be used to challenge the extent of the debt. Advisers should also check whether Part 13.6.4 of the *MCOB* applies (see p148).

It may be necessary to contact the lender to obtain information (taking care not to acknowledge the debt and restart the limitation period). The information required may include:

- copies of any letters written by the lender to the client (which could confirm whether or not the CML Agreement applies);
- a copy of the lender's 'completion statement' following the sale of the property (which will confirm the breakdown of the shortfall);
- a full statement of account (which will confirm when the last payment was made into the account by any of the borrowers); *and*
- copies of any letter(s) received by the lender from the client (which could be acknowledgements).

Additional information may also be required, and advisers may wish to seek specialist advice if unclear how to proceed.

Checklist for action

Advisers should take the following action.

- Check liability, including whether the debt is unenforceable because the creditor has not taken recovery action within the appropriate time limit.
- Assist the client to choose a strategy from the list below or one of the other strategies in Chapter 9 as this is a non-priority debt. See also Chapter 15 for insolvency options.

Consider the following strategies.

- **Write-off.** A total write-off is likely to be the most appropriate strategy if it can be demonstrated that the client has no available income or assets and that the position is unlikely to improve (see p244). In other cases, pressure should be brought (perhaps by using publicity or local politicians) to highlight the unfairness of seizing a person's home and also expecting repayment of the shortfall.
- **Bankruptcy** (see Chapter 15). Personal bankruptcy will legally and finally end the shortfall debt recovery process. It will usually be appropriate when the lender/insurer insists on pursuing the claim, bankruptcy would not adversely affect the client, and s/he needs the peace of mind and fresh start that follows.
- **Individual voluntary arrangements** (see Chapter 15). An individual voluntary arrangement is usually only appropriate if the shortfall is modest

and in proportion to other unsecured debts, and the client can afford substantial repayments and/or owns a home that would be at risk in bankruptcy proceedings, or if the lender obtained a charging order (see p301).

- **Full and final settlement.** Most lenders and insurance companies will agree to accept a smaller sum than the full outstanding shortfall debt. How much will be acceptable varies according to individual circumstances. Settlements in the region of 10 per cent to 50 per cent are not uncommon. Advisers should ensure that any full and final settlement agreement includes the claims of both the lender and any insurer, and it is binding on them. For more information about full and final settlements, see p249.
- **Instalment payments.** Many lenders will accept modest monthly payments towards a substantial debt, where personal circumstances show this to be reasonable. The client may find it daunting to be asked to pay, for instance, £20 a month towards a debt of £35,000 because s/he cannot see an end. On the other hand, many lenders see token payments as recognition that the client is being responsible about the shortfall. Debt advisers should suggest that, provided the client keeps up the payments for, say five years, the lender should accept this in full and final settlement and agree to write off the balance. For more information about partial write-offs, see p246. If the client has other non-priority debts and the mortgage shortfall is to be included in a pro rata payment arrangement, the debt adviser should attempt to agree a total figure that the lender is prepared to accept for inclusion in the financial statement, on the basis that the balance will be written off on completion of the payment arrangement.

When preparing a strategy, bear in mind that if there was a mortgage indemnity guarantee, there may be two separate demands to negotiate – one from the lender and one from the insurer.

National insurance contributions

National insurance (NI) contributions are a compulsory tax on earnings and profits above certain levels (set annually).

The legal position

National insurance contributions are payable under s2 of the Social Security Act 1975, as amended by the Social Security Contributions and Benefits Act 1992.

Special features

Employed people pay Class 1 NI contributions directly from their wages and thus do not build up arrears. Class 2 contributions must be paid by self-employed earners unless they have a certificate of exception on the grounds of low income. Self-employed people have to pay Class 2 NI contributions by monthly direct debit or quarterly bill. In addition, self-employed people may have to pay Class 4 contributions, calculated as a percentage of their profits above a certain level (set annually). After the year end, HMRC sends out demands to self-employed people from whom it has not received the required Class 2 contributions.

If a self-employed person has also employed someone else, s/he may be liable for Class 1 NI contributions for the employee, as well as Class 2 and perhaps 4 for her/himself.

Demands for payment should be distinguished from the notice sent to people whose contribution record is insufficient to entitle them to use it towards a retirement pension or bereavement benefits. In such cases, HMRC sends a notification giving the insured the opportunity to make up the deficit for a particular year with voluntary (Class 3) contributions. This is not a demand for payment.

It is vital that the client pays any ongoing contributions on time and makes arrangements to repay any arrears, otherwise HMRC can seize essential goods without a court order and so close down the business. In addition, if contributions remain unpaid, the client's eventual entitlement to retirement pension will be affected.

Checklist for action

Advisers should take the following action.
- Consider whether emergency action is necessary (see Chapter 8).
- Consider whether the client should be referred to a specialist agency – eg, TaxAid.
- Otherwise, assist the client to choose a strategy from Chapter 8 as **this is usually treated as a priority debt if the business is continuing to trade.** If the business is no longer trading, the arrears are a non-priority debt. Assist the client to choose a strategy from Chapter 9.

Non-domestic rates

Non-domestic rates (business rates) is a charge levied on most commercial property by local authorities. It is based on a national valuation and fixed amounts are charged across England and Wales in proportion to this.

The legal position

Non-domestic rates are payable under the Local Government Finance Act 1988.

Special features

Arrears are recovered through a liability order in the magistrates' court. If bailiffs are used by a local authority after it has obtained a liability order, there is no exemption for tools, books, vehicles or goods which are necessary for use in the client's business (as there is for council tax arrears).[38] Once a business ceases trading, it may be able to claim local discounts or reliefs from non-domestic rates and advisers should check with the local authority what is available. If the business is renting premises under a lease, it will continue to be liable for the non-domestic rates for as long as the lease exists.

Local authorities have the power to reduce or write off arrears of non-domestic rates in situations of severe hardship.[39] This is most appropriate in cases of business failure and should always be sought before considering payment.

Checklist for action

Advisers should take the following action.
- Consider whether emergency action is necessary (see Chapter 8).
- Check liability for the debt, including any associated bailiff's charges. Consider whether there are any grounds for a complaint.
- Assist the client to choose a strategy from Chapter 8 as **this is a priority debt if there is a risk of the client losing essential goods.** Otherwise, the arrears are a non-priority debt. Assist the client to choose a strategy from Chapter 9.

Regulated mortgage contract

Since 31 October 2004 most mortgage lending (including arranging and administering mortgages) is regulated by the FSA, the regulator set up by the government to look after the financial services industry under the Financial Services and Markets Act 2000.[40]

The legal position

Firms involved in these activities must be authorised by the FSA. If not, they will commit a criminal offence and any regulated mortgage contract will be unenforceable. To check whether a lender or intermediary is authorised, see www.fsa.gov.uk/register/home.do and follow the instructions. However, the court can allow enforcement if satisfied that it is 'just and equitable' to do so.[41]

A mortgage is a regulated contract if it was taken out on or after 31 October 2004 and:
- the borrower is an individual;
- the loan is secured by a first mortgage on a property;
- the property is at least 40 per cent occupied by the borrower or her/his family.

The purpose of the loan is not relevant. Secured loans that would have been regulated by the Consumer Credit Act if made before 31 October 2004 are now regulated mortgage contracts if they meet the above criteria.

The FSA has detailed rules covering:
- advising on and selling mortgages;
- financial promotions;
- disclosure requirements;
- calculating the annual percentage rate;
- responsible lending;

- unfair or excessive charges;
- arrears and repossession (including mortgage shortfall debts).

Special features

Generally, lenders and intermediaries must conduct their business with integrity, consider the interests of clients and treat them fairly. The detailed rules are set out in the *Mortgages and Home Finance: conduct of business sourcebook* (*MCOB*), available online at www.fsahandbook.info/FSA/html/handbook/mcob. It is not worth downloading this document as it is subject to frequent change and the adviser will need to insert the date at the top of the screen in order to ensure s/he is reading the version in force at the relevant date.

Before the client is offered a mortgage, s/he must be provided with a 'key facts illustration' – a personalised illustration setting out specified information. Any mortgage offer subsequently made must incorporate this, updated as necessary. The offer must include a tariff of fees and charges the client could incur. Arrears charges must not be excessive, but should be a reasonable estimate of the cost of the additional administration required as a result of the client being in arrears. The lender must be able to demonstrate that it has taken into account the client's ability to repay the loan by keeping adequate records (but these need only be retained for a year). Lenders must operate a written policy setting out the factors it will take into account when assessing ability to repay. The policy should be written on the assumption that any regular payments will be made out of the client's income and, therefore, lenders should take account of the client's actual and/or reasonably anticipated income. Lenders should only rely on self-certification of a client's income where this is appropriate (eg, where proof of income is not readily available) – there have been cases where non-status lenders, in particular, have accepted inflated income figures based on self-certification from clients in regular employment where proof of income was readily available.[42]

Lenders must deal fairly with clients in arrears and not only have a written arrears policy in place, but also follow it. This requires the lender to use reasonable efforts to reach an agreement with the client over repayment, liaise with advisers and apply for repossession only where all other reasonable attempts to resolve the situation have failed. Within 15 business days of the account falling into arrears (defined as the equivalent of two monthly payments), the lender must send the client a copy of the FSA's information sheet on mortgage arrears, together with a statement of account, including details of the arrears, charges incurred and the outstanding balance. This information must be provided at least quarterly and, even if a repayment arrangement is in place, the information must still be sent out quarterly if the account is attracting charges.

From 30 June 2010, lenders must not charge arrears fees if the client is complying with an arrangement to pay those arrears. Lenders must not put pressure on clients through excessive telephone calls or letters and must not contact them at unreasonable hours ('reasonable hours' are defined as 8am–9pm).

Lenders must not use documents that look like court forms or other official documents containing unfair, unclear or misleading information designed to coerce the client into paying.

If a property is repossessed, the lender must market it as soon as possible and obtain the best price that might reasonably be paid, although the lender is entitled to take account of market conditions or other factors that might justify deferring a sale – eg, the repayability of a grant if the property is sold by a certain date. In the event of a mortgage shortfall, the lender should inform the client of this as soon as possible, but has six years in which to notify the client of its intention to recover the shortfall debt (in line with the position for pre-31 October 2004 mortgages to which the rules discussed on pp141–45 still apply).

Breach of the above rules does not make any transaction void or unenforceable.[43] Lenders and intermediaries must have a written complaints policy and the client will be able to complain to the Financial Ombudsman Service if the matter cannot be resolved with the lender or intermediary.[44]

In October 2008, the Council of Mortgage Lenders issued industry guidance on arrears and possessions to assist lenders comply with Part 13 of the *MCOB* and their duty to treat customers fairly. It can be found at www.cml.org.uk/cml/policy/guidance. As well as guidance, this document contains examples of good practice and is an essential reference for advisers (see p327).

Checklist for action

Advisers should take the following action.
- Consider whether emergency action is necessary (see Chapter 8).
- Check liability. If possession proceedings have started, see Chapter 12.
- Assist the client to choose a strategy from Chapter 8 as **this is a priority debt if the mortgage is on the client's current home**. Otherwise, the arrears are a non-priority debt. Assist the client to choose a strategy from Chapter 9.

Rent

Rent is payable by tenants to landlords in exchange for the use of their property. A landlord may be either a private individual or property company, or a public sector landlord, such as a local authority or housing association.

The legal position

Rent is payable under a tenancy agreement (whether written or oral). For more details, see *Defending Possession Proceedings* (see Appendix 2).

Special features

After the termination of a tenancy (eg, because a notice to quit is served), a tenant is allowed to remain in possession of the home because of protection given by legislation. In these circumstances, the landlord may refer to the money due in exchange for possession of the home as 'mesne profits'. For practical purposes, this is the same as rent. Similarly, if a person is a licensee rather than a tenant, what s/he pays will not strictly be rent, but will be a charge for use of the property. Arrears of payment due under a licence are treated in the same way as rent when giving debt advice.

Checklist for action

Advisers should take the following action.
- Consider whether emergency action is necessary (see Chapter 8).
- Check liability. If possession proceedings have started, see Chapter 12.
- Assist the client to choose a strategy from Chapter 8 as **this is a priority debt if the rent is due on the client's current home**. Otherwise, the arrears are a non-priority debt. Assist the client to choose a strategy from Chapter 9.

Social fund repayments

Social fund loans (budgeting loans and crisis loans) are available to claimants who need to borrow money for essential items. Budgeting loans are only available to those getting income support (IS), income-based jobseeker's allowance (JSA), income-related employment and support allowance (ESA) or pension credit (PC) for 26 weeks. Social fund loans are normally repaid by a direct deduction from the claimant's weekly benefit. However, when a person stops getting benefit before having repaid the entire loan, s/he will still owe money to the social fund.

For further information about social fund loans, see p178 and CPAG's *Welfare Benefits and Tax Credits Handbook*.

The legal position

Social fund repayments are required by s78 of the Social Security Administration Act 1992. The *Social Fund Guide* lays down the procedures that the Department for Work and Pensions (DWP) uses to collect loans from claimants.

Special features

The DWP tells the client how the loan is to be repaid. Claimants on IS, income-based JSA, income-related ESA or PC have a fixed proportion of their benefits deducted, depending on their other commitments. Deductions can also be made from other benefits, including, from October 2013, universal credit. The debt adviser should consider asking for these deductions to be reduced (but the loan must be repaid over 104 weeks), especially if the DWP was unaware of the financial problems. If the client is no longer in receipt of benefit, the adviser should ask for the loan to be rescheduled. **Note:** deductions from benefit can be made even where an order for bankruptcy or a debt relief order has been made. Since 19 March 2012, social fund loans have been excluded debts for the purpose of those two debt remedies.

See CPAG's *Welfare Benefits and Tax Credits Handbook* for further details.

The DWP can take court action to recover the money if no arrangement is made. If the client is unable to afford repayment, it may consider writing off the debt. The debt should be treated as a normal unsecured loan and is not a priority unless the client is in receipt of a benefit from which deduction can be made (see p223).

Checklist for action

Advisers should take the following action.

- Check liability.
- Assist the client to choose a strategy from Chapter 9 as, unless the client is in receipt of a benefit from which deductions can be made, this is a non-priority debt.
- If the loan is being recovered by deductions from benefit, consider whether the rate of deduction can be reduced on the grounds of hardship.

Tax credit overpayments

Child tax credit (CTC) and working tax credit (WTC) are means-tested tax credits administered by HMRC.

Overpayments of tax credits can arise because initial awards are usually based on annual income over the previous tax year – 6 April to 5 April (although they can be based on an estimate of the current year's income). Some changes in circumstances must be reported straightaway and are taken into account by HMRC. However, changes in income do not have to be reported immediately and can be notified at the end of the tax year when the award is finalised. Clients faced with this choice may need specialist advice.

For further information about tax credits, see Chapter 7 and CPAG's *Welfare Benefits and Tax Credits Handbook*.

The legal position

If there is likely to be an overpayment during a tax year, or HMRC realises during the year that an award is too high (sometimes referred to as an 'in-year' overpayment), it can revise an award and reduce payments for the remainder of the year.[45] There are maximum amounts by which an award can be reduced.

Overpayments that come to light when an award is finalised at the end of the year are sometimes referred to as 'end-of-year' overpayments.[46] In the case of joint claims by couples, each partner is jointly and severally liable to repay any tax credit overpaid during the year. HMRC must issue an overpayment notice stating the amount to be repaid and the method of repayment it intends to use.[47] Recovery can be:

- by reducing an ongoing tax credits award. There are maximum amounts by which an award can be reduced.[48] This is the method HMRC prefers; *or*
- from the person(s) overpaid, in one lump sum, or by monthly payments over 12 months or for between three and 10 years so long as the payments are at least £10 a month (payments of less than £10 a month should only be accepted if the overpayments can be cleared in full within three years); *or*

- from 30 April 2010, from IS, JSA, ESA and PC, provided the client consents; *or*
- through the PAYE system if the debt does not exceed £3,000.

The overpayment can be remitted (ie, written off) if HMRC accepts that it is unlikely that the client will ever be in a position to repay, or if the client is currently unemployed with no savings or realisable assets and there is little prospect of her/him returning to work within two years.

Former partners could be asked to repay different amounts, but, as a concession, HMRC has agreed that partners will only be asked to pay a maximum of 50 per cent each (although any unpaid balance is not formally written off). However, this policy could change.

Interest can be added to an overpayment if HMRC considers the overpayment occurred as a result of the claimant's fraud or neglect.[49] The interest is recovered using the same methods as for overpayments.

Note: penalties can be imposed in some circumstances – eg, if someone makes an incorrect statement or supplies incorrect information and this is done fraudulently or negligently. Different procedures apply for the recovery of penalties.

Special features

All overpayments are recoverable, whatever the cause, although HMRC has the discretion not to recover and can decide to write off an overpayment. It has a code of practice on the recovery of tax credit overpayments, *What Happens if We've Paid You Too Much Tax Credit?*, available at www.hmrc.gov.uk/leaflets/cop26.pdf.

The code of practice was changed on 31 January 2008 and the decision on whether to recover any overpayments notified to the claimant on or after this date should be made according to this amended version. The code of practice says that HMRC will not pursue repayment if:

- the overpayment was caused by HMRC failing to meet its 'responsibilities'; *and*
- the claimant has met all of her/his 'responsibilities'.

Note: from 18 January 2010, HMRC has had a policy of offsetting some overpayments if the client failed to notify that s/he had ceased to be a single claimant and was now part of a couple, or had ceased to count as a couple and was now a single claimant.

See CPAG's *Welfare Benefits and Tax Credits Handbook* for more details and the 2007/08 edition for recovery of overpayments decided before 31 January 2008.

HMRC has agreed to stop recovery action of overpayments from 2003 to 2009 either if there has been no contact for 12 months or the client cannot be traced, but it has not formally written off these overpayments. However, this policy could change.

There is a right of appeal against HMRC's decisions about entitlement to tax credits. It is, therefore, vital to check that entitlement has been correctly calculated (ie, that there has been an overpayment), appealing any incorrect decisions within the time limit.

There is *no* right of appeal against a decision to recover an overpayment. However, such a decision can be disputed. It is best practice to use HMRC's official dispute form (TC846). HMRC suspends recovery when it receives this, pending its decision on whether to write off any of the overpayment. If a client is appealing an incorrect decision, it is important to dispute recovery at the same time to ensure that recovery is suspended pending the outcome of the appeal.

HMRC can remit (ie, write off) the overpayment if a client:

- has no means to repay an overpayment; *or*
- has no assets; *or*
- would be caused 'hardship' if recovery were to go ahead.

Specifically:

- if medical information or evidence is received that the client has a mental health problem, HMRC may agree not to pursue her/him for repayment. It will refer to the Money Advice Liaison Group guidelines for guidance;
- if an overpayment cannot be recovered from a deceased person's estate, it can be remitted if the surviving partner was jointly and severally liable and recovery from her/him would cause hardship.

An additional means of challenging recovery of an overpayment is to use HMRC's complaints procedure and/or to complain to the independent Adjudicator's Office (see Appendix 1). The only legal challenge to a decision to recover an overpayment is by judicial review.

If clients refuse to pay or do not keep to any payment arrangement, HMRC will consider taking legal proceedings to recover the debt. Unlike for income tax, there is a six-year time limit for taking court action (see p274). There is no time limit for recovery by making deductions from ongoing tax credit awards.

Checklist for action

Advisers should take the following action.

- Check liability.
- Assist the client to choose a strategy from Chapter 9 as **this is a priority debt**.

Value added tax

Value added tax (VAT) is a tax charged by HMRC on most transactions of businesses with an annual taxable turnover of more than a certain limit, set annually. A business must be registered for VAT unless its turnover is below the limit.

The legal position

VAT is payable under the Finance Act 1972 and the Value Added Tax Act 1994, and subsequent regulations and amendments. Its scope and level are reviewed each year and changes are often made to the Act following the Budget.

Special features

VAT is a tax on the value added to goods and services as they pass through the registered business. Thus, although VAT is payable on purchases, this amount can be offset against the tax on the business's own sales. For example, if the total purchases in a year were £100,000 and the total sales were identical, there would be no value added and no tax payable.

A debt adviser will generally encounter VAT debts after a business has ceased trading and the partner or sole trader is left responsible for VAT (see Chapter 16). Some goods are exempt and the calculation of the amount of VAT is complicated. Help should normally be sought from an accountant specialising in VAT. If VAT is overdue, a surcharge, which will be a percentage of the VAT owed, will be added to the debt. This amount can be appealed.

Checklist for action

Advisers should take the following action.
- Consider whether emergency action is necessary (see Chapter 8).
- Consider whether the client should be referred to a specialist agency – eg, TaxAid.
- Otherwise, assist the client to choose a strategy from Chapter 8 as this is **usually treated as a priority debt if the business is continuing to trade**. If the business is no longer trading, the arrears are a non-priority debt. Assist the client to choose a strategy from Chapter 9.

Water charges

Water companies charge for water, sewerage and environmental services on the basis of either a meter or the rating system, which was abolished as the basis of a local tax in April 1990 in England and Wales. Under the rating system, every dwelling was given a rateable value. Each year, water companies set a 'rate in the pound', which converts this rateable value into an annual charge. For example, a rate of 20p in the pound converts a rateable value of £300 to an amount of water rates payable of £60.

If a water meter is installed, a client pays for the actual amount of water used. Charges are per cubic metre at a rate set by the water company. A standing charge is also payable. There may also be installation and inspection charges. Separate charges are levied for sewerage and environmental services. These charges are based either on the rateable value of the property or on the amount of water used as recorded by the meter.

The legal position

Water charges are payable under the Water Industry Act 1991. Water companies will initially use county court action to recover arrears. They have no discretion to waive charges if there is an ongoing supply.

Special features

Bills for unmetered water charges are sent out in April and payment is due in advance unless the client takes advantage of one of the payment options offered by all the water companies. For example, payment can be made in eight to 10 instalments or weekly/monthly in cases of financial hardship. If the client defaults, the water company can take action to recover the outstanding balance for the remainder of the year. However, many of the companies' charges schemes allow them to apportion the bill in the event of the client including her/his water charges in bankruptcy or a debt relief order and recover the post-bankruptcy/debt relief order charges to the end of the current year. This practice should be challenged, as it clearly conflicts with the definitions of 'bankruptcy' and 'qualifying debt' in the Insolvency Act (see p469).

It is important to check that the bill refers to a property in which the client actually lives, or lived, and that the dates of occupation and name(s) shown on the bill are correct. The occupier of the property is the person liable to pay the bill. If there is more than one occupier, each is jointly and severally liable.

If there is a meter, bills are issued every three or six months based on meter readings carried out by the company's staff or the client. If this is not possible, an estimated bill will be issued. Bills should be checked and queried if they seem too high as there may be a hidden leak or the meter may be faulty.

Since 30 June 1999, water companies cannot disconnect for arrears of domestic water charges and, therefore, this is a non-priority debt (see Chapter 9), but the realistic cost of current water charges must be in the financial statement to avoid ongoing enforcement action.[50]

Ofwat guidelines, *Dealing With Household Customers in Debt,* available from www.ofwat.gov.uk, set out the following principles, which companies should include in their own codes of practice.

- Companies should be proactive in attempting to contact clients who fall into debt as early as possible and at all stages of debt management.
- Companies should provide clients with a reasonable range of payment frequencies and methods. The entire range of options should be properly and widely advertised to ensure that clients can select the arrangement which best suits their circumstances.
- Paperwork sent to clients should be written in plain language and in a courteous and non-threatening style, but should clearly set out the action the company will take if the client fails to make payment or contact the company, along with the possible consequences for the client.

- When agreeing payment arrangements, the client's circumstances (including her/his ability to pay) should be taken into account wherever possible.
- Clients whose accounts have been passed to collectors should receive the same treatment as if the account had remained with the water company and the potential consequences should be no more severe than if the service were provided by the water company – ie, the collector should comply with its own industry codes of practice as well as the water company's code of practice. Although the guidelines recognise this may not be possible if the debt is sold, which should only be done if all other debt recovery methods have been attempted, they seem to assume that such clients will be 'won't pays' and so not entitled to the same level of 'service'.
- Some water companies use local authorities or housing associations as 'billing agents' to bill and collect water charges from their tenants. The guidelines state that service standards should be agreed and notified to the tenants, but do not spell out what those standards should be. If the water charges are collected as part of the rent, the guidelines state that where eviction for non-payment of rent (including unpaid water charges) is a possibility, alternative solutions should be found (although it may well be that such provisions in a tenancy agreement could be challenged under the Unfair Terms in Consumer Contracts Regulations 1999). In such situations, specialist housing advice should be sought.

Advisers should be aware that there are vulnerable groups schemes (known as the WaterSure scheme) available for clients on low incomes. Many water companies have set up trust funds to assist clients with paying arrears of water charges. Advisers should check their local company's website for details of any scheme operating in their area.[51]

Auriga publishes a leaflet summarising the schemes or services water (and energy) companies can provide to help customers, available from Auriga Services, Emmanuel Court, 12–14 Mill Street, Sutton Coldfield B72 1TJ, Tel: 0121 321 1324.

Checklist for action

Advisers should take the following action.

- Check liability. Consider whether the client is eligible for assistance under the water company's consumer assistance scheme(s).
- Assist the client to choose a strategy from Chapter 9 as this is a non-priority debt.

Traffic penalties

A number of traffic penalties, particularly parking charges and certain other fixed penalty notices such as bus lane contraventions and (in London) the congestion charge, are recovered by local authorities using the county court under Part 75 of the Civil Procedure Rules.

The legal position

The current legislation is the Traffic Management Act 2004, which came into force on 30 March 2008. The enforcement authority (either the local authority or Transport for London) issues a 'penalty charge notice' which gives the registered owner 28 days in which to pay. **Note:** generally, the person or organisation registered at the *Driver and Vehicle Licensing Agency* (DVLA) as the registered keeper is responsible for payment of any penalty charge, regardless of who was driving the vehicle at the time, although a prior change of ownership would be a defence so long as the DVLA confirms this. If payment is made within 14 days, the amount due is reduced by 50 per cent.

If payment is not made within 28 days, the enforcement authority issues a 'notice to owner' and the client has a further 28 days in which to pay the full amount or make representations on specified grounds. The enforcement authority has 56 days in which to respond. If the client's representations are rejected, s/he has a further 28 days in which to appeal to the Parking and Traffic Appeals Service (in London) or the Traffic Penalty Tribunal (elsewhere). The grounds for appeal are the same as the grounds for representations. If the appeal is rejected (or any recommendation to the enforcement authority to withdraw the penalty charge notice is not accepted), the client has a further 28 days to pay. If the appeal is withdrawn before a decision is made, the time limit is 14 days. The statutory provisions relating to challenging traffic penalties are complex. There is valuable information on the Parking and Traffic Appeals Service website at www.patas.gov.uk and on the Traffic Penalty Tribunal website at www.trafficpenaltytribunal.gov.uk.

If the amount due is not paid, the penalty is increased by 50 per cent and a charge certificate is issued. If the amount due is not paid within 14 days, the enforcement authority can register the charge certificate for enforcement in the county court.

It is important to distinguish between traffic penalties (usually under the Road Traffic Regulation Act 1984) registered in the magistrates' court for enforcement, which are recoverable as fines (see p133) and are, therefore, priority debts and penalty charges recoverable through the Traffic Enforcement Centre, currently attached to Northampton County Court.[52] Once the penalty charge has been registered in the county court, it is passed to private bailiffs for collection. If the bailiff is unable to collect the debt, the local authority can then use other county court enforcement methods but, in practice, appear not to do so, preferring instead to leave the warrant with the bailiffs for the full 12 months.

If the client claims s/he is not liable to pay the penalty (eg, s/he was not the owner of the motor vehicle at the time), s/he should complete either the form of statutory declaration (PE3) or the witness statement (TE9) which accompanies the court order registering the charge. This must be returned to the court before the end of the period of 21 days beginning with the date of service of the order. The court can extend this time limit if it considers it reasonable to do so.

There are two potential liabilities for having no road tax. One is being the registered keeper of an unlicensed vehicle (criminal) and the other is late renewal of the licence (civil). Both arise under the Vehicle Excise and Registration Act 1994. The civil penalty is imposed under section 7A and the criminal offence under section 31A.

The section 31A penalty can be registered in the magistrates' court for enforcement. It is then recoverable as if payable under a conviction and is treated as a fine (see Chapter 13).

The £80 penalty under section 7A is recoverable as a debt due to the Crown – ie, by civil proceedings (see Chapters 10 and 11).

Special features

A traffic penalty enforced through the county court does not have the sanction of imprisonment for non-payment, but the county court has no power to suspend bailiff action by applying on an N245 (see p319), nor does the court have power to make an instalment order to prevent enforcement action.

In certain circumstances, the client can complain to the Local Government Ombudsman (in England) or the Public Services Ombudsman (in Wales) (eg, if there was a failure to consider compelling reasons for cancelling the penalty charge), but is usually expected to use the appeal procedure where appropriate.[53]

Guidance issued by the Department for Transport says that the Ombudsman cannot consider the issue of a warrant of execution or the recoverable sum as these are matters for the court, but can consider the level of bailiffs' costs or the reasonableness of their actions – eg, if there has been an excessive levy or the bailiffs have made undue threats.

Checklist for action

Advisers should take the following action.
- Consider whether emergency action is necessary (see Chapter 8).
- Check liability for the debt and any associated bailiff's charges. Consider whether there are any grounds for making representations and/or a complaint.
- Assist the client to choose a strategy from Chapter 9 as this is a non-priority debt unless the client is at risk of losing essential goods (see Chapter 8).

Notes

1. Regulated debts

1 For a discussion on various aspects of bank transfers, see J Wilson, 'Consultancy Corner', *Advisers* 107 and 108. See also report of a complaint to the FOS (*Adviser* 107 abstracts)
2 See FOS decision in *Ombudsman News* 84 (*Adviser* 140 abstracts)
3 *Lee v Barnes* [1886] 17 QBD 77
4 *Re Morritt ex parte Official Receiver* [1886] 18 QBD 222 (CA)
5 s7 Bills of Sale Act (1878) Amendment Act 1882
6 s1(1)(b) Law of Property (Miscellaneous Provisions) Act 1989
7 Although a party may not attest the bill, a party's agent, manager or employee may do so; *Peace v Brookes* [1895] 2 QB 451
8 s113 CCA 1974
9 s13 Bills of Sale Act 1882
10 For further discussion of the provisions of the code, see G Skipwith, 'Bills of Sale: codes of practice', *Adviser* 145
11 s8 CCA 1974
12 s8 CCA 1974
13 *Office of Fair Trading v Lloyds TSB and others* [2007] UKHL 48 (*Adviser* 125 consumer abstracts)
14 A creditor is required to give seven days' notice of its intention to enforce a term of the agreement allowing it to demand early payment of any sum in cases where this right arises, even though the client is not in default.
15 OFT leaflet, *Hire Purchase: making the right choice*, includes a section on the client's right to terminate.
16 See P Madge, 'Take it Back', *Adviser* 106
17 *First Response v Donnelly*, Durham County Court, 16 October 2006 (*Adviser* 122 consumer abstracts). For a discussion on challenging this approach to creditor termination, see C Meehan and P Madge, 'Letters', *Adviser* 125 and 127

18 Creditors could avoid this by including two principal agreements in the same document, each containing its own consumer credit heading and signature box.
19 s127(3) CCA 1974 (repealed from 6 April 2008, but not retrospectively, by s15 and Sch 3 para 11 CCA 2006)
20 *Ombudsman News* 82, 2003
21 See A MacDermott, 'CPAS: the facts behind the myths', *Adviser* 150
22 See *Ombudsman News* 103, June/2012
23 ss14 and 17 CCA 1974

2. Other debts

24 *R (on the application of Sutherland) v SSWP* [2004] EWHC 800 (Admin)
25 *A Retailer v Ms B and Ms K*, Oxford County Court, 9 May 2012, HHJ Harris QC. See also, R Dunstan and G Skipwith, '(Un)civil Recovery', *Adviser* 142
26 s76 LGA 2003 and see 'Complaint against Redcar and Cleveland Borough Council' (*Adviser* 126 money advice abstracts)
27 s35 MCA 1980
28 Sch 6 para 2 EA 1989; Sch 2B paras 6A and 7 GA 1986, as amended by the Utilities Act 2000
29 s1 MOA 1958
30 *Bradford and Bingley v Cutler* [2008] EWCA Civ 74 (*Adviser* 128 money advice abstracts)
31 *Hopkinson v Tupper*, 30 January 1997, CA, unreported (*Adviser* 63 abstracts)
32 s20(1) LA 1980
33 s20(5) LA 1980
34 *Bristol and West plc v Bartlett*, 31 July 2002, CA, unreported (*Adviser* 94 abstracts). For a full discussion of the issues, see P Madge, 'Out of the Blue', *Adviser* 61 and P Madge, 'About Face', *Adviser* 94.
35 *Scottish Equitable v Thompson* [2003] EWCA Civ 225 (*Adviser* 98 abstracts)
36 *West Bromwich Building Society v Wilkinson* [2005] UKHL 44 (*Adviser* 111 abstracts)

37 *West Bromwich Building Society v Crammer* [2002] EWCA 2618 (ChD) (*Adviser* 97 abstracts)

38 Reg 14(1A) Non-Domestic Rating (Collection and Enforcement) (Local Lists) Regulations 1989, No.1058

39 s49 LGFA 1988

40 See R Rosenberg, 'Mortgage Day: the final countdown', *Quarterly Account* 73, IMA, Winter 2003/04

41 s28 FSMA 2000

42 Part 11.3 MCOB

43 s151(2) FSMA 2000

44 See P Bristow, 'One-stop Complaints Shop', *Adviser* 107, and S Quigley, 'Removing the Barriers', *Adviser* 109

45 s28(5) TCA 2002

46 s28(1) TCA 2002

47 s29 TCA 2002

48 Reg 12A TC(PC) Regs

49 s37 TCA 2002

50 s1 and Sch 1 Water Industry Act 1999

51 *Adviser* 105 contains a series of articles on dealing with water debt. See also, J Guy, 'Maximising Income: using utility trust funds', *Quarterly Account* 4, IMA, Spring 2007

52 Part 75 CPR

53 See P Madge, 'No Waiting', *Adviser* 68, and T Redmond, 'Parking Complaints', *Adviser* 108

Chapter 7

Maximising income

This chapter covers:
1. Introduction (below)
2. How to use this chapter (p163)
3. A–Z of benefits and tax credits (p165)
4. Calculating entitlement (p182)
5. Other help (p189)

- - - - - - - - - -

Future changes

Major changes are taking place that affect the tax credits and benefits system. For more information, see CPAG's *Welfare Benefits and Tax Credits Handbook*.

- - - - - - - - - -

1. Introduction

It is important to ensure that a client's income is raised as high as possible by checking:

- s/he receives all the benefits and tax credits to which s/he is entitled, and that these are paid at the correct amount;
- tax liability is as low as possible;
- all possible sources of income have been explored.

Maximising income is not the same as increasing it. Maximisation means that income is not only increased, but that it cannot be increased any further.

If a debt adviser is not a welfare rights specialist, s/he should consult with colleagues who are, or refer cases to someone who is able to undertake this work.

The debt adviser's approach to income maximisation must be systematic in order to be comprehensive. Advisers must be familiar with the benefits and tax credits system and the books on income maximisation listed in Appendix 2. This chapter assumes general advice knowledge, but cannot explain all the ways in which income can be maximised. Instead, it describes some common ways of increasing income for people in debt.

The rules of entitlement to benefits are laid down in law, mostly very detailed rules in regulations. Many legislative terms are not described fully here and the adviser who is unfamiliar with them should consult the relevant CPAG handbooks (in particular, the *Welfare Benefits and Tax Credits Handbook*), which are fully referenced to the law and caselaw.

The criteria for entitlement are very strict and must be met. In particular, these include the following.

- **Claims.** Most benefits and tax credits must be claimed, which usually means completing a paper form or making a telephone claim to the Department for Work and Pensions (DWP) or HM Revenue and Customs (HMRC). Satisfying the rules of entitlement is not enough; if a claim is not made for a benefit, the client cannot receive it.
- **Time limits.** All benefits have strict time limits for claiming, which must be met or the client will lose money to which s/he would otherwise be entitled. Some benefits can be backdated, but the rules vary and some important basic benefits, like income-based jobseeker's allowance (JSA), are extremely difficult to backdate.
- **Appeals.** Most decisions on benefits, including whether to award or not, carry a right of appeal. Clients must appeal against decisions in writing and within strict time limits, usually one month, if they disagree with a decision. Errors by the DWP and HMRC in awarding and calculating benefits and tax credits are common, but if the client does not appeal an incorrect decision, s/he may find s/he loses out. Decisions about whether an overpayment of benefit can be recovered can also be appealed (but not for tax credits).
- **Changes in circumstances.** A client is under a duty to notify the authority that pays her/him benefits about any changes of circumstances that might affect her/his entitlement or the amount – eg, if s/he is claiming a benefit on the basis of being out of work and then gets a job. Failure to notify relevant changes of circumstance is a common cause of overpayments.

Note: most benefits have residence, presence and immigration tests. Clients who are 'persons subject to immigration control', sponsored migrants or asylum seekers have very limited access to most of the benefits referred to in this chapter. Specialist advice should always be sought for such clients. In addition, most means-tested benefits are subject to 'habitual residence' and 'right to reside' tests. These tests mainly affect European Union nationals.

The benefits system is complex, and there are many ways of categorising benefits. It can be helpful to think of benefits as falling into three types.

- Earnings-replacement benefits, such as contribution-based JSA or retirement pension. Typically, these are based on national insurance contributions and are not means tested. If a client has worked or been self-employed in the recent past, s/he may qualify for a contribution-based earnings-replacement benefit.

- Benefits that depend on a person's circumstances, such as disability living allowance and child benefit. These are paid because the client has certain needs or falls into a certain category – eg, s/he has a disability or a child.
- Means-tested benefits or tax credits that top up a client's benefit and/or other income, such as income support, income-related employment and support allowance, income-based JSA, pension credit (PC), housing benefit and council tax benefit. These are paid to bring a client's income up to a certain level, sometimes referred to as the 'safety net'. Which means-tested benefits a client can claim depends on her/his circumstances – eg, a client over pension age can claim PC and a client looking for work can claim JSA.

2. How to use this chapter

The table on p164 lists common circumstances that apply to people and the benefits and tax credits that may be appropriate for those circumstances. Many of the suggestions are also appropriate for groups other than those under which they are described. Many people fit into more than one category, so the adviser should check all the categories that could be relevant.

The A–Z of the most common benefits (see p165) outlines the main eligibility criteria for each benefit. This chapter cannot describe fully the entitlement conditions for every benefit; rather it is a guide to which benefits the debt adviser should consider may be appropriate for a client.

Following the A–Z is a brief explanation of how benefits are calculated, including, in particular, how the means test works. Means tests are complex and cannot be described fully in this *Handbook*. This chapter explains the basics so the debt adviser can judge whether further enquiries or an application for benefit should be made. Other sources of financial help that may be available to clients are listed on p189.

The amounts of benefits, thresholds and capital limits referred to in this chapter are for 2012/13. Benefit rates are updated annually and are included in CPAG's *Welfare Benefits and Tax Credits Handbook*.

Which benefits and tax credits can a client claim

The following table gives an overview of the possible benefits and tax credits to which a client may be entitled depending on her/his circumstances. More than one circumstance may apply to a particular client (eg, s/he may have a child, a disability, a mortgage and work part time), in which case the adviser should refer to each circumstance.

Note: whichever category a client fits into, some benefits and tax credits can be paid if s/he does not have enough money to live on, either in addition to other benefits and tax credits, or on their own. These are:

- income-based jobseeker's allowance (JSA) or income support (IS) if s/he is not in full-time paid work;
- income-related employment and support allowance (ESA) if s/he has 'limited capability' for work;
- working tax credit (WTC) if s/he is in full-time paid work;
- pension credit (PC) whether s/he is in or out of full-time paid work.

Circumstance	Potential benefits and tax credits
Bereaved	Bereavement payment
	Widowed parent's allowance
	Bereavement allowance
	Funeral expenses payment
Carer	Carer's allowance
Responsible for a child	Child tax credit
	Child benefit
	Guardian's allowance
	Statutory maternity pay
	Statutory paternity pay
	Statutory adoption pay
	Maternity allowance
	Health benefits
Disabled	Disability living allowance
	Attendance allowance
	Industrial injuries benefits
Has a mortgage	Income support
	Income-based jobseeker's allowance
	Income-related employment and support allowance
	Pension credit
	Council tax benefit (until April 2013, when it is abolished)
Need to meet a specific one-off cost	Community care grant (until April 2013, when it is abolished)
	Budgeting loan
	Crisis loan (until April 2013, when it is abolished)
Pensioner	State retirement pension
	Pension credit
	Winter fuel payment

Pregnant	Statutory maternity pay
	Maternity allowance
	Sure Start maternity grant
	Health benefits
	Employment and support allowance
	Statutory sick pay
Sick and not able to work	Incapacity benefit
Tenant	Housing benefit
	Council tax benefit (until April 2013, when it is abolished)
Unemployed and seeking work	Jobseeker's allowance
Unemployed and not seeking work	Income support
Working, but on a low income	Working tax credit
	Child tax credit
	Housing benefit
	Council tax benefit (until April 2013, when it is abolished)

3. **A–Z of benefits and tax credits**

Unless otherwise stated, all the benefits referred to in this section are claimed from and paid by the Department for Work and Pensions (DWP).

Future changes

The benefits system is undergoing substantial change. Most of the changes affect clients of working age; benefits for pensioners remain largely unaffected.

From October 2013, universal credit (UC) will start to replace the following means-tested benefits and tax credits:
– income support (IS);
– income-based jobseeker's allowance (JSA);
– income-related employment and support allowance (ESA);
– housing benefit (HB);
– child tax credit (CTC);
– working tax credit (WTC).

UC will be a means-tested benefit for people under the pension credit (PC) qualifying age who are in or out of work. It will have allowances for adults, and additions for children, childcare costs, limited capability for work, caring responsibilities and housing costs (for both owners and renters). It will be administered by the DWP.

From October 2013, therefore, clients moving in or out of work, or whose circumstances mean they need to claim a means-tested benefit, may have to claim UC.

UC will be rolled out on a regional basis and will be available nationally by April 2014. Existing claimants of the above benefits that are due to be abolished will be transferred to UC by 2017.

Attendance allowance

Attendance allowance (AA) is a benefit for clients who are aged 65 or over when they first claim and who have care needs as a result of either a physical or mental disability. They must need:

- frequent help with personal care throughout the day; *or*
- continual supervision throughout the day to avoid danger to themselves or others; *or*
- repeated or prolonged supervision at night to help with personal care or to avoid danger to themselves or others.

Clients must satisfy the disability conditions for at least six months. However, those who are 'terminally ill' (ie, who have a progressive disease from which it would not be unexpected for her/him to die within six months) should be awarded the higher rate of AA immediately. This is known as a claim under the 'special rules'.

An award of AA always makes a client better off. It is not means tested and does not count as income when calculating means-tested benefits and tax credits. In fact, entitlement to AA may give rise to an entitlement to a means-tested benefit, or a higher amount if benefit is already being paid. In particular, an award of AA means that a client's carer could claim carer's allowance (CA – see p167) for looking after her/him, or the client could qualify for an extra amount of a means-tested benefit (called a severe disability premium/additional amount – see p184).

AA cannot be backdated. It is not taxable.

Bereavement benefits

Bereavement benefits are benefits for widows, widowers or surviving civil partners. The three types of bereavement benefit are:

- **bereavement payment** – a lump-sum payment of £2,000;
- **widowed parent's allowance** – a weekly benefit paid if the client has at least one child, or is pregnant, when her/his spouse or civil partner dies;
- **bereavement allowance** – a weekly benefit paid for up to 52 weeks for clients who are at least 45 years of age when their spouse or civil partner dies.

The late spouse or civil partner must have paid national insurance (NI) contributions, unless s/he died as a result of an industrial accident or disease, and the client must usually have been under state pension age when her/his spouse or civil partner died. Entitlement to bereavement allowance and widowed parent's allowance ends on remarriage or a new civil partnership, and is suspended if the client is cohabiting. Bereavement payment must normally be claimed within 12 months of the death of the late spouse or civil partner.

A client cannot get both widowed parent's allowance and bereavement allowance at the same time.

Bereavement benefits are not means tested, but they normally count as income for mean-tested benefits and tax credits. Bereavement allowance is not taxable. Widowed parent's allowance and bereavement allowance are taxable, apart from any amounts in widowed parent's allowance for children.

Note: the government has announced that bereavement benefits will be substantially changed. This will not be until 2015 at the earliest. Existing claimants are unlikely to be affected.

Carer's allowance

CA is a benefit for clients who are providing regular and substantial care (35 hours a week or more) for someone who is in receipt of AA or the middle or highest rate of disability living allowance (DLA) care component, or constant attendance allowance for an industrial or war disablement. This includes caring for a relative or a member of the family – eg, a partner or child.

Clients who get CA (even if this is not paid because of special rules on 'overlapping benefits') may be entitled to an extra amount in a means-tested benefit, called a carer premium (see p183).

Note, however, that a claim for CA can have a negative effect on the means-tested benefits of the cared-for person and so a detailed better-off calculation is often needed. Clients should be referred for specialist advice if required.

CA is not means tested, but clients cannot get it if they count as in 'gainful employment', which means having earnings above a set limit (£100 a week in 2012/13). However, CA is taken into account in full as income for means-tested benefits and tax credits. CA is taxable; any increases for children are not.

Child benefit

Child benefit is a benefit for clients who are responsible for a child or a 'qualifying young person'. A 'child' is someone under 16; a 'qualifying young person' is someone aged 16 to 19 (20 in some cases) who meets certain conditions, including being enrolled on a course of full-time non-advanced education or on approved training.

To be responsible for a child or qualifying young person, the client must live with the child or contribute to the cost of supporting her/him of at least the child benefit rate. Once a client is awarded child benefit, s/he is usually considered as the person with responsibility for the child by other authorities – eg, a local authority when calculating HB or assessing the client's housing needs.

Child benefit is not means tested, and can be paid in addition to other benefits and tax credits. Child benefit is not taxable. Child benefit is claimed from and paid by HM Revenue and Customs (HMRC).

Note: from January 2013 a client who earns, or whose partner earns, £50,000 or more a year will pay extra income tax if s/he gets child benefit.

Child tax credit

Note: CTC will be affected by the introduction of UC from October 2013 (see p165).

CTC is paid to clients who have responsibility for a child or 'qualifying young person'. The rules on who counts as a child or qualifying young person are the same as for child benefit (see p167). A client counts as responsible for a child if s/he normally lives with her/him. CTC is usually paid to the person who has been awarded child benefit for the child.

CTC is paid in addition to child benefit and can also be paid with most other benefits. People entitled to IS, income-based JSA, income-related ESA or PC are automatically 'passported' to maximum CTC, but it counts as income for HB and council tax benefit (CTB), except for people who are at least the qualifying age for PC (see p176).

CTC is claimed from and paid by HMRC and is means tested. The means test for tax credits is different from that for benefits, and is based on annual income (see p186). CTC is not taxable.

Council tax benefit

Note: council tax benefit (CTB) is due to be abolished in April 2013. It will be replaced by local rebate schemes, so the help that is available with council tax bills will depend on where the client lives. See p191 for more details.

CTB is a means-tested benefit that helps with council tax payments. It can be claimed by clients who are liable for council tax and can be paid to those who are working or out of work.

Clients entitled to IS, income-based JSA, income-related ESA or the guarantee credit of PC are normally entitled to have all their council tax paid by CTB, but they still have to make a separate claim. Clients not on a means-tested benefit can still qualify for CTB if their income is sufficiently low and they have capital below a certain amount (£16,000 for most clients). There is no capital limit for clients on the guarantee credit of PC.

Some people, known as 'non-dependants' (eg, relatives or friends), living with the client can affect the amount of CTB paid. The amount of the deduction depends on the non-dependant's income. It is, therefore, vital that the correct details of the non-dependant's income are disclosed to ensure the maximum amount of CTB entitlement is paid. This is a common problem area.

Claims for CTB can be backdated for a maximum of six months if a client can show continuous 'good cause' for claiming late. Clients or their partners not in receipt of IS, income-based JSA or income-related ESA who are at least the qualifying age for PC can get CTB backdated without needing to show 'good cause', but only for up to three months.

CTB is not taxable.

Some clients may qualify for what is called 'second adult rebate' if they are the only person liable for council tax in the home and an adult on a low income lives with them. It is assessed at the same time as the claim for CTB. It does not matter how much income or capital the client has.

Even if a client does not qualify for CTB, s/he might qualify for a reduction in the council tax bill – eg, if s/he is the only adult living in the household (25 per cent reduction) or if s/he has a disability for which the house has special features (in which case, the property is taxed as if it is one band below its actual band). Discounts are not means tested and can be backdated. See CPAG's *Council Tax Handbook* for more details and p131 if the client has council tax arrears.

Disability living allowance

Note: DLA will be replaced for working-age claimants by a new benefit, personal independence payment (PIP), from April 2013. From this date, no new claims can be made; clients will have to claim PIP instead (see p177). Clients under 16 can still claim DLA and clients over 65 in receipt of DLA can continue to receive it.

DLA is a benefit for people who are under 65 when they first start to claim and have care needs as a result of either a physical or mental disability. DLA has two components.

To qualify for the '**care component**' the client must:
- need frequent help with personal care throughout the day; *or*
- need continual supervision throughout the day to avoid danger to her/himself or others; *or*
- need repeated or prolonged attention at night to help with personal care or to avoid danger; *or*
- need frequent or prolonged supervision at night to avoid danger; *or*
- be unable to prepare a main meal – known as the 'cooking test'.

To qualify for the '**mobility component**', the client must:
- be unable or virtually unable to walk; *or*
- face danger to her/his life or health by walking; *or*
- have a 'severe visual impairment'; *or*
- need supervision on unfamiliar routes.

DLA care component is paid at three different rates and the mobility component at two different rates. Clients can get one or both components if they satisfy the relevant conditions. Many clients are paid at a rate below that to which they might be entitled, or are not paid at all, and so there is often scope for increasing a disabled person's income via DLA. However, getting an increase in the rate of DLA is not something which should ordinarily be undertaken without the client seeking specialist advice, as there is always the risk that the rate awarded could decrease.

Clients must satisfy the disability conditions for at least three months before the start of the award and be likely to continue to satisfy them for at least the next six months. However, a client who is 'terminally ill' (ie, who has a progressive disease from which it would not be unexpected for her/him to die within six months) should be awarded the higher rate of DLA care component immediately. This is known as a claim under the 'special rules'.

Children can claim DLA. They can get DLA mobility component at the higher rate from age three and at the lower rate from age five. There is no lower age limit for DLA care component, but they cannot qualify via the 'cooking test' until they are 16.

An award of DLA always makes a client better off, is not means tested and does not count as income when calculating means-tested benefits and tax credits. In fact, entitlement to DLA may give rise to an entitlement to means-tested benefits (or higher amounts if they are already being paid).

DLA cannot be backdated. It is not taxable.

Employment and support allowance

Note: income-related ESA will be affected by the introduction of UC from October 2013 (see p165).

ESA is a benefit for clients who cannot work because of an illness or disability. Employees usually claim statutory sick pay (SSP) for the first 28 weeks of illness rather than ESA. Self-employed and unemployed people claim ESA straightaway.

There are two types of ESA.
- Contributory ESA is paid if a client satisfies the national insurance (NI) contribution conditions. It is not means tested. It is only paid for 52 weeks.
- Income-related ESA is means tested and has no NI contribution test. It is possible to receive contributory ESA, topped up with income-related ESA. It can be paid indefinitely.

A basic allowance of ESA is paid during an initial 'assessment phase' of 13 weeks. The amount of income-related ESA paid could be higher if, for example, it includes premiums (see p183) or housing costs (see p185). The client's ability for work is assessed by the DWP under a 'work capability assessment'. A small number of people are treated as having limited capability for work and do not have to undergo this – eg, people who are terminally ill, those receiving or recovering from certain types of chemotherapy and hospital inpatients.

After the assessment phase, clients who pass a medical assessment go on to the 'main phase' of ESA and are paid an extra amount, called a 'component', because of their inability to work. Clients are put into one of two groups:

- the work-related activity group for clients who must attend work-focused interviews and undertake work-related activity;
- the support group for clients with the most severe illnesses or disabilities.

The general rule is that people cannot work and claim ESA. Clients can do some limited work (called 'permitted work') while on ESA, but they must notify the DWP and they can lose entitlement if they earn more than a certain amount. Clients affected by these rules may need specialist advice.

Contributory ESA is not means tested, but it is affected by any income from a pension scheme/plan or an income protection insurance policy, and is subject to the 'overlapping benefit' rules (see p187).

Income-related ESA can be paid in addition to contributory ESA in some circumstances – eg, if a client has a partner. Amounts for children are not included, but clients getting income-related ESA can claim and get the maximum amount of CTC for their children. Income-related ESA is a 'passporting' benefit, which means it can help the client to get maximum HB and CTB, free prescriptions, free school lunches for her/his children and help from the social fund. Extra amounts can be paid depending on the circumstances of the client and her/his partner – eg, premiums for carers or because of a disability (see p183).

Income-related ESA includes an amount for housing costs (see p185).

Contributory ESA is taxable; income-related ESA is not.

Guardian's allowance

Guardian's allowance is a benefit paid to clients who are responsible for a child who is effectively an orphan. Clients can be paid it if they are entitled to child benefit for a child whose parents have died, or one has died and the whereabouts of the other is unknown, or one has died and the other has been sentenced to a term of imprisonment of two years or more or is detained in hospital by a court order. Guardian's allowance is not means tested, does not count as income for other benefits and tax credits, and can be paid in addition to child benefit. It is claimed from and paid by HMRC.

Health benefits

Note: it is not yet known who will qualify for the following health benefits after UC is introduced in October 2013.

Clients can qualify for the following health benefits if they receive IS, income-related ESA, income-based JSA, the guarantee credit of PC, CTC and have income below an income threshold, or WTC that includes a disability or severe disability element and they have income below an income threshold. There is also a scheme for people on a low income. Clients apply directly to the NHS Business Services Authority on Form HC1.

- **Free prescriptions**. Clients also qualify if they:
  - are pregnant or have given birth in the last 12 months;
  - are under 16 (or under 19 and in full-time education);
  - are aged 60 or over;
  - have certain medical conditions; *or*
  - live in Wales.
- **Free dental treatment**. Clients also qualify if they:
  - are pregnant or have given birth in the last 12 months;
  - are under age 18 (or under 19 and in full-time education);
  - live in Wales and are under 25, or 60 and over (examinations only).
- **Free sight tests**. Clients also qualify if they:
  - are under 16 (or under 19 and in full-time education);
  - are aged 60 or over;
  - are registered blind or partially sighted;
  - have prescribed complex or powerful lenses;
  - have diabetes or glaucoma or they are at risk of glaucoma;
  - are aged 40 or over and the parent, brother, sister or child of someone with glaucoma.
- **Vouchers towards the cost of glasses or contact lenses**. Clients also qualify if:
  - they are under 16 (or under 19 and in full-time education);
  - their eyesight changes often, making their current glasses or contact lenses inadequate;
  - they have been prescribed complex or powerful lenses;
- Travel to and from hospital for treatment or services.

Healthy Start food and vitamins

Note: it is not yet known who will qualify for the following after UC is introduced in October 2013.

The Healthy Start scheme provides vouchers that can be exchanged for healthy foods, such as fresh fruit and vegetables, and milk. Those who qualify for vouchers can also get free vitamins. Clients qualify if they:

- are under 18 and pregnant;
- are 18 or over and pregnant or if they have a child under one (or it is less than a year since her/his expected date of birth). They must also be entitled to IS, income-related ESA or income-based JSA, or to CTC (but not WTC) and have an annual taxable income below an income threshold;

- have a child under four, and they are entitled to IS, income-related ESA or income-based JSA, or to CTC (but not WTC) and have an annual taxable income below an income threshold.

Housing benefit

Note: HB will be affected by the introduction of UC from October 2013 (see p165).

HB is a means-tested benefit, claimed from and paid by local authorities to tenants. HB can be paid to people in and out of work.

Clients in private-rented accommodation may have their HB restricted if the rent exceeds a local housing allowance for their area. The local housing allowance for a particular client is based on the number of bedrooms s/he is allowed under the rules (the 'size criteria') and the average rents for the cheapest 30 per cent of properties in the area. There are fixed maximums for each number of bedrooms and an absolute maximum of £400 per week for a four-bedroom property.

The local housing allowance system was introduced on 7 April 2008. Clients who have been receiving HB continuously since before this date may be on an older system of rent restriction. Specialist advice should be sought.

Clients in local authority or housing association accommodation cannot have their rent restricted under the local housing allowance rules; all their rent is normally 'eligible rent' for HB. However payments made to their landlord may include non-eligible charges, such as fuel, water or some service charges.

Note: from April 2013 the 'size criteria' will also be applied to local authority and housing association tenants. If their accommodation is deemed to be too big, they will not get all their rent covered.

Clients entitled to IS, income-based JSA, income-related ESA or the guarantee credit of PC are normally entitled to have all their 'eligible rent' met by HB, but they still have to make a separate claim. Clients not on a means-tested benefit can still qualify for HB if their income is sufficiently low and they have capital below a certain amount (£16,000 for most clients). There is no capital limit for clients on the guarantee credit of PC.

Some non-dependants (eg, relatives or friends) living with the client can affect the amount of HB paid. The amount of the deduction made depends on the non-dependant's income. It is, therefore, vital that the correct details of the non-dependant's income are disclosed to ensure the maximum amount of HB entitlement is paid. This is a common problem area.

Claims for HB can be backdated for a maximum of six months if a client can show continuous 'good cause' for claiming late. Clients or their partners not in receipt of IS, income-based JSA or income-related ESA who are at least the qualifying age for PC can get HB backdated without needing to show 'good cause', but only for up to three months.

Clients left with a shortfall in their rent despite getting the maximum HB to which they are entitled can apply for a discretionary housing payment to help make up the shortfall. Discretionary housing payments are paid from a cash-limited budget, so they are not guaranteed.

HB and discretionary housing payments are not taxable.

Incapacity benefit

Incapacity benefit (IB) is a benefit for clients who are sick and unable to work. It was replaced for new claims by ESA on 27 October 2008, but clients who started to claim IB before this date may still be getting it. Clients getting IB can continue to receive it, but they are being transferred to ESA. This means that they are invited for a medical. If they pass they can move onto ESA; if they fail their entitlement to IB ends, and they will have to try to claim another benefit.

Income support

Note: IS will be affected by the introduction of UC from October 2013 (see p165).

IS is a means-tested benefit that provides basic financial support for clients on a low income who are not expected to 'sign on' as available for work. To qualify, the client must:

- not be in full-time work – ie, work less than 16 hours a week. If s/he has a partner, the partner must not be in full-time work (less than 24 hours per week);
- not be a full-time student (there are some exceptions);
- pass the means test;
- have capital below £16,000;
- fall into a specified category of person who is eligible to claim IS (see below).

The main categories of people eligible to claim IS are:

- lone parents – ie, a single people responsible for a child under five;
- certain lone parents who are foster parents or who are adopting a child;
- carers – ie, people getting CA or 'regularly and substantially' caring for a disabled person;
- people unable to work because of illness or disability. No new claims can be made from 27 October 2008 (unless client is also getting IB or severe disablement allowance (SDA)), but many clients may already be claiming on this basis;
- pregnant women for the 11 weeks before and 15 weeks after giving birth;
- people receiving statutory sick pay (SSP).

The list above is not exhaustive. See CPAG's *Welfare Benefits and Tax Credits Handbook* for more details.

IS pays a basic amount for the client and her/his partner if s/he has one. Amounts for children are not included in new claims, but clients getting IS can claim and get the maximum amount of CTC for their children. IS is a 'passporting' benefit – ie, it can help the client get maximum HB and CTB, free prescriptions, free school lunches for her/his children and help from the social fund. Extra amounts can be paid depending on the circumstances of the client and her/his partner – eg, premiums for carers or because of a disability (see p183).

IS includes an amount for housing costs (see p185).

IS is not taxable.

Industrial injuries benefits

Industrial injuries disablement benefit is for clients who:
- while working as an employee have had a personal injury – eg, from an accident at work; *or*
- have a prescribed industrial disease contracted during the course of their employment – eg, asbestosis.

Clients have to be assessed as having a 'degree of disablement' (eg, '20 per cent disabled') resulting from a loss of faculty – eg, reduced ability to walk because of arthritis. Clients can get industrial disablement benefit if they are still in work. It can be paid on top of IB, contributory ESA and other non-means-tested benefits. Industrial injuries benefits are not taxable. They generally count as income for the purposes of calculating means-tested benefits and are disregarded as income for tax credits.

Jobseeker's allowance

Note: income-based JSA will be affected by the introduction of UC from October 2013 (see p165).

JSA is a means-tested benefit that provides basic financial support for people who are expected to 'sign on' as available for work and actively seek work. There are two types of JSA:
- contribution-based JSA, paid for six months to those who have recently paid NI contributions;
- income-based JSA, which is means tested with no requirement to have paid NI contributions.

To qualify for income-based JSA, the client must:
- not be in full-time work – ie, working less than 16 hours a week. If s/he has a partner, the partner must not be in full-time work (less than 24 hours a week);
- not be a full-time student (there are some exceptions);
- pass the means test;
- have capital below £16,000;
- be available for and actively seeking work.

Income-based JSA pays a basic amount for the client and her/his partner if s/he has one. Amounts for children are not included in new claims, but clients getting income-based JSA can claim and get the maximum amount of CTC for their children. Income-based JSA is a 'passporting' benefit – ie, it can help the client get maximum HB and CTB, free prescriptions, free school lunches for her/his children and help from the social fund. Extra amounts can be paid depending on the circumstances of the client and her/his partner – eg, if the client is caring for someone or has a disability (see p183).

Some couples (eg, those without children) have to claim what is known as 'joint-claim JSA' and both have to be available for work.

Income-based JSA includes an amount for housing costs (see p185). These payments are only paid for two years if the claim was made on or after 4 January 2009.

Contribution-based JSA pays a basic amount for the client and is only paid for six months. People can get both contribution-based and income-based JSA at the same time.

Payments of JSA can be reduced or entitlement can end if the client fails to comply with what are known as the 'jobseeking conditions'. As well as being available for and actively seeking work, clients must comply with certain directions given to them and attend regular interviews. Clients can be sanctioned for failing to attend interviews and for other things, such as losing a job because of misconduct, giving up work without 'just cause' or for failing to participate in specified training or employment schemes. JSA is either not paid or is paid at a reduced rate.

Clients can appeal against sanction decisions, and can also apply for 'hardship payments' if their JSA is not paid. Hardship payments can only be paid to clients who are in a vulnerable group or if they (or their partner) would experience hardship were the hardship payment not made. Vulnerable groups include carers, and people who have a disability or children.

JSA is taxable.

Maternity allowance

Maternity allowance (MA) is a benefit for women who are pregnant or who have recently given birth. It is normally claimed by women who do not qualify for statutory maternity pay (SMP) – eg, self-employed women, those not currently in work or those who have not worked for long enough to get SMP. To qualify for MA, the client must have been employed or self-employed for at least 26 of the 66 weeks before the week in which the baby is due, and have had average weekly earnings of at least £30 a week. MA is not taxable.

Pension credit

Note: PC will be affected by the introduction of UC from October 2013. As a result of the phasing out of HB and CTC (see p165), help with housing costs for tenants and amounts for children will be included in PC. Couples with one member below the qualifying age will not be able to claim PC and will have to claim UC instead.

PC is a benefit for people on a low income who have reached the qualifying age. This is basically the 'pension age' for women (see p178), which will rise from 60 to 65 between 2010 and 2018 as the pension age for men and women is equalised. Then the pension age for both women and men will rise to 66 by 2020.

PC is made up of a guarantee credit and a savings credit. The guarantee credit is the basic amount paid for the client and her/his partner. It is means tested, but there is no upper capital limit.

Extra amounts can be paid depending on the circumstances of the client and her/his partner – eg, if she is caring for someone or has a disability (see p183). Amounts for children are not included but clients getting PC can claim and get the maximum amount of CTC for their children. PC is a 'passporting' benefit – ie, it can help the client get maximum HB and CTB, free prescriptions, free school lunches for her/his children and help from the social fund.

PC includes an amount for housing costs (see p185).

The savings credit is an additional amount, paid to clients who have 'qualifying income' (eg, retirement pension) over a threshold. The rules are complicated, but many clients who fail the means test for the guarantee credit may qualify for the savings credit instead.

PC is not taxable.

Personal independence payment

PIP will be introduced for new claimants from April 2013. It will be similar to DLA (see p169), but will be less generous and fewer people will qualify.

Clients under 16 will not be affected by PIP and will still be able to claim DLA. Clients already 65 and getting DLA will not be affected. Clients of working age already getting DLA will be transferred to PIP between 2014 and 2016.

PIP has two components – a daily living and a mobility component. Each component has two rates – a standard rate, and an enhanced rate paid if a client's ability to carry out certain activities is 'severely limited' by her/his physical or mental condition.

Entitlement to PIP is determined by the difficulty a client has performing a specified list of activities. Points are given for each activity and benefit awarded once a specified number of points is reached.

PIP is not means tested, taxable or based on NI contributions, and is available to clients both in and out of work.

Retirement pension

There are three main types of retirement pension:
- Category A, based on a client's own NI contribution record. People who are divorced or who have had a civil partnership dissolved may be entitled to a

Category A pension based on their former spouse or civil partner's contribution record;

- Category B, based on the NI contribution record of a spouse or civil partner (or late spouse or civil partner) for those with an incomplete NI record of their own;
- Category D, which is non-contributory and payable to those over 80.

Although there is a basic amount of retirement pension, each person's entitlement is based on her/his own specific contribution record, so some clients receive less than the basic state retirement pension. Amounts can also be paid above the basic amount – this is called the additional pension or SERPS, so some clients get more than the basic amounts. Some clients may have been in contracted-out occupational or personal pension schemes and so cannot receive any, or receive only very little, additional pension despite having a full work record.

Retirement pension is not means tested, but counts as income for other benefits and tax credits.

A client usually has to make a claim for retirement pension – it is not paid automatically. In some circumstances, payment can be deferred and a higher amount paid in future, or a lump sum accrued. Retirement pension can be backdated for up to 12 months. Before 2003, people could claim additional amounts for dependent children, so some clients may still be receiving these.

Note: between 2010 and 2018, the pension age for women born after 6 April 1950 is being increased gradually to 65, and women will generally have to wait longer to be entitled to retirement pension. The pension age for both women and men will increase to 66 between 2018 and 2020.

Retirement pension is taxable.

Social fund

Note: crisis loans and community care grants are being abolished in April 2013 and will be replaced by 'local welfare provision' delivered by local authorities. The help a client can get will therefore depend on where s/he lives. Budgeting loans will still be available to claimants who are not getting UC. The rules about who qualifies for payments from the regulated social fund (see p179) will also be affected by the introduction of UC in October 2013.

There are two sections to the social fund – the regulated and the discretionary. Maternity grants, funeral expenses, winter fuel payments and cold weather payments are part of the regulated social fund. If a client satisfies the conditions of entitlement, s/he is entitled to a payment. Budgeting loans, community care grants and crisis loans are part of the discretionary social fund; there is no guarantee of a payment, or for the amount requested.

Discretionary fund

- **Community care grants** help meet the cost of starting or continuing to live independently in the community. They do not have to be repaid. The client must be on a qualifying benefit (see below).
- **Budgeting loans** are for specified types of expenses, such as an item of furniture or household equipment. The amount paid is determined by a formula based on the size of the client's family and the amount of outstanding budgeting loan debt. They are repaid through weekly deductions from benefits, but are interest free. The client must be on a qualifying benefit (see below).
- **Crisis loans** help meet urgent needs. They are repaid through weekly deductions from benefit, but are interest free.

Regulated fund

- **Sure Start maternity grant**. This is a £500 lump sum payable to clients on a low income to help with the costs of a new baby (expected, born, adopted or if a client has a residence or a parental order). If the client is already getting benefit for another child under 16, they will probably be excluded from getting the grant. The client must be on a qualifying benefit (see below). It must be claimed within three months of the birth, adoption or residence or parental order.
- **Funeral payment**. This is a lump sum to cover the basic costs of a funeral plus some other related expenses. The client must be responsible for the funeral arrangements and be on a qualifying benefit (see below). The payment may be recovered from any money or assets left by the person who died. There are also some complicated rules which exclude some people from claiming if someone else, not on benefit, could have paid for the funeral.
- **Winter fuel payment.** This is a lump-sum payment to help pay fuel bills, although it can be spent on anything the client wants. Clients must be at least the qualifying age for PC to qualify (see p176). It is usually paid automatically, but men aged under 65 and not on any benefits may have to make a claim as the DWP may not know they are entitled to a payment.
- **Cold weather payments** are paid to people on certain means-tested benefits during recorded periods of cold weather.

Qualifying benefits

For community care grants and budgeting loans, a client must be in receipt of a qualifying benefit and, in the case of budgeting loans, have been in receipt of a qualifying benefit or tax credit for 26 weeks. A qualifying benefit is IS, income-based JSA, income-related ESA and PC. For the regulated social fund, except winter fuel payments, a client must have been awarded IS, income-based JSA, income-related ESA, PC, CTC of more than just the family element, or WTC including the disability or severe disability element. Cold weather payments also have other conditions attached. HB and CTB are also qualifying benefits for funeral payments. In some cases, someone can claim if her/his partner has an award of the qualifying benefit or tax credit.

Statutory adoption pay

Statutory adoption pay (SAP) is paid to clients who are (or have recently been) employees and who take adoption leave.

Average gross weekly earnings must be equal to or above the NI 'lower earnings' limit (£107 a week in 2012/13). The client must have worked continuously for her/his employer for 26 weeks by the end of the week in which s/he is notified that s/he has been matched for adoption. SAP can be paid to both women and men.

SAP is claimed from the client's employer and is paid in the same way as the client's normal pay. The employer must be given relevant notice and information within a strict time limit. SAP is paid for 39 weeks. It is not means tested, but counts as earnings for means-tested benefits and tax credits. SAP is taxable.

Statutory maternity pay

SMP is paid to clients who are (or have recently been) employees and who take maternity leave.

Average gross weekly earnings must be at least equal to the NI lower earnings limit (£107 a week in 2012/13). The client must have worked continuously for her employer for 26 weeks up to and including the 15th week (called the 'qualifying week') before the week in which her baby is due.

SMP is paid for a maximum of 39 weeks. For the first six weeks, clients get a higher rate of 90 per cent of average weekly earnings and a further 33 weeks at the lower rate. These are the minimum amounts of maternity pay; the client's employer might operate a more generous scheme. Clients who do not qualify for SMP may be able to claim MA. Entitlement to SMP does not depend on the client returning to work.

SMP is claimed from the client's employer and is paid in the same way as her normal pay. The employer must be given relevant notice and information within a strict time limit. SMP is not means tested, but counts as earnings for means-tested benefits and tax credits. SMP is taxable.

Statutory paternity pay

Statutory paternity pay (SPP) is paid to clients who are (or have recently been) employees and are taking paternity leave because their partner has just given birth. Clients can also get SPP if they are adopting a child and their partner is claiming SAP.

Average gross weekly earnings must be equal to or above the NI 'lower earnings' limit (£107 a week in 2012/13). The client must have worked continuously for her/his employer for 26 weeks up to and including the 15th week (called the 'qualifying week') before the week in which her baby is due.

SPP is claimed from the client's employer and is paid in the same way as normal pay. The employer must be given relevant notice and information within a strict time limit. 'Ordinary' SPP is paid for a maximum of two consecutive weeks. 'Additional' SPP can be paid in some circumstances for up to 19 weeks if the mother has returned to work 'early' and the client is now the main carer of the child. Both are paid at the lower of a standard rate or 90 per cent of average weekly earnings.

SSP is not means tested, but counts as earnings for means-tested benefits and tax credits. SPP is taxable.

Statutory sick pay

SSP is paid to employees who are sick and unable to work for at least four consecutive days. SSP is not paid during the first three days of illness. Clients cannot get ESA or IB while they are entitled to SSP, but can claim IS to top up SSP if their income and capital are sufficiently low. If a client does not qualify for SSP, s/he may be able to claim ESA instead.

Clients must have average earnings of at least the NI lower earnings limit (£107 a week in 2012/13) to qualify.

SSP is claimed from the client's employer and is paid in the same way as her/his normal pay. It is paid at a standard rate for a maximum of 28 weeks for each episode of illness. If a client is still off work sick after SSP has expired, s/he may then qualify for ESA. SSP is not means tested but it counts as earnings for means-tested benefits and tax credits. SSP is taxable.

Universal credit

From October 2013, UC will start to replace the following means-tested benefits and tax credits:
- IS;
- income-based JSA;
- income-related ESA;
- HB;
- CTC;
- WTC.

UC is a means-tested benefit for people under PC age who are in or out of work. It has allowances for adults, and additions for children, childcare costs, limited capability for work, caring responsibilities and housing costs (for both owners and renters). It will be administered by the DWP. It is not taxable.

It is not yet clear whether UC will be a 'qualifying benefit' and so 'passport' a client onto free school lunches (see p191), regulated social fund payments (see p179) and health benefits (see p172).

Budgeting loans are replaced by 'advances' of UC, which are repayable loans. A client who experiences a delay in payment at the start of her/his claim for UC can claim an 'alignment payment' instead of a crisis loan.

Working tax credit

Note: working tax credit will be affected by the introduction of UC from October 2013 (see p165).

WTC is paid a client who is, or whose partner is, in full-time paid work. The client must be:
- a lone parent with a dependent child and working at least 16 hours a week;
- part of a couple with a child, one who works at least 16 hours a week, and the other is disabled, in hospital or in prison, or a carer;
- part of a couple with a child. The couple must work 24 hours between them, with one partner working at least 16 hours a week. If only one partner works 24 hours, s/he will qualify;
- disabled and work at least 16 hours a week;
- aged 25 or over and work at least 30 hours a week;
- aged 60 or over and work at least 16 hours a week.

WTC is claimed from and paid by HMRC. It is means tested, and counts as income for the purposes of means-tested benefits. It is claimed and assessed at the same time as CTC. WTC is not taxable.

4. **Calculating entitlement**

This section looks at how the means tests for benefits and tax credits work. There are a number of common rules for the different benefits, but tax credits are calculated differently. It also refers to other issues which affect how much money the client is actually paid.

Future changes

From April 2013, the total amount of benefits that can be received by a client (and her/his partner) will be limited to around £350 for single people without children and £500 for couples and lone parents with children. A client's benefit income will not be able to be maximised above this amount.

This benefit cap will initially be administered by local authorities via reductions in housing benefit (HB). The following benefits will be included in the cap: bereavement allowance, carer's allowance (CA), child benefit, child tax credit (CTC), employment and support allowance (ESA), guardian's allowance (GA), HB, incapacity benefit (IB), income support (IS), jobseeker's allowance (JSA), maternity allowance (MA), severe disablement allowance (SDA), widowed mother's allowance, widowed parent's allowance and widow's pension.

Clients who are (or whose partner or child is) getting attendance allowance (AA), working tax credit (WTC), disability living allowance (DLA), ESA support component, war widow's pension or industrial injuries disablement benefit will be exempt. Also, if a client has worked for 12 months and loses her/his job, the cap will not be applied for nine months.

When universal credit (UC) is introduced in October 2013, it will be included in the cap. Clients on UC earning at least £430 a month, however, will be exempt.

Means-tested benefits

The basic formula for calculating means-tested benefits is as follows. See p186 for UC.
- Work out the applicable amount (see below).
- Calculate the client's income and capital.
- For IS, income-based JSA, income-related ESA and PC, deduct the income from the applicable amount. The remainder (if any) is the amount of benefit. HB and CTB can still be awarded if income is above the applicable amount by applying a 'taper'. Sixty-five per cent of the amount of income above the applicable amount is deducted from eligible rent. Any remaining rent will be met by HB. Twenty per cent of income above the applicable amount is deducted from council tax liability, with the remainder met by CTB.

Applicable amounts

Applicable amounts are made up of a basic allowance for the client and her/his partner if s/he has one, plus additional amounts (called 'premiums') to take account of their circumstances. Advisers should check that the client's applicable amount includes all the premiums that are appropriate.

Eligible housing costs for clients who are homeowners can be added. Amounts are included in HB and CTB for children.

The terms used for PC are slightly different; the applicable amount is called the 'appropriate minimum guarantee', and the premiums are called 'additional amounts'. The extra amounts in ESA are called 'components'.

Carer premium and carer's additional amount

This is paid if the client is entitled to CA, even if s/he is not getting it because s/he is getting an 'overlapping' benefit (see p187).

Family premium

This is paid in HB and CTB if the client has a child or qualifying young person in the family. Clients still getting IS and income-based JSA for their children should have a family premium included as well.

Disabled child premium

This is paid if a child receives DLA or is blind. It is available in HB and CTB. It can be included in IS and income-based JSA if the client still gets those benefits for her/his children.

Disability premium

This is paid if the client is registered blind or receiving a 'qualifying benefit'. These include DLA, the long-term rate of IB, and the disability or severe disability element of WTC.

Since the introduction of ESA in October 2008, the disability premium is generally not available on grounds of incapacity for work in any new claims for IS, income-based JSA, HB or CTB. Clients who were getting it on 27 October 2008 may still do so.

There is no disability premium in PC or ESA. There is also no disability premium in HB and CTB if a client is getting ESA. Instead, either a 'work-related activity component' or a 'support component' is included in her/his applicable amount.

Severe disability premium and severe disability additional amount

This is paid if a client receives a 'qualifying benefit' (AA, the middle or highest rate care component of DLA, constant AA, or an equivalent war pension) and no one gets CA for looking after her/him. S/he must not have a non-dependant aged 18 or over normally living with her/him.

The rules for couples are more complicated. See CPAG's *Welfare Benefits and Tax Credits Handbook* for more details.

Enhanced disability premium

This is paid if the client or her/his partner is under the qualifying age for PC and receives the highest rate care component of DLA. For HB and CTB only, it can also be paid in certain circumstance for each of the client's children who receive the highest rate care component of DLA.

Pensioner premiums

Pensioner premiums can be paid to clients on IS, income-based JSA and income-related ESA if the client's partner has reached the qualifying age for PC (see p176).

As PC is more generous, clients in these situations should claim PC instead.

Employment and support allowance components

ESA has two additional components. Both are paid once the initial assessment phase is over. They are paid at the same rate for couples as for single people. A client can only be paid one. The work-related component is paid to people who have limited capability for work. The support component is paid to people who are more severely disabled and those assessed as having limited capability for work-related activity.

Eligible housing costs

Clients who are homeowners can have an amount for their housing costs included in their IS, income-based JSA, income-related ESA or PC. The rules are complex. Costs that can be covered include help with the interest on a mortgage or eligible home repair or improvement loan, ground rent and some service charges. The amount paid might not be the full housing cost because payments are:

- based on a standard rate of interest, not the rate paid;
- reduced if the client has a non-dependant (eg, a relative or friend) living with her/him;
- restricted to loans below an upper limit (either £200,000 or £100,000 depending on circumstances – but see below);
- restricted if they are considered excessive, or if the client took out the loan while on IS, JSA, income-related ESA or PC (or during certain periods between claims);
- in most cases (but never with PC), subject to a 'waiting period' of 13 weeks (but see below).

If entitlement to benefit ends because the client starts work or her/his hours or pay increase, housing costs can continue to be paid for four weeks. This is known as 'mortgage interest run-on'.

Note: it is likely that, at some point in 2013, the waiting period will be extended, the upper limit reduced to £100,000 and a two-year limit on payments applied to everyone.

Capital

A client cannot get means-tested benefits if her/his (and her/his partner's) capital is more than an upper limit. Capital below a specified lower limit is ignored. Any capital between the two limits is assumed to produce a certain amount of income, called 'tariff income'. This counts towards the client's income when working out how much benefit s/he gets.

There is no upper capital limit for PC (and for HB and CTB if the client is entitled to the guarantee credit of PC), but 'tariff income' is still taken into account.

Capital includes:

- cash;
- the balance in any bank or building society current account or savings accounts;
- the value of any National Savings and Investments products, including premium bonds;
- the value of any shares, gilts, bonds, unit trusts.

Under what is known as the 'notional capital' rule, clients can be treated as still owning capital if it is decided that they have deliberately deprived themselves of it in order to claim benefits or increase the amount to which they are entitled. Clients affected by this rule may need specialist advice.

Some forms of capital are ignored – eg, the client's home and personal possessions.

Income

Each of the means-tested benefits has different rules on what income and how much of income is taken into account. The rules are, on the whole, more generous for PC (and for HB and CTB if the client is at least the qualifying age for PC) than for the other means-tested benefits. The income of couples is aggregated.

Most types of income are taken into account – eg:

- earnings from a job;
- profits from self-employment;
- retirement pension;
- other pensions;
- income from annuities;
- some benefits, such as CA and bereavement allowance;
- WTC.

Under what is known as the 'notional income' rule, clients can be treated as still having income if it is decided that they have deliberately deprived themselves of it in order to claim benefits or increase the amount to which they are entitled. Clients affected by this rule may need specialist advice.

There are many types of disregarded income, including some benefits – eg:

- DLA and AA;
- social fund payments;
- CTC and child benefit. However, for IS and income-based JSA, child benefit is taken into account unless the client is getting CTC.

Some of the client's earnings can also be disregarded, depending on her/his circumstances. For HB and CTB, an amount is disregarded from earnings for childcare costs (up to £175 a week for one child or up to £300 a week for two or more children), if s/he works at least 16 hours a week, or if both partners do in a couple. If only one partner works, they can still qualify if the other is incapacitated, or in hospital or prison.

Universal credit

UC is calculated as follows.

- Add together the various 'elements' to which a client is entitled (see p187) to arrive at a 'maximum amount'.
- Deduct any unearned income (see p187).
- Deduct 65 per cent of net earnings after disregards (see p187).
- The remainder (if any) will the amount of UC payable.

There will also be transitional additions paid to clients who are transferred from other benefits to UC.

Universal credit elements

UC is made up of:

- a personal ('standard') allowance for a single person or a couple;
- an amount for each child or qualifying young person for whom a client is responsible, with additions if they are disabled;
- an amount for childcare costs;
- an amount for limited capability for work or for work-related activity;
- an amount for caring for a 'severely disabled person' (the rules are likely to be the same as for carer premium – see p183);
- housing costs, including rent and mortgage interest payments.

Income

A client's income is assessed in a similar way to the current means-tested benefits, but on a monthly basis. In most cases, actual income received during a month is taken into account. A couple's joint income counts. Children's income is ignored.

Unearned income taken into account includes JSA, ESA, CA, pensions, annuities, notional income (see p186), student income, spousal maintenance, tariff income from capital of between £6,000 and £16,000.

Some income, including DLA, personal independence payment (PIP), child benefit and child maintenance, is disregarded.

Unearned income is calculated as a monthly amount and reduces the client's UC entitlement on a pound for pound basis.

Earned income from employment and self-employment is assessed net of tax, national insurance contributions and 50 per cent of any occupational pension contributions. Statutory sick pay and statutory maternity, paternity and adoption pay count as earnings. UC entitlement is reduced by 65 per cent of net earnings – ie, every £1 of earnings will reduce a client's entitlement by 65 pence.

Some earnings are disregarded, depending on the client's circumstances and whether s/he is receiving payments for housing costs.

Capital

Capital is assessed in a similar way to other means-tested benefits (see p185).

Overlapping benefit rules

Special rules mean that a client sometimes cannot be paid more than one of the following non-means-tested benefits at the same time:

- contribution-based JSA;
- IB;
- contributory ESA;

- MA;
- retirement pension;
- widow's pension or bereavement allowance;
- widowed mother's or widowed parent's allowance;
- SDA;
- CA.

Clients entitled to more than one of the above benefits are paid the benefit that takes priority, with a top-up of any other of the benefits if appropriate.

Deductions from benefits

Clients can have deductions made from their benefit for a variety of reasons, which means the amount they are paid is less than their entitlement.

Benefit penalties for failing to take part in work-focused interviews can apply to a number of different benefits depending on the client's circumstances. Benefit sanctions can apply to JSA. In both cases, a client's benefit can be reduced.

Overpayments of benefits are normally recovered by making deductions from a client's ongoing entitlement to benefit. If a client is challenging the overpayment, s/he should ask for deductions to stop.

Deductions for a wide variety of charges or debts (eg, for fuel or rent arrears) can be made from benefits, normally the means-tested benefits: IS, income-based JSA, income-related ESA and PC. For more information, see p223.

Tax credits

The basic formula for calculating tax credits is as follows.
- Work out the number of days in the client's 'relevant period'. Both CTC and WTC are awarded for the tax year, so a claim made in July runs until 5 April – the number of days in this period is the 'relevant period'.
- Work out the 'maximum amount'. Add together all the elements of CTC and WTC to which the client is entitled.
- Work out relevant income. Income is annual income and is calculated in accordance with the tax rules – basically, all taxable income is counted. There is no capital limit, but taxable income from capital counts as income.
- Compare this with a 'threshold figure'.
- Calculate entitlement. If the income figure is below the threshold, the client gets the maximum amount. If it is above, it is reduced by a taper. Forty-one per cent of the client's income above the threshold is deducted from the maximum amount. The remainder is the amount of tax credits paid.

Note: clients on IS, income-based JSA, income-related ESA or PC are passported to maximum entitlement.

The amounts that make up CTC are:
- family element;

- child element;
- disabled child element;
- severely disabled child element.

The amounts that make up WTC are:
- basic element;
- lone parent element;
- couple element;
- 30-hour element;
- disabled worker element;
- severe disability element;
- childcare element.

HM Revenue and Customs (HMRC) uses the previous tax year's income to make an initial award for the year (although it can use an estimate of income for the current tax year instead). At the end of the tax year, HMRC finalises the award by comparing the client's actual income over the year of the award with that of the previous year. This could result in an underpayment, which HMRC pays back in a lump sum, or an overpayment that may have to be repaid. Decreases in income of less than £2,500 are ignored. Increases in income of less than £10,000 from one year to the next can be ignored. Note: before April 2011, increases of less than £25,000 were ignored. From April 2013, the £10,000 disregard will be reduced to £5,000.

Overpayments of tax credits are common and many clients have some kind of adjustment to their award. This, combined with the complexity of the system, means it is often difficult to establish whether or not a client is being paid the correct amount. Specialist advice may be needed.

Some changes of circumstances must be reported and taken into account during the year and carry a potential penalty if not reported. Other changes can be reported at the end of the year, but may result in underpayments or overpayments. Advisers should bear this in mind when giving advice about whether and when to report a change during the year.

5. **Other help**

Charities

There are thousands of charities that can provide payments to individuals in need. Some are open to all and others are for certain groups only, such as armed service personnel or people with certain disabilities. Many have a committee that sifts through applications and meets on a cyclical basis. Some of the very large charities receive thousands of applications a year and may place limits on people from whom they are prepared to accept applications – eg, from social workers only.

It is worthwhile investigating less well-known charities to approach, in addition to the major ones. These are either locally based or specialise in helping particular people. Some charities expect a person to have exhausted other statutory provisions before approaching them. The organisation Turn2us has a website (www.turn2us.org.uk) with an A–Z of all the charities that can provide financial help and, in many cases, applications for support can be made directly from the website.

The publication *The Guide to Grants for Individuals in Need* provides a list of local and national charities, advises on the most appropriate charity and gives guidance on how to make a successful application.

Most charitable payments are ignored for means-tested benefits and tax credits if they are made regularly. Most that are made irregularly are treated as capital and so only affect the benefit if it takes the client above the capital limit.

Child maintenance

Clients may be able to get child maintenance for their child/ren if they are not living with her/his other parent. Child maintenance may be paid voluntarily, following a court order or following an application to the Child Support Agency (CSA).

Child maintenance is disregarded as income for all means-tested benefits and for tax credits.

Civil compensation for damages

Personal injury claims can be made against an individual or organisation if they have been negligent in causing damage, either by doing something or by failing to do something. Injury caused by negligence can be an issue in road traffic accidents or accidents at work, in the street or other public places. Damages for personal injury can be substantial, but can be reduced by the amount of social security benefit paid as a consequence of the injury.

If the injury occurred at work, the client should contact her/his trade union, if a member. Other clients may need to be referred to a solicitor. More information is available at:

- the Solicitors Regulation Authority for details of the Personal Injury Accreditation Scheme on 0870 606 2555 or at www.sra.org.uk;
- the Association of Personal Injury Lawyers on 0115 958 0585 or at www.apil.org.uk;
- Accident Line on 0800 192 939 or at www.accidentlinedirect.co.uk;
- The Motor Accident Solicitors Society on 0117 925 9604 or at www.mass.org.uk.

Equal pay rules

Equality legislation provides that a woman should not be paid less than a man for work of equal value or for the same work. If a woman is in debt, it is always worth checking whether these rules might help increase her income. If a client is being paid less than others doing similar work because of her/his age, gender, disability, race, religion and belief, or sexual orientation, it could constitute unlawful discrimination. Specialist help is necessary to pursue a claim. For further details, contact the Equality and Human Rights Commission Helpline on 0845 604 6610 (England) or 0845 604 8810 (Wales), or see www.equalityhumanrights.com.

Foodbanks

Clients who are without any means to obtain food may be able to be helped by a foodbank. Most foodbanks operate on a referral basis, to find a local one see www.trusselltrust.org/foodbank-projects.

Free school lunches

Children are entitled to free school lunches if their family receives:
- income support, income-based jobseeker's allowance or income-related employment and support allowance;
- child tax credit (CTC) (but not if also receiving working tax credit) and their gross annual income is below the threshold;
- the guarantee credit of pension credit.

Also entitled are 16–18-year-olds receiving the above benefits and tax credits in their own right, and asylum seekers in receipt of support provided under Part VI of the Immigration and Asylum Act 1999.

Guarantee pay

If an employer fails to provide work for (lays off) an employee, in most cases, s/he must pay guarantee pay for five days of lay-off in any period of three months. The right to guarantee pay can be enforced through an employment tribunal. Specialist help should be sought. A client who is dismissed for seeking to enforce this right is entitled to claim unfair dismissal to an employment tribunal, regardless of the length of her/his service.

Guarantee pay is taken into account as earnings for means-tested benefits.

For further details, see the guidance on guarantee pay at www.direct.gov.uk.

Local authority payments

From April 2013 local authorities will be responsible for delivering 'local welfare provision'. This replaces community care grants and crisis loans form the social fund (see p178). The help available will vary, depending on where the client lives.

Local authorities are unlikely to make as many cash payments as the social fund and are more likely to provide goods in kind and refer people to furniture projects and charities.

From April 2013, council tax benefit (CTB – see p168) will be replaced by payments from local authorities. Each local authority will have its own scheme. The new payments will be means tested in the same way as CTB, but there will be differences in the way that payments are calculated.

The applicable amounts used are likely to be lower than those used for means-tested benefits, so some clients on very low incomes are likely to have to pay something towards their council tax.

National minimum wage

Most employees are entitled to be paid at a rate equivalent to at least the national minimum wage. A client who is entitled to the minimum wage and is being paid less than this can complain to the Pay and Work Rights Helpline or to an employment tribunal. For more information, contact the Helpline on 0800 917 2368 or visit www.direct.gov.uk.

Notice pay

An employee is entitled to be paid during the notice period if s/he works during that period or cannot work because of illness, pregnancy or childbirth, or because s/he is on adoption, parental or paternity leave or holiday, or the employer does not wish her/him to work. An employee who is dismissed without being given the correct notice is entitled to be paid her/his normal wages 'in lieu' of notice, unless the dismissal is due to gross misconduct. Notice rules are laid down in the law and these depend on length of service. Some employees may be entitled to a longer period of notice under the terms of their contract with the employer. The contract may be written or unwritten.

For further details, see www.direct.gov.uk.

Payments for war injury

There are a number of different schemes providing benefits for those disabled, or for the dependants of those killed, in either the First World War or any conflict since 3 September 1939. Some of these schemes only cover members of the armed forces, but there are others that apply to auxiliary personnel, civil defence volunteers, merchant mariners and ordinary civilians. Who qualifies and what payments they can receive are complicated. For who may be eligible, visit www.veterans-uk.info or contact the Veterans Helpline on 0800 169 2277 or write to the Service Personnel and Veterans Agency, Norcross, Thornton Cleveleys, Lancashire FY5 3WP or email veterans.help@spva.gsi.gov.uk.

Private and occupational pensions

Clients who are members of an employer's (occupational) pension scheme or a private pension plan may be entitled to take benefits from these plans before the normal retirement age if, for instance, they become permanently incapable of work. Benefits available from pension schemes should be closely examined and independent financial advice should be sought before making a decision to take benefits early from a private scheme.

Redundancy pay

An employee who has two years' continuous service and is not in an excluded occupation, and who loses her/his job through redundancy, might be entitled to statutory redundancy pay. If a statutory redundancy payment has not been made or is not for the correct amount, the employee can apply to an employment tribunal. There is a strict six-month time limit from the date of termination for making such an application. A client in need of advice in this situation should be referred to an employment law adviser.

Some clients may be entitled to a larger redundancy payment under the terms of their contract.

For further details, see www.direct.gov.uk.

Return-to-work help

Note: in-work credit, return-to-work credit and job grants will be phased out from October 2013 to coincide with the introduction of universal credit (see p165).

Jobcentre Plus administers a number of schemes for those who are returning to work. Clients must normally have been unemployed for a specified length of time or have participated in one of the various training or employment schemes. The schemes change from time to time, as do the eligibility criteria. The current range of help is:

- job grant of £100 for single people or members of a couple without children, or £250 for lone parents or members of a couple with children;
- a payment from the Adviser Discretionary Fund, at the discretion of the personal adviser at the Jobcentre Plus office, to help overcome barriers to work – eg, for initial travel and childcare costs or the cost of work clothes;
- return-to-work credit of £40 a week for the first 52 weeks in a new job if a client earns no more than £15,000 a year and has or has had a health condition or disability;
- for lone parents, an in-work credit of £40 a week (£60 a week in London), for the first 52 weeks in a new job.

For further details, see www.direct.gov.uk.

School clothing grants

Local authorities have a discretionary power to give grants for school uniforms or other clothing needed for school – eg, for sportswear. Policies vary across the county. Some school governing bodies or parents' associations also provide help with school clothing.

School transport

Local authorities have a duty to provide free transport for a pupil under 16 if it is considered necessary to enable her/him to get to the 'nearest suitable school'. This might be because a pupil lives beyond walking distance or if s/he cannot walk because of a disability.

Social services

Local authority social services departments have statutory duties to provide a range of practical and financial help to families, children, young people, older people, people with disabilities and asylum seekers.

Special funds for sick or disabled people

A range of help is available for people with an illness or disability to assist with things like paying for care services in their own home, equipment, holidays, furniture and transport needs.

Student support

See Chapter 17 of this *Handbook*, and also CPAG's *Student Support and Benefits Handbook*.

Tax allowances

A higher personal allowance can be claimed by those aged 65 to 74, and an even higher amount by those aged 75 or over. This age-related personal allowance is reduced once a person's income exceeds a certain limit, but can only be reduced back down to the rate of the basic personal allowance. **Note:** the higher allowance for those over 65 will be restricted from April 2013.

Clients aged 65 or over before 6 April 2000 may still be entitled to a married couple's allowance. Those eligible have to be married and be living together.

A client who is registered blind can claim a blind person's allowance for the whole tax year. This is in addition to the personal allowance. Any unused allowance can be transferred to her/his spouse or civil partner. If both spouses and civil partners are registered blind, they can claim an allowance each.

A backdated claim can be made for up to six years for any allowances, so the adviser should check to see whether the client has not received an allowance to which s/he is entitled.

Tax rebate

A client who is unemployed or is laid off may be entitled to a tax rebate at the end of the tax year. However, this is reduced or may be cancelled out if s/he receives a taxable benefit. In some cases, if HM Revenue and Customs has delayed paying the tax rebate, it must pay interest on it.

Tax reliefs

Tax reliefs are amounts that are deducted from taxable income in recognition of money that is needed to be spent by the taxpayer in working. They can be claimed in addition to a personal allowance and can be backdated for up to six years. Tax reliefs for self-employed people should be calculated by a specialist adviser.

For employed people, it is possible to claim relief on any money that is spent to enable a job to be done, but which is not paid for by the employer. The expenses have to 'wholly, exclusively and necessarily' incurred in order to do the work.

Items for which tax relief can be claimed include:
- membership of professional bodies;
- special clothing for work;
- using heating/lighting or the telephone at home for work;
- buying tools.

Another form of tax relief is the 'rent-a-room' scheme. This enables someone to let out a main room in their home and not pay tax on the rental income, provided the rent stays below a certain level. Even if the client cannot benefit from this scheme, there are other forms of tax relief that may be applicable if s/he lets out property. Specialist advice should be sought.

Trade unions

Many trade unions have hardship funds for members or ex-members. Unions may also be involved in various benevolent funds and charities associated with particular industries. If a client has been a member of a union, it is worth approaching the union to enquire about possible lump-sum payments or, in some cases, ongoing support.

Chapter 8

Dealing with priority debts

This chapter covers:
1. Deciding on priorities (below)
2. The general approach to priority debts (p199)
3. Strategies for dealing with priority debts (p203)
4. Emergency action (p227)

1. Deciding on priorities

After dealing with any emergencies and checking the client is liable for the debts, advisers need to identify which debts must be dealt with first – ie, which debts are priority debts. The criteria for deciding which debts are priorities are, for the most part, 'objective' – the severity of the legal remedies available to creditors determines the degree of priority. If non-payment would give the creditor the right to deprive the client of her/his home, liberty, or essential goods and services, that debt will have priority. For a discussion of other debts which may need to be treated as priority, see Chapter 9.

Clients often believe that priorities must be decided on the basis of the amount owed, or that any debt that is subject to a court order should be a priority. The existence of a court judgment does not automatically give priority status to a debt and there are many judgments given by courts in England and Wales each year for debts that remain unpaid. These debts only become a priority if the enforcement methods open to a creditor through a court pose a serious threat to the client's home, liberty or essential goods.

Penalties for non-payment of priority debts

Debt	*Ultimate penalties*
Mortgage arrears	Repossession/eviction
Rent arrears	Eviction
Council tax arrears	Imprisonment
Unpaid fine/maintenance	Imprisonment
Gas/electricity arrears	Disconnection

Income tax/VAT arrears	Goods seized
	Bankruptcy
Hire purchase arrears	Goods repossessed

Recognising priority debts

Using the criteria outlined above, the following are priority debts.

Secured loan

Mortgages and all other loans secured against a client's home are priorities because non-payment can lead to possession action by the lender, and homelessness. One of the strategies outlined in this chapter must be adopted immediately for any secured loan in arrears. For emergency action, see p227. If the lender has already begun possession proceedings, see Chapter 12.

Rent arrears

Rent arrears are a priority because they can lead to possession action by the landlord, and homelessness. If the landlord has already begun possession proceedings, see Chapter 12.

A client who is a tenant may find that water charges are paid as part of the rent so that the client could be evicted for non-payment. In such cases, water charges should be considered as a priority. If a client is threatened with possession proceedings for non-payment of water charges, see Chapter 6.

For emergency action, see p227.

Council tax

Council tax arrears are a priority because non-payment could lead to imprisonment. If the magistrates' court has issued a liability order (which allows the council to use bailiffs) or the client is facing a committal hearing or a warrant has been issued that could result in imprisonment, see p230 and p233. If the local authority has a liability order and the amount outstanding is at least £1,000, it can apply for a charging order in the county court (see p301). If the local authority has served a statutory demand on the client or issued a bankruptcy petition, see p231.

Fines, maintenance and compensation orders

Unpaid fines, maintenance and compensation orders are a priority because non-payment could lead to imprisonment. If the client is in arrears with any of these debts, even if no bailiff or other enforcement action has been taken, see Chapter 13. For emergency action, see p227.

Charges for utilities

Payment for gas and electricity are priorities because suppliers have powers to disconnect for non-payment of bills. Such sanctions do not apply to arrears on non-fuel items (eg, cookers or the cost of central heating installation) purchased from gas and electricity suppliers, and thus debts for such items are not a priority.

Help with arrears may be available from one of the energy company's trust funds, and all energy companies are required to have social tariffs which may be able to help with high bills (see p137).

Until the passing of the Water Industry Act 1999, water companies also had powers to disconnect for debt and so were considered priorities. This is no longer the case and attempts by water companies to retain priority status should be resisted, as this would be inequitable to other creditors. A realistic amount for current consumption of water must be included in the financial statement, but not for arrears. As with energy bills, help with arrears may be available from one of the water industry's trust funds, or the WaterSure scheme may be able to help with high bills (see p154).

If disconnection is threatened, make immediate contact with the supplier to challenge this and discuss ways of paying for the supply (see p228).

TV licence

A colour TV licence costs £145.50 a year. Payment plans are available to spread the cost (see www.tvlicensing.co.uk). Although not a debt as such, because it is a criminal offence to use a television without a licence (for which the usual penalty is a fine), if a client either does not have a licence (but does have a television) or is behind with a payment plan, this should be treated as a priority.

Some people qualify for a concession on the cost of the TV licence – eg, clients who are aged 74, have sight impairments, or who are living in residential care. A person aged 75 or over is entitled to a free licence.

Tax and VAT

These debts are a priority if the client is continuing to trade because HM Revenue and Customs (HMRC) can seize goods from the client to cover unpaid tax without requiring a court order (known as 'levying distraint'), or could make the client bankrupt and put her/him out of business. If the client has ceased trading, each case must be looked at on its merits. If:

- bailiffs are involved, see Chapter 14;
- action has been started in the magistrates' court, see Chapter 12;
- action has been started in the county court, see Chapter 10;
- emergency action is required, see p233.

See also Chapter 16.

Hire purchase and conditional sale agreements

Some hire purchase or conditional sale agreements will need to be treated as priority debts if they are for goods that are essential for the client to retain (eg, a car for work in the absence of suitable public transport), because the creditor has powers to repossess the goods if payments are not kept – see pp114–15.

National insurance contributions

Class 4 national insurance contributions for self-employed earners are a priority because they are assessed and collected by HMRC along with unpaid income tax.

Tax credit overpayments

These debts are a priority because, in addition to being able to recover an overpayment from an ongoing tax credit award or through amending the client's PAYE code, HMRC can levy distraint (see p198) against the client's goods without a court order (and prefers to do this rather than using the county court to recover the debt). The client could even be imprisoned for non-payment.

2. **The general approach to priority debts**

Once identified, priority debts must be dealt with quickly and effectively. General rules about how this should be done are listed below. There are also specific ways of dealing with particular types of debts.

Immediate contact should be made with the creditor. If it is not possible to make a definite offer of payment immediately, ask for more time (eg, 14 or 28 days) and ask the creditor either to take no further action or to suspend any existing action during this period. If possible, the client should be advised to pay at least the current instalments in the meantime.

Generally, it is not appropriate to make offers to priority creditors on a pro rata basis (see p255) or to include priority debts in a debt management plan (see p242) and it will be necessary for advisers to negotiate with them individually. It must first be decided whether to make payment:

- either as soon as possible; *or*
- over as long a period as possible.

The following should be taken into account.

- If the debt is accruing interest or charges, it may be in the client's best interests to pay it off quickly.
- It might be in the client's best interests to pay off a small priority debt as soon as possible.
- The creditor's collection policies – eg, the local authority's policy may be to send council tax liability orders straight to the bailiffs, which will increase the debt.
- The creditor may insist on arrears being cleared before the next bill is due to be delivered or payment made.

- If the client is currently earning above her/his average wage, it may be in her/his best interests to make higher payments while s/he can.
- If capital or lower-cost finance is available, the debt can be cleared more quickly.
- The client's age or state of health may lead to a reduction in income. It could be in her/his best interests to make a payment before this happens.
- If the client is considering moving, it may be necessary to make a payment before doing so.
- If the client has any non-priority debts, s/he will usually need to make some provision for these (see Chapter 9).

Advisers should also further prioritise the debts in the light of:
- what the client wants;
- the existence of more than one priority debt;
- the severity of the sanction available to the creditor;
- the potential consequences of using a particular strategy;
- the stage the recovery process has reached.

Although the decision to give one debt priority over another is to some extent a subjective one, advisers should always discuss with the client the range of options available and the possible consequences.

Advisers should work through the following list of tasks.
- In the case of secured loans and hire purchase/conditional sale agreements, check whether the client has payment protection insurance to cover the repayments in the event of sickness or incapacity, unemployment, accident or death. If the client does have insurance and her/his situation is covered by the policy, advise the client to make a claim. If the claim is refused, consider whether this can be challenged and/or also whether the policy may have been mis-sold (see p102). If the client's situation is not covered by the policy, also consider whether the policy may have been mis-sold – eg, the client's circumstances were such that s/he could never have made a claim. If the agreement is regulated by the Consumer Credit Act 1974 and the client says that taking out payment protection insurance was a condition of being granted the credit, the agreement may be unenforceable (see p71).
- In the case of secured loans and hire purchase/conditional sale agreements, investigate whether the lender complied with its duty to assess the client's ability to repay either under *The Lending Code*, the Financial Services Authority's *Mortgages and Home Finance: conduct of business sourcebook (MCOB)*, the OFT's *Second Charge Lending Guidance* (or its predecessor, the *Non-status Lending Guidelines)* or the *Irresponsible Lending Guidance* produced by the Office of Fair Trading (OFT).
- In the case of tax, VAT or tax credit overpayments, consider what method of enforcement HMRC is using or threatening to use. Bear in mind in the case of

tax credit overpayments that recovery from an ongoing award or by amending the client's PAYE code will reduce the amount of surplus income the client has available to make offers to other creditors.

- Consider whether the client has any other grounds for challenging either the debt or the creditor's conduct (see Chapters 5 and 6).
- The adviser should telephone the creditor as soon as possible, even if s/he does not have all the necessary information on which to base a strategy. This may help prevent further action and alert the priority creditor to the involvement of an independent agency. Invoke the 30-day 'breathing space' provisions referred to in paragraph 7.12 of the OFT's *Irresponsible Lending Guidance*.
- If necessary, take emergency action to prevent the immediate loss of home, liberty, essential goods or services (see p227).
- Negotiate the amount, manner and time of repayments.
- Ensure the client is clear about whom to pay, when to pay and how much to pay.
- Encourage the client to seek further assistance from the adviser if s/he is facing practical difficulties with repayment arrangements.
- Monitor the initial strategy with the client. If the client's circumstances change or the original strategy is unsuccessful, the adviser and the client must decide whether to adopt a new strategy or whether the details of the original strategy can be modified.

Consider carefully the amount of income included as 'available' to the client. The fact that a debt is priority may influence the way in which a partner's income is treated. A partner may not wish to pool her/his income and liabilities if only non-priority debts have been accrued (and there is no need to – see p43). However, if serious consequences, such as loss of home, could be experienced by the client's partner, s/he may wish to contribute towards repaying a debt for which s/he is not legally liable. This situation can also occur when a debt arose while someone was with a previous partner.[1]

Points to note

- Although many priority creditors have their own collection policies which act as guidelines for their officers, these can always be negotiated. A refusal to negotiate could give rise to a formal complaint.
- It may be necessary to contact someone in a position of authority within the relevant organisation before policies can be changed.
- Accounting periods, such as local authority financial years or other periods between quarterly bills, should not be taken as absolute dates by which current liabilities must be met.
- Secured lenders often argue that arrears should be repaid in short periods. However, in an important decision, the Court of Appeal suggested that a reasonable period to clear arrears might be the whole of the remaining term of

the mortgage.[2] Thus, if a possession action was started half way through a 30-year mortgage, it would be possible for the court to suspend an order on payment of an amount which would repay the mortgage together with the arrears over the next 15 years. On the other hand, if the secured loan is regulated by the Consumer Credit Act, the client may be able to apply for a time order (see p220 and p340). If the loan is a regulated mortgage contract (see p147), the lender should have complied with section 13 of the *MCOB*. This requires the lender to use reasonable efforts to come to an agreement with the client on payment of the arrears over a reasonable period (in appropriate cases, the remaining term of the mortgage), to repossess the property only as a last resort, where there is no other realistic alternative.

The client should be advised to:
- start making payments immediately the strategy has been decided, as this will encourage the creditor to accept the arrangements; *and*
- where possible, set up a direct debit or standing order to ensure a payment arrangement is kept.

Creditors should be asked to confirm the agreed strategy in writing. They may often require a financial statement (see p50), list of debts and written proposal from the adviser before providing such confirmation. However, a delay in providing confirmation is not a reason for withholding agreed or offered payments.

Negative equity

'Negative equity' occurs when the value of a client's property falls below the amount due under her/his mortgage or other loans secured on it. This means that, even if her/his property were sold, the client would not be free of debt and would still owe an amount (the negative equity) to the creditor. If a client wants to sell a property in negative equity, s/he will need the permission of any secured creditors who are not going to be repaid out of the sale proceeds. Section 13.3 of the *MCOB* requires Financial Services Authority-regulated lenders to treat clients 'fairly'. If a creditor unreasonably refuses to agree to a sale, the court can overrule it.[3] In this situation, the adviser should seek specialist advice.

Many lenders now offer support to clients so that they can sell their homes and so avoid repossession. These schemes are known as 'voluntary' or 'assisted voluntary' sales. Shelter and the National Homelessness Advice Service have produced guidance for advisers, available at www.tinyurl.com/ca62ml7.

The strategies that follow depend on the housing market. If houses cannot be sold easily, creditors may not want to repossess and a sale by the client could be undesirable or impossible. However, advisers should not necessarily rely on this, as lenders will sometimes decide to cut their losses and repossess regardless.

If possible, it is important to reach an agreement to avoid such a situation. Section 13.3.2A(5) of the *MCOB* says that, if a payment arrangement cannot be made, the lender should consider allowing the client to remain in the property in order to sell the property.

Negative equity will affect whether some of the following strategies apply. However, in most circumstances, the approach remains the same, either because a lender is prepared to ignore the negative equity or because it becomes an unsecured and non-priority debt (see Chapter 9).

The mortgage shortfall on the sale of the property

For what to do if there is a 'mortgage shortfall' or a claim from a mortgage indemnity insurer, see p141. These debts, though non-priority at present, need to be dealt with because they represent a potential future problem if an attachment of earnings, bankruptcy or charging order were to be used at a future date.

3. **Strategies for dealing with priority debts**

Interest-only payments (for mortgages and secured loans)

A large proportion of secured borrowing is repaid by means of monthly payments that combine interest with a repayment of capital. In such cases, a client can reduce the payments if the creditor will agree to accept payment of only the interest without any capital repayment. Creditors will need to be persuaded that a request to make interest-only payments is not just a delaying tactic or an excuse for being unable to pay anything. If a client can afford to pay the interest which is accruing on an agreement, advisers are not asking for anything that is either out of the ordinary or generous.

Payments towards the capital can be resumed if the client's financial circumstances improve in the future. Some creditors are prepared to wait until property is sold for the capital to be repaid. Creditors will need to be satisfied either that the arrangement is a temporary one and that the client will be able to resume making the full contractual payments or that repayment of the capital by some other method is adequately assured.

When applicable

Paying interest only is appropriate if the client cannot afford to pay both the interest and capital. Interest-only payments cannot be used for:

- any agreement where the total interest has already been added at the beginning of the loan period and the whole amount secured against the property, because no interest is accruing on a daily basis (but see reduced payments, on p204); *or*
- an endowment mortgage, because payments are already for interest only and the capital is repaid in a lump sum at the end of the period of the loan by an endowment insurance policy (see p140).

Advantages

- It is easily accepted by priority creditors as a temporary forbearance measure.
- It prevents further action.
- It may avoid a bad credit rating.

Disadvantages

- The debt may take longer to clear than it would if full payments were maintained, or if a reduction in capital or charges could be negotiated and so the client may pay more in the long run.
- The Administration of Justice Act 1973 requires the arrears to be cleared in a 'reasonable time'.[4] Although the court could use its powers to order an adjournment or a suspended possession order to allow payments of interest only,[5] this would only be possible for a short period (eg, six months), after which time an increased payment would be necessary to clear the arrears in a reasonable time (see p208). Similarly, the court could not make a time order on this basis as it would not provide for payment of the loan (see p220 and p340).

Useful arguments

- Most mortgage or other secured lenders have policies that allow interest-only payments on a temporary basis (perhaps six months). These can often be arranged over the telephone (although any such arrangement must be confirmed in writing and a financial statement may be required).
- If a client is receiving income support (IS), income-based jobseeker's allowance (JSA), income-related employment and support allowance (ESA) or pension credit (PC) that does not yet cover the whole mortgage interest, many creditors will accept half the interest until s/he becomes eligible for the full interest to be met by her/his benefit.

Checklist for action

- Telephone/write to the creditor to propose the strategy and request written confirmation that the strategy is accepted.
- Explain the cause of the client's inability to pay – through a change of circumstances or economic factors such as high interest rates.
- Advise the client of how much to pay and when.
- Consider direct payments for clients on IS, income-based JSA, income-related ESA or PC (see p223).
- Consider advising the client to set up a direct debit or standing order to ensure payments are kept up.

Reduced payments

A creditor can be asked to renegotiate the contract that has been made so that a client can afford the payments. There are three main ways in which payments can be reduced.

- Ask the creditor to charge a lower rate of interest, either for a period of time (eg, the next year) or for the rest of the loan, even if interest has already been added to the amount payable over the whole period of the loan.
- Ask the creditor to agree to reduce the amount outstanding on a loan so that future payments (perhaps of interest only) are affordable by the client.
- Ask the creditor to allow repayments to extend over a longer period, thereby reducing the capital portion of the repayments. There would need to be enough equity to allow this – the amount of equity can be calculated by deducting the total amount of all loans secured on the property from the market value of the property.

When applicable
- If the client cannot meet her/his original contractual obligations.
- If interest rates have risen significantly since the contract was taken out, or if the interest originally charged was significantly higher than available elsewhere or if, despite a general fall in interest rates, a high rate of interest continues to be charged. This is particularly true if a time order would be appropriate (see p220).
- If the outstanding balance includes capitalised arrears of interest/charges, particularly where these have accrued at a high rate.
- If the property against which the loan is secured is worth less than the capital outstanding, some lenders will reduce their capital outlay rather than continue to chase something which is effectively no longer a fully secured debt.
- If there is another secured loan against the same property, the first mortgagee may reduce the amount outstanding on its loan in order that the client can borrow enough to be able to pay off the second mortgagee and then have one remaining loan. This might be a likely option if the second mortgagee is considering repossession, and the first mortgagee wishes to continue with the business it has with its customer.
- If adverse publicity would be attracted by a repossession.
- If the property market is slow and, therefore, repossessed properties are unlikely to be saleable.

This strategy is not appropriate for endowment mortgages.

Advantages
- It reduces the amount payable and protects the client's home and essential goods.

Disadvantages
- It will be difficult to gain agreement to this as a long-term strategy from creditors, particularly if the loan is more than fully secured.

- The lender may only defer interest and so the client may be faced with substantially higher payments at the end of the arrangement, which may lead to further default in the future.
- Repaying an interest-bearing debt over a longer period may result in additional interest being paid, unless the payments are sufficient to cover this or the rate of interest is reduced accordingly.
- If mortgage rescue is not practicable (see p212), it is sometimes better to allow the home to be lost if it will end indebtedness and ensure appropriate rehousing by a local authority or housing association (see p216). The local authority may argue, however, that the client has made her/himself intentionally homeless and, if the sale results in the client having equity, this could affect entitlement to certain benefits.
- If the capital outstanding is to be reduced, it may require changes to the legal charge, which is registered on the property. The client will be liable for the costs associated with this.

Useful arguments

- If a time order would be possible (see p220), a creditor may prefer to negotiate changes voluntarily rather than have them imposed by the court, especially if adverse publicity is likely to be attracted by a case.
- Point out any failure by the creditor to prevent the build-up of arrears, to send the client regular statements of account or to inform the client of the need to increase payments to cover the ongoing arrears/charges.
- If the alternative for the creditor is repossession of a house, point out that under paragraph 7.14 of the Office of Fair Trading's (OFT) *Irresponsible Lending Guidance* and paragraph 6.3 of its *Second Charge Lending Guidance*, repossession of the client's property should be a last resort and that the strategy being offered may be cheaper, as possessing and reselling a property is time-consuming and, therefore, expensive.
- In the case of regulated mortgage contracts, section 13 of the Financial Services Authority's (FSA) *Mortgages and Home Finance: conduct of business sourcebook (MCOB)* requires the lender to contact the client within 15 days of the account falling into arrears and to provide her/him with prescribed information, including the likely charges that will be incurred should the arrears not be cleared. Any failure to comply with this could be pointed out to the lender if it has contributed to the build-up of arrears. From 1 October 2008, additional post-contract information requirements have been imposed on creditors under agreements regulated by the Consumer Credit Act 1974 (see p78).
- In all cases, point out mis-selling of any part of the loan, such as payment protection insurance, or failure to assess the client's ability to repay, in order to support arguments to reduce the amount outstanding, and for reduced payments. For example, mis-selling of payment protection insurance may give

rise to an argument for a rebate of some or all of the premium or that the loan agreement itself is unenforceable (see p102).

- Payments are more likely to be maintained if set at a lower level, which is affordable by the client.
- The sums already paid by the client have given the creditor a more than adequate return on the loan.

Checklist for action

- Telephone/write to the creditor to propose the strategy and request written confirmation of its acceptance.
- Advise the client of how much to pay and when.
- Consider a time order in Consumer Credit Act cases (see p220 and p340).

Capitalise arrears

If arrears have built up (particularly on a repayment mortgage), a creditor can be asked to add these to the capital outstanding and simply charge interest on the new capital amount. This can then be rescheduled over the remaining period of the mortgage, although it may be possible to extend the repayment period.

When applicable

- This strategy is particularly useful when there is an improvement in the client's circumstances following a period in which arrears have built up. For example, if a client has recently become employed after a period of unemployment or returned to work after a long strike or period of sickness, provided her/his payment record was previously satisfactory, most creditors will agree to capitalise the arrears.
- Creditors will only capitalise arrears if the market value of the property is significantly greater than the amount of capital currently outstanding. They will not usually do so if it would lead to the capital outstanding being more than the value of the property.

Advantages

- It regularises the situation.
- It prevents further action.
- It can avoid a bad credit rating as the client will no longer have arrears.
- The repayments are affordable.

Disadvantages

- The repayments on the loan will be increased if the loan is to be repaid within the original contractual period.
- The debt may take longer to pay off, in which case the client would pay more.
- If interest charges rise, the effect is greater than when capital was less.
- Interest is, in effect, paid on the arrears throughout the term of the mortgage.

- IS, income-based JSA, income-related ESA or PC will not usually meet the cost of additional interest because arrears have been capitalised.

Useful arguments

- Some creditors will only consider capitalising arrears after a trial period in which a client makes regular repayments, particularly if there is little prospect of an improvement in circumstances. The adviser can, therefore, suggest that the lender reviews the strategy after an agreed period in which the client is able to demonstrate that s/he is able to maintain the repayments.

Checklist for action

- Telephone/write to the creditor to propose the strategy and request written confirmation that this is agreed.
- Advise the client of any change in repayments.
- Advise clients on IS, income-based JSA, income-related ESA or PC to notify the Department for Work and Pensions (DWP) of changes in repayments.

Scheduled payment of arrears

Secured loans

Arrears may be repayable over a period of time. This may be a set amount each month, calculated to repay the arrears over a period of time acceptable to the creditor/lender and/or court. Proposals to clear arrears over three years are regularly accepted. In one case, the court said that it is acceptable to repay arrears over the amount of time remaining until the end of the loan.[6]

However, advisers should be imaginative in their suggestions for repayment schedules. A staggered offer, in which initially a smaller amount is offered towards the arrears, followed by increased payments, is useful if it is anticipated that the client's circumstances will improve. Such an arrangement may be made directly with the creditor or may need to be ratified by the court if proceedings have already started.

If there is no spare income immediately available, so that only the normal contractual payment can be met, creditors can sometimes be persuaded to accept no payments towards the arrears for several months, particularly if there is plenty of equity (see p238) in the property. In extreme circumstances, they may be persuaded to accept no payments at all for one or two months where inability to pay is clearly temporary.

Some mortgages may allow for a 'payment holiday' (usually for no more than six months), but may require the client's payments to be up to date at the start of the period. Interest continues to accrue during any period of non-payment and is added to the outstanding balance, so that the client will pay more in the long term in return for taking advantage of this concession.

Many creditors have their own internal rules about the time period over which they will spread the repayment of arrears on secured borrowing, but these periods can generally be increased by contacting regional or head offices or formally complaining when necessary. Most lenders are subject to codes of practice which require them to treat clients 'sympathetically and positively' and section 7 of the OFT's *Irresponsible Lending Guidance* requires creditors to treat clients in default or arrears with understanding and due consideration, and with forbearance. If an adviser believes a creditor is allowing a policy to stand in the way of its duty to consider every case individually, s/he should consider using the complaints procedure and referring the matter to the Financial Ombudsman Service (FOS), if appropriate.

Rent, fuel and council tax

Creditors use various criteria to decide whether the repayments are acceptable, including the level of arrears, the client's previous payment record and the likelihood of the client remaining as a tenant, consumer or council tax payer in the same location.

When applicable
- After there has been an improvement in financial circumstances.
- After a debt adviser has helped the client to prioritise payments of debts.

Advantages
- Provided the income is available to repay both contractual payments and something towards the arrears, this should be readily acceptable to creditors.
- It prevents further action.

Disadvantages
- It increases the client's outgoings at a time when the financial shortage may not be over.
- In the case of loans, interest will accrue not only on the capital outstanding but also on the unpaid arrears so that, unless the creditor agrees to freeze interest and other charges, the repayments will continue beyond the original contractual period, sometimes, on unregulated agreements, at a penalty rate which is higher than that normally charged. Check the agreement to find out if this is the case.

Useful arguments
- Creditors will need to understand why payments have not been made in the past and why they are now possible.
- Advisers must explain any changes of circumstances and the fact that the client has now reorganised her/his financial affairs to give priority to these debts.
- Advisers should explain to creditors that ability to pay needs to be the guiding factor in deciding on repayment of arrears. Point to any relevant code of

practice which supports this. A carefully drawn up financial statement will be the adviser's most useful tool.

- The strategy is considered appropriate by a reputable money advice agency.
- If the creditor or court is reluctant to accept that payments will be made, the arrangement can be made subject to a review after a set period (eg, six months), so that the creditor's position is not prejudiced.

Checklist for action

- Telephone or write to the creditor to propose the strategy and request written confirmation of the repayment schedule.
- Advise the client of how much to pay and when.
- If necessary, make the appropriate application to court.

Change to a repayment mortgage

An endowment mortgage is a secured loan on which only interest is payable, accompanied by an endowment life assurance policy which is intended to pay off the capital borrowed either at the end of the agreed term or on the death of the borrower (whichever is the sooner).

For the borrower in debt, it is essential that the full amounts of both the endowment insurance payments and the interest on the loan itself are repaid on, or shortly after, the due date. The creditor relies on the insurance company to repay the capital amount lent at the end of the loan period and, if payments to the insurance company stop, the creditor is likely to call in its loan on the basis that its security is at risk, unless acceptable proposals for repayment of the capital at the end of the loan can be made. If, on the other hand, payments to the creditor are not kept up, the amount outstanding on the loan rises and is likely to become more than the amount which will be produced by the insurance policy at its maturity. Thus, endowment mortgages are less flexible than repayment ones.

To have flexibility to capitalise arrears, extend the period of a loan or negotiate repayment of arrears over several years, an endowment mortgage needs to be changed to a repayment mortgage. For some clients, the creditor will do this automatically once the endowment premium is significantly in arrears.

However, to cease paying, surrender or sell an endowment policy is a major financial decision and should not be taken without specialist advice from an independent financial adviser.

When applicable

- A client is in arrears with an endowment mortgage, or likely to go into arrears, and therefore a renegotiation on the terms of the mortgage is necessary.
- A client is unable to maintain the payments on the endowment policy.
- A client is facing a substantial period of low income and needs to achieve more flexibility.

- The endowment policy has been running for several years, in which case it may be beneficial to cash it in or sell it and use the lump sum to pay off arrears. Advice from a number of independent financial advisers should always be taken before surrendering an endowment policy. Some insurers charge significant fees for early surrender and, in addition, the value of the policy depends on the state of the stock market. The surrender value of a policy is frequently much less than the amount of the payments made into it to date. A sale of the policy instead usually produces a better return. However, even if changing to a repayment mortgage, it is better if possible to keep the endowment policy (without making any new payments into it) until it matures.
- The client can afford the new repayments.

Advantages
- Increased flexibility in the long term.
- Ensures that the home is not lost.
- Possible reduced monthly outgoings.

Disadvantages
- There may be an arrangement fee to convert the mortgage to a capital repayment type.
- The client will have to arrange separate life insurance cover.
- Some or all of the money already invested in the endowment policy may be lost (especially if it is relatively new).
- If a policy is 'assigned' to the lender, the surrender/sale value may be taken by it in full (although negotiation is possible).
- Possible increased monthly outgoings.

Useful arguments
- Creditors may be sympathetic if this is the only way of paying the mortgage as it ensures the loan is repaid.

Checklist for action
The client should get independent advice from a specialist in this field (but not from a broker who was involved in setting up the endowment mortgage as s/he may be motivated by the knowledge that s/he will probably lose commission if a recently taken-out endowment policy is cancelled).

If, after taking financial advice, the client decides on this course of action, do the following.
- Telephone/write to the creditor to propose the strategy and request details of new instalments and the surrender/sale value of the endowment policy.
- Advise the client of how much to pay and when.

- If disposing of the endowment policy, ensure the full surrender value of the policy is paid to the client. Selling it rather than merely surrendering may produce a larger sum.
- Advise the client to take advice to arrange new life assurance cover for the mortgage, if necessary.
- Advise clients on IS, income-based JSA, income-related ESA or PC to notify the DWP of changes in repayments.

Mortgage rescue schemes

Before the 'credit crunch', many people were encouraged to take out expensive loans from sub-prime lenders secured on their homes, which were clearly risky and, from the outset, were not affordable. The credit crunch, together with the collapse of the property market and the recession which followed, raised the spectre of mortgage repossessions returning to the levels of the early 1990s.

In response, the government announced a number of initiatives including:

- the mortgage rescue scheme (see below);
- repossession prevention funds (see p215).

These are intended as schemes of last resort, after all other support and forbearance options available from a mortgage or secured lender have been explored and/or exhausted.

Mortgage rescue scheme

The mortgage rescue scheme was launched in January 2009 to prevent households at risk of repossession because of mortgage arrears becoming homeless, if they would be in 'priority need' if they applied as homeless to a local authority.

The mortgage rescue scheme in England is funded by central government and administered by local authorities in conjunction with registered social landlords, lenders and money advisers. The scheme is now due to close in spring 2013. Since April 2011, local authorities in Wales have assessed and prioritised the need for help in their area. The local authority decides whether to help clients with mortgage rescue and what eligibility criteria to use.

The scheme has two options.

- **Shared equity.** A registered social landlord (eg, a housing association) makes a low-interest loan to enable the client to reduce her/his mortgage or secured loan. The aim is to reduce the payments on the existing loan(s) to an affordable level. There must be between 25 per cent and 40 per cent equity in the property. The maximum loan is 25–75 per cent of the outstanding mortgage and is paid directly to the lender. The equity loan is secured on the property and the client pays interest in monthly instalments at 1.75 per cent a year for the first year and the retail prices index plus 0.5 per cent a year thereafter. These loans cannot be used to clear unsecured debts. Very few clients have taken up this option.

- **Mortgage to rent.** Most clients have chosen this option. A registered social landlord purchases the property at 97 per cent of its market value and the former homeowner is granted a three-year assured shorthold tenancy at 80 per cent of the open-market rent. The client will be eligible to apply for housing benefit (HB) to cover this. Before May 2009, a client must have had between 3 per cent and 25 per cent equity in her/his property, but since this date clients with negative equity of up to 120 per cent loan to value can be considered. In such cases, it will be necessary to negotiate with any lenders either to reduce the shortfall or convert it into an unsecured non-priority debt. Lenders have been encouraged to waive early redemption charges and other fees in order to reduce any shortfall. It may be possible to clear the shortfall using repossession prevention funds (see p215). If there is sufficient equity in the property, the client may receive a lump sum, which can be used to deal with her/his non-priority debts.

Money advice is an essential part of the process of being accepted on the scheme. All the other options for dealing with the client's arrears discussed in this *Handbook* should have been explored and the lender should have exhausted all its forbearance options. The client's financial position must be assessed using the common financial statement (see p51) and any other priority and non-priority debts must be dealt with.

Citizens Advice Bureaux can access a supported money advice scheme via the National Homelessness Advice Service online consultancy. This offers:
- consultancy on money advice/housing options for clients with mortgage arrears up to and including mortgage rescue;
- help with negotiating with lenders or local authorities if cases may be held up in the process;
- funding to assist with the costs of assessing eligibility for mortgage rescue and for providing post-rescue advice where required.

Mortgage rescue and bankruptcy

If the client goes bankrupt in the five years following the transaction, the trustee in bankruptcy may challenge the arrangement as a transaction at an undervalue (see p467). This might put the client's home at risk if the new owner decides to sell it to pay off the trustee.

However, the Insolvency Service has said that the mortgage rescue scheme is unlikely to give rise to a transaction at an undervalue if the client enters the scheme before bankruptcy and the registered social landlord pays the market value. However, if the client receives a lump sum and uses this to clear unsecured debts, the question of a preference might arise (see p467). Any shortfall will be a bankruptcy debt (although if the lender only agreed to mortgage rescue on the basis of the client entering into a new arrangement to pay the shortfall, questions of fraud will arise if the client entered into the arrangement with the intention of going bankrupt and avoiding payment). The reduction in housing costs may increase the chances of an income payments agreement/order being made (see pp458–60).

Entering the mortgage rescue scheme post-bankruptcy and while undischarged will not give rise to a transaction at an undervalue, but the trustee in bankruptcy will need to be satisfied that the market value is paid for the property. Any surplus will be an asset and will be claimed by the trustee. If the lender will only agree to the scheme post-bankruptcy if the client enters into new arrangements to pay any shortfall, the trustee should not object, provided the client has taken independent advice (as should be the case).

When applicable
- The client is a homeowner, whose household is at risk of repossession because of mortgage arrears and who would be in 'priority need' if s/he applied as homeless to a local authority. **'Priority need'** households are those with children, someone who is pregnant, older people (eg, over 60) or a household in which someone is vulnerable for some other reason (eg, because of a disability or long-term illness) and repossession would be detrimental to her/his health. As this is not a homelessness application, local authorities should not take such a strict approach to questions of vulnerability and should not consider whether or not a household is intentionally homeless.
- The value of the property is below a maximum figure specified for the region in which the property is situated (although this figure is only indicative).
- The household's total income is £60,000 or less a year and there are no assets which could be realised to reduce the debt.
- The client's property has no more than 120 per cent of its value secured against it.
- The client does not have a second home.

Advantages
- The scheme allows the client to remain in her/his home.
- The rent (which is 80 per cent of the open-market rent for the property) is likely to be lower than the mortgage/secured loan payments and HB may be available.
- The client may receive a lump sum, which can be used to make a full and final offer to her/his creditors (see p249).
- The landlord will be responsible for the ongoing repairs to, and maintenance of, the property rather than the client/homeowner.

Disadvantages
- The client stays in her/his home as a tenant rather than as a homeowner.
- The client will have an assured shorthold tenancy and can be evicted if s/he does not keep to the tenancy's terms.

- The client must make a contribution of 3 per cent of the value of the property in order to enter the scheme.
- The client has no right to buy back the property if her/his financial circumstances improve.
- If the client is in negative equity, the lender(s) may not agree to write off the shortfall unless s/he makes an arrangement to pay off the shortfall.

Useful arguments
- Repossession should be a last resort.
- The scheme enables the lender to avoid the costs of repossessing and selling the property.
- It is likely to provide a quicker and (if the property is in negative equity) a better return for the lender than repossession.
- Any shortfall could be covered from the repossession prevention funds (see below).

Checklist for action
- Contact the lender(s) to confirm that all available forbearance tools have been applied.
- Arrange for any repossession proceedings to be adjourned pending the scheme process (see p335).
- Contact all the other creditors to request that no further action be taken pending the client's joining the scheme.
- Refer the client to the local authority and inform the lender(s) of the referral.
- Advise the client to make any payments required by the lender(s) while the application is processed.
- If an offer under the mortgage rescue scheme is made, ensure the client seeks independent financial advice and obtains advice on the tenancy arrangements and any benefit implications (the client may have to be referred).

Repossession prevention funds

These funds are administered by local authorities in England and operate on the basis that relatively small amounts of money can make a significant difference in preventing repossessions and evictions.

Although it is not intended that clients should apply for loans, advisers can approach local authorities on their behalf in order to prevent a client from losing her/his home because of mortgage arrears.

Welsh local authorities may also have funds available that they can use to prevent repossessions and the potential costs of rehousing and the resettlement of clients.

Sale and rent-back schemes

These are commercial, non-government schemes that allow an owner-occupier who is unable to meet her/his mortgage repayments and who is possibly facing repossession to sell her/his home and remain in the property as a tenant. Before 1 July 2009, such schemes were not regulated by the FSA and clients who were the victims of mis-selling had little redress.

Following concerns raised by Citizens Advice, Shelter and the Council of Mortgage Lenders, the FSA introduced a regulatory regime on 30 June 2010. All existing firms who wished to continue operating were required to register for authorisation. Any complaints arising after authorisation can be considered by the FOS in accordance with its normal rules (see p268).

Following a review published in February 2012, which identified widespread poor practice, the sale and rent-back market has effectively been closed. No homeowner should be offered a sale and rent-back product until further notice.[7]

Sale of the property

There are a number of circumstances in which it may be advisable to sell a home in order to repay priority creditors.

When applicable

There are circumstances in which the loss of a home may be inevitable and, indeed, the best option.

- A client has somewhere else to live as well as the property in question.
- A client has considerable equity in the home, but now the property is too large or in the wrong place for her/his current requirements and a more suitable home could be purchased at a lower price.
- Repossession is inevitable. For example, if the client's available income is too low to make an acceptable repayment proposal, a better price may be paid to an owner-occupier than a mortgagee in possession. This can give a client equity, but her/his need for a suitable home must be paramount (see disadvantages on p217).

This strategy, although superficially tempting, is not generally applicable merely to repay priority debts. When other circumstances make the sale of the home inevitable or even desirable, however, clearing the debts can be achieved in this way and there may even be sufficient capital to make a full and final offer to non-priority creditors (see p249). As it is such a major decision, it is important that the client and her/his family reach it for themselves. The debt adviser must ensure that the advantages and disadvantages of this strategy are understood and that the client has time to consider all the implications.

If the client is a former local authority tenant who has exercised her/his right to buy, it is worth checking whether the local authority or housing organisation to whom its stock is now transferred operates a 'buy-back' scheme, whereby the owner sells the home back to the local authority and remains as a tenant. Check whether the client is still within the discount repayment period. If so, a proportion of the purchase price will have to be repaid to the local authority.

Advantages

- It is easily accepted by priority creditors and courts. Time may be given for the sale to go through if necessary.
- It prevents further action.
- It may avoid a bad credit rating.
- It may release capital for other purposes.
- A better price will generally be achieved by a voluntary sale than by a financial institution selling the property after it has repossessed it.
- It is an alternative to bankruptcy proceedings, either as part of an individual voluntary arrangement (see Chapter 15) or an informal arrangement with creditors.
- It may avoid court costs if the strategy is agreed before repossession action.
- It can be seen by the client as an opportunity for a fresh start.

Disadvantages

- The client is forced to move home. This is costly and disruptive.
- Unless the client has a buyer, it may be seen by the creditor and the court as a way of delaying possession/eviction proceedings.
- If rehousing by a local authority is required, it may be difficult to persuade it that the client has not made her/himself intentionally homeless.
- It may not be possible to find alternative suitable housing.
- The client may lose money if the housing market is depressed and s/he has only recently bought the property.

The client or adviser must explain the circumstances to the local authority in advance and gain its approval of the strategy, in writing, and its acceptance that homelessness is inevitable rather than intentional. For further details, see the *Manual of Housing Law* (see Appendix 2).

Useful arguments

- Creditors prefer to avoid repossessing and selling property and so can be persuaded of the advantages of not having to sell an empty property. A property is likely to sell more quickly if inhabited.
- The loan will be repaid in full. If it is not and the creditor is unreasonably refusing to agree to a sale, the court can override the creditor's objections.[8]

Checklist for action

- Ensure that the client has suitable alternative accommodation.
- Inform the creditors of the proposed strategy.
- Advise the client to put the house on the market. If a quick sale is required, the client should explain this to the estate agent.

- Discuss with the client how much to pay, if anything, towards the mortgage until the house is sold, particularly if there is negative equity.

Refinancing

Refinancing means taking out a loan or other credit agreement to repay an existing debt.

When applicable

When a priority debt (often a second mortgage) has terms that are very expensive, it can be worth refinancing it. It is common for possession of homes to be sought by second mortgagees (who may have lent money for double glazing or other home improvements) from clients who had always managed to pay their first mortgage. The repayments on a medium-term loan from a finance company may be greater than those on a mortgage from a high street lender.

In these circumstances, the first mortgagee may be sympathetic to the client and will not want to lose her/his business simply because s/he has become unable to repay the high rate of interest charged by the second mortgagee.

Even though possession action is not threatened, it may be obvious that a client's financial problems are caused by excessive repayment on a particular priority debt. Refinancing may, therefore, be more appropriate than asking the creditor to capitalise arrears, as this could result in higher repayments than if the loan were refinanced.

Refinancing should be used when a cheaper form of borrowing is available to replace a priority debt. A variety of credit products can be used – eg:

- an unsecured loan;
- an additional advance from an existing secured lender;
- a secured loan from a new lender;
- a remortgage;
- a transfer of balances to a credit card. Some credit card companies offer 0 per cent interest for a temporary period on balances transferred from other creditors.

It should only be considered if:

- the client's monthly outgoings will be reduced; *and*
- the client can afford the new repayments; *and*
- the client will also be able to meet her/his essential expenditure and any other financial commitments.

When refinancing is not applicable

Many advertisements for refinancing or debt consolidation also promote the 'feel-good factor' by suggesting that people can borrow extra spending money in addition to paying off their debts. Many people do this and, for those in financial difficulties, the effect is to exacerbate their problems. The 'churning' of loans (ie, where debts are consolidated and then consolidated again) can be very expensive because of the way the interest is apportioned; the amount of capital paid off is small and so the debt increases. The churning of loans could give rise to an unfair relationship (see p98).

Advantages

Clients can benefit from refinancing or consolidating their debts on more advantageous terms – ie:

- lower interest rates;
- lower monthly payments;
- having to deal with only one creditor.

Disadvantages

Refinancing or debt consolidation is often seen as an easy way of obtaining more credit or as a short-term solution to debt problems. The possible long-term implications may not always be understood and, without clear information on the costs involved, problems can occur – eg:

- the costs of settling existing loans (eg, early settlement charges) and finding and arranging new loans (eg, a broker's fees) can be significant;
- clients can pay more for their credit overall and have a larger debt for a longer period if the new loan is spread over a longer period of time.

A report published by the OFT in March 2004 found that most consumers did not 'shop around' for new finance; many were unaware of alternative solutions to their debt problems – eg, negotiating with their creditors or getting help from the free debt advice sector; and most did not take proper account of the length of the term of the new loan or the total cost of the repayments.[9] The study also identified potentially unfair practices – eg, creditors requiring existing customers to take out consolidation loans as a way of dealing with their debt problems and inappropriate selling of payment protection insurance on such loans, for instance, to borrowers who were unlikely to be able to claim on it.

Useful arguments

- If the first mortgagee is being asked to refinance a second secured loan, whenever possible emphasise the client's good payment record.
- Point out the business advantages to the creditor of refinancing the loan rather than allowing another secured lender to take possession.
- If they will not agree immediately, it is worth advising creditors to review their decision after three to six months of regular payments.

Checklist for action

- Advise the client to take independent financial advice and obtain full details of the refinancing, including new monthly instalments, arrangement fees, interest rates and annual percentage rate.

- Inform the existing creditor of the proposed action.

Refinancing should be distinguished from rescheduling existing repayments, which does not involve taking on (further) credit.

Time orders

A time order is granted by the county court and sets new repayment terms and possibly lower interest rates/charges for an agreement if the court believes that the original terms should be altered. See p340 for further details.

When applicable
- A time order can only be granted for loans, credit cards, overdrafts and any other type of agreement regulated by the Consumer Credit Act 1974.[10]
- Time orders are most likely to be granted if the borrower's circumstances have changed during the period of the loan. Time orders will usually be granted if the change in circumstances is expected to be temporary, but can be made for a longer period if the court accepts that it is 'just' to do so.[11]

Advantages
- The agreement of the creditor is not required if the court can be persuaded that an order should be made.
- Any possession order will be suspended by the court on the terms of the time order.
- Once made, the creditor can take no further action as long as payments are maintained.
- It can reduce interest rates/charges (possibly retrospectively) and set payments at an affordable level.

Disadvantages
- Time orders are difficult to get and, because they are still rarely applied for, many judges are not familiar with the principles. The court is required to draw a distinction between a 'deserving' and an 'undeserving' client.
- The client will have to wait until the creditor issues an arrears notice (on or after 1 October 2008) or a default notice, or takes court action before applying for a time order.
- Creditors' costs may be added to the debt.

Useful arguments
See Chapter 12.

Checklist for action
See Chapter 12.

Voluntary charge

Most unsecured debts are not priorities. However, very occasionally it may be advisable to offer to turn an unsecured debt into a secured one – eg, if there is a real risk of a creditor applying to make a client bankrupt. This is achieved by offering the creditor a 'voluntary charge' secured on the client's property. Many advisers routinely dismiss creditors' requests for a voluntary charge without considering whether it would be in the client's best interests to agree.

When applicable

Although often requested by creditors, a voluntary charge is only very rarely in the client's best interests. The only circumstances in which it may be advisable are the following.

- It is the only means of stopping HM Revenue and Customs (HMRC) from taking action to commit a person to prison.
- It is the only means to stop someone issuing undesirable bankruptcy proceedings. **Note:** although many creditors threaten bankruptcy proceedings, including issuing a statutory demand (see p444), this very rarely results in an actual petition for bankruptcy. However, a statutory demand should always be taken seriously and should never be ignored.
- It is essential to the client that no county court judgment is made – eg, because s/he would lose her/his job if this happened. **Note:** a time order may be a more appropriate way of stopping a county court judgment.
- The creditor refuses to accept any other strategy, and if the creditor obtains a county court judgment, it is likely the court will make a charging order (see p301).
- The creditor has an automatic right to impose a charge – eg, in the case of the Legal Services Commission's statutory charge, which can incur higher costs than a voluntary charge.
- It is known that when a person's current home is sold, s/he will not need the proceeds of sale – eg, if s/he is terminally ill. In this situation, a voluntary charge could reduce the stress of lengthy negotiations with creditors.

It is essential that the client seeks legal advice before signing a voluntary charge in order to safeguard her/his position should the creditor decide to enforce the charge and apply for an order for sale. As a minimum, the adviser should ensure that the charge document is worded so that the creditor's right to do so is removed altogether (or is at least restricted), in order that that the property cannot be repossessed and sold against the client's wishes. In addition, the client must ensure almost always that the creditor will agree to freeze interest so that the charge is against a fixed sum that will not swallow up the equity.

Agreement also needs to be reached about whether any instalments are required by the creditor in addition to the charge. All these issues need to be agreed before a voluntary charge is made, and must be part of a written agreement.[12]

In the case of jointly owned properties where the joint owner has no liability for the debt, her/his agreement may also be required and s/he should be advised to seek separate and independent advice.

Advantages
- A voluntary charge is likely to satisfy a creditor and therefore mean that no further action is taken.
- Once their capital outlay is secured by a voluntary charge, many creditors will agree to add no further interest/charges until the property is sold, and to accept the client's repayment offer or even no (or only token) payments.
- Lenders can be persuaded to agree not to enforce their charge – ie, not to force a sale but to wait for payment until the client sells the property (or remortgages).

Disadvantages
- By changing the status of a debt, a client is potentially putting her/his house under threat.
- There may be costs incurred by the client seeking legal advice to ensure a watertight agreement is drawn up.
- If the client has a partner who is a co-owner of the property, the partner will have to sign the charge document and make her/himself liable for the debt.
- The creditor may still insist on payments being paid in addition to the charge.

Useful arguments
From the client's point of view, the voluntary charge is only ever the lesser of two evils. To the creditor, the adviser may need to argue the following.
- In practice, it is the only way the creditor will get any money.
- Making people bankrupt does not often produce money, but a voluntary charge will do so.
- If house prices increase, so too will the equity against which the charge is made.

Checklist for action
- Consider whether any other strategy would be more appropriate – eg, a time order.
- Advise the client to obtain full details of the terms of the charge in writing from the creditor.
- Ensure the client receives legal advice about the agreement before signing.
- Check that interest is frozen and all the other terms are acceptable.

Deductions from benefits

Certain priority arrears can be deducted from a claimant's IS, income-based JSA, income-related ESA and PC at a set weekly amount and paid directly to creditors.[13] If this is done, the creditor concerned can demand that payments for current liabilities also be met in full from benefit. Deductions can also be made from contribution-based JSA, contributory ESA and some other benefits in limited circumstances. See CPAG's *Welfare Benefits and Tax Credits Handbook* for further information.

The maximum amount of deductions is £10.65 a week. If the client has more debts than can be paid within these limits, they are paid in set order of priority as follows: [14]

- housing costs;
- rent arrears;
- fuel charges (in the case of both gas and electricity arrears, the DWP chooses which one to pay);
- water charges;
- council tax arrears;
- fines, costs and compensation orders;
- repayment of integration loans;
- repayment of eligible loans made by certain 'not-for-profit' lenders – eg, credit unions;
- repayment of tax credit overpayments and self-assessment tax debts.

Note: the rules for universal credit will be different. See CPAG's *Welfare Benefits and Tax Credits Handbook* for more details.

Deductions from benefits are commonly used to pay off arrears of gas and electricity charges as an alternative to disconnection, or rent arrears as an alternative to eviction. In some circumstances, direct payments can be made without the claimant's consent – eg, for council tax arrears and fines.

When applicable

- Deductions from IS, income-based JSA, income-related ESA or PC can be made to pay for rent arrears, residential accommodation charges, hostel payments, fuel, water charges, council tax arrears, community charge arrears, fines, repayments of eligible loans and child support maintenance. Deductions can also be made for the cost of home loans, loans for repairs and improvements and other housing costs, and paid to the lender.
- Deductions from benefit are useful if the alternative is either the disconnection of a fuel supply, or an impending eviction.
- Because of the statutory maximums on the amount that can be deducted for arrears, it is often a cheaper method of paying off arrears than a repayment schedule, or than token or slot meters that have been recalibrated to recover arrears along with current consumption. Gas and electricity suppliers often seriously overestimate current use and request an amount from the DWP far in

excess of the amount actually required to cover consumption. If they do, advise the client to take daily or weekly meter readings. It is the appropriate decision maker at the DWP who decides how much to deduct for current consumption, so the client can ask for a lower deduction to be made based on her/his own readings. If the DWP refuses, the client can appeal to the First-tier Tribunal.

- Some gas and electricity suppliers insist on installing a token meter to cover current consumption and will only collect arrears through deductions from benefit.
- Full help with the cost of home loans is not usually available until a client has been claiming IS, income-based JSA or income-related ESA for a period. There are no waiting periods for PC claimants. See CPAG's *Welfare Benefits and Tax Credits Handbook* for further details. The housing costs element of IS/JSA/ESA/PC is usually paid automatically to the creditor under the mortgage payment scheme as soon as the claimant qualifies for full help, even if there are no arrears. Lenders may agree to adjourn a claim for possession if they are receiving payments directly from the DWP. If they have already obtained a possession order, they can be asked not to enforce it so long as deductions from benefit are paid.

Advantages

- If the client fits the criteria for deductions from benefit, it is a simple and quick way to ensure that no further action is taken by the creditor and that arrears are paid at a relatively modest rate – £3.55 per debt per week in 2012/13 – particularly if money is owed to several creditors (but see below).
- Creditors are assured of payments.

Disadvantages

- Only certain debts can be paid for in this way (and council tax only at the request of the local authority, fines at the request of the magistrates' court and eligible loans at the request of the lender). If the client has more than one such debt, deductions might not be made for all of them. If this happens, there is a set order of priority.
- By reducing subsistence-level benefits, they reduce the flexibility with which a claimant can juggle her/his weekly budget.
- Fuel suppliers may demand a large amount for current consumption.
- If the client is likely to cease claiming benefit in the near future (even if only for a temporary period), payments will have to be replaced with another strategy. The client may be faced with a demand for the full amount when her/his benefit ends.
- The DWP often pays amounts collected on a quarterly basis. This can mean long delays for creditors in receiving their money.
- If the client is getting help with her/his mortgage (or loans for repairs or improvements) in her/his IS, income-based JSA, income-related ESA or PC,

payment is usually made directly to the lender under a mortgage payment scheme. If the client's lender is participating in this scheme, no amount for mortgage arrears can be deducted from benefit and paid to the lender.

Checklist for action

- Telephone the creditor to find out how much is required and, if the client can afford this amount, try to obtain the creditor's agreement to payments by deductions from benefit.
- Assist the client in her/his request for the DWP to arrange deductions.

Gas and electricity pre-payment meters

Both electricity and gas companies must provide a pre-payment meter to a customer to prevent disconnection of her/his supply, if it is safe and practicable to do so.[15] If someone has arrears on fuel bills, a pre-payment meter will collect money not just for the fuel used, but also towards the arrears. For a discussion of the different types of meters available, see CPAG's *Fuel Rights Handbook*.

When applicable

- Pre-payment meters allow arrears to be collected over a period of time and are, therefore, a way of avoiding disconnection.

Advantages

- A client continues to have some access to fuel supplies and will not be pressed further for the debt.
- Pre-payment meters can assist budgeting.

Disadvantages

- A pre-payment meter is often a do-it-yourself disconnection kit, because it may not be possible to keep it running at all times.
- In some cases, the amount of money recovered towards the arrears varies in relation to the amount of fuel used and thus, in winter, not only does a client have to spend more money on fuel, s/he also has to contribute more towards her/his arrears.
- With token meters the client has to remember to buy enough tokens. There may be costs incurred (eg, bus fares) in buying tokens/cards or charging credit keys, or it may be difficult for the client to get to a charging point or point of sale (eg, in the case of illness), and such places may be closed.
- Fuel is more expensive per unit if paid for in this way. It should, therefore, be considered as a last resort.
- A pre-payment meter is not always technically possible. This applies if gas appliances have pilot lights that could go out when the pre-payment ends and are not protected by a fail-safe device when payment is resumed.

- Coin meters have to be positioned somewhere safe, which normally means they cannot be placed in buildings that do not have inside meters.

Useful arguments

Fuel suppliers are required to offer pre-payment facilities if this is the only means of avoiding disconnection. However, it may be necessary to argue with a fuel supplier about the level at which the arrears will be collected through the pre-payment meter. If a client is on IS, income-based JSA, income-related ESA or PC, the amounts deducted by the DWP from benefit should be used as a maximum level of recovery (currently, £3.55 a week).

Checklist for action

- Check exactly what type of meters are available locally.
- Contact the fuel supplier to request installation of a meter.
- Advise the client to monitor fuel consumption to check the calibration of the meter. This will involve taking a meter reading each week and comparing the number of units with the amount paid.

See also Chapter 6.

Writing off debts

Both the magistrates' court (in respect of fines and council tax) and the local authority (in respect of non-domestic rates and council tax) have powers to remit (ie, write off) amounts owing in cases of hardship. HMRC can also remit taxes (although it does not formally write them off).

Advantages

- It reduces or removes the debt.

Disadvantages

- The client will often need to attend a means enquiry (see p374).
- The magistrate will need to consider whether there has been 'wilful refusal or culpable neglect' (see p383) and may therefore look at other alternatives to remittance, such as imprisonment.

Useful arguments

- **Non-domestic rates.** The closure of a business may adversely affect the amenities or employment prospects of an area. Only 25 per cent of the cost of relief is borne by the authority; the remainder is borne by central government.
- **Fines.** Magistrates need to see how the client's circumstances have changed since the fine was imposed or that the client's financial situation was not taken into account when the fine was originally set. Guidelines state that fines

should be paid in a reasonable period, and that two to three years would be exceptional.

- **Council tax.** Local authorities have complete discretion and should be encouraged to use it in all cases of hardship which fall outside the exemption, discount and benefits rules. Paragraph 4.741 of the *HB/CTB Overpayments Guide* to local authorities says that financial hardship is proved if a client's income minus priority debts gives a figure which is more than £9 a week below her/his applicable amount for these benefits. The guidance recommends that, in such cases, the local authority should consider a write-off. Advisers should encourage local authorities to apply the same criteria to council tax arrears.
- **Tax.** Remission is usually only available if the client is on a low income and has no, or insignificant, savings. HMRC will need to be satisfied that the client's financial circumstances are unlikely to improve sufficiently to make future recovery action worthwhile. It is unlikely to be offered to a client who is currently self-employed, although collection could be suspended in cases of serious illness.

Checklist for action

- Write to the creditor to request remittance.
- Enclose a financial statement.
- Point out any additional factors – eg, terminal illness, severe medical conditions or disability.

4. Emergency action

The need for debt advice very often arises as a result of a priority creditor threatening to take immediate action against someone's fuel supply, property or liberty. In such circumstances, a debt adviser must always be prepared to take emergency action. In some cases, enough information and time will be available to use one of the strategies outlined above. In other cases, neither time nor information is immediately available and, therefore, action by the creditor needs to be halted or delayed. This may be possible by making a telephone call to a creditor explaining that the client has approached the agency seeking advice and assistance, and indicating when an offer will be made.

Paragraph 4(n) of the *Credit Services Association Code of Practice* provides for a 30-day 'breathing space' if requested by an advice agency, and paragraphs 201–203 of *The Lending Code* make similar provisions for credit card debts. Paragraph 7.12 of the Office of Fair Trading's *Irresponsible Lending Guidance* extends this to all cases in which an adviser is helping a client to agree a repayment plan. However, this may not be the case when adjournments or delays have already been granted. In such situations, other emergency action will have to be taken.

Preventing fuel disconnection

The legislation governing the supply of gas and electricity states that supplies should not be disconnected while there is a genuine dispute about the amount due.[16] When there is any question about the amount claimed, such a dispute should immediately be registered with the relevant supplier and confirmed in writing. The supplier should be asked not to disconnect the supply until the dispute has been resolved.

Before being offered a pre-payment meter, the consumer should have been offered some form of repayment option to pay the arrears and cover the ongoing consumption. If this breaks down, some suppliers automatically offer a pre-payment meter as the only remaining option. Advisers should consider offering an explanation about why the arrangement broke down (eg, it was unrealistic in the first place) and urge the supplier to enter into a new arrangement based on a financial statement.

Before disconnecting, the supplier must:

- comply with its code of practice (including information about reconnection);
- fit a pre-payment meter where it is safe and practical to do so;
- provide seven days' notice of the date of disconnection;
- obtain a warrant of entry if the client refuses access;
- give a further seven days' notice of intention to use it.

A warrant of entry is granted by the magistrates' court and allows the supplier to enter the client's home (by force if necessary) in order to disconnect the supply. Although the supplier must give the client written notice that it intends to apply for a warrant, it does not have to give the client notice of the actual application. Advisers can, however, phone the court in advance of an application, ask to speak to the magistrate who would deal with any application and make representations on behalf of the client – eg, that s/he is a vulnerable person and the supplier has unreasonably refused to agree to a repayment arrangement.

The client cannot be disconnected if:

- the bill is genuinely disputed;
- the debt is owed to a different supplier. A supplier who wants to retain the power to disconnect should object to the supplier being switched;
- the debt is due from a previous occupier and the client has agreed to take over the supply;
- the debt is for something other than the supply of gas or electricity – ie, it does not relate to fuel consumption. Note, however, that the supply can be disconnected for non-payment under a 'green deal plan' for energy efficiency improvements to the property made under the Energy Act 2011;
- a repayment plan has been agreed. Under its licence conditions, when arranging a repaying plan, the supplier is required to take into account the client's ability to pay;

- the client has agreed to have a pre-payment meter fitted and it is safe and practicable to do so. The meter should be calibrated to recover the arrears at the rate the client can afford, taking into account her/his ability to repay;
- it is between 1 October and 31 March, and the supplier either knows or has reason to believe there is someone of pension age living either alone in the property or with others over pension age or under 18;
- it is between 1 October and 31 March and someone living in the property is either severely disabled or chronically sick, unless all other reasonable steps have been taken to recover the arrears.

Clients in the last two categories are likely to be on the Priority Services Register.

Energy UK members have signed up to a 'safety net for vulnerable customers', under which they are committed never knowingly to disconnect a vulnerable customer at any time of year 'where for reasons of age, health, disability or severe financial insecurity that customer is unable to safeguard their personal welfare or the personal welfare of other members of the household'.

No one who is prepared to have a pre-payment meter or who is eligible for direct payments from her/his benefits or who can afford to pay for current consumption plus a payment towards the arrears should ever be disconnected. Energy trust funds or other charities may be able to help with payment of bills or to prevent self-disconnection – ie, if clients do not use gas or electricity because they cannot afford to pay for it. In the case of pre-payment meters, self-disconnection can be as a result of arrears being recovered at too high a rate. Suppliers can always be asked to confirm how arrears are being recovered, and asked to recalibrate the meter where appropriate.

If negotiations with the fuel supplier are proving unsuccessful, the adviser should contact Consumer Focus or the Ombudsman Services: Energy (see Appendix 1), which have the power to intervene when disconnection is threatened. See also CPAG's *Fuel Rights Handbook* for more information.

Preventing the home being lost

When a possession order has already been granted and is followed by a warrant of possession (see p352), an immediate application may need to be made to the court on Form N244 to suspend the warrant. If the eviction is not due to take place for several days, the debt adviser should attempt to negotiate directly with the lender (or the lender's solicitor) or the landlord, to obtain a binding agreement that the property will not be repossessed. If this is not possible or appears unlikely, or the eviction is due to take place that day or the following day, Form N244 needs to be submitted to the court. Form N244 must state the grounds of the application and, if possible, include an offer of payment. The fee is court fee 2.9 – ie, £40 (and not £80 as some courts argue). See p273 for how to apply for a remission. For further information about a warrant of possession and how to complete Form N244, see p271.

In the case of local authority or registered social landlord tenants, there will usually be an internal procedure that must be followed before a warrant is applied for, which may involve considering representations from the tenant. The adviser should check that procedure has been complied with and challenge the landlord if it has not.[17]

Such an application will always stop county court bailiffs executing a warrant (ie, carrying out its instructions) until the court has heard the application, although the court is usually very quick in arranging a hearing. The success of an application depends largely on:

- whether several arrangements have already been made but not kept to;
- the adviser's and the client's ability to present the case;
- how many previous warrants have been suspended;
- how long the client has been seeking help from an advice agency;
- the client's ability to pay.

If it is too late to make the application to the court because the bailiffs are already on their way to carry out the eviction, the adviser should ring the creditor immediately and negotiate with the bailiff, on the doorstep if necessary, for more time. Bailiffs normally have a mobile phone with them and so can be contacted right up to the point of eviction.

Preventing goods being seized by magistrates' court bailiffs

Bailiffs working for the magistrates' court cannot act without the authority of a distress warrant. This is a document issued by the court allowing them to take goods belonging to the client, that can then be sold and the money used to pay for the unpaid debt.

If a distress warrant has been issued by a magistrates' court because of arrears in the payment of fines and bailiffs are about to seize goods, there is some doubt as to whether magistrates are entitled to hear an application to give further time to pay (see p369). Occasionally, bailiffs will agree to give a debt adviser a few days in which to produce an offer of repayment. This is always worth trying, but success is limited.

See Chapter 14 for further details of bailiffs' powers.

Council tax arrears

Private bailiffs (see p387) are used by a local authority after a liability order has been granted to collect the amount owing. Different local authorities give different instructions to their bailiffs. In some areas a clear code of conduct exists, preventing the seizure of goods from people on benefit or in certain other circumstances. The good practice protocol on collection of council tax arrears agreed by the Local Government Association recommends that local authorities and advice agencies should work together to develop a fair collection and enforcement policy, highlighting examples of vulnerable people and specifying clear procedures about how they should be dealt with – eg, contractual arrangements between local authorities and bailiffs should set out procedures for the local authority to take back cases involving vulnerable people. An adviser must know what rules (if any) her/his own local authority uses. If an action by bailiffs breaches these, the relevant section of the local authority should be contacted immediately so that its order to the bailiffs can be withdrawn. The protocol recommends the use of dedicated contacts accessible on direct lines and by electronic means so that issues can be taken up quickly.

In appropriate cases, advisers should refer bailiffs to the Ministry of Justice's *National Standards for Enforcement Agents*, particularly if the client is a 'vulnerable person' (see p394).[18] In addition, the local authority may (and, arguably, should) have its own policy on when someone should be considered vulnerable and how s/he should be treated.

Even where there is no clear policy, the adviser should contact the local authority and ask it to consider withdrawing the warrant from the bailiffs or, if that is not possible, instructing the bailiffs to accept a lower payment offer. Bailiffs themselves may occasionally agree to delay action, but this is unlikely. There may be no need for the client to let the bailiffs into her/his home. See p395 for the rules about bailiffs' powers to enter property.

In appropriate cases, the local authority could be asked to write off council tax arrears.

Preventing the local authority taking bankruptcy proceedings

Many local authorities now use bankruptcy proceedings to recover council tax arrears from homeowners. There is no government guidance on this. However, local authorities should bear in mind the principles of proportionality and reasonableness in deciding whether to use bankruptcy, particularly the client's potential liability for substantial 'trustee in bankruptcy' costs. Charging orders are likely to be a more proportionate recovery method in relation to the sums involved and should not be rejected purely on the basis that the court might not order a sale in the event of payment not being forthcoming.

The Local Government Ombudsman has made the following points.
- Bankruptcy should only be used as a 'last resort' and local authorities should have a policy to this effect.
- Local authorities should record their reasons for not pursuing alternative collection methods.
- Local authorities should send out letters containing clear and detailed warnings of the potential consequences of bankruptcy for the client in terms of not only the costs of the petition itself and possible loss of the home but also the far greater costs that would be incurred if a bankruptcy order was made.

- The policy should also deal with charging orders and require their use to be considered as an alternative to bankruptcy. Charging orders should not be rejected on the grounds that they do not provide a practical recovery method.
- Local authorities must act proportionately and take into account the client's personal circumstances.
- Local authorities must proactively make enquiries about vulnerability.[19]

The Ombudsman is likely to find maladministration if a local authority:[20]
- does not have a formal debt recovery policy that has been published;
- has not gathered and considered information about the client's circumstances;
- does not include in its debt recovery policy the steps it must take before deciding on bankruptcy, committal or charging orders;
- pursues bankruptcy without clearly recording that each of these steps has been taken.

Local authorities must also take account of their duties under the Equality Act 2010, particularly if the client may have mental health issues.

Advisers should, therefore, obtain their local authority's collection policy to ensure it complies with the Ombudsman's recommendations and point out any shortcomings. Advisers should also use the recommendations to challenge any inappropriate use of bankruptcy proceedings by local authorities.[21]

Note: while complaining to the Local Government Ombudsman (or the Public Service Ombudsman for Wales) is a cheap remedy, it is an after-the-event remedy and is not quick. Because of restrictions on its jurisdiction, the Ombudsman can only investigate a local authority's actions up to the issue of proceedings, although the Ombudsman retains the right to investigate in cases in which the client has unsuccessfully applied to annul a bankruptcy order.[22] Outcomes of complaints about local authority council tax collection can be viewed at www.lgo.org.uk/complaint-outcomes/local-taxation. In cases where the client is eligible for public funding and the petition has not yet been issued, an application for judicial review could be considered.[23]

Advisers should also bear in mind that, before the local authority can take bankruptcy proceedings, it must have a liability order for the amount in question and be able to prove the existence of that liability order to the satisfaction of the court. The local authority's own computer records are not sufficient for this purpose; it must either be able to produce a sealed copy of the liability order or a statement from the magistrates' court that an order was made.[24]

Advisers should seek specialist advice if a client has received either a statutory demand or a petition from the local authority, or if a bankruptcy order has been made on the local authority's petition.

Preventing goods being seized by county court bailiffs

If a creditor has instructed the court to issue a warrant of execution for an unpaid county court judgment, the client can make a combined application to the county court to suspend the execution of the warrant and to vary the judgment. This is done on Form N245. See p319 for details of how to do this and Chapter 14 for details of county court bailiffs' powers.

If the bailiff is threatening to seize goods subject to a hire purchase/conditional sale agreement or bill of sale, specialist advice should be sought.

Preventing goods being seized by High Court enforcement officers

Enforcement officers enforce High Court judgments (including county court judgments transferred to the High Court for enforcement). Before 1 April 2004 this task was carried out by sheriff officers. They are private bailiffs authorised by the court to enforce debts in the High Court. See Chapter 14 for details of the powers of enforcement officers.

If an enforcement officer is threatening to seize goods, specialist advice should be sought.

Preventing goods being seized by tax bailiffs

Officials from HM Revenue and Customs have the powers of bailiffs to take and sell goods to pay for unpaid tax debts.[25] If they are unable to gain access to a property, they can apply for an order to force entry. Normally, a private bailiff accompanies the collector on such visits.

It is possible to negotiate with the collector directly and either suggest a repayment arrangement or submit a late return if the client does not agree with the amount of the debt and is out of the normal time limit for appealing (see Chapter 16). If the client has no goods, the collector is likely to seek an alternative means of enforcement, such as court action or bankruptcy.

Preventing imprisonment

Magistrates' courts have the power to imprison people who refuse to pay financial penalties, maintenance, community charge, council tax or rates. See Chapter 13 for the circumstances in which they can use this power and the arguments to use against them.

Warrant with bail

When a client has failed to attend a court hearing, or sometimes just failed to keep up the payments, a warrant can be issued for her/his arrest by magistrates. In most cases this will be a warrant with bail which requires the client to surrender her/himself and be given a time and date for a court hearing.

Warrant without bail

Occasionally (usually where previous warrants have been ignored), a warrant without bail is issued. This requests the police to arrest the client and hold her/him in custody until a court hearing can be arranged (within 24 hours). Such warrants have a very low priority for the police and are often left for weeks or months before being discovered when the adviser rings the court.

If a warrant without bail has been issued, the client should report to the court at a time, depending on local circumstances, when it is likely not to be busy so that s/he will not be held in the cells for too long. This may be after lunch, if the court sits then, or first thing in the morning before other prisoners have been brought from police stations. Some courts demand that people surrender themselves to the police station rather than the courts, but there is no legal foundation for this and advisers should ensure that police and other court staff accept a client's surrender in court buildings.

Committal hearing

Most magistrates' courts do not imprison people until they have been given a number of opportunities to pay by instalments. Whenever someone is brought before court after the issue of an arrest warrant, s/he should be represented, if possible. S/he cannot lawfully be imprisoned if legal representation has not been made available to her/him. If a solicitor (perhaps from the duty solicitor scheme) is to provide representation, an advice agency should brief her/him first and provide a full financial statement, as it is common for unrealistic offers to be made by solicitors, which then cause the client to be brought back before the court and treated with even less sympathy because s/he has broken a previous undertaking to pay. In some courts, probation officers are able to obtain adjournments so that they can produce a statement of the client's means for the courts. For further information about committal hearings, see p381.

After imprisonment

If magistrates have imprisoned someone for debt, it is possible that they have done so improperly, in which case an application for judicial review should be made immediately. An application for bail pending a hearing can also be made (to a High Court judge in London). The applications will always have to be made by a solicitor or barrister specialising in this field. The most likely improprieties are procedural irregularities (eg, if the court failed to consider the question of wilfulness, culpability or alternatives to imprisonment) or unreasonableness (eg, if the court expected someone on income support to pay £20 a week towards a fine), natural justice (eg, if legal representation was denied to the client) or acting *ultra vires* – eg, if the resolution setting council tax was not signed by the appropriately authorised officer of the council.

Notes

2. The general approach to priority debts

1 See P Madge, 'Till Debt Do Us Part', *Adviser* 71

2 *Cheltenham and Gloucester v Norgan* [1996] 1 All ER 449, CA (*Adviser* 53 abstracts)

3 s91 LPA 1925

3. Strategies for dealing with priority debts

4 s8(2) AJA 1973

5 s36 AJA 1970

6 *Cheltenham and Gloucester v Norgan* [1996] 1 All ER 449, CA (*Adviser* 53 abstracts)

7 For further discussion, see M Mackreth, 'Home Buy-back Schemes: rescue or rip-off?', *Adviser* 123; V Smith, 'Sale and Leaseback Schemes', *Quarterly Account* 9, IMA, Summer 2008, and M Robinson, 'Housing Casebook: rescue me!', *Adviser* 138

8 *Palk v Mortgage Services Funding*, 31 July 1992, CA (*Adviser* 34 abstracts)

9 OFT, *Debt Consolidation*, OFT 705

10 s129 CCA 1974

11 *Director General of Fair Trading v First National Bank* [2001] UKHL 52 (*Adviser* 89 abstracts)

12 For a further discussion, see J Wilson, 'Consultancy Corner', *Adviser* 95

13 Reg 35 and Sch 9 SS(C&P) Regs

14 Child support payments under the new rules are always payable regardless of what other deductions are being made.

15 Condition 27.9 Standard Conditions of Electricity Supply Licence; condition 27.9 Standard Conditions of Gas Supply Licence

4. Emergency action

16 Sch 6 EA 1989; Sch 2B GA 1986

17 See B Fisher, 'Eviction Appeal Panels' and D Durden, 'A Landlord's Perspective', *Adviser* 114

18 See A Hobley, 'Reasonableness and Bailiff Action', *Adviser* 146; p9 of the *National Standards for Enforcement Agents* deals with vulnerable people.

19 Complaint against Wolverhampton City Council, 06/B/16600 (*Adviser* 128 money advice abstracts). See also Complaint against Camden London Borough Council, 07/A/12661 (*Adviser* 129 money advice abstracts), where the revenue department's failure to make internal enquiries resulted in bankruptcy proceedings against a vulnerable person. The Ombudsman said: 'The dire and punitive consequences of bankruptcy, involving a multiplication of the original debt many times over and frequently incurring the loss of the debtor's home, must be a factor to be taken into account in deciding that the 'last resort' is indeed appropriate.'

20 Local Government Ombudsman, *Local Can't Pay? Won't Pay? Using bankruptcy for council tax debts*, October 2011, available at www.lgo.org.uk/publications/fact-sheets/complaints-about-bankruptcy

21 The Local Government Ombudsman has also issued a fact sheet, *Complaints about Bankruptcy*, available from www.tinyurlcom/cwshekj. See also A Hobley, 'Using Bankruptcy for Council Tax Debts', *Adviser* 150

22 Complaint against Newham London Borough Council, 08019113 (*Adviser* 137 abstracts)

23 See R Barnwell, 'Local Government Ombudsman and Complaints About Bankruptcy', *Adviser* 131; R Low-Beer, 'Council Tax Arrears and Bankruptcy', *Quarterly Account* 12, IMA, 2009

24 *Smolen v Tower Hamlets London Borough Council* (*Adviser* 126 money advice abstracts)

25 s61 TMA 1970

Chapter 9

....

Dealing with non-priority debts

This chapter covers:
1. Choosing a strategy (below)
2. The general approach to non-priority debts (p240)
3. Strategies for dealing with non-priority debts (p243)
4. Court-based strategies (p263)

---

1. Choosing a strategy

The majority of a client's debts are likely to be non-priority ones. These are debts where non-payment will not result in the loss of the client's home, liberty, essential goods or services. They vary from an unpaid bill of a few pounds to a loan of several thousand pounds. Non-priority debts will not usually include any of the debts listed in Chapter 8.

Advice given to a client on non-priority debts should take account of:
- the nature of the debt;
- the client's financial position;
- the powers of the creditor;
- whether interest or charges on the debt have been frozen or reduced.

All options identified as being available to the client in her/his individual circumstances should be discussed with her/him, including: [1]
- the advantages/disadvantages;
- any eligibility criteria;
- the debts covered; *and*
- any costs and risks associated with each option.

The client must agree to the strategy chosen. It is not usually an appropriate option for the client to do nothing, although there are some occasions when doing nothing is in the client's best interests – eg, if a debt is about to become 'statute-barred', it is not in the client's best interests to acknowledge the debt by sending out a 'holding letter' to the creditor and so start time running again (see p142). Doing nothing, however, usually leaves the client uncertain as to the status of the debt.

Occasionally, a client will have not only a large amount of non-priority debt but also a high disposable income. It is not usually in her/his best interests to put such a client through the debt advice process discussed in this *Handbook*.[2] S/he may just need some money guidance to reduce her/his monthly outgoings. It is probably not in any client's best interests for an adviser to contact creditors (except when dealing with an emergency), even by sending out holding letters, until the extent of the debt problem has been investigated, as some creditors may react inappropriately – eg, by terminating facilities and registering defaults with credit reference agencies.

A number of criteria are important when deciding which strategy will be the most appropriate for dealing with each of these debts.

Availability of income

Once the financial statement (see p50) has been produced, the adviser will know whether there is any income left over for non-priority debts after payments have been arranged with priority creditors and all the other essential items of expenditure have been taken into account. In many cases, there will not be enough income, even after income maximisation, to meet essential expenditure, but in others a significant amount may be available.

Insurance

In the case of credit debts, check whether the client has payment protection insurance to cover the repayments in the event of sickness or incapacity, unemployment, accident or death. If the client does have payment protection insurance and her/his situation is covered by the policy, advise her/him to make a claim.

If the claim is refused, consider whether this can be challenged and/or whether the policy has been mis-sold. If the client's situation is not covered by the policy, again consider whether the policy may have been mis-sold – eg, the client's circumstances were such that s/he could never have made a claim. If the agreement is regulated by the Consumer Credit Act 1974 and the client says that taking out payment protection insurance was a condition of being granted the credit, the agreement may be unenforceable if it was made before 6 April 2007 (see p71).

Availability of capital

It should have been established at the initial interview whether a client has any significant capital or savings available. These can include:
- bonds, savings certificates and shares;

- money put aside for specific items – eg, a holiday;
- capital that will become available in the near future – eg, a tax-free payment from a pension provider, expected redundancy pay and proceeds from the sale of a house or business;
- legacies under a relative's will.

Realisable assets

A client may have assets which are reasonable to realise. These will be valuable items that could be sold to raise money – eg, antiques or works of art, cars and life assurance policies with an appreciable surrender value. Such a list should only include items of a non-essential nature. For example, a recently acquired and fairly new car that is only used for weekend trips may be a realisable asset, while one that is necessary for work is not. The client must be adequately advised about her/his options before coming to a decision about disposing of assets – eg, to ensure that a car is not subject to a bill of sale or a hire purchase or conditional sale agreement, or that sale or surrender of an insurance policy is in the client's best interests. The client should be advised to obtain independent financial advice where appropriate.

Equity in the home

The equity in a person's home is the total value of the property less the amount required to pay any loans or debts secured against it, including any 'charges' and the costs of a sale. 'Charges' include mortgages and secured loans, charging orders and statutory charges owed to the Legal Services Commission in connection with publicly funded legal work. For example, to calculate the equity on a property saleable for £145,000:

Deduct solicitor's fee on sale	£2,000
Deduct estate agent's fee	£1,400
Deduct first mortgage (building society)	£115,000
Deduct second mortgage (after early-settlement discount)	£15,000
Total deductions	**£133,400**
Total equity = £145,000 – £133,400 = £11,600	

If the property is jointly owned, the equity is shared in proportion to the amount each person owns (usually equally).

In many cases, there may be no equity in the property (see p202) and the amount owed may exceed the value of the property, particularly if the client has defaulted on a high-interest, non-status secured loan. In other cases, however, it is likely that the 'equity position' will be favourable, particularly if the property has no outstanding mortgage.

It is important to establish whether or not there is equity at an early stage since many creditors now seek to secure their debts (eg, by obtaining a charging order – see p301), while others seek preferential status by resorting to threats of bankruptcy (see p444). For this reason, advisers should stress to clients the urgency of dealing with any court papers. While advisers should make it clear to clients that enquiries about equity do not necessarily mean they should sell their house, they should bear in mind that, unless the circumstances are wholly exceptional, creditors are unlikely to agree to, for example, writing off a debt (see p244) if there are realisable assets or equity in the home. A creditor may accept, for example, a token payment (see p254) on the basis that the amount due will be repaid out of the sale of the asset/property in due course.

Change of circumstances

It is important to know whether the client's current circumstances are likely to change. For example, if a client's income was until very recently quite high, but has now been reduced by a period of illness that is not expected to last very long, this must be taken into account. Similarly, if someone is about to retire or begin a new job with higher wages, these factors are vital to the strategy selected.

The amount owed

The choice of strategy is affected by the amount owing. Some strategies cost money to set up (eg, a voluntary charge – see p221) and would be too expensive for a small debt. In addition, large companies often have policies to write off small amounts owed if they are not paid after a final warning. Very large debts may also be written off in appropriate cases. Debt advisers should not assume that very large debts 'simply must be paid'. Creditors do write off sums of several thousand pounds.

It will sometimes be obvious to a debt adviser, particularly where a small debt is concerned, that a large company has already written off an amount owed because it has not communicated with the client for several years and the client has not been contacted by a collection agent acting on behalf of the creditor. In such circumstances, it is probably best to take no action and assume that the creditor has decided not to pursue the debt. However, there has been a tendency for some creditors to sell on debts where there has been no contact for many years (a practice which the Office of Fair Trading regards as unfair).[3]

Note: if there has been no contact for more than six years, the debt is probably unenforceable (see p31).

Type of debt

Some debts, although not priority debts (see Chapter 8), do not fit into the usual debt advice process and so cannot be treated as straightforward non-priority debts (see p240). Separate strategies may need to be made for such debts.

Repayment period

In the case of instalment arrangements, the shorter the repayment period, the more likely it is that the strategy will have a successful outcome. The longer the repayment period the more likely the client's circumstances are to change – and possibly deteriorate – and the more disheartened the client is likely to become. Advisers should, therefore, consider whether it is in the client's best interests to propose open-ended repayment arrangements or whether s/he should request there should be a time limit on the repayment period.[4]

Enforcement issues

If a debt is legally unenforceable, the client will be in a strong negotiating position as s/he can decide whether or not to repay the debt, and, if so, on what terms. This may make income available for payment of other debts. On the other hand, if the creditor is in a position to take enforcement action – or has already done so – the client could be at risk of losing her/his home or essential goods. For example, a creditor may have obtained a charging order on the client's home which has substantial equity but the client has little available income with which to make a reasonable offer. This debt may have to be treated as a priority debt as the creditor could apply for an order for sale in these circumstances (see p307).

Even where a debt is legally enforceable, it may be possible to persuade the creditor to write off some or all of the debt. Advisers should point out:
- any mis-selling of any part of a loan, such as payment protection insurance; *or*
- failure by a lender to assess the client's ability to repay; *or*
- 'churning' of loans (see p260).

2. The general approach to non-priority debts

If the suggested strategy is to be accepted by creditors, it is important that it is based on a consistent set of criteria and that all creditors are treated alike. Treating all creditors alike does not mean that a particular creditor should not be challenged if, for instance, the debt is unenforceable, or the creditor is adopting unacceptable lending or debt collection practices. The credit industry is competitive and individuals within it are likely to reject any strategy that appears to favour another creditor. The strength of a debt adviser's negotiating position lies in the ability to present a strategy that is empirically based and businesslike. Thus, all offers to creditors must be made on the same basis, using the same criteria when making choices with regard to their debts. Where appropriate, creditors may need reminding of their obligations under the relevant industry code of practice (eg, to treat cases of financial difficulty sympathetically and positively) and also under the Office of Fair Trading's (OFT) *Debt Collection*

Guidance – eg, not to pressurise clients to make payments which they are unable to afford, to sell property or increase their borrowing. Also, under the OFT's *Irresponsible Lending Guidance*, creditors should treat clients in default or arrears with understanding, due consideration and forbearance and should not unreasonably require that all arrears are paid in one payment, or in unduly large amounts, and/or within an unreasonable period.[5]

If a debt has a special importance to the client, there may need to be an exception to this. Some debts that *may* need to be treated differently are as follows. **Note:** if there is any possibility of the client becoming bankrupt or applying for a debt relief order in the foreseeable future, the adviser should advise the client about the implications of preferring such debts (see p467).

- **Debts created by a loan from a family or community member, or an employer.** These may, on strict legal criteria, be no different from money owed to a finance company. However, if failure to repay this debt will lead to serious financial or personal problems elsewhere in the family (eg, if a loan has been taken out to consolidate the client's non-priority debts which is secured on a family member's home) or at work (eg, dismissal), it may be necessary to give it priority over other non-priority debts.
- **Unsecured debts that have been guaranteed** (see p85). These may need to be given priority in order to protect the guarantor.
- **Mail order catalogues.** These may be essential to someone on a low income as a way of budgeting for essentials such as household items and clothing, provided a low balance is maintained.
- **Bill paying services** (also known as budgeting accounts), perhaps through a credit union (see p37) or a commercial lender. The client makes monthly payments to the credit union or lender, who in turn pays various agreed household bills on the client's behalf. These bills are likely to be for essential expenditure in terms of including them on the client's financial statement and, if they fall into arrears, will then be priority debts. It may, therefore, be in everyone's best interests to maintain these payments if this means there will be more money available for other non-priority creditors.
- **A debt incurred through the fraud** of the client or her/his partner or a relative, where s/he could face prosecution if the debt is not paid.
- **Debts which do not fit into the usual debt advice process** – known as 'square peg' debts because they do not fit neatly into the priority/non-priority categories – eg, credit union loans (see p37), mortgage shortfalls (see p141) and traffic penalties (see p156).[6]
- **'Loan sharks'.** This expression tends to refer to illegal moneylenders who make loans at extortionate rates and enforce payment through violence or threats of violence. Once involved with a loan shark, people often find themselves permanently in debt, with late payment resulting in substantial penalties being added to the debt. As well as not having a consumer credit licence, loan sharks are often involved in other criminality and sometimes

coerce their victims into committing criminal offences as a way of repaying their debts.

Clients rarely admit to being indebted to a loan shark and often use money intended for essential expenditure in order to make their repayments. They may even claim that money is being used to repay a 'family friend'.

If an adviser discovers a client is a loan shark victim, it is likely s/he will be reluctant to report the matter, fearing for her/his own safety or that of her/his family. As ever, the decision as to the next step is the client's but it should be an informed one. The adviser could refer the client to the Illegal Money Lending Team (Tel: 0300 555 2222 in England or 0300 123 3311 in Wales). These can offer the client support and arrange to meet her/him at a safe venue (in the presence of the adviser, if necessary) to discuss what remedies are available, what action can be taken and the protection that can be provided.[7]

Debt management plans

A 'debt management plan' is an informal arrangement, under which the client agrees to repay her/his creditors. The term is usually used to describe an arrangement made on the client's behalf by a third party who also manages the plan. The arrangement normally involves an equitable distribution of the client's available income (after priority payments) (see p255). The client makes a single regular payment (usually monthly) to the third party, who may be:

- a debt management company. It negotiates the debt management plan, collects the payments from the client and distributes them to the creditors in return for a fee paid by the client (often referred to as 'fee chargers');
- the Consumer Credit Counselling Service or Payplan. They can arrange a debt management plan and distribute the payments to the client's creditors, but do not charge the client a fee. They are paid by the creditors through deducting a percentage of the money recovered (known as 'fair-share' arrangements). For this reason, they are part of the free money advice sector. Both have minimum criteria for setting up a plan (eg, relating to amount of available income) and can also help clients to set up individual voluntary arrangements (se p427).

If a client's agreed strategy is to make pro rata payments to her/his creditors (see p255), a debt management plan under which s/he only has to make one monthly payment instead of a number of individual payments may be in the client's best interests.

Note: some debt management companies do not deal with emergencies and/ or priority debts. The adviser will therefore need to assist the client to deal with these before s/he can be referred for a debt management plan.

Debt management companies have individual consumer credit licences and, from 6 April 2007, fall within the Financial Ombudsman Service's consumer credit jurisdiction. If a client is dissatisfied with the service provided, s/he should consider making a complaint.

3. **Strategies for dealing with non-priority debts**

This section describes the available strategies for non-priority debts. They are not mutually exclusive. The adviser may use several strategies to deal with each debt – eg, a moratorium of three months followed by a partial write-off and the freezing of interest/charges with instalments by equitable distribution. Alternatively, different strategies (or combinations of strategies) may be needed for individual debts – eg, some requests for write-offs, some token payments and one voluntary charge.

Strategy selection often is not a single process, but may be done initially and reviewed later. The criteria described here should be equally applicable to initial or review strategies. The strategy chosen for each debt will need to be reviewed:
- if a creditor refuses to accept a particular strategy; *or*
- at the end of the time agreed by the creditor. For example, the creditor may agree to accept no payments for six months and then review the position; *or*
- if the client's financial circumstances change.

Often strategies will not be accepted on first application (eg, write-offs – see p244) and debt advisers should always urge creditors several times to accept a realistic strategy. Second and third letters can be strengthened by details of how other creditors have come to agree to a particular strategy. If the adviser considers a creditor is not complying with its obligations under a relevant code of practice or Office of Fair Trading (OFT) guidance (eg, is not treating the client's individual and particular financial situation 'sympathetically and positively' or demonstrating understanding, due consideration and forbearance), s/he should consider using the creditor's complaints procedure and threaten to refer the case to the Financial Ombudsman Service (FOS) to resolve the matter in a 'fair and reasonable' way.

Clients should not routinely be advised to stop payments to all their non-priority creditors while negotiations are taking place. In many multiple debt cases, it will be appropriate for the client to reduce payments to non-priority creditors or even stop them altogether. If the client is able to make payments to non-priority creditors while still servicing her/his essential commitments, including priority debts, s/he should be advised to do so.

If s/he is unable to do so, the adviser should point out that the client's default will be registered with credit reference agencies and may eventually lead to court action by the creditor, but that it is still in the client's best interests not to make those payments because there is no, or very little, available income after meeting essential expenditure and payments to priority creditors.

A long period without any payments at all to creditors is undesirable, unless a strategy involving non-payment has been proposed in the meantime. On the other hand, a short period during which no payments are made may be inevitable while the adviser works out a strategy with the client.

Request a write-off

A write-off should be considerd if:

- there is no available income or capital and a client's circumstances are unlikely to improve in the foreseeable future (or may even worsen); *or*
- the debt is uneconomical for the creditor to collect – eg, a small amount is owed or the pro rata payment would be less than £1 a month (see p255); *or*
- there is some available income, but this will not repay the debt within a reasonable time (see also partial write-offs on p246); *or*
- the client's circumstances are exceptional and unlikely to improve – eg, s/he has a terminal illness or mental health problems that affect her capacity to make a contract (see p89).

A write-off means the creditor agrees not to collect any further payments and removes the account from its records. The client makes no further payments. If the debt is large, any realisable assets or equity in the client's home must be considered as it is unlikely that creditors will agree to write off the debts of 'asset-rich, income-poor' clients unless the circumstances are wholly exceptional. It is likely that, if the creditor took court action and the client could not make payment as ordered by the court, the creditor could either apply for a charging order against the equity in the client's home (see p301) or ask the court to make a bankruptcy order (see p444) so that goods owned by the client or the home could be sold.

The question of write-offs has generated much discussion among debt advisers. Every creditor recognises the need to write off some debts, and makes provision for this in its accounts and the interest rates it sets. Advisers, exposed to a society whose prevalent moral code is one which lays emphasis on the importance of repaying one's debts, may well have personal anxieties about requesting a write-off. These should not be allowed to prejudice advice. Clients, too, may be anxious about the consequences of this strategy, so the adviser may need to explain the reasoning behind the suggestion, and that it is being proposed to the creditor as the most economic and realistic solution available in order to financially rehabilitate the client. However, the decision whether or not to request a write-off is ultimately one for the client. A client who initially says s/he wants to pay something may change her/his mind in the light of creditors' responses to her/his financial difficulties and so the possibility of proposing this strategy to creditors should be kept under review.

Advantages

- It removes the financial and emotional stress caused by that debt.
- It enables the client to make a fresh start.
- It acknowledges that further action against the client is not appropriate.

Disadvantages

- Creditors will not agree easily to write off debts, particularly if the debt has been incurred recently.
- When creditors write off debts, they often report this to a credit reference agency. This is an agency that collects evidence, such as county court judgments or evictions, and sells details of individuals who have experienced these to creditors. If a debt is reported as written off, it may be difficult for a client to get credit in the future. For more details on credit reference agencies, see p8.
- Many creditors never formally agree to write off a debt, even when they have received a request to do so. They will take no further action on it and at some point will write it out of their accounts. This can mean that the client is left uncertain as to whether or not the creditor has agreed to her/his request, and s/he can be vulnerable either to a change of company policy or to pursuit of a debt if her/his circumstances improve.

Useful arguments

- The circumstances of the client will need to be outlined carefully and attention drawn to the fact that s/he has no property or goods of significant value, no income except benefits/low wages and there is no prospect of improvement in the foreseeable future. This will help creditors to see that court action is unlikely to be successful. Explain that if bankruptcy were pursued, the outcome would be the same. Medical evidence confirming, for example, the nature of any disability or that the client is unable to work may also be persuasive.
- Inform the creditor of the total amount of debt owing to all creditors to show the hopelessness of the client's situation.
- Most creditors have a set of criteria for deciding when to abandon debt recovery, which will be determined by the cost of recovering the money. The adviser should suggest that writing off a debt is likely to be the most economic solution for the creditor. For example, *The Lending Code* suggests that a write-off should be considered if the client's financial and personal circumstances are exceptional and unlikely to improve. The creditor must give reasons for refusing a write-off request and advisers should press for these to be provided as this may enable the adviser to ask the creditor to reconsider its position.
- Creditors may be more willing to write off a debt after repeatedly withholding action on the account for three or six months (see p252).
- It will be easier to get smaller debts written off.

Checklist for action

- Write to the creditor(s) proposing the strategy, enclosing any supporting evidence, and request written confirmation that the strategy is agreed.
- Advise the client to stop paying.
- A creditor may not initially accept a write-off. The adviser should ask the creditor to reconsider after, say, three to six months, and repeat the request at subsequent reviews.

Request a partial write-off

If there is some money available to meet a creditor's demands, but this will not pay off the whole debt in a realistic period of time (in line with what a court would consider reasonable), creditors can be asked to reduce the balance owing immediately or to accept agreed instalments for a set period of years, after which the balance will be written off.

Partial write-off should be seen as a means of coming to an arrangement similar to an individual voluntary arrangement and which accords broadly with what a court would order if an income payments order in bankruptcy application were being considered. A period of at least three to five years, but no more than seven to 10 years, should be suggested. A request should also be made that further interest is stopped (see p247). Partial write-off is appropriate when:

- there are no realisable assets or substantial equity that could be charged;
- the client's circumstances are such that s/he cannot repay the whole debt within a reasonable period of time;
- there is no expectation of capital or extra income becoming available soon.

Advantages

- It reduces the amount owed and gives the client a realistic target to aim for and, therefore, a framework in which s/he can regain a sense of control over her/his financial affairs.
- The client repays less money.

Disadvantages

- When creditors write off debts, they often report this to credit reference agencies and it may, therefore, be difficult for a person to get credit in the future.
- It may be difficult to get all creditors to agree to the strategy.

Useful arguments

- It can be argued that the creditor will receive more than if the client were made bankrupt, and thus it is quicker, cheaper and less stressful to the client for the creditor to limit demands to that amount now.
- A partial write-off is also very similar to a composition order in an administration order (see p421) or an individual voluntary arrangement (see

p427) and so creditors are only being asked to take a similar course of action to that taken in those legally binding situations, but on an informal basis. Again, as there are no attendant court/supervisor costs, the creditor is likely to see a higher return than in an administration order or individual voluntary arrangement.

- The creditor may be persuaded that it is better to go for something shorter term and realisable, rather than longer term but potentially expensive to collect and unlikely to be paid. Unless creditors reduce their demand to something the client can pay in the foreseeable future, the client is likely to lack the motivation to keep up with payments. It is unrealistic for both sides to set up repayment schemes which will last more than about five years and the likelihood is that such money will eventually be written off.
- If the creditor refuses to agree to this strategy initially, it is worth requesting it again after, say, 12 months of regular payments if there is still no improvement in the client's circumstances.

Checklist for action
- Agree with the client the amount of income available to creditors.
- Calculate offers and decide a payment period.
- Write to the creditor(s) proposing the strategy, with details of the offers and requesting written confirmation that this is accepted.
- Advise the client to start making payments. Consider direct debits or standing orders if the client has a current account.
- Request that interest or charges are stopped, using the arguments in the following section.
- Consider whether any steps need to be taken to ensure that the arrangement is legally binding on creditors (see full and final settlements on p249).

Request that interest is frozen or reduced

If a client is unable to pay the contractual payments due under an agreement, adding interest and other charges, especially if s/he is not even repaying any capital due, will only increase the total balance and the debt will never be repaid. This fact has long been recognised by the county court where statutory interest is not charged after judgment on debts regulated by the Consumer Credit Act (but see p293 for when interest can be charged after a judgment).

Whenever a repayment schedule of less than the original contractual payments is envisaged, or if no payment can be afforded at present, a request should be made to stop (or freeze) all interest and any other charges accruing on the account. This strategy should always be used in conjunction with another strategy.

The request to stop interest should be made in most cases immediately the client contacts a debt adviser. However, the adviser must explain to the creditor why it is considered necessary – eg, the payments the client is likely to be able to afford will not cover the ongoing interest.

The Lending Standards Board has issued guidance to creditors to consider reducing or freezing interest and charges.[8] Creditors often complain that advisers 'automatically request creditors to freeze interest in all cases'. Requests to freeze interest should be appropriate and justified. In cases where a creditor believes the level of the client's repayments warrants it, the creditor may refuse to freeze interest, but may instead agree to reduce it. If the loan is regulated by the Consumer Credit Act, an application for a time order may be appropriate (see p340).

Advantages
- Realistic repayment schedules can be created under which debts will be repaid in a known time.
- All payments made reduce the debt. The client can see that s/he is repaying her/his debts.

Disadvantages
- Creditors may not accept the strategy, particularly if there is substantial equity in a property or the client has realisable assets which it is reasonable to expect her/him to use to pay her/his debts.
- It is not appropriate for loans where all interest is added at the beginning of the loan and there are no default interest/charges. In these cases, a partial write-off may achieve the desired result.

Useful arguments
- If a county court judgment were awarded, in practice interest would be stopped for all regulated consumer credit agreements (see p65).
- Excessive default charges (ie, charges which are more than any actual or anticipated loss which the creditor has or may face as a result of the loss) are almost certainly unenforceable either as a penalty at common law or as an unfair contract term, and so the creditor should either reduce them or remove them altogether and should consider doing so retrospectively (see p91).
- It is a necessary incentive to the client because otherwise s/he will not be prepared to lose valuable income in pursuit of a completely hopeless goal.
- Many other creditors are being asked (or have agreed) to stop interest and, therefore, fairness demands that this creditor does too.
- Make any offer of payment conditional upon interest stopping.

Checklist for action
This strategy should always be used with another strategy.
- Write to the creditor and include a request to freeze interest and other charges, together with some justification for the request.
- Request written confirmation that this has been done.

- If the strategy is not successful initially, ask the creditor to reconsider. It may be useful to provide evidence of other creditors' agreement to freeze or reduce interest and other charges.

Offer a reduced capital sum in full and final settlement

If there is available capital or saleable assets, or if the client will have such assets in the near future (eg, because s/he intends to sell a house for reasons unrelated to the debt, or a third party, such as a friend or relative, has a lump sum s/he is willing to give to the creditor), the creditor may accept an offer of an amount less than that which is actually due as early settlement. This is particularly likely if there is little or no available income and the client's financial position is unlikely to improve or may even worsen. Creditors are likely to recognise that acceptance of a cash lump sum makes commercial sense. When the client's income is low and unlikely to improve, it could be an attractive alternative to waiting to see if s/he gets more over a long period. If there is more than one creditor, lump sums should usually be apportioned between them in proportion to the amount owing to each.

Ask the client if there are essentials s/he needs to purchase, or essential repairs that need to be carried out, before the lump sum is allocated to creditors.

The key to using this strategy successfully is to ensure that the lump-sum payment is not made until the creditor has agreed in writing to accept this in full and final settlement of all the money owed. Ideally, no payments should be made until all creditors have agreed and offers can – initially at least – be made on this basis, but advisers should be prepared to adopt a flexible approach to prevent the whole strategy from failing. For example, creditors who are reluctant to accept may be persuaded by knowing that other creditors have already agreed to accept it. Other creditors may threaten the whole strategy by demanding more than their fair share, leaving insufficient funds to tempt the remaining creditors.

There is no set amount that needs to be offered and, in fact, a promise by a creditor to accept part-payment is not a legally binding contract unless the client has provided what the law regards as fresh 'consideration' for the creditor's promise to forgo payment of the balance. The FOS, however, may take the view that a creditor that goes back on its word is not behaving 'fairly and reasonably' unless the client misrepresented her/his true financial situation.

There will be a legally binding agreement if either:
- an arrangement is made with all the client's unsecured creditors; *or*
- the funds are made available by a third party (eg, a relative) and the offer is made by her/him on the client's behalf; *or*
- the agreement is embodied in a formal document known as a 'deed'. The client will need to be referred to a solicitor if s/he wants a deed drawn up – eg, if there is any doubt about the trustworthiness of a particular creditor.

Advantages

- The client pays less than s/he would if repaying over a longer term.
- The client has the opportunity of a fresh start.
- It is a more immediate and convenient solution than setting up a repayment schedule over a number of years.
- Even if not all creditors accept, the client's total indebtedness will be reduced and this may in turn enable another strategy to be adopted to deal with these.

Disadvantages

- The client loses the advantage of having a lump sum which could have been used for other purposes.
- Once aware of the existence of a lump sum, the creditor may attempt court action to obtain all the money for itself.
- If all available funds are distributed among only some of the client's creditors, the client may subsequently have little room to manoeuvre if put under pressure by other creditors.

Useful arguments

- Contact the creditor before the money is available and suggest that this is the only chance that the client will have of paying a substantial amount and that because the client wants to pay her/his debts, s/he is prepared to hand all (or if there are several debts to be treated in this way, a proportionate share) of the money over to the creditor.
- It is worth pointing out that the creditor is not going to get more by refusing the offer and taking enforcement action, and that acceptance of the offer makes more commercial sense than the client's continuing to make small payments over a long period of time. Such an arrangement may have to be made with senior staff in a creditor organisation and the adviser should ensure s/he is writing or speaking to senior credit control managers.

Checklist for action

- Write to the creditor(s) with details of the offer and request acceptance in full and final settlement to be confirmed in writing.
- If the money is coming from a third party, it should be made clear that the offer is being made by her/him on behalf of the client.
- Consider specialist legal help to draw up the agreement.
- Once written confirmation is received, advise the client (or third party) to send the payment(s).
- Any covering letter sent with a cheque should explain exactly what it is for and state that it is in 'full and final settlement'. Cashing a cheque sent 'in full and final settlement' is never binding on a creditor unless it has previously agreed to accept it on this basis (although cashing a cheque is strong evidence of acceptance unless it is accompanied by a swift rejection of the offer).

- If money is being made available from the sale of a house, it may be necessary to obtain a solicitor's undertaking that the money will be paid to the creditor once the house is sold.
- If fewer than 25 per cent in value of a client's creditors will not agree a full and final settlement, even though the remaining creditors have accepted the offer, the client could consider an individual voluntary arrangement (IVA) – see p427). However, because of the costs involved, the creditors will receive less money. This could be pointed out and the creditors asked to reconsider their position.

In the unlikely event of a creditor threatening to go back on a full and final settlement if the client has made the payment, specialist advice should be sought.

Offer payment by a capital sum and instalments

When a client has capital or assets together with stable available income, but there are substantial arrears, the threat of further action can often be avoided by paying a single capital sum towards the arrears and then paying instalments towards part or all of the contractual payments. This often needs to be linked to another strategy, particularly freezing interest/charges (see p247) or a partial write-off (see p246). This is different from paying a capital sum in full and final settlement in that the payments will have to continue. It could be the fall-back position if a full and final strategy is rejected because the amount offered is insufficient to gain acceptance from the client's creditors and there is a reasonable amount of surplus income available.

Advantages
- The creditor is no longer pressing.
- Payments made towards the debt out of available income will be lower than otherwise.

Disadvantages
- The flexibility to use the capital sum elsewhere is lost.

Useful arguments
- If this tactic is being used to prevent imminent court action, the adviser can argue that the creditor will obtain its money more quickly than by going to court, and more money will be available to repay the debt as there will be fewer costs. An agreement such as this will have to be made in writing.

Checklist for action
- Contact the creditor proposing the strategy and request acceptance in writing.
- Calculate the instalments on a pro rata basis (see p255).

- Once written confirmation is received, advise the client to send payment of the capital sum, followed by regular instalments. It may be helpful for the client to set up a direct debit or standing order for these if possible.
- Ensure that interest is stopped. If not, consider advising the client to withhold instalments until agreement is given to stop interest.
- An IVA could be considered as an option if most, but not all, of the client's creditors will not accept the strategy (see p251 and p427).

Holding tactics (moratorium)

It may sometimes be important for the adviser to gain time for the client when:
- there is some available income, but this is immediately required to deal with priority debts;
- there is no available income, but shortly there will be;
- available assets are being sold;
- the full situation is not yet known.

There are two types of holding tactic (also known as a 'moratorium'):
- **Asking creditors to suspend collection or enforcement action.** Paragraph 4(n) of the *Credit Services Association Code of Practice* provides a 30-day 'breathing space' if requested by an advice agency. Paragraphs 201–203 of *The Lending Code* make similar provisions for credit card debts. Paragraphs 7.12 and 3.7(m) of the OFT's *Irresponsible Lending Guidance* and *Debt Collection Guidance* respectively extend this to all cases in which an adviser is assisting a client to agree a repayment plan.

  It may be useful to request a short delay if the adviser needs to check a credit agreement or its enforceability. Some agencies write automatically to all creditors asking them to withhold action for a short period when their advice is first sought. This is not necessary if a strategy can be formulated quickly or if the debt adviser will be asking the creditor to write off the debt or to accept no payments for three months. It is wasteful of resources to employ this device automatically and can increase the stress faced by the client, as it lengthens the time before agreement with creditors about a long-term strategy is reached, and may lead to creditors routinely refusing requests.

  If a delay is needed because balances are required before a strategy can be implemented, ask the client to contact the creditors to obtain these where possible.

  If a debt is queried or disputed, the creditor (or debt collector) should investigate/provide details (as appropriate) and should cease collection activity in the meantime.[9]
- **Asking creditors to accept no payments for a specified period.** If no money is available at present to pay any non-priority debts, the creditor should be asked to accept no payments for three or six months and then review the situation.

This is invariably a temporary strategy and so will be subject to review, usually after three or six months. It will always be used with another strategy – eg, asking a creditor to withhold for three months and then follow this with a request for a write-off. This can be useful where it is known that the creditor is unlikely to accept a write-off immediately. If a request is made to a creditor to withhold any action and accept no payments, the creditor must always be asked, at the same time, to stop interest/charges in order to prevent the debt increasing even further.

The length of time for which the adviser requests no payments will depend on:

- any known future changes in the client's financial position which might allow payments to begin;
- the length of time needed to repay priority debts;
- the stress faced by the client and how much breathing space s/he needs.

If the creditor agrees to withhold action and collect no payments for six months, it gives the client a substantial period of relief.

However, as this strategy can never be a permanent solution, it means that a request for a six-month delay prolongs the process of reaching one.

Advantages

- Time can give the adviser space to gather all the necessary facts and work out the best strategy.
- It removes the immediate pressure from the client, and enables payments to be made for priority debts.
- It gets creditors used to the idea that there are problems, but does not leave them in the dark.
- Almost as a matter of routine, many creditors will accept a request from a debt advice agency to withhold action for a short period.

Disadvantages

- It does not actually solve anything. Some creditors will refuse to stop interest and thus the debt grows while no action is taken.
- It can create extra work for the adviser.

Useful arguments

- Explain that considerable debts have arisen and outline the client's circumstances.
- Explain that time is required for professional debt advice.

Checklist for action

- Telephone/write to the creditor to explain the situation and request written confirmation that the account is held in abeyance. Enclose a financial statement if requesting that more than a month's payments are withheld.
- Ensure that interest/charges will be stopped.
- Advise the client not to make payments.

Offer token payments

When there is little available income, no assets or capital and the situation is unlikely to change, but it is impossible to get agreement on any other strategy, payment by instalments of a nominal or token nature may be necessary to satisfy the administrative systems of a creditor and may be the only way to prevent it from taking further action.

Clients initially seeking advice often want to make token payments rather than withholding payments or asking creditors to write off their debts, out of fear or ignorance of enforcement action, or because of previous harassment by creditors, or because they want to make some payment, however small, towards their debts. The adviser must ensure that clients do not make payments they cannot afford or which are at the expense of making payments towards their essential expenditure and any priority debts. A nominal or token payment is usually £1 a month. Even £5, £20 or more a month is regarded as a token payment by some creditors because, in reality, the debt will never be repaid at that rate.

The strategy need not be used for all creditors and should only be offered as a last resort where the creditor has refused to either write off the debt or accept no payments, or to freeze interest/charges and where court action by the creditor would be undesirable. The creditor must be asked to agree to take no further action and to stop interest in return for token payments being made. Token payments do not resolve the client's debt problems and so it is necessary to review the strategy at a later date to choose a more suitable long-term option.

If a creditor has already taken court action, but there is no available income and the court is unwilling to order no payments, the client will need to make a token offer to pay by instalments (eg, £1 a month) in order to prevent further enforcement action.

Token payments are essentially a short-term strategy. *The Lending Code* recommends that offers of token payments may be accepted where the client has demonstrated that there is no available income for non-priority creditors, but there is a realistic prospect of her/his circumstances improving.[10] This guidance reflects not only the difficulty of persuading creditors to accept no payments at all but also the belief of creditors that, firstly, people can always find some money and, secondly, that something will turn up.

All advice must be in the best interests of the client and it is not generally in the client's best interests to make payments at a higher level than s/he can afford or to make any payments at all if the client either has no surplus income or a deficit budget. However, if a creditor will not agree, for example, to a moratorium and/or freeze interest/charges unless token payments are made, the adviser must consider whether it is nevertheless in the client's best interests to make those payments.

Many clients whose financial circumstances mean that they are only able to afford token payments may be eligible for a debt relief order or should consider bankruptcy as a debt relief option (see Chapter 15).

Advantages
- Paying a token amount may be the only way to obtain a creditor's agreement to take no further action and stop interest/charges.
- The client feels s/he is paying something towards her/his debts and creditors can see the habit of payment being re-established.

Disadvantages
- It uses up income that is not really available.
- It encourages creditors to take an unrealistic view of people's ability to pay.
- It can be expensive for the client as it may cost as much in postage and other charges to make the payment as the payment is worth.
- The debt will never be repaid at this rate and it hangs over the client.
- Creditors can continue to apply pressure on clients to pay more.

Useful arguments
- A request for payments may be made by the creditor after the adviser has made it clear there is no (or only a nominal amount of) available income as shown by the financial statement. The adviser should explain that, in fact, the only payment possible is a token payment because the client is cutting back on essential spending, such as food or fuel, in order to make the payment.
- If creditors are threatening court action, draw their attention to any recent low judgment amounts awarded by the county court in similar cases and suggest that even if they go to the trouble of going to court, they will get no more than a nominal amount (or a general stay).

Checklist for action
- Telephone/write to the creditor and await written confirmation of the strategy.
- Ensure that further action, and interest and other charges, are stopped.
- Advise the client to make payments. Ask for a payment book if this facilitates payments without cost.
- Review at an agreed date with the client.

Equitable distribution of available income (pro rata payments)

If there is available income, a number of debts, and no capital or realisable assets, this income should be distributed among all the non-priority creditors in a fair way. Apportioning the available income fairly is best done by a method known either as 'equitable distribution' or 'pro rata payments', where the amount of each instalment is directly proportionate to the total amount owing to that particular creditor (see example below). Clients who are using the CASHflow self-help process (see p18) are likely to be making offers on this basis and so may find the information in this section useful.

Some creditors seek a distribution that is proportionate to the payments due under their agreement rather than the capital outstanding. This is popular with those creditors that lend smaller amounts over short periods at very high rates of interest. Such arrangements should be rejected because:

- this is not the way in which a court would define an equitable offer if an administration order (see p419) or other insolvency procedures were being considered;
- the creditors owed large sums are unlikely to agree to it and may go to court and obtain an order for repayments based on capital outstanding;
- short-term lenders of small sums have already allowed for the high risk associated with such lending and this is reflected in the rates of interest charged.

The adviser must calculate the amount due to each creditor per week or month. The calculation is based on the following formula:

Amount owed to creditor ÷ total amount owed x total income available for distribution

---

Example

The client owes money to three creditors:

Creditor A	£1,000
Creditor B	£800
Creditor C	£250
Total amount owing	**£2,050**

(The client's total available income is £12 a month.)

Calculation:

Creditor A	$1,000 \div 2,050 \times 12 = £5.85$ a month
Creditor B	$800 \div 2,050 \times 12 = £4.70$ a month
Creditor C	$250 \div 2,050 \times 12 = £1.45$ a month
Total repayments to creditors	**$= £12.00$ a month**

(Amounts may be rounded up or down for convenience, but not if this results in payments which the client cannot afford.)

If the adviser does not use the common financial statement or some other computer-based financial statement which automatically calculates pro rata offers, this sum must be worked out for each creditor. Even if the exact balances are not known, it may be worth calculating a distribution on the basis of good estimates, as the weekly variation will probably be very small and may be acceptable to creditors.

If the calculation gives rise to a very low payment to a particular creditor (eg, less than £1 per month), the adviser may wish to include in the offer letter a request that, in view of the high collection costs for such a small sum, the creditor should consider writing off the debt (see p244) or at least agreeing to a moratorium (see p252). Any payment arrangement must be sustainable and so, when calculating the amount of available income on offer to creditors, the adviser should ensure some leeway in the financial statement to cope with unexpected events (eg, short periods of sickness) so that payments can still be maintained.

In paragraphs 3.27 and 3.28(b) of its *Debt Management Guidance* the OFT points out that clients should not usually be advised to cancel contractual payments to their creditors before a debt repayment plan has been agreed or make payments that do not cover ongoing interest or other charges unless it is demonstrably in their best interests – eg, if someone has insufficient available income due to the need to meet essential expenditure and/or payments to priority creditors.

Unless the client has sufficient available income to be able to maintain the contractual payments on these debts, as well as servicing her/his other debts, it will be in the client's best interests to offer pro rata payments, provided this is accompanied by a request for any ongoing interest and any charges to be stopped so that each payment made by the client actually reduces the debt. On the other hand, if the creditor refuses to stop interest or reduce it sufficiently, pro rata payments will almost certainly not be in the client's best interests and the creditor must be urged to reconsider, or the strategy reviewed with the client.

It is usual to send to each creditor details of the amounts owed to all creditors, together with the offers made. This should not be done if the client wishes confidentiality to be maintained. However, it will be helpful for the creditors to know that they have been given the whole financial position of the client as they would in an administration order or bankruptcy. If the creditor has already obtained a court order that is higher than the offer calculated, the client should consider applying to the court on Form N245 to vary the order if s/he cannot obtain the creditor's written agreement to accept the offer made and to take no further action to enforce the debt (see p317 for how to do this).

Advantages
- Equitable distribution is widely accepted by the credit industry. Many creditors think it is the only strategy that money advisers should use.
- It ensures that all non-priority debts are dealt with together.
- It is based on court practices. This is how money is distributed to creditors when an administration order is granted (see p419).
- Many creditors automatically freeze interest/charges once an offer is accepted.

Disadvantages

- A client may be left with little financial flexibility and money only for basics.
- Unless coupled with a partial write-off (see p246), many debts may take years to clear.
- If the payments do not cover ongoing interest/charges the debt will never be repaid.

Useful arguments

- The strongest argument in favour of this strategy is its fairness. It can be presented as a business-like response to a difficult situation, ensuring that every creditor will be treated in a way which will give them the maximum possible amount.
- Paragraphs 7.16 and 7.18 of the OFT's *Irresponsible Lending Guidance* states that creditors should allow for 'alternative, affordable, payment amounts when a reasonable proposal is made', and should not unreasonably require that 'all arrears are paid in one payment, or in unduly large amounts and/or within an unreasonably short period'.
- It is exactly what would happen if a court were to grant an administration order or in bankruptcy, and is the kind of order which a court should make every time it makes an instalment order. The creditor cannot expect to do better.
- This strategy has often been used successfully where it can be shown that the person is starting to pay her/his creditors and wishes to treat them all fairly. In addition, consideration should be given to asking for a partial write-off where offers will be paid for two or three years only (see p246 for details).
- If the creditor subscribes to the British Bankers' Association/Money Advice Trust common financial statement (see p51), it has been agreed that 'in general' a pro rata offer should be accepted (but not necessarily that interest/charges will be frozen). Non-acceptance would suggest the creditor has other information about the client, which it should be asked to disclose.
- Many creditors now have strict criteria for automatically accepting repayment offers based either on a minimum payment or percentage of the debt or repayment over a maximum period in exchange for concessions on interest/charges.

Checklist for action

- Agree with the client the amount of income available for creditors.
- Calculate offers to creditors. Consider a partial write-off where the suggested repayment period will not clear the debts within a reasonable time (see p246).
- Write to the creditors with offers. Suggest a write-off where offers are low.
- Ensure that interest and other charges are stopped.
- Advise the client to make payments (consider direct debit or standing order if the client has a current account). Ask for a payment book if this allows payment

without cost. The client should not wait until all the creditors have accepted before starting to make payments.

- Consider whether a referral to a non-fee-charging debt management company might be in the client's best interests – ie, s/he would have to make one monthly payment for distribution among her/his creditors (see p242).

Consolidate the debts

Debt consolidation involves the client either taking out a new loan or increasing existing borrowing in order to pay off multiple debts. Debts can be consolidated by:

- an unsecured loan. These are likely to be small and so of limited potential;
- a further advance from an existing mortgage or secured lender, also secured on the client's property;
- a secured loan from a lender other than the existing mortgage provider, in addition to the existing mortgage;
- a remortgage with a new lender to replace any existing mortgage or secured loan;
- the transfer of balances to a credit card (including the use of credit card cheques).

Debt consolidation loans are the subject of extensive advertising, particularly on television. Much of this advertising encourages people to borrow extra cash to have more spending money as well as paying off their debts. For people in financial difficulties, this is likely to make the situation worse. There is some evidence of financial institutions offering consolidation loans to their customers as the only solution to their financial difficulties and solely to clear debts owed to them, so placing them in an advantageous position over the client's other creditors.

Paragraph 3.6(b) of the OFT's *Debt Collection Guidance* states that it is an unfair practice to pressurise a client into taking on further borrowing in order to raise funds to pay off debts.

Clients who are not in arrears and can meet their monthly commitments have the option of either carrying on with their existing agreements or refinancing them individually on more advantageous terms. However, for the average client struggling to meet her/his commitments, the other options discussed in this *Handbook* are likely to be more suitable. The client should always be advised to obtain independent financial advice.

Advantages

- Multiple agreements are replaced by a single agreement. The client only has to deal with one creditor.
- The consolidation loan is likely to be on better terms than the agreements it replaces, such as lower interest rates and monthly repayments.

- Where the balance transfer is on the basis of a low or zero interest rate and the client can settle the balance before any balance transfer offer expires, the flexibility of a credit card enables consolidation to take place without incurring any additional costs.
- The client's credit rating can be improved or the creditors prevented from registering defaults by the debts being repaid.

Disadvantages

- Debt consolidation often involves replacing unsecured non-priority debts with a secured priority debt with the client's property at risk if s/he defaults.
- Loans to clients with impaired credit ratings (non-status loans) are likely to be at higher rates of interest than those available to people with a clean credit record (status loans).
- There are usually costs associated with switching debts – eg, brokers' fees and early settlement charges.
- Although debt consolidation tends to involve lower monthly payments, it is often over an extended period, increasing the total amount payable by the client.
- Many debt consolidation loans are refinanced before running their full term (a process known as 'churning'), which means that the client often has to borrow more as most of the repayments on the original loan will have been interest rather than capital and there will be early settlement charges. There may also be further costs (eg, a broker's fee), which will often be added to the new loan.

Equity release loans

An equity release or lifetime mortgage enables a property-owning client to release equity from her/his home. It is secured on the client's property and is a way of raising capital to repay debts. The term of the loan is the client's lifetime, at the end of which all the capital becomes due. The interest is rolled up and the client is not required to pay anything while s/he is alive. These loans are only available to clients over 60 and the older the client is the more s/he can borrow (depending on the amount of equity in the property). The interest rate is usually fixed. If at the time of death there is a shortfall because there is no longer equity, the lender must write the outstanding balance off and cannot pursue it from other funds the client may have in her/his estate.

This type of loan may involve the conversion of unsecured borrowing into secured borrowing and is only appropriate if there is plenty of equity in the property. It will be most useful if the client is finding it particularly stressful owing money to a number of different creditors, or if creditors are proving difficult to negotiate with. Clients must always be advised to obtain independent financial advice.

Advantages

- The loan prevents further action by the creditors.
- It may be a means of releasing equity from the house to use for other purposes, such as insulation or heating, which in turn can reduce living costs.

Disadvantages

- The equity in the home is reduced by the value of the loan and will be steadily eroded by the accruing interest.
- On the client's death, the property will have to be sold to repay the loan, which may result in dependants who lived with the client being left homeless.

Checklist for action

- Advise the client to obtain independent financial advice.
- Ensure the client obtains full details about the terms and conditions and the cost of the loan before signing any agreements.
- Inform creditors of the proposal and ask them to take no further action to enable the loan to be set up.

Selling the home

When there is no available income, capital or realisable assets other than a home, sale may be considered. It should not be considered if the financial situation is likely to improve or if the sale of the home would result in homelessness. It is only appropriate as a way of dealing with non-priority debts if there is sufficient equity to satisfy most creditors' demands and to cover the costs of selling and moving, and when the stress of debts is creating unacceptable problems for the household.

The sale of a house is often recommended to people who are in debt as an easy way out of the situation, but it should be remembered that courts rarely order a property to be sold to satisfy unsecured borrowing and only after a charging order (see p301) has been made and an order for sale subsequently applied for (see p307), or a bankruptcy order made. If, however, an expensive house can be sold and a more modest one, which would nonetheless satisfy the client's needs, can be bought, this can be an acceptable way of coping with a debt problem and perhaps having money left over for other purposes as well.

A client may have been advised (sometimes by family or friends) that s/he has no alternative other than to sell her/his house and s/he will, therefore, approach an adviser at a stage where this process has already begun. By examining the other strategies outlined here, it may be possible to demonstrate that the sale of the house in these circumstances is not the only option. The state of the housing market may also mean that this strategy is not easily achievable.

If a local authority or housing association re-houses people following a sale of their home, it will normally only do so if it is clear that the sale is the only means to prevent eviction. Some local authorities still consider that the sale of a house makes someone intentionally homeless and, therefore, not eligible for rehousing under homelessness legislation. However, the code of guidance for local authorities states that a person should not be treated as intentionally homeless if her/his house was sold because of financial difficulties, and advisers should draw attention to this if necessary.[11]

A successful mortgage rescue (see p212) may mean that funds are raised for non-priority creditors.

Advantages
- It can clear the debts.
- It may raise capital for other purposes.
- The client may see it as providing the opportunity for a fresh start.

Disadvantages
- It releases equity held in the property to satisfy unsecured creditors in a way a court may not order.
- It may not be possible to find alternative suitable housing.
- Moving house is a major disruption and costs a lot of money.
- The client may lose money if the housing market is depressed.
- The sale may take a long time or, in the midst of a recession, prove impossible, and the benefits of choosing this strategy may be lost.

Useful arguments
- Creditors will receive a lump sum, either paying the debt in full or partially in full and final settlement (see p249).

Checklist for action
- Discuss the pros and cons of selling a house with the client.
- Telephone/write to creditors to inform them of the strategy and obtain written confirmation that they will take no further action.
- Advise the client to put the house on the market with a reliable estate agent.
- Check that suitable alternative accommodation is available.
- Once it has been decided to put the house on the market, letters should be written informing the creditors of this and asking them to withhold interest charges or any other action until sale prices are available. Creditors may require a letter from an estate agent and, if a confirmation of a request to sell a property is available, this can be photocopied and sent. They may also want a letter from the client's solicitor confirming her/his share of the proceeds of sale will be forwarded directly to them.

Voluntary charge

Occasionally, but only as the 'lesser of two evils', it is advisable to turn an unsecured loan into a secured one in order to prevent any further action being taken. This is a very high-risk strategy and should not be undertaken lightly. It is described in detail on p221.

4. **Court-based strategies**

General stay

If a court order has been made, or is about to be made, and there is no available income, capital or assets, the county court can make an order for a general stay of judgment or enforcement. See p319 for an explanation of the court's power to make such an order and how the adviser can help the client make an application for no payment.

Administration order

If a client already has at least one county court (or High Court) judgment against her/him and her/his total debts do not exceed the limit for an administration order (currently £5,000), s/he can apply to the county court for the court to 'administer' payments to all her/his creditors. The client makes one monthly payment to the court, which will divide it equitably among all creditors. See p419 for details.

Bankruptcy and debt relief orders

Bankruptcy is a legal procedure in which the inability of a client to pay her/his debts is acknowledged and the majority of unsecured creditors can no longer pursue their debts, which are eventually written off. A third party (known as the trustee in bankruptcy) takes over the handling of the client's financial affairs for the benefit of her/his creditors. The trustee will distribute a proportion of any available income and/or capital resources to creditors. Bankruptcy may be a suitable strategy for a client if:
- debts have arisen which creditors will not write off;
- s/he does not own a home or has little or negative equity;
- s/he does not have any available assets or capital;
- s/he has a low available income compared with the amount of debt, which means it would take many years to repay her/his creditors.

Although not strictly a court-based option, a debt relief order operates in a similar way to bankruptcy and may be an appropriate option for clients who have:
- total debts of £15,000 or less;
- available income of £50 a month or less;
- gross assets worth £300 or less (the client can also own a motor vehicle worth less than £1,000).

See Chapter 15 for further details, including the advantages, disadvantages, consequences and procedures involved in bankruptcy.

Individual voluntary arrangement

An individual voluntary arrangement is a means whereby a client can protect her/himself from further action from creditors by entering into a legally binding arrangement with them, supervised by an insolvency practitioner. They are often described as informal bankruptcy and should be considered before bankruptcy itself. See Chapter 15 for further details.

Time order

An application for a time order may be appropriate either to prevent the creditor from obtaining a judgment or to freeze interest or other charges. See p340 for further details.

Notes

1. Choosing a strategy

1 OFT, *Debt Management Guidance,* March 2012
2 See J Phipps, 'It's Debt Jim, But Not As We Know It', *Adviser* 88
3 OFT, *Debt Collection Guidance,* October 2011, para 3.15(b)(i)
4 See J Kruse, 'The Death of Pro Rata?', *Adviser* 115

2. The general approach to non-priority debts

5 OFT, *Debt Collection Guidance,* October 2011, paras 3.7(b) and (i); OFT, *Irresponsible Lending Guidance,* February 2011, paras 7.3, 7.4 and 7.18
6 See D Shields and M van Rooyen, 'Square Peg Debts', *Adviser* 99
7 See also P Richardson, 'Help Us Stop Loan Sharks Now', *Adviser* 141

3. Strategies for dealing with non-priority debts

8 *The Lending Code,* March 2011, paras 224–27
9 OFT, *Debt Collection Guidance,* October 2011, paras 3.8(i) and (k). The *Credit Services Association Code of Practice* contains similar provisions in para 4(n)
10 *The Lending Code,* March 2011, para 213
11 Department for Communities and Local Government, *Homelessness Code of Guidance for Local Authorities,* July 2006, s11.18. There is similar guidance in Wales.

Chapter 10

The county court

This chapter covers:
1. Introduction (below)
2. Before starting court action (p266)
3. Taking court action (p270)
4. Court fees (p273)
5. Time limits (p274)
6. Appeals and adjournments (p276)

---

1. Introduction

The majority of cases involving debt are dealt with by a network of county courts throughout England and Wales. Cases are heard by district judges and circuit judges, assisted by part-time judges, with some decisions being delegated to court staff. Judges are drawn from the ranks of experienced barristers and solicitors. The county court was originally intended to provide a cheap and simple system for the recovery of small debts, but its jurisdiction has gradually increased.

The county courts derive their powers from the County Courts Act 1984, as amended. Since 26 April 1999, the Civil Procedure Rules 1998 (as amended) have governed the procedures in the county court.

The Ministry of Justice and HM Courts and Tribunals Service (HMCTS) are the government agencies responsible for the courts. HMCTS publishes various leaflets and guides on court procedure and these are available free from court offices and www.justice.gov.uk/forms/hmcts. There is also a Courts Charter, a series of leaflets covering all the courts and offices run by HMCTS, which sets out the standards of performance court users can expect and how to complain. All forms of discrimination should be challenged and taken up with the court as part of the debt adviser's social policy work.

The court manager and her/his staff are responsible for carrying out the court's administrative functions – eg, processing applications and fixing hearing dates. It is a good idea for debt advisers to establish a working relationship with their local court. Many courts operate users' groups and/or court desks for unrepresented parties. Debt advisers have no right to represent their clients in courts except at hearings allocated to the small claims track (see p297), but judges have increasingly recognised the value of such representation and rarely refuse to allow debt advisers to speak on behalf of their clients. However, only legal representatives can sign court forms on behalf of clients.[1]

2. **Before starting court action**

The Civil Procedure Rules include pre-action protocols and a pre-action conduct practice direction. These are codes of practice that the parties are expected to follow before starting court action. There is currently no protocol for debt cases. There are separate protocols for possession claims for rent arrears and for mortgage arrears. Regardless of whether there is a protocol for the specific type of case, the practice direction expects the parties to act 'reasonably and proportionately' in exchanging sufficient information to enable them to understand each other's position, make informed decisions and to attempt to resolve the matter without starting proceedings, including considering the use of alternative dispute resolution (see p267).[2]

The Civil Procedure Rules (including the protocols and practice direction) are available at www.justice.gov.uk/courts/procedure-rules and are published in *The Civil Court Practice*.[3] This is an expensive two-volume publication (plus a separate volume containing prescribed forms) which, like its predecessor, is known as the 'Green Book' and is published annually with supplements. In addition to the rules, the Green Book contains annotations and commentary, tables summarising various common procedures, details of court costs and fees, the pre-action protocols and excerpts from relevant legislation.

Parties to a potential dispute should follow a reasonable procedure, which intended to avoid litigation. This should usually include:

- the creditor writing to give details of the claim (a 'letter before claim');
- the client giving a detailed written response within a reasonable period (14 days is suggested in the case of undisputed debts);
- the client acknowledging the letter within 14 days if s/he cannot provide a detailed response within that period and then providing a full response within 30 days if third-party involvement is required (or possibly longer if specialist advice is required).

Two annexes to the practice direction provide more detailed guidance. Annex A is intended to apply in cases where there is no specific pre-action protocol and the debt is likely to be disputed. It is not intended to apply to undisputed debt claims. Annex B sets out specific information that should be provided in a debt claim by a company against an individual:

- details of how the money can be paid – eg, payment methods and the address to which it can be sent;

- that the client can contact the creditor to discuss repayment options and provide contact details;
- the availability of free, independent advice and assistance from organisations listed in Annex B. The creditor should allow the client a 'reasonable time' (14 days is suggested) to get that advice. Annex B discourages this if the client has previously obtained advice or has failed to do so after asking for time.

If the practice direction is not complied with, the court can 'stay' (ie, suspend) the proceedings until the required steps have been taken or make an order not to allow costs or to pay costs to the other party (see p296). The court is not concerned with minor or technical infringements and will look at the overall effect of the non-compliance on the other party when deciding whether to impose sanctions.

There is no requirement to exchange documents in all cases. If the creditor is aware of a potential dispute, Annex A stipulates that the letter before claim should contain a considerable amount of information and detail. If the creditor is not aware of a potential dispute, it merely has to comply with the lesser requirements of Annex B (it is likely that the above information required by Annex B will have been provided at an early stage in the process). If a client who receives an Annex B letter before a claim disputes it, her/his response must contain the level of information and detail to comply with Annex A. It is only then that the creditor must comply with a request for copies of documents (or explain why they will not be provided).

The wording of the practice direction suggests that:

- creditors who follow Annex B only are unlikely to be criticised by the courts for failing to comply with Annex A (unless the creditor is aware of a potential dispute);
- creditors are unlikely to be sanctioned for taking court action if the client has failed to respond to the letter before the claim (regardless of whether the claim is disputed or not);
- the courts will not support 'fishing' expeditions for possible defences through requests for documents, unless a potential dispute and the basis for it have been identified.

If a creditor's claim is disputed, this should be made clear at the earliest opportunity in order to obtain maximum disclosure from the creditor about its case. This is in order for it to be in accordance with Annex A and also to persuade the creditor to avoid court proceedings in favour of other methods of resolving the dispute.[4]

Alternative dispute resolution

There is an increasing emphasis on the use of alternative dispute resolution, with some courts offering the services of local court-based mediation schemes. The objective is to encourage parties to a dispute to use some form of alternative resolution and, even after a county court claim has been issued, the court can 'stay' (ie, halt) the proceedings to enable the parties to attempt to settle their dispute by mediation or other means. Although the courts have no power to compel parties to do so, when deciding the amount of any costs to be awarded, they can take into account the efforts made before and during the proceedings to resolve the dispute (see p296).

Using the Financial Ombudsman Service

The Financial Ombudsman Service (FOS) is a form of alternative dispute resolution and, if a complaint has been (or could be) referred to the FOS, the court may agree to stay the proceedings.[5]

The FOS has been able to consider complaints against banks and building societies since December 2001 and against all other holders of consumer credit licences since 6 April 2007 (known as its 'consumer credit jurisdiction'). This means that debt collectors, sub-prime lenders and debt purchasers are all likely to be covered. The FOS is not a regulator (these are the Financial Services Authority and the Office of Fair Trading). Its role is to resolve individual disputes between clients and businesses.

Businesses that fall within FOS jurisdiction are required to have a written complaints procedure in place, and to publicise and operate it. The FOS cannot consider a complaint unless the business has had an opportunity to deal with it first. The client should therefore initially complain in writing to the company concerned. On receipt of a complaint, the creditor should:
● acknowledge the complaint promptly;
● keep the client informed of progress; *and*
● send a 'final response' in writing within eight weeks.

A 'final response' is one which:
● either accepts the complaint and offers redress; *or*
● does not accept the complaint, but offers redress anyway; *or*
● rejects the complaint and gives reasons for this; *and*
● informs the client that if s/he remains dissatisfied, s/he has a right to refer the matter to the FOS within six months, and encloses a consumer leaflet.

If no final response has been received after eight weeks, the client can refer the complaint to the FOS, provided it is within its jurisdiction (see p269). Even if it does not contain referral rights, provided a letter is clearly the business's last word on the matter, the FOS will accept the complaint even if fewer than eight weeks have elapsed.

Unless the circumstances are exceptional or the business does not object, a complaint to the FOS must be made within:
● six months of the date of the final response (this time limit must have been made clear in the final response otherwise it will not apply); *and*

- six years of the matter complained of taking place or, if later, three years of the client's reasonably becoming aware s/he might have grounds for complaining.

The FOS does not consider complaints about the way businesses reach their commercial decisions and, in consumer credit cases, cannot consider complaints about events that occurred before 6 April 2007, although it can 'take account' of them. This means that if the complaint is about, for example, excessive charges added to an account before 6 April 2007 which the client did not find out about until after this date, the FOS cannot provide a remedy. On the other hand, if the complaint relates to excessive charges added to an account after 6 April 2007, the FOS can look at the agreement to see what it says, even if it was made before 6 April 2007. Banks and building societies within FOS jurisdiction before this date are not subject to this restriction, even if the complaint against them relates to a consumer credit agreement.

The FOS will not determine whether or not a relationship is unfair. It decides disputes on the basis of what is 'fair and reasonable'. It is there to resolve disputes; it is not on anyone's 'side'. The FOS looks at the relevant legislation, regulations, any official guidance, relevant codes of practice and standards, and good industry practice at the time of the conduct complained about. This means it can take into account the same issues that a court would consider, but can come to a different conclusion. The FOS has an inquisitorial remit and so conducts its own enquiries rather than just relying on what the parties tell it.[6]

A complaint to the FOS should contain the following information:
- the client's details;
- details of the business complained about;
- reference/account numbers;
- copies of the final response (if any) and of any other relevant documents – eg, the agreement and correspondence;
- a summary of the complaint. This should set out the 'story' in the client's own words, if possible, rather than take the form of a legal-type submission (this can be done later in the process, if necessary);
- how the client wants the business to address the issue. The FOS does not grant a remedy just because a business has broken rules – this is the job of a regulator. There must be some consumer detriment, not necessarily financial, such as distress, inconvenience, injury and damage to reputation;
- a letter of authorisation if the adviser is submitting the complaint on behalf of the client.

The complaints form is available online at www.financial-ombudsman.org.uk/consumer/complaints.htm. It must be downloaded and posted. If the FOS accepts the complaint, it will attempt to resolve the dispute through mediation – ie, assisting the parties come to an agreement. If not, an adjudicator will form a preliminary view, which will be circulated to the parties. If they accept this, the dispute is settled. If they do not, the case is referred to an Ombudsman for determination. If the Ombudsman upholds the complaint, the business can be ordered to:

- pay compensation for financial loss (up to a limit of £100,000); *and/or*
- pay compensation for non-financial loss (this tends to be a few hundred pounds maximum); *and/or*
- take appropriate action to remedy the issue complained about – eg, remove excessive charges from an account.

FOS decisions are binding on the business, but not on the client, who can still take the matter to court if s/he remains dissatisfied. There is no appeal against an FOS decision. If the business fails to comply with the decision, it can be enforced through the courts. Advisers should seek specialist advice if this becomes necessary.

More information can be found on the FOS website (www.financial-ombudsman.org.uk). In the publicity section, advisers will find *Ombudsman News,* a monthly newsletter which often contains features and case studies of interest and relevance to money advisers. Informal guidance on FOS practice and procedure is available by telephoning 020 7964 1400 or emailing technical.advice@financial-ombudsman.org.uk.[7]

3. **Taking court action**

The person or organisation bringing court action is called the 'claimant'. The person or organisation against whom court action is brought is called the 'defendant'. Most forms used in court proceedings are prescribed and can be identified by their number and title in the bottom left-hand corner. It is important for debt advisers to familiarise themselves with these. The forms debt advisers most commonly encounter are available online at www.justice.gov.uk/forms/hmcts.

Cases can be classified as follows:

- money-only claims – eg, for repayment of an amount due under a loan, overdraft or credit card agreement. See Chapter 11;
- claims relating to agreements regulated by the Consumer Credit Act 1974 which are not for money only – eg, for possession of goods supplied under a hire purchase agreement. See Chapter 12;
- claims relating to land – eg, for possession of a house by a mortgage lender or landlord. See Chapter 12;
- all other claims – eg, a claim for the return of goods supplied under an agreement not regulated by the Consumer Credit Act 1974. These differ from money-only claims in that, if the client does not respond to the claim, the creditor must make a formal application to the court for judgment and submit

supporting evidence. The court will decide whether the creditor is entitled to judgment.

Applications: Form N244

Part 23 of the Civil Procedure Rules deals with applications. Form N244 is the prescribed form that must be used. There are guidance notes to help complete the form, available from www.justice.gov.uk/about/hmcts.

- **Section 1** should be completed with details of the client's name (unless s/he has a solicitor acting for her/him).
- **Section 2** should usually indicate that the client is the defendant (unless s/he has a solicitor acting for her/him or, exceptionally, s/he is the claimant).
- **Section 3** asks what order the client is seeking and why s/he is seeking the order. This information must be supplied.[8] The following are suggested wordings for some common applications.
  - **Redetermination/reconsideration:** 'The judgment be paid by instalments of £x per month because I cannot afford to pay at the rate determined.'
  - **Variation:** 'Payment of the judgment debt be varied to £x per month because my circumstances have changed and I can no longer afford to pay at the rate ordered.'
  - **Suspension:** 'Payment of the judgment debt be suspended under s71(2) of the County Courts Act 1984 on the ground that I am no longer able to pay it because…'
  - **Stay of enforcement:** 'Any enforcement proceedings against me be stayed until further order (Rule 3.1(2)(f) of the Civil Procedure Rules).'
- **Section 4** asks whether a draft of the order being applied for has been attached. This will not usually be required unless the application is being made by consent.
- **Sections 5 and 6** ask for information about the application. The client must indicate whether or not s/he wants the court to deal with the application with or without a hearing or at a telephone hearing. If a hearing is requested, the court will fix a time and date and notify the parties at the same time as it serves the N244. Debt advisers should use their experience to estimate hearing times, but can just leave the box(es) blank. If no hearing is requested, the application is referred to a district judge to consider whether the application is suitable for consideration without a hearing. There is no advantage in asking the court to deal with the application without a hearing since the district judge may disagree and order a hearing anyway and the other party can apply to set aside or vary any order made without a hearing.[9] Debt advisers should only ask the court to deal with an application without a hearing if the application is one that will not automatically be transferred to the client's local court, and should also ask the court to exercise its discretion to transfer the case to the client's

local court if it decides that a hearing should take place, quoting Rule 30.2(1) of the Civil Procedure Rules.

If it is not going to be possible (or will be extremely difficult) for the client to attend a hearing in person, it is possible to ask the court to arrange a telephone hearing. The N244 should indicate whether the client is seeking a telephone hearing. If it is the creditor or lender's application, the client can request a telephone hearing in writing.[10]

- **Section 7** should contain details of any hearing date already allocated for the case.
- **Section 8** should usually specify a district judge for the hearing.
- **Section 9** should usually specify the other party/ies as the persons to be served with the application.
- **Section 10** should indicate whether the client is relying on a separate witness statement, her/his statement of case – ie, the claim form, particulars of claim or defence, or the evidence set out in the box on the N244 in support of the application. The amount of text that can be fitted into the box is limited and so, in many cases, a separate witness statement may be needed. Evidence is required in certain cases (eg, set-aside applications) and the court can always ask for evidence of facts in support of an application. The client will not usually have served a defence and so any facts that the client wishes the court to consider should be set out in the box and any written evidence referred to and attached – eg, a financial statement. The client should sign the statement of truth (see particulars of claim on p283) at the foot of the box. There is no need for a financial statement to contain a statement of truth.
- **Section 11** should be signed and dated and the details of the client's address completed.

An application should be made as soon as the adviser realises that one is going to be necessary. Applications can be made at a hearing that has already been fixed (eg, for an application by the creditor) and can be made without using an N244, but the creditor and the court should be informed (if possible in writing) as soon as possible.[11]

Clients with mental health problems.

A client who 'lacks capacity' for the purposes of the Mental Capacity Act 2005 is a 'protected party' in any county court proceedings and can only take part in these proceedings through another person, known as a 'litigation friend'.

A creditor can issue a claim and it can be served on a client who is a protected party even if s/he does not have a litigation friend, but any further steps taken before a litigation friend has been appointed (eg, entering default judgment (see p292) or taking enforcement action (see p298) is of no effect unless the court subsequently ratifies it.[12]

4. **Court fees**

Most steps taken in court proceedings have a fee to cover administrative costs, which must be paid to the court before the step can be taken. The fees are set annually by statutory instrument and details can be obtained from any court office or the HM Courts and Tribunals Service (HMCTS) website or leaflet EX50 (www.tinyurl.com/ce5tuoc or http://hmctsformfinder.justice.gov.uk).

Remission of fees

A client who is not being funded by the Legal Services Commission for the proceedings can claim a full or partial remission of the fees if one of the following applies. **Note:** remission cannot be applied for in the case of consolidated attachment of earnings orders (see p311) or administration orders (see p419).

- If s/he is in receipt of income support, working tax credit with no child tax credit, income-based jobseeker's allowance, income-related employment and support allowance or the guarantee credit of pension credit, the client can get a full remission of the fees. To qualify, the client must be the person receiving the benefit and not the claimant's partner. Partners of benefit claimants must claim remission under one of the other grounds.
- A client will get a full remission of the fees if her/his gross annual income (including that of any partner) is below a certain limit. The calculation is based on all income received from any source (excluding certain benefits and other payments but including tax credits) and takes into account whether the client has children.
- A client may qualify for full or partial remission on the basis of the amount of her/his disposable monthly income (including that of her/his partner). To calculate entitlement, a list of deductions is made from the client's net monthly income from all sources (excluding certain benefits and other payments, but including tax credits) to arrive at her/his disposable monthly income. No fee is payable if the client's disposable monthly income is less than £50. If it is above this amount, her/his contribution to the fee is assessed according to fixed amounts.
- If none of the other grounds apply, the court has discretion to allow full or partial remission of a fee if, because of exceptional circumstances, the client would face undue financial hardship in paying it. Guidance suggests that the client must satisfy the court that paying a fee would seriously impact on her/his day-to-day life – eg, if s/he has financial commitments that are not taken into account under the other grounds, but which are likely to have serious consequences if not paid on time.

Note: tax credits are taken into account in full as income, but childcare costs are only taken into account in assessing monthly disposable income and not gross annual income. Also, although a client may be included in her/his partner's benefit claim, s/he cannot rely on her/his partner's receipt of benefit to claim remission. Disability living allowance and attendance allowance are both disregarded when calculating income, but there is no allowance for the costs of disability.[13]

The application should be made on Form EX160 (available from www.justice.gov.uk/about/hmcts), together with evidence of eligibility. HMCTS publishes an accompanying leaflet (EX160A) (also available from the website) and detailed guidance has been issued to court staff on assessing applications (available from any court office).

The guidance makes clear that joint litigants are jointly and severally liable for payment of the fee. If one qualifies for full or partial remission, the other must pay the full fee, unless s/he also qualifies for full or partial remission.

If the client has no money with her/him to pay the fee and does not apply for remission, the court may nevertheless process the court action in an emergency (ie, if the interests of justice would be compromised if a delay occurs) – eg, to suspend an eviction the following day. The client must undertake to apply for fee remission within five days and to pay the fee if this application fails. If the client fails to do so, the matter is referred to the district judge who may revoke any order made in the court action.

A refusal of full or partial remission can be appealed to the court manager in writing within 14 days. The letter should state why the client believes the decision is wrong and can include further information and evidence. The court manager should notify the decision on the appeal within 10 days. There is a further right of appeal to the area director, again within 14 days. There is no further appeal, and, because fee remission is an administrative matter, the judiciary is not involved.

If the application is not made at the same time as the court action is taken, any fee can be refunded retrospectively, provided an application is made within six months of the fee being paid. This time limit can be extended for good cause.

5. **Time limits**

There are time limits in which to take court action to recover debts.[14] These are mainly contained in the Limitation Act 1980, although some debts have their own time limit – eg, council tax. These time periods are known as '**limitation periods**'. Most limitation periods run from the date the 'cause of action accrued' – ie, the earliest time at which court action could be taken against the client.[15] The following are some of the most common limitation periods advisers will encounter.

Common limitation periods
- **Unsecured borrowing:** six years from default unless repayable 'on demand' when the time period does not start until the date of the demand.

- **Interest:** six years from default in payment. Each amount of interest charged to an account has its own six-year limitation period.
- **Fuel debt:** six years from the date of the bill.
- **Telephone charges:** six years from the date of the bill.
- **Water charges:** six years from the date of the bill.
- **Council tax:** six years from the date of the bill (demand notice).
- **Rent arrears:** six years from the date the rent became due. Each amount of rent due has its own six-year limitation period.
- **Possession of land** – ie, by a mortgage or secured lender or landlord: 12 years from default in payment.
- **Mortgage shortfall:** six years for arrears of interest from the date the interest became due; 12 years for the outstanding capital from the date the right to receive the money accrued (usually after default in payment of one or more contractual instalments). See p141.

Once the relevant limitation period has expired, a debt is said to be '**statute-barred**'. When calculating the limitation period, the date the cause of action accrued is ignored. For example, if the client defaulted on 30 November 2000, a six-year limitation period would have ended on 30 November 2006. If the limitation period has already started, but the law requires the creditor to serve a notice on the client before taking court action (eg, a default notice), the creditor cannot claim that the limitation period only starts when the notice is served, as otherwise the creditor could defer the start of the limitation period indefinitely.[16]

Note: if a loan (eg, an overdraft) is repayable 'on demand', until the demand is made there is no cause of action. Limitation periods are only relevant to when the creditor must take the initial court proceedings. Time ceases to run once court proceedings are issued. If the creditor obtains a judgment, the law on limitation periods does not apply to the enforcement of that judgment.

A limitation period that has already started can be repeatedly restarted by an 'acknowledgement' or 'part-payment'.

If a client receives a claim form for a debt which is statute-barred or partly statute-barred (eg, in the case of rent or interest), and the client wishes to avoid a judgment being made against her/him, s/he must defend the claim on the ground that the debt is statute-barred.[17] Although the client must raise a limitation defence, once s/he has done so, the onus switches to the creditor to prove that the claim is not statute-barred.

Acknowledgements

In this context, an acknowledgement means that the client has, in effect, admitted liability for what is being claimed. No amount need be specified. An acknowledgment must be in writing and signed by the client (or her/his agent – eg, a debt adviser). The debt must be acknowledged either to the creditor or its agent. This means the client cannot acknowledge a debt on the telephone and letters from the creditor to the client cannot restart the limitation period. On the other hand, an adviser could inadvertently acknowledge a debt when writing to a creditor on behalf of the client.

An admission of part of a debt coupled with a denial of liability for the balance is not an acknowledgment of the disputed balance. The phrases 'outstanding amount' and 'outstanding balance' have been held to be acknowledgments.[18] An acknowledgment by one co-debtor only restarts the limitation period against that debtor and not any co-debtors. Once a debt becomes statute-barred, it cannot be revived by any subsequent acknowledgment.

Part-payments

In order to restart the limitation period, a payment must be made by the client (or a co-debtor) or agent, to the creditor or agent and must be in respect of the particular debt in question. For this purpose, the Department for Work and Pensions (DWP) is treated as the client's agent when making payments of mortgage interest to lenders.[19] If part of the debt is disputed and a payment is made, the client must make clear that the payment relates to the undisputed part of the debt and ask the creditor to appropriate the payment to that part of the debt.[20]

A payment of interest restarts the limitation period for the capital, but not the interest. In practice, payments are usually allocated first to interest and then to capital. **Note**: once the capital is statute-barred, so is any claim for interest, even if that interest was added to the account less than six years ago. Similarly, a payment of rent arrears does not restart the limitation period for any other rent outstanding. Writing off part of a debt does not count as a payment. Once a debt has become statute-barred, it cannot be revived by any subsequent payment. However, the client cannot recover the payment, as the effect of a debt being statute-barred is only to prevent court action; the debt still legally exists and can be recovered by any other lawful method.

Note: payments by co-debtors restart the time limits against every other debtor, unlike acknowledgments by co-debtors which only restart the time against the acknowledger.

6. **Appeals and adjournments**

Appeals to a judge

If a client disagrees with a judgment or order made by a district judge and none of the ways of preventing enforcement (see p314 and p355) are applicable, the client must appeal if s/he wishes to challenge the judge's decision. The client may appeal to a circuit judge against any decision made in a county court by a district judge (unless it was made by consent) on the grounds that the decision was:[21]

- wrong – eg, the district judge wrongly decided a legal issue or wrongly exercised her/his discretion by reaching a decision which no reasonable judge could have made; *or*
- unjust – ie, there was a serious procedural or other irregularity in the proceedings before the district judge.

An appeal must be made on a point of law, not on things like a change in the client's circumstances. If new evidence becomes available, this may be a ground for appeal if the court considers it would be in the interests of justice to hold a rehearing.[22]

The client must obtain permission to appeal:
- verbally from the district judge at the end of the hearing; *or*
- if permission was refused or not applied for, to the circuit judge in the notice of appeal.

Permission will only be given if:
- the court considers that the appeal would have a real prospect of success; *or*
- there is some compelling reason why the appeal should be heard. The Civil Procedure Rules contain no guidance on when this might apply.

The district judge must give written reasons for granting or refusing permission to appeal on Form N460.

The notice of appeal must be filed: [23]
- within the time specified by the district judge when granting permission verbally; *or*
- within 21 days of the date of the decision being appealed.

An appeal must be made on a Form N161 (N164 in small claims cases). A fee of £135 (£115 for small claims) is payable. See p273 for details about applying for full or partial fee remission. If the claim is on the small claims track (see p297), the restrictions on cost orders also apply to appeals.

If an adviser has identified possible grounds of appeal, specialist advice/ assistance will be required and the client will usually need to be referred to a solicitor.

Adjournments

An adjournment is a court order to delay a hearing, either for a specified amount of time or indefinitely. The county court can, at any time, either adjourn or bring forward the date of a hearing. It can decide to do this itself or because one or both of the parties have applied.[24]

An application for an adjournment on the grounds of illness should be accepted, provided it is supported by a sick note, unless there is evidence that the illness or medical evidence is not genuine. Similarly, if an important witness cannot be present, a district judge should adjourn a hearing. It is reasonable to grant an adjournment if there would otherwise be a miscarriage of justice. For example, if a client comes into an advice agency at 10am to ask for representation at a possession hearing a quarter of an hour later, it should be argued that there are (or may be) legal points which the court will need to hear and which cannot be adequately presented without further preparation. However, there will need to be some explanation of why the client has left it until the last minute to obtain advice or representation.

It is not a sufficient reason to adjourn a hearing simply because one (or even both) of the parties is not yet ready. Judges will often be impatient or suspicious of applications to adjourn which they believe are merely means to prolong an action in which they believe the creditor should succeed.

A district judge should consider the merits of an adjournment, whether or not one or both parties are requesting one. However, it is clearly much easier to get an adjournment if the creditor agrees, and it is always worth contacting the creditor or its representative before applying for one.

It is important, if possible, to attend court to make the application in case it is not granted. One of the main aims of the Civil Procedure Rules is to avoid delays in hearing cases. Judges can, therefore, be expected to be more reluctant to adjourn cases than previously. In a recent case, the Court of Appeal upheld the trial judge's refusal to grant an adjournment on the basis of the unavailability of an expert witness on the grounds that another expert should have been instructed.[25] If the adjournment is being sought precisely because no one is available to represent the client and it is not opposed by the creditor, a letter (or fax) should be sent to the court explaining that this is the case and that no one will be attending. In such circumstances, if a court decided not to adjourn, an application should be made to set the decision aside (see p314) on the grounds that both sides had not been properly heard.

Notes

1. Introduction
1 Barristers, solicitors and their employees, and people authorised by the Lord Chancellor to conduct litigation under s11 CLSA 1990

2. Before starting court action
2 para 6 PD CPR
3 Published by LexisNexis.
4 For a detailed discussion, see J Phipps, 'What's the Catch?', Adviser 136 (also contains the full text of Annex A)

5 In *Derbyshire Home Loans v Keaney* (*Adviser* 124 abstracts), Bristol County Court stayed possession proceedings for two months to enable the borrower to pursue a possible complaint in view of the lender's failure to respond to his proposals.

6 *R (on the application of Williams) v FOS* [2008] EWHC 2142 (Admin)

7 For further information, see B Philbey, 'The FOS and Consumer Credit Complaints', *Quarterly Account* 4, IMA, Spring 2007; S Quigley, 'Ombudsman Takes on Consumer Credit Cases', *Adviser* 121

3. Taking court action

8 r23.6 CPR

9 Part 23 para 2.4 PD CPR

10 Part 23A para 6 PD CPR

11 Part 23 paras 2.10 and 3(5) PD CPR

12 r21.3(4) CPR. See also C Bradley, 'The MCA 2005 and Litigation Issues', *Adviser* 127

4. Court fees

13 For further details, see S Edwards, 'Fee or Free?', *Adviser* 125

5. Time limits

14 For a discussion of tactics when dealing with statute-barred debts, see C Wilkinson, 'Consultancy Corner', *Adviser* 109, including a suggested response letter to a demand for payment.

15 *Reeves v Butcher* [1891] 2 QB 509

16 *Swansea County Council v Glass* [1992] 2 All ER 680

17 Part 16 para 13.1 PD CPR

18 *Bradford and Bingley v Rashid* [2006] UKHL 37 (*Adviser* 117 abstracts)

19 *Bradford and Bingley v Cutler* [2008] EWCA Civ 74 (*Adviser* 128 money advice abstracts)

20 *Ashcroft v Bradford & Bingley* [2010] EWCA Civ 223, CA (*Adviser* 140 abstracts)

6. Appeals and adjournments

21 r52.11(3) CPR

22 r52.11(1)(b) CPR

23 r52.4 CPR

24 r3.1(2)(b) CPR

25 *Rollinson v Kimberley Clark Ltd, The Times,* 22 June 1999, CA

Chapter 11

The county court: money claims

This chapter covers

This chapter deals with court action by creditors who are claiming money only from the client. See Chapter 12 if the creditor is taking action to recover property, or goods as well as money, from the client.

1. Starting a money claim

Court proceedings start when the county court issues a 'claim form' at the request of the creditor (the 'claimant').

A claim form can only be issued in the High Court if the creditor expects to recover more than £25,000 and can justify the matter being dealt with by a High Court judge. This will rarely be possible in ordinary debt cases, and so there should be no reason for creditors to issue proceedings in the High Court.[1]

Debts regulated by the Consumer Credit Act 1974

Note: the High Court cannot deal with claims related to secured or unsecured agreements regulated by the Consumer Credit Act 1974, or actions linked to such agreements, regardless of the amount of the claim.

If an adviser encounters a case involving a regulated consumer credit agreement (or any other case) being dealt with in the High Court, s/he should seek specialist advice.

Default notice

A default notice is a form which must be issued by a creditor for all debts regulated by the Consumer Credit Act 1974 before court action can start for early payment of money due under an agreement. It is usually required in debt cases where arrears are claimed along with the money which would become due if the agreement ran its course. It is not required if the time allotted to an agreement is already over but arrears remain, or if only arrears are claimed.

The default notice must contain details of:
- the type of agreement, including the name and address of creditor and client;
- the terms of the agreement which have been broken;
- for fixed-sum credit, the early settlement figure;
- the action needed by the client – eg, to pay arrears in full by a certain date;
- the action the creditor intends to take if the client is unable to comply with the default notice – eg, refer to debt collection or start court action.

A default notice served on or after 1 October 2008 must contain the following further information.
- If the notice relates to a hire purchase or conditional sale agreement, information on the client's right to terminate the agreement (including the amount of her/his liability if s/he exercises this right) (see p117).
- Where applicable, a statement that the client may have to pay post-judgment contractual interest in the event of the creditor obtaining a judgment (see p79).
- A copy of the current Office of Fair Trading (OFT) information sheet on default.

The client must be given at least 14 days to carry out the required action, and if the default notice requests payment, it must contain a statement about time orders (see p340) and about seeking advice from a Citizens Advice Bureau, solicitor or trading standards department.

If a default notice is not complied with, a creditor can:
- terminate the agreement; *and*
- demand earlier payment of money due under an agreement.

If a default notice is not completed correctly (eg, it does not give the client sufficient time to respond or the arrears figure is incorrectly stated), it is invalid and the creditor will have to issue a fresh notice before taking action.[2]

Creditors will not always automatically initiate court action if a default notice is not complied with and, even if the time limit has expired, it is always worth negotiating with a creditor in order to try to prevent court action. Clients often claim not to have received default notices and so advisers should bear in mind that a default notice is treated as served for this purpose if it is sent by post to the client's last known address.[3]

Which court deals with the claim

Claims for the recovery of money only are started by creditors in the County Court Money Claims Centre based in Salford, but the claim is issued in the name of Northampton County Court. Such claims are known as **'designated money claims'**. Large creditors which issue county court claims in bulk and prepare claims on computer can use the Claim Production Centre or County Court Bulk Centre at Northampton County Court, which charges a lower court fee (see p273). The court that issues the claim (the originating court) deals with the matter either by post or electronically unless it is transferred to another court.

Automatic transfer

The case will automatically be transferred to the client's 'home court' (ie, the county court for the district in which the client lives) if:[4]

- the client defends the action (see p295); *or*
- there is a request for redetermination of a decision by the court (see p291); *or*
- the district judge decides that a request for an instalment order should be dealt with at a hearing; *or*
- there is an application to set aside a default judgment (see p314); *or*
- there is an application by a creditor to increase the amount payable under a judgment (see p317); *or*
- there is a request for reconsideration of a decision by the court relating to a client's application to vary the amount payable under a judgment or to suspend a warrant of execution (see p317 and p319).

If the client's defence is that s/he paid the debt before the claim was issued, this will be checked with the creditor before the case is transferred. In County Court Bulk Centre cases, all defences are checked with the creditor before the case is transferred. Automatic transfer is only available if the defendant is an individual. If automatic transfer does not apply, the court has the discretion to transfer the case if:

- it would be more convenient or fair for a hearing to be held in another court; *and/or*
- the facilities available at the court where the case is currently being dealt with are inadequate because a party or witness has a disability.

The claim form

The claim form (Form N1) must contain a concise statement of the nature of the claim and a 'statement of value'. This states the amount the creditor is claiming and whether s/he expects to recover:

- not more than £5,000;
- more than £5,000, but not more than £25,000; *or*
- more than £25,000.

The amount claimed includes the court fee paid by the creditor to issue the proceedings and, if a solicitor has been instructed, an amount for the solicitor's costs. The court fee and solicitor's costs vary with the amount claimed. The claim form must state the amount of any interest included.

Details of the court of issue and of the unique reference number allocated to the case appear in the top right corner of the claim form.

The claim form must be served on the client within four months of issue. This will usually be done by the court and will be by first-class post. The claim form is usually deemed to have been received on the second business day after it was posted – ie, if posted on Monday it is deemed to have been received on Wednesday (Saturdays, Sundays, Bank Holidays, Christmas Day and Good Friday are not counted).[5] However, in Claim Production Centre or County Court Bulk Centre cases, the claim form is deemed to be served five days after issue.

See p314 if the client states that s/he did not receive the claim form before judgment was entered or any enforcement action taken by the creditor.

Particulars of claim

The claim form must be accompanied by 'particulars of claim' or these must be sent to ('served on') the client by the creditor within 14 days of the claim form being served. The particulars of claim must include a concise statement of the facts relied on by the creditor (including the details of any contract) and must be verified by a 'statement of truth' – ie, that the creditor believes the facts stated are true. A copy of any written agreement should (but not must) be attached (this is not required where the claim form and particulars of claim are issued by the Claim Production Centre or County Court Bulk Centre).[6]

If the claim form includes particulars of claim, it must be accompanied by:

- a response pack, including an acknowledgement of service (N9);
- a form for admitting the claim (N9A);
- a form of defence and counterclaim to be used if the client disputes the claim (N9B);
- notes for the client on replying to the claim form (N1C).

If the particulars of claim are served separately from the claim form, the forms must be served with the particulars of claim. This may be important as the client's time for responding to the claim runs from the deemed date of service of the particulars of claim.

Responding to the claim form

The client must respond to the claim form/particulars of claim within 14 days of service – ie, the response must be received on or before the 16th day after the date of posting (or within 19 days of issue if issued by the Claim Production Centre or County Court Bulk Centre). S/he can:

- send ('file') a defence or counterclaim to the court (see p295); *or*

- file an acknowledgement of service at the court within the 14-day period if s/he is unable to file a defence in time or wishes to dispute the court's jurisdiction – eg, if a creditor has issued proceedings for an amount due under a regulated consumer credit agreement in the High Court rather than, as required, in the county court (see p280). Once an acknowledgement of service has been filed, the client must file the defence within 28 days of the date of service of the claim form/particulars of claim; *or*
- send ('serve') an admission to the creditor, admitting the whole of the claim (see p285); *or*
- still send the admission to the creditor outside the 14-day period, provided the creditor has not requested a default judgment (see p292); *or*
- file an admission and defence at the court, admitting part of the claim but disputing the balance or making a counterclaim (see p295).

Electronic communication

The Civil Procedure Rules enable the parties to file documents at court by fax. A document is not treated as filed until it is actually delivered by the court office's fax machine, so it is good practice for advisers to telephone the court and check it has been received. A fax delivered after 4pm is treated as filed the following day. Fax should not be used for routine or non-urgent documents or, unless it is unavoidable, to deliver documents which attract a fee and documents relating to a hearing less than two hours ahead.[7]

Parties to a claim in a court or court office which has published an email address for the filing of documents on HM Courts and Tribunals Service website can send a document listed on the website to the court by email. This is not possible if a fee is payable for the particular step in the proceedings. Documents that can be filed by email include the acknowledgement of service, partial admission, defence and allocation questionnaire.[8]

If a claim has been issued electronically using either the money claims online procedure or the Claim Production Centre/County Court Bulk Centre, clients can file an acknowledgement of service, part admission and defence electronically online. The claim form contains a password to enable her/him to access the case. A document is not filed until the transmission is received by the court. The time of receipt is recorded electronically. If a transmission is received after 4pm, the document is treated as filed on the next day the court office is open.

All parties to a claim can be served with documents, including the claim form, electronically if they have given prior written consent to accept electronic service and a fax number or email address to which they should be sent. A fax number or email address included on a letterhead, claim form or statement of case is sufficient.[9]

2. **Admitting a money claim**

The admission and statement of means form

The admission and statement of means form (Form N9A) provides the creditor and the court with information about the client's financial circumstances, and allows the client to admit the amount owing and make an offer to pay the debt. See p295 if the client only agrees that part of the amount claimed is due.

The statement of means accompanying any admission is a vital document. It may be all the creditor knows of the client's ability to pay. Apart from any information provided by the creditor, it is the sole basis for the court's decision about the rate of payment if the creditor does not accept the offer made by the client (see p288).

Completing Form N9A

Note: this section is also relevant to completing Form N245 (Application to Suspend a Warrant of Execution or Reduce an Instalment Order) and Form N56 (Reply to Attachment of Earnings Application). See p319 and p309.

Form N9A does not always fit the circumstances of the particular client. Advisers should be prepared to amend it as necessary in order to give the creditor and the court as complete and accurate a picture as possible of the client's situation. In addition, the headings in the income and expenditure sections do not always reflect the headings on a financial statement. Also, if a couple pool their income, it is often not possible to say who is paying for what. In such a case, the proportion of the partner's income which is contributed to the expenditure listed should be shown as 'other income' unless the offer is being made on the basis of a joint financial statement, in which case the partner's income should be shown.

When the N9A has been completed, it should be photocopied and sent by 'recorded signed for' post to the address shown on the back of the claim form (Form N1). The copy should be kept on file.

- **Personal details.** This section should show the name, address and date of birth of the client. If there are joint defendants, separate N9As should be completed and it should be made clear whether the offer made in Box 11 is a joint one as, otherwise, it will be assumed that the offers are separate even though they are for identical amounts. Alternatively, if the income and expenditure are joint, each N9A could offer half of the available income.
- **Dependants.** This information is needed to explain the level of expenditure. A heterosexual or same-sex partner should be included on the form as a dependant even if s/he has an independent source of income. If a partner does not wish to be considered as a dependant, this fact should be noted either in the box or in an accompanying letter. S/he must, however, be included on the

form because s/he is a member of the household and her/his presence may affect the level of instalment payments.

- **Employment**. Every employment status of the client should be shown (s/he may have more than one). If the client believes the standard boxes do not accurately describe her/his status, an additional description can be inserted. Take-home pay is entered in the income section. Courts do not take account of information provided by self-employed clients in Section 3 when determining a rate of payment and the question about annual turnover for self-employed people appears unnecessary. The information may, however, influence the decision the creditor makes on whether or not to accept the offer of payment. However, if the information is not easily available, it will be sufficient to indicate employment status only.

  Details of any tax or national insurance arrears should be included in Sections 8 or 9. Other business debts should be included in Sections 8, 9 or 10, although the N9A is not really suitable for a business which is still trading to make payment. Guidance to court officers suggests that, if a client is still trading, unless the creditor is prepared to accept the client's payment offer, the papers should be referred to the district judge.

- **Bank accounts and savings**. Court officers are instructed to see whether sums are available to pay either a large lump sum towards a debt or a regular amount. They should ignore any amounts that are less than one-and-a-half times a client's monthly income or seven times her/his weekly income.

  If the amount shown is more than the ignored amount and some, or all, of the money in an account is needed to pay a priority creditor, it is important that the money is not shown as being available for a non-priority debt. So, if the amount is intended to meet the expenses detailed in Section 7 this should be made clear, as otherwise the court officer will assume it is available to pay the debt.

  If the client has a joint bank account, only her/his share of any savings need be declared.

- **Property**. This section provides background information to the creditor and may indicate whether the debt could ever be enforced by a charging order in the event of default on the judgment (see p301). The client could fit into more than one category (eg, rented and council property), so could tick either or both boxes.

- **Income**. This section requires details of the client's income from all sources (including any disability or incapacity benefits, and benefits paid for children). See p43 for how to treat clients who are couples to help decide whether to show joint income and expenses (see notes to Section 7) on the form.

  The decision is further complicated by the instruction at the top of Section 7. If, for example, a partner (or any other member of the household) pays all fuel bills, those items should not be included as an expense unless that person's contribution is included in 'Others living in my home give me'. Court officers are instructed to convert all figures to either weekly or monthly amounts for consistency, and so the form should be completed in the same way.

- **Expenses.** Unless joint income and expenditure figures are being used, only include items of expenditure actually paid for by the client out of her/his income disclosed in Section 6 (see notes for Section 6). A major problem with this section is the absence of many categories of essential expenditure. These can be added in the space marked 'Others' and need not be limited to the three lines given – eg, telephone or mobile phone bills, insurance premiums and childcare costs. Always explain what 'other' expenditure is and use a covering letter to explain its importance if necessary. The expenses figure at the end of Section 7 should be accurate and the items a court may consider 'non-essential' should be included, where possible, in one of the named categories listed on the form. If disability/incapacity benefits, or benefits paid for children cannot be fully accounted for in Section 7, a note should be added to explain that these payments are intended to meet the costs associated with disability, incapacity or bringing up children and are not intended to be used for payment of unrelated debts. This should only be done with the client's agreement following discussion; it is not the adviser's role to decide how clients spend their money.

  Travelling expenses need to cover either fares or vehicle running costs plus petrol. Mail order catalogues are often used to budget for clothing, bedding and small household items, and so expenditure for these items can be listed in that section if the client pays for these items this way.

  Section 7 should include details of payments to meet the regular costs of ongoing services provided by priority creditors, including water charges (but any arrears of water charges should appear in Section 10, regardless of the instruction in Section 8).

  Expenditure figures need to reflect accurately the actual spending as far as possible.[10]

- **Priority debts.** This section requires information about offers which have already been accepted to prevent action by priority creditors in pursuit of arrears. Thus, it is desirable before submitting Form N9A that arrangements with priority creditors have been made. If an arrangement has not yet been made with one or more priority creditors, state the total arrears outstanding to that creditor and amend the form by adding, for instance, 'payment to be arranged' or 'offering £x a month'. Otherwise, if the total arrears figures are given, court officers are advised to assume repayment of arrears in three months, except for hire purchase and mortgage arrears which might be spread over one to two years. If offers have been made, but a reply is awaited, they should be included on the form. Include priority business debts, such as VAT or income tax, here.

  Clients may be uncertain about what proportion of payments to priority creditors are to cover arrears. In this case, to save time, total payments,

11

Chapter 11: The county court: money claims
3. The judgment.

including arrears, could be entered in Section 7 'Expenses' and a note written in Box 8 to indicate this.

- **Court orders.** Only existing court orders should be listed, except the one subject to the present action. Use a separate sheet or financial statement if there is not enough room on the form.
- **Credit debts.** This section requires details of payments already arranged with other non-priority creditors who have not obtained a court order. The three spaces provided for such debts are unlikely to be adequate and another sheet may be needed. Only the amounts currently being paid should be included, but an accompanying financial statement is useful information to indicate the level of indebtedness and offers made to other creditors, as well as indicating how the offer on the N9A has been calculated.
- **Offer of payment.** An offer of payment should always be made in Box 11. If there is available income, an offer should normally be made on a pro rata basis, but some kind of offer should always be made even if it is only a nominal figure – eg, 50p or £1 a month.

3. **The judgment.**

'Judgment' is the formal term for the court's decision in a case. Before judgment, the creditor is trying to establish that the client owes the money. After judgment, liability cannot be denied unless the client appeals (see p276) or applies to set the judgment aside (see p314).

The court can order the client to pay:
- by monthly instalments; *or*
- in one instalment – eg, within 14 or 28 days; *or*
- immediately ('forthwith'). This means the client is inevitably unable to comply with the order and is automatically in arrears with the judgment.

If a client is unable to pay at the rate ordered by the court, s/he can take action to change the terms of the judgment (see pp317–20).

The creditor's response

When the creditor receives Form N9A (see p285), it decides whether to accept or reject the offer of payment. If the creditor accepts, it requests the court to enter judgment . on Form N205A/225 for the sum claimed to be paid as offered and the court sends the client a copy (N30(1) Judgment for Claimant (Acceptance of Offer)) The creditor is not required to send a copy of the N9A to the court when accepting the offer and so the court has no information on the client's ability to pay the judgment.

If the client fails to comply with the terms of the judgment, the creditor can decide whether to use one or more means of enforcement in order to obtain

Chapter 11: The county court: money claims
3. The judgment.

11

payment (see p298). Some creditors request orders for immediate payment (or 'forthwith') as a matter of course so they can take enforcement action immediately.

If the client does not 'request time to pay', the creditor may specify the terms of the judgment (s/he could specify immediate payment) and the court enters judgment accordingly. If the creditor does not specify any terms of payment, the court enters judgment for immediate payment.[11] A 'request for time to pay' is defined as a 'proposal about the date of payment or a proposal to pay by instalments at the times and rate specified in the request'.[12] Thus, if the client wishes to avoid a judgment for immediate payment, s/he must make an offer of payment on the N9A – however small – in order to trigger the next step in the procedure.

If the creditor rejects the offer, s/he must inform the court and supply reasons for the refusal and a copy of the N9A. The court then enters judgment for the amount admitted and 'determines' the rate of payment.

How courts calculate instalment orders

The amount is not more than £50,000

If the amount involved is not more than £50,000, the rate of payment may be 'determined' by a court officer.

Court officers carry out a determination without a hearing. HM Courts and Tribunals Service provides guidance on how to do this.[13] The following is a summary. The references are to the box numbers on Form N9A. The total income (Box 6) is the starting point. To this may be added any savings (Box 4). From this total income, the following are deducted:

- expenses (Box 7);
- priority debts (Box 8);
- court debts (Box 9);
- credit debt repayments (Box 10).

Court officers are instructed to use common sense when assessing essential items of expenditure and to allow a reasonable amount for items not listed in Box 7, but which are essential to the client's household – eg, payments for a vehicle or childminder to enable the client to work, or the cost of travelling to and from work. Although court officers are not expected to assess whether any of the amounts are too high, 'frivolous' and 'non-essential' items will be disregarded. These are specified as:

- children's pocket money;
- money for gambling, alcohol or cigarettes;
- money for newspapers or magazines (unless essential to the client in her/his work);
- holiday money.

11

Chapter 11: The county court: money claims
3. The judgment.

The guidance does, however, give the court officer discretion to allow £15 a week for 'sundries' (presumably per household).

The client should be allowed sufficient resources and time to pay priority debts, although court staff are instructed to make certain assumptions about what is a reasonable period for clearing such arrears. Although court officers are instructed to take a common-sense approach to credit debts, the guidance also states that 'there is no logical reason why these debts should take precedence over a county court judgment'.

The guidance reminds court officers that creditors must state reasons for rejecting offers. Rejecting an offer because of the amount of the debt or the length of time it has been outstanding or because the offer is 'too low' is not sufficient unless the creditor can demonstrate inaccuracies in the information provided by the client.

The resulting figures are then transferred to a 'determination of means calculator' (EX120) and the court officer works out the rate of payment based on the amount of 'disposable (available) income'. In some courts, the creditor is expected to complete the EX120 electronically, but this does not mean the creditor decides which figures to allow or disallow, or what order is made. The guidance states that if the disposable income is: [14]

- higher than the offer but lower than the figure the creditor is prepared to accept, the instalment order should be for the amount of disposable income;
- higher than the figure the creditor is prepared to accept, the instalment order should be for the amount the creditor is prepared to accept;
- lower than the offer, the instalment order should be for the amount the client has offered unless this is 'unrealistically high';
- nil or a negative figure, either the instalment order should be for the amount the client has offered (unless unrealistically high) or the matter should be referred to the district judge for advice or a decision.

When the court has decided on the rate of payment, it notifies both the creditor and client of the order made (on Form N30(2)). Either party can apply to the court for a reconsideration of this decision (known as 'redetermination' – see p291).

The guidance recognises that Form N9A is designed for individual, rather than business, debts and that, unless a business has provided information about its financial position, it will be difficult for court officers to make a decision on the rate of payment. If the creditor has indicated the terms on which s/he will accept payment by instalments, the court officer can enter judgment accordingly. Otherwise, s/he is instructed to refer the matter to the district judge.

If the amount is more than £50,000

If the amount involved is more than £50,000, the rate of payment must be determined by a district judge.

Chapter 11: The county court: money claims
3. The judgment.

11

A district judge may carry out a determination with or without a hearing (although hearings are very rare). In some courts, claims for less than £50,000 are referred to the district judge for determination. In carrying out the determination, the district judge must take into account:

- the client's statement of means;
- the creditor's objections;
- any other relevant factors – eg, increasingly this includes the fact that the client is a homeowner but the instalment offer is so low that it will not pay off the judgment within a reasonable period.[15]

The district judge is not required to follow the guidelines issued to court staff. If the district judge decides to hold a hearing, the case will be automatically transferred to the client's home court.

When the court has decided on the rate of payment, it notifies both the creditor and client of the order made (on Form N30(2)). Either party can apply to the court for a reconsideration of this decision (known as 'redetermination' – see below).

Redetermination by a district judge

If the rate of payment has been decided without a hearing, either the creditor or the client can ask for the amount to be reconsidered (redetermined) by a district judge within 14 days of the order being served. No court fee is payable.[16] The client can request a redetermination regardless of whether the original determination was made by a court officer or the district judge (provided there was no hearing).

District judges are not bound by the determination of means guidelines and can make whatever order they think fit. If there is available income, the N9A should be carefully completed so that a decision can be made from the form alone, and the decision is more likely to be upheld by a district judge if the creditor asks for a redetermination. This is particularly important where large amounts are owed or a creditor feels particularly aggrieved for some other reason – eg, no payments have so far been made under an agreement.

However, there is an increasing trend for district judges to reject low or nominal offers of payment and make an order for immediate payment to enable the creditor to enforce it, if possible, usually by a charging order (see p301). Such offers may be seen as unrealistic and the creditor may not be regarded as being unreasonable in refusing to accept an offer of payment which will take many years to pay off the judgment, if ever. If the client has property, assets or savings, they may be at risk. On the other hand, if the client's financial difficulties are temporary, it is worth pointing this out to the court as, in these circumstances, the district judge may be more willing to make an instalment order at a low rate on the basis that it will be reviewed.

11

Chapter 11: The county court: money claims
3. The judgment.

A client whose position is unusual may benefit from the wider discretion of a district judge if, for instance, payment could be made from money which s/he expects to receive in time or if s/he is seriously ill and likely to gain sympathy. All such arguments should be made clearly, and the application should be made by letter (or on Form N244 – see p271) giving reasons why the matter should be reconsidered. The court will arrange for the case to be transferred to the client's local court.

If the original determination was made by a court officer, the redetermination may take place without a hearing unless one is requested. If the original determination was made by a district judge, the redetermination must be made at a hearing unless the parties agree otherwise. There is usually no indication on the judgment as to who carried out the original determination. Although the adviser can establish this by a phone call to the court office, it is usually better to ask for a hearing so that the client's case can be put to the district judge in person. The decision is one for the client, not the adviser.

The request should always refer to redetermination under Rule 14.13 of the Civil Procedure Rules, specify whether or not a hearing is required and set out why the original determination should be reconsidered – eg, the client cannot afford to pay the judgment at the rate ordered by the court but can pay at the rate of £x a month in accordance with the attached financial statement. If the client asks for the matter to be dealt with without a hearing, the request could be accompanied by a witness statement from the client setting out her/his case.[17]

If the determination was made by a district judge at a hearing, there is no right to request a redetermination. If circumstances change, either party can apply for a variation in the rate of payment ordered (see p317).

Default judgment

If the client fails to reply to the claim form (including a 'nil' or no offer of payment), the creditor can request the court to enter judgment in default on Form N205A/225. Default judgment cannot be entered if the client has, within the specified time limits:[18]

- filed a defence; *or*
- filed an acknowledgement of service; *or*
- filed or served an admission together with a request for time to pay (even if this is outside of the time limit).

The creditor must specify the date by which the whole of the debt is to be paid (which may be immediately) or the rate at which it is to be paid by instalments. If none is specified, the judgment will be for payment immediately.[19]

A debt adviser who thinks that default judgment has been entered, or is about to be, should check with the court of issue. If it has not been entered, the client can still respond. However, if judgment has already been entered, s/he should apply either to vary it (see p317) or set it aside (if appropriate, see p314).

Chapter 11: The county court: money claims
3. The judgment.

11

If the creditor does not apply for judgment within six months of the expiry of the client's time for responding to the claim, the action is 'stayed' and the creditor must apply to the court for permission to proceed with it.[20]

After judgment, if the amount required is not paid within a month, details are entered in the Register of Judgments, Orders and Fines. This information is publicly available and is used by many credit reference agencies. Entries are cancelled six years after the date of judgment.

Interest charges after a judgment

In some cases dealt with by a debt adviser, no interest is chargeable after a county court judgment is made. This is important, not only because it means that any payments the client is able to make will reduce the amount outstanding, but also because, if the creditor knows that interest charges will have to stop once the matter is taken to court, s/he may be persuaded to stop charging interest once a client begins to experience difficulties in repaying.

The court can include in any judgment simple interest, at such a rate as it thinks fit, from the date the debt fell due to:[21]

- in the case of a debt paid before judgment, the date of payment; *or*
- in the case of debt for which judgment is entered, the date of judgment (**'discretionary interest'**).

Discretionary interest must be claimed specifically by the creditor in the particulars of claim and included in the 'amount claimed' figure on the N1 claim form. It cannot be claimed in addition to any other interest, nor can it be awarded to run after the date of judgment. Provided the creditor restricts her/his claim to the rate of interest payable on judgment debts (currently 8 per cent a year – see below), the claim for interest can be included in a default judgment or judgment on admission. Such a claim is not subject to the Limitation Act 1980, but the client can ask the court to reduce the amount of interest included in the judgment if there has been a long delay in starting the proceedings with no satisfactory explanation for that delay.

- As a general rule, interest should be allowed from the date the right to sue for the relevant payment arose.
- The existence of and need to investigate a genuine dispute does not prevent interest running.
- If the creditor has been guilty of excessive delay in making or pursuing the claim, either the starting point or the rate of interest can be adjusted in favour of the client.[22]

If a client wants to challenge a claim for discretionary interest, s/he must file a defence (see p295).

11

Chapter 11: The county court: money claims
3. The judgment.

Some judgments carry simple interest from the date of judgment to the date of payment at the rate specified from time to time (currently 8 per cent a year since 1 April 1993; 15 per cent prior to this date). This is known as '**statutory interest**'.[23]

Since 1 July 1991, county court judgments for £5,000 or more have carried statutory interest unless:

- under the terms of the judgment, payment is either deferred to a specified date or is to be made by instalments. Interest does not accrue until either the specified date or the date the instalment falls due; *or*
- the judgment arises out of a consumer credit agreement regulated by the Consumer Credit Act 1974;[24] *or*
- a suspended possession order is made; *or*
- an administration order or attachment of earnings order is in force.[25]

Interest ceases to be due when enforcement proceedings (other than charging orders) are started, but if these do not recover any money, interest accrues as if the proceedings had never started. It seems that, if the client defaults under the terms of the original judgment and then obtains a variation or suspension of the judgment, interest does not accrue.

Some credit agreements contain provisions for lenders to charge interest on the amount borrowed and additional interest in the event of default by the client ('**contractual interest**'). The general rule is that, once the lender obtains judgment, the right to any further contractual interest ceases. However, an agreement may contain a clause stating that the creditor can continue to charge contractual interest after a judgment is made. The House of Lords has ruled that such a clause is 'fair'.[26] Following the judgment in *Forward Trust v Whymark*,[27] which allowed lenders to obtain judgment for the outstanding balance of a loan without giving credit for any early settlement rebate, many lenders issue proceedings for the full sum owed (including interest pre-calculated to the end of the agreement). Other lenders (where the interest rate is variable) limit the claim and the judgment to the principal amount outstanding plus accrued interest to the date of judgment, while reserving the right to issue separate proceedings for the ongoing interest.

Clients who are paying off the judgment can be confused and alarmed to receive statements showing the debt increasing and demands from the creditor for additional payments. The judgment is satisfied once the amount sued for (plus costs) has been paid. Creditors who claim to be able to 'add' contractual interest to the judgment should be challenged.

Before 1 October 2008 (or subsequently if the judgment does not relate to an agreement regulated by the Consumer Credit Act), if creditors wished to include ongoing contractual interest in a judgment, they should have sought a judgment for the amount of interest to be decided by the court.[28] Although the House of Lords in *Director General of Fair Trading v First National Bank* declared that judgments should take account of accruing contractual interest so that courts could consider making time orders (see p340), it declined to decide whether the rules then in force actually allowed such judgments to be made.[29]

If a judgment is made on or after 1 October 2008 in relation to a regulated consumer credit agreement and the creditor wishes to pursue a claim for post-judgment contractual interest, it must serve a notice on the client stating its intention to charge interest after judgment and informing the client of her/his right to apply for a time order (known as the 'first required notice'). This notice cannot be given until after the judgment has been made.

Subsequently, the creditor must serve further notices, containing details of the interest charged, at six-monthly intervals as well as annual statements (see p79). The creditor cannot charge post-judgment contractual interest for any period before the service of the first required notice or during any period when the creditor has failed to serve a subsequent notice.

Although these provisions only apply to judgments made on or after 1 October 2008, they apply to regulated agreements whenever made (provided the agreement contains a provision specifically allowing the creditor to charge interest after judgment).[30] If the agreement does not include such a provision, the creditor cannot charge contractual interest after judgment. Default notices served on or after 1 October 2008 (see p281) must contain a statement of the creditor's right to claim post-judgment contractual interest.

Once the judgment is paid off, the creditor must issue fresh proceedings to recover any post-judgment contractual interest to which it claims to be entitled. To avoid this, the client could apply for a time order in Box 11 of the N9A as follows: 'I ask the court (1) to make a time order in the terms of my offer and (2) amend the loan agreement in consequence so that no further contractual interest accrues after the date of judgment.'

Alternatively, the client can wait until the first required notice is served and then apply for a time order as above.

If a creditor threatens to pursue additional interest by taking further proceedings, the debt adviser should obtain specialist advice.[31]

---

4. **Defending a money claim**

The defence and counterclaim form

Form N9B provides the client with an opportunity to explain the circumstances and facts of any dispute, which should be stated clearly and in sufficient detail. A defence should be submitted where there is one – eg, if the debt has already been paid. It is not a defence that the client cannot afford to pay the debt. In these circumstances, the client should follow the admission procedure described on pp285–91. A counterclaim can be made if the client has lost money because the creditor has failed to carry out her/his legal obligations, although a court fee is payable (unless the client is able to obtain remission – see p273).

The N9B should be returned to court within 14 days of service. If the defence cannot be prepared within this time, the client should return the acknowledgement of service (N9) to the court. S/he will automatically have a further 14 days in which to file a defence – ie, 28 days from the date of service of the claim form/particulars of claim. The client may need to obtain specialist consumer or legal advice before completing the N9B.

If some of the claim is admitted and time is required to pay that amount, but some is disputed, both Forms N9A and N9B should be completed and returned to court (not the creditor).

Challenging the creditor's costs

This procedure may be used to challenge the creditor's costs if it is thought that paragraph 6 of the pre-action conduct practice direction (see p266) has not been complied with. This imposes a general obligation to act reasonably in negotiations and avoid unnecessary court action. The client needs to show that:
- s/he has made reasonable attempts to avoid court action; *and*
- issuing proceedings was not a proportionate response by the creditor to the client's attempt to settle the matter.

Examples of where this might be successfully argued include if:
- the client has made a payment arrangement with the creditor before proceedings were started and has complied strictly with that arrangement;
- the client has made what the adviser regards as a reasonable payment offer but the creditor has unreasonably demanded higher payments – eg, other creditors have accepted offers made on the same basis and the creditor is unable to demonstrate where any additional payments are to come from;
- the creditor has not warned the client that it intends to take court action by sending her/him a 'letter of claim' (also called a 'letter before action'), setting out details of the debt and warning the client that, unless payment is made within a stated period – eg, 21 days, court action will be taken without further notice;[32]
- the creditor has acted unreasonably – eg, refused to negotiate or breached a code of conduct.

The court is required to take account of the conduct of both parties and also to assess the reasonableness of any offer made.

Advisers should beware of substituting what they consider reasonable for what a district judge is likely to consider reasonable, as it is the client who will have to pay any additional costs incurred. As a general rule, district judges do not consider it unreasonable for a creditor to seek a judgment which the client appears unable to pay. On the other hand, the district judge may consider it unreasonable for a creditor to refuse an offer of payment, issue proceedings and then accept the same offer made on an N9A.

Advisers should be aware that just because the creditor has failed to comply with the letter of the practice direction, the court will not necessarily deprive the creditor of its costs. The practice direction says that the court 'is likely to look at the effect of non-compliance on the other party when deciding whether to impose sanctions'. If the court decides the default has made no difference to the client's position, it is unlikely to deprive the creditor of its costs.

Allocating the case to the appropriate track

If the client disputes the debt on grounds other than that it was paid before the issue of the claim form (see p282) and the claim is a 'designated money claim' (see p282), the court will send both parties an allocation questionnaire on Form N149 (small claims track) or N150 (other cases).[34] This must be returned to the court within 14 days, together with a fee of £40 payable by the creditor if the case is on the small claims track (unless the claim is for £1,500 or less) or £220, if the case is on one of the other tracks (see below). On receipt of the questionnaire, the case will be automatically transferred to the client's home court and that court will:

- allocate the case to a track (see below); *or*
- set a hearing date to consider allocation; *or*
- make orders on the future conduct of the case ('case management directions'); *or*
- summarily dispose of the case (see p298); *or*
- if requested on the questionnaire by both parties, suspend further action for up to one month to enable the parties to try and settle the case.

Tracks

The '**small claims track**' is the normal track for cases with a financial value of not more than £5,000.[35] On allocating the case, the court gives standard directions for its future conduct and fixes a hearing date at least 21 days ahead. The case is normally heard in private by a district judge. Debt advisers have the right to represent clients at the hearing. Even if the value of the claim is more than £5,000, the parties can still agree to the case being allocated to the small claims track. The court will not usually allow more than a day for the hearing and so cases which are likely to last longer may not be considered suitable for this track by the court.

The '**fast track**' is the normal track for cases with a financial value of no more than £25,000, which the court estimates can be tried in a day.[36] On allocating the case, the court gives case management directions and sets a timetable in which those steps are to be taken. At the same time, the court also fixes either a hearing date or a period within which the hearing is to take place. The hearing of the case should take place within 30 weeks.

The '**multi-track**' is the normal track for all other cases – ie, cases with a higher financial value that cannot be heard in a day or more complex cases requiring individual directions.[37] On allocating the case, the court either gives case management directions with a timetable in which those steps are to be taken (although no trial date or period is fixed) or fixes a hearing to consider the issues in the case and the directions that will be required.

Summary disposal

One of the key features in the Civil Procedure Rules is the duty of the court actively to manage cases, with scope to act on its own initiative. The court can 'strike out' (see below) the particulars of a claim or defence if: [38]

- no reasonable grounds are disclosed in the particulars of the claim (eg, 'money owed £1,000') or defence ('I do not owe the money') for either bringing or defending the claim; *or*
- it is an abuse of the court's process – eg, where it raises issues which should have been dealt with in a previous case involving the same parties; *or*
- the court is satisfied that a case either has no real prospects of success or is bound to succeed or fail on a point of law and there is no other compelling reason for the matter to go to trial. To have a 'realistic prospect of success' the case must be a convincing one and not be merely arguable. Where there are significant factual issues between the parties, summary disposal is not appropriate.

If either the particulars of claim or defence are struck out (literally deleted), this means that it cannot be relied on and the party will be unable to proceed. The court can then enter 'summary judgment' for the other party.[39] The court can take this step either on its own initiative or on the application of a party. Courts are now more proactive in this area than in the past and debt advisers should, therefore, exercise great care when preparing defences and counterclaims. Defences which lack detail are likely to be struck out – ie, the defence must set out the relevant facts and reasons for disputing the claim.

5. **Enforcing a judgment**

Once judgment has been given, it is the responsibility of the creditor (and not the court) to collect payments. It is, therefore, important for the client to record all payments made and obtain receipts. If the client fails to pay in accordance with the judgment, the creditor can attempt to enforce payment through the court by obtaining:

- a warrant of execution (see p300);
- a charging order (see p301);
- an attachment of earnings order (see p309);
- a third-party debt order (see p312).

Debt advisers should explain to clients that, provided they keep to the terms of the judgment, the creditor cannot take enforcement action however unhappy it may be with the terms of the judgment. The adviser should also emphasise that, if the judgment states that a certain payment should be made each month, it is important this amount is paid every single month by the date stated in the judgment. If payments are made in advance in a lump sum to cover future months and no payments made in the following months, the client will have defaulted on the terms of the judgment and the creditor can take enforcement action against her/him. For example, if a judgment states that payment must be made at the rate of £2 a month, the client pays £6 to cover three months. If no payment is made in the second month, the client will have defaulted.

The creditor can use any available method of enforcement, and can use more than one method either at the same time or one after the other.[40] However, while an attachment of earnings order is in force, the creditor cannot take any other type of enforcement action against the client unless the court gives permission.[41]

See p314 for how to prevent enforcement.

Information order

Commonly known as an 'oral examination', an order to obtain information from a judgment debtor (an 'information order') is an order for the client to attend the court, in person, to be interviewed by a court official about her/his means or any other matter about which information is needed to enforce a judgment. It is not a way of enforcing a judgment, but more an information-gathering process. A creditor can apply for an order at any time to obtain information, even where enforcement of the judgment has been stayed or the client has not defaulted or missed payments, as an order to obtain information is not itself regarded as enforcement.[42] The procedure is contained in Part 71 of the Civil Procedure Rules.

A creditor who has obtained a judgment against someone can apply to court on Form N316 for an information order requiring that person to attend a hearing at her/his local court before either a district judge (if there are 'compelling reasons') or, more usually, a senior court official. The order is on Form N39 and must be served personally on the client at least 14 days before the hearing. Within seven days of service, the client can require the creditor to pay her/his reasonable travel expenses to and from the court. These are likely to be added to the judgment and so ultimately paid by the client, but it is always worth the client requesting travel expenses from the creditor because if they are not paid, the client cannot be committed to prison for non-attendance at the hearing). The N39 contains a list of documents which the client is required to bring to court – eg, pay slips, rent book, credit agreements and outstanding bills. The creditor can ask the court to add further documents to the list.

At the hearing, the court officer asks the client a set of standard questions contained on Form EX140 (available from www.justice.gov.uk/forms/hmcts).

This is a 12-page questionnaire designed to find out what money, goods, property or other resources the client has to satisfy the judgment, in order for the creditor to decide what action to take next. The creditor can ask additional questions. The client must answer on oath. The client must attend the hearing. If s/he does not appear, refuses to take the oath or to answer any questions, or possibly if s/he fails to bring any documents listed on Form N39 to the hearing, the court can make a suspended order committing her/him to prison unless s/he attends a further hearing and complies with the other terms of the original order – ie, produces documents and takes the oath. If s/he again fails to comply, s/he will be arrested and brought before the judge to decide whether or not s/he should be committed to prison. In practice, the client will not be sent to prison provided s/he co-operates in the process, and cannot be committed if s/he requested travel expenses for the first hearing and these were not paid by the creditor.

The adviser can help a client who has been served with an information order by providing a financial statement and a list of other debts and capital resources (including any equity in a house) in accordance with the information required by Form N39, together with a letter of explanation if the client is unable to obtain any of the required information. The adviser can also help by going through the questions on Form N39 with the client before the hearing.

An information order will almost certainly be followed by further action, if any is possible – eg, the creditor may apply for an attachment of earnings order or a charging order. It is therefore important to pre-empt this if possible by submitting the above information to the creditor, implementing the most appropriate strategy for all the debts, and agreeing this with the creditor who has requested the information order before the hearing, which may no longer need to take place. If this cannot be agreed, nevertheless, it may be appropriate to offer the strategy to all the other creditors, and this fact (along with any responses available) can be reported at the hearing. If the client has defaulted on payments, an application for variation of the judgment should be made to prevent enforcement. The court can also treat the hearing as an application for an administration order (see p419).[43]

Warrant of execution

The warrant of execution is a document that allows the county court bailiff to take and sell goods belonging to the client to pay a judgment debt plus the court fees and costs. If the client does not keep to the payments ordered by the court, the creditor can ask the court to issue a warrant of execution once a payment is missed and remains unpaid. The warrant can be for the whole amount of the judgment outstanding or just the arrears, which must be at least £50. Goods can be taken unless the amount shown on the warrant plus costs are paid. Certain goods are exempt from seizure (see p400). The client has an opportunity to apply for the warrant to be suspended (see p319). A creditor who wishes to issue a warrant more than six years after the date of the judgment must obtain the prior permission of the court. Ordinarily, the delay will itself justify the refusal of permission unless the creditor can explain the delay and show that the circumstances take the case out of the ordinary.[44]

A county court judgment may be transferred to the High Court for enforcement by execution against the client's goods if the judgment is between £600 and £5,000. It must be transferred to the High Court for enforcement if it is for more than £5,000. Judgments relating to agreements regulated by the Consumer Credit Act 1974 cannot be transferred to the High Court regardless of the amount of the judgment.[45] If an adviser comes across a judgment which has been transferred to the High Court for enforcement, s/he should seek specialist advice.

Even though the numbers are declining, warrants of execution remain the preferred enforcement method for many creditors.

Charging order

A charging order is a court order that secures the amount owed under the judgment, usually against the client's interest in a property, in which case an entry is made on the Land Register to this effect. Charging orders are governed by the Charging Orders Act 1979.

When the property is sold, the judgment debt, together with court fees/costs plus any statutory interest (but not contractual interest),[46] must be repaid out of the balance of the proceeds of sale after payment of any prior mortgages or charges. A charging order can only be made if judgment has been entered and the client has defaulted. Even if only one instalment under a judgment has not been paid, the creditor can apply for a charging order, unless the client has applied for a variation, obtained an instalment order and maintained the payments (see p317).[47]

Note: s93 of the Tribunals Courts and Enforcement Act 2007 was brought into force on 1 October 2012. This enables a charging order to be made even though the client has not defaulted in payment of the instalment order. When deciding whether or not to make a charging order, the court is required to take into consideration the fact that the client has not defaulted. Section 93 does *not* apply to any judgment or order under which the client is required to pay a sum of money by instalments made before 1 October 2012. In such cases, a charging order cannot be made unless the client defaults on the instalment order.

The effect of a charging order is to turn an unsecured debt into a secured one. Many creditors request the court to make judgments for immediate payment simply so that they can apply straightaway for a charging order. Some district judges regard this as reasonable, especially in cases of nominal offers, or if it appears that the client's offer of payment will not clear the debt for many years. Advisers should, therefore, follow the admission procedure as far as redetermination (see p291), if necessary, in order to demonstrate to the district judge that the client's offer is a reasonable one and that a charging order should not be made.

Although the client can apply for a variation at any time (see p317), if, in the meantime, the creditor applies for a charging order and obtains an interim order (see below), the variation may not prevent the charging order being made.

Although charging orders are normally made against a person's home (including a part-share in a home) or business premises, they can also be made against shares or the client's interest under a trust.

Charging orders are increasingly sought by creditors and this trend is likely to continue.

Office of Fair Trading requirements

The Office of Fair Trading (OFT) has said that creditors must use charging orders 'proportionately'.

In November 2010, the OFT issued requirements on charging orders to a number of creditors. Although these requirements are company-specific, they were issued in the context of an OFT investigation which identified sector-wide failures and so, before applying for a charging order, all creditors should consider:

- the extent to which the client has responded to reasonable requests by the creditor and whether or not the client has been making payments in accordance with the court order;
- the client's personal and financial circumstances, including her/his ability to pay the sum owed;
- the amount owed and the length of time that sum has been owed to the creditor;
- how long it is likely to take the client to repay the sum owed compared with how long it would have taken had s/he made payments in accordance with the credit agreement;
- whether it is reasonable for the creditor to take steps other than obtaining a charging order.

The less ability the client has to repay, the larger the outstanding amount, the longer it has been outstanding and the longer it is going to take the client to repay, the more proportionate it is for the creditor to resort to a charging order.

Interim charging orders

The creditor must first apply to the court to obtain an interim charging order on Form N379. If the creditor is applying to enforce a judgment made in Northampton County Court in respect of a designated money claim (see p282) and the case has subsequently been transferred to a different court, the application must be made to that court. Otherwise, the application must be made to the client's home court.[48] Northampton County Court Bulk Centre does not deal with charging order applications and in such cases the creditor must arrange for the case to be transferred to a court of its choice.

The application must demonstrate either that the client is in arrears with instalment payments due under a judgment or that the judgment is a 'forthwith judgment', which is unpaid. The creditor must also provide details of the client's interest in the property to be charged, and details and addresses of all other creditors if this information is known to the creditor – eg, if the adviser has previously sent the creditor a financial statement containing details of the client's other debts.[49] Provided the papers are in order, the court sends the client a copy of Form N379 and the interim charging order, together with notice of the date and time of the hearing at which the court will consider making the order final. These must be sent at least 21 days before the hearing. Copies are also served on any joint owner and creditor the court directs, so they have the opportunity to object.[50]

The creditor also applies to the Land Registry to register a 'notice' or 'restriction' on the property. This is a warning that an application is about to be made for a final charging order and means that, if the client attempts to dispose of the property or her/his interest in it, the creditor will be informed and can object to the transaction. The Land Registry sends a copy of the registration to the client as soon as it is received. This effectively 'blocks' any transfer or sale of the property made with the intention of avoiding the charge.

Final charging orders

The second stage in the charging order process is for the creditor to obtain a final charging order. At the hearing, the district judge decides whether to make the interim charging order final, or to discharge it. S/he should take into account both the personal circumstances of the client and whether any creditors would 'be likely to be unduly prejudiced by the making of the order'.[51]

Objecting to the order

If the client wishes to object to the final order being made, s/he can apply to have the hearing transferred to her/his local court.[52] The client must also file at court and serve on the creditor written evidence stating the grounds of objection not less than seven days before the hearing.[53] Any relevant documents (including a financial statement) should be attached. In many cases, debt advisers will want to present a defence but, in practice, most district judges appear to make final charging orders automatically. If the client wants to defend the charging order, the following arguments could be used.

- Some creditors believe they can apply for a charging order at any time, so check whether any of the instalment payments due under a judgment have been missed. If not, the court cannot grant a charging order, unless the judgment was made on or after 1 October 2012 (see p301).[54]

- Check whether an application to vary the judgment was submitted and the variation order granted before the interim order was made. If it was, provided the new payments have been maintained, the application for a charging order should fail, unless the judgment was made on or after 1 October 2012 (see p301). However, a variation order made after the date of the interim order does not bar making a final order.[55]

- Once a request for redetermination has been received by the court, the original determination does not have any effect as it must be replaced by a new judgment – ie, it is only a final judgment if no application is made for redetermination, which is the end of the process. There is no rule preventing creditors from applying for charging orders pending a redetermination request or hearing. In fact, this frequently happens.[56] If the client has applied for redetermination, courts usually list the redetermination hearing and the charging order hearing together. The application for redetermination should be dealt with first, regardless of which application was actually filed first, because it is the judgment made on redetermination (N30(3)) which will be enforced. If the client's application for redetermination is successful and an instalment order is made, this is *not* a variation but a new judgment. As the client will not have defaulted, the court has no jurisdiction to make the charging order and the creditor's application should be dismissed, unless the judgment was made on or after 1 October 2012 (see p301). In the past, district judges have usually accepted this argument (but see 'hybrid orders' on p305). However, if the original determination is confirmed and the client has not paid in accordance with that determination, the Civil Procedure Rules would seem to enable the court to deal with the final charging order application immediately, rather than require the creditor to start all over again.[57]

- Check whether other creditors have been notified of the charging order application, as the charging order could unduly prejudice their rights and, therefore, should not be made final. If the court was not given details in the charging order application of other creditors of which the creditor in question was aware (eg, because they had been included on a financial statement), it could be argued that the creditor has not complied with the rules and the client has been denied a fair hearing, as prejudice to creditors is one of the matters which the Charging Orders Act specifically requires the court to take into account. Alternatively (and more usually), the district judge may adjourn the case while other creditors are notified. If none of the creditors lodges an objection, this 'prejudice to other creditors' argument may fail.

- The client is technically insolvent and thus a charge in favour of one creditor prejudices the rest. This will be the case if there was insufficient equity in the property to cover all the debts in full and there is, or is about to be, an arrangement to distribute the proceeds of sale on a pro rata basis among the client's creditors. However, a final charging order made after a bankruptcy petition has been presented against the client will not necessarily be set aside once a bankruptcy order is made, unless the court was expressly made aware of the existence of the petition before the final charging order hearing.[58]

A client cannot object to a charging order on the grounds that the application was made more than six years after the date of judgment or that the property is in negative equity.[59]

Hybrid and instalment orders

'Hybrid orders' were made for several years by the district judges at Northampton County Court in County Court Bulk Centre cases where the creditor had rejected the client's offer on Form N9A and asked the court to make an immediate judgment expressly for the purpose of obtaining a charging order. A judgment was made without a hearing on Form N24 stating:

> '1. Judgment against defendant payable forthwith.
> 2. The claimant may apply for a charging order at once.
> 3. Apart from a charging order, all other execution is stayed as long as the defendant pays £x per month (as offered on N9A). [This is not an instalment order, but merely a stay (or halt) of any other type of enforcement action by the creditor. Provided the client complies, s/he is protected from multiple enforcement action by the creditor.]
> 4. Any party affected by this order may apply within seven days after service to vary, amend or set it aside.'

Similar types of order are now made by a number of district judges at redetermination hearings with one crucial difference: paragraph 1 is an instalment order. It is arguable that if the judgment was made before 1 October 2012, the court could not override statutory rules by leaving the existing instalment order in place/making an instalment order on the one hand and giving leave to the creditor to issue a charging order on the other, in the absence of default under the instalment order.

If a client wishes to object to this type of order being made, s/he could argue that:

- the court has no jurisdiction to make either an interim or a final charging order if it has already made an instalment order and the client has not defaulted, unless the judgment was made on or after 1 October 2012 (see p301);[60] *and*
- instalment orders are made under s71(1) of the County Courts Act 1984. Unlike s71(2) (under which the stay of execution in para 3 of the so-called 'hybrid orders' are made), s71(1) does not allow the court to make an instalment order 'on such terms as the court thinks fit'.

If an adviser comes across a hybrid order or an instalment order giving leave to the creditor to apply for a charging order, s/he should seek specialist advice.

Conditions attached to a charging order

A charging order can be made either with or without conditions.[61] A client could apply at the hearing for a condition to be imposed to prevent the charging order being used as a basis for an order for sale, or for it only to be used as such in certain circumstances – eg, after the youngest child of the family ceases to be in full-time education. If a court is determined to impose a charging order, such conditions can mitigate the worst effects of its decision. Debt advisers should point out to the court that, when making a final charging order, it should consider the possibility of enforcement by the creditor and should either attach conditions or suspend it on terms (see below).

If the client intends to ask the district judge to attach conditions to the final order or to suspend it on terms, written evidence in the form of a witness statement should be submitted together with a financial statement. If a final order has already been made, it is still possible to make an application to the court to vary or discharge the order if it seems the court did not consider the client's circumstances at the time the order was made or the circumstances have since changed . A co-owner or a joint occupier who is a spouse or civil partner can also apply.[62]

After a charging order has been made, the creditor can wait until the property is sold, in which case it will be paid out of the proceeds of sale. Alternatively, it can apply to the court for an order for sale (see p307).

Some creditors argue that a charging order allows them to enforce payment of accrued contractual interest even though it forms no part of the judgment. If a creditor tries to argue this, the debt adviser should seek specialist advice.

Suspending a charging order

Enforcement of a final charging order may be suspended on payment of instalments.[63] The client can apply for these payments to be suspended or varied if her/his circumstances change. Some district judges say that they cannot suspend the charging order or they cannot consider the application at the final charging order hearing. The county court's power to suspend an order is in s71(2) of the County Courts Act 1984 and because the court should attempt to deal with as many aspects of the case as it can at the same hearing, the court should be asked to deal with the application at the same time.[64]

Because a charging order is an indirect method of enforcement (ie, it only secures payment but does not actually produce any money at the time), a creditor may decide to use (an)other method(s) of enforcement as well. It is, therefore, good practice to apply for a variation of the judgment (see p317) as well as suspension of, or the attachment of conditions to, the charging order (see p319).[65] In fact, an application at the final charging order hearing for an order suspending enforcement of the charging order and all other enforcement action, so long as the client pays instalments as ordered will, in practice, achieve the same result.

Order for sale of the property

Note: an application for an order for sale is both serious and legally complex. Specialist advice should always be sought.

An order for sale is a court order to sell a property that is the subject of a charging order so that the debt can be paid out of the proceeds. It is only possible after a charging order has been made final and if any conditions or terms attached to the order have not been met.

The Charging Orders Act 1979 requires a district judge to use her/his discretion to decide whether to order a sale.[66] It is an extreme sanction and would be a draconian step to satisfy a simple debt and is likely only to be used if a client's failure to pay has been intentional or where a sale is the only realistic way in which the debt will be paid.

In the past, applications for orders for sale have been very rare, but advisers report that numbers appear to have increased.

The creditor must apply using the procedure under Part 8 of the Civil Procedure Rules. This requires a hearing in all cases. The application is made to the court that made the charging order, which may not be the client's local court. The client should complete and return the acknowledgement of service not more than 14 days after the service of the claim form, together with a request for transfer to the client's local court (where appropriate) and any written evidence, indicating that s/he intends to oppose the order for sale and her/his reasons for doing so. It is vital that clients attend and are represented at this hearing. Strictly, if the judgment debt is more than £30,000, the application for an order for sale should be heard in the High Court, but the High Court can transfer all these cases to the county court.[67]

Even if a sale is ordered, the court can suspend the order on terms (eg, payment by instalments) or postpone the order for sale until a future date – eg, when the youngest child of the family reaches 18. The debt adviser will need to discuss with the client a way of ensuring that the charging order creditor is paid and this debt must now be treated as a priority (see Chapter 8). A full financial statement should be completed and an offer of payment made if possible. If not, the adviser should consider whether there are any exceptional circumstances that could be used to prevent an order being made. Always recheck that the client's income is maximised (see Chapter 7).

If the court accepts the client's offer of instalments, the adviser should ask the court to adjourn the application for an order for sale on condition that the client makes the payments. If an order for sale is made and not suspended, the client is normally given 28 days to pay the debt or leave the property. If this does not happen, the creditor can apply for a warrant of possession (see p352).

Note: when s93 of the Tribunals, Courts and Enforcement Act 2007 is implemented on 1 October 2012, no order for sale can be made unless the client has defaulted on the instalment order and the arrears remain unpaid. Section 94 enables the Lord Chancellor to set financial thresholds for orders for sale. Although this was brought into force on 17 May 2012, at the time of writing, no regulations have yet been made.

Joint ownership of property

A charging order can be made against a client's 'beneficial interest' (her/his share) in a property. If a client owns only a part-share of a property, a charging order can still be made, but it will apply only to her/his share.

If a charging order is made, the creditor becomes a party with an interest in the property and can apply for an order to sell the property so that the creditor's interest can be realised.[68] The court is required to take into account:

- the intentions of the owners at the time of the original purchase – ie, the purpose for which the property was bought. For example, it may be that a court should not order the sale of an asset, which was bought for a specific purpose, until the need for it has ceased to exist. If this is a correct interpretation, a family home should not be sold until all members of the family have ceased to need it;
- the welfare of any child who occupies the property as her/his home;[69]
- the interests of any secured creditor. In one case, the Court of Appeal ordered the sale of a property where there was sufficient equity to pay only part of the debt and the client was apparently unable to make any offer of payment.[70]

All the circumstances should be considered, including the size of the judgment debt and the value of the property. The personal circumstances of the client and other occupiers should be explained to the court in detail. Point out:

- that it is not equitable (or fair) for a whole family or group of occupants to be evicted for the debt of one of their members;
- any special factors – eg, age, disability, illness, need for stability at work or school, availability of alternative housing, and the effect on children;
- the history of the loan.

Human rights issues have not so far had much effect on applications for orders for sale. It is arguable that a court faced with an application for an order for sale should always consider whether it is proportionate to deprive the client of her/his home in order to satisfy a modest debt. In assessing proportionality, the court should also consider whether the creditor seeking the order has bought the debt and how much they are actually out of pocket.[71]

If an application for an order for sale is made, a claim form is sent to all co-owners of the property. This may include someone who does not owe money to the creditor who has obtained the charging order. However, because that person owns part of the property against which the debt is secured, the court must treat her/him as a joint defendant in the case. This means s/he is entitled to be heard at the hearing of the application and to put forward her/his own case, if necessary.

If a divorce petition has been served, any application for an order for sale (or a charging order) should normally be considered along with the finances and property of the couple.[72]

One important side effect of a charging order on a jointly owned property is that it 'severs' any joint tenancy. This means that, if either of the joint owners dies, her/his share no longer passes automatically to the survivor but, instead, is dealt with as part of her/his estate (see p87). One of the consequences of this is that any creditors will have an estate against which to claim.

Attachment of earnings order

An attachment of earnings order requires an employer who is paying wages, statutory sick pay or an occupational pension to a client to deduct some of it and make payments to the court to meet the debt. It cannot be used to attach state benefits or tax credits. Attachment of earnings orders are governed by the Attachment of Earnings Act 1971 and can be made either by the magistrates' or the county courts. The following information relates to county court judgments, not to magistrates' court fines or attachment of earnings orders made under liability orders.

The county court can make attachments to cover default on any judgment debt (including High Court judgments, which must be transferred to the county court for enforcement[73]) or administration orders.

A creditor can request an attachment of earnings order for any unpaid judgment debt over £50. The client receives a notice of the application (Form N55), together with Form N56 to complete, showing a statement of her/his means. The N56 is similar to the N9A (see p285), except there is provision to include a partner's income. **Note:** the time limit for returning the N56 is only eight days. If s/he does not return Form N56, the court can order the client to complete a statement of means and the client's employer can be ordered to supply a statement of earnings. This must always be completed and returned to the court, as failure to do so can lead to a summons for a personal appearance. Failure to comply can lead to imprisonment.

Responding to the application

There is space on Form N56 to request that a suspended attachment of earnings order be made. This allows the client to agree to make regular payments. A request for a suspended order should always be considered. A client may decide to make a request where an attachment of earnings order could lead to the client's dismissal by her/his employer.

How the order is made

A court officer uses the information supplied on the N56 together with a formula contained in the protected earnings calculator (EX119), to make an attachment of earnings order and set a 'protected earnings rate' in accordance with the determination of means guidelines (see p289). This is an amount that the court considers is the minimum the client, and any dependants, need to live on. The income support level is considered the minimum required plus housing costs, essential work-related expenses and other court orders. If, after taking into account any partner's income or other sources of income, the client has less than this amount (the protected earnings rate), the order will not be made. The guidance instructs court officers to disregard disability living allowance and attendance allowance when calculating income. The guidance suggests that deductions (the 'normal deduction rate') are set at between 50 per cent and 66 per cent of the client's 'disposable income' – ie, the difference between the client's net earnings and the protected earnings rate. It also recommends that a suspended attachment of earnings order should only be made if the client requests one, but that the request should be granted unless an attachment of earnings order is already in force. If the client does not give sufficient information on Form N56, the court officer will refer the matter to the district judge to make an order.

Both the client and the creditor have 14 days in which to give notice to the court that they object to the terms of the attachment of earnings order, whether the order has been made by a court official or a district judge. If an objection comes from either side, a hearing will be arranged in the client's local court at which the district judge can make any order s/he thinks appropriate. An objection can be made by letter stating the grounds – eg, if the protected earnings rate or the normal deduction rate does not leave the client with sufficient income for essential expenditure.

A court can decide to make an administration order (see p419) when considering attachment of earnings if the total indebtedness is below the limit for administration orders.[74] The court should always consider this if there are other debts. If attachment of earnings is to be accepted by the client, converting it to an attached administration order can simplify repayments.

Effect of an attachment of earnings order

An attachment of earnings order reduces a client's flexibility to manage her/his own affairs and it may endanger her/his employment because it notifies the employer of debts. Employers (eg, security firms or those where money is handled) may have a policy of dismissing anyone against whom a judgment is made. If this happens, the client should seek the advice of an employment specialist.

An attachment of earnings order tells the employer the total amount due under the judgment(s) concerned, and gives the normal rate to be deducted each week or month and states the protected earnings rate. The employer can only make deductions from any earnings in excess of the protected earnings rate. If the client's earnings are insufficient to enable the full, or any, deduction to be made, any resulting shortfall cannot be carried forward to the next pay day.

Even if the principle of an attachment is accepted, the adviser could argue against the normal deduction figure suggested. An offer could be made in Box 10 of the N56 on a pro rata basis if the client has more than one non-priority debt. A good financial statement is the basis of this argument, showing how repayment of priority creditors represents essential expenditure and that amounts to cover these should be included in the protected earnings rate.

If an attachment of earnings order is made, a fee (currently £1) can be added to each deduction by the employer to cover administrative costs. If a client leaves a job, s/he must notify the court within seven days of any new employment and income. Failure to do so is an offence which could be punishable by a fine. If the client becomes unemployed or self-employed, s/he should write to the court immediately.

A county court attachment of earnings order does not take priority over an attachment of earnings order made to recover fines, maintenance or local taxes or a deduction from earnings order made to recover child support arrears, even if made earlier. The combined effect may be to reduce the client's resources to a very basic level. In such a case, the client should be advised to apply to vary the attachment of earnings order on Form N244, quoting s9(1) of the Attachment of Earnings Act 1971 (there are no rules in either the Civil Procedure Rules or County Court Rules dealing with such applications) (see p317).

An attachment of earnings order prevents the creditor from enforcing the debt by a warrant of execution, charging order (and, arguably, an order for sale) or third-party debt order without first obtaining the permission of the county court.[75]

Although the courts cannot make an attachment of earnings order against the pay or allowances of a member of the Armed Forces, arrangements can be made through the Defence Council for compulsory deductions to be made from the client's pay, even where the client is stationed outside the UK.

Consolidated attachment of earnings order

If:
- there are two or more attachment of earnings orders for debt; *or*
- one attachment of earnings order is in force and a second one is applied for; *or*
- one attachment of earnings order is in force and the client has at least one other county court judgment,

the client can ask the court to consolidate these two debts and all other debts on which there is a judgment. The court can also make such an order on its own initiative.[76]

No procedure is specified, but the client should provide the court with details of the other judgments and a financial statement. There is no limit on the number of judgments or the amount owed. The advantage of this procedure is that there is only one protected earnings rate and one deduction figure. Some clients welcome this opportunity to avoid making several payments each month themselves.

Third-party debt order

Formerly known as a 'garnishee' order, a third-party debt order instructs someone (the 'third party') who owes money to the client (eg, a bank holding her/his savings) to pay it instead to the creditor. A third-party debt order may only be given to a creditor who has already obtained a judgment that is not being complied with.[77] The procedure is contained in Part 72 of the Civil Procedure Rules.

The order is made in two stages. An interim third-party debt order is given on application by the creditor on Form N349 either to the court which made the judgment or, if the proceedings have since been transferred, to the court being used. This temporarily prohibits the third party from making any payment which reduces the amount s/he owes the client to less than the amount specified in the order – ie, the balance of the debt plus the costs of the application. However, it should be noted that any funds paid into the account following the interim order being served are not affected.

This is followed by a final order after a hearing in front of a district judge, which must be not less than 28 days after the making of the interim order. If the client wishes to object to the final order being made, s/he can apply to have the hearing transferred to her/his local court. The client (and also the third party) must file at court and serve on the creditor any written evidence in the form of a witness statement setting out the grounds of objection not less than three days before the hearing. When making a final order, the district judge has a full discretion and should consider the position of both the client and any other creditors (if known).[78] If, for instance, an attempt is made to seize a client's only monthly income, the debt adviser should argue this would be unreasonable and would cause hardship to the client and her/his family, as well as preventing payments to other (possibly priority) creditors.

If the third party is a bank or building society, on receipt of the interim order it must search for all accounts held in the client's name, freeze them and give details to both the court and the creditor within seven days. The bank or building society is entitled to deduct £55 from the client's account balance towards the costs and expenses of responding to the order, regardless of the amount in the account. Similarly, the bank or building society is required to inform the court within seven days if the client has no account. If the bank or building society claims to be entitled to any of the money in the account, it must inform the court within seven days and state its grounds. The court cannot make a third-party debt order in relation to a joint account if the other account holder is not liable for the debt under the judgment.

Note: although the Department for Work and Pensions (DWP) cannot itself be subject to a third-party debt order in relation to benefit payments, once the payment is in the client's bank or building society account, the bank or building society can be the subject of a third-party debt order in relation to the funds in that account.

An order cannot be made in respect of a debt owed jointly to the client and another person where the judgment is against the client alone. However, a third-party debt order could be used if, for example, a client had told a creditor that an amount of capital would shortly be due from an endowment insurance policy in her/his sole name. The creditor could obtain a third-party debt order against the insurance company after the amount became due but before it had been paid out. For this reason, it is important for a debt adviser not to reveal details of future money available to a client if it is required to pay priority creditors or to be shared among a number of creditors.

Note: in a recent case, the High Court decided that a third-party debt order could be made against a tax-free lump sum that the debtor was entitled to draw from his pension fund but which he had elected to defer.[79] The court made an order under s37 of the Senior Courts Act 1981 requiring the debtor to authorise the creditor's solicitor to exercise his right to elect to withdraw the lump sum. Once made, the lump sum was due for payment and a third-party debt order could be made at that point.

Hardship payment order

If, because of an interim third-party debt order (see 312), a client finds her/his bank account frozen and s/he or her/his family is experiencing 'hardship in meeting ordinary living expenses' as a result of not being able to withdraw money from the account, s/he can apply to her/his local county court for a hardship payment order. The client must produce written evidence to prove both her/his financial position and the need for payment. Applications are made on Form N244 (see p271). The fee is £80 (full or partial remission can be applied for). Two days' notice of the hearing must be given to the creditor, but the court can dispense with this in cases of 'exceptional urgency'. The court can permit the bank or building society to make one or more payments out of the account either to the client or some other specified person.[80]

Bailiffs

Chapter 14 discusses bailiffs' powers in detail.

6. **Preventing enforcement**

Setting aside a judgment

If a judgment is 'set aside', its effect is cancelled and the client and creditor are put back into the position they were in before judgment was obtained. This includes the creditor cancelling any enforcement action.[81]

Part 13 of the Civil Procedure Rules deals with setting aside and varying the amount of (but not the rate of) payment a judgment entered in default. The following are '**mandatory grounds**' for setting aside a default judgment – ie, the court *must* do so if:

- judgment was entered before the client's time for filing an acknowledgement of service or a defence had expired (see p283); *or*
- the client served an admission on the creditor together with a request for time to pay before the judgment was entered (see p283); *or*
- the client paid the whole of the claim (including any interest or costs due) before judgment was entered. If the client paid the whole of the claim before the claim form was issued, s/he should have filed a defence (see p295).

The following are '**discretionary grounds**' for setting aside a judgment – ie, the court *may* do so if:

- the client has a real prospect of success in the claim; *or*
- the court is satisfied that there is some other good reason why the judgment should be set aside/varied or the client allowed to defend the claim; *or*
- there has been an error of procedure, such as a failure to comply with a rule or practice direction.

Serving the claim form

Note: provided the claim form was served in accordance with the Civil Procedure Rules, the fact that the proceedings only came to the client's attention after judgment was entered is not a ground in itself for it to be set aside, even if the client alleges s/he did not receive the claim form.

If the claim form was issued before 1 October 2008, it is treated as having been served in accordance with the Civil Procedure Rules, provided it:[82]

- was sent by the court to the client's usual or last known address; *and*
- has not been returned by the Post Office as undelivered.

If the claim form was issued on or after 1 October 2008, it is treated as having been served in accordance with the Civil Procedure Rules even if it is returned undelivered to the court, provided it was sent to the client's 'relevant address'. This is the client's usual or last known address unless:

- the creditor has reason to believe it is no longer the client's current address; *and*

- the creditor is able to establish the client's current address; *or*
- the creditor is unable to establish the client's current address, but considers there is an alternative place or method of service.

If the creditor has reason to believe that the client's usual or last known address is not her/his current address – eg, because letters have been returned marked 'gone away', the creditor is required to take reasonable steps to find out the client's current address. If the creditor is able to establish the client's current address, the claim form must be served at that address. Provided this is the client's current address, the claim form will be treated as having been served even if the client does not actually receive it or it is returned to the court.

If the creditor is unable to establish the client's current address, it must consider whether there is an alternative place or method of service and, if so, must ask the court to authorise service at that place or by that method. The creditor must be able to satisfy the court that the claim form is likely to reach the client if it is served at the place or by the method proposed. For example, if the adviser contacts the creditor stating that s/he is acting for the client, but is not authorised to disclose the client's current address, the creditor could ask the court to authorise the claim form to be sent to the adviser's agency. The Civil Procedure Rules also suggest that leaving a voicemail message stating where the document is could be an alternative method of service, provided the creditor can satisfy the court that the client uses that telephone number and is likely to receive the message. If the court agrees to the creditor's request, it will make an order specifying:

- the method or place of service;
- the date the claim form is treated as served; *and*
- the period the client has to respond to the claim form.

The claim form is treated as having been served by the alternative method or at the alternative place, even if it does not reach the client or is returned to the court. If the creditor is both unable to establish the client's current address and there is no suitable alternative place or method of service, the client's usual or last known address is still the relevant address (even though it is unlikely that the claim form will come to the client's attention) and a claim form sent to that address will be treated as having been served even if it does not reach the client or is returned to the court.

If the claim form is treated as having been served under one of the above rules, unless one of the mandatory grounds applies (see p314), if the client wants to apply for a set-aside, one of the discretionary grounds will have to be relied on (see p314).[83]

On the other hand, if the claim form has not been properly served, the client can apply to have the judgment and any enforcement action set aside. In the usual case, the court can only refuse a set-aside either if there has been no prejudice to the client or possibly if the client has been guilty of 'inexcusable delay', in making the application.[84]

Applications

If the application is made on a discretionary ground, the court must take into account whether or not the client acted promptly in making the application – ie, with all reasonable speed once s/he found out about the existence of the judgment. When applying for a judgment to be set aside, the client should always try to find an argument based on the facts or law of the case (eg, 'I do not owe the money because the goods supplied under a linked agreement were of unsatisfactory quality'), rather than personal circumstances – eg, 'I did not know how to reply to the claim form'. Although not strictly required by the Civil Procedure Rules, the client should explain why s/he failed to respond to the claim form – eg, although failure to receive the claim form may not be a set-aside ground in itself, it could be a valid explanation for failing to respond. The onus is on the client to show the defence is a 'convincing' one as opposed to merely 'arguable'.

Unless the client wishes to defend the claim or the creditor has already taken enforcement action (which would also be cancelled), it may be preferable for the client to apply to vary or suspend the terms of payment of the judgment (see below). Applying to set aside a judgment does not automatically prevent or delay any enforcement action by the creditor.

The application to set aside should also contain an application for a stay of enforcement pending the hearing, quoting Rule 3.1(2)(f) of the Civil Procedure Rules. Application is made on Form N244 and must be supported by the client's statement in Section 10 of the form. A fee of £80 is payable (see p273 for applying for full or partial fee remission). The case will be transferred to the client's local court.

If the client is seeking to set aside a county court judgment transferred to the High Court for enforcement, it seems that the application must still be made to the county court.[85] However, an adviser faced with this situation should seek specialist advice.

If the client has admitted the debt and judgment was entered on the basis of an N9A, the correct application is for permission to withdraw the admission under Rule 14.1(5) and defend the claim under Rule 3.1(2)(m). The N244 must also contain a request for transfer to the client's local court (where appropriate) (see p282) plus a request for a stay of enforcement.

If there has been a hearing in the county court, the client can apply to have the order set aside and the matter reheard if s/he did not attend the hearing and an order was made in her/his absence. The court will want to know why the client did not attend and whether there has been a miscarriage of justice. The court is unlikely to order a rehearing if the client deliberately failed to attend or if the court is satisfied that there is no real prospect of the original order being changed.[86] The court will not allow an application for a rehearing purely on the grounds that the client did not receive notice of the hearing date without enquiring as to why s/he did not receive it. On the other hand, the court should not refuse an application for a rehearing just because s/he failed to provide the creditor or lender with a forwarding address. In general: [87]

- if the client is unaware that proceedings are imminent or have been served, s/he will have a good reason for not attending any hearing;
- if the client knows of the existence of proceedings but does not have a system in place for receiving communications about the case, s/he is unlikely to have a good reason for not attending any hearing.

Suspending a charging order

If a final charging order has been made but no application was made at the hearing to suspend its enforcement by an order for sale on payment of instalments, the client can still make this application, if necessary, on an N244 (see p271). A fee of £40 is payable (see p273 for applying for full or partial fee remission).

Alternatively, the adviser could contact the creditor and ask if it intends to apply for an order for sale. In many cases the creditor has no intention of applying for an order for sale and so, provided an instalment arrangement can be agreed, in most cases, the creditor will be prepared to confirm that no order for sale will be applied for, provided the payments are maintained.

If an instalment order is in place, it is unlikely that the court will make an order for sale if there has been no default, although (strictly) if the judgment was made before 1 October 2012, non-default on an instalment order does not prevent an application for an order for sale being made. If the judgment or order under which the client is required to pay a sum of money by instalments is made on or after 1 October 2012, the court cannot make an order for sale unless the client has defaulted on the instalment order *and* any arrears of instalments remain unpaid.[88]

Varying payments due under an order

If the decision on the rate of payment was made by the court without a hearing, the procedure for redetermination on p291 should be followed if the client is unable to afford the rate of payment. If judgment was either entered in default or on acceptance of the client's offer of payment, the following procedures apply. **Note:** the procedure on p291 does *not* apply in these situations.

If the creditor believes s/he can persuade the district judge that the client can afford to increase her/his payments, s/he can apply for the rate of instalments to be increased. Application is made on Form N244 (see p271) and the case is automatically transferred to the client's home court for a hearing. The determination procedure on pp289–91 does not apply.[89]

Once an order for payment has been made, either in default or on acceptance of the client's offer of payment, the client can apply to the court that made it to have it varied at any time. S/he does not need a particular reason for making this application, although it will normally be because the original instalment order can no longer be afforded because of a change in circumstances or because the original order was made in ignorance of some material fact. In the case of default judgments for immediate payment, a successful application for variation prevents the creditor from taking subsequent enforcement action, so long as the client complies with the terms of the variation order.

The variation can include changes to either the amount of instalments or their frequency and is made on Form N245, which is very similar to Form N9A (see p285 on how to complete this). The N245 should be sent to the court that made the judgment. If it is also being used to apply to suspend a warrant of execution, it should be sent to the enforcing court (see p319). If the N245 is being used to apply to suspend a warrant of execution, an application for variation should be made at the same time by ticking both boxes. A fee of £40 is payable to cover both applications. See p273 for details about full or partial remission.

When helping a client to apply for a variation order, it is helpful to send a letter to accompany the N245, with a copy to the creditor, outlining the reasons for the application, especially if this is the first contact the debt adviser has had with the creditor.

The court sends a copy of the N245 to the creditor and if s/he does not respond within 14 days, the variation *must* be granted in the terms applied for.[90] If the creditor objects within 14 days, a court officer will use the determination of means guidelines to decide what the order should be.

Once the variation order has been made, either the creditor or client has 14 days to apply to the court for a reconsideration if they do not agree with the terms (see p291). The case will automatically be transferred to the client's local court and a hearing arranged. At the hearing, the district judge can make whatever order s/he thinks just.

Not all courts follow the above rules for dealing with an N245. For example, some have failed to follow up the application because, for instance, the creditor has applied for a charging order, or they have allowed considerably more than 14 days for the creditor to send objections. Advisers should keep a copy of the N245. Clients may wish to ask the court for a receipt or, if the N245 is to be posted, send it by special delivery or obtain a certificate of posting. Advisers should follow up applications which are not dealt with within 21 days of the N245 being posted to, or filed at, the court.

If the order for payment was made by a court officer or the district judge without a hearing and the client is out of time to apply for a redetermination, or it was made by the district judge at a hearing, the client can only apply to vary the order on the grounds of a change of circumstances (including information not previously before the court). The application is made on an N244 (see p271).[91] A fee of £40 is payable. See p273 for applying for full or partial fee remission. The case will not be automatically transferred to the client's local court and so an application for this will have to be included on the N244, quoting Rule 30.2(1) of the Civil Procedure Rules.

If the order for payment of the judgment was made in the High Court either in default or on acceptance of the client's offer of payment, the adviser should seek specialist advice on how to apply for a stay of execution and a variation of the judgment.

Suspensions and stays

An application for a variation on Form N245 must include an offer of payment. If even a nominal sum cannot be found, the client can apply for the judgment to be 'suspended' or 'stayed' (see also p285 on the N9A). A 'suspension' is usually on terms (eg, so long as payments are made) and a 'stay' is usually until an event occurs – eg, until a particular date. In practice, the terms seem to be interchangeable. Applications should be on Form N244 (see p271). Applications are more likely to be accepted if there are compelling reasons – eg, if the client has serious mental or physical ill health or is in prison. A fee of £40 is payable on the basis that the application is 'to vary a judgment or suspend enforcement'. See p273 for details about full or partial fee remission. The case will not automatically be transferred to the client's local court and so an application for this will have to be made on Form N244, quoting Rule 30.2(1) of the Civil Procedure Rules.

Suspension of a warrant of execution

If payments ordered under a judgment are missed and the creditor applies to the county court for bailiffs to enforce the debt, the client will receive a notice from the court warning that a warrant for the seizure of goods has been issued and giving a date after which it will be executed. Bailiffs may call at the client's home to try to take goods to sell (see Chapter 14 for details of the powers of county court bailiffs). Form N245 should be completed in order to suspend the warrant. The client should not only tick the box requesting 'suspension of the warrant' but also the box requesting 'a reduction in the instalment order' (even if the current terms of the judgment are for immediate payment). **Note:** the bailiffs can continue to attempt to seize goods until the application has been heard and a decision given. The N245 should be sent to the enforcing court, which will be the client's local court. A fee of £40 is payable, which covers both applications. See p273 for details about applying for full or partial fee remission.

The client could apply to have the matter stayed (see above). However, in order to prevent seizure of goods, an offer of payment must be made on the N245, but this need only be a token amount (eg, £1 a month) if the client is realistically unable to afford payments. The debt adviser should write to the creditor and explain the client's circumstances. If payments cannot be afforded, explain why such enforcement is not appropriate.

An offer of payment may not be appropriate if the client has no goods that could be seized (see p400 for excluded items) and there are no other methods of enforcement open to the creditor – eg, charging orders and attachment of earnings orders (see p301 and p309). In these circumstances, the debt adviser should ask the creditor to consider writing off the debt (see p244).

Once the court receives Form N245, a copy is sent to the creditor, who has 14 days to agree to the client's proposal or not. If the creditor agrees with the proposal, the warrant is suspended and the client is ordered to pay the amount offered. If the creditor does not agree to suspension on any terms, a hearing will be arranged at the client's local court, where the district judge will decide whether or not to suspend the warrant and on what terms. If the creditor agrees with a suspension but not the proposed terms, the determination procedure described above for varying an order will be followed.

Note: in some cases, county court judgments may (and in others, must) be enforced in the High Court. Once the adviser is aware that High Court bailiffs (known as enforcement officers) have been instructed, s/he should seek specialist advice.

Administration order

If the client has a judgment (either a county court or High Court judgment) and her/his total debts do not exceed £5,000, s/he should consider applying for an administration order (see p419).

Notes

1. **Startng a money claim**
   1 Part 7 para 2 PD CPR
   2 *Brandon v American Express* [2011] EWCA Civ 1187, CA (*Adviser* 149 abstracts)
   3 s176(2) and (3) CCA 1974; *Lombard North Central v Power-Hines* [1995] CCLR 24
   4 r2.3(1) CPR
   5 r6.14 CPR; *Anderton v Clwyd County Council* (*Adviser* 93 abstracts)
   6 Parts 7C para 1.4 and 16 para 7.3 PD CPR
   7 Part 5A PD CPR

   8 Part 5B PD CPR. For further information, see www.justice.gov.uk/courts/procedure-rules
   9 rr6.3(d) and 6.20(1)(d) and Part 6A para 4 PD CPR

2. **Admitting a money claim**
   10 For a discussion on drafting separate financial statements, see P Madge, 'Till Debt Do Us Part', *Adviser* 71

3. **The judgment**
   11 r14.4(6) CPR
   12 r14.9(2) CPR
   13 LCD, *Determination of Means: guidelines for court staff*, revised April 2011
   14 r3.2 CPR
   15 Part 14 para 5.1 PD CPR

16 Advisers should refer court staff who query this to item 3.4.5, 'What Happens Next?' in LCD, *Determination of Means: guidelines for court staff*, revised April 2011

17 For more information about the use of witness statements and how to draft them, see G Smith, 'Keep Your DJ Happy', *Adviser* 109

18 r12.3 CPR

19 r12.5 CPR

20 r15.11 CPR

21 s69 CCA 1984; s35a SCA 1981

22 *Adamson v Halifax plc* [2002] EWCA Civ 1134 (*Adviser* 115 abstracts); *Socimer International Bank v Standard Bank* [2006] EWHC 2896 (Comm) (*Adviser* 121 abstracts)

23 s17 JA 1838

24 Many district judges seem to be unaware that statutory interest cannot be charged on county court judgments arising out of agreements regulated by CCA 1974 – even if the judgment is for £5,000 or more. They can find confirmation in Art 2(3)(a) County Courts (Interest on Judgment Debts) Order 1991 (the text of which is in the commentary to s74 CCA 1984 in vol 2 of the 'Green Book' (*The Civil Court Practice*).

25 CC(IJD)O 1991

26 *Director General of Fair Trading v First National Bank* [2001] UKHL 52, 25 October 2001, unreported (*Adviser* 89 abstracts)

27 *Forward Trust v Whymark* [1989] 3 All ER 915, CA

28 rr12.6, 12.7 and 14.14 CPR. In the *First National Bank* case the House of Lords assumed the creditor could take further court action, but the point was not argued and so the issue remains unclear, at least so far as pre-1 October 2008 judgments are concerned.

29 *Director General of Fair Trading v First National Bank* [2001] UKHL 52, 25 October 2001, unreported (*Adviser* 89 abstracts)

30 s130A CCA 1974, as inserted by s17 CCA 2006

31 For further discussion of these issues, see P Madge, 'Interest After Judgment Under Regulated Consumer Credit Agreements', *Legal Action,* December 1990; P Madge, 'A Point of Interest', *Adviser* 59; P Madge, 'No Further Interest', *Adviser* 79; P Madge, 'Full Circle', *Adviser* 89; R Rosenberg, 'Interest After Judgment: is it the end of the road?', *Quarterly Account* 62, IMA

4. Defending a money claim

32 *Phoenix Finance Ltd v Federation Internationale de l'Automobile, The Times,* 27 June 2002

33 See P Madge, 'Using the Overriding Objective', *Adviser* 96

34 Para 5.3 PD CPR. Para 7C sets out a different procedure for claims issued by the Bulk Centre: all defences are referred by the court to the creditor who has 28 days to confirm whether or not it wishes to proceed. If so, the case is automatically transferred to the client's home court. If there is no response, the claim is stayed.

35 Part 27 PD CPR

36 Part 28 PD CPR

37 Part 29 PD CPR

38 *ED and F Man Liquid Products Ltd v Patel* [2003] EWCA Civ 472 (*Adviser* 101 abstracts)

39 Parts 3 and 24 PD CPR

40 r70.2(2) CPR

5. Enforcing a judgment

41 s8 AEA 1971

42 *Sucden Financial v Garcia* [2009] EWHC 3555 (QB) (*Adviser* 139 money advice abstracts)

43 CCR 39; Rule 2 Sch 2 CPR

44 r5 26 CCR; Sch 2 CPR; *Patel v Singh* [2002] EWCA Civ 1938 (*Adviser* 105 abstracts)

45 Order 8(1A) HCCCJO 1991, as amended

46 See also P Madge, 'Charging Interest', *Adviser* 76

47 *Ropaigealach v Allied Irish Bank* [2001] EWCA Civ 1790 (*Adviser* 90 abstracts)

48 Part 70 paras 8–11 PD CPR

49 Part 73 para 1.2 PD CPR

50 r73.5 CPR

51 s1(5) COA 1979

52 Part 73 para 3 PD CPR

53 r73.8 CPR. 'Written evidence' is a person's evidence set down in writing and signed to the effect that the maker of the statement believes the facts stated are true. See Part 32 PD CPR for the formalities of witness statements. Unless specifically required, an affidavit should not be used in preference to a statement.

54 *Mercantile Credit Co Ltd v Ellis, The Times,* 1 April 1987, CA, confirmed in *Ropaigealach v Allied Irish Bank* [2001] EWCA Civ 1790 (*Adviser* 90 abstracts)

55 *Ropaigealach v Allied Irish Bank* [2001] EWCA Civ 1790 (*Adviser* 90 abstracts)

56 Arguably, if the charging order application was made after the client applied for redetermination, the court had no jurisdiction to make an interim order as there was no judgment on which the client could default.

57 r1.1(2) CPR; see also P Madge, 'Charging On', *Adviser* 115

58 *Rainbow v Moorgate Properties* [1975] 2 All ER 821; see also *Nationwide BS v Wright* [2009] EWCA Civ 811 (*Adviser* 136 money advice abstracts)

59 *Fraenkl-Rietti v Cheltenham & Gloucester* [2011] EWCA Civ 524, CA (*Adviser* 146 abstracts)

60 s86(1) CCA 1984; *Ropaigealach v Allied Irish Bank* [2001] EWCA Civ 1790 (*Adviser* 90 abstracts)

61 s3(1) COA 1979

62 s3(5) COA 1979; r73.9 CPR

63 s71(2) CCA 1984 gives the county court power to suspend or stay any judgment or order on such terms as the court thinks fit.

64 r1.4(2)(i) CPR. Also, if a date has already been fixed for a hearing, any other applications should be dealt with at that hearing; Part 23 paras 2.8 and 2.10 PD CPR

65 Alternatively, an additional term or condition could be requested in the witness statement submitted for the final charging order hearing that all other enforcement action is stayed provided the client pays instalments as ordered.

66 s3(4) COA 1979

67 *National Westminster Bank v King* [2008] EWHC 280 (ChD) (*Adviser* 128 abstracts)

68 Under s14 TLATA 1996

69 s15 TLATA 1996. These provisions do not apply if the client is the sole owner of the property, even if it is the family home; *Wells v Pickering* [2000] EWHC 2540 Ch (*Adviser* 96 abstracts)

70 *Bank of Ireland v Bell* [2001] 2 FLR 809, CA

71 See M Robinson, 'Home Page', *Adviser* 146

72 *Harman v Glencross* [1986] 1 All ER 545, CA

73 r70.3 CPR

74 s4(2) AEA 1971

75 s8(2) AEA 1971

76 Part 27 rs18-22 CPR

77 *Mercantile Credit Co Ltd v Ellis, The Times,* 1 April 1987, CA

6. Preventing enforcement

78 *Rainbow v Moorgate Properties* [1975] 2 All ER 821

79 *Blight and others v Brewster* [2012] EWHC 185 Ch (*Adviser* 152 abstracts)

80 r72.7 CPR

81 r70.6 CPR

82 *Adam v Akam* [2004] EWCA Civ 1601, CA (*Adviser* 108 abstracts)

83 rr6.9, 6.15 and 6.18 and Part 6 para 9 PD CPR. The rules allow the creditor to take steps to effect service at an alternative place or by an alternative method and ask the court to validate it retrospectively. Provided the court makes the order, the claim form will be treated as served.

84 *Nelson v Clearsprings (Management) Ltd* [2006] EWCA Civ 1252 (*Adviser* 119 abstracts)

85 s42(6) CCA 1984, which says that the county court's powers to set aside a judgment continue to apply

86 The application is made 'in the interests of justice' under r3.1(2)(m) and (7) CPR; *Forcelux v Binnie* [2009] EWCA Civ 854 (*Adviser* 137 money advice abstracts)

87 *Estate Acquisition and Development v Wiltshire* [2006] EWCA Civ 533 (*Adviser* 118 abstracts)

88 s93(3) TC&A 2007. Note: rules of court can provide otherwise. At the time of writing, no such rules have been made

89 r10(3) and (4) Sch 2 CPR

90 r10(7) Sch 2 CPR

91 Part 14 para 6 PD CPR

Chapter 12

∙∙

The county court: possession of goods and property

This chapter covers:
1. Recovering goods on hire purchase or conditional sale (below)
2. Recovering property (p326)
3. Recovering owner-occupied property (p327)
4. Recovering rented property (p346)
5. Preventing enforcement (p355)

This chapter deals with court action by creditors when they wish to recover goods or property from a client. See Chapter 11 if the creditor is claiming money only.

Note: in some cases, in addition to making an order for payment of money, the court can order a client to give up possession of goods or property to the creditor. However, it can usually suspend the order if the client makes payments to the creditor as ordered by the court. See p325, p336 and p351 for more details.

Debts regulated by the Consumer Credit Act 1974

If the agreement to which the court action relates is regulated by the Consumer Credit Act 1974, the creditor must send the client a default notice before it can take action to repossess goods or land (see p281).

The High Court cannot deal with claims related to secured or unsecured agreements regulated by the Consumer Credit Act 1974, or actions linked to such agreements, regardless of the amount of the claim.

If an adviser encounters a case involving a regulated consumer credit agreement (or any other case) being dealt with in the High Court, s/he should seek specialist advice.

1. Recovering goods on hire purchase or conditional sale

A creditor requires a court order to repossess goods on hire purchase or conditional sale if at least one-third of the total cost has been paid (see p114 or p116) or if

∙∙∙∙

12

Chapter 12: The county court: possession of goods and property
1. Recovering goods on hire purchase or conditional sale

the client has paid less but has refused to allow the creditor to enter private property in order to take back the goods.

The creditor must first serve a default notice and include in the section on what action may be taken that goods can be repossessed. See p281 for further information about default notices. In these cases, the 'Consumer Credit Act procedure' applies.

- The claim must be started in the county court for the district in which the client either lives or carries out her/his business (or did when s/he made her/his last payment).
- The court fixes a hearing date when it issues the claim form (Form N1 – see p282) and notice of the hearing date is given when the claim form is served.
- The particulars of claim (containing the prescribed information – see p283) must be served with the claim form.
- The claim form and particulars of claim are accompanied by Forms N1(FD) (Note for Defendants), N9C (Admission and Statement of Means) and N9D (Defence/Counterclaim). There is no acknowledgement of service.

The client's response

The client is not required to file either an admission or a defence, although s/he should do so as the court can take account of a failure to do so when deciding on its order for costs in the case – eg, if an unnecessary hearing has to take place as a result. The creditor cannot request a default judgment. Form N9C enables the client to admit the claim and make an offer on which the court can make an order for the return of the goods suspended, provided the client makes payments in accordance with her/his offer (a 'time order').[1] The statement of means is similar to the N9A (see p285).

The client should complete Form N9C by:

- indicating whether or not s/he still has the goods in her/his possession;
- admitting liability for the claim; *and*
- offering to pay the unpaid balance of the total price. This figure is contained in the particulars of claim.

The admission should be returned to the court, not sent to the creditor. A copy is sent by the court to the creditor. If the creditor accepts the amount admitted and the offer of payment, it informs the court, which enters judgment and sends a copy to the client (Form N32(2) HP/CCA). No one need attend the hearing. If nothing is heard from the court, the client should attend the hearing. If the creditor does not accept the amount admitted or offer of payment, or the client does not respond, the hearing proceeds.

Negotiating before the hearing

An adviser should always try to negotiate with the creditor to reach an agreement before the court hearing. Most creditors prefer to receive payments rather than

Chapter 12: The county court: possession of goods and property
1. Recovering goods on hire purchase or conditional sale

12

repossess goods. Resuming the contractual payments will often be enough to persuade the creditor to withdraw or adjourn the court action. If no agreement can be reached, a hearing will take place and the client should attend, with a financial statement indicating her/his ability to pay. A court is unlikely to accept a long-term substantial reduction in payments (eg, £20 a month when the contractual agreement is for £120), but may accept a short-term reduction – eg, £20 a month for three months, then £120 a month. Unless a time order application is made (including completing Form N9C – see p324) or the hearing is adjourned, the court appears to have no power to make an order for payment of less than the contractual instalments.

Decisions the court can make

The court has a general power to adjourn for a short period if required, but will only exercise this power if it has compelling reasons (see p277). If the client can make an offer of payment in respect of the balance of the total price which the court finds acceptable, it will order the return of the goods but suspend the order, provided the payments are maintained.[2] If there is no acceptable payment offer, the court will order that the goods be returned. The judgment is on Form N32(1) and gives the date for delivery – ie, for the client to return the goods. If the goods are no longer in the client's possession, the court cannot order their return.[3] The creditor will have to obtain a judgment for the total balance due under the agreement.

Alternatively, the client could make an application for a time order once the default or arrears notice has been issued (see p340).

If the client fails to make payments or return the goods as ordered, it is arguable that the creditor cannot repossess the goods if they are 'protected goods' (see p400). The creditor should ask the court to issue a warrant of delivery (see below).

Note: returning the goods to the creditor is not the end of the matter. The creditor will sell the goods and set the proceeds of the sale against the remaining balance due. There may well be a shortfall that the client will be liable to pay. The creditor must apply to the court for a further hearing date to obtain an order for payment of the money.[4]

If the client's circumstances change, s/he can apply to vary the order.

Unless the client is merely disputing the amount s/he has already paid, the adviser should obtain specialist advice on any other potential defences. If the client disputes the claim, the court will either:
- deal with the case at the hearing; *or*
- allocate the case to a track (see p297) and make directions; *or*
- give directions to enable it to make a decision on allocation (see p297).

Warrant of delivery

A warrant of delivery is a document that allows the county court bailiff to seize goods that are the subject of a hire purchase or conditional sale agreement if the court has ordered that the goods be returned to the creditor. It is issued by the court following a request from the creditor that the client has not returned the goods as ordered by the court or is in breach of a suspended return of goods order. The warrant may allow the client to pay the value of the goods as an alternative to allowing them to be taken by the bailiffs. The client can apply for this warrant to be suspended and for delivery of the goods to be postponed (see p355). It is always worth approaching the creditor to negotiate an agreement before applying back to the court.

2. **Recovering property**

Note: this chapter only covers possession action taken on the grounds of unpaid payments due under a mortgage (or other secured loan) or unpaid rent due under a tenancy. It cannot cover the details of all the law in these areas and advisers should therefore refer to specialist books (see Appendix 2) and refer to a housing specialist where necessary.[5]

A landlord or a mortgage lender can start action in the county court for possession of a tenant's or owner occupier's home by completing a claim form (Form N5) and particulars of the claim (Form N119 for tenants and N120 for mortgages). The creditor cannot request a default judgment (see p292) or apply for summary judgment (see p298) in this type of action. There must be a hearing to consider the merits of the claim. The procedure is contained in Part 55 of the Civil Procedure Rules. Possession claims are normally brought in the county court for the area in which the property is situated. A claim may only be brought in the High Court in 'exceptional circumstances' and an adviser who encounters a possession claim or order made in the High Court should seek specialist advice.

Note: a client cannot be forced to leave her/his home against her/his will unless a court order and warrant have been obtained.

Negotiating before the hearing

The debt adviser should always try to negotiate with a creditor and reach a satisfactory agreement before going to court. This is preferable to relying on the decision of a district judge and avoids the possibility of things 'going wrong' at the hearing. In addition:

- if an order is made for possession of the property and/or payment of rent arrears, the client is usually ordered by the court to pay the landlord's costs;
- most mortgages allow the creditor to charge all her/his costs to the client in connection with default and repossession without needing a specific order for costs made by the court;
- it is important to avoid unnecessary court hearings or delays;

- ideally, both parties will apply for the matter to be adjourned generally (ie, without a future hearing date) on the agreed terms.

Often landlords and lenders insist on a suspended possession order (see p336) being made rather than agreeing to the case being adjourned on the basis of the agreed terms. This puts the client's home at risk, but it may result in a better order for her/him than if the matter had been left to the discretion of the district judge. If the creditor agrees to a suspended possession order (see p336), the adviser should check that any solicitor representing the landlord or lender has been informed and obtain written confirmation of the terms of the proposed suspended order so this can be produced at the hearing if there is any dispute. See Chapter 8 for possible strategies.

If the agreement to clear the arrears was made before the landlord or lender issued court proceedings and the client has not defaulted under the agreement, the adviser should ask the court to adjourn the matter and not allow the landlord's/lender's costs. This is because the Civil Procedure Rules and paragraph 6 of the pre-action conduct practice direction require people to act reasonably in trying to avoid the need for court proceedings (see p266).

In addition, a lender that issued proceedings in these circumstances would be in breach of the spirit of the mortgage arrears pre-action protocol (see p329). In the case of social landlords, if the payment agreement is made before the issue of proceedings, under paragraph 12 of the rent arrears pre-action protocol, the landlord should agree to postpone proceedings, provided the client keeps to the agreement. If the payment arrangement was made after proceedings were issued, the landlord should agree to an adjournment (see p357).

3. **Recovering owner-occupied property**

If the loan is a regulated agreement under the Consumer Credit Act (see p65), a default notice (see p281) must first be issued. The lender must obtain a court order before it can take possession, but the client could give her/his informed consent to the lender taking 'peaceable possession'.[6] In the case of other mortgages, the lender can take peaceable possession if the client has abandoned the property and left it empty. If the client returns the keys to the lender, this is known as a 'voluntary surrender' and the lender takes peaceable possession by accepting the keys.

Guidance to lenders

If the mortgage was made on or after 31 October 2004, it may be regulated by the Financial Services Authority (FSA) (see p147). If so, the lender is required by the *Mortgages and Home Finance: conduct of business sourcebook* (*MCOB*) to deal 'fairly' with borrowers in arrears and have a written arrears policy and procedures.[7] These should include:

- providing clients with details of missed payments, the total amount of arrears, the outstanding balance due under the mortgage, any charges incurred to date, an indication of possible future charges and a copy of the Money Advice Service's leaflet *Problems Paying Your Mortgage* (available from www.moneyadviceservice.org.uk);
- making reasonable efforts to come to an agreement with the client about repaying the arrears;[8]
- liaising with an adviser or agency if the client arranges this;
- allowing a reasonable time for repayment, bearing in mind the need to establish, where feasible, a practical repayment plan in the client's circumstances (in appropriate cases, arranging repayments over the remaining term of the mortgage);
- granting the client's request for a change to the payment date or method of payment (unless the lender has a good reason for not agreeing to this);
- if no reasonable repayment arrangement can be made, allowing the client to remain in possession of the property to enable it to be sold;
- repossessing the property only where all other reasonable attempts to resolve the situation have failed.

The lender must take into account the client's circumstances and consider whether it is appropriate to agree to:

- extend the term of the mortgage;
- change the type of mortgage – eg, repayment mortgage to interest-only mortgage;
- defer interest payments;
- capitalise the arrears;
- make use of any government forbearance initiatives (see p212).

The lender should also have given the client certain prescribed information (see p147). In addition, many mortgage lenders will not seek possession until payments of mortgage interest are three, or even six, months in arrears.

In October 2011, the Council of Mortgage Lenders issued industry guidance on arrears and possession to assist lenders comply with their duty to treat customers fairly. It can be found at: www.cml.org.uk/cml/policy/guidance. This includes examples of good practice for lenders, including:

- encouraging clients at the earliest opportunity to contact independent free money advice providers, and providing a dedicated contact point within the arrears handling department for money advisers;
- when agreeing repayment arrangements, assessing income and expenditure including using financial statements prepared by money advisers, ensuring staff have the flexibility to agree repayment periods suitable for individual

circumstances and taking into account repayment levels ordered by the courts and other priority debts;

- if no reasonable repayment can be made, informing clients that they can stay in the property to sell it, explaining how this will work and considering:
  - ways of helping clients to end their home ownership, including through an assisted voluntary sales scheme; *and*
  - when they will allow sales at shortfall to proceed – ie, if the client is in negative equity;
- applying for a possession order only when:
  - all attempts to contact or liaise with the client have failed;
  - it has not proved possible to agree an affordable repayment arrangement;
  - the client has not been able to maintain the agreed repayments;
- not applying for a possession order:
  - when a reasonable negotiated settlement is possible;
  - to discipline clients into maintaining payment arrangements;
  - if an arrangement is in place to which the client is adhering;
  - if an arrangement to pay is entered into after the proceedings have started, and consider agreeing to the hearing being adjourned instead;
- checking that the mortgage pre-action protocol has been complied with (see below), including completing the compliance checklist before the hearing.

Pre-action conduct

The **mortgage arrears pre-action protocol** (which came into force on 19 November 2008 and was amended in April 2011) makes it clear that starting a possession claim should 'normally' be the last resort and should not 'normally' be started unless all other reasonable attempts to resolve the situation have failed. The protocol aims to encourage lenders and borrowers to reach an agreement without the need for proceedings. The parties (or their advisers) should take all reasonable steps to discuss with each other the reasons for the arrears, the client's financial circumstances, whether the client's financial difficulties are temporary or long term and the client's proposals to clear the arrears 'in a reasonable time'. There is no guidance in the protocol on what this might be (unlike for rent arrears – see p346). Lenders must consider postponing possession action if the client:

- has made a claim:
  - to the Department for Work and Pensions (DWP) for a benefit that includes an amount for housing costs – eg, income support (IS); *or*
  - under a payment protection insurance policy; *or*
  - to a local authority under the mortgage rescue scheme.
  S/he must have supplied all the information necessary to process a claim and have a reasonable expectation that the claim will be successful;
- can demonstrate that s/he has taken (or will be taking) reasonable steps to sell the property at an 'appropriate price' (presumably one which will clear the

mortgage and any other loans secured on it) and the client continues actively to market the property;

- has made a 'genuine complaint' to the Financial Ombudsman Service (FOS) about the possession claim. As a complaint has to be made first to the lender and is only referred to the FOS if the lender either fails to issue a final response or rejects the complaint, it is unlikely that lenders will accept that complaints are genuine unless the Ombudsman agrees to investigate.

If the lender decides not to postpone issuing possession proceedings, it must inform the client at least five business days before doing so.

If a lender does not comply with the mortgage arrears pre-action protocol, the court does not have grounds to refuse to make a possession order. However, the lender must be able to explain to the court what actions it has taken to comply (as must the client).

From 1 October 2009, a lender must have two copies of Form N123 available at the hearing. This is a checklist verified by a statement of truth in which the lender confirms that it has taken various steps to comply with the protocol. Failure to produce an N123 would give the court grounds to strike out a possession claim for failure to comply with a rule under Rule 3.4(2)(c) of the Civil Procedure Rules (although it might prefer to adjourn the hearing to enable the lender to comply). There are, however, sanctions for non-compliance in the pre-action conduct practice direction (see p266). If the court believes the lender has not complied with the substance of the relevant principles and requirements (as opposed to minor or technical shortcomings which have had no overall effect on the situation), it can:

- 'stay' (ie, suspend) the proceedings until the steps which ought to have been taken have been taken; *and/or*
- order that the party at fault pays the costs (or part of the costs) of the other party (or, in this context, disallows some or all of the lender's costs that would otherwise be payable).

If the lender appears not to have complied, advisers should point this out and argue that no further action should be taken, provided the client complies with her/his obligations under the protocol, such as by making payments or actively pursuing a claim for payment protection insurance, benefits or a proposed sale of the property (including the Mortgage Rescue scheme). Advisers should also point this out on the N11M form of defence (see p333) and put the arguments to the district judge at the hearing for any dismissal, or (more likely) adjournment of the possession claim, or in relation to costs.

Advisers should bear in mind that, if the client has not complied with the protocol, the court will take this into account.

The claim form

The possession claim form (Form N5) includes the date and time of the hearing. It must be accompanied by a particulars of claim (Form N120), although the lender can use its own particulars of claim provided it contains details of:[9]

- the identity of the property to be recovered;
- whether the claim relates to residential property;
- the ground(s) on which possession is claimed;
- the mortgage or charge;
- every person in possession of the property (to the best of the lender's knowledge);
- whether any charges or notices have been registered under the Family Law Act 1996 or Matrimonial Homes Acts 1967–1983;
- the state of the account between the client and lender, including:
  - the amount of the advance, any periodic payments and any repayment of interest required to be made;
  - the amount which would have to be paid, taking into account any allowance for early settlement, to redeem the mortgage at a stated date not later than 14 days after the start of proceedings, including solicitors' costs and administrative charges;
  - if it is a regulated consumer credit agreement, the total amount outstanding under the terms of the mortgage;
  - the rate of interest payable originally, immediately before any arrears accrued and at the start of proceedings;
  - a schedule of arrears, showing all amounts due and payments made together with dates and a running total of the arrears either for the previous two years or from the date of default, if later;
  - details of any other payments required to be made as a term of the mortgage (such as insurance premiums, legal costs, default interest, penalties, and administrative and other charges), whether any of these payments are in arrears and whether or not they are included in the periodic payment;
- whether or not the loan is a regulated consumer credit agreement and the date(s) on which the appropriate notices under the Consumer Credit Act have been served;
- information that the lender knows about the client's circumstances and, in particular, whether s/he is in receipt of benefits and whether direct mortgage interest payments are being received from the DWP;
- any previous steps taken by the lender to recover either the money secured under the mortgage or the property itself, including dates of any court proceedings and the terms of any orders made;
- the history of arrears (if longer than two years). This should be stated in the particulars and a schedule of the arrears should be exhibited to a witness statement and served separately, at least two days before the hearing.

All the above requirements are covered in paragraphs 1 to 9 on Form N120. The lender may also include a money-only claim arising out of an unsecured loan agreement. Although the lender can obtain a money judgment in respect of such a debt, it cannot be enforced as part of any possession order.[10] The lender will not normally be seeking an order for costs, as the mortgage normally allows for these to be added to the outstanding balance automatically.

The particulars of claim must be verified by a statement of truth.

'Possession claim online'

Certain specified county courts can now operate a scheme known as 'possession claim online', which enables lenders to issue claims for possession electronically via https://www.possessionclaim.gov.uk/pcol.

The particulars must contain the same information referred to above with one exception. If the lender has already provided the client with a schedule of arrears showing all amounts due and payments made, together with dates and a running total of the arrears either for the previous two years or from the date of default, if later, the particulars of claim may contain a summary of the arrears stating:

- the amount of the arrears on the date of the lender's pre-action letter;
- the dates and amounts of the last three payments (or, if less than three payments have been made, the dates and amounts of those payments); *and*
- the arrears on the date possession proceedings are issued.

However, if the lender only includes the summary information listed above in the particulars of claim, it must serve a full arrears history on the client within seven days after the issue of the claim and verify this by a witness statement or verbally at the hearing.

Proceedings are issued according to the property's postcode supplied by the lender. If this is not the client's local court, s/he can ask the court to transfer the case.[11]

Before 'possession claim online' was introduced, courts could send information of details of local advice agencies and the availability of a court helpdesk with possession claims. Courts can signpost local advice agencies within the claim pack generated by online possession claims. Individual courts are responsible for keeping this information up to date, so advisers should inform their county court of any new developments.

After the claim form is issued

The hearing (which takes place in private) will normally be fixed for not less than 28 days or more than eight weeks after Form N5 is issued. The claim form and particulars of claim must be served on the client not less than 21 days before the hearing. Not less than 14 days before the hearing, the lender must send a notice to the property addressed to 'the occupiers' containing details of the claim. The purpose of this is to alert anyone living at the property who is not the borrower but who may be in a position to oppose the claim for possession.

Since 1 October 2009, the lender must also write to the local authority for the area in which the property is situated and inform it about the hearing. The lender must be able to confirm at the hearing that these steps have been taken (a witness statement is sufficient). The Department for Communities and Local Government has provided guidance to local authorities on what to do with this information to enable them to include it within their overall strategy on preventing homelessness.[12]

There is no acknowledgment of service. Written evidence may be given at the hearing and should be filed at court and served on the other side at least two days before the hearing date. Evidence of the arrears, including interest, should be up to the date of the hearing and refer to a daily rate, if necessary. If the claim cannot be dealt with on the hearing date because there appears to be a substantial dispute, the district judge should give directions and allocate the case to a track (see p297).

Responding to the claim

There is a 'defence' form (N11M) which is supposed to be completed and filed at court within 14 days of service, but which may be filed at any time before the hearing. The questions are straightforward, although they are not cross-referenced to the numbered paragraphs in the particulars of claim. It is not a defence as such, but a reply to the claim. It is not essential to respond, but it is advisable to do so, as any delay caused by the client's failure to file the defence may mean further liability for costs. Although there will be a hearing, it is helpful if the district judge has been prepared for the client's circumstances and arguments by submitting a well completed reply form. A copy of the form is also sent by the court to the lender.

In the case of online claims, the claim is accompanied by a covering letter containing details of the user name and password to access the website where the client can complete and file the form online. The website contains a user guide, although most of the information is only relevant to lenders and there is no guidance on how to complete Form N11M.

Completing Form N11M

Form N11M should be completed as follows.
- **Question 1** requests details of the client's personal circumstances including her/his date of birth.
- **Question 2** relates to paragraphs 2 to 4 on Form N120, which should be confirmed as correct, or details of any disagreement given.
- **Question 3.** Check the level of arrears as carefully as possible. The court may not make an order if it is unsure that the arrears figure is correct.

- **Question 4** needs completing only in cases where possession is sought (perhaps partly) on grounds other than arrears.
- **Questions 5 and 6** are primarily addressed to borrowers whose loans are regulated agreements.

  Question 5 asks whether the client wants the court to consider whether the terms of the loan agreement are 'fair'. This appears to apply to the unfair relationship provisions of the Consumer Credit Act 1974 (which do not apply to mortgage contracts regulated by the FSA), as well as to unfairness under the Unfair Terms in Consumer Contracts Regulations (which apply to all agreements, not just Consumer Credit Act-regulated agreements). Although one of the main principles of FSA regulation is that lenders must treat their customers fairly (see p148), it is not clear to what extent a court could address a breach of the FSA's rules as a defence to possession proceedings.

  Question 6 asks whether the client intends to apply for a time order (see p340). An application may be made either on this form (which does not have a fee) or by notice of application (Form N244) (which has a fee, but full or partial remission may be possible – see p273).[13] As there is only room to tick a box on the N11M, any applications will need to be supported by written evidence in the form of a witness statement, setting out the grounds.
- **Question 7.** If the arrears have been paid in full by the date of the hearing, the case should be adjourned.[14]
- **Question 8.** If an agreement has been reached, details should be included. In this case, the reply should ideally be accompanied by a letter requesting a general adjournment. If the lender agrees, it should also write to the court indicating its agreement to a general adjournment. If the agreement has been running since before the action started, the client may argue there was no need to take court action, and ask for the matter to be adjourned generally and challenge any costs the lender seeks to charge.[15] S/he should send proof of payments, or include a written request from the lender that an order be made and suspended on payment of whatever sum has been agreed.
- **Question 9** should be completed in the affirmative if agreement has not been reached. Note that clients who fail to ask the court to consider instalments might later find this used against them if a local authority is considering the question of the intentionality of their homelessness.
- **Question 10** asks for the amount, in addition to the contractual payments, being offered. This question may not be relevant as it is not always necessary for the client to be able to afford the contractual payments for the court to make a suspended possession order. For the position if the client is applying for a time order, see p340; for other cases, see pp335–40.
- **Questions 11–13** relate to IS, income-based jobseeker's allowance (JSA), income-related employment and support allowance (ESA) and pension credit (PC). It is important to check with the DWP what payments have been made before attending court, so that any misunderstandings with the lender can be

resolved. Remember to convert weekly benefit amounts to calendar monthly amounts to compare with monthly mortgage payments.

- **Questions 14–25** relate to dependants (and non-dependants), bank accounts and savings, income and expenditure, priority debts, court orders and credit debts similar to those required on Form N9A (see p285) and should be filled in similarly.
- **Question 26.** The client should not answer 'yes' to Question 26 ('If an order is made will you have somewhere to live?') unless the accommodation is absolutely certain. The date given, even in such cases, should always be realistic.
- **Question 27** is important because it gives the client the opportunity to explain:
  - any breaches of the FSA rules, especially the principle of treating clients fairly and any breaches of the *MCOB*;[16]
  - the circumstances in which the loan was made, if relevant – eg, to refinance unsecured borrowing in response to high-pressure selling;
  - why the arrears arose;
  - what circumstances were beyond her/his control;
  - why it would cause particular hardship if eviction was ordered.

Powers of the court to deal with possession action

If a court is considering an action for the possession of a private house, it has wide-ranging powers in relation to the protection it can potentially give a client with a mortgage or a secured loan not regulated by the Consumer Credit Act 1974.[17] These include:

- adjourning the proceedings (see below); *or*
- suspending a possession order (see p336); *or*
- postponing the date for the delivery of possession (see p337).

If an agreement is regulated under the Consumer Credit Act 1974 (see p65), the court should consider making a time order. This can be specifically requested by the client. See p340.

Adjournment

The court has a general power to adjourn any proceedings for a short period.[18] For example, if the client needs more time to seek money advice or the lender is required to clarify the arrears, the court may adjourn the matter, usually for 28 days. The court may attach terms to the adjournment – eg, that basic instalments are paid or that no further interest is added to the loan. The court can also adjourn the proceedings for a short time to enable the client to pay off the mortgage in full – eg, by selling the property, or otherwise satisfying the lender.[19]

The court sends out a written notice giving the date and time of the next hearing. If the property is about to be sold or the arrears cleared in full in some other way, the court may adjourn with 'liberty to restore'. There will not be another hearing, provided the expected action happens. However, if the expected action fails, the lender can ask for a hearing to be restored.

Advisers may wish to argue that the matter should be adjourned, rather than have a suspended possession order granted, in one of the following ways:

- **adjourn with liberty to restore** – eg, because the arrears have been, or are about to be, paid in full, or the property is in the process of being sold or an agreement to pay the arrears has already been agreed;
- **adjourn for a fixed period** (eg, 28 days) for the client to get further advice or for the lender to produce correct particulars of claim;
- **adjourn generally** because there is a repayment plan agreed and working.

Terms may be attached to an adjournment – eg, that basic payments be maintained. An adjournment is preferable because no further action, including enforcement, can be taken without a further court hearing. For clients who are vulnerable because of age or disability, this can be a valuable tactic.

Suspended possession orders

Under s36 of the Administration of Justice Act 1970 and s8 of the Administration of Justice Act 1973, provided the client can pay both the arrears and the future contractual payments within a 'reasonable period', the court can suspend any possession order on such 'conditions with regard to payment by the mortgagor [the borrower] of any sum secured by the mortgage or the remedying of any default as the court thinks fit'.[20] The terms of the order will usually be for basic instalments plus £x towards the arrears. However, a number of court cases show this is not always necessary.

In one case, an order was made for payment of £250 for one month and £500 for two months, with a review thereafter on the basis that the client had good prospects of obtaining employment within that period.[21] In another case, the client offered £150 a month until mortgage interest became payable by the DWP, which would cover the current payments.[22] Although the arrears would increase meanwhile, they would be cleared within three-and-a-half years. The court made an order accordingly. In each case, the court held that the test was not whether the client could pay the contractual payments now but whether s/he would, within a reasonable period, be able to clear the arrears and pay the contractual instalments.

In 1996, in the case of *Cheltenham and Gloucester v Norgan*, the Court of Appeal said that a starting point for 'reasonable period' should be the remaining period of the mortgage.[23] This valuable precedent strengthens the money advice case for setting repayments at a level the client can afford. In exceptional cases, a 'reasonable period' could be longer than the remaining mortgage.[24] The decision also guides the court on points it should take into consideration, including the means of the client and the value of the lender's security.

On the whole, courts appear satisfied that, for a long-term agreement, such as a mortgage, the security is safe. A clear financial statement is an essential tool. Identify the basic mortgage instalment separately from the payment towards the arrears to demonstrate to the court that the client is able to afford the contractual mortgage payments as well as being able to pay off the arrears within the period requested.

Tactically, advisers should still look for an affordable sum rather than spreading the arrears over as long a period as possible, just in case further difficulties arise in the future. Do not be intimidated by creditors and solicitors who say they want the arrears cleared in a shorter fixed period – eg, three years. The court will make its own decision and it should be familiar with the *Norgan* case.

If the arrears cannot be paid by instalments and the mortgage can only be repaid out of the proceeds of sale of the property, the *Norgan* decision does not apply. In *Bristol and West Building Society v Ellis,* however, the Court of Appeal held that the 'reasonable period' for a suspended order could be the time it would take to organise the sale of the property.[25]

What is a reasonable period depends on the circumstances of each case. Factors the court could take into account are:
- the extent to which the balance of the mortgage, as well as the arrears, is secured;
- if there is little equity and the value of the security is at risk, in which case a short period of suspension might be appropriate;
- if there has already been delay and/or there is negative equity or insufficient evidence of the property's value, in which case an immediate possession order might be appropriate.

Note: advisers should check the wording of any suspended or postponed possession order carefully to see whether it provides for the order to cease to have effect once the client has paid the arrears in accordance with its terms. If the client then falls into arrears again, the lender will need to obtain a further order and will not just be able to issue a warrant of possession.

Suspended possession orders for mortgage arrears) currently do not contain such a provision, but the lender will need to apply to the court for permission to enforce the order if more than six years have elapsed since the date of the original possession order.[26]

Postponing possession

A court should grant either a deferred or suspended possession order if the proceeds of the sale will fully cover the mortgage to allow the client to remain in her/his home while it is sold.[27] In a county court case decided a few years ago, the judge 'stayed' a warrant of possession for three months to allow the client to sell the property, pointing out that there would be no disadvantage to the lender because of the amount of equity.[28]

Creditors have challenged suspended orders made to allow time for properties in negative equity to be sold. The Court of Appeal has held that if the mortgage cannot be cleared from the proceeds of the sale, the court has no jurisdiction to suspend the order,[29] but the court may adjourn the proceedings for procedural reasons.[30] However, in the case of *Cheltenham and Gloucester v Booker*, the Court of Appeal confirmed the court's jurisdiction to postpone, giving possession to the lender for a short period to enable the client to sell the property.[31]

Advisers should be in a position to produce written evidence from, for instance, an estate agent that the property is on the market and of the sale price, details of any offers received and, if an offer has been accepted, evidence about how far the conveyancing process has reached, including any proposed completion date from the client's solicitor.

Orders for possession

If there is no real chance of clearing the arrears or the mortgage, the court will make a possession order, which will usually be effective in 28 days. If the client has special reasons (eg, ill health or a new home not yet available), the court may extend this to 56 days. At the end of the specified period, the lender can apply back to the court for bailiffs to execute a 'warrant of possession' (also known as a 'warrant of eviction'). See p352. The order states that if the client does not leave the property, the lender can ask the court to instruct the bailiff to evict her/him without a further hearing. It also states that the client can apply to the court to postpone the eviction.

A warrant of possession allows the county court bailiff to evict the occupants from their home. The client will receive notification that a possession warrant has been obtained on Form N54. It states the exact date and time when the bailiffs will carry out the eviction. The bailiffs can physically remove the occupants from their home, if necessary, and hand over possession of the property to the mortgage company. This is usually followed by the lender's agent changing the locks to prevent the client moving back in. Form N54 informs the client that:
- a possession warrant gives the bailiff authority to remove anyone still in the property when the eviction takes place;
- s/he should act immediately to get advice about the eviction or rehousing from an advice agency, solicitor or local housing department;
- s/he can apply on Form N244 (see p271) for the court to suspend the warrant and postpone the date for eviction;
- s/he must attend the hearing of the application or it may simply be dismissed, incurring further costs;
- if s/he can pay off any arrears, s/he should contact the lender or the lender's solicitor immediately.

The N54 must also contain details of the bailiff and the client or the her/his solicitor.

When dealing with a warrant of possession, the debt adviser should either negotiate directly with the lender or help the client make an application to the court to suspend the warrant (see p356). County court bailiffs acting for a mortgage company which has issued an eviction warrant can change the locks and evict the client if no application has been made to suspend it. They can use necessary reasonable force to carry out the eviction.

Granting a possession order should not, however, be seen as the end of the line. Even when this has occurred, lenders still do not want to repossess homes unnecessarily and it may be possible to negotiate terms directly with the creditor that are more acceptable than those imposed by the court. Such variations should at least be agreed in writing and the court asked to vary the relevant order, with the consent of the other party if possible (see p355).

Arguing against a possession order

In some cases, the situation when the loan was made is relevant. In particular, if a client was badly advised to take out a new secured loan by a financial adviser or the lender itself, this should be pointed out to the court – eg, if there has been irresponsible lending (see p63). The early history of the loan can be vital in enlisting the sympathy of the court.

If mortgage interest should have been paid by the DWP but has not been or if a claim is pending, this should be brought to the court's attention. Similarly, if penalties have followed slow payments from the DWP, these should be challenged (and compensation sought from the DWP with the help of an MP if necessary).

If the loan is regulated by the Consumer Credit Act, the adviser should check whether the agreement has been drawn up correctly and, if not, whether this makes it irredeemably unenforceable or enforceable only if the court gives permission (see p104).

Debt advisers sometimes agree to a suspended possession order on the grounds that this is a technicality and does no more than safeguard the lender's position. This is a very dangerous view and means that any future default in payment or the accruing of further mortgage arrears puts the client at serious risk of losing her/his home. If a suspended order is going to be made, the amount of instalments towards arrears should be set at a level that provides some leeway for the client faced with an unexpected and essential item of expenditure.

It is unnecessary to argue against a possession order if a time order is made instead (or as well). If this is the case, the order for possession should be suspended, provided the time order is complied with. A time order should, therefore, always be considered (see p340) in cases of regulated agreements.

For agreements made after 1 July 1995, so-called 'arrears charges' and 'fines', and interest penalties on early settlement are also possible areas where the terms of a loan could be challenged under the Unfair Terms in Consumer Contracts Regulations 1999 to reduce the amount payable by the client. It may also be possible to challenge the lender's legal charges on the grounds that they were unreasonably incurred and/or unreasonable in amount.[32]

Time orders

A 'time order' is an order made under ss129–36 of the Consumer Credit Act 1974 which allows the court to reschedule the payments under a credit agreement regulated by that Act. If a time order is made, a client can pay any sum owed under a regulated agreement by instalments, payable at whatever frequency the court thinks 'just', having regard to the means of the client and/or any surety.[33] In the case of possession action, the 'sum owed' is the outstanding balance of the loan. **Note:** the provisions of the Administration of Justice Acts 1970 and 1973 (see p336) do not apply to regulated agreements[34] and debt advisers should challenge district judges who still insist on making orders for payment of contractual instalments plus arrears instead of time orders.

If the only reason a secured loan (eg, a loan for home improvements secured by a first charge over the property) is not regulated by the Consumer Credit Act is because it is a regulated mortgage contract (see p147), the Act says that the loan must be enforced by a court order and that 'related provisions' apply to the loan.[35] According to the FSA, the 'related provisions' include time orders. Advisers should seek specialist advice if they are considering using this argument.[36]

Time orders are unpopular with the credit industry. Some lenders prefer to negotiate out of court rather than have a time order, so the threat of an application can be part of the client's negotiating tactics.

Creditors often argue that courts can only make time orders in cases of 'temporary financial difficulty', but this no longer appears to be the case. In *Southern and District Finance v Barnes* the Court of Appeal clarified the court's powers in relation to time orders, but it suggested that:

> If, despite the giving of time, the client is unlikely to be able to resume payments by at least the amount of the contractual instalments, no time order should be made.

However, the House of Lords decision in the *First National Bank* case suggests that the fact that a borrower's difficulties are not temporary is not necessarily an obstacle to making a time order: '… the broad language of s129 should be so construed as to permit the county court to make such an order as appears to it just in all the circumstances' (including any amendment to the loan agreement – eg, freezing/reducing interest as it considers just to both parties).[37]

Although time orders extending over a long period are generally regarded as undesirable, in the same case, the House of Lords confirmed that the court has the discretion to make whatever order it considers 'just' in the circumstances of the case.[38]

In the *Barnes* case, the Court of Appeal made it clear that a court 'must first consider whether it is just to make a time order' in all possession cases involving regulated agreements.[39] This accords with the Consumer Credit Act 1974's grant of discretion to award a time order in such cases 'if it appears to the court just to do so'.[40] To use this discretion properly, the court must consider the justice of an order in each case. The circumstances and terms of the loan, the reasons for default and the client's payment record are relevant circumstances.

Some creditors argue that, once judgment has been entered, the court no longer has the power to make a time order as there is no longer any 'sum owed' under a regulated agreement – ie, the debt is now owed under the judgment. However, s129(2)(c) of the Consumer Credit Act 1974 says that a time order can be made 'in an action … to enforce a regulated agreement' and s130(1) specifically allows the court to make a time order where a client has made an instalment offer in response to a county court claim. Finally, none of the House of Lords' judgments in the *First National Bank* case (see p294) suggest that the court cannot make a time order in relation to a judgment debt. If an adviser comes across a case in which the creditor denies that the court has the power to make a time order, specialist advice should be sought.

If a time order is granted, the client's full liability to the creditor will be discharged when s/he has made all the payments ordered. If a hearing is required, the court should transfer the hearing to the client's local court on its own initiative.[41]

When a time order is appropriate

A client can apply for a time order if money is owed under a regulated agreement and:[42]

- the creditor has served:
  - a default notice; *or*
  - a notice of intention to recover goods or land; *or*
  - a notice requiring early payment because of default; *or*
  - a notice seeking to terminate an agreement; *or*
- enforcement action has been taken by the creditor (including an application for an enforcement order); *or*
- from 1 October 2008, an arrears notice has been served by the creditor and the client has given the creditor 14 days' notice of her/his intention to apply for a time order and made a repayment proposal.

A time order application is generally appropriate if:

- current circumstances make payments impossible, but the client's income is likely to increase – eg, if s/he is currently on short-time working or experiencing a period of unemployment, benefit disqualification or a reduction in IS during the early months of a claim or illness. A time order can still be considered, however, if there is no foreseeable improvement in circumstances;
- the original agreement was harsh on the client (eg, s/he was disadvantaged in negotiations or ignorant of its implications) or there is evidence of irresponsible

lending (see p63). In these circumstances, the court may be sympathetic to using a time order in the interest of justice;
- an application might persuade the creditor to negotiate realistically and reduce the payments due under a regulated agreement.

Time order applications can be made for both secured and unsecured debts. In *Director General of Fair Trading v First National Bank*, the House of Lords recommended that a time order application could be made where a creditor was continuing to charge contractual interest after judgment. This can be done by adding in Box 11 of the N9A: 'I ask the court to (1) make a time order in the terms of my offer and (2) amend the loan agreement in consequence so that no further contractual interest accrues after the date of judgment.'

Applications

An application can be made by the client after receiving a relevant notice using Form N440 or on the defence form (Form N11M). A fee of £175 is payable. See p273 for details about how to apply for full or partial fee remission. The borrower is the claimant and the lender is the defendant.

An application can be useful when a lender is demanding very high payments towards the arrears, or in other ways pressurising the client, but does not start court action itself and refuses to negotiate. It is much more common for an application for a time order to be in response to a claim for possession.

Applications from lenders are made on Form N244.

The application must show that a time order is just to both the creditor and the client and indicate the terms that are required. Include: [43]
- the circumstances of the client at the time s/he took out the loan, the situation now and her/his likely prospects for the future;
- the purpose of the loan;
- the client's payment history;
- the amount of the loan, the interest rate charged and any extra charges because of the default;
- the value of the security;
- the payments that can be made now, and if and when these can be increased in the future, including a financial statement;
- the implications the time order will have on any changes required to the original agreement, particularly the extra time required and the reduction in interest rate required.

The court is required to be just to both parties and it will, therefore, consider the client's position, including whether s/he was able to afford the agreement when s/he entered into it (and, if not, whether there is evidence of irresponsible lending – see p63), whether the cause of the arrears is temporary and whether s/he will be able to afford to resume at least contractual payments at a foreseeable future date.

Positive responses to these questions suggest it is just for the client. The court will also consider whether there is adequate security for the lender and how the interest rate charged compares with other that of other lenders.

> **Example**
> A couple took a secured loan at 28 per cent APR to pay for double glazing and maintained payments for 18 months. The wage earner then had a serious accident and was unable to work. He should be fully recovered in about nine months when he will resume employment and the contractual payments. The loan is secured against the couple's home, which has adequate equity. On these facts, a court should grant a time order.

The amount due

A time order can be made for 'the sum owed'. This phrase has been the subject of much dispute, but has now been clarified by the Court of Appeal. It means 'every sum which is due and owing under the agreement'. If possession proceedings have been brought, this is the total indebtedness, and this was confirmed in the *Barnes* case (see p340). In the case of unsecured regulated loans, it will also usually be the total amount due.

The amount due (and subject to a time order) is therefore the sum of:
- the amount borrowed;
- the total charge for credit (early settlement rebates should not be applied to this);
- any default interest properly charged up to the hearing date; *less*
- all payments made to date.

The lender should make clear to the court the total sum owed and the present arrears as well as the contractual instalments. The debt adviser should, if possible, check these calculations. The lender should also be asked to confirm in writing:
- if the client makes the contractual payments plus £x towards the arrears, how much s/he will still owe at the end of the loan repayment period; *and*
- the monthly payment the client needs to make to repay the loan by the end of the contractual period.

How much to offer

The offer of payment will be according to the client's ability to repay and her/his personal circumstances. In the *Barnes* case, an order was made for £25 a month for six months, then nearly £100 a month for the remaining 174 months.

Varying other terms

Having decided the instalments and their timing, the court is left 'inevitably', according to the Court of Appeal, with the need to amend either the rate of interest or the length of the loan. It can do this provided it is 'just to both parties and a consequence of the term of the order'.[44] It is, therefore, important for the debt adviser to demonstrate that a reduction in interest is a necessary consequence of a reduction in payments in order to prevent a loan running for too long. This may simply be a reduction in interest on the arrears, or a reduction in interest on the arrears and principal during the period of reduced payments, or a longer term reduction. The court does not have the facilities to calculate interest charges. Advisers may consider approaching their local trading standards office for assistance with this or asking the court to include in the order that the lender adjusts the interest rate for payments to be completed in a fixed period.

Reviews

A time order can be varied or revoked by the court on the application of a creditor or client.[45] This power to review should be sufficient to persuade district judges who resist time orders that one can safely be granted because it can later be reviewed.

After property has been repossessed

A warrant of possession is executed on the date and time stated in the warrant. A court bailiff comes to the property accompanied by a locksmith and a representative from the lender. The bailiff may use force to enter the property and evict all occupants. If opposition is expected, the bailiff may be accompanied by a police officer to prevent a breach of the peace (not to enforce the eviction). The locksmith will change the locks. Any of the client's property left in the home will therefore be locked inside. The client can ask the lender for access to the home to remove her/his property within a reasonable period, usually two weeks. Once a warrant has been executed, the court cannot suspend the possession unless:

- the original possession order itself is set aside; *or*
- the warrant has been obtained by fraud; *or*
- there has been oppression or abuse of process in its execution. Court staff providing misleading information could amount to 'oppression', but unless there has been 'fault' on the part of the lender or the court, there will be no abuse of process.[46]

Otherwise, the property will be sold by the lender. The following is a brief summary of the responsibilities of the lender (called the 'mortgagee in possession').

- The lender must take proper care of the property. This includes making essential or emergency repairs (eg, mending a leaking pipe) and may include simple maintenance (eg, mowing the lawn, painting the windows), but not include improvements – eg, refitting the kitchen.
- The lender must sell the property at the best price reasonably possible. Most lenders get at least two valuations to ensure the price is fair and sell through an

estate agent in the usual way. Sale by auction is usually considered to achieve a fair market price, although a reserve price is set.

- The lender should sell the property as soon as possible. The lender is not under an obligation to delay the sale in the hope of obtaining a better price. The lender has to balance the need to prevent the debt increasing with market factors.
- The lender must account to the client for money received and charged in respect of the property (see below).

After the sale of the property, the lender will balance the payments and proceeds of the sale against the outstanding mortgage (the 'account'). The sale proceeds are applied first to any arrears of interest and are usually sufficient to cover these, so that any shortfall is likely to consist of the capital borrowed.

If the mortgage is less than the payments and proceeds of sale, the balance should be paid to the client as soon as reasonably possible. If the mortgage is more than the payments and proceeds, the client should be informed as soon as possible and asked to make up the difference, usually referred to as a 'mortgage shortfall' debt. In order to recover any debt, the lender must produce an account to show all payments made and proceeds of the sale versus the amount of the mortgage and its other costs to show the balance outstanding. The client is bound by law and contract to repay the mortgage and all the costs associated with recovering the debt. Once the property has been sold, the shortfall debt will be unsecured. Although the lender should inform the client of the amount of the shortfall as soon as possible after the sale, inevitably the client will have moved and, in the absence of a forwarding address, it may take some time to trace her/him. It is not unusual for people to remain unaware of the shortfall debt for several years.[47]

To lose a home is not necessarily the end of the line for a client. Many lenders do not take any action immediately following a forced sale because they recognise the client is likely to have financial problems that caused the arrears and therefore could not afford to pay anything anyway. However, many lenders keep records of repossessed borrowers and are likely to attempt to recover any shortfall at a later date when either her/his situation is known to have improved or the general economic situation is better. It is also possible that such lenders could sell these debts at a later date to companies whose standards of collection are more draconian than those of the original mortgage lender. If the lender decides to recover the shortfall from the client, it must inform her/him of this decision within six years of the date of sale.

It is, therefore, vital that the debt adviser advise any client whose home is sold by a secured lender that there may be future attempts by the lender to recover this money. For more details on dealing with mortgage shortfall debts, see p141.

4. **Recovering rented property**

Guidance to social landlords

Since October 2006, social landlords (ie, local authorities, housing associations and housing action trusts) have been required to follow certain steps before issuing claims for possession based on rent arrears alone. The aim of this **rent arrears pre-action protocol** is to reduce homelessness by encouraging social landlords to work with their tenants to deal with rent arrears. The protocol does not apply to the private-rented sector.

The protocol requires the following.

- The landlord should contact the client as soon as reasonably possible to discuss the reason for the arrears, the client's financial circumstances (including any entitlement to benefits) and repayment of the arrears by affordable amounts based on her/his ability to repay. The landlord should also advise the client to seek advice from the free money advice sector.
- The landlord must provide comprehensible rent statements on a quarterly basis.
- If the landlord is aware that the client is under 18 or particularly vulnerable (eg, has mental health issues or a disability), it should take appropriate steps to ensure the client's rights are protected.
- If there is an outstanding housing benefit (HB) claim, the landlord should work with the client to resolve any problems and, in most circumstances, should not issue possession proceedings (see p350).
- After serving the statutory notice seeking possession the landlord should continue to try to contact the client to discuss the matter and, if an arrangement is made for payment of the current rent and an amount towards the arrears, should agree to postpone the issue of proceedings so long as the client complies with the agreement.
- At least 10 days before the possession hearing, the landlord must provide the client with an up-to-date rent statement, confirm the details of the court hearing and of the order the landlord is seeking, and advise the client to attend the hearing.
- If, after the issue of proceedings, an arrangement is made for the payment of the current rent and an amount towards the arrears, the landlord should agree to adjourn the hearing so long as the client complies with the agreement.
- If the client fails to comply with any payment arrangement, the landlord should warn her/him of its intention to start, or continue with, possession proceedings and give the client a clear time limit within which to bring her/his payments up to date.

Courts should take into account the conduct of both landlord and client when considering whether the protocol has been followed and what orders to make. If the landlord has unreasonably failed to comply, the court may:

- order the landlord to pay the client's costs; *and/or*
- adjourn, strike out or dismiss the claim (unless it is brought on a mandatory ground).

If a client has unreasonably failed to comply, the court may take this into account when considering whether it is reasonable to make a possession order.

Advisers should be prepared to bring the terms of the protocol to the attention of landlords and district judges and point out that it is not a voluntary code of practice but part of the county court rules of procedure. Advisers can download a copy from: www.justice.gov.uk/courts/procedure-rules/protocol/prot_rent.

The claim form

The particulars of claim, on Form N119, in a possession action for rented property must include:[48]

- what property is to be recovered;
- whether the claim relates to a dwelling house;
- full details of the tenancy agreement;
- the grounds on which possession is claimed;
- details of every person living in the property (to the best of the landlord's knowledge);
- the amount due at the start of proceedings;
- a schedule showing all amounts of rent due and payments made over the previous two years, or from the date of first default if within the two-year period;
- the daily rate of rent and any interest;
- any previous steps the landlord has taken to recover the arrears, including dates of any court proceedings, and the dates and terms of any order made;
- any relevant information known about the tenant's circumstances, including whether s/he is in receipt of benefits and whether any deductions from benefit are being paid to the landlord.

If the landlord uses the 'possession claim online' process (see p332), the particulars must contain the same information as above with one exception. If, before proceedings are issued, the landlord has provided the client with a schedule of arrears showing all amounts due and payments made, together with dates and a running total of the arrears, either for the previous two years or from the date of default (if later), the particulars of claim may contain a summary of the arrears stating:

- the amount of the arrears on the date of the landlord's notice of seeking possession;

- the dates and amounts of the last three payments (or, if fewer than three payments have been made, the dates and amounts of those payments); *and*
- the arrears at the date of issue of the possession proceedings.

As a notice of seeking possession is a statutory requirement for secure and assured tenancies, most landlords should be able to take advantage of this provision. However, if the landlord only includes the summary information in the particulars of claim, it must serve a full arrears history on the client within seven days after the issue of the claim and verify this by a witness statement or verbally at the hearing.

Responding to the claim

The reply is on Form N11R.

- **Question 1** requests details of the client's personal circumstances, including date of birth.
- **Question 2** relates to paragraphs 2 and 3 of Form N119 and should either be confirmed as correct or details given of any disagreement.
- **Question 3** asks about the service of the 'notice seeking possession' or equivalent. The debt adviser should always ensure this has been done in the prescribed manner.
- **Question 4** asks the client to check the rent arrears as stated by the landlord. This should be done carefully.
- **Question 5** only needs completing if possession is being sought on grounds other than rent arrears – eg, for nuisance.
- **Question 6** asks for any counterclaims that the client may have. There are a series of counterclaims or 'set-offs' that can be made by a tenant when a landlord claims possession.
  - Under a tenancy created before 15 January 1989, a landlord may be charging more than the fair rent set by the rent officer. In such cases, not only is the excess over the fair rent not recoverable or counted as arrears for the purposes of seeking possession of the property, but the client can also claim back all the overpaid money for up to two years.[49]
  - A counterclaim can be made for disrepair if a landlord has failed to keep her/his statutory obligations to repair the exterior or main structure of the property or facilities for the supply of water, gas, electricity or removal of sewage. The client can claim the rent arrears should be reduced by an amount to compensate her/him for this loss, which can be done by completing the defence part of the reply to the possession claim form. However, in order to safeguard their rights, clients should either pay the rent or open an account into which to pay it. In one case, a county court judge still made an order for possession because of rent arrears despite awarding an amount for damages for disrepair that was greater than the actual arrears.

The decision to order possession was subsequently overturned by the Court of Appeal.[50]

Consider seeking the advice of a specialist housing adviser if a landlord has failed in some contractual obligation – eg, has not provided furniture as agreed or redecorated a property as regularly as promised. In such cases, it may be necessary to refer the matter to a solicitor before proceeding.

- **Question 7** asks for details of payments made since the claim form was issued.
- **Question 8**. If an agreement has been reached, details should be included and the reply should ideally be accompanied by a letter requesting a general adjournment. The landlord should be asked to write separately, if the landlord can be persuaded to agree to this course of action rather than to an order suspended on payment of whatever sum has been agreed. If an unrealistic offer was previously made (perhaps under pressure) and broken, this should be made clear. If the landlord is a social landlord, the adviser should refer to the rent arrears pre-action protocol to check whether the landlord has complied with it (see p346).
- **Question 9** should be completed in the affirmative if agreement has not been reached. Note that clients who fail to ask the court to consider instalments might later find this used against them if a local authority is considering the question of the intentionality of their homelessness.
- **Question 10** asks for the amount in addition to the rent that is being offered. If money is not yet available for the arrears, the court can be asked (probably on a separate sheet) to make an order suspended on payments of £x extra each week or month, with the first payment on a specified date in the foreseeable future. Alternatively, a token offer could be suggested for the first months' payments, followed by something more realistic.
- **Questions 11–15** relate to income support (IS) or HB. In preparation for any hearing, it is important for the debt adviser to know the up-to-date position on these (particularly if rent is paid directly to a landlord or if non-dependant deductions vary with the movement of non-dependants). If the landlord is a social landlord and is aware that an HB claim is pending, the adviser should refer to the rent arrears pre-action protocol (see p346).
- **Questions 16–27** relate to dependants (and non-dependants), bank accounts and savings, income and expenditure, priority debts, court orders and credit debts similar to those required on Form N9A (see p285) and should be completed in the same way.
- **Question 28**. The client should not answer 'yes' to this question ('If an order is made will you have somewhere to live?') unless the new accommodation is absolutely certain. The date given, even in such cases, should always allow for 'slippage'.
- **Question 29** is important because it gives the client the opportunity to explain:
  - why the arrears arose;
  - what circumstances were beyond her/his control;

– why it would cause particular hardship if eviction were ordered;
– why an expensive property was rented (if applicable).
If the landlord is a social landlord, any breaches of the rent arrears pre-action protocol can be pointed out here (see p346).

What counts as rent arrears

In many cases, particularly when the local authority is landlord, some of what is claimed as rent arrears may not, in fact, be so. For example, amounts of overpaid HB that an authority wishes to recover may be added to a client's rent account as though they were arrears. In fact, even where such an amount has properly become payable (and the client has been given the right of appeal),[51] such amounts do not constitute unpaid rent. They can be included in a rent account, provided they are clearly distinguished from rent that is owed to the authority, but should not appear on a claim form as rent arrears. However, in non-local authority tenancy cases, if HB has been paid directly to the landlord and the local authority has exercised its right to recover any HB overpayment directly from the landlord, the amount recovered can be treated as rent arrears.[52]

In some cases, a client may also have amounts of water charges, rent arrears from a previous tenancy or other non-rent charges included in her/his rent arrears. These amounts should not appear on a claim form, unless they are specifically included in the rent for the client's home. If the tenancy agreement provides not only for water charges to be collected by the landlord but also for them to be treated as rent, it may be possible to argue that this is an unfair term within the meaning of the Unfair Terms in Consumer Contracts Regulations (see p92) because it creates the possibility of the client being evicted on the basis of arrears of water charges. As an unfair term is unenforceable, this would be a full or partial defence to the possession proceedings, depending on whether the arrears also include any 'true' rent.

Powers of the court to deal with possession action

There are a number of grounds on which possession may be sought when rent is unpaid and these differ slightly according to whether the client has a private or public landlord and whether her/his tenancy began before or after 15 January 1989. A debt adviser must be certain about the status of the client's occupancy before giving advice about a possession claim. For example, some clients who consider themselves tenants may, in fact, be licensees.

A client may receive a possession claim form on grounds that are not connected to a debt. This *Handbook* does not cover these matters. For a detailed explanation of all the grounds upon which possession might be sought, see *Defending Possession Proceedings* (see Appendix 2), or consult Legal Action Group or a specialist housing advice service, such as Shelter.

The court's role in every case of arrears, except those of some assured tenants who are more than 13 weeks in arrears (see below), is to decide whether or not it is 'reasonable' to make an order for possession and whether or not to suspend this on particular terms (usually payment of the normal rent plus an amount towards the arrears). This means that, as long as the client keeps to the payment ordered by the court, the landlord cannot regain possession of the property. If a client is in receipt of IS, income-based jobseeker's allowance, income-related employment and support allowance or pension credit, offers of the direct deduction rate of £3.50 a week may be accepted by the court. If the client does not attend the hearing or there is no request for time to pay the arrears from her/him, the order may be made absolutely – ie, for possession to be given up in a certain period of time – for a minimum of 14 days or a maximum of 42 days, but usually for 28 days.

Since 25 March 2002, courts have been able to award fixed costs (instead of assessed costs) in all cases where a possession order is made and not just in cases where the possession order is suspended.

Assured tenants

The Housing Act 1988 created a new mandatory ground on which a court must make a possession order. This applies only to assured tenants (eg, of housing associations and private landlords) and thus to no one except previously protected tenants, whose tenancy began before 15 January 1989. It requires a court to grant a possession order to a landlord if, at the date of the hearing, at least eight weeks' or two months' rent (three months' if paid quarterly) is unpaid. The landlord has to prove there was two months' rent in arrears (or three months' if paid quarterly) both at the time when the notice of seeking possession was served and at the date of the hearing, which need be only two weeks later.

There is no requirement for the court to consider reasonableness when this ground is used. Therefore, even if delays in the payment of HB caused the arrears (see p390), this could still lead to a possession order being granted, as the court has no power to adjourn, except for procedural reasons or in exceptional circumstances.[53] In such a case, the adviser should pressure the local authority to make an emergency payment before the hearing and, if it fails to do so, local politicians and the Local Government Ombudsman or Public Services Ombudsman for Wales should be informed.

This ground will fail if, by the date of the hearing, the arrears are reduced to even a nominal amount (eg, £1) below two or three months' rent. It may sometimes be worthwhile for a client to borrow money, particularly from family or friends, to ensure s/he does not become subject to this mandatory ground. See also Chapter 7 for ways of maximising income.

The warrant of possession

Note: advisers should check the wording of any suspended or postponed possession order carefully to see whether it provides for the order to cease to have effect once the client has paid the arrears in accordance with its terms. If the client then falls into arrears again, the landlord will need to obtain a further order and will not just be able to issue a warrant of possession.

The new form of postponed order (rent arrears) (N28A) (see p354) provides for the order to cease to be enforceable once the arrears are paid. However, Form N28 (rent arrears suspended) does not.

A warrant of possession gives county court bailiffs the power to evict the occupiers and change the locks (see Chapter 14). It is issued by the court following a request from the landlord if the client has not voluntarily left the property by the date ordered by the court at a possession hearing or has not kept to the terms of a suspended order for possession. In order to prevent eviction, an application must be made for the warrant to be suspended (see p356). The notice of eviction (Form N54) informs the client about this (see p338).

Tenants of properties with mortgage arrears

A client may pay rent to someone who is buying the property with a mortgage. If the client became a tenant after the date the mortgage started but the lender's permission was not sought or granted in accordance with the terms of the mortgage, she is known as an 'unauthorised' tenant of a mortgage borrower and will rarely have a defence to a possession claim brought against her/his landlord. From 1 October 2010, such tenants can apply to the court to 'stay' or suspend execution of possession orders for a period not exceeding two months to allow them sufficient time to obtain suitable alternative accommodation.[54]

The client can apply at the hearing of the possession claim or subsequently. S/he must have first approached the lender for a written undertaking not to enforce the order for two months and the lender must have refused to give this undertaking. It is arguable that a failure to respond, even after reminders, counts as a refusal as there is no time limit within which the lender is required to respond. Such a request could be made verbally or in writing. The court can only postpone execution of the order once. The court must take account of the client's circumstances, including any breaches of the tenancy agreement. The court can order the client to make payments to the lender. The client's application should be made on Form N244 (see p271). The fee is £45. See p273 for details on applying for full or partial fee remission.

In the case of buy-to-let lending, the terms and conditions of the loan usually incorporate consent to tenancies being created. Provided the terms and conditions have been complied with, guidance from the Council of Mortgage Lenders issued in June 2009 on buy-to-let arrears and possessions advises lenders that the tenancy is binding and the lender will take possession of the property, subject to the terms and conditions of the tenancy. The lender will only be able to evict the tenant in accordance with landlord and tenant law. The position is the same for other tenancies created after the loan was entered into to which the lender has specifically consented.

Arguing against a possession order

An outright possession order is not necessarily a breach of a client's human rights under Article 8 of the European Convention on Human Rights (respect for family and private life).[55]

A variety of arguments can, however, be used to demonstrate that it is 'unreasonable' to make a possession order. Note, however, that courts take into account the view that a landlord is entitled not only to the increase in capital value of her/his property but also to revenue from rent. A debt adviser should argue that the existence of an agreement to clear the arrears or even a reasonable offer coupled with an ability to pay the ongoing rent makes a possession order unnecessary and, therefore, unreasonable.

Arguments can be based on the client's circumstances (eg, s/he has children, or is sick or disabled) or her/his finances – eg, s/he has been dependent on benefits for some time. If an improvement in circumstances can be shown (eg, s/he is about to get a job), this will probably help convince the court that it is unreasonable to make a possession order. Other arguments could be based on the position of the landlord – eg, the landlord's identity was unknown or s/he had failed to collect rent or arrange for an agent to do so.

Any defence the client offers may be helped if s/he has begun to pay the contractual rent and something towards the arrears by the time the hearing takes place. Such payments should have been recorded by the landlord or, if the landlord has refused to accept payments before the court hearing, the money should have been paid into a separate account. Proof of payment made should be taken to the hearing.

Arrears because of non-payment of housing benefit

If a client should have been getting HB but was not, or is waiting for the outcome of a claim, this can be a powerful argument for saying it is unreasonable to make an order, particularly if it is a social landlord. In addition, the rent arrears pre-action protocol says that the landlord should make every effort to establish effective ongoing liaison with the HB department and should also offer to assist the client with her/his HB claim, in particular, if s/he has:

- provided the local authority with all the evidence required to process her/his HB claim;
- a reasonable expectation of eligibility for HB; *and*
- paid any other sums due to the landlord that will not be covered by the HB claim.

The landlord should not only refrain from issuing possession proceedings on the grounds of rent arrears but should also (with the client's consent) make direct contact with the HB department.

If the landlord is not a local authority, the client can ask the court to consider making a third-party costs order against the local authority – ie, for the local authority to pay the landlord's costs. This can only be done if the local authority is: [56]

- made a party to the proceedings for the purposes of costs only; *and*
- given a reasonable opportunity of attending the hearing for the court to consider the question.

This requires action to be taken before the possession hearing itself and advisers should consider obtaining specialist housing advice. A threat to seek an order for costs may prompt the local authority to expedite the HB claim and clear the arrears. Otherwise, if possible, the client should obtain a letter from the local authority explaining when HB will be paid and take this to the hearing.

Order postponing the date of possession

Until the Court of Appeal's decision in *Harlow District Council v Hall,* it was thought that, provided the client did not default in her/his payments on a suspended possession order, any secure tenancy would continue. However, in this case, the Court of Appeal held that, once the date for possession specified in the order had passed (usually after 28 days) the tenancy ended and the client became a 'tolerated trespasser' and, consequently, lost many of the rights of a secure tenant.[57] However, an order deferring or postponing possession does not have this effect, provided the client complies with the conditions on paying the arrears and current rent.

Since 1 July 2006, the standard form for a suspended possession order in rent arrears cases has been the N28A. It is, in fact, not a suspended possession order, but a postponed possession order. It does not set a date for possession, but allows the landlord to apply to the court to fix a possession date in the event of the client defaulting on the order. However, the landlord must first give the client 14 days' notice of its intention to apply and invite her/him to bring the arrears up to date or provide an explanation for her/his non-payment. The landlord's application can be dealt with without a hearing, although the court could list it for a hearing. If the court grants the application, a date for possession will be fixed (usually the next working day). The landlord still needs to issue a warrant of possession if the client does not leave the property voluntarily and the client can still apply to suspend the warrant (see p356).[58]

The N28 suspended possession order is still a prescribed form. Advisers should check the practice in their local county court. However, the N28A gives the client greater protection and so advisers should encourage courts not to use the N28.

5. **Preventing enforcement**

Setting aside a judgment

If there has been a hearing in the county court, the client can apply to have the order 'set aside' (see p314) and the matter reheard if s/he did not attend the hearing and an order was made in her/his absence. The court must consider whether the client:

- acted 'promptly' – ie, with all reasonable speed once s/he found out that the court had made an order against her/him;
- had a good reason for not attending the hearing; *and*
- has a reasonable prospect of success at any rehearing.

The court is unlikely to order a rehearing if the client deliberately failed to attend or if the court is satisfied that there is no real prospect of the original order being changed.[59]

The court will not allow an application for a rehearing purely on the grounds that the client did not receive notice of the hearing date without enquiring why s/he did not receive it. On the other hand, the court should not refuse an application for a rehearing just because s/he failed to provide the creditor or lender with a forwarding address. In general: [60]

- if the client is unaware that proceedings are imminent or have been served, s/he will have a good reason for not attending any hearing;
- if the client knows of the existence of proceedings but does not have a system in place for receiving communication about the case, s/he is unlikely to have a good reason for not attending any hearing.

Suspending a warrant of delivery (hire purchase or conditional sale)

If the client wants to keep goods that are the subject of a hire purchase or conditional sale agreement, an application can be made on an N244 (see p271) to suspend the warrant. A financial statement should be supplied. The N244 should be sent to the enforcing court. A fee of £40 is payable. See p273 for details about full or partial fee remission. An offer of payment must be made that will realistically repay the agreement and arrears. A court is unlikely to agree to very small payments compared with the original contractual sum. If this is not possible, the debt adviser should try to renegotiate with the creditor the payments due under the agreement, or consider a time order (see p340).

Varying the terms of a suspended or postponed possession order

If the repayments under a suspended order, or any other terms of an order, require a change, the client can apply back to the court for the order to be changed or varied. Application is on Form N244 (see p271). A fee of £40 is payable. See p273 for details on applying for full or partial fee remission. It is always better to apply to vary an order if circumstances have changed, rather than be served with a warrant and have to apply to suspend it. For example, if the client is on maternity leave, and therefore has a reduced income for a period, s/he could apply for a reduction in payments, or if a client unexpectedly finds employment, s/he can apply for a possession order to be suspended because s/he can now make payments.

Suspending a warrant of possession

Following the issue of a warrant, a notice of eviction on Form N54 will be sent or delivered from the court, stating a date and time when the bailiffs will evict the client from her/his property. The client can apply for a warrant of possession to be suspended at any time before the date and time specified on the warrant, although it is preferable to apply as early as possible.

An N244 should be completed (see p271), showing:
- how the client's circumstances have changed since the possession order (see p338) was made;
- that the equity or rental revenue of the creditor is not threatened by a suspension;
- a well-supported offer of payment and a lump sum (or first payment) if possible;
- if the client does not wish to remain in the property, that arrangements are in hand for sale of the property or rehousing, but that this will take time.

Form N244 should be accompanied by a financial statement. **Note:** a fee of £40 (*not* £80 as many courts claim) is payable. See p273 for details on applying for full or partial fee remission. If possible, take the form to the court rather than posting it as there will be little time available.

If the lender or landlord issued the possession action using the 'possession claim online' process and the client wants to make her/his application online, any court fee must be paid either by debit card or credit card. The possession claim online website contains a list of organisations through which the client can claim full or partial fee remission online. Otherwise, the N244 must be filed, and any application for fee remission must be made, in person.

A hearing will be granted almost immediately and the client must attend. A debt adviser should always try to negotiate directly with the creditor before the hearing and ensure that if an agreement has been reached, the details are communicated to the solicitor or agent who will be representing the creditor at the hearing. If possible, arrange for confirmation in writing so the client can take this to the hearing in case there is any dispute. If no agreement can be reached, the matter must be presented clearly before the district judge, using similar arguments to those covered on p276. At the same time, it may be necessary to ask for the payment order to be varied (reduced) to a level the client can afford.

In theory, there is no limit to the number of applications that can be made to suspend a warrant, but if the client persistently applies and then fails to make payments, the application may be refused and s/he may be told s/he cannot make any further applications without leave of the court. In this case, assuming that the application is realistic, the client must ask for leave of the court to apply, on an N244, before continuing on the same application to explain the reasons. The court will usually consider granting leave to apply first then, if granted, continue in the same hearing to consider the application for suspension.

If the application is refused, the eviction will usually take place on the date and time on the warrant. The client may ask for a short suspension (eg, two weeks) to find alternative accommodation.[61] Alternatively, in mortgage cases, if repossession is granted, the client could ask to stay in the property while the lender sells it (see p338).[62] After the execution of a warrant (eviction), no order for suspension can be made unless:

- the possession order itself is set aside (see p314); *or*
- the warrant was obtained fraudulently; *or*
- there had been an abuse of the process or oppression in the execution of the warrant.[63] It appears that 'oppression' is not limited to conduct by the creditor but can extend to conduct by the court – eg, misleading information from court staff on the procedure for suspending a warrant.[64]

Appealing to a judge

If a client disagrees with a judgment or order made by a district judge and none of the options discussed above are applicable, s/he must appeal if s/he wishes to challenge the judge's decision.

If the judgment or order with which the client disagrees was made in her/his absence, s/he should consider applying to set aside the order and for a rehearing, as described on p316. An appeal might be appropriate if, for instance, the client did not act 'promptly' or did not have a good reason for not attending the hearing but not, for example, if her/his case has no reasonable prospect of success.[65]

Adjournment

An adjournment is a court order to delay a hearing either for a specified amount of time or indefinitely. The county court can, at any time, either adjourn or bring forward the date of a hearing. It can decide to do this itself or because one or both of the parties have applied (see p277).

If a client unsuccessfully applies for an adjournment and the case it dealt with in her/his absence, s/he should normally apply to set aside the judgment or order and for a rehearing on the grounds discussed above rather than appeal. However, the client could appeal a refusal to set aside the judgment or order, provided there are grounds.

See p276 for more information.

Notes

1. Recovering goods on hire purchase or conditional sale
1 s130(1) CCA 1974
2 s135 CCA 1974
3 s135(2) CCA 1974
4 Part 7B para 3.3 PD CPR

2. Recovering property
5 For a summary of recent developments in mortgage arrears cases, see M Robinson, 'Mortgage Possession Update', *Adviser* 147

3. Recovering owner-occupied property
6 ss92 and 173(3) CCA 1974
7 See *MCOB* 13 on the FSA's website at http://fsahandbook.info/FSA/html/handbook/MCOB/13. Home finance plans provide finance for buying a home complying with Islamic law which forbids the charging of interest. See J McShane and J Wilson, 'Consultancy Corner', *Adviser* 134, p45
8 Under *MCOB* 12.4, if the client has a payment shortfall, any payments received must be allocated first to paying off the balance of the shortfall (excluding interest and charges). If the client has a payment arrangement for the arrears and is keeping to it, the lender should not impose any arrears charges.
9 Part 55 para 2 PD CPR
10 Part 55 para 1.7 PD CPR
11 r30.2(1) CPR
12 Available at www.communities.gov.uk/publications/housing/lendernotificationrepossession
13 Part 55 para 7.1 PD CPR
14 *Halifax Building Society v Taffs*, CA (*Adviser* 81 abstracts)

15 See C Evans, 'The New Rules are Working!', *Adviser* 79
16 For a discussion on how this might be applied in mortgage possession proceedings, see N Clayton, 'Mortgage Conduct of Business Rules and Mortgage Repossessions', *Quarterly Account* 8, IMA, Spring 2008
17 s36 AJA 1970 and s8 AJA 1973
18 r3.1(2)(b) CPR
19 See *Birmingham Citizens Permanent Building Society v Caunt* [1962] 1 All ER 163
20 See *Zinda v Bank of Scotland* [2011] EWCA Civ 706 (*Adviser* 147 abstracts). These powers are unlikely to apply to 'all monies charges' securing a debt repayable on demand (eg, a bank overdraft), since the client will have to pay the whole outstanding balance within a 'reasonable period'; see *Habib Bank v Taylor* [1982] 1 WLR 1218, CA
21 *Royal Bank of Scotland v Elmes*, Clerkenwell County Court (*Legal Action*, April 1998, p11)
22 *Halifax plc v Salt and Bell*, Derby County Court, 29 December 2007 (*Adviser* 127 abstracts)
23 *Cheltenham and Gloucester v Norgan* [1996] 1 All ER 449, CA (*Adviser* 53 abstracts)
24 See for example, *Abbey National v Padfield*, Bristol County Court, 26 July 2002 (*Adviser* 96 abstracts)
25 *Bristol and West Building Society v Ellis* [1996] 29 HLR 282, CA
26 r26 CCR; r17(6) Sch 2 CPR. See also *Zinda v Bank of Scotland* [2011] EWCA Civ 706, CA (*Adviser* 147 abstracts)
27 *Target Home Loans v Clothier* [1993] 25 HLR 48, CA

28 *Cheltenham and Gloucester plc v Frasca,*
Gloucester County Court, 16 June 2003
(*Legal Action*, April 2004, p15)

29 *Cheltenham and Gloucester Building
Society v Krausz* [1996] 29 HLR 597, CA

30 *State Bank of New South Wales v Harrison*
[2002] EWCA Civ 363 (*Adviser* 95
abstracts)

31 *Cheltenham and Gloucester v Booker*
[1996] 29 HLR 634, CA

32 For a general discussion of the court's
powers, see M Robinson, 'Mortgage
Possession in the County Court', *Adviser*
123

33 s129(2)(a) CCA 1974

34 s38a AJA 1970

35 S16(6D) CCA 1974

36 Part 4.17.2(G) *The Perimeter Guidance
Manual*, FSA

37 See P Madge, 'Full Circle', *Adviser* 89 for
a full discussion of the implications of
the *First National Bank* decision. For a
summary of the development of time
orders, see P Madge, 'Time Goes By',
Adviser 148

38 *Director-General of Fair Trading v First
National Bank* [2001] UKHL 52 (*Adviser*
89 abstracts)

39 *Southern and District Finance v Barnes,
The Times,* 19 April 1995, CA

40 s129(1) CCA 1974

41 r3.1(2)(m) CPR

42 s129(1) CCA 1974, as amended by s16
CCA 2006

43 For practical guidance on making a time
order application, see S Coles, 'Time
Orders: what's all the fuss?', *Quarterly
Account* 11, IMA, Winter 2008/09

44 s136 CCA 1974

45 s130(6) CCA 1974

46 *Cheltenham and Gloucester Building
Society v Obi* [1996] 28 HLR 22, CA
(*Adviser* 65 abstracts)

47 For a full discussion of this issue, see D
McConnell, 'No Equity?', *Adviser* 53

4. Recovering rental property

48 Part 55 para 2 PD CPR

49 ss44 and 57 RA 1977

50 *Trevantos v McCullough* [1991] 19 EG
18, CA

51 *Welfare Benefits Handbook 2002/03,*
CPAG, 2002

52 Reg 93(2) HB Regs, as amended by
SI.1997/65 from 7 April 1997

53 *North British Housing Association v
Matthews* [2004] EWCA Civ 1736
(*Adviser* 109 abstracts)

54 Mortgage Repossessions (Protection of
Tenants etc) Act 2010

55 *Lambeth London Borough Council v
Howard,* 6 March 2001, CA (*Adviser* 88
abstracts)

56 r48.2 CPR; Part 19 contains the
procedure for adding parties.

57 *Harlow District Council v Hall* [2006]
EWCA Civ 156 (*Adviser* 115 abstracts).
The concept of the 'tolerated trespasser'
was abolished on 1 December 2008 and
a secure or assured tenancy now only
comes to an end when the possession
order is actually executed, regardless of
when the possession order was
originally made. Possession orders made
before 1 December 2008 remain in
effect in all other respects.

58 Part 55 para 10 PD CPR. For a discussion
of the background to, and implications
of, the new procedure, see J Gallagher,
'The Tolerated Trespasser: an
endangered species?', *Quarterly Account*
4, IMA, Spring 2007

5. Preventing enforcement

59 The application is made 'in the interests
of justice' under r3.1(2)(m) and 3.1(7)
CPR; *Hackney London Borough Council v
Findlay* [2011] EWCA Civ 8, CA (*Adviser*
145 money advice abstracts)

60 *Estate Acquisition and Development v
Wiltshire* [2006] EWCA Civ 533 (*Adviser*
118 abstracts)

61 For issues to consider when dealing with
warrants of possession for rent arrears,
see M Robinson, 'Hard Times', *Adviser*
149; see also J Luba and D Malone,
'Staying, Suspending and Setting Aside
Possession Warrants', *Legal Action,* June
2012

62 *Cheltenham and Gloucester Building
Society v Booker* [1996] 29 HLR 634, CA

63 *Hammersmith and Fulham London
Borough Council v Hill, The Times,* 25 April
1994, CA; see also *Cheltenham and
Gloucester Building Society v Obi* [1994]
28 HLR 22, CA

64 *Hammersmith and Fulham London
Borough Council v Lemeh,* 3 April 2000,
CA (*Adviser* 83 abstracts); *Lambeth
London Borough Council v Hughes,* 8 May
2000, CA (*Adviser* 84 abstracts)

65 *Bank of Scotland v Pereira* [2011] EWCA
Civ 241, CA

Chapter 13

. . . .

The magistrates' court

This chapter covers:
1. Introduction (below)
2. Financial penalties (p361)
3. Compensation orders (p377)
4. Council tax (p378)
5. Wilful refusal and culpable neglect (p383)

1. Introduction

This chapter looks at how the magistrates' court operates as a creditor, or collector of other people's debt, and discusses how the debt adviser should proceed when advising on such debts as financial penalties (eg, fines) and local taxes – eg, council tax.

The magistrates' court

The magistrates' court is best known as the first tier of the criminal justice system. Its decisions are made by magistrates. Magistrates have traditionally been lay volunteers (ie, unpaid and not legally qualified), although it is increasingly common for them to be full time and paid, particularly in London and urban areas. Paid magistrates are called district judges and are either barristers or solicitors. Lay magistrates depend on their legally qualified clerks (known as justices' clerks) in much of their decision making. A justices' clerk, who is a qualified barrister or solicitor, is present at all hearings to direct the way the hearing proceeds and to advise the magistrates on the law and procedure, on the penalties available and any guidance on their use, but should not otherwise take any part in the proceedings.

The administration of magistrates' courts in England and Wales is the responsibility of Her Majesty's Courts and Tribunals Service (HMCTS), part of the Ministry of Justice. A justices' clerk acts as chief executive of the court and makes arrangements for the efficient and effective administration of the individual magistrates' court. This includes allocating responsibilities to assistant justices' clerks and other magistrates' court staff, such as issuing summonses, timetabling hearings, collecting payments (eg, fines) and conducting means enquiries. S/he is required to arrange for the justices' clerks to discuss matters of law (including practices and procedures) in order to ensure the advice given to the magistrates themselves is consistent. Fines officers are court staff with powers to enforce fines. Since the implementation of the Courts Act 2003, many decisions on fines enforcement that used to require court hearings (such as applications for further time to pay and deciding the enforcement action in cases of default) are now dealt with by fines officers.

The law on fines enforcement is in the Magistrates' Courts Act 1980, the Courts Act 2003, the Fines Collection Regulations 2006 and Part 52 of the Criminal Procedure Rules. The current fines collection scheme has been in place since 2006.

The role of the adviser

In relation to the court itself, the debt adviser's role is predominantly to prepare a financial statement and list of debts for the client to take to court hearings and perhaps a letter explaining her/his circumstances.

The adviser may represent the client or act as a 'McKenzie Friend' (see p23). Advisers should check local practice to see whether they are allowed to represent clients. The justices' clerk is likely to be a useful contact at the magistrates' court. Sometimes, the adviser will need to liaise with probation staff or solicitors, particularly in respect of unpaid fines. It will be helpful to establish links between the advice agency and the probation service so that once the adviser has produced the financial statement and details of debts, the client can be put in touch with the probation service for assistance and support at the court hearing. Probation officers and assistants are normally based at the court. Some advice agencies now staff help desks at their local magistrates' courts.

If a committal warrant has been issued for the client to be imprisoned (see p233), it is usually advisable to obtain good legal representation for her/him. Free legal representation is now available at committal hearings.

2. **Financial penalties**

A fine is the most common penalty imposed by magistrates' courts in criminal cases. Magistrates can also make costs and compensation orders (see p377). These are all known as 'financial penalties'. The client may be required to complete a means enquiry form (available from the court office), although many clients who plead guilty and ask the court to deal with the matter in their absence do not provide information about their means.

When setting financial penalties, the court must take account of the seriousness of the offence and the offender's financial circumstances.[1] There is a reduction for a guilty plea. In cases where both a fine and compensation cannot be paid, the court should order compensation (see p377) rather than a fine.

Costs are at the discretion of the court, but are usually ordered and fixed at the time. If the offence was committed after 1 April 2007 and the client is ordered to pay a fine, or a fine and compensation (in either case with or without costs), s/he may also be ordered to pay a 'victim's surcharge' of £15. This is used to fund services for victims, and also witnesses, rather than being paid to them direct. If the client does not have the means to pay both compensation and the surcharge, priority is given to compensation and the surcharge can be reduced to nil, if necessary. If the client does not have the means to pay both the fine and surcharge, the fine should be reduced to enable payment of the surcharge.

Payments

When imposing a financial penalty, the court can order:
- immediate payment; *or*
- payment within a fixed time; *or*
- payment by instalments.

Magistrates' courts are discouraged from inviting applications for time to pay and will usually ask the client how much can be paid immediately. The court can search the client for any money that could be used to meet the financial penalty, but this power is rarely used.

The court can only order imprisonment in default of immediate payment if:
- the offence is imprisonable and the client appears to have sufficient means to pay immediately; *or*
- the client is unlikely to remain long enough in the UK to enable other enforcement methods to be used; *or*
- the client is already serving a prison sentence (known as 'lodging' the financial penalty); *or*
- the client is sentenced to imprisonment by the court for the same, or another, offence.

Financial penalties should generally be capable of being paid within 12 months. This is not a fixed rule, but the period should not exceed two to three years.[2] If the client is unable to do this, it suggests that either there has been a change of circumstances since the penalty was imposed or that it was fixed without adequate financial information. In either case, the debt adviser should consider asking for all or part of the financial penalty to be remitted – ie, totally or partially written off at a means enquiry (see p374).

However, when making an application (either for further time to pay or remission), the adviser should bear in mind not only that financial penalties are a priority debt, but also that they were imposed as a punishment and this affects the court's attitude to their recovery. Non-payment of a fine can be viewed as an attempt to avoid punishment.

The current fines enforcement scheme attempts to remove the need for hearings by giving fines officers the power to decide on the level of instalments and the enforcement step(s) to be taken. Once the fine has been imposed, obtaining a hearing before the magistrates is likely to happen only if the client appeals against a decision of the fines officer or if the fines officer refers the matter to the magistrates following a number of unsuccessful attempts to enforce the fine.

Payments are applied by the court in the following order:
- compensation orders;
- costs;
- fines.

If the client defaults on payment, this will affect any term of imprisonment s/he is ordered to serve and also any remission. It is also relevant to the collection of Crown Court fines in the magistrates' courts, since the Crown Court will already have fixed the term of imprisonment the client is to serve for defaulting on the payment of the fine, but not of any costs or compensation. Although the sentence can be reduced proportionately by part payment or remission, the magistrates have no power to vary the actual sentence.

Problems can also arise if a client has more than one fine or compensation order. Courts do not always make it clear to clients how their payments will be applied, which can lead to enforcement action being taken on one matter, even though regular payments are being made in respect of another. Financial penalties can be paid either:
- consecutively, with the client allowed to clear the oldest first with no enforcement action taken on later ones; *or*
- concurrently, and payments credited to each outstanding financial penalty.

The client should be advised to request whichever method is in her/his best interests.

Debt advisers are likely to be concerned with the client's difficulty in paying financial penalties after they have been imposed, rather than with the conditions attached on the day of sentence. Advisers may, therefore, find themselves being required to negotiate with the fines officer or the bailiffs concerning unpaid financial penalties.

Fines (except parking or other fixed penalty offences) can be paid online using a debit or credit card The client will need the notice of fine letter to make payment in this way as it contains the relevant references.

Varying and setting aside a financial penalty

A magistrates' court may vary or even rescind a sentence or other order imposed or made by it (but not a sentence or order made by the Crown Court) if it appears to be in the interests of justice to do so.[3] Although discretionary, this could be a speedy and effective means of cancelling or reducing a financial penalty that has been wrongly imposed or is demonstrably too high, as there is no time limit on making the application and the client does not have to show any change of circumstances since the financial penalty was imposed.

In addition, if the case was dealt with in the client's absence and s/he had no knowledge of the summons or the proceedings, s/he can make a statutory declaration to this effect, which will result in the conviction being rendered void and the financial penalty being set aside. There will be a new hearing and so this option needs to be carefully considered.[4] The statutory declaration must be delivered to the magistrates' court within 21 days of the proceedings first coming to the client's knowledge. There is discretion to extend the time limit if the court decides it was not reasonable to expect the client to comply with it.[5]

If either of these options is being considered, the client should be referred to a solicitor. If neither of the above applies and the client maintains her/his innocence of the offence(s), s/he should be referred to a solicitor for a possible appeal or application for judicial review. There are short time limits.

Registration of the financial penalty

Registration in the Register of Judgments, Orders and Fines means that information about the client's default is available to credit reference agencies and may affect her/his ability to obtain credit. The entry must be cancelled if:
- the financial penalty is paid within a month of being registered;
- the client's conviction is set aside or reversed;
- the financial penalty has been remitted in full;
- five years have elapsed since the date of the client's conviction.

Transfer of fines

If a client moves to a different magistrates' court's area but still has a financial penalty to pay at the magistrates' court where s/he used to live, it may be advisable to apply to the original court for a fine transfer order to the new local court.[6] This should make payments easier to arrange.

Enforcement methods

Collection order

A magistrates' court that is either imposing a new financial penalty or enforcing payment of an unpaid financial penalty must make a collection order, unless it is impracticable or inappropriate to do so – eg, if the court has no information about the client's financial situation. The collection order sets out:

- a breakdown of the sum due – ie, the amount of the fine and/or compensation order and/or costs;
- whether the client is an 'existing defaulter' – ie, whether s/he has already defaulted on payment of another financial penalty and, if so, whether that default can be disregarded;
- whether an attachment of earnings order or application for deductions from benefits has been made and, if so, the repayment terms that apply if the order or application fails ('reserve terms'). If not, the payment terms;
- which fines office will deal with the case; *and*
- the consequences of default.

The client is an existing defaulter

If the client is an existing defaulter and has failed to show the court there was an adequate reason for the default, the court must:

- make an **attachment of earnings order** (see p366) if the client is in employment, provided it is not impracticable or inappropriate to do so; *or*
- apply to the Secretary of State to make **deductions from benefits** (see p366) if the client is in receipt of income support (IS), income-based jobseeker's allowance (JSA), income-related employment and support allowance (ESA) or pension credit (PC), provided it is not impracticable or inappropriate to do so.

If a fixed penalty has been registered in the magistrates' court for enforcement, the client is deemed to have no adequate reason for default, so that the first enforcement condition will be satisfied automatically. If the client is in employment or entitled to a relevant benefit, the court can either make an attachment of earnings order or a request for deductions from benefit, but cannot do both.

There is no guidance on the meaning of 'impracticable or inappropriate'. It could include situations where the court has no information about the client's financial circumstances or where, for example, there is an existing council tax attachment of earnings order and the client would be left with insufficient income to meet essential expenses if another order were made. In the case of deductions from benefits, it could include a case where deductions were already being made from the client's benefit for debts with a higher priority.

If the court is satisfied the client has shown an adequate reason for her/his default, an attachment of earnings order or application for deductions from benefits can still be made, but only if the client consents, unless the financial penalty consists solely of (or includes) a compensation order. If it does, the court must make an attachment of earnings order or an application for deductions from benefits, unless it is impracticable or inappropriate to do so.

If a client does not want an attachment of earnings order or deductions from benefit, the adviser should check whether s/he has any outstanding financial penalties before a magistrates' court hearing and, if so, either advise her/him to bring her/his payments up to date or to provide the court with an explanation of the default and of the possible adverse financial consequences of any attachment of earnings order or make a request for deductions from benefits.

Attachment of earnings orders made in the magistrates' courts are not made in the same way as those made in the county court (see p309). Instead, fixed deductions are made from the client's net earnings using the percentage deductions in the table below.

Net earnings			
Monthly	Weekly	Daily	Deduction rate
Up to £220	Up to £55	Up to £8	0%
£220.01 to £400	£55.01 to £100	£8.01 to £15	3%
£400.01 to £540	£100.01 to £135	£15.01 to £20	5%
£540.01 to £660	£135.01 to £165	£20.01 to £24	7%
£660.01 to £1,040	£165.01 to £260	£24.01 to £38	12%
£1,040.01 to £1,480	£260.01 to £370	£38.01 to £53	17%
£1,480.01 and over	£370.01 and over	£53.01 and over	17% of this threshold and 50% of the remainder

Attachment of earnings orders for fines take priority over existing attachment of earnings orders for payment of judgment debts or administration orders, but have equal priority with other attachment of earnings orders – eg, for council tax arrears. Employers are required to deal with such priority orders in date order. The client's net earnings are calculated after making the deductions due under previous orders. If the client has more than one fine, they can be collected through a consolidated attachment of earnings order and so the client should be advised to contact the fines officer and ask for this to be arranged.

The court can apply to the Secretary of State for Work and Pensions to **deduct payments** towards a financial penalty from the client's IS, income-based JSA, income-related ESA or PC. The amount that can be deducted is £5 a week. When universal credit is introduced in October 2013, the amount will be between £5 and £25 a week. Fines have low priority, however, and deductions can only be made in respect of one application at a time. If the client is likely to experience hardship as a result of the deductions being made, the adviser should consider making written representations to the Secretary of State not to enforce the court's application.

The client is not an existing defaulter

The collection order sets out the terms on how payment of the financial penalty is to be made. An attachment of earnings order or request for deductions from benefits can only be made if the client consents, unless the financial penalty consists solely of (or includes) a compensation order. If it does, the court must make either an attachment of earnings order or an application for deductions from benefits, provided it is not impracticable or inappropriate to do so. Where appropriate, clients should be advised to resist pressure to agree to such a course of action in favour of voluntary payments.

Varying the terms of a collection order

The client will be sent a copy of the collection order. Providing s/he has not defaulted on the payment terms, s/he can contact the fines officer and ask to vary the order on the grounds that there has been a change in her/his circumstances since the collection order was made (or last varied), or that s/he is making further information available about her/his circumstances. This could be useful if there has been no change of circumstances, but the client did not provide full information about her/his financial circumstances on a previous occasion. The fines officer can require the client to provide a statement of her/his financial circumstances in connection with the request. It is an offence not to comply with such a requirement. There is no limit to the number of times a client can ask for variation. There is right of appeal against the fines officer's decision to the magistrates' court within 10 working days (see p368).

If the attachment of earnings order or deduction from benefits fails

If the attachment of earnings order or application for deductions from benefits fails (eg, if the client leaves her/his employment or the DWP is unable to comply with the request because of prior deductions), the fines officer must send the client a 'payment notice' informing her/him:

- the order (or request) has failed;
- the reserve terms in the collection order now have effect;
- what s/he must do to comply with the reserve terms;
- of her/his right to apply to vary the reserve terms.

The client can contact the fines officer and ask to vary the order on the grounds that there has been a change in her/his circumstances since the reserve terms were set (or last varied), or that s/he is making further information available about her/his circumstances. The fines officer can require the client to provide a statement of her/his financial circumstances in connection with the request. It is an offence not to comply with such a requirement. There is no limit to the number of times the client can ask for a variation, provided the fines officer has not issued a 'further steps notice' (see p368). There is a right of appeal against the fines officer's decision to the magistrates' court within 10 working days (see p368).

If the client defaults on the collection order

The client will be in default of the collection order if s/he fails to comply with the payment terms (or, if they have taken effect, the reserve terms). The fines officer may refer the case back to the magistrates' court or decide to enforce payment her/himself. Providing there is no outstanding request to the fines officer to vary the reserve terms or appeal to the magistrates about a previous decision of the fines officer on a request to vary the reserve terms, the fines officer can send a 'further steps notice', setting out which of the following steps s/he intends to take:

- make an attachment of earnings order or request deductions from benefits;
- issue a warrant of distress (see p369);
- register the financial penalty in the Register of Judgments, Orders and Fines;
- make a clamping order (see p371);
- apply to have the financial penalty enforced in the High Court or the county court (see p373).

Appeals and referrals

The client can appeal to the magistrates' court within 10 working days (ie, excluding Saturdays and Sundays, Christmas Day, Good Friday and bank holidays) against a fines officer's decision:

- to vary the terms of a collection order;
- to vary reserve terms;
- to issue a further steps notice.

On an appeal, the magistrates' court may:

- confirm or vary the payment terms (or any reserve terms);
- confirm, quash or vary a further steps notice;
- discharge the collection order and exercise any of its standard powers (see below).

On a referral to the magistrates' court by the fines officer, the magistrates can:

- confirm or vary the payment terms (or any reserve terms);
- discharge the collection order;
- exercise any of the powers referred to in this chapter.

By discharging the collection order, the court retains control of the collection and enforcement process itself rather than delegating it to the fines officer. The 'standard powers' given to the magistrates are much wider than the powers given to fines officers, although some of the powers can be exercised by both.

If a fines officer refers the case to the magistrates' court either instead of issuing a further steps notice or after taking any of the steps listed in it, the magistrates may increase the fine (but not any other part of the financial penalty) by 50 per cent, provided the magistrates are satisfied that the client's default on the collection order is due to her/his 'wilful refusal or culpable neglect'. The increase is enforced as if it were part of the fine.

To ensure the client attends a referral hearing, the fines officer may issue a summons directing her/him to attend the magistrates' court at a specified time and place. If the client fails to attend, the court will issue a warrant for her/his arrest by a civil enforcement officer. The warrant is either with or without bail – ie, the client is either bailed to attend court, or is arrested and brought before the court. Before executing the warrant, the enforcement officer will seek to obtain full payment. If an adviser discovers a client is subject to a warrant without bail, s/he should advise her/him to surrender her/himself to the court on a day when the court is sitting to deal with fine defaulters, and prepare a financial statement for the client to take with her/him.

Advisers should always contact the fines officer immediately if there are arrears on an order as it may be possible to agree a new payment arrangement, particularly if the financial penalty can still be paid within the original period allowed by the court.

Distress warrant

The court can issue a distress warrant against the client's money and goods if s/he fails to pay as ordered by the court.[7] Although there is now more emphasis on the use of attachment of earnings and deductions from benefits, distress warrants are frequently the first enforcement method used. This is because many financial penalties are imposed in the offender's absence, with the court having no information about her/his means.

No hearing is required before a distress warrant is issued, although the court can postpone its issue if it wishes.[8] There is no requirement to hold a means enquiry before issuing a distress warrant,[9] but if there is evidence the client has sufficient assets to pay the debt, the magistrates should use distress rather than committal.[10]

The use of bailiffs

HM Courts and Tribunals Service (HMCTS) has national contracts with private bailiffs firms to execute distress warrants. Since 18 July 2005, bailiffs collecting financial penalties (but not other debts) can use reasonable force, if necessary, to enter and search any premises if it is reasonably required.[11] This power, however, is rarely used and should only be exercised in accordance with HMCTS instructions.

Bailiffs should not attempt to levy distress without referring back to the magistrates' court if the client:

- is in a hospital or nursing home;
- appears to have a severe physical, or any mental, disability;
- is an elderly person who has difficultly dealing with her/his affairs;
- has a long-term sickness, or serious or acute illness or frailty which has resulted in a recent period of hospitalisation, or s/he is housebound;
- has had a recent bereavement of a close/immediate family member;
- is heavily pregnant. No period of weeks is suggested and so it is a matter for the bailiff's discretion;

- has a genuine communication problem. There is no definition of this and so is a matter for the bailiff's discretion;
- produces evidence to show the 'account' has been paid. Once the warrant is with the bailiffs, the court should not accept any payment from the client and should refer any offers of payment to the bailiffs;[12] *or*
- claims to have made a statutory declaration to set aside the conviction (see p364).

The bailiffs should refer back to the court if they have doubts about the identity of the client or in any other circumstances if the bailiff considers it would be 'prudent' to do so. No examples or guidance are provided, but the *National Standards for Enforcement Agents* include lone parents and unemployed people in its list of potentially vulnerable people.

Rule 52.8(3) of the Criminal Procedure Rules lays down a more restrictive list of exempt goods than that which applies to most other debts. The bailiff may not seize bedding or clothes belonging to the client or any member of the client's family, or the tools, books, vehicles or other equipment which the client personally needs to use in her/his employment, business or vocation. In addition, under their contract, bailiffs must not seize goods that:

- may be necessary to maintain the 'core of life'. This is not defined and so is left to the bailiff's discretion, but examples include the only cooking facility, and an item of heating or storing food; *or*
- are clearly identifiable as 'children's items'; *or*
- are tools, books, vehicles and other items of equipment that are necessary for the client to use personally in her/his job or business (broadly mirroring the statutory requirements).

Under their contract, bailiffs are given a timescale for collecting financial penalties, and the financial penalty must be paid before the bailiffs can take their own fees. The bailiffs' fees are in the contract between the bailiffs' firms and HMCTS.

There is no legal time limit within which a warrant must be executed. However, full payment of both the financial penalty and costs is expected within 180 days, but the court can recall the warrant if the bailiff has taken no steps within 90 days from the issue of the warrant. This means the bailiffs may refuse the client's offer of instalments and press for payment at a rate the client clearly cannot afford. A client may, therefore, want to ask the court for further time to pay after a distress warrant has been issued. Whether or not this can be done is a 'grey' area.

Although the High Court has held that the magistrates' court cannot suspend or cancel a warrant after it has been issued,[13] it has been pointed out in another High Court case that magistrates may be able to review the situation under s142 of the Magistrates' Court Act 1980 on the basis that it is 'in the interests of justice to do so' (see p364).[14] The last government's view was that this can only be used to correct an error in the actual sentence or order and cannot be used to affect the way the sentence (in this case, the financial penalty) is enforced. The contract does not allow the court to withdraw a warrant unless the fine becomes subject to an appeal or other application to set aside the conviction. The court does reserve the power to recall the warrant if there is evidence that the client is vulnerable and that enforcement would either not be in the interests of justice or might bring the process into disrepute.

The bailiff must make a minimum of two visits before returning the warrant to the court. Although there are no legal restrictions on times, visits should begin at a reasonable time and at least one attempt must be made outside 'normal' working hours – ie, 8am to 6pm, Monday to Friday. Visits should not be made on Sundays, Good Friday, Christmas Day, bank holidays or at a time that is likely to be inappropriate to the client's religious beliefs (if these are known). The court should not accept full or a part-payment from the client so long as the warrant is with the bailiff, but should instead refer any offers of payment directly to the bailiff.

The bailiff will return the warrant to the court if:

- the bailiff is unable to make contact with the client after a minimum of two visits; *or*
- the bailiff is unable to obtain payment; *or*
- there are insufficient goods, or all the goods are in one or more of the categories listed above; *or*
- the client is identified as being in one of the categories listed above.

For more details on bailiffs, see Chapter 14.

Clamping order

A clamping order is an order made by the fines officer or the magistrates' court that a motor vehicle registered in the client's name is fitted with an immobilisation devise ('clamped'). A clamping order is made to obtain payment of the financial penalty and includes the costs of carrying out the actual clamping of the vehicle.

Before the magistrates' court or the fines officer can make a clamping order, it must be satisfied that:

- the client has the means to pay the financial penalty; *and*
- the value of the vehicle(s) is likely to exceed the amount of the financial penalty plus the likely charges due and estimated costs of sale.

It is not clear exactly what is meant by 'has the means to pay'. The natural meaning of the words is that the client must be in a position to pay the financial penalty immediately. As a client will always have at least 10 days' warning of the possibility of a clamping order being made, s/he will have the opportunity either to remedy the default or demonstrate that one or both of the conditions is not satisfied.

A copy of the order must be sent to a clamping contractor who, if payment is not made, is required to execute the order on or after the date specified within a period of 60 days (which can be extended by the court to 90 days). The copy sent to the clamping contractor must be accompanied by details of the client's last known address, the vehicle and, if known, the likely whereabouts of the vehicle to be clamped.

The clamping contract is part of the contract agreed between the HMCTS and bailiffs' firms (see p369).

Vehicles may be clamped at any place (including on any highway or road) to which the public has access or on any private land to which access may be had at the time of clamping without opening or removing any door, gate or other barrier. The contractor may enter any such place (with a vehicle if necessary) in order to clamp a vehicle, release it from clamping or remove it for storage.

A vehicle cannot be clamped if:

- it is not registered in the client's name under the Vehicle Excise and Registration Act 1994;
- a current disabled person's badge is displayed on it, or there are reasonable grounds for believing it is used to carry a disabled person;
- it is used for police, fire or ambulance purposes;
- it is being used by a doctor on call away from her/his usual place of work, and a British Medical Association badge or other health emergency badge showing the doctor's address is displayed on it.

The contractor must ensure that members of staff engaged in clamping operations are dressed in an identifiable uniform with an identification card attached to it in a prominent position. In the event of a complaint by the client in connection with the clamping, removal or storage of a vehicle, the contractor must give her/him a leaflet about the company's complaints procedure.

The contractor's office where payment of the fine and the charge(s) due is made must be readily accessible from the place where the vehicle is clamped during all hours when the contractor undertakes clamping and for at least two hours thereafter. Once the fine and charge(s) have been paid in full, the vehicle must be released from clamping or storage within:

- four hours of the time of payment, if payment is made at or to the contractor's office or the court; *or*
- two hours of the time of payment, if payment is made to a member of the contractor's staff.

Payment must be accepted by cash, cheque (up to the amount specified on the payer's debit card or cheque guarantee card) or credit card (up to the credit limit for which the card is valid). If full payment is not made, it will first be applied towards payment of the charges and the balance towards the financial penalty.

Unless released, the vehicle must remain clamped for up to a maximum of 24 hours, after which the contractor removes the vehicle to secure premises for storage. The contractor must notify the client and the fines officer of the vehicle's new location. If this does not result in payment, the contractor must refer the matter back to the court.

If the fine has not been paid in full and 10 clear working days have elapsed since the date the vehicle was clamped, the fines officer must apply in writing to the court (and send a copy of the application to the client) for an order to sell the vehicle. **Note:** although either the magistrates' court or fines officer can make a clamping order, only the magistrates can order the actual sale of the vehicle. The application must not be listed for hearing until 21 days have elapsed.

When considering whether or not to order the sale of the vehicle, the magistrates' court must consider the history of the case, in particular whether the clamping order was justified, reasonable and proportionate. If the court decides the vehicle should not be sold, it may direct the vehicle to be released, either with or without liability for payment of the charges due. If the court makes an order for sale, the fines officer must send a copy of the order for sale to the contractor who will arrange for the vehicle to be sold by an agent or by auction (unless the client makes full payment in the meantime).

When the vehicle has been sold, the contractor must first deduct from the net proceeds of the sale the charges due for the clamping, removal and storage. The fines officer will then deduct an amount that is sufficient to discharge the client's liability for the fine from the remaining balance. S/he must then send the client a cheque for any balance remaining within 10 working days of the date of sale of the vehicle, accompanied by a written statement of account.

If the net proceeds of the sale are not sufficient to meet the amount of the fine and any charges due, the net proceeds must first be put towards meeting the charges due and then, if a balance remains, towards discharging the client's liability for the fine. The fines officer must then seek to recover the outstanding amount of the fine under the collection order and the powers available under it, including the power to refer the case to the magistrates' court.

Complaints about making the clamping order and its content must be made to the fines officer. Complaints about its execution or the removal or storage of the vehicle must be made to the contractor's senior manager. If the client is dissatisfied with the outcome of the complaint, s/he has 10 working days to ask for the matter to be referred to the magistrates' court. A hearing will be arranged at which the magistrates can make whatever decision they think fit.

High Court and county court orders

The fines officer may apply to the High Court or a county court for an order only available in these courts – eg, a third-party debt order or charging order.[15] Such an application is unlikely to be made unless the fines officer believes that none of the other available collection methods is likely to be successful, but a High Court or county court remedy is.

For more information on these enforcement methods, see Chapter 11.

Enforcement methods following a means enquiry

Before the court can take certain types of enforcement action, it must enquire into the client's ability to pay the financial penalty and reason for default at a hearing at which the client is present. For example, unless a person was sentenced to a term of imprisonment in default of immediate payment, there must be a means enquiry before imprisonment can be considered.[16] The client can be questioned by the magistrates' clerk.[17]

Clients are often required to complete a means enquiry form, which may be similar to a debt adviser's financial statement. Magistrates may have little knowledge of the benefits system and of many items of ordinary expenditure, and advisers should ensure that a full financial statement is prepared and given to the magistrates, even if this means adding considerably to the court's own form. This should include an explanation of any essential expenditure that the debt adviser believes may be questioned by the court. In addition, magistrates may not take into account items of expenditure that the client has prioritised over payment of the financial penalty, but which the magistrates regard as non-essential. Magistrates usually take account of expenditure on housing (including fuel), clothing and food for the client and her/his dependants, water charges and council tax. However, there is no consistent approach and debt advisers should establish the local practice.

Information should also be made available about the reason for non-payment, the financial position at the time of the previous order and future prospects, as appropriate.

Following a means enquiry, the court has the power to:
- remit a fine (see below);
- fix a return date (see p375);
- make a money payments supervision order (see p375);
- order the client to be imprisoned or detained (see p375 and p377);
- make an attendance centre order (see p377);
- make an fines payment work order (see p377).

Remitting fines

To remit a fine means that the fine is cancelled, either in full or in part. Provided that circumstances have changed since the fine was imposed, it can remit all or part of the fine.[18] The court can also remit a fine that was imposed in the absence of information about the client's means and, as a result, was set too high.

Debt advisers should always argue for a full remission of a fine if a person is on benefit or in serious debt (although the court may take into account the client's financial position at the time the financial penalty was imposed (or warrant suspended) and any other resources available to her/him). The magistrates should be urged to consider full or partial remission if the guidelines on the time for payment of a financial penalty have not been observed.

The magistrates do not have the power to remit costs or a victim's surcharge and can only remit compensation orders in limited circumstances.

Fixing a return date

Magistrates may also order payment of the amount due by a certain date or fix an amount to be paid periodically and give a date when the client must return if s/he has not paid either the amount due or all the instalments. If the client fails to appear, a warrant of arrest can be issued. Debt advisers should try to ensure that the order is one with which the client can realistically comply or, if s/he defaults, that they can show this was not due to the client's 'wilful refusal' or 'culpable neglect' (see p383).

Money payments supervision order

The court can also make a money payments supervision order, appointing someone to 'advise and befriend the defendant with a view to inducing him to pay the sum adjudged to be paid' – ie, supervise the client during the payment of the financial penalty.[19] This is normally a probation officer or a fines officer. The court is not required to hold a means enquiry before making an order, nor is the client's consent required, but since the client's co-operation is essential to the working of the order, it is normally required. As a matter of good practice, the money payments supervision order should specify the terms of payment.

Imprisonment

If a client falls into arrears with payment of a financial penalty, the court may order her/his imprisonment.[20] There is a similar power to detain under-21-year-olds in a young offenders' institution, but there are additional restrictions.[21] The minimum term of imprisonment is five days and the maximum term that can be imposed by a magistrates' court is 12 months.

The court can only issue a warrant to imprison someone:[22]

- if a distress warrant is returned to the court by the bailiffs because there are insufficient goods or money to cover the amount owing; *or*
- instead of issuing a distress warrant.

Once a distress warrant has been issued, imprisonment cannot be considered unless the warrant is returned with an endorsement stating there were no goods. Debt advisers should consider asking solicitors to argue that, if a warrant has been returned because the bailiffs were unable to gain access to the client's property, imprisonment is not an option open to the court, but this argument has not been tested in the higher courts.

There must also be a means enquiry,[23] at which the court must be satisfied:

- if the original offence was punishable by imprisonment, that the client appears to have sufficient means to pay the sum immediately; *or*
- that the default is due to the client's 'wilful refusal' or 'culpable neglect' (see p383); *and*
- that all other methods of obtaining payment have been considered or tried, but have been either inappropriate or unsuccessful, including a money payments supervision order (see p375) or a fines payment work order if available (see p377).

The Divisional Court has stressed to magistrates that the second bullet above is mandatory.[24] In practice, the court will often assume that, if a person has paid nothing, this is deliberate. Debt advisers should encourage solicitors and other representatives to argue strongly that it is impossible to find money from a client's low income, even for priorities like financial penalties. However, even if the court is 'satisfied' that the client had the means to pay, a prison sentence will be quashed unless the court can demonstrate it has considered all the non-custodial alternatives discussed above. Over the past few years there has been considerable publicity about the number of wrongful committals. This has generally been due to inadequate means enquiries and/or failure to follow the above rules.

Any term of imprisonment must be proportional to the size of the financial penalty. The period is determined by a statutory scale and depends on the amount of the financial penalty outstanding. A stay in prison can be avoided by immediately paying the outstanding balance. Any costs of unsuccessful bailiff action can be added to the amount the client must pay to obtain her/his release. The length of any period of detention (whether actual or suspended) can be reduced by paying a proportion of the outstanding balance.[25] The financial penalty and any costs are wiped out if the prison sentence is served.

If the court decides to impose a period of imprisonment, it can be postponed in certain situations – eg, if the client keeps to a payment arrangement.[26] This is known as a 'suspended committal'. The conditions can be varied if, for example, the client's circumstances change and s/he can no longer comply with the terms of the suspended committal.

A suspended committal order cannot be combined with any other enforcement order since, by implication, they have all been considered inappropriate and any attempt to do so could be challenged on the basis that no period of imprisonment should have been imposed in the first place.

If the client fails to comply with the conditions of postponement, another hearing must be held before s/he can be sent to prison. The client must be given the opportunity to attend the hearing in order to make representations on why the committal warrant should not be issued. This will involve attempting to persuade the magistrates that circumstances have changed since the previous hearing (including new facts). The court can still consider remission at this stage. Although the rules state that notice of the hearing is deemed to be served if sent by 'special' or 'recorded signed for' delivery to the client's last known address, the High Court quashed a sentence of imprisonment where a notice of hearing had been returned to the court as undelivered. The High Court said that the magistrates should have adjourned the hearing until the client had actually been served with notice of the hearing.[27]

Short local detention

Instead of imposing imprisonment, the magistrates can order the client to be detained for the remainder of the day, either in the court building or at a police station up until 8pm. S/he must be released in time for her/him to get home on the same day. The magistrates can also order the client to be detained overnight at a police station until 8am the next morning.[28] This is not imprisonment and so the restrictions on imprisoning clients do not apply, but (as with imprisonment) the financial penalty is wiped out (see p375).

It might be appropriate to ask the magistrates to consider this option if they have ordered the financial penalty to be paid immediately, the client is unable to do so and the magistrates are not prepared to allow her/him time to pay.

Attendance centre order

If the court has an attendance centre available to it and the client is under 25 years old, the magistrates can order her/him to attend the centre for between 12 and 36 hours.[29] Attendance can be required for two to three hours at a time, usually on Saturday afternoons.

Fine payment work order

The magistrates' court can allow defendants over 18 liable to pay a fine (but not amounts due as compensation or costs) to discharge it by doing unpaid work, if it appears to the court that the amount owed cannot be collected by any of the other available methods.[30] The court makes a fine payment work order. This means that, in some cases, the courts make unpaid work orders rather than remit fines. Advisers should check the position with their local courts.

3. Compensation orders

A magistrates' court can impose a compensation order alongside a fine or other sentence and must give reasons for not making an order in cases in which it is empowered to do so.[31] The compensation order is intended to be a simple way for the injured party in a criminal case to get compensation without having to sue in the county court. Compensation orders are often made in cases such as criminal damage or petty theft. They are collected by the court and paid to the victim. The powers to remit a fine (see p374) do not apply to compensation orders. The only circumstances in which a compensation order could be altered are if:[32]

- a client appeals against either the conviction or the compensation order. A solicitor is needed for this and there are strict time limits; *or*
- subsequent civil proceedings demonstrate that the loss in respect of which the order was made was less than that stated in the order; *or*
- a compensation order is made for stolen goods which are later recovered; *or*
- the client has experienced a substantial reduction in her/his means, which was unexpected at the time the order was made and they seem unlikely to increase for a considerable period.

Compensation orders are difficult to change. If a client is appearing in a criminal court on a charge that might result in a compensation order, the debt adviser should advise her/him to take a clear statement of means with her/him. A representative should also be prepared to argue that, in view of the client's other debts, s/he should not have a compensation order awarded against her/him. The court must consider a client's financial statement and debts when making a decision.[33]

Costs awarded along with a fine or compensation order are treated in exactly the same way as the compensation order – ie, they cannot be remitted by the court.

4. **Council tax**

Magistrates' courts have two distinct roles in relation to the collection of council tax. These are:
- to decide about the issue of a liability order;
- to decide about committal to prison.

Issuing a liability order

The court can issue a liability order against an individual at the request of a local authority. The local authority cannot apply for a liability order after a period of six years beginning with the date on which the tax became due. The duty to pay does not arise until the demand notice (ie, the bill) is served.[34] Demand notices should be served 'as soon as practicable' after the date on which the local authority first sets the amount of council tax for the year in question. This suggests that Parliament intended that there should be no unnecessary delay. However, late service of a demand notice does not automatically invalidate it and it is only a defence to an application for a liability order if the client can establish that s/he has experience substantial 'prejudice' as a result.[35]

The client is summonsed to attend a hearing. The summons must be served at least 14 days before the hearing date. The summons will have been properly served by:

- delivering it to the client; *or*
- leaving it at the client's usual or last known place of abode; *or*
- posting it to the client's usual or last known place of abode; *or*
- leaving it at, or posting it to, an address given by the client as an address at which service of the summons will be accepted.

This means the client does not necessarily have actually to receive the summons.[36] The order states that an amount of tax is due from the client, that s/he has not paid it and that s/he is therefore liable. Issues concerning liability for, or exemption from, the tax cannot be raised at the hearing, but must be dealt with through the appropriate appeals procedure, although the court will probably adjourn if an appeal is pending.[37] Failure by the local authority to follow the rules on billing and reminder notices can be raised as a defence), as can the fact that the demand has actually been paid.

If the client is disputing liability, the adviser should consider an appeal to a valuation tribunal. This can determine appeals about banding, whether the client is liable for the council tax, entitlement to a discount or exemption, and the calculation of the amount of council tax claimed to be due. The valuation tribunal cannot consider wider issues, such as whether the council sent out the council tax bill at the correct time.[38] An appeal must be made to the local authority in the first instance.[39]

Although the fact that a claim for council tax benefit or rebate is pending is not a defence, the magistrates could adjourn the matter. However, the Local Government Ombudsman has repeatedly found local authorities guilty of maladministration where council tax arrears wholly or mainly arose as a result of their failure to determine council tax benefit claims and the client has provided the information requested or a reasonable excuse for any delay.[40]

If payment is made after the liability order has been applied for, the local authority can ask for an order for payment of its reasonable costs.[41] The magistrates cannot be asked to allow time to pay at this stage.

The order allows the authority to pursue collection of the debt by:

- a payment arrangement; *or*
- a distress warrant (see p369 and Chapter 14); *or*
- an attachment of earnings order in accordance with the scales set out in the regulations. The costs of unsuccessful distress or applications for committal to prison can also be included in the order); *or*
- deductions from the client's income support (IS), income-based jobseeker's allowance (JSA), income-related employment and support allowance (ESA) or pension credit (PC) currently at the rate of £3.55 a week (see p366);
- a charging order in the county court, provided there is at least £1,000 outstanding under one or more liability orders (see p301); *or*
- bankruptcy (see p231 and Chapter 15).

The local authority can also request that information about the client's means be supplied.

Enforcement of a liability order is done by the local authority, unless it chooses to return to the magistrates' court to seek the imprisonment of the client.

Local authorities can only use one of the above enforcement methods for one liability order at a time.

Although, in theory, once the local authority has obtained a liability order there is no time limit on enforcement,[42] in practice, however, if the client disputes the existence of a liability order, the local authority will either have to produce a copy or some evidence from the magistrates' court that one has been made. Its own internal computer records should not be accepted as sufficient.[43]

Setting aside a liability order

Since 22 April 2004, local authorities (but not council tax payers) have had the power to apply to the magistrates' court to quash the liability order on the ground that it should not have been made.[44] If the magistrates' court is satisfied that the liability order should not have been made, it must quash the order.

In addition, if the magistrates' court is satisfied that the local authority is entitled to a liability order for a lesser amount, the magistrates' court must make a liability order for:

- that lesser amount; *plus*
- any sum included in the quashed order for the costs reasonably incurred by the local authority in obtaining that order.

In the case of *Liverpool City Council v Pleroma Distribution,* the Administrative Court held that magistrates' courts have the power to reopen matters where they have acted 'in excess of jurisdiction' – ie, where they have made an order that they had no power to make.[45] In this case, the magistrates had not been informed of Pleroma Distribution's application for an adjournment to enable it to contest the application.

In *R (on the application of Newham London Borough Council) v Stratford Magistrates' Court,* the Administrative Court set out three criteria to be considered by magistrates' courts faced with set-aside applications.[46]

- There must be a genuine and arguable dispute about ability to pay.
- The liability order must have been made as a result of some substantial procedural error, defect or mishap.
- The set-aside application must have been made promptly once the client had notice of its existence.

The application is made by letter, requesting the magistrates' court to re-list the local authority's application for the liability order and setting out the grounds on which it is being argued that the original liability order should not have been made. This is appropriate in cases where the local authority does not accept there are grounds for a set-aside and refuses to apply itself.

If the summons for the liability order was not properly served (see p378), the Administrative Court has recommended a procedure for setting aside the liability order to avoid expensive litigation.

- On discovering the existence of the liability order, the client should promptly inform both the local authority and the magistrates' court that the summons was not properly served.
- The local authority should then satisfy itself as to whether or not the client's assertion is correct.
- If this is established, the client and the local authority should co-operate in making a joint application to the magistrates' court to have the liability order set aside.[47]

If the local authority accepts that the order should not have been made, but refuses to apply to set it aside, the client can consider making a complaint to the Local Government Ombudsman or Public Services Ombudsman for Wales, particularly if s/he is out of time to apply her/himself.

Committal to prison

If an application to commit someone to prison is made, the court must arrange a hearing and hold a means enquiry.[48] These proceedings can only begin once a distress warrant has been issued and returned because insufficient or no goods of the client could be found (for whatever reason, including if it was because the bailiffs could not gain entry).[49]

The adviser should not rely on the court to produce paperwork and must prepare a full statement of income, expenditure and debts, as well as a clear explanation of any particular difficulties facing the client.

The court must decide whether the client has shown 'wilful refusal' or 'culpable neglect' in failing to pay (see p383). The magistrates should consider the issue for the whole period up to the date of the committal hearing. In all cases, the magistrates must also consider the client's ability to pay at the date of the actual committal hearing. Courts often equate failure to pay with refusal or neglect to pay regardless of the client's financial situation. For this reason, a debt adviser who acts as a representative in the magistrates' court should ensure that the court understands that poverty, rather than politics, is the cause of the non-payment, by producing evidence about the client's income and spending and other priority debts. Free legal representation is available to assist clients at these hearings as well as at committal hearings regarding financial penalties.

Note: many magistrates' courts do not allow lay representatives in committal hearings. If the magistrates do not accept a debt adviser as a representative, s/he can act as a 'McKenzie Friend' (see p23).

The High Court has repeatedly advised magistrates that the purpose of committal in such cases is to obtain payment and not to punish the client. Therefore, although there is no statutory obligation to do so, local authorities, as well as magistrates, should consider alternative viable methods of enforcement and not refuse reasonable offers of payment.[50] However, a suspended committal order is regarded as a method of enforcement in its own right.[51] Orders should not be suspended for more than two to three years and partial remission should be considered in order to reduce the sum in respect of which the order is being made.[52] The magistrates must take account of the principle of proportionality, with the maximum term being reserved for the most serious cases. The magistrates should use the tables of sentences provided for fines as a guide to the appropriate level of sentences. See *Anthony and Berryman's Magistrates' Court Guide* for more information.[53] The magistrates must consider the question of wilfulness/culpability separately from the question of how they are going to deal with the case.

The number of people committed to prison for non-payment of local taxes has steadily fallen over the past 12 years or so. The increasing reluctance of magistrates' courts to make committal orders has led many local authorities to resort to bankruptcy proceedings as an enforcement method if the client is a homeowner – in many cases, for debts that are only just above the £750 bankruptcy limit. For more details, see p231.

Outcome of the committal hearing

If the court decides there has not been either 'wilful refusal' or 'culpable neglect' (see p383), it can either remit (write off) all or some of the arrears,[54] or make no order at all. **Note:** since 18 November 2003, local authorities have had the power to write off council tax arrears themselves (see p226). Although there is no time limit in which a local authority must enforce a liability order, the High Court has said that magistrates should consider remitting the debt on their own initiative where more than six years have elapsed between the date of the original default and the committal hearing.[55]

If the magistrates decide there has been 'wilful refusal' or 'culpable neglect', they can issue a warrant committing the client to prison for up to three months. They can (and usually do initially) suspend this warrant on payment of regular instalments. This means that, so long as the agreed payments are kept, the client will not be imprisoned. However, unlike financial penalties, the court no longer has the option to remit the debt. If the client fails to comply with the terms of the suspended order, the magistrates must satisfy themselves that s/he had the ability to pay before they can activate the committal order by arranging a further means enquiry.[56]

If the arrears and costs to date are paid in full after the local authority applies for committal, no further recovery action can take place and, if the client has been imprisoned, s/he must be released. If partial payment is made, the period of imprisonment is reduced proportionately. If the part-payment is made after the term of imprisonment has been fixed but before the client begins to serve the sentence, the period to be served is also reduced proportionately. From 6 April 2010, the maximum fee for committal has increased from £85 to £305 and this is added to the arrears and other costs, imposing an even greater burden of debt on clients, particularly those on a low income.

If a client is sent to prison, no further enforcement action can be taken for any arrears and costs that remain unpaid. They are still owed, but cease to be priority debts.

The High Court has repeatedly advised magistrates that the purpose of committal in such cases is to obtain payment and not to punish the client. Therefore, although there is no statutory obligation to do so, local authorities, as well as magistrates, should consider alternative viable methods of enforcement and not refuse reasonable offers of payment.[57] However, a suspended committal order is regarded as a method of enforcement in its own right.[58] Orders should not be suspended for more than two to three years and partial remission should be considered in order to reduce the sum in respect of which the order is being made.[59] The magistrates must take account of the principle of proportionality, with the maximum term being reserved for the most serious cases. The magistrates should use the tables of sentences provided for fines as a guide to the appropriate level of sentences. See *Anthony and Berryman's Magistrates' Court Guide* for more information.[60] The magistrates must consider the question of wilfulness/culpability separately from the question of how they are going to deal with the case.

5. **Wilful refusal and culpable neglect**

There are a number of situations in which magistrates acting as debt collectors are required to decide whether a client's non-payment is due to her/his 'wilful refusal' or 'culpable neglect'.

Although magistrates' courts have been making decisions based on their interpretation of this important phrase for many years, the two phrases are not defined by statute or regulation. There is little guidance on what factors should be taken into account when making a decision, but the client's conduct must be 'blameworthy' in some way.

The client should only be found guilty of **'wilful refusal'** if s/he has made a deliberate decision not to pay the amount due, even though s/he is able to do so – eg, on a point of principle. However, a finding of 'wilful refusal' does not automatically justify a sentence of imprisonment; the two questions must be considered separately.

'**Culpable neglect**' is more difficult. It means a reckless disregard of the court order and usually involves the situation where the client spends any available income on non-essential items rather than on paying the financial penalty. It is not sufficient for the magistrates to find the client had available income and did not pay; they must also find out why it has not been paid.[61] If a couple are in receipt of benefits intended for both of them, the non-claimant client can be found guilty of 'culpable neglect' if there has been a 'household' decision not to pay.[62]

To prove 'culpable neglect', it must be shown that:

- money was available, but it was not paid to the court or local authority; *and*
- this was due to a failure which demonstrates an avoidable choice to use the money for other purposes.

Evidence in the form of a financial statement should demonstrate to the court that the client's 'choices' were impossible and that a failure to pay was not 'culpable'.

Most courts assume that, if a person has ignored reminders or suspended committals, s/he has culpably neglected payment. This assumption should be challenged. The debt adviser should argue that a client:

- did not have any money available after paying for essential items; *or*
- was too stressed to be culpable; *or*
- did not understand the need to pay; *or*
- was not skilful enough to balance a very difficult budget; *or*
- was wrongly advised not to pay.

When representing a client, it is helpful for the adviser to begin by presenting a financial statement and evidence about her/his debts and social circumstances before asking the court to make a specific decision on the question of wilfulness or culpability. After the court has decided this, the adviser can argue about an affordable instalment arrangement, if necessary. It is useful to secure the court's agreement to conduct proceedings in this format because it encourages the court to think about wilfulness and because it allows the adviser to rescue something if the initial decision is unfavourable. The financial argument about the payment of a weekly amount by the client should be based on the scales in the regulations for attachment of earnings, although as these make no allowances for dependants or other commitments, they will often require modification.

Notes

2. Financial penalties

1 If no information is available, the court is entitled to assume a weekly income of £400. The court can remit all or part of the fine if the client subsequently provides evidence of means: ss164 and 165 Criminal Justice Act 2003. If the client is on a low income (including benefits), s/he is deemed to have a weekly income (currently £110).
2 *R v Olliver & Olliver* [1989] 11 Cr App R (Sentencing) 10
3 s142 MCA 1980, as amended by CAA 1995
4 s14 MCA 1980
5 See G Skipwith, 'Consultancy Corner', *Adviser* 148
6 s89 MCA 1980
7 s76 MCA 1980
8 s77(1) MCA 1980
9 *R v Hereford Magistrates ex parte MacRae, The Times,* 31 December 1998
10 *R v Birmingham Justices ex parte Bennett* [1983] 1 WLR 114
11 s27 and Sch 4 Domestic Violence, Crime and Victims Act 2004 was brought into force by SI.1821/2005
12 Under r52.8(5) CPR, a warrant ceases to have effect if the bailiff is paid the sum for which the warrant was issued, together with any extra sum payable in connection with the distress, or a receipt for the sum for which the warrant was issued is produced to the bailiff and the bailiff is paid any extra sum payable in connection with the distress.
13 *Crossland v Crossland* [1992] 2 FLR 45, confirmed in *R v Hereford Magistrates' Court ex parte MacRae, The Times,* 31 December 1998
14 *R v Sheffield City Justices ex parte Foster, The Times,* 2 December 1999
15 s87(1) MCA 1980
16 s82(3)(b) MCA 1980
17 *R v Corby MC ex parte Mott, The Times,* 12 March 1998
18 s85 MCA 1980
19 ss56(2) and 88 MCA 1980
20 s76 MCA 1980, restricted by s82

21 s88(5) MCA 1980 and ss1(5) and 5A CJA 1982
22 s76(2) MCA 1980
23 s82 MCA 1980
24 *R v Stockport Justices ex parte Conlon, The Times,* 3 January 1997
25 s79 MCA 1980
26 s77 MCA 1980
27 *R v Doncaster Justices ex parte Harrison* [1998] 163 JP 182
28 ss135 and 136 MCA 1980
29 s60 Powers of Criminal Courts (Sentencing) Act 2000
30 Sch 6 CA 2003

3. Compensation orders

31 ss1(1) and 35(1) PCCA 1973
32 s37 PCCA 1973
33 s35(1)(a) PCCA 1973

2. Council tax

34 Reg 34(3) CT(AE) Regs; *Regentford Ltd v Thanet District Council* [2004] EWHC 246 Admin (*Adviser* 103 abstracts)
35 Reg 19(1) CT(AE) Regs; *Regentford Ltd v Thanet District Council* [2004] EWHC 246 Admin (*Adviser* 103 abstracts); *North Somerset District Council v Honda Motors and others* [2010] EWHC 1505 (QB) (*Adviser* 148 abstracts)
36 Reg 35(2) and (2A) CT(AE) Regs, as amended
37 *R v Bristol Justices ex parte Wilson and Young* [1991] 156 JP 409
38 *Hardy v Sefton Metropolitan Borough Council* [2006] EWHC 1928 (Admin) (*Adviser* 125 abstracts)
39 For a discussion on the role and jurisdiction of valuation tribunals, see A Murdie, 'Computer Says No!', *Adviser* 118. Since 1 April 2008, the new 'appeals direct' system means clients have to appeal directly to the tribunal. See A Murdie, 'Local Taxation Update', *Legal Action,* April 2008.
40 For a more detailed discussion of the role of the Local Government Ombudsman, see A Hobley, 'Local Taxation and Bailiffs', *Adviser* 129
41 Reg 34(5)(b) and (8) CT(AE) Regs

42 *Bolsover District Council v Ashfield Nominees Ltd* [2010] EWCA Civ 1129
43 See *Adviser* 104, letters; see also *Smolen v Tower Hamlets London Borough Council* [2006] EWHC 3628 (ChD) (*Adviser* 126 money advice abstracts)
44 Reg 36A CT(AE) Regs, as inserted by Reg 5 CT(AE)(A) Regs
45 *Liverpool City Council v Pleroma Distribution* [2002] EWHC 2467 (Admin) (*Adviser* 96 abstracts)
46 *R (on the application of Newham London Borough Council) v Stratford Metropolitan Council* [2008] EWHC 125 (Admin); see A Murdie, 'A Low Key Anniversary', *Adviser* 130, p56
47 *R (on the application of Tull) v (1) Camberwell Green Magistrates' Court (2) Lambeth London Borough Council* [2004] EWHC 2780 (Admin) (*Adviser* 113 abstracts). If the magistrates refuse the application, the court pointed out they will have acted unreasonably and could have a costs order made against them if an application for judicial review were necessary.
48 Reg 41(2) CC(AE) Regs; reg 44(2) CT(AE) Regs
49 Reg 41(1) CC(AE) Regs; reg 44(1) CT(AE) Regs
50 *R v Sandwell Justices ex parte Lynn*, 5 March 1993, unreported; *R v Alfreton Justices ex parte Gratton, The Times,* 17 December 1993
51 *R v Preston Justices ex parte McCosh, The Times,* 30 January 1995
52 *R v Newcastle upon Tyne Justices ex parte Devine,* 23 April 1998, QBD; *R v Doncaster Justices ex parte Jack and Christison, The Times,* 26 May 1999
53 *R v Warrington Borough Council ex parte Barrett,* 18 November 1999, unreported
54 Reg 42(2) CC(AE) Regs; reg 48(2) CT(AE) Regs
55 *R v Warrington Borough Council ex parte Barrett,* 18 November 1999, unreported; *R v Gloucestershire Justices ex parte Daldry,* 12 January 2000, unreported
56 *R v Felixstowe Justices ex parte Herridge* [1993] Rating Appeals 83
57 *R v Sandwell Justices ex parte Lynn,* 5 March 1993, unreported; *R v Alfreton Justices ex parte Gratton, The Times,* 17 December 1993
58 *R v Preston Justices ex parte McCosh, The Times,* 30 January 1995
59 *R v Newcastle upon Tyne Justices ex parte Devine,* 23 April 1998, QBD; *R v Doncaster Justices ex parte Jack and Christison, The Times,* 26 May 1999
60 *R v Warrington Borough Council ex parte Barrett,* 18 November 1999, unreported

5. **Wilful refusal and culpable neglect**

61 *R v Watford Justices ex parte Hudson,* 21 April 1999, unreported
62 *R v Ramsgate Magistrates ex parte Haddow* [1992] 157 JP 545

Chapter 14

. . . .

Bailiffs

This chapter covers:
1. Types of bailiff and the seizure of goods (below)
2. How bailiffs become involved (p391)
3. Bailiffs' powers (p394)
4. Powers of arrest (p409)
5. Complaints against bailiffs (p410)
6. Emergency action (p415)

A bailiff is someone who acts on behalf of creditors or courts to collect debts, repossess homes or goods, and execute certain arrest warrants. This chapter looks mainly at the role of bailiffs in the seizure of goods to enforce debt and also outlines their powers of arrest. Because of their broadened powers, the government now prefers to refer to bailiffs as 'enforcement agents'. Advisers should bear in mind two points. Firstly, bailiffs are employed to seize goods, not to collect debts by instalments. Arranging affordable repayments on behalf of a client in multiple debt may, therefore, be very difficult. Secondly, bailiffs seldom have to remove or sell goods, as it is the threat of this that is effective in eliciting payments from a client.

1. Types of bailiff and the seizure of goods

There are several different types of bailiff operating in England and Wales. The most meaningful distinction that can be made between them is on the basis of their powers to seize goods (known as **'distress'** or **'distraint'**). This determines both their duties and liabilities as enforcement agents, and their powers as bailiffs. The main areas of business for bailiffs, and the main areas for abuse and dispute, are enforcement of council tax, road traffic penalties and fines. Particular attention is given to these in this chapter.

Note: some bailiff firms undertake debt collection work as well as enforcing warrants by seizing goods. Their powers in these two functions are distinct. Bailiffs only have a right to take goods to recover an outstanding liability in the circumstances described in the following paragraphs. If a firm of bailiffs is collecting an unsecured consumer debt or a benefits overpayment, it does not have any special powers, despite the fact that the firm may describe itself as 'bailiffs' in its letterhead.

Many firms also hold licences under the Consumer Credit Act and must therefore comply with the Office of Fair Trading's debt collection guidelines (see p30).

Common law distress

There has always been a power in English law for a landowner to levy distress in respect of certain liabilities arising from, or associated with, her/his land. The surviving forms today are as follows.

Distress for rent

Arrears of unpaid rent can be collected by means of distraint, either by the landlord personally or by using a **private 'certificated' bailiff**. Many private bailiffs hold a certificate, although firms described as certificated bailiffs often employ other staff who are not certificated to undertake most of their work.

In order to be certificated, an individual bailiff must apply to a county court. Applicants must have a bond of £10,000 lodged either with the court or in a bank (or indemnity insurance for the same amount), must know the law of distress sufficiently, and must be a 'fit and proper person to hold a certificate'. From 2009, prospective bailiffs must also supply a copy of a Criminal Records Bureau check to the court. Once a certificate has been granted, it will be recorded on a central online register, which can be checked to confirm whether a bailiff holds a certificate and, if so, from which court.[1]

In practice, certification means very little, as the courts do not investigate a person's suitability or check the information on the application form. There is no monitoring of certificated bailiffs and, although most certificates are renewable every two years, this process is largely a formality. However, the certification system does mean that complaints can be heard by the court. The view of the HM Courts and Tribunals Service (HMCTS) is that complaints may be made against individual bailiffs levying distress for rent, and also against those levying other forms of distress and execution and their managers (see p410).

'Distress damage feasant'

'Distress damage feasant' is a remedy that permits the seizure and impounding of 'trespassing chattels'. The power was generally regarded as obsolete until recently. However, if wheel-clamping becomes illegal under the Protection of Freedoms Act 2012, distress damage feasant may be used increasingly by landowners to deal with unauthorised parking.

Distress damage feasant give the landowner the right to tow away, impound and detain a vehicle parked without permission until compensation for the trespass has been paid. Sufficient and adequate signs must be in place, warning the motorist of the risk of removal and the likely costs. These may include a fair charge for towing and impounding the vehicle and an amount for damages, reflecting the nature of the parking infringement.

In this form of distress, there is no right to sell the seized goods. It cannot be levied on vehicles after they have left the land in question.

Execution

'Execution' is the enforcement of civil court judgments by seizing and selling goods. An adviser may encounter three different types of execution.

High Court execution

The High Court uses bailiffs (**High Court enforcement officers**) to enforce the following judgments by seizing and selling the defendant's goods:

- High Court judgments of any amount;
- county court judgments over £5,000 where the debt has not arisen from an agreement regulated by the Consumer Credit Act 1974;
- county court judgments between £600 and £5,000 that do not arise from an agreement regulated by the Consumer Credit Act 1974 if the creditor chooses to transfer them.

High Court enforcement officers are private bailiffs, organised on a county basis. They have similar powers to county court bailiffs, but are preferred by some creditors because, being private bailiffs, they are considered more effective.

County court execution

HMCTS employs bailiffs in each county court (**county court bailiffs**), responsible for enforcing all warrants in that court's area. The bailiff may enforce the following judgments by seizing and selling the defendant's goods:

- all judgments based on agreements regulated by the Consumer Credit Act 1974;
- all judgments under £600;
- any other judgment up to £5,000, unless the creditor chooses to transfer to the High Court for enforcement.

Road traffic penalties

Local authorities may use **private bailiffs** to enforce unpaid orders for road traffic penalties – eg, parking charges. Any sum payable for such a violation is recoverable by a form of warrant of execution as if it is payable under a county court order. Road traffic execution is complex, but is essentially county court execution levied by a private certificated bailiff.

Statutory distraint

Many public bodies have a statutory power to seize and sell goods if money is owed to them. There are many forms of 'statutory distraint', but debt advisers will most often encounter the following.

Local taxes

Both council tax and non-domestic rates (business rates) are enforceable by the seizure and sale of goods. Distraint may be levied by either **local authority officers** or by **private bailiffs**, provided in both cases they are certificated.

Income tax, national insurance and tax credits

HM Revenue and Customs (HMRC) can levy distraint to collect any unpaid taxes, Class 1 and 4 national insurance (NI) contributions and overpayments of tax credits. A **private bailiff** may attend, but only to assist and advise HMRC staff. The power of distraint is generally only used against businesses still trading, although occasionally it is used to collect tax or NI contributions from someone who is no longer trading, but who has property in the home being levied against.

VAT

HMRC may use its **own officers** or **private bailiffs** to levy for arrears of VAT. About 75 per cent of its collection work is now in private hands.

Magistrates' court orders

Distraint may be used by magistrates' courts to collect unpaid civil debts (ie, tax and NI contributions), damages, compensation orders and fines, including those from the Crown Court, Court of Appeal and Supreme Court. Many courts restrict distraint for fines to fixed penalty offences (eg, fines for driving offences) or to sums under £100 to £150.

Magistrates' courts use either their own '**civilian enforcement officers**' or firms of **private bailiffs** to collect unpaid fines. These bailiffs are appointed by HMCTS.

Child support maintenance

The Secretary of State for Work and Pensions has the power to levy distraint to collect arrears of maintenance due to the Child Support Agency under a magistrates' court liability order. **Private bailiffs** are employed.

In a recent case, the enforcement of child support arrears by distraint was challenged by the non-resident parent on two grounds.[2] He argued that use of bailiffs could prejudice the welfare of the children in his household and that it was a violation of Article 8 of the European Convention on Human Rights (protection for home and family life). The Court of Appeal rejected both arguments. The arrears were an unpaid debt to be recovered and it was reasonable to seek to enforce it. There was already a charging order against his home and it was preferable for the family to face the loss of non-essential household items than to face the loss of the home.

2. **How bailiffs become involved**

Whatever the type of bailiff or debt involved, the process of seizure is started by the issue of a warrant to the bailiff for the specific sum due from the client. The details of how warrants are issued (and how they may be stopped, if that is possible) depend on the type of warrant.

Distress for rent

The way a warrant is issued depends on the client's tenancy agreement. Landlords of assured, protected or statutory tenants cannot levy distraint without first obtaining permission from the county court. Generally, the courts are reluctant to grant permission. In addition, at this stage the court has the power to suspend or adjourn the order (see p356 and p357).

Landlords of secure or commercial tenants or of long leaseholders can seize goods without a court order. If the landlord is not an individual, a certificated bailiff must be used, although this could be a member of staff of a local authority.

A warrant may be issued and distress levied the day after a rent payment falls due. No prior demand is needed.

This remedy can be used only for the collection of rent and other amounts collected as rent, such as service charges. Housing benefit overpayments or council tax arrears, which may appear on a tenant's rent account, should not be enforced in this way.

County court warrants of execution

A warrant of execution (see p300) may be issued by a creditor when a client has defaulted on the terms of payment of a judgment debt. A warrant may be issued for the whole of the balance due under the judgment, or just the arrears (known as a part-warrant). If the judgment was payable by instalments, the bailiff may be asked to levy for one-monthly instalments (or four-weekly instalments, as appropriate) or for not less than £50, whichever is the greater. Consumer credit lenders often prefer to issue part-warrants, as these are considered more likely to be effective. As a result, lenders may repeatedly use execution to threaten the client following default on an instalment order.

The client does not have an opportunity to oppose a warrant being issued, but the bailiff must deliver a warning notice telling her/him that a warrant has been issued. The levy is then delayed for seven days to allow payment to be made. A warrant is valid for 12 months and may be executed at any time within that period.

At any time after the issue of the warrant, the court can suspend or 'stay' its execution. The client should also apply to the court to vary the judgment on Form N245 (see p317).

High Court execution

If a judgment of the High Court (and some county court judgments – see p300) is unpaid, it may be enforced by execution by issuing a writ of *fieri-facias* (commonly known as *'fi-fa'*). This instructs the High Court enforcement officers to seize sufficient goods to cover the full amount of the judgment debt, plus interest and the costs of execution. Unlike in the county court (see above), no part-warrants are possible. The client should receive a warning note from the High Court enforcement officer that the writ has been issued, although this is not compulsory and does not always happen.

The client should apply immediately on Form N244 for a stay of execution in order to suspend the writ and then for variation of the judgment. See p271 for how to do this.

Road traffic penalties

If a penalty imposed by a parking attendant is not paid, the relevant local authority can obtain an order from the Traffic Enforcement Centre, based at Northampton County Court, confirming liability. The local authority can enforce this by issuing a warrant to private certificated bailiffs with whom it has a contract.

It can often be difficult to negotiate, as the bailiffs' instructions will usually be to collect the whole debt and not to accept instalments. Although the order is made by the county court, it cannot intervene to suspend the warrant. Normally, the only way of challenging the warrant is to challenge the original charge or order. Various means of appeal exist, initially through the Traffic Enforcement Centre, and then through the Parking and Traffic Appeals Service.

Note: the Civil Procedure Rules specify that, if the order is cancelled, the bailiff's warrant 'shall cease to have effect'. Further enforcement is, therefore, not permitted, although it is less clear whether a previous levy and costs are rendered null and void. However, threatening to sue for a refund may persuade the bailiffs to reimburse the client.

Income tax

The use of distraint for income tax arrears does not have to be sanctioned by a court. Initially, demands for payment are made from the computer collection centres and then by the local collector. If the client is still seen to be 'neglecting or refusing' to pay, a warrant is issued internally by a senior HM Revenue and Customs (HMRC) officer.

If the debt adviser is dealing with the threat of bailiffs for unpaid tax, s/he should contact the relevant tax office. If the offer is accompanied by a financial statement, the collector will probably accept a reasonable offer to clear the debt (though possibly only over a period of between six and 12 months) and stay the warrant. The collector may also be persuaded to take no action if a debt is clearly unrecoverable.

VAT

HMRC may use distraint to recover a debt or to close down a business in order to prevent the problem reoccurring. Little warning is given once the final demand for payment has been ignored, and it is often difficult to negotiate anything but the severest terms of repayment.

The distraint process is started when a VAT return is made by a trader without enclosing full payment of the VAT due or, if a return has not been made, s/he has been assessed as owing over the prescribed figure of £200. At this stage, the HMRC officer collecting VAT arrears will often try to negotiate directly with the client. If this fails, a final demand notice is issued. If the client still neglects, or refuses, to pay and at least £200 is still due, a warrant is issued. In either case, the adviser may be able to agree a stay on enforcement while instalment payments are made, although the timescale allowed to negotiate may be short.

Magistrates' court orders

If a client defaults on a magistrates' court order for payment, the whole sum ordered to be paid falls due and may be enforced by distraint. In the case of fines (which are most commonly enforced by distraint), if the court allowed time to pay or set instalments, or if the client was absent at the hearing, a warrant cannot be issued until the court serves written notice on her/him stating the total balance due, the instalments ordered and the date when payment begins. Once these conditions have been satisfied, a warrant may be issued on default.

If there is a hearing before the issue of a warrant, either because a review date has been set by the court or because (eg, with maintenance) the legislation requires the client to appear, the client may have a chance to prevent distraint. S/he can apply to have the warrant postponed by the magistrates' court at the hearing. This may be done on further terms of payment. It is, however, almost impossible to suspend or withdraw a warrant once it is with the bailiffs. However, the bailiff has the power to postpone the sale of goods for up to 60 days if repayments can be agreed with the client.

Decisions about how and when to enforce a fine are taken by the fines officer at each magistrates' court. A 'further steps notice' will be issued after a default in payments and this determines how the fine will be pursued. If the procedure before the issue of a distress warrant is unlawful, the warrant itself will also be unlawful. For instance, in one case, it was decided that a distress warrant had been illegally issued because the preceding further steps notice was invalid.[3]

The bailiffs are normally instructed to collect the whole debt forthwith and not to agree to instalment payments.

Local taxes

The magistrates' court issues a 'liability order' (see p378) that enables the local authority to use a variety of enforcement measures, including distraint. The court has no power to intervene in the enforcement, either at this stage or later, nor can it set terms of payment.

A warrant is then issued by the local authority to bailiffs to levy the amount due. The debt adviser can either come to an agreement directly with the bailiffs or persuade the local authority to withdraw its warrant. Many local authorities will wish to come to reasonable arrangements with clients if these result in regular payment. Bear in mind the local authority's own code of practice on local tax enforcement when negotiating on these debts, especially when seeking to have the warrant withdrawn.

3. **Bailiffs' powers**

In addition to bailiffs' specific legal powers, in January 2012 the Ministry of Justice issued a revised version of the *National Standards for Enforcement Agents* (NSEA). This provides minimum standards of business management and best practice in enforcement work. Copies can be downloaded from www.justice.gov.uk/ downloads /courts/bailiffs-enforcement-officers/national-standards-enforce-ment-agents.pdf. Unfortunately, the NSEA does not include a mechanism for monitoring or enforcing its application. Complaints may be made to the Ministry of Justice, but will not be followed up. However, the adviser could raise a failure to comply with the NSEA in any complaint to one of the bailiffs' trade bodies, to a creditor, to the Ombudsman or against a bailiff's county court certificate (see p410).

People whose goods cannot be seized

Certain people may be protected from having their goods seized. They include the following.

- **Third parties**. In most cases (rent is the main exception) the warrant only entitles the bailiff to take goods owned solely or jointly by the debtor. Goods that are the property of a third party (including those leased or subject to hire purchase) should not be seized.
- **Children**. Property belonging to a child is protected, as children count as third parties. This is confirmed by the NSEA, which also extends protection to goods

'for the exclusive use of a child'. It does not matter whether the goods were given to the child as a present or were bought with pocket money. They are the child's property and not that of a parent.

- **Vulnerable people**. The NSEA requires bailiffs and creditors to protect vulnerable and socially excluded people, and to have procedures to deal with cases where it appears that someone may fall into such a category. The NSEA lists older people, lone parents, people with a disability, people who are seriously ill, recently bereaved or unemployed, and people who have difficulty speaking or understanding English as all potentially vulnerable. This is not an exhaustive list and advisers should always raise suitable cases with bailiffs to consider whether it is appropriate to proceed with enforcement.

Entering premises

The first crucial stage in the procedure is for the bailiff to enter the client's premises. In most cases, whether or not goods can be seized will depend on whether the bailiffs have gained entry. The client has a number of legal rights. If the bailiff breaches one of these basic principles, the whole levy may be illegal and the bailiff company will be unable to recover its fees. See p410 for remedies. The NSEA reminds bailiffs that unlawful force should not be used – presumably against either property or people.

Time

The rules on the time of levy are as follows.

- Most forms of distraint and execution can be levied at any time of day and on any day of the week.
- Distress for rent cannot be carried out between sunset and sunrise, nor on a Sunday.
- VAT distraint levies must begin between 8am and 8pm. If the client trades partly (or wholly) outside these times, the levy may start at any time and on any day when the business is trading.
- Execution cannot be levied on Sundays, Good Friday or Christmas Day.

Codes of practice may further restrict when distraint may be levied. The NSEA requires that levies should generally not occur outside the hours of 6am and 9pm, nor on Sundays and public holidays. Bailiffs tend to call at varying times and on different days in order to have a good chance of finding a person at home. **Note:** many bailiffs enforcing fines and road traffic penalties habitually call on clients very early in the morning to attempt to seize cars. Pay special attention to the above rules in such cases.

Place

In theory, bailiffs may go anywhere in England and Wales where the client's goods may be found. In practice, they will have either a business or home address on the warrant and this will be the only place they will visit.

Landlords can only levy at the rented premises for which the arrears are due, although there is a right to pursue goods they know have been removed to avoid distress.

Method of entry

Most bailiffs do not have the right to force their way into a property to execute a warrant: they may only enter *peaceably* and *with the permission* of the occupier. '**Permission**' can be an express invitation to enter, or may be implied from the person's words or conduct. For example, the courts have said that there is a general right for people on lawful business to come onto premises, and this principle has also been used to explain why bailiffs may open closed doors or climb through open windows (see below).

A client can refuse bailiffs entry or can ask them to leave. The bailiff must comply promptly with this request, provided s/he has not actually started listing goods. This rule applies to the vast majority of warrants, but there are a few exceptions.

- HM Revenue and Customs (HMRC) can obtain a warrant to force initial entry, but this is very rare.
- Civil court bailiffs can force initial entry to non-domestic premises in order to levy execution – this too is rare.
- Since July 2005, bailiffs and officers executing arrest and distress warrants issued for magistrates' court fines have the power to force entry.[4] These powers should only be exercised if it is 'reasonable' and 'necessary', and advisers should monitor bailiffs acting for magistrates' courts to ensure this is so. Check with your local magistrates' court committee to see if it is permitting its bailiffs to use this provision – not all are.

Any other use of force by a bailiff makes a levy illegal. 'Force' may be as little as placing a foot in the door to prevent it being closed. In theory, therefore, a well-informed client may simply deny most bailiffs access and that will be the end of the matter. Bailiffs are, of course, aware of the limitations on their powers and will try various tactics. They may attempt to walk straight into a house as soon as a door is opened to them, or they may simply decide not to try to enter the house itself but to seize goods outside, such as a car parked on the driveway. Bailiffs may also use one of the wide range of entry rights they have – eg, entering through doors, windows and skylights that are left open, and using ladders to climb in windows or over back walls. It is not normally necessary for bailiffs to use any of these possible entry routes as they are frequently admitted into the property by people anxious to avoid embarrassment or confrontation.

Once entry has been gained, bailiffs may break open internal doors. This may be to open cupboards or attics or, if they have entered a house shared by a group of people with no single 'householder' (ie, in multiple occupation), the bailiff is entitled to use force to enter parts of the house that may be exclusively used by the client even if they are locked. However, the use of these powers is usually unnecessary. **Note:** if the client lives in a block of flats, or similar property, and the bailiffs enter by the common doorway, this does *not* constitute lawful entry to the client's home. The bailiff must still legally enter the flat itself.

Note: bailiffs *cannot* call the police to assist them to enter someone's home. The police can only be called to prevent a breach of the peace that is either taking place or is genuinely feared. A breach may be caused by either the bailiff or the client. In the latter case, the bailiff may summon police support in advance if s/he has a genuine expectation of difficulty, or may call for help while conducting the levy. A bailiff acting unlawfully may well be in breach of the peace and could be arrested. However, in practice, this is unlikely to happen as police officers tend to side with bailiffs in such situations. A bailiff acting lawfully is not liable to arrest.

Identification

The rules on identification are as follows.
- Bailiffs levying distress for rent and for road traffic penalties must produce their certificate to the tenant or other person responsible for the house.
- A bailiff collecting local taxes must carry written authority from the collecting local authority.
- Enforcement agents acting for magistrates' courts in the execution of warrants of distress and arrest must carry identity cards at all times. These must be shown to the client when executing the warrant and to any other person on demand. Warrants should also be shown to the client on request.

There are no rules for other bailiffs, though it would be normal to expect them to produce the warrant on request (whether a hard copy or a digital document). If the bailiff cannot produce the warrant because s/he does not have it with her/him and it is not nearby in the van or car, any subsequent levy will be illegal.[5] The NSEA requires that agents should always produce identification and a copy of their warrant/instruction. If a bailiff falsely identifies her/himself to gain entry, it should be argued that the entry is illegal – s/he has been given permission to enter for a specific purpose and has no right to be there for other reasons.

Levying goods

Bailiffs have the power to 'levy' – ie, to seize, secure and, if necessary, sell goods in order to discharge the debt due (including the bailiffs' accruing charges). The levy process can generate many disputes.

Seizure

Seizure involves a bailiff selecting certain specified goods with a view to taking and selling them later. If the goods to be seized are household items, it is essential that the bailiff has first entered the home (see p395). However, once this has been achieved, the bailiffs will merely need to make a claim to the goods to assert the creditor's rights.

A verbal declaration of intent may be enough to constitute seizure, but a written inventory is usually taken. This lists the goods that have been seized. Ideally, it should specify items individually, but a statement of 'all goods on the property', although very bad practice and possibly excessive, has been held to be legal. However, this decision was before the introduction of statutory classes of exempt basic items (see p400), so it may be argued that this form of inventory makes a levy unlawful (unless the bailiff genuinely intends to seize everything in the property and this is justifiable and not disproportionate). Inventories that seize 'all goods except those exempt' are illegal.[6] This is because the purpose of an inventory is to inform the client and others exactly what has been seized and what has been exempted, so that proceedings may be taken to contest that seizure if necessary. Seizures of 'all goods except those exempt' are too vague to be acceptable; a specific list of the items seized should ideally be provided.

Note: bailiffs may claim to be able to levy without entry and formal seizure. This process is sometimes known as a **'constructive levy'**. Often a notice is put through a person's door saying that certain goods have been levied, presumably merely by looking through the window. The courts have rejected levies of household goods by such means. Advisers should assume that seizure requires the bailiff to be physically capable of removing the goods. The emphasis on having had this physical ability at some time indicates that seizure without being in the building in which goods are kept is a nonsense and that such an alleged seizure gives the bailiffs no rights or claim over the goods.

Sometimes bailiffs merely enter and discuss the debt with a client. There is no levy (ie, no change in the status of the goods and no right to make any charge for a levy) unless steps are taken to list or seize goods, or there is a declaration that this has been done. It is important for advisers to check exactly what has taken place and to see what documentation has been given to the client by the bailiff.

Some bailiffs, to save time, will levy on a motor vehicle parked outside a client's property. This is done simply by noting the make, model and registration number. No details of this alleged seizure are given to the client and no checks are made to establish ownership. It is often only when an adviser checks the fees charged on the account that the purported levy comes to light. Advisers should be vigilant for such tactics and, if a car has been listed, should always check with the client that it is her/his property and is not owned by a hire purchase company, a partner or relative, or someone else. If the vehicle has been levied incorrectly, the levy should be cancelled and the fees should be deducted from the account.

Impounding

Impounding is when goods are placed in the 'custody of the law'. This legal custody is important as it gives the bailiff the right to return at a later date (forcing entry to the client's premises if necessary) and remove and sell them. It also protects the goods from seizure or interference by others, whether this is the client or another bailiff seeking to levy on the goods.

There are a number of ways in which the goods may be impounded.

- The bailiff leaves the goods with the client, subject to a **'walking possession agreement'**. This is an agreement in which the client acknowledges that the property is now in the control of the bailiff and is liable to be removed if the debt is not paid. The client is allowed to continue to use the goods while s/he arranges payment. A nominal fee is usually charged for walking possession. Bailiffs prefer to have a written agreement to secure their rights and fees, although a verbal agreement could be adequate to impound the goods. Any 'responsible person' in the property may sign an agreement – eg, a spouse or adult dependant. Walking possession is a personal commitment by the signatory, so if the client subsequently moves home with the affected goods, the bailiff can remove them from the new address if payments are not made. **Note:** if an agreement is one for which a fee may be charged under local tax regulations, it must be personally signed by the client at the time of the levy.

If the bailiff is claiming 'constructive seizure', it is not advisable to sign a walking possession agreement. In other cases, if the bailiff has gained entry, the client should be advised to sign a walking possession agreement if s/he does not want to risk the goods being removed immediately. In addition, county court bailiffs often require a walking possession agreement as security before they allow time to make an application to suspend the warrant and to vary a payment order. Private bailiffs also often refuse to consider instalment payments until an agreement has been signed. In these cases, although this procedure may not be strictly correct, it may be advisable to agree to walking possession if it is the only way to avoid removal of property. In either case, signing the agreement gives the client a few days to negotiate instalments, to raise a lump sum of money to pay the debt, or to try to have the warrant withdrawn or suspended. If a bailiff cannot obtain a signature and is not in a position to remove immediately, s/he will often give the client a notice of distress and then leave the goods in the property. This constitutes a lawful seizure of the goods, but only for a temporary period of a week or so. If this seizure is not followed up by regular and frequent visits (ie, every few days), the seizure will be 'abandoned' and the bailiffs' rights and costs lost. Their only option is to start again from the beginning. There will be no abandonment if an instalment arrangement has been agreed with the client and s/he is adhering to it – the question only arises when a payment has been missed. In this situation, the bailiff must act promptly to follow the matter up. Advisers should remember that impounding on the premises (eg, by walking possession) is only permissible if the relevant legislation gives the bailiffs that power. In the absence of such a provision, walking possession or other methods cannot be used.

- In the case of magistrates' court distraint, unless the warrant specifies otherwise, household goods can only be removed from the client's property on the day of sale, having been seized and impounded by means of a **'conspicuous mark'**. There is no provision for 'walking possession' in magistrates' court cases and if advisers encounter walking possession being used in respect of magistrates' court levies, they should argue that the levy is ineffective – ie, no seizure has taken place, the bailiff has no right to remove and sell, no costs may be charged and the bailiffs' only option is to give up and start again.

- **Wheel clamps** are frequently used by bailiffs to impound motor vehicles. Some seek to justify this as an intermediate stage between seizure and removal, to 'immobilise' the vehicle while waiting for a removal truck. It is debatable whether this practice is lawful. Clients faced with such a situation need urgent specialist advice to consider their options, which may include simply removing the clamp from the vehicle if this can be done without damaging it.[7]

- **Immediate removal**. This is most common with vehicles or with easily disposable business assets. Walking possession is preferred in almost every other case.

- **Close possession**. It is lawful to leave a bailiff as a 'possession man' on the premises in 'close possession' of the goods, guarding them against interference. A charge can be made for this activity. It is, however, extremely rare.

- **Securing in a room** or other location on the premises. This is only lawful for distress for rent, but might (in that context) justify the use of clamps.

Note: advisers should always check any walking possession agreement signed by the client and investigate the circumstances in which seizure and impounding took place in order to be certain that a legal levy has occurred. If it appears this is not the case, see p410.

Goods

The general rule is that a bailiff may seize any property belonging to the debtor. Certain goods are exempt from seizure and advisers should go through any inventory with the client to establish which (and whose) goods have been seized.

In **most forms of distraint and execution** the following cannot be seized:

- 'such tools, books, vehicles and other items of equipment as are necessary to that person for use *personally* by him in his employment, business or vocation'; *and*

- 'such clothing, bedding, furniture, household equipment and provisions as are necessary for satisfying the basic domestic needs of that person and his family'.

A self-employed trader's essential and basic tools are thus protected, but only if these are not used by an employee or business partner. A motor vehicle is only protected as a 'tool of the trade' if it is absolutely essential to the continuation of the business – eg, a motorbike was not considered essential to a sociology lecturer, even though it helped him get to work quickly and cheaply.[8] Guidance issued in the past to county court bailiffs suggested that a three-piece suite may be seized in a home if dining chairs remained, or a microwave may be taken if an oven was also available. Furthermore, a couple of recent county court decisions have caused the Insolvency Service to revise its position on the treatment of motor vehicles for domestic purposes in bankruptcies. As the same categories of exemption apply in both distress and execution and in bankruptcy, it may be possible to apply this guidance to cases of seizure of vehicles by bailiffs (see p457 for more details). In some cases, it may be possible to argue successfully that a vehicle is required because a client is 'vulnerable' under the NSEA (see p395). **Note:** these are *subjective* categories of exemption and the adviser should establish the client's exact domestic or business circumstances and whether the different exemptions apply to her/him.

In **distress for VAT** a different list of exemptions applies, which is generous in protecting the home, but exempts little at a business.

- Household items that are reasonably required to meet the domestic needs of any person living in the home are exempt. The exempt goods are:
  - beds and bedding;
  - household linen;
  - chairs and settees;
  - tables;
  - food;
  - lights and light fittings;
  - heating appliances;
  - curtains;
  - floor coverings;
  - furniture, equipment and utensils used for cooking, storing and eating food;
  - refrigerators;
  - articles for cleaning, pressing and mending clothes;
  - articles for cleaning the home;
  - furniture used for storing clothing, bedding or household linen, cleaning articles or utensils for cooking and eating food;
  - articles used for safety in the home;
  - toys for the use of any child in the household;
  - medical aids and equipment.
- In business premises, the only exempt goods are fire fighting equipment and medical aids for use on the premises.

In **magistrates' court distraint** the following goods are exempt:
- clothing, beds, bedding; *and*
- tools of a person's trade, as above. See also p369.

In **distress for rent** the general rule is that everything on the rented premises may be seized, but this is subject to a wide range of exemptions, including:

- things in use at the time of the distraint – eg, electrical goods that are turned on;
- perishable items.

These categories of exemptions are known as 'privileges' and are lengthy and, in some cases, complex. If dealing with a client facing distress for rent, especially at business premises, it is important to seek specialist advice.

In addition to the statutory exemptions, other general rules on seizable goods apply to most forms of distress and execution.

- **Fixtures and fittings** from a property cannot be seized in either distress or execution because they are part of the property itself. The definition is difficult, and is complicated by modern building techniques and materials. Basically, a fixture is not merely something fixed, but something that has become part of the property and without which the home would be incomplete. Light fittings are fixtures, whereas shades are not; kitchen units are fixtures, but shelf units may not be.

- **Goods belonging to third parties** cannot generally be seized (except in some circumstances for distress for rent. This includes goods belonging to partners, spouses and relatives as well as to hire and hire purchase companies. In practice, many bailiffs attempt to seize any goods at a particular property, irrespective of their ownership, and will deal with adverse claims to ownership later. If receipts of purchase or other documents can be produced, these should be enough to prove the ownership of goods. If there is a possibility that another person's goods may be seized, the client or the owner of the goods could draw up an inventory and threaten legal action if any goods are wrongly taken and retained. Bailiffs may decide not to risk seizing goods if there is serious claim to their ownership. Such an inventory could also be drawn up as a statutory declaration, made on oath by the owner in the presence of a commissioner for oaths. Items that are hired, or subject to hire purchase or conditional sale agreements, are not the property of the client and should not be seized – a copy of the relevant agreement should be sufficient to satisfy the bailiff. The NSEA also requires that goods belonging to *or used by* a child should not be taken. The bailiff should always treat such claims seriously and should take time to consider and assess them.[9]

- **Items of no value**. The bailiffs should not list goods whose value is so low that it does not cover the cost of their seizure and removal. Nevertheless, this does happen, as it enables the bailiffs to charge fees and to collect money from the client.[10] Sometimes these seizures are part of a so-called 'two-tier levy'. Some firms claim they will make an initial cursory levy of a few visible items to secure the creditor's position (but avoiding disturbance for the client) but this may be revised later if it is necessary to remove, relying on a claim to 'all goods on the property' made in the inventory. This procedure is not lawful. Only a first levy is possible – the bailiff may take fewer goods than listed on a later occasion, but never more. Furthermore, initial levies often include seizure of exempt goods, such as all forms of seating in a property. These levies require careful scrutiny and often need to be challenged with the bailiffs.

If goods have been wrongfully seized, the owner of the goods has a number of remedies (see p410). In cases of execution for judgments or road traffic penalties, a client can apply for an 'interpleader' if exempt goods or a third party's property have been seized (see p414). Initially, the matter should be taken up informally with the bailiff or creditor, if necessary backed with the threat of court action.

Always check inventories to confirm what has been seized. In particular, check whether the bailiffs have seized any exempt goods, or only a few items inadequate to cover the costs, or whether they have claimed to levy 'all goods except those exempt'.

Forms and documents

At the conclusion of a levy the bailiff usually gives the client a number of documents. These will typically include a 'notice of seizure,' comprising details of the debt and an inventory of the seized goods, and a copy of any walking possession agreement that has been signed. In some cases, regulations specify what information should be provided – eg, in council tax levies copies of the relevant regulation and fee scale must be presented. The client is entitled to receive these forms and should ask to be sent them if the bailiffs do not have copies. The revised NSEA now requires bailiffs to leave an inventory following a levy.

In some cases, the legislation specifies the form that these documents should take. For instance, a form of walking possession agreement is prescribed for High Court enforcement officers and for county court bailiffs. In distress for rent, forms are prescribed for the notice of seizure, walking possession agreement and notice of removal expenses. These same forms also apply with modifications to road traffic penalties. If the bailiffs do not use these forms, or make alterations to them, this is an irregularity for which damages might be recoverable.

However, at least one large national bailiffs' company has altered the notice of seizure and walking possession used in road traffic executions. More importantly, bailiffs collecting road traffic penalties are required to issue a breakdown of their removal fees on a prescribed form (Form 9). In practice, it seems that very few ever issue this form. This is irregular and may mean that these fees cannot be lawfully charged to the client.

Selling goods

The purpose of seizure is to give the creditor security over the client's goods and to put the client under pressure to settle the debt. The ultimate conclusion of the process is to sell the goods, but this is seldom reached because of the costs, inconvenience and low returns. Except perhaps for motor vehicles, most second-hand goods are of no, or negligible, value and it is the threat of sale that is effective, not the remedy itself.

If sale becomes necessary, the bailiff must remove the goods seized previously and can, at this stage, use force to re-enter the client's property to gain access to the goods. Prior warning is generally given of an intended visit to remove, and entry can only be forced if the client has received this. If this is the case, failure to permit access may be construed as deliberate obstruction. Only what was previously seized can be removed. The NSEA requires bailiffs to handle goods with reasonable care and have insurance in place to cover against damage in transit. A receipt for goods removed should be left at the premises.

Note: the power to force re-entry depends on there having already been a valid seizure of goods. Bailiffs cannot force entry if the seizure has been abandoned or if they did not previously take an inventory and walking possession agreement (or the equivalent in the form of a valid verbal seizure and impounding of goods).

The goods are stored for a few days while the sale is arranged. At this stage, the client has the opportunity to pay the amount due.

Normally there must be at least five days before sale. In most cases, this is by public auction. The bailiffs are expected to raise the best price possible, although returns from auction sales tend to be very low. In most forms of distress and execution, the client may request that the goods be 'appraised' or valued before the sale. This may lead to a slightly higher reserved price being set, but as fees are charged for the process, any gain may be offset by the extra expense incurred.

It is usual for the bailiff to deduct her/his fees from any sale proceeds (or payments made to her/him) before passing the sums on to the instructing creditor. Goods cannot be sold merely to cover the bailiffs' fees if the debt is paid directly to the creditor. Creditors normally try to avoid receiving payments directly from a client, which bypasses the bailiffs and circumvents their fees. However, in cases in which a debt *is* cleared in full with the creditor, and/or the warrant is withdrawn from the bailiffs, the latter will be left without any recourse against the client for any unpaid fees.

If the bailiff damages the goods while removing or selling them, or could be shown to have mishandled the sale so that the goods were sold for too little, s/he could be sued for damages in the county court.

Fees

Bailiffs are allowed to recover money from the client to cover the cost of their action. The charges can inflate the amount due considerably and are the cause of much complaint. Some bailiffs add charges that are not allowed and advisers should, therefore, examine bailiffs' bills carefully to ensure that the burden of debt on a client is not being added to improperly.

The rules for charging for distress are varied. In most cases, the amount bailiffs can charge is regulated by legislation. The exception is in magistrates' courts, in which no statutory scale is laid down. Fees are negotiated by HM Courts and Tribunals Service (HMCTS) with the bailiff companies to whom regional contracts are granted. Advisers should request a copy of the scale in operation from the bailiffs or from the court.

Note: under the NSEA, bailiffs are required to issue a notice every time a fee is incurred and must provide a breakdown of their fees if they are asked in writing for one. Advisers should request a detailed breakdown of the fees charged to a client, check the fees against the appropriate scale and compare the dates given with the actual events of a case.

All scales tend to include the same elements. Fees are charged for certain actions such as visits, seizure and removal, and reasonable disbursements for storage and advertising are permitted. Charges tend to be a mixture of flat-rate fees, sums calculated as a percentage of the amount due, and 'reasonable' amounts. **Note:** the fees charged in the county court, although set by legislation, are much lower than those found in the private sector. There is a standard charge for the issue of the warrant, which is added to the debt. This covers all visits made by bailiffs, plus seizure and possession. Only if the matter reaches the stage of removal and sale are any other fees charged.

Disputed fees

Any charges that the adviser does not consider reasonable may be reviewed by the county court or by the High Court in the case of High Court enforcement officers. The court has a power to examine and reassess, if necessary, disputed bailiffs' charges. The process was formerly called 'taxation', but is now known as 'detailed assessment'. A client can apply to the court under Part 8 of the Civil Procedure Rules for a district judge to review the sums demanded by, or paid to, the bailiff. **Note:** this power only applies to charges made under the scales set by the legislation. As magistrates' bailiffs charges are set by their contract with HMCTS, these fees are not 'taxable', although the legislation permits the magistrates' court to fine bailiffs whose fees are 'improper or undue'. Another legal remedy could be for the client to pay the disputed fees and then use the county court to recover the balance by issuing a small claim. S/he would protect her/his goods from seizure or even removal and sale, but would have to be able to pay up front the whole sum due.

Although legal remedies are available, a more accessible and useful method of redress is to use the bailiffs' trade body complaints procedure (see p412). This is valuable if the level or necessity of the fee is being challenged, but is not suitable if the interpretation of the fees regulations is being questioned.

A 'reasonable' fee recoverable by a bailiff is one that is calculated correctly, is applied at the correct stage of the process, is for a fair amount and is legal. Some bailiffs' bills contain fees that may be questioned on all these points. The adviser should check the amounts demanded with the amounts permitted on the statutory scale. Advisers should be aware of:

- fees made too early in the process, before the proper point for making them has been reached – eg, charges for attending with a vehicle when none was present or the costs of preparing for a sale when goods had not been seized or removed;

- fees for a sum disproportionate to the work done or debt due. The meaning of 'reasonable' charges was examined in a case in Birmingham County Court in the mid-1980s. The judge decided that any question about 'reasonableness' should be resolved in favour of the payer. A reasonable charge must be related to the value of goods taken. Thus, it cannot be reasonable to remove goods if their sale value is unlikely to cover the costs of removal and sale. The amount charged for bailiffs' services must also be spread across all those against whom they hold warrants issued by a particular creditor. In the case in question, a charge for a removal van was 'taxed down' on the basis that a van could be hired privately for considerably less than the billed sum, and any overheads incurred by the bailiffs could be spread across all those subject to removals on that day;

- fees for work that is not actually or necessarily undertaken. For example, if a bailiff conducts only one levy for a debt, but produces three or four identical inventories for each sum due and makes a separate charge for each, this should be challenged on the basis that only one set of fees should be allowed.[11] Similarly, clients often allege they have been billed for visits that never took place. The bailiff is under a duty to deliver a notice whenever a charge is incurred. Ask for copies of these and challenge the failure to supply them;

- fees not allowed for on the scale – eg, fees for administering accounts, for negotiating with the client or collecting payments from her/him and for clamping vehicles. Note that, in the case of distress for rent, the Distress for Rent Rules 1988 specifically prohibit the charging of 'any fees, charges or expenses for levying... or any related act' other than those authorised in the applicable fee scale. This same rule applies to the recovery of road traffic penalties. Therefore, in the case of both of these debts, there is an explicit statutory prohibition against charging anything not specifically allowed for in the scale;

- fees that cannot be justified. In an assessment hearing, the bailiff must be able to show how each separate fee was calculated – eg, the hourly rate of the staff employed, the cost of the vehicles used, and the fact that letters and notices were issued. In a couple of recent cases, bailiffs have seen large reductions made in their bills because they did not retain adequate records and were charging arbitrary amounts for certain activities.

In levies for council tax, advisers should also bear in mind:
- the use by bailiffs' firms of their right to charge for 'attendance to remove' at premises. In the council tax regulations these charges are only allowed *after* a levy has been made – ie, there has been an entry and seizure of goods. Some firms appear to charge *before* there has been any levy. What seems to happen is that the statutory fees allowed for visits are used to cover basic administrative overheads and are added on as soon as an instruction is received, so that the bailiff has then to use the 'attendance' charge to cover initial visits to premises. In road traffic enforcement there is no clear limit on when and how often these charges can be applied. As a result, multiple and substantial charges are often added to an account. Advisers should examine accounts carefully. In council tax cases, they should challenge attendance fees that are made too early or more than once. In road traffic and fines cases, the adviser should challenge charges made for attendances to remove when no levy has been made (or walking possession has been taken). Although the context in which these fees can be charged is not as well defined as in council tax distraint, separate fees are allowed in the scale for visits. This implies it was intended that attendance fees should apply to separate and later calls to the premises;
- redemption fees. The fee scale allows a charge of £24.50 (or 5 per cent of the balance) to be made where 'no sale takes place by reason of payment or tender' of the debt due. Some firms seem to charge this fee in every case where a levy takes place. The regulations, however, appear to envisage a situation in which goods have been removed for sale, but the sale is cancelled at the last minute because the debtor comes up with the full council tax arrears plus the costs; they refer to the goods being made 'available for collection'. Charging this sum earlier in the process, especially if payment of the full debt has neither been made nor offered, seems unjustifiable. The bailiffs' industry has a different interpretation of this fee but, having obtained legal counsel's opinion on its meaning, it has accepted that it can only be charged once the debt has been cleared *in full*. The bailiffs argue that the fee could be added to the final instalment payable on an account, rather than being deducted from a lump-sum settlement of the debt. This may not be correct as the regulations refer to the 'tender' of the debt, which is usually understood to mean an offer of full payment of the sum outstanding. The bailiffs also believe that this fee should be charged where nothing more than walking possession has been taken. It is difficult to reconcile this with the reference to goods being made available for collection, which implies some change in their location. In a recent decision, the Local Government Ombudsman said that goods had to be removed for this

fee to arise. There may still be scope for debate as to *when* exactly in the process the fee may be added, but it is clear that it can only follow *full payment* of the council tax arrears and charges.[12]

Note: for many years, advisers have encountered problems with the fees charged by private bailiff companies for levying distress. Recently, similar problems have arisen with certain firms of High Court enforcement officers. All the issues described above are the subject of disputes, coupled with the fact that the fees charged can be substantially higher than those charged by private bailiffs. The legal remedy is a detailed assessment in the court. An application must be made to the High Court.[13]

Codes of practice

Future changes

Following the 2010 election, the government promised action on 'aggressive bailiffs'. As well as amending the NSEA, a further consultation on the Tribunals, Courts and Enforcement Act 2007 was issued in February 2012. This sought views on powers of entry, exempt goods and a new scale of fees.

The powers described in this section are those laid down in law. In addition, some creditors (mostly local authorities) operate codes of practice. These regulate the conduct of their bailiffs (eg, by specifying certain goods to be treated as exempt from seizure) and specify the circumstances in which it is considered inappropriate to levy distraint – eg, if a client is on means-tested benefits, has a disability or is recently bereaved.

As warrants are often issued against those whom the local authority has voluntarily exempted from distress, it is important for advisers to be familiar with any code the local authority operates and to lobby for warrants to be withdrawn in cases where they should not have been issued. Some local authorities, however, are reluctant to release their codes, stating they are part of their contract with their bailiffs and are, therefore, confidential. This argument should not be accepted. Compliance with the European Convention on Human Rights requires that any measure governing the interference with individuals' rights should be made accessible to them. Codes dealing with bailiffs' rights to enter property and seize goods fall into this category and must be made public.

The Child Support Agency used to operate a code of practice that gave additional protection to clients facing distress proceedings. This is now largely incorporated into the contracts and service-level agreements agreed with the three enforcement agencies it uses. Other creditors, although not having explicit codes, will often be prepared to withdraw warrants in cases of severe personal and/or financial hardship.

The Freedom of Information Act can be used to obtain copies of codes of practice, as well as copies of a public body's contracts and service-level agreements with the enforcement agencies it uses. Often an adviser may discover there is no written agreement in place, but nonetheless the Act can be a useful tool for finding out the local criteria within which bailiffs are expected to work.

The NSEA requires enforcement agents to ensure that all information and documentation supplied to debtors is clear and unambiguous, that bailiffs act without any form of discrimination, that they are aware of potentially vulnerable individuals, taking special care when proceeding against them, and that they treat debtors' information confidentially. Bailiff firms are required to operate complaints procedures and to make details of these readily available. It is sometimes argued by bailiffs that the NSEA is only a guideline. It is, however, more significant than this, as all the main bailiff trade bodies, plus the Local Government Association, are signatories. Bailiffs must have very good reasons for failing to comply – and should be able to justify their decision.

The revised NSEA, issued in February 2012, includes new clauses that seek to address the problem of 'aggressive bailiffs'. It states that bailiffs should not be deceitful by misrepresenting their powers, qualifications, capacities, experience or abilities. Specifically, they should avoid stating or implying that they can take certain action when they legally cannot, that certain consequences will follow when it is not yet possible to know this or that certain steps have been taken when they have not. In addition, bailiffs should not act in a threatening manner, whether by words or gestures causing clients to fear harm.

Bailiffs' companies holding a consumer credit licence must also comply with the Office of Fair Trading (OFT) *Debt Collection Guidance*. Many of the larger firms are licensed, but if you are not sure, ring the OFT on 020 7211 8608 to check. The OFT guidelines complement and reinforce the NSEA in many areas of practice. A copy can be downloaded from the OFT's website at www.oft.gov.uk.

4. **Powers of arrest**

Since April 2001, private bailiffs have had the power to enforce a range of magistrates' court warrants previously executed by the police. These include warrants of arrest to ensure attendance at means enquiries following default in payment of fines and local taxes, and warrants of committal to prison made following such means enquiries.

When choosing the firm to work for the court, possession of a distress for rent certificate from a county court, convictions and being the subject of complaints, damages claims and insolvency proceedings are all considered. Advisers should note that, as part of this scheme, bailiffs and courts are required to operate and publish complaints procedures.

Bailiffs' powers when executing these warrants are broadly similar to those for distress. Warrants may be executed anywhere in England and Wales at any time of day. Under amendments made to the Magistrates' Court Act 1980 in 2004, an officer has a right to enter premises in search of a person against whom an arrest warrant has been issued, provided there are reasonable grounds for believing s/he is on the premises. Reasonable force may be used to gain entry. A person may be physically seized or touched, and informed that s/he is under arrest, or arrest may be by words alone (provided the person submits to these). The arresting officer is also entitled to search an arrested person for items that could be used either to cause harm to her/himself or to others, or to escape from custody. The arresting officer must have reasonable grounds for conducting a search, and any items found may be seized and retained. As soon as possible after being arrested, a person must be given full and clear details of the reason for her/his arrest and how to complain. Defendants are not liable for any fees for the execution of these warrants.

Resisting a lawful arrest can be an offence. While it may be lawful to resist an unlawful arrest, it is generally more advisable for clients to make a civil claim for damages for false imprisonment and/or assault after the event, and they should be encouraged to seek legal advice.

5. Complaints against bailiffs

In recent years, the action of bailiffs has been subject to increasing public scrutiny. It is possible that this may lead to changes in certification and regulation. Meanwhile, media interest remains high and such pressure may be effective. The media, however, often wants stories of gross wrongdoing, especially physical violence, by bailiffs – these are rare.

Wrongful seizure

Broadly speaking, the law recognises three categories of bailiffs' offence.
- **Illegal levies**, where the bailiffs do something (generally at the outset of the levy) that they have no power to do – eg, to force entry on a first visit or to seize exempt goods. Because the whole action is rendered unlawful as a result, the client can often recover substantial damages, and the bailiff will have to give up on the levy (forgoing any charges made to that point) and attempt to conduct a further, lawful levy.
- **Irregular levies**, which are seizures where something is done incorrectly later in the process. Most forms of enforcement have regulations stating that such mistakes are *not* to be treated as illegalities. In other words, an error in the conduct of a sale or in leaving a required notice does not invalidate the whole

procedure and only entitles the client to recover any identifiable and provable losses arising from the mistake.

- **Excessive levies**, where the bailiff takes far more than is necessary to cover the debt and costs by sale at auction. The client can sue to recover the value of the excess. Excessive levies are rare. Many clients believe they have been the victims of such levies because they do not appreciate that bailiffs value their goods at auction value, which may only be 10 per cent of their face value. However, in the case of seizures of cars, it may be possible to claim an excessive seizure. Cars are worth more than household goods and hold their value better at auction. They are often seized for fines and road traffic penalties, which are relatively small debts (at least before charges are added). Bailiffs should establish if other goods are available first, but they tend to take cars because they are available and valuable. Such a procedure is open to challenge. If there was genuinely nothing else worth seizing on the property except the very expensive item, the bailiff will have a defence to the claim that the levy was excessive.

Except in the case of excessive levies, it is usually only worthwhile taking action against illegal acts.

Threatening court action

If there has been a procedural error, threatening county court action could help a client negotiate or have the levy withdrawn. Bailiffs may be reluctant to have their procedures tested in court and may, in any event, find it more advantageous to settle the matter than be involved in the expense of litigation. If negotiations are not progressing, it can be effective to draft a claim form, send it to the bailiffs and threaten to issue in the county court unless payment is made within a set time scale. Frequently a 'commercial decision' will be taken to settle the case at this stage.

Complaining to the bailiffs

If there is a problem, the adviser should also complain to the bailiff firm itself. Direct contact with the bailiff is seldom fruitful, other than to agree a stay on recovery, and the adviser should find out who the complaints manager is and write to her/him directly. Firms have a duty to deal with complaints promptly under their trade body complaints procedures (see p412). In addition, if they are acting for a public authority such as a local authority or government department, the bailiffs should also be treated as 'public authorities', with all the duties this implies. For example, they should give reasons for their decisions, so that if they refuse to treat a person as vulnerable under a code of practice, they should explain why.

Complaining to creditors

While it is always worthwhile contacting the bailiffs to complain about their actions, it may be unproductive if the point at issue is whether they should have been instructed at all or if the terms of repayment set by the contract with the creditor are impossible for the client to meet – eg, council tax contracts often require the bailiff to collect within three months. In such cases, the bailiffs are bound by the contract with the instructing creditor to enforce the warrant issued to them, and other than asking them to stay the action while negotiations are conducted, little else may be possible.

Creditors should always be notified about wrongful acts by their agents, as this may help bring pressure to bear in individual cases and may lead to improved monitoring more generally, but direct contact with a creditor is particularly important where matters such as the personal circumstances of the client are at issue. A complaint may be made about either the incorrect use of legal powers or a failure to follow a code of practice. If the complaint is not properly dealt with, it may be possible to use the organisation's internal complaints procedure. If this is unsatisfactory, it may be possible to complain to an independent adjudicator, such as the Local Government Ombudsman (Public Services Ombudsman for Wales) or the Parliamentary and Health Service Ombudsman.

Complaining to trade and professional bodies

If a complaint to a firm of bailiffs is not dealt with satisfactorily, a complaint could be made to the bailiffs' professional or trade organisation. When making such a complaint, it should be remembered that these bodies exist to promote their members' interests and are not entirely independent or impartial. Several bodies may be responsible, depending on the type of enforcement agent involved. The relevant bodies to which advisers may turn are the High Court Enforcement Officers Association and the Civil Enforcement Association (CIVEA) (see Appendix 1). All operate disciplinary codes linked to complaints procedures. Serious breaches of professional ethics or of procedure may lead to investigation and the imposition of penalties, such as being excluded from membership and, as a result, from the profession (although this is rare). A complaint can also lead to at least an apology and perhaps compensation, such as a refund of fees. CIVEA also has a code of practice regulating members' business practices, which may be of some assistance. These and the complaints procedures can be found on its websites. The complaints procedures can be particularly effective in cases of poor administration and customer care by bailiffs' firms and where fees are disputed as unnecessary or incorrect.

Complaining to the Ombudsman

There is not yet a regulator for the enforcement industry (although this may change. However, most creditors for whom bailiffs act are public sector bodies and are subject to supervision by an Ombudsman. The creditors themselves operate their own complaints procedures, but if this fails to produce a satisfactory outcome for the client, a complaint can be made to the Local Government Ombudsman (or Public Services Ombudsman in Wales) or the Parliamentary and Health Service Ombudsman or to the Adjudicator's Office (about HM Revenue and Customs).

In the case of local authorities, before a complaint is made to the Ombudsman (or applying for judicial review in the High Court), the case can be taken up by the local authority's monitoring officer. This person is usually the chief legal officer and must consider whether there has been maladministration or whether the local authority has acted unlawfully. It can sometimes be helpful to refer a case to the monitoring officer if the department in question is unwilling to intervene or negotiate, but the adviser believes its bailiffs have acted unlawfully.

Court proceedings

If non-judicial action or pressure fails, court proceedings can be initiated against the bailiffs in order to recover seized goods or gain financial redress. The form of action taken depends on the bailiffs' offence (see p410). However, in most cases, the value of the claim involved will be well within the small claims limit and so legal action can be taken for relatively little expense and at little risk of legal costs.

If threatened with legal action or having received a claim form, bailiffs will often choose to settle the matter to avoid the expense of litigation or the scrutiny of the court.

An injunction can also be made by the county court to prevent a bailiff's re-entry and removal of goods or their subsequent sale. Injunctions can be applied for at the same time as issuing a claim form, or in advance in urgent cases.

The client or owner of the seized goods may be able to start one of the following claims. **Note:** there are detailed procedural requirements for all of these, plus court fees and the risk of substantial legal costs if a case is lost.

- **Sue for wrongful interference with goods**. The owner of goods may be able to get an order for their return if they were illegally seized (although an award of damages for their value is more likely) plus an award of damages for any other losses incurred, such as loss of use. As the courts rarely order the return of the goods themselves, other remedies may be preferable.
- **Sue for the recovery of sums already paid to the bailiffs**. This could be a payment made by the client in order to prevent an illegal seizure of goods or for the recovery of disputed fees. This may seem an unlikely occurrence for debt clients, but it often arises in levies on motor vehicles – the client will raise the money to continue to have use of her/his car.

- **Start 'replevin'.** This is an obscure and ancient remedy where the goods are immediately ordered to be returned to the client, who then takes court action to prove the levy was illegal and s/he was consequently entitled to have her/his goods back. It is not recommended except to use as a threat, as it is not covered by the costs protection of the small claims procedure. (The same is true for complaints about local tax or child support levies to the magistrates' court, unless the client can get legal aid.)

- **Challenge the certificate.** If the bailiff is certificated, it is possible to apply to the court that granted the certificate for it to be revoked on the grounds that the bailiff no longer appears to be a fit or proper person to hold it. The complaint must be on the prescribed form. An officer at the court is then required to send a copy to the bailiff. The bailiff must respond within 14 days and, if the judge is dissatisfied that the bailiff has adequately explained the incident and remains fit to hold a certificate, s/he is summonsed to show why the certificate should not be cancelled. At this hearing the judge can proceed as s/he thinks fit – generally the court allows the complainant to make representations. If a certificate is revoked, the client may also be awarded compensation, generally by forfeiture of all or part of the indemnity insurance or bond which the bailiff is required to hold. Unfortunately, there is very limited experience of complaints against certification. Another problem that advisers may encounter is that the rules on certification complaints relate solely to distress for rent. Some judges question whether they have any jurisdiction either to hear complaints at all, or to award any compensation, if the complaint is about the bailiffs' activities in other fields, whether or not they require a certificate. Clients should be aware that, if a complaint is unsuccessful, the court may award costs against them and some bailiff companies vigorously contest such proceedings, being represented by barristers. The procedure is under-used, but should only really be used for serious or repeated abuses by a bailiff. It can, however, provide a quick and effective means of redress for an aggrieved client and is worth considering as a threat if a bailiff has acted badly – eg, by ignoring codes of practice. If the bailiff's name is known, the adviser can check the certificate details online at http://certificatedbailiffs.justice.gov.uk/certificatedbailiffs or by telephoning 0845 408 5302. If unsure whether a particular bailiff is certificated, the adviser should ask the firm to provide full details.

- **Interpleader.** If a third party's goods have been seized in execution, a special remedy known as 'interpleader' exists to enable the third party to prove ownership and recover them. Specialist help should be sought.

6. **Emergency action**

People often seek advice only when the 'crunch' comes, such as a visit from a bailiff. In order to buy time for a client's finances to be investigated and an overall repayment strategy devised, it may be necessary to consider some of the emergency measures described here.

Refuse the bailiffs access

Often a debt adviser is first consulted when a client hears from bailiffs. The best advice to protect goods from seizure is to ensure that bailiffs are not given access to property and for the client to remove any goods that are outside the home (especially cars) to a place where they will not be seen. **Note:** in the case of distress for rent, removing goods in this way is an offence.

Bailiffs will try to visit more than once to gain access, so clients should be advised to be vigilant, and keep doors and windows locked. If the bailiffs are unable to gain entry, they will eventually return the warrant to the court, indicating whether or not there are sufficient goods to satisfy the debt. They rely on what they can see through a window to decide this.

If the bailiff fails to raise the sums due, this will not be the end of the debt's recovery; other means are tried. With fines and local taxes, the debt often goes back to the court for it to consider committal to prison (see p375). A client may be sentenced for 'wilful refusal' or 'culpable neglect' to pay (see p383) and may be threatened that failure to give access to the bailiffs will be construed by the court as wilful refusal. There are no reported instances of anyone being committed on this ground.

If bailiffs have already gained access, they can subsequently force their way in to remove goods for the same debt (see p396).

Get the warrant withdrawn from the bailiffs

In every case, the aim of the debt adviser should be to remove the matter from the hands of the bailiffs and place it back for consideration by the creditor.

In the civil courts, the client should make an immediate application to suspend the warrant. For county court action, this is done on Form N245 (see p319). For High Court action, an application for variation of the judgment and a stay of execution should be made. Magistrates' courts do not have such a power, but it may be worthwhile speaking to the court's fines officer to see what scope s/he has to intervene. It may be possible for the fines officer to refer the case back to the magistrates for a further hearing.

In situations where there is no power to suspend through the courts and the client cannot afford to pay a lump sum, the only option may be to persuade the issuing creditor that the warrant should be withdrawn because of the client's personal or financial circumstances. This may also be because s/he falls into one of the categories of people exempt from distraint by the code of practice operated by that creditor. In many cases, terms of payment will have to be negotiated at the same time, and often these will be for instalments of sums much lower than it would have been economic for the bailiff to collect.

Threaten court action

If there has been an error in procedure, a lever for negotiation or withdrawal may be to threaten court action (see p413). Bailiffs may be reluctant to have their procedures tested in court and may find it more advantageous to settle the matter than be involved in the expense of litigation.

Raise a lump sum to clear the debt

If the above tactics have been unsuccessful, or if the goods have been seized already, it may be necessary for the client to pay the debt to avoid goods being sold (see Chapter 7 for ways of maximising income). This may be in violation of certain basic principles of money advice, but will often be the only option that the client is prepared to consider. It may also make financial sense, as the replacement cost of the items in question may be much more than the total required by the bailiffs.

Note: the Court of Appeal has clarified a debtor's rights to make payments to a bailiff. This may happen either before a levy (or removal) takes place, or afterwards, but payment cannot be offered during a levy or removal, as the sums due cannot be calculated.[14]

Notes

1. Types of bailiff and the seizure of goods
1 http://certificatedbailiffs.justice.gov.uk/certificatedbailiffs
2 *Brookes v Secretary of State for Work and Pensions and Child Maintenance and Enforcement Commission* [2010] EWCA Civ 420

2. How bailiffs become involved
3 *R (Guest) v Woking Metropolitan Council* [2008] EWHC 2649 (Admin)

3. Bailiffs' powers
4 s27 Domestic Violence, Crime and Victims Act 2004 and Sch 4 MCA 1980
5 *Olukotun v London Borough of Southwark* [2011] *The Times*, 16 April 2011; *Andrews v Bolton Borough Council* [2011], unreported, but see J Kruse, *Sources of Bailiff Law*, PP Publishing, 2012, p230
6 *Ambrose v Nottingham City Council* [2004] (*Adviser* 107 abstracts, and J Kruse, *Sources of Bailiff Law*, PP Publishing, 2012, p119

7   For further details, see J Kruse,
    'Clamping Motor Vehicles', *Adviser* 138,
    pp43-47
8   *Thompson v Bertie* [2007] EWHC 2238
    (QBD)
9   *Rai and Rai v Birmingham City Council*
    [1993], unreported, but see J Kruse,
    Sources of Bailiff Law, PP Publishing,
    2012, p112; *Huntress Search v
    Canapeum Ltd and DSI Foods* [2010]
    EWHC 1270 (QBD)
10 See LGO decision on a complaint
    against Slough Borough Council, 2011,
    Arian 30, June 2011, Caselaw Update
11 See LGO decision on a complaint
    against Blaby District Council, 2012
12 See J Kruse, 'Bailiffs' Charges: recent
    developments', *Adviser* 135, pp43-46
    There is an abstract of the case *Culligan v
    Marstons Group* [2008] in the same
    issue, or see J Kruse, *Sources of Bailiff Law*,
    PP Publishing, 2012, p188. See LGO
    decision on a complaint against Blaby
    District Council, 2012
13 J Kruse, 'Challenging High Court
    Enforcement Officers' Fees', *Adviser* 140,
    pp41-44

6. Emergency action
14 *Wilson v South Kesteven District Council*
    [2000] EWCA Civ 218

Chapter 15

Personal insolvency

This chapter covers the formal debt relief options available to clients who are unable to pay their debts. It includes:

1. Last resort or a fresh start (below)
2. Administration orders (p419)
3. When to use bankruptcy and individual voluntary arrangements (p423)
4. Individual voluntary arrangements (p427)
5. Bankruptcy (p437)
6. Debt relief orders (p472)

1. Last resort or a fresh start

Someone is said to be 'insolvent' if s/he is unable to pay her/his debts as they fall due. In many cases, people are able to resolve their financial problems by coming to the informal arrangements with their creditors discussed earlier in this *Handbook*. Apart from these arrangements, there are currently four ways in which a client can reach a formal arrangement with her/his creditors.

- **Administration order (AO)** (see p419). However, this is currently not a viable option for someone whose total unsecured debts exceed £5,000.
- **Individual voluntary arrangement (IVA)** (see p427). An IVA is a formal arrangement made between the client and her/his creditors that creates a legally binding agreement between them. However, secured creditors cannot be included unless they agree. Student loans and child support cannot be included at all. The arrangement provides either for the client to defer payment of her/his debts and/or for the creditors to accept less than 100 per cent of their debts. Provided a certain percentage of the creditors agree to accept the arrangement, on completion of the IVA, the balance of the debts is written off. In the meantime, the creditors agree not to take recovery action. The arrangement is set up by a nominee (usually an insolvency practitioner who is an approved accountant or solicitor) who is likely to be appointed as supervisor to oversee the arrangement.
- **Bankruptcy** (see p437). Either the Official Receiver or an insolvency practitioner is appointed to handle the client's financial affairs for the benefit

of her/his creditors. This person is known as the 'trustee in bankruptcy' (the trustee). This can be done by a request from the client, by one or more creditors or by the supervisor of a failed IVA. Bankruptcy generally lasts for 12 months, after which the client is discharged and released from all her/his unsecured debts other than those specified in the legislation.

- **Debt relief order (DRO)** (see p472). These are suitable for clients who do not own their own homes and have total debts not exceeding £15,000 (other than some specifically excluded debts), available income not exceeding £50 a month, total assets (apart from some motor vehicles and other basic assets) worth no more than £300 and who are not currently subject to a bankruptcy order or an IVA. A DRO is made by the Official Receiver, but the client must apply via a skilled money adviser, known as an 'approved intermediary', appointed by a 'competent authority' (see p480). Following a 12-month moratorium, during which the DRO can be revoked on a number of specified grounds, the client is discharged from all debts included in the DRO (other than those incurred fraudulently).

The law on AOs is contained in the County Courts Act 1984 and Schedule 2 of the Civil Procedure Rules. The law on IVAs, bankruptcy and DROs is contained in the Insolvency Act 1986, as amended by Part 10 of the Enterprise Act 2002 and Part 5 of the Tribunals, Courts and Enforcement Act 2007. The detailed rules and forms are contained in the Insolvency Rules 1986, as amended by secondary legislation. The Civil Procedure Rules (which include an Insolvency Practice Direction) apply, provided they are consistent with the bankruptcy rules.

It will be useful for a client who chooses one of the above remedies to resolve her/his financial difficulties to have a session with a money adviser. This is a preventative measure to attempt to ensure that her/his debt problems do not reoccur (see p33).

2. Administration orders

An administration order (AO) is a county court order which prevents individual creditors taking enforcement action without permission from the court and which requires that all a person's debts be dealt with together.[1] It is applied for by the client, who must have at least one judgment against her/him in either the county court or High Court. This includes a traffic penalty registered for enforcement in the Traffic Enforcement Centre at Northampton County Court. The client makes a single monthly payment to the court, which then distributes it equitably among the creditors. An AO is applied for on Form N92. There is no fee for the application, but costs will be added to the sum the client repays, at 10p per pound repaid.

Making the application

County court Form N92 requires a list of all the client's debts. These must not exceed £5,000. This limit has been the subject of much criticism. AOs can only be given to individuals, but debts that are jointly owed must be included. If a person is jointly and severally liable, s/he should include the whole value of the debt. Even if finances are shared, couples cannot apply together and should make individual applications if both want to deal with their debts in this way.

Guidance on completing Form N92 states that the client should list in Part B (list of creditors) arrears of:

- mortgage;
- council tax;
- hire purchase;
- consumer credit debts (including cards).

This does not appear to fit with the legal requirement that the AO should cover the 'whole indebtedness'. Courts' practice on this matter appears to differ and it may be advantageous (for instance, to stay within the £5,000 limit) to apply for an order on the basis of arrears alone if this will be granted by a local court (and another strategy is available for the rest of the debts). In addition, the guidance appears to require arrears of priority debts to be included in Part A (statement of means) as part of the client's expenditure, even when it is intended that the debt should be included in the AO. It is suggested that such debts should not be listed both in Part A and Part B. They should be listed in Part A only where the client is asking the court not to include the debt(s) in the AO, and should be listed in Part B where the client is asking the court to include the debt(s) in the AO.

Some courts have queried the inclusion of debts such as council tax arrears and debts that would not be covered by bankruptcy, such as fines, but these debts can all be included.[2] Social fund loans and benefit overpayments can be included in an AO even if the client is in receipt of a benefit from which deductions can be made, since deductions cannot be made while the AO is in force. Once the AO is completed, any outstanding balance will no longer be payable.

An attachment of earnings order will usually be made if the client is employed unless the client asks the court not to make one on Form N92, setting out her/his reasons – eg, if her/his employment will be affected once her/his employer finds out about the AO. See p309 for more on the advantages and disadvantages of attachment of earnings orders. Most clients prefer not to have an attachment of earnings order.

AOs are registered at the Registry Trust and will probably affect a client's ability to get credit.

The proposed order

Some AOs are decided by court officers without a hearing. A notice of the application and a calculation are sent to creditors explaining what they can expect to receive (the proposed order). A district judge will only be involved if the amount offered by the client is insufficient to repay the debts in a 'reasonable time'. Guidance to court staff suggests this is three years.

If court staff cannot make an order, a district judge will decide the matter. S/he can either propose a longer repayment period or make a composition order (see below). S/he can do this with or without a hearing. **Note:** the rules allow a district judge to make an order without a hearing, but do not permit a district judge to either dismiss an application for an AO or exclude any debts from the AO without a hearing.[3] If a court hearing is required, the client and all the creditors will be sent notice of the hearing, details of the debts and the proposed terms of the order. The creditors must send a corrected balance to the court, if required. See p422 for details about the hearing.

If the court staff prepare the order, a copy is sent to the client and all the creditors, who then have 14 days in which to object to the AO being granted. This is an opportunity for the client to object to the level of instalments, as well as for the creditors to object to being included. If no objections are received, a 'final order' is made. If objections are received, a hearing must be arranged to consider them.

Composition orders

A district judge can order that a client pays only a proportion of her/his debts (a composition order). This should be considered if the debts cannot be cleared in a 'reasonable time' (see above).

The debt adviser should help the client to work out the monthly amount available to offer creditors. If this amount will not clear the debts plus the 10 per cent charge made by the court in three years, s/he should suggest a composition order in the box under Section C of the N92.

The percentage of each debt offered is calculated by establishing the total time available for payments (ie, 36 – the number of months in three years) multiplied by the monthly payment offered, deducting 10 per cent from this total, and then dividing the resulting figure by the total of the debts owed, and finally showing this as a percentage.

Example

A person has £75 a month available income and owes a total of £4,500. A suggested composition would be to offer:

36 x £75 = £2,700 total amount to be paid (less 10% handling (£270)) = £2,430
2,430 divided by 4,500 = 0.54 (the proportion to be paid)
0.54 = 54% (the percentage to be paid)

In this case, the following wording can be inserted in the box: 'I ask that the court considers making a composition order at the rate of 54 pence in the pound.' The client should also use this box to explain her/his reasons for not wanting an attachment of earnings order, where applicable.

In many cases, the actual order will not be opposed, but a composition may be. However, provided the debt adviser is prepared with facts and figures to justify the financial necessity of what s/he argues, such orders are increasingly acceptable to courts. An application for a composition order can only be decided by a district judge (and not court officers) and cannot be rejected without a hearing.

The court hearing

There will be a court hearing if a judge thinks one is necessary – eg, if s/he may refuse the application, or either the client or a creditor objects to the terms of the proposed order. Creditors may attend the hearing (but rarely do), at which a district judge will decide whether or not to grant the order. The court will normally grant an AO unless the information given is incorrect or it appears that the order would unreasonably deny a creditor another type of remedy. If creditors object merely because they want to take action in pursuit of their debt, the debt adviser should argue that this would result in other creditors being treated less fairly.

Note: some local authorities object to the inclusion of council tax arrears in an AO on the ground that they have an attachment of earnings order and that this will continue regardless. This is incorrect and should be challenged.[4]

Once an AO is granted, it is unlawful for any creditor to approach the client for payment of any debt included in the AO without the permission of the court (including resorting to 'self-help' remedies such as deductions from benefits). Interest and charges are effectively frozen on all debts included in the order. The court charges a percentage handling fee (currently 10 per cent) for all the money collected and distributes this quarterly. Provided the client makes all the payments required by the AO, s/he is discharged from all the debts in it, including any debts subject to a judgment.

Reviewing an administration order

An AO can be reviewed at any time by the court. The client, any creditor included in the order or the court itself can request a review. Some orders contain provision for periodic reviews. If the client applies, a letter should be used explaining why the review is being requested (usually because of a change in circumstances) and enclosing a financial statement. The court will then arrange a hearing.

On review, the court may:[5]
- reduce the payments;
- suspend all payments for a specified amount of time;

- add or vary a composition order, including theoretically varying it to 0 pence in the pound;
- reinstate a revoked order (but see below);
- make an attachment of earnings order to secure payments due under the order;
- revoke the AO.

Although creditors can apply to be added to an AO, there is no specific provision allowing clients to add a creditor. New creditors can sometimes be included by a review on the basis of a 'material change of circumstances', although some courts apply the rules strictly and only allow the creditors to apply. Once made, an AO is not invalidated because the debts are found to exceed the £5,000 limit, but the court can revoke the AO. The court might take this step if it thought the client had 'abused' the AO by obtaining further credit.[6] If a client misses two consecutive payments or persistently fails to pay on time, the court should send a notice requiring either:

- payment;
- an explanation;
- an application for a variation;
- a proposal for payment of arrears.

If the client fails to do one of the above, the AO is revoked in 14 days. If the client replies, the matter is referred to the district judge who may either order a hearing or revoke, suspend or vary the AO. If the order is revoked, suspended or varied without a hearing, creditors or the client can object within 14 days and a hearing must be held.

At a hearing, the district judge will consider all circumstances of the case and make one of the decisions listed above.

If the district judge decides to revoke the order, the court will no longer collect and distribute payments. The creditors will be informed that they are free to pursue their debts individually. In practice, only a small proportion of creditors contact clients following the revocation of an AO.

3. **When to use bankruptcy and individual voluntary arrangements**

Bankruptcy is likely to be the preferred option only if a client has a number of debts, no assets (or little or no equity in her/his home), low available income to pay creditors so that it would take more than three years to clear her/his debts, and it is unlikely that her/his situation will change in the foreseeable future. S/he must also have no need for credit in the medium term.

An individual voluntary arrangement (IVA) is likely to be the preferred option if the client has a number of debts plus a particular reason for wanting to avoid bankruptcy (eg, to avoid losing the family home) and is able to make a substantial offer, but s/he is either unable to persuade her/his creditors to accept an informal arrangement or the only informal arrangement they will accept is open-ended and likely to take many years to complete. However, IVAs do not end in automatic discharge, as bankruptcy does (usually after a maximum of 12 months) (see p469). If the client fails to keep to the arrangement, s/he could still face bankruptcy if s/he is unable to reach agreement with her/his creditors to vary the IVA.

Advisers should take the following factors into account.

Risk to current assets

Some property solely owned by a client is put directly at risk in bankruptcy. In practice, many things which a person uses may be owned by someone else – eg, a partner. Jointly owned property or property in which the client has a beneficial interest, particularly the family home, will be indirectly at risk because the trustee may be able to sell it in order to realise the bankrupt client's share (see p461). In bankruptcy, any transactions involving gifts of property or transfers where the client did not receive the market value in return will be investigated by the trustee who may be able to reclaim the property (see p467). Similarly, if payments have been made to some creditors but not to others, the trustee may be able to reclaim the money (see p467). This may particularly affect members of the client's family or friends.

There is more flexibility with an IVA, as creditors are usually offered regular payments. Although most IVAs require clients who are homeowners to obtain a valuation of the family home towards the end of the IVA, with a view to raising a lump sum by remortgaging against the equity in the property (see p429), clients are not expected to sell their homes unless they choose to agree this as part of the IVA. However, other assets are at risk if the creditors do not agree to exclude them from the IVA.

Risk to future assets

When considering either bankruptcy or an IVA, the client should bear in mind the potential risk to any future assets, particularly if s/he expects to inherit property in the near future or already owns assets, which may have no or little value now, but which are likely to have a realisable value within the next few years.

IVAs usually contain 'windfall' clauses – eg, stating that any assets with a value of more than £500 the client acquires during the term of the IVA can be claimed for the IVA. It is, however, possible to make arrangements with potential donors – eg, by asking them to change their wills. Bankruptcy usually lasts for a maximum of only 12 months, whereas IVAs tend to last for around five years.

Effect on future credit

Both bankruptcy and IVAs are a matter of public record. The Individual Insolvency Register contains details of bankruptcies, IVAs (including post-bankruptcy IVAs) and bankruptcy restriction orders (BROs) and bankruptcy restriction undertakings (BRUs). Bankruptcy records remain on the Register for three months after the date of the client's discharge. IVA records remain until the IVA ends (plus a further three months if an insolvency practitioner agrees to act as nominee in respect of an IVA proposal made on or after 6 April 2010). Records of BROs (which last for between two and 15 years) remain on the Register until they come to an end. Credit reference agencies keep details on file for six years.

It is unlikely that a lender will give credit to a bankrupt person and it is likely to be more expensive to obtain credit after discharge. In addition, it is an offence for either an undischarged bankrupt, or a person who has been discharged from bankruptcy but is subject to a BRO/BRU, to obtain credit of £500 or more without disclosing her/his status (including ordering goods on credit).[7] This declaration may make it impossible for a person to run her/his own business because s/he is unlikely to be given further credit.

Although there are no legal restrictions on a client with an IVA obtaining credit, most IVAs state that the client cannot obtain credit of more than £500 without the supervisor's permission. If s/he does, it is a breach of the IVA.

Effect on employment or office

Being an undischarged bankrupt prohibits someone from:
- engaging in business in a name other than that in which s/he was judged bankrupt without disclosing that name to people with whom s/he has business dealings;[8]
- acting as a director of, or directly or indirectly promoting, forming or managing, a limited company without permission from the court;[9]
- acting as an insolvency practitioner.[10]

These restrictions end on discharge unless a BRO/BRU is made (see p452). A BRO/BRU may also affect her/his ability to belong to a professional body. This should always be checked before proceeding with bankruptcy. If it appears there is a risk that post-bankruptcy restrictions may be imposed, a client should be advised to consider whether any of these restrictions would affect her/him.

The professional rules of solicitors and accountants make it virtually impossible for people who have been made bankrupt to work in these professions. Other employers may be unwilling to employ a bankrupt person, especially if s/he is responsible for handling money. Charity law limits the ability of people who have been made bankrupt and subject to BROs/BRUs to serve on management committees. The bankruptcy of a sole trader does not necessarily mean the business will close, but it will be difficult for it to continue in view of the above restrictions and the following factors.

- If there are items of business equipment used by the person's employees rather than by her/him personally in the business, s/he will not be able to claim exemption for them (see p456) and the trustee may insist on a sale. Stock in trade is not exempt from sale by the trustee.
- The bankruptcy (and any BRO/BRU) may be advertised and publicised locally, and this may damage the reputation of the business as well as of its proprietor. All bankruptcy orders are advertised in the *London Gazette*.
- The person will find it extremely difficult to operate a bank account, not only because of the credit restrictions, but also because of the possibility of the trustee making a claim against any credit balance in the account.

These restrictions do not apply to someone with an IVA.

Effect on housing

Bankruptcy may well result in the loss of the family home (see p461). Many tenancy agreements contain provisions allowing the landlord to end the tenancy and repossess the property in the event of the tenant's bankruptcy. If the client has rent arrears, the landlord can still apply for a possession order even though the rent arrears are a bankruptcy debt (see p346).

In the case of a bankrupt homeowner, if there is sufficient equity, the trustee will usually be able to force a sale unless the family can raise a sufficient amount to buy out the trustee's interest (see p462).

In the case of an IVA, although creditors expect the value of the person's interest in the family home to be taken into account, there is little likelihood of the property having to be sold. The IVA protocol (see p428) says that clients should not be required to sell their property instead of releasing equity.

Effect on reputation and stress

Bankruptcy can be a humiliating experience for many people. There is a possibility of a public examination of the client's conduct and financial affairs in open court, although this is very rare. There may be an advertisement in the local paper. If the client's conduct is considered blameworthy, s/he may be made the subject of a BRO/BRU with the possibility of local publicity. Bankruptcy has the potential to add considerably to a person's stress. On the other hand, there is a certainty about bankruptcy, which can reduce stress – most creditors are forced to accept the situation and can no longer pursue the client for payment.

IVAs do not carry any stigma, but can be time consuming to draw up and gain agreement for, which could add to stress. In addition, the situation is not finally resolved until the last payment is actually made, and they can fail if there is an adverse change of circumstances.

Costs

If a client wants to petition for her/his own bankruptcy, s/he must pay a deposit (currently £525) in addition to a court fee (currently £175). It may be possible to have the court fee waived (see p273). Lack of resources sometimes prevents someone from obtaining a bankruptcy order, although if the client is unable to raise the court fee/deposit, a charity or trust fund may help.

There should be no need for a client to pay any fees for an IVA in advance as a free initial interview may be available and most insolvency practitioners collect their fees out of the payments made into the IVA. A person may pay more for the 'privilege' of avoiding bankruptcy. The fee for arranging the IVA and supervising it will probably be in the region of £4,000 to £5,000, with the typical fee for arranging the IVA being £2,000 and 15 per cent of realisations during the period of the IVA (plus VAT). Some IVA providers argue that the client does not actually pay the fees because they come out of the total 'pot' paid into the IVA. In practice, however, only part of the money paid into an IVA actually goes to creditors. However, creditors – particularly the banks – have increasingly expressed their dissatisfaction with the level of fees, which in turn has led to downward pressure on fees. Fees are generally based on the amount paid into the IVA rather than on an hourly rate for work done.

4. Individual voluntary arrangements

Who can make an individual voluntary arrangement

Only an individual can enter into an individual voluntary arrangement (IVA), including someone who is currently bankrupt for whom an IVA is a more attractive option (see p470). At the hearing of a debtor's petition (see p440), the court must consider whether an IVA might be a more appropriate option.

An IVA should be explored as an alternative to bankruptcy if the client has at least £100 to £200 a month and/or a lump sum or non-essential asset available to pay her/his creditors. An IVA lasts for a fixed period. This is usually not more than five years, unless a single payment IVA is agreed involving a lump sum, and so should also be considered if an informal payment arrangement is likely to last longer. If a client has no assets that are at risk in bankruptcy, s/he may want to consider bankruptcy, because monthly payments will only last for a maximum of three years (see p458).

There is no maximum or minimum level of debt for an IVA, but, in view of the costs involved, it is unlikely to be appropriate unless the client has two or more debts totalling at least £10,000.

A client faced with being made bankrupt by a creditor (see p444) should always consider an IVA as an alternative option if s/he does not want to become bankrupt and is not in a position to challenge the creditor.

Straightforward consumer individual voluntary arrangements

The individual voluntary arrangements protocol

In 2008, the Insolvency Service and the British Bankers' Association set up the IVA Forum, which agreed a protocol for creditors and IVA providers. The protocol provides a standard framework for straightforward consumer IVAs and includes standard documentation and standard terms. The protocol has been updated and the current version has applied to all protocol-compliant IVAs entered into since 1 July 2012. Details can be found at www.tinyurl.com/6u9w3y5.

The protocol sets out a standard approach to:

- the content of the proposal to the client's creditors;
- assessing the client's income and expenditure;
- dealing with the equity in the client's home; *and*
- the terms and conditions to be included in the IVA.

Creditors are expected to accept a protocol-compliant IVA, not propose unnecessary modifications and, if they vote against, to disclose their reasons to the IVA provider.

Clients are likely to be suitable for a protocol-compliant IVA if they:

- are receiving a regular income, either from employment or a pension; *and*
- have at least three debts with two or more creditors.

A reasonably steady income stream is necessary in order for the client to be suitable to be dealt with under the protocol. Self-employed clients are suitable if that self-employment produces a regular income. If income is uneven/ unpredictable, this should be highlighted in the proposal. Clients with more than 20 per cent of their income from bonuses or commission or who are unemployed may not be suitable.

The client should not have any disputed debts. In order to give creditors confidence that the proposed IVA is the most appropriate solution to the client's debt problems, IVA providers carry out a 'due diligence' process. This means the client is given appropriate advice, including information on the advantages and disadvantages of the various options available for resolving her/his particular debt problem. Previous attempts to resolve the client's financial difficulties must be included in the proposal, together with an explanation of their failure and details of any payments made to an advice provider. The protocol also reassures creditors that the IVA provider has verified the information contained in the proposal. Creditors generally accept financial statements drawn up in accordance with the Consumer Credit Counselling Service and the common financial statement (see p51) guidelines. **Note:** if the client is under the age of 55, only minimum pension contributions should be allowed – there are some restrictions on the pension contributions made by clients aged 55 or above.

IVAs usually last for five years. If an IVA proposal is 'protocol compliant', it is expected that creditors will accept it without putting forward unnecessary modifications.

The client's home

The protocol applies whether or not the client is a homeowner. If the client is a homeowner, the IVA must deal with the equity in the home. Six months before the end of the IVA, the client is expected to remortgage to release any equity above £5,000 up to a maximum of 85 per cent of the 'loan-to-value' – ie, 85 per cent of the valuation less any outstanding mortgage, provided the increased remortgage payments are not more than 50 per cent of the monthly payment into the IVA and that the remortgage term does not extend beyond the date of the client's state retirement age or the existing mortgage term. The remortgage repayments are deducted from the client's contribution to the IVA. If, as a result, the client's payments into the IVA fall to below £50 a month, the IVA will be concluded. If the client is unable to remortgage in this way, the IVA is extended for up to 12 months.

Standard terms and conditions

In addition to the protocol, there are standard terms and conditions.

The supervisor carries out a review of the client's income and expenditure every 12 months and the client is expected to increase her/his contributions to the IVA by 50 per cent of any net surplus. Overtime, bonus and commission payments in excess of 10 per cent of the client's normal take-home pay must be disclosed and 50 per cent of the excess paid to the supervisor. If the client is made redundant during the IVA, s/he must pay any amount in excess of six months' take-home pay into the IVA.

The supervisor can also reduce the dividend payable by up to 15 per cent without referring back to creditors to reflect changes in the client's income and expenditure. The client is allowed one payment break of up to six months and the IVA is then extended accordingly. In addition, the client may be allowed a 'payment holiday' of up to three months if, because of an emergency or other unforeseen circumstances, s/he is unable to make her/his full contributions or anything at all. The IVA is extended accordingly.

The supervisor can extend the IVA for up to six months if the client has failed to disclose income.

Many IVAs provide that, if the client defaults, the arrangement automatically comes to an end and/or the supervisor must make the client bankrupt. The standard terms state that, if the client's contributions fall more than three months in arrears (unless this has been agreed – see above) or the client has failed to comply with any of her/his other obligations under the IVA, the supervisor should give the client up to three months to remedy or explain any default. If the client fails to do this, the supervisor must either issue a certificate of termination bringing the arrangement to an end or refer the matter to the creditors within 28 days to:

- vary the terms of the IVA; *or*
- bring the arrangement to an end by issuing a certificate of termination; *or*
- make the client bankrupt.

Advantages and disadvantages

Advantages

- The client avoids the stigma or publicity that is attached to bankruptcy.
- An IVA can be drawn up to meet the client's situation, so that assets are not automatically lost if the creditors agree – eg, because, overall, they will be better off than in bankruptcy.
- Creditors should receive higher payments than they would in a bankruptcy.
- Unsecured creditors who voted against the IVA are still bound by it.
- The client is not subject to the restrictions imposed in bankruptcy and so can still be a company director without the court's permission, and may find it easier to obtain credit for the business than s/he would following bankruptcy.
- The client could be in a profession where s/he could lose her/his job in the event of bankruptcy – eg, accountancy or the legal professions.
- An IVA is time-limited and does not involve any investigation of the client's affairs (although the client does have to confirm that s/he has not entered into any 'antecedent transactions' – see p467).

Disadvantages

- The client must have two or more unsecured creditors and unsecured debts of at least £10,000 for an IVA to be a viable option.
- The client will generally be required to make higher payments over a longer period than in a bankruptcy.
- The costs of an IVA are relatively high and may have to be paid in advance (although it should be possible to find an insolvency practitioner who does not require upfront fees).
- Assets are at risk if the creditors do not agree to exclude them.
- The client may still be made bankrupt if the IVA fails and the costs of the unsuccessful IVA will be added to the debts.
- The client will be closely monitored by the supervisor during the period of the IVA and will have to report any changes of circumstances.
- If the client's circumstances change, the IVA may fail if the supervisor cannot persuade the creditors to agree to a new arrangement.
- IVAs are a matter of public record and future applications for credit could be affected.

Applying for an individual voluntary arrangement

The first step for the adviser is to find an insolvency practitioner prepared to act for the client. Many advice agencies have referral arrangements with insolvency practitioners and can arrange an initial free consultation. If the adviser has no contacts, the local Official Receiver's office keeps a rota of insolvency practitioners to whom they refer cases. The local county court may also be able to supply advisers with a list. Otherwise, details of insolvency practitioners in the area can be obtained online from the Association of Business Recovery Professionals (R3) at www.r3.org.uk (8th Floor, 120 Aldersgate Street, London EC1A 4JQ). Avoid companies who say they can refer clients to an insolvency practitioner in return for a fee. Insolvency practitioners are required by their regulators to give a leaflet (*Is a Voluntary Arrangement Right For Me?*) to everyone who consults them about an IVA. This is available online at www.r3.org.uk. The insolvency practitioner's fees are agreed as part of the IVA. Most insolvency practitioners do not charge upfront fees, but are paid on an ongoing basis, typically taking the client's first few contributions as fees and then a percentage of the remaining contributions.

The proposal

The insolvency practitioner draws up a 'proposal' for the client's creditors. S/he has a duty to ensure a fair balance between the interests of the client and the creditors. In the proposal, the client makes a repayment offer to the creditors. The proposal has to be accepted by creditors owed more than 75 per cent of the total amount of the client's debts. Only the debts of the creditors who actually vote, however, are counted. For example, if the client has total creditors of £20,000, but only £10,000 worth vote, the proposal can be approved, provided more than £7,500 worth of creditors vote in favour. To gain acceptance, a proposal should contain a more attractive financial offer than the creditors could expect to receive in a bankruptcy. This means paying a higher dividend to creditors, and the proposal sets out how the client intends to achieve this. It is an offence for a client to make any false representations or to act (or fail to act) in a fraudulent manner in connection with an IVA proposal.[11]

If both members of a couple want to enter into IVAs covering debts in their sole and joint names, they cannot make a joint proposal. They could make separate proposals that run in conjunction with one another, containing sole and joint debts based on one financial statement and involving only one set of fees (which is therefore cheaper than two unrelated IVAs). However, in order to obtain approval of their IVAs, each proposal must be considered separately and each member of the couple must obtain the required majority of her/his own creditors in favour.

The client should take as much information on her/his financial affairs as possible to the insolvency practitioner, including details of:
- debts;

- assets;
- income; *and*
- expenditure.

The proposal must include:

- details of the proposed arrangements, including why an IVA is the appropriate solution and likely to be accepted by creditors. IVAs do not usually provide for payment of the client's debts in full. They normally provide for her/his available income and the proceeds of the sale of any assets to be distributed to creditors on a pro rata basis, with the balances being written off – ie, a composition;
- the anticipated level of the client's income during the period of the IVA;
- details of all assets (and their estimated value) and of any assets available from third parties, such as a relative or friend;
- details of any charges on property in favour of creditors and of any assets that the client proposes to exclude from the IVA. It is usual to make some arrangement for realising the client's share in any equity in the family home and, if this provision is included in the IVA, the client should be aware of its significance;
- details of the client's debts and of any guarantees given for them by third parties;
- the proposed duration of the IVA and the arrangements for payments to creditors, including the estimated amounts and frequency. IVAs do not normally last longer than five years;
- details of the supervisor, and of the fees to be paid to the nominee and the supervisor;
- whether the client has previously made any IVA proposal in the previous 24 months and, if so, whether:
  - that proposal was approved and the IVA has been completed; *or*
  - that proposal was rejected or the IVA was terminated and, if so, how that proposal differs from the present one.

Note: student loans cannot be included in an IVA. Similarly, a student loan cannot be included as part of the client's income for the purposes of an IVA.[12] Child support arrears cannot be included in an IVA.[13]

In the case of a protocol-compliant IVA (see p428), the proposal should also contain details of any other previous attempts to deal with the client's financial problems and the reasons why these were unsuccessful. The IVA provider should give the client advice and information on the advantages and disadvantages of all available debt solutions (including bankruptcy). The proposal may contain details of any recommendations made to the client and the reasons s/he has decided to propose an IVA.

An experienced insolvency practitioner will be aware of the proposals likely to be acceptable to creditors and the court, and will ensure the proposal complies with the requirements of the Insolvency Act. The insolvency practitioner is required to endorse the notice of the proposal to indicate s/he is prepared to act and will not do so unless s/he is satisfied that the proposal is viable. Once the insolvency practitioner has signed the proposal, s/he becomes the client's 'nominee'. Once the proposal is made, the client must prepare a statement of affairs, containing details of the matters contained in the proposal.

Within 14 days, the nominee must submit a report to the client's creditors stating in her/his opinion:

- whether the proposed IVA has a reasonable prospect of being approved and implemented;
- whether a meeting of the client's creditors should be held to consider the proposal and, if so, the date, time and place proposed.

At the same time, the nominee should also submit: [14]

- her/his comments on the client's proposal;
- a copy of the proposal;
- a copy of the statement of affairs;
- a copy of the endorsed notice of proposal of the nominee's agreement to act;
- a statement that no application is to be made for an interim order (see below).

Interim orders

Until the IVA is approved, the client is vulnerable to enforcement action by creditors. To avoid this, once the insolvency practitioner has become the nominee, the client can apply to the court for an 'interim order'.[15] If an interim order is granted:[16]

- a creditor cannot attempt to make the client bankrupt;
- a landlord cannot repossess the client's property without permission of the court;
- court proceedings or other enforcement action (including distress) cannot start or continue against the client or her/his property without the permission of the court.

The application is made to the court to which the client would be entitled to present her/his own bankruptcy petition (see p440) (or if the client is an undischarged bankrupt, the court which has conduct of the bankruptcy). It must be accompanied by a witness statement and a copy of the notice of the proposal endorsed with the nominee's consent to act. A court fee of £155 is payable.

The court sets a hearing date to consider the matter and gives two business days' notice. The court can freeze (or 'stay') any other court proceedings or enforcement action against the client pending consideration of the application, and usually does so. If the client is an undischarged bankrupt, notice must be given to the Official Receiver and any trustee.

The court can make an interim order provided that:

- it is satisfied that the proposal is 'serious' and viable – ie, that it has not been made just to delay making a bankruptcy order and with no benefit to creditors;
- the insolvency practitioner is prepared to act as the nominee;
- there has been no application for an interim order in the previous 12 months; *and*
- the client is either an undischarged bankrupt or could petition for her/his own bankruptcy (see p440).

An interim order initially lasts for only 14 days but is usually extended to allow sufficient time for the creditors' meeting (see below) to take place and for the nominee to report back to the court.

In most cases, the nominee's report is presented at the same time as any application for an interim order. Provided the court is satisfied that the proposals should be put to the creditors, the court will usually endorse the recommendation and extend the interim order for seven weeks after the proposed date of the meeting. (If the matters are dealt with together, the order is known as a 'concertina order'.)

If the court rejects the nominee's recommendations, the interim order is discharged and any proceedings or enforcement action can continue. The client cannot apply for another interim order for 12 months.[17]

The client can, however, put forward her/his proposal without applying for an interim order, but will be vulnerable to any enforcement action by a creditor until the IVA is actually agreed. Applications for interim orders are rare and where, for example, a creditor included in the proposal has a hearing date for a final charging order before the date fixed for the creditors' meeting, the client can apply for this to be adjourned so that the creditor's debt can be paid under the IVA if it is approved.

The creditors' meeting

The nominee must inform all creditors of the date and time of the meeting, which is normally held in the nominee's offices and chaired by her/him. The client is usually required to attend. **Note:** a client is not required to attend in person in order to participate in the meeting, which can be held, for example, by teleconference. The creditors consider the proposal and vote on it. Although the proposal can be amended, the client must consent to any modifications. It is usual for IVAs to contain provisions for any 'windfall' payments (eg, assets received by the client during the term of the IVA) to be taken into account. Protocol-compliant IVAs also make specific provisions to deal with receipt of redundancy payments. It is also usual to include specific proposals about any beneficial interest the client may have in the family home.

The proposal must be approved by more than 75 per cent of the creditors (in value of debts owed to them) who vote on it. Many creditors do not attend the meeting, but instead send their vote to the nominee. Certain creditors, such as banks and HM Revenue and Customs, always vote at meetings and, as they also tend to be the largest creditors, any proposal is unlikely to be approved unless these creditors agree. The practice of some banks of referring all proposals they receive to a voting house (which will recommend an acceptance or refusal) means these firms can influence the content of the proposal and its eventual outcome, even if, taken individually, the individual creditor would not be in position to block the IVA.

The nominee may discuss the proposal with creditors before the meeting to obtain agreement. The meeting cannot approve a proposal that would affect the rights of a preferential creditor in bankruptcy (such as arrears of wages owed to employees of the client) or the rights of secured creditors (such as a mortgage lender) without their consent.[18] Unless the IVA specifically excludes a secured lender's right to enforce its security, it may still be able to do so even if it has agreed to being included in the IVA.[19]

Usually, the nominee's appointment is approved at the meeting and s/he becomes the supervisor (see p437) of the IVA. If the proposal is approved, it takes effect immediately and is binding not only on every creditor who had notice of the meeting and was entitled to vote, but also on any other creditor who would have been entitled to vote if s/he had received notice of the meeting. Such creditors are entitled to claim from the client the amounts they would have received under the IVA and the client will have to make these payments in addition to those made under the IVA. Alternatively, such creditors may challenge the IVA (see p436).[20]

After the meeting

If an interim order is made, the outcome of the meeting must be reported to the court within four business days – ie, any day other than a Saturday, Sunday or bank holiday. The court records the effect of the report and discharges any interim order. The outcome of the meeting must also be reported to the creditors within four business days or, if an interim order is made, as soon as possible after the report is filed in court.

No later than 14 days after the date of the meeting, the supervisor must send details of the IVA and of the client to the Secretary of State to enter on the Individual Insolvency Register.

If disclosure of the client's current address might reasonably be expected to lead to violence against her/him or a member of her/his family who normally lives with her/him, a court may order that:

- details of the client's address be removed from any court file;

- the client's details entered on the Register must not include details of her/his current address;
- if a post-bankruptcy IVA is made which results in the bankruptcy order being annulled (see p470), any notice permitting this must not include details of the client's address.

The application to withhold disclosure can be made by either the client, the supervisor, the Official Receiver or the Secretary of State, but such applications are likely to be made only by the client. The application is made on Form 7.1A and must be accompanied by a witness statement containing sufficient evidence to support the application. If there are already court proceedings, the court fee is either £35 or £70 depending on whether or not the court is prepared to deal with the application without giving notice to the supervisor. Otherwise, the court fee is £155. Remission for fees is available (see p273).[21]

Challenging an individual voluntary arrangement

The client, or any creditor, can appeal to the court against the IVA within 28 days of the report of the creditors' meeting being made to the court, including those who did not receive notice of the meeting (who have 28 days from when they found out about it), but only on the grounds that:

- there were irregularities in the way the meeting was held – eg, the proposal contained misleading or inaccurate information; *or*
- the arrangement unfairly prejudiced the rights of a creditor – eg, if the meeting approved a proposal to include a debt which is not provable in bankruptcy, such as a magistrates' court fine, thus preventing the creditor from taking action to recover full payment.

Because an IVA is an agreement between the client and her/his creditors, in theory any debt can be included (apart from secured creditors who can only be included if they specifically agree, child support arrears and student loans). However, in the case of other debts which cannot be proved in bankruptcy and/or are still payable by the client after discharge from bankruptcy (see p469), it may be necessary to replicate their treatment in bankruptcy in order to avoid creditors successfully challenging the approval of an IVA in which they find themselves unwilling participants. This can be done either by agreeing to exclude them altogether and leaving them to be paid outside the IVA or by including them with their agreement.

If a creditor challenges an IVA and the court considers the challenge is justified, it may:[22]

- revoke (or suspend) the IVA; *or*
- direct that a fresh creditors' meeting is held to consider a new agreement or reconsider the existing agreement (and renew any interim order).

Completing the individual voluntary arrangement

The insolvency practitioner's role as supervisor of the IVA is to implement it and ensure the client carries out her/his side of the arrangement as agreed, seeking guidance from the court, if necessary. The supervisor arranges the sale of any assets that need to be sold, and collects the payments due from the client and distributes them to the creditors. If the client's circumstances change, s/he should be advised to contact the supervisor immediately, as it may be possible for the original agreement to be 'modified' at a creditors' meeting. The supervisor may be able to extend the period of the IVA to enable the client to complete the payments. IVAs often make provision for such eventualities either by giving the supervisor a degree of discretion and/or by making specific provision for variation/extension of the IVA. Protocol-compliant IVAs provide for both. If the IVA contains no such provisions, even though more than a 75 per cent majority was needed for its original approval, it is likely that all the creditors included in the IVA would have to agree to any variation.

Provided the client complies with the IVA, s/he will be discharged from her/his liability to all creditors covered by it at the end of the period. The IVA will not, however, automatically discharge any co-debtor, including the client's spouse or partner, and provision for this will have to be specifically included and agreed. However, unless the joint income is used to fund the IVA (or the partner/spouse has no income), creditors may challenge the IVA.

If the terms of the IVA are not complied with, the supervisor will usually be able to petition for the client's bankruptcy. If the supervisor decides it is not worth doing this (eg, because there are insufficient funds paid into the IVA), individual creditors may decide to do so instead. The client will have to negotiate with them separately if s/he wants to avoid bankruptcy.

5. **Bankruptcy**

Who can become bankrupt

A client may become bankrupt if:
- s/he is unable to pay her/his debts and applies for her/his own bankruptcy (see p440); *or*
- a creditor is owed at least £750 (or two or more creditors are owed a total of at least £750 between them) and applies to have her/his made bankrupt (see p444); *or*
- s/he has defaulted on an individual voluntary arrangement (IVA) and the supervisor applies to the court for her/his bankruptcy (see p448).

People who are 'domiciled' in England and Wales, or who have been resident or carried out a business in England or Wales at some time in the three years before the presentation of the bankruptcy petition, are covered by the bankruptcy provisions described in this chapter.

People who live in another European Union (EU) member state (apart from Denmark) and who do not administer their financial affairs on a regular basis in England and Wales are only subject to the provisions described in this chapter if they have an 'establishment' in England or Wales. An 'establishment' is the place where the client carries out her/his business. Business carried out on an occasional basis does not count, nor does merely having a property, such as a holiday home, in England or Wales.[23] See p440 for more information.

Advantages and disadvantages

Advantages

- It can remove the uncertainty and anxiety caused by negotiating with a large number of creditors simultaneously.
- There can be a sense of relief for the client.
- The client usually pays less. There is one payment to the trustee rather than individual payments to creditors. Payments will usually last for three years.
- It can be a fresh start; the process is intended to rehabilitate the client.
- Creditors have to accept the situation and contact with the client will stop. Most creditors are unable to take further action against the client (see p468).
- The process is certain.
- After discharge, most types of debt are written off and can no longer be pursued by creditors (see p469).

Disadvantages

- The client will almost certainly lose any assets of value that can be sold, unless they are exempt (although even then the client may have to accept a replacement of lower value).
- If there is equity in the family home (ie, it is worth more than the mortgage), the trustee will want to realise the client's share of this. This may lead to the home being sold. However, this cannot happen if the value of the client's share (after-sale costs) does not exceed £1,000.
- If the client owns a business and employs people, or the business has a value, the employees may have to be dismissed and the business sold.
- If the client has mortgage or rent arrears, the home will still be at risk. Bankruptcy does not prevent a secured lender from taking possession proceedings. A landlord can also take possession proceedings on the grounds of rent arrears even though those arrears are covered by the bankruptcy. In addition, the landlord may be able to enforce a suspended possession order if the arrears are not paid or find some grounds other than rent arrears to start possession proceedings – eg, persistent delay in paying rent.
- The client cannot obtain credit of £500 or more without disclosing her/his status if s/he is an undischarged bankrupt or subject to a bankruptcy restriction

order (BRO) or bankruptcy restriction undertaking (BRU) and s/he may find it more difficult to open a bank account, even a basic one (see p456).

- The process is expensive. A client who wishes to pay off the debts in order to preserve an asset (eg, the family home) will also have to pay post-bankruptcy costs and these could be substantial.
- The client must allow her/his financial affairs to be scrutinised by officials who may take criminal action if irregularities are found. S/he may also become subject to a BRO/BRU. However, apart from the restriction on obtaining credit, this may have no effect on her/him.
- The client may be barred from certain public offices or may be unable to practise certain professions – eg, as an accountant or solicitor.
- The client's credit rating will continue to be adversely affected after discharge and this will probably make running a business or buying a home in future very difficult.
- The client may feel judged and humiliated. Some clients may feel there is a stigma attached to bankruptcy and this could be reinforced in cases where a BRO/BRU is made.
- The client's immigration status may be affected and specialist immigration advice should be obtained. Sources of immigration advice available locally can be found in the 'legal adviser finder' section of the Community Legal Advice website at http://legaladviserfinder.justice.gov.uk/AdviserSearch.do.
- While undischarged or subject to a BRO/BRU, the client cannot be a company director without the leave of the court (which may be granted on condition that the client makes payments from her/his income for the benefit of creditors) and cannot trade under any name other than the one used at the date of the bankruptcy order without disclosing the name under which s/he went bankrupt to everyone with whom s/he does business.
- The names of people who are made bankrupt are published in the *London Gazette* and may also be published in the local press. BROs/BRUs may also attract local publicity, and friends and neighbours may find out about the client's financial difficulties and, if a BRO is made, that s/he has been found to have acted irresponsibly in relation to her/his financial affairs.
- Not all debts will be written off at the end of bankruptcy – eg, social fund loans, fines, maintenance and child support.
- Secured creditors are not affected by bankruptcy and can still enforce their security.
- Joint debts are not written off, as creditors can still pursue the non-bankrupt co-client. If s/he is the client's partner, the family will still be in financial difficulties unless s/he has taken separate action to resolve her/his debt problems.

If a client wants to make her/himself bankrupt

The debtor's petition

In order to make her/himself bankrupt, a client must 'petition' the court on the grounds that s/he is 'unable to pay her/his debts' (although it is possible to become bankrupt for only one debt which the client is unable to pay).[24] This involves completing a court form, called the debtor's bankruptcy petition (Form 6.27), together with a statement of affairs (Form 6.28). These can be obtained from the county court or downloaded from the forms section of the Insolvency Service website at www.bis.gov.uk/insolvency.

Although these can be completed online, they currently cannot be submitted online and so must be printed and filed at the court. An example of a completed debtor's petition (Form 6.27) can be found at www.bis.gov.uk/assets/insolvency/docs/forms/ew/6-27example.doc.

If a client wants to petition for her/his own bankruptcy, a court fee of £175 is payable together with a deposit of £525. The court can remit the fee (see p273), but not the deposit.

The petition and statement of affairs, together with three copies of the petition and one copy of the statement of affairs, must be presented to the appropriate court with bankruptcy jurisdiction. This is the client's 'own county court' (see below) if s/he:

- is *either* resident in England or Wales *or* not currently resident in England and Wales but was resident or carrying out business in England and Wales at some time within the previous six months; *and*
- has neither lived nor carried on business in the London insolvency district for most of the six months before the presentation of the petition.

This will apply to most clients.

The appropriate court is the High Court if the client:

- is not currently resident in England or Wales and has neither resided nor carried out a business in England or Wales within the six months before the presentation of the petition; *or*
- has *either* resided *or* carried out business in the London insolvency district for a longer period in those six months than in any other insolvency district and has debts of £100,000 or more. If her/his debts are less than £100,000, the petition must be presented in the central London county court.

If the client has carried out a business within the previous six months, her/his 'own county court' is the county court for the insolvency district where *either* s/he carried out the business *or* where the principal place of business was located (if the business was carried out in more than one insolvency district).

If the client has not carried out a business in the previous six months, the client's own county court is the county court for the district where the client has resided for the greater part of that period. If it is not possible to present the petition to that court (eg, if s/he has left the area because of violence), in order to expedite the presentation of the petition, the client may instead present the petition to the court for the insolvency district where s/he currently resides.[25]

The debtor's petition requires the client to certify either that s/he has her/his 'centre of main interests in England and Wales' or an 'establishment in England and Wales' or that her/his centre of main interests is not in an EU member state. If the client administers her/his financial affairs on a regular basis in another EU member state (other than Denmark), s/he must usually petition for bankruptcy in that member state.[26] According to the Insolvency Service:

> The court will usually regard the country where you carry on a business or otherwise earn your living as your centre of main interests. If you are not employed or self-employed your centre of main interests will be the country you normally live in at the date of the petition. Therefore, if you do not live or work in the UK you cannot go bankrupt here.

A person who only has an 'establishment' in England or Wales but whose centre of main interests is in another EU member state (other than Denmark) cannot petition for her/his own bankruptcy in England or Wales unless s/he would be unable to present her/his petition in that other state.

If a client has previously lived abroad, s/he may not be able to petition in England or Wales. Specialist advice should be obtained.

The statement of affairs

The statement of affairs requires a considerable amount of information to be supplied, much of which, such as asset valuations, may not be readily available. Guidance notes are available at www.bis.gov.uk/insolvency/about-us/forms/england-and-wales. If not typed, the statement of affairs should be completed in capital letters using black ink. All amounts should be to the nearest pound. The following points should be borne in mind when assisting the client to complete the statement of affairs.

- **Section 1** asks for personal details. Question 1.14 does not require information to be included about any informal attempts to come to a payment arrangement with creditors. Details of any pending court action should be included in the answer to Question 1.15, including magistrates' court proceedings.
- **Section 2** only needs to be completed if the client is or has been self-employed at any time in the previous two years.
- **Section 3** asks for details of assets and their valuation. Examples of assets are listed at the start of the section. Approximate values only should be given, using the amount the client would get if s/he sold them rather than their new or replacement value. If any valuable items are listed, they are likely to be claimed by the trustee. Perishable items or items which will diminish in value

if not disposed of quickly are likely to be claimed by the Official Receiver before a trustee is appointed.[27]

- **Section 4** asks for details of secured and unsecured creditors. If the client is unsure who all her/his creditors are, it may be helpful to obtain a copy of her/his credit reference file.

- **Section 5** asks for details of bank accounts and credit cards. Any bank or building society accounts which the client has may be frozen and so any money needed to cover everyday living expenses should be withdrawn before the application for a bankruptcy order is made. Any cash that the client has on the day s/he petitions for bankruptcy should be included as 'cash in hand' in Section 3.

- **Section 6** asks for details of employment and income. Only details of regular income should be included. Question 6.7 asks for the amount of contribution from other members of the household to the household expenses (listed at Question 7.1) and this should be worked out on a proportionate basis where it is not possible to identify an exact figure. Question 6.8 asks for 'total household income' calculated as the total of the client's income and contributions. No pence should be included. Any attachment of earnings orders referred to in Question 6.10 should be 'stayed' (ie, halted) once the petition is presented.

- **Section 7** asks for details of the client's outgoings, but the total household expenditure should be shown to correspond with the response to Question 6.7 (contributions). The list given only contains the usual household expenses. Any other essential items should also be included.

- **Section 8** asks for details of current properties owned or rented by the client, either solely or jointly. Advisers should be aware that, where an owner-occupied property is in the sole name of the client's partner, this does not necessarily mean that the client does not have an interest in it. If the client has made a direct contribution to the purchase price, either by paying a deposit or making mortgage repayments, s/he may have an interest in the property and the adviser should seek specialist advice.

- **Section 9** asks for details of property disposed of in the previous five years. If the client has either given property away or has transferred it but not received the cash value or equivalent in return, the trustee may be able to reopen the transaction to restore the position to what it was before the disposal took place (see p467).

- **Section 10** asks for details of members of the client's household and dependants. In deciding the amount of any income payments order, the trustee is required to take into account the reasonable domestic needs of the client and her/his family (see p458).

- **Section 11** is headed 'Causes of Bankruptcy' and asks the client when s/he first had difficulty paying her/his debts, the reasons why s/he is unable to pay her/his debts and whether s/he has lost money through betting or gambling in the previous two years. Great care needs to be taken in completing this section as the replies may lead the Official Receiver to consider applying for a BRO (see p452).

- **Section 12** is a declaration that all the information provided is true and accurate to the best of the client's knowledge and belief.
- **Section 13** is a continuation sheet.

Once the forms are completed, they must be taken to the court to be filed, together with the fee (or an application for remission on Form EX160) and the deposit. The statement of affairs sworn must be verified by a statement of truth. The court will arrange for the papers to be put before a district judge. Some courts arrange a hearing either immediately or later in the day; other courts insist on a prior appointment being made. Advisers should find out the local practice.

Is an individual voluntary arrangement or debt relief order more appropriate?

In some cases, the court is required to refer the case to an insolvency practitioner for a report. This happens if: [28]

- the client's unsecured debts are less than £40,000;
- the client has money and/or property worth at least £4,000;
- the client has not been the subject of bankruptcy proceedings in the previous five years;
- the court considers an IVA might be a more appropriate option.

The client does not have to pay the fee for this report. In practice, there are usually insufficient assets for the insolvency practitioner to recommend an IVA and the bankruptcy proceeds.

Even if the case is not referred to an insolvency practitioner, the court will still not automatically make a bankruptcy order. If it appears, for example, that the client's assets exceed her/his liabilities or that the client is otherwise able to pay her/his debts, the district judge can dismiss the petition and the bankruptcy deposit will be returned to the client. Sometimes, petitions are adjourned for the client to take advice on alternatives to bankruptcy – eg, a repayment arrangement. Otherwise, the bankruptcy order is made.

If the court thinks it would be in the client's interests for a debt relief order (DRO) to be made instead, it may 'stay' (ie, halt) proceedings on the petition and make an order referring the client to an approved intermediary (see p480). If a DRO is subsequently made, the petition is dismissed.[29] As the court is likely to consider that anyone who is not a homeowner who has debts of less than £15,000, available income not exceeding £50 a month and no assets is suitable for a DRO, the adviser should consider writing a letter confirming her/his advice that bankruptcy is a more appropriate option for the client than a DRO so that this can be handed in to the court if necessary. For the differences between DROs and bankruptcy, see p482.

If a creditor wants to make a client bankrupt

Creditors who are considering making a client bankrupt need to bear in mind that the process is intended to benefit all creditors, not just themselves. They could bear all the costs of obtaining a bankruptcy order only to find that other creditors receive more and they could even end up with nothing at all if the client has no income or assets.

The creditor's petition

A creditor can apply for someone to be made bankrupt if s/he is owed at least £750, which the person 'appears' unable to pay. Two or more creditors who are owed a total of at least £750 between them can petition together. The creditor must satisfy the court of the client's inability to pay by either: [30]

- serving a 'statutory demand' on the client with which s/he fails to comply (see below); *or*
- unsuccessfully attempting to enforce a court judgment against the client by using bailiffs or other enforcement process. The bailiffs must have made serious attempts to enter the client's home and seize property. It is not enough that the bailiff has merely visited the client's home and been unable to gain access.[31]

Essentially, if the enforcement method chosen by the creditor produces no or insufficient money, the creditor can petition for bankruptcy.[32]

Serving a statutory demand

Serving a statutory demand is the most common method used by creditors to satisfy the court of the client's inability to pay. This is a document demanding that the client either pays the debt in full or comes to an agreement for payment with the creditor, or offers security for the debt which is acceptable to the creditor. Form 6.1 is used where there is no judgment; Form 6.2 is used where there is a judgment.

The statutory demand does not have to be issued by the court or even seen by it at this stage. If the client does not comply with the statutory demand within 21 days, the creditor can issue a creditor's petition and ask the court to make a bankruptcy order. A creditor does not need a judgment in order to be able to serve a statutory demand for the debt. However, without a judgment the creditor might find the client is able to challenge the existence of the debt. A creditor who has a judgment is not required to attempt to enforce it; the creditor can serve a statutory demand instead.

Responding to a statutory demand

Some creditors use statutory demands as a method of debt collection. The courts have said that this is only an abuse of process if the creditor is aware the debt is

reasonably disputed.[33] The Office of Fair Trading has discouraged the use of a statutory demand unless:
- it is commercially viable; *and*
- its use is considered reasonable; *and*
- there is a realistic prospect of bankruptcy proceedings being taken.

Circumstances in which the use of a statutory demand is not considered reasonable include where:
- the debt is known to be 'statute-barred' (see p275); *or*
- a valid dispute remains unresolved; *or*
- the client has provided adequate proof that s/he is unemployed and has no assets; *or*
- the client has demonstrated that there is no (or minimal) equity in her/his home, that s/he has no other assets and has made a reasonable payment offer; *or*
- bankruptcy would result in the client losing her/his job and s/he has provided a financial statement and made a reasonable offer of payment.

Although the creditor may have no intention of making the client bankrupt, statutory demands should never be ignored. On receipt of a statutory demand, the client should be advised about the consequences of bankruptcy. If s/he does not want to become bankrupt, s/he should consider:
- applying for an administration order or proposing an IVA as an alternative to bankruptcy;
- making payment(s) either to clear the debt in full or reduce it below the £750 bankruptcy limit so that the creditor will not be able to ask the court to issue a bankruptcy petition (see p447);
- offering a payment in full and final settlement of the debt or in full. This could either be in a lump sum or by instalments. The client should be prepared to demonstrate either that s/he has no assets (including if the home has no or only minimal equity) or that it would not be reasonable to expect her/him to realise them. If the debt is subject to a judgment, as well as trying to negotiate with the creditor, the client should apply to the court to vary this to enable payment by instalments with a view to arranging this before the creditor can obtain a bankruptcy order.
- applying for a time order if the debt is regulated by the Consumer Credit Act 1974 (see p340);
- offering a voluntary charge over her/his property as security for the debt (see p221);
- applying to set aside the statutory demand within 18 days of service.[34]

Setting aside a statutory demand
If the statutory demand has been 'set aside' (ie, cancelled), the creditor cannot apply for a bankruptcy order. The client can apply for the demand to be set aside:

- on the grounds that there is dispute about the money said to be owed. If the debt is a credit debt and the client asserts there is an unfair relationship (see p98), unless the creditor can show that there is nothing the client could say which would lead the court to decide that the relationship is unfair, the statutory demand should be set aside. In the context of a set-aside application, this is a virtually impossible exercise for a creditor.[35] If the creditor has obtained a judgment, at this stage the court will not enquire into the validity of the debt. If this is an issue, the client should be advised to consider applying to set aside (see p314) or appeal the judgment (see p276);[36]
- on the grounds that the client has a counterclaim against the creditor, which equals or exceeds the amount of the debt;
- on the grounds that the creditor holds security, which equals or exceeds the amount of the debt;
- on 'other grounds' – eg, the debt is 'statute-barred' (see p275) or the demand has not been signed.[37] A statutory demand based on a judgment debt is not statute-barred even if the judgment was made more than six years ago.[38]

The application is made on Form 6.4, supported by a witness statement on Form 6.5 to which a copy of the statutory demand must be attached. The application is made to the court in which the client would present her/his bankruptcy petition (see p440). Three copies of each form must be filed. There is no court fee. If the judge considers there are no grounds for the application, s/he can dismiss it without a hearing. Otherwise, a hearing will be arranged at which the district judge will consider the application.

The court will not set aside a statutory demand on the grounds that the creditor has unreasonably refused an offer of payment or security, or even on the grounds that the creditor has refused to consider such an offer. Nor will the court set aside a demand on the grounds that it is for an excessive amount. In such a case, the client is supposed to pay the amount admitted to be due and only apply to set aside the amount in dispute. The court will not 'do a deal' with the client to set the statutory demand aside on condition that s/he makes a payment. The court can set aside a statutory demand for a disputed debt, provided it is satisfied there are reasonable grounds of success.

If the application to set aside the statutory demand is dismissed, the creditor will be given leave to present her/his bankruptcy petition. [39]

The bankruptcy petition

The creditor must present a bankruptcy petition on the appropriate form to the court. There are different forms depending on whether the creditor is an unsatisfied judgment creditor or has served a statutory demand. The creditor must file at court the petition, plus:

- a witness statement that the facts stated in the petition are true;

- a court fee of £220; *and*
- the deposit of £700.

Responding to the petition

The petition must be served personally on the client. It is still not too late to prevent a bankruptcy order being made, but the client must give at least five business days' notice to the court and to the creditor of her/his intention to oppose the bankruptcy order. The client can still raise any 'genuine triable issue' even if s/he did not apply to set aside the statutory demand, but s/he cannot put forward any matter on which the court has already ruled against her/him unless there has been a relevant change of circumstances.

Note: a client cannot be referred to an approved intermediary for a DRO to be made instead of a bankruptcy order without the consent of the creditor (see p474). As the effect of a DRO is that no further payments are made to the creditor, the creditor is unlikely to agree to one unless it is satisfied that the client has no assets and no income and will never be in a position to make payments towards the debt.

The bankruptcy hearing

The hearing is before a district judge. At the hearing, the creditor must prove s/he has delivered the petition to the client (and, if relevant, that the statutory demand has been brought to the client's attention) and file a certificate that the debt is still outstanding. If the client has paid the debt (excluding any creditor's costs) in full before the hearing date, it will be dismissed, but the district judge may still order that the client pay the creditor's costs. If not paid, these will have to be the subject of fresh enforcement proceedings (which could be bankruptcy proceedings if the order is for £750 or more). If the client has reduced the debt (excluding any creditor's costs) to less than £750 in between the issue of the petition and the hearing date, the court has the discretion to make a bankruptcy order, taking into account the client's previous conduct.[40] Even if the petition is dismissed, the client could be ordered to pay the creditor's costs.

The court has discretion to refuse to make a bankruptcy order in certain circumstances, including where execution on a judgment has been stayed (including an instalment order for payment), or if the creditor has unreasonably refused to accept an offer to pay the debt by instalments, a reduced sum in full and final settlement, or an offer to secure the debt.[41] The High Court has pointed out that a creditor is entitled to take into account any history of default, partial payments and broken promises on the part of the client and to consider its own interests. The High Court also pointed out that 'acting reasonably' is not the same as 'acting justly, fairly or kindly'.[42]

It is not unusual for the parties to reach an agreement about payment of the debt and the hearing of the petition can be adjourned, but repeated adjournments should not be allowed unless there is a reasonable prospect of payment within a reasonable time.[43] If an agreement is reached and the creditor does not want to proceed with the bankruptcy, the petition can be dismissed with the permission of the court. The client may, however, find her/himself being ordered to pay the creditor's costs if the court decides that it was reasonable for the creditor to resort to bankruptcy to recover the debt.

If a supervisor wants to make a client bankrupt

If the client is subject to an IVA, the supervisor can petition for a bankruptcy order on the grounds that: [44]

- the arrangement was based on false or misleading information supplied by the client; *or*
- the client has failed to comply with the terms of the IVA.

In the case of protocol-compliant IVAs (see p428), the supervisor must obtain the creditor's approval before taking this step.

After a bankruptcy order is made

The role of the Official Receiver

When a bankruptcy order is made (either because the client has petitioned for her/his own bankruptcy or a creditor or supervisor has successfully petitioned), the court will notify the Official Receiver. The Official Receiver will contact the client soon after the bankruptcy order is made, which could be on the same day.

The Official Receiver's main role is to:

- investigate the client's conduct and financial affairs, and report to the court; *and*
- obtain control of the client's property and any relevant documents.

The client may be asked to complete a questionnaire (Form B40.01). This replicates many of the questions in her/his statement of affairs (Form 6.28) and so s/he should keep a copy of this document to assist in completing the questionnaire. If a client petitioned for her/his own bankruptcy (unless s/he has recently traded or been bankrupt previously), s/he will usually be offered a telephone interview with an examiner (a member of the Official Receiver's staff). The examiner will check the client's answers and ask questions to obtain any additional information. In other cases, the client will be required to attend an interview at the Official Receiver's office.

The client is required to co-operate with the Official Receiver. S/he must give up possession of her/his assets (with limited exceptions) and hand over any papers that are reasonably required.[45] Failure to do so could result in her/his discharge being delayed. The Official Receiver can arrange for her/him to be examined in public by the court about her/his financial affairs and the causes of her/his bankruptcy, although this rarely happens if the client has co-operated fully with the Official Receiver. The Official Receiver can arrange for her/his mail to be re-directed, if appropriate.[46] In appropriate cases, the Official Receiver can apply to the court to impound the client's passport to prevent her/him leaving the country. It is a bankruptcy offence for the client to leave (or attempt to leave) with assets of £1,000 or more which should have been given up to the Official Receiver.[47]

The Official Receiver has a duty to investigate every bankruptcy unless s/he considers such investigation is unnecessary.[48] Any criminal offences revealed must be reported to the authorities (see p451). S/he will usually visit any business premises, and may also visit the client's home, but this is rare. If the Official Receiver does visit, s/he may remove any items of value which are not exempt (see p456).

Within 12 weeks of making the bankruptcy order, the Official Receiver must decide whether or not to call a meeting of creditors to appoint a trustee in bankruptcy (see p450). If no trustee is appointed, the Official Receiver will become the trustee.[49]

Preventing the client's address being disclosed

The Official Receiver registers the bankruptcy at the Land Registry, advertises it in the *London Gazette,* inserts details in the Insolvency Register and may advertise it in one local paper.[50]

If the disclosure of the client's current address or whereabouts might reasonably be expected to lead to violence to her/him or other members of the family who live with her/him, the court may order that:

- details of the client's address be removed from any court file;
- the client's details entered in the bankruptcy order must not include details of her/his current address;
- the details of the client's current address given to the Chief Land Registrar be removed. This is important if the client still owns an interest in a previous address through which s/he might be traced;
- any gazetted or advertised notice must not include details of the client's current address;
- the details entered onto the Individual Insolvency Register must not include details of the client's current address (or that such details must be removed).

The application not to have details disclosed can be made by either the client, the Official Receiver, the trustee in bankruptcy or the Secretary of State, but is most likely to be made by the client. The application is made on Form 7.1A and must be accompanied by a witness statement containing sufficient evidence to support the application. The court fee is either £35 or £70, depending on whether or not the court is prepared to deal with the application without giving notice to the Official Receiver. Otherwise, the court fee is £155. Remission may be available (see p273).

If a client does not want to become bankrupt unless an order to have her/his address withheld is made, both applications should be made at the same time, with a request that the court does not make a bankruptcy order unless it is prepared to make an address withheld order.[51]

The role of the trustee

Once a trustee is appointed, or the Official Receiver becomes the trustee, the client is deprived of ownership of all her/his 'estate' – ie, all her/his property (except certain items – see p456). The estate 'vests' in the trustee – ie, ownership passes automatically to the trustee. The client cannot sell anything, but if arrangements have already been made to sell something (eg, the home), the trustee will almost certainly approve, provided it is a proper commercial transaction. The proceeds will then be used to satisfy the creditors. The trustee is responsible for handling the client's affairs and getting as much money as possible for her/his creditors. The trustee is charged with gathering and selling all the property previously owned by the client and distributing the proceeds among her/his creditors. Property that vests in the trustee include property in countries outside England and Wales, although there may be practical issues for a trustee in taking control of and realising this.

The client may have property which either cannot be disposed of and/or is subject to obligations which would involve expenditure to the detriment of the estate, and hence the creditors – eg a business lease. The trustee can dispose of such 'onerous property'.[52]

If the client attempts to give away or sell 'her/his' property after the bankruptcy petition is issued but before the property passes to the trustee, this transfer is void – ie, of no effect. The court can confirm a sale but, in the absence of this, the property still forms part of the client's estate and can be recovered and sold by the trustee.

The sale of jointly owned property requires the consent of the co-owner or a court order. If a client acquires any property before discharge, s/he must inform the trustee within 21 days. The trustee then has 42 days (during which the client must not dispose of the property) in which to claim the property for the estate.[53]

How money is paid

Once a bankruptcy order is made, the trustee takes over many of the functions of the debt adviser. The client may need considerable personal support, and the debt adviser may need to ensure the trustee acts correctly. However, until discharge, the debt adviser is largely powerless to affect decisions.

The Official Receiver will contact her/his creditors and invite them to 'prove' their debts – ie, submit claims. Creditors must, therefore, contact the trustee and demonstrate that they are owed the money. This must be done on a prescribed form.[54] The court can prevent any creditor who is entitled to prove a bankruptcy claim from attempting to recover the debt in any other way. This power arises as soon as the bankruptcy petition is presented and continues until discharge.[55]

The only debts which cannot be proved are:[56]

- fines;
- maintenance orders (other than orders for payment of a lump sum or costs) and Child Support Agency orders;
- debts from certain other orders of the criminal courts;
- student loans; *and*
- social fund loans (where the bankruptcy petition was presented on or after 19 March 2012).

Secured loans do not need to be proved because the rights of a secured creditor are not affected by bankruptcy. Secured creditors can, theoretically, remove their security and ask to be included in the list of creditors. If they have already forced a sale of the home, they can be included as creditors for any unsecured balance due.

The trustee will work out the value of the debts and any assets. S/he will list the following, which are priorities to be paid first:[57]

- bankruptcy expenses (including amounts due to the trustee, the court or the Insolvency Service, which charges for the Official Receiver's services). This often leaves creditors with nothing;
- expenses of, for instance, estate agents to realise assets;
- contributions owed by the client to occupational pension schemes;
- arrears of wages to employees for four months before the bankruptcy (up to a maximum of £800 each);
- other ('ordinary') creditors. These creditors receive nothing until the other 'preferential' creditors have been paid in full. If paid at all, these creditors generally receive only a percentage of the value of their debt;
- deferred debts – eg, debts due to the client's spouse;
- interest on any of the above from the date of the bankruptcy order.

Any surplus will be returned to the client.

Offences

It is an offence for the client to do anything that intentionally conceals information or property from the Official Receiver or trustee, or to deliberately mislead the Official Receiver or trustee about property which s/he had either before or after the bankruptcy. Criminal charges can be brought against a client, leading to a fine and/or imprisonment. However, if the client can show that there was no intention to mislead or defraud, this counts as a valid defence. Other so-called 'bankruptcy offences' include obtaining credit of £500 or more without telling the creditor s/he is bankrupt, and trading under a different business name without informing people with whom s/he comes into contact through the business the name under which s/he was made bankrupt (see p452).[58]

Restrictions during bankruptcy

Pre-discharge restrictions

A client who is an **undischarged bankrupt** cannot:

- obtain credit of £500 or more from a creditor without disclosing her/his status as an undischarged bankrupt;
- engage in business in a name other than that in which s/he was made bankrupt without disclosing that name to people with whom s/he has business dealings;
- act as a director of, or directly or indirectly promote, form or manage a limited company without leave of the court;
- act as an insolvency practitioner or an intermediary for DROs (see p480);
- act as a charity trustee (unless s/he is a director of the charity and has obtained leave of the court).

Breach of any of these is a criminal offence, but the restrictions usually end on discharge.

Post-discharge restrictions: bankruptcy restriction orders and undertakings

People who are regarded as 'culpable' because they have acted recklessly, irresponsibly or dishonestly may be made subject to an extended period of restrictions through a bankruptcy restriction order (BRO) or bankruptcy restriction undertaking (BRU). The court can make a BRO or BRU if it thinks it 'appropriate having regard to the conduct of the bankrupt' (see p453). If the court makes a BRO or BRU, the above restrictions on obtaining credit, engaging in business, involvement in a limited company and acting as an insolvency practitioner continue for a minimum of two years and a maximum of 15 years from the date the order or undertaking was made.[59]

In addition, being subject to a BRO/BRU may affect a client's employment or her/his ability to hold certain offices. For example, a person subject to a BRO/BRU cannot:

- serve as an MP, local councillor, a member of the Welsh or Northern Ireland Assembly, or sit in the House of Lords;
- act as a school governor;
- exercise any 'right to buy'.

Breach of a BRO/BRU is punishable as a bankruptcy offence (see p451).[60]

According to the Insolvency Service, the vast majority of BROs/BRUs are for two to five years. Most are BRUs. BROs/BRUs are most commonly made because the client has:[61]

- contributed to the bankruptcy by neglectling her/his business affairs (usually, tax affairs);

- entered into transactions either to prefer friends or relatives ahead of other creditors or at an undervalue;
- incurred debts with no reasonable prospect of being able to repay them.

The Secretary of State maintains a register of BROs, interim BROs and BRUs, open to public inspection at no charge at www.bis.gov.uk/insolvency. It may also be in the client's local press. The client can apply to the court to order that details of her/his current address be withheld on the grounds that there is a reasonable risk that disclosure could lead to violence towards her/him or a member of her/his family who lives with her/him (see p449).

Example

A 34-year-old man was running a music business and had debts estimated by the Official Receiver of around £38,298. He received £300 a week from the business, which fell to £200 and then to nothing when the business ceased trading. Despite this, he spent at least £14,284 in just under six months (after which he filed his petition), which he had no reasonable prospect of being able to repay. Of this, £10,728 went on credit cards, £1,767 on a widescreen TV and he increased his overdraft by £1,789. The credit card spending included a payment towards his wedding in Florida, a holiday to Greece, jewellery and designer goods, gym membership, home improvements and driving lessons. He took out a £12,000 bank loan, which he said was used to pay a £5,000 gambling debt and repay a £7,000 loan from his partner made the previous year. By the time he went bankrupt, his debts were £52,582. He admitted he spent £120 a week on cocaine and then subsidised his income with credit cards. He was made the subject of a six-year BRU.

Bankruptcy restriction order applications

When considering an application for a BRO, the court can take any behaviour of the client into account, but must specifically take into account whether s/he has:[62]

- failed to keep records which account for a loss of property by the client, or by a business carried out by her/him. The loss must have occurred in the period beginning two years before the petition and ending with the date of the application;
- failed to produce records of this kind on demand by the Official Receiver or the trustee;
- entered into a transaction at an 'undervalue' (see p467);
- made an excessive pension contribution;
- failed to supply goods or services which were wholly or partly paid for and which gave rise to a provable claim in the bankruptcy;
- traded before the start of the bankruptcy when s/he knew, or ought to have known, that s/he would be unable to pay her/his debts;

- incurred before the start of the bankruptcy a debt which s/he did not reasonably expect to be able to pay (which appears to include increasing the amount of debt on a credit card);
- failed to account satisfactorily for a loss of property or for an insufficiency of property to meet bankruptcy debts;
- carried on any gambling, 'rash and hazardous speculation' or 'unreasonable extravagance', which may have contributed to or increased the extent of the bankruptcy or which took place between the presentation of the petition and the start of the bankruptcy;
- neglected her/his business affairs, which may have contributed to or increased the extent of the bankruptcy;
- been fraudulent;
- failed to co-operate with the Official Receiver or the trustee.

The conduct that the court is required to take into account addresses behaviour by consumers as well as by traders, and behaviour both before and after the bankruptcy order. If no period is specified, it is likely that the more serious the misconduct, the longer the period over which it will be taken into account.

The court is also required to consider whether the client was an undischarged bankrupt at some time during the six years ending with the date of the bankruptcy to which the application relates. However, it is understood that the existence of two bankruptcies is not considered to be misconduct in itself, but it allows the court to put misconduct in context.

Only conduct on or after 1 April 2004 (the date the BRO regime came into force) can be taken into account.[63]

The application must be made by the Secretary of State or by the Official Receiver acting on the direction of the Secretary of State. The application must normally be made within one year from the date of the bankruptcy order, even if the client is discharged before this. An application for a BRO must be supported by a report and evidence from the Secretary of State.

The hearing date must be fixed for no earlier than eight weeks from when the court decides on the venue. Since the application is made as part of the bankruptcy proceedings – rather than in separate proceedings – the hearing takes place in the client's local bankruptcy court. The hearing is in public. The Secretary of State must serve the application on the client not more than 14 days after the application was filed at court, together with:

- at least six weeks' notice of the hearing;
- a copy of the Secretary of State's report;
- any further evidence in support of the application in the form of a witness statement; *and*
- an acknowledgement of service.

The client must:
- return the acknowledgement of service to the court, indicating whether or not s/he intends to contest the application, not more than 14 days after the application is served. Otherwise, s/he may attend the hearing, but cannot take part unless the court agrees;
- file at court any evidence opposing the application which s/he wishes the court to consider, within 28 days of being served with the application and supporting evidence;
- serve copies on the Secretary of State within a further three business days.

Within 14 days, the Secretary of State must file at court any further evidence and serve a copy on the client as soon as reasonably practicable.

The court may make a BRO regardless of whether or not the client attends the hearing or submitted any evidence.[64]

This is an application within the bankruptcy proceedings and is a civil, not a criminal, procedure. The Secretary of State only needs to satisfy the court on the (lower) civil standard of proof (ie, 'on the balance of probabilities') rather than the (higher) criminal standard – ie, 'satisfied beyond a reasonable doubt'.

In order to avoid the need for court proceedings, the Secretary of State may instead accept the client's offer of a BRU, which has the same effect as a BRO (including the consequences of a breach) from the date it is accepted by the Secretary of State.

The Official Receiver informs the client of the period s/he thinks the court will make the BRO for and the client will have to decide:
- whether or not s/he accepts there is a case for a BRO; *and*
- whether or not s/he wants to avoid going to court and risk a longer period.

The client can also apply to the court to annul a BRU or for an order that it should cease to have effect from an earlier date than originally agreed.[65]

Interim bankruptcy restriction orders

Because the client must be given at least six weeks' notice of the application for a BRO and an application must be made within 12 months of the bankruptcy order (unless the court gives leave to apply later), there may be a gap of several months between the date of discharge and the date of hearing when the client is not subject to any restrictions. The Secretary of State can apply to the court to make an interim BRO.

An interim BRO has the same effect as a full BRO and lasts from when it is made until:[66]
- the application for the BRO is determined; *or*
- the Secretary of State accepts a BRU; *or*
- it is revoked.

Only two business days' notice of the application is required and the hearing will be in public. The Secretary of State must file a report and evidence.[67]

How bankruptcy can affect a client

Protected goods

Some goods do not pass to the trustee and cannot be taken. These include:[68]

- tools of the trade, including a vehicle, which are necessary and used personally by the client in her/his 'employment, business or vocation'. Stock is not protected, which will almost certainly mean that the business has to close down if it depends on stock;
- household equipment necessary to the basic domestic needs of the client and her/his family. This should include all clothing, bedding, furniture and household equipment and provisions, except perhaps particularly valuable items (eg, antiques and works of art) or luxury goods with a high resale value – eg, expensive TVs or music systems.

If the value of any protected goods exceeds the cost of a 'reasonable replacement', the trustee can require them to be sold for the benefit of the creditors. In practice, this rarely happens but, if so, the trustee must provide the funds to enable the client to replace the goods.

The trustee can visit a bankrupted person and remove goods or close a business. In practice, however, this is mainly done in cases of businesses or domestic properties in which there may be valuable goods. Generally, trustees do not dispose of items unless there will be at least £500 benefit to the estate, as it is not usually economical to do so. If the client acquires any asset which is not protected in the period between the bankruptcy order and her/his discharge, the trustee may claim it within 42 days of becoming aware of it.[69]

Bank accounts

The client's bank account may be frozen.

There is no legal reason why a client cannot have a bank account. However, despite their expressed commitment to financial inclusion, the majority of banks and building societies do not offer basic bank accounts to undischarged bankrupts, even though these are considered suitable because they involve no credit facilities. Post Office card accounts are not suitable for all clients. There is, however, the possibility of being able to open a credit union current account, although not all credit unions offer these.

If the client's bank honours a cheque after the date of the bankruptcy order, the transaction will not be void if either:[70]

- the bank did not have notice of the bankruptcy order before honouring the cheque; or

- it is not reasonably practicable to recover the payment from the person to whom it was made.

Utility companies

Although utility companies cannot insist on payment of pre-bankruptcy arrears as a condition of continuing to supply services, they may require a security deposit or insist on installing a pre-payment meter. It may, therefore, be necessary to transfer the accounts to a non-bankrupt member of the family. The policies of a client's utility suppliers should be checked before petitioning for bankruptcy so that the client knows what to expect.

Motor vehicles

The trustee must deal with any motor vehicle owned by, or in the possession of, the client as a matter of urgency, as it is a potential source of liability for the trustee. If the client claims the vehicle is exempt, s/he must complete Form B50.10. If a car is essential for her/his employment (eg, if there is no reasonable alternative transport to and from work), the client may be allowed to keep it, although if it is particularly valuable the trustee may order it to be sold to allow a cheaper replacement to be bought. The trustee does not usually do this unless there will be at least £500 profit for the benefit of creditors. A maximum of £1,000 is usually allowed for a replacement vehicle, but could be more depending on the circumstances.

Insolvency Service guidance has widened the definition of 'employment, business or vocation' to include bankrupt clients who are informal, full-time carers of a disabled friend or relative (including a child) who use the motor vehicle in connection with that role. Although receipt by the client of carer's allowance is not essential, the Insolvency Service regards this as indicative that the client is pursuing a 'vocation' as a carer.

Previous Insolvency Service guidance said that a motor vehicle could never be regarded as an item of 'household equipment'. Current guidance now allows the Official Receiver to consider claims from bankrupt clients that a motor vehicle is necessary to meet basic domestic needs. 'Necessary' in this context means that no reasonably practical alternative exists to meet a genuine need. The test of necessity is not satisfied just because use of a motor vehicle is more convenient than the alternatives, unless these are likely to be more expensive.

According to the Insolvency Service, the people most likely to come within the guidance are clients who are disabled and need a vehicle for mobility. The vehicle must be used personally by the client. If s/he requires assistance to travel in the vehicle, it will not fall within the guidance.

Clients who live in urban areas with reasonable public transport are unlikely to be able to benefit from the 'domestic needs' guidance (other than because of disability). Even in an urban area, it might be possible to claim exemption on the grounds that a vehicle is necessary to transport children to school where there is no public transport alternative or if children attend different schools and the distance to travel would make walking or cycling an impractical alternative. If the motor vehicle is of high value, the trustee can still require a cheaper replacement.

If a motor vehicle is not exempt, a member of the client's family or a friend may be able to negotiate to buy the vehicle to enable the client to retain it. Any other asset can be treated in the same way if the trustee regards it as a 'luxury' item.

If the vehicle is subject to a hire purchase or conditional sale agreement, the finance company may be able to terminate the agreement and repossess the vehicle if the client becomes bankrupt. The trustee will always contact the finance company and so, even if the trustee agrees that the vehicle is exempt, the finance company may seek to repossess it. In other cases where there is insufficient equity to make it worth the trustee's while selling the vehicle her/himself, s/he may invite the finance company to repossess the vehicle.[71]

A mobile home that is not parked on a protected site (ie, a site registered by the local authority under the Caravan Sites Act 1968), but under an informal arrangement, is more likely to be regarded as a 'motor vehicle' than a 'house' even if it is the client's permanent residence. The question of whether it is exempt under the 'domestic needs' category therefore arises. A mobile home parked on a registered site with a degree of immobility may be regarded as a 'house'. A caravan used as a permanent residence with a degree of site permanence and immobility is also likely to be regarded as a house.

Income payments order

If the client has at least £20 a month available income, the trustee may suggest a weekly or monthly payment from a client's earnings. If payment is not agreed, s/he can apply to the court for an income payments order. This must be applied for before the client is discharged and the order must specify the period for which it is to last. This must be no longer than three years from the date of the order. These payments will be ordered to be paid to the trustee and can be required of either the client or employer under an attachment of earnings order.[72] Either the client or the trustee can apply to vary the order (both before and after discharge). The court must leave sufficient money for the reasonable domestic needs of the client and her/his family – the client is not restricted to basic income support levels. An income payments order should not be sought if the client's only source of income is state benefits but, if the client also has non-benefit income, the trustee can consider applying for an order.

Calculating the order

The trustee should calculate the client's available income by deducting from her/his actual income the household outgoings (less contributions from other members of the household towards these, either actual or assumed).

Chapter 31.7 of the Insolvency Service's Technical Manual (available in the freedom of information section of the Insolvency Service website at www.bis.gov.uk/insolvency/contact-us/foi-intro/foi) lists various types of expenditure and discusses the different factors to be taken into account when deciding whether (and, if so, how much) to allow as expenditure. This has links to a spreadsheet which contains typical figures for certain items of expenditure for different households based on the annual expenditure survey. These figures are used to help assess whether a client's expenditure is 'reasonable'. Advisers should familiarise themselves with these resources which can be accessed at www.tinyurl.com/6ea3doy.

Note: when calculating the household's expenditure, an allowance for sundries and emergencies of £10 a month for the client and £10 a month for each dependent member of the household should be made.

Guidance in the Insolvency Service Technical Manual says that, when assessing the client for an income payments order, the Officer Receiver should not include any amounts payable for rent arrears under a suspended possession order. However, the client should be allowed time to apply to the court to vary the possession order to pay current rent only. In the meantime, 'under no circumstances should the bankrupt be advised to cease making payments under the terms of the suspended possession order before it has been varied by the court'.[73]

If there is no court order, but the client has made an informal arrangement to pay the rent arrears, the Technical Manual advises that no allowance should be made for such payments, which should stop immediately even if this might trigger possession action. However, if the client does not have sufficient surplus income for an order to be made, there is no objection to the client making payments towards rent arrears out of her/his surplus income or, in cases where there is an income payments agreement or order, out of the £10 month 'sundries and emergencies' allowance.

Note: the trustee does not use the common financial statement 'trigger figures' (see p52).[74]

Any surplus is available income and, provided this is at least £20 a month, the order is assessed at the full amount of the surplus income. If the client has both benefit and non-benefit income, the amount of the order should not exceed the non-benefit income figure – ie, payment should not come out of the client's benefit income.

The client may apply to the court to vary an income payments order or for it to cease before its specified date.[75]

Income payments agreement

The client can come to an agreement with the trustee about a payment arrangement and incorporate it into a written income payments agreement without applying to the court. An income payments agreement is enforceable as a court order just like an income payments order and can be varied by either:[76]

- a further written agreement; *or*
- the court, on the application of either the client or the trustee.

In the first instance, clients are offered an income payments agreement. If the client thinks that the household expenditure claimed is reasonable but the trustee does not agree, the client does not have to sign an agreement, but can leave the decision to be made by the court. Provided the client has not acted unreasonably, it is unlikely that the court will order the client to pay any costs of the application even if the court ultimately agrees with the trustee.

Pensions

If the bankruptcy order was made on a petition presented to the court before 29 May 2000, personal pensions are part of the bankrupt client's estate and must be paid to the trustee by the pension company. This is the case whether the payments fall due during or after the bankruptcy.[77]

In the case of occupational pensions, trustees may argue that pensions pass to them as a matter of course, and so the position should be checked with the pension company. However, although an occupational pension cannot normally be claimed directly by the trustee, the income could be made the subject of an income payments order (see p458).[78]

If the bankruptcy order was made on a petition presented on or after 29 May 2000, all rights under an 'HM Revenue and Customs-approved pension arrangement' are excluded from the client's estate (ie, they do not vest in the trustee), including personal pension plans. However, if the client becomes entitled to the pension (including a lump sum) during the period of the bankruptcy, it could be made the subject of an income payments order (see p458).[79]

The High Court has held that, if a client is entitled to receive payments (usually a tax-free lump sum and/or monthly pension payments) from a scheme and can do so merely by asking for it, the trustee can treat the client as being entitled to payment under the scheme and can take this into account when assessing the client for an income payments order or agreement.[80]

Insurance policies

Ordinary term life assurance policies or endowment policies are not exempt and will usually pass to the trustee in the normal way. If a policy has been assigned or charged to the lender in connection with a mortgage or secured loan, it will be treated as part of the security and will not vest in the trustee (see p450). If a third party is named as beneficiary under the policy, the policy does not normally vest in the trustee. If a client was originally the beneficiary under the policy and the transfer of the right to receive the proceeds is a transaction at an undervalue (see p467), however, the trustee will claim the benefit of the policy.

Student loans

Student loans, whether made before or after the bankruptcy order, are not part of the client's estate and so cannot be claimed by the trustee.

Loans made under the Teaching and Higher Education Act 1998 are not part of the client's estate and cannot be part of an income payments order or agreement.

The Student Loans Company does not carry out credit checks as part of its loan application process. Any clients who are considering bankruptcy and intend to become students can be reassured that their bankruptcy will not affect any student loan application.

Owner-occupied homes

If the client has a beneficial interest in her/his home, that interest automatically becomes the property of the trustee in bankruptcy on her/his appointment. The trustee protects her/his interest by registering either a notice or a restriction at the Land Registry. If the home is solely owned by the client, the legal title vests in the trustee and the client's interest, which passes to the trustee, is the whole value of the property. If it is jointly owned, only the client's share vests in the trustee, but this does not prevent the trustee from taking action to realise that share. The trustee can realise the value of that interest (eg, by selling it to a joint owner or forcing a sale of the property) and this does not have to be done before the client's discharge from the bankruptcy.

The trustee has a three-year 'use it or lose it' period from the date of the bankruptcy order to deal with the client's interest in a property which, at the date of the bankruptcy order, is the sole or principal residence of the client, or her/his spouse/civil partner or former spouse/civil partner. Otherwise, the interest will no longer form part of the client's estate and will transfer back to her/him. It will, therefore, no longer be available to pay the client's bankruptcy debts. However, this will not happen if, during the three-year period, the trustee: [81]

- realises the interest – eg, by selling her/his interest to the client's partner or some other third party. The full sale price must be paid to the trustee before the end of the three-year period; *or*
- applies for an order for sale or possession; *or*
- applies for a charging order in respect of the client's interest; *or*
- comes to an agreement with the client about her/his interest.

If the trustee decides to take the third option, the charging order is for the value of the client's interest in the property at the date of the charging order plus interest at the prescribed rate (currently 8 per cent a year). The client will, therefore, retain the benefit of any subsequent increase in the value of the property.

Low-value exemption

If the value of the client's interest is less than the prescribed amount (£1,000), the court *must* dismiss any application by the trustee in bankruptcy for:[82]

- an order for the sale or possession of the property; *or*
- a charging order on the client's interest in the property.

In valuing the client's interest in the property the court must disregard:[83]

- any loans secured by mortgage or other charge against the property;
- any other third-party interest – eg, a joint owner's share of equity;
- the reasonable costs of sale, currently estimated at 3 per cent of the gross value of the property.

Realising a client's interest in the property

If another person shares ownership of the home and there is sufficient equity, the trustee will try to sell the client's share to that person. S/he will have to obtain an up-to-date valuation at her/his own expense, plus details of any outstanding mortgages or secured loans, and pay her/his own legal costs (at least £250). If the property is jointly owned, the trustee will require the value of the client's share (usually, 50 per cent of the equity) plus her/his legal costs, but will allow some discount to take account of the savings made from not having to take possession of the property and conduct the sale. Any increase in the value of the property as a result of expenditure by either party after the date of bankruptcy should also be taken into account.

If the property is solely owned by the client, s/he may be able to buy back her/his interest from the trustee. If there is equity, the purchase money will have to come from a third party – eg, a friend or relative. Mortgage lenders are reluctant to agree to people buying an interest in property, unless they take some responsibility for the mortgage. In the case of jointly owned properties, the co-owner(s) is already responsible for the mortgage. In the case of solely owned properties, however, before agreeing to transfer her/his interest to a partner or third party, the trustee must ensure that arrangements have been made between the proposed transferee and the mortgage lender(s) for future payment of the mortgage.

The trustee will probably seek a court order for the sale of a jointly owned property if the non-bankrupt owner will not/cannot purchase the beneficial interest and there is sufficient equity. If there is a partner and/or children, their interests should be considered, but after a year these are overridden by the interests of the creditors unless the circumstances of the case are exceptional (see p463). This means that, in practice, homes are not sold for at least a year after the bankruptcy.

In deciding whether to order the sale of a house, the court must consider:[84]

- the creditors' interests;
- whether the spouse/civil partner contributed to the bankruptcy;

- the needs and resources of the children and spouse/civil partner;
- other relevant circumstances (but not the client's needs).

At the outset of the bankruptcy, if there is negative, or very little, equity, the case will be reviewed after two years and three months.[85]

- If the value of the client's share in the property is valued at less than £1,000, steps will be take to transfer that share back to the client.
- If the value of the client's share in the property is worth more than £1,000, the trustee will invite the client or a third party such as a co-owner or family member to buy back the client's share.
- If it is not possible to sell the client's share in this way and there is not sufficient equity to attract an insolvency practitioner to act as trustee, the Official Receiver as trustee should consider applying for a charging order on the client's share of the property (see p301).

If a charging order is obtained on the client's share in the property, the trustee is not subject to any limitation period for seeking an order for its sale – ie, s/he can apply to the court for an order for sale at any time in the future.[86]

If a property is sold, the trustee will send any money due to the co-owner or other person with an interest in the property on completion. It is important that people who share a home with a bankrupt person are independently advised by a solicitor, particularly if they have made direct contributions to the purchase price, because they may have an equitable or beneficial interest in the property for which they should be paid, even if they are not an 'owner' on the deeds.

Endowment policies

If there is an endowment policy in place to pay a mortgage, it may vest in the trustee who can arrange for it to be sold. The policy is treated as an asset and taken into account when valuing the client's interest in the property if:[87]

- it has been formally assigned to the mortgage lender; *or*
- the policy document is held by the mortgage lender; *or*
- the mortgage lender's interest in the policy for repayment of the mortgage has been noted with the insurance company; *or*
- there has been a specific agreement between the mortgage lender and the client that the policy will be used to pay the mortgage.

This may result in there being sufficient equity for the trustee to realise the property.

Exceptional circumstances

If an application is made for the sale of a property which is, or has been, the home of the client or the client's spouse or civil partner or former spouse or civil partner, and it is more than one year after the date the client's estate vested in the trustee, the court must assume that the interests of the bankrupt's creditors outweigh all other considerations, unless the circumstances of the case are exceptional.[88]

Before the Human Rights Act came into force on 2 October 2000, caselaw established that circumstances could only be exceptional if they were unusual. However, the recent case of *Ford v Alexander* contains a useful summary of this test. [89]

- Although exceptional circumstances are needed to displace the assumption that the creditors' interests prevail, even if there are exceptional circumstances, the court can still make an order for sale.
- Exceptional circumstances relate to the personal circumstances of one of the joint owners and/or their children, such as a physical or mental health condition.
- Exceptional circumstances cannot be categorised or defined. The court must make a judgement after considering all the circumstances.
- To be exceptional, the circumstances must be 'outside the normal melancholy consequences of debt and improvidence'.
- It is not an exceptional circumstance that the spouse and children are faced with eviction because there are insufficient funds to provide them with a comparable home.
- Creditors have an interest in an order for sale being made even if the whole of the net proceeds go towards the expenses of the bankruptcy and they receive nothing. This situation is not an exceptional circumstance.

The court has the power to defer the sale of the property to a future date which it considers 'fair and reasonable'.[90]

Beneficial interest

If the property is in the sole name of the bankrupt client, the non-bankrupt partner could argue that s/he has a beneficial interest in the property – ie, s/he is entitled to a share in the proceeds of sale of the property. If this can be established, the trustee will have no claim against the non-bankrupt partner's share of the property so that:

- if the property is sold, the partner will be entitled to be paid the value of her/his share;[91]
- the partner will not have to make any payment to the trustee in respect of her/his share in order to buy out the trustee.

On the other hand, if the property is in the sole name of the non-bankrupt partner, the trustee may try to establish that the client has a beneficial interest. The trustee will also investigate whether the property was put into the partner's sole name in circumstances that amount to a transaction at an undervalue (see p467).

The general rule is that the beneficial interest is presumed to be the same as the legal interest.

If a family home has been bought in the joint names of a cohabiting couple who are both responsible for any mortgage but there is no express declaration of their beneficial interests, they are both equally entitled to the beneficial interest unless:

- they had a different common intention at the time when they acquired the home; or
- they later intended that their respective shares would change.

The onus of proving that the parties intended their beneficial interests to be different from their legal interests is on the party seeking to establish this.

If the property is in the sole name of one of the partners, joint beneficial ownership is not presumed. The trustee will look at whether it was intended that the non-owner party should have any beneficial interest in the property and, if so, what it is.

The other partner may have acquired a beneficial interest either by:

- a court order confirming the existence of a beneficial interest; or
- an agreement at the time the property was acquired, or subsequently, that s/he should have a beneficial interest *plus* acting to her/his detriment or significantly altering her/his position in relation to the agreement – eg, by making substantial contributions to the household expenditure; or
- making a direct contribution to the purchase of the property – eg, by:
  - paying some or all of the deposit out of her/his own money unless it was made as a gift or a loan. This includes a right-to-buy discount; or
  - making direct, regular and substantial contributions to the mortgage repayments out of her/his own money; or
  - subject to any contrary agreement, paying for, or making a substantial contribution towards, identifiable improvements to the property out of her/his own money.

Living in someone else's house (even as a partner, civil partner or spouse), sharing household expenses and ordinary domestic duties, such as looking after the property and bringing up children, do not entitle the client to a beneficial interest on their own.

Assuming the other partner does have a beneficial interest, the value of her/his share depends on the value of her/his contributions, any agreement between the parties and any inferences that can be drawn from their conduct.[92]

Even if the trustee is dealing with a jointly owned property, there may be a question about whether one of the parties has more than a 50 per cent share in it. If the property is held in joint names as joint tenants, this is considered to be conclusive evidence of an intention to hold the property in equal shares, unless one of the parties can demonstrate fraud or that there has been a mistake in the conveyance, or that there has been undue influence (see p89) or a declaration of trust of the beneficial interests. If Land Registry Form TR1 has been used (compulsory for all transfers since 1 April 2008), there is a specific declaration of trust tick box. The House of Lords has said that, where there is no declaration of trust, the presumption should be that properties in joint names are owned in equal shares rather than in proportion to the parties' financial contributions to its purchase.[93] If a party seeks to argue otherwise, the onus is on her/him, and unequal contributions to the purchase will not be sufficient on their own.

Specialist advice should always be sought if the adviser has grounds for believing that either the client or someone else may have a beneficial interest in a property which could be the subject of a claim by the trustee.[94]

Rented accommodation

Assured, protected and secure tenancies do not automatically vest in the trustee, but can be claimed within the 42-day period, if they have a value, but this is relatively rare.

Pre-bankruptcy rent arrears are a 'bankruptcy debt', which cannot be excluded from the bankruptcy and are provable like any other bankruptcy debt. The landlord has no 'remedy' in respect of that debt.[95]

However, the Court of Appeal has recently ruled that the phrase 'remedy in respect of the debt' means 'remedy for the debt'.[96] As a result, the following applies.

- An order for possession based on rent arrears which are a bankruptcy debt is not a remedy in respect of the debt whether the order is an outright order or a suspended order.
- A landlord can take possession action based on those rent arrears and any possession proceedings pending at the date of the bankruptcy order should not be put on hold ('stayed').
- At the hearing, the court can suspend the possession order but cannot suspend the order on condition the client pays those arrears; nor can the court give judgment for those arrears.
- Any suspended possession order should be made on condition that the client pays the current rent (plus any costs awarded after the date of the bankruptcy order.

In the case of assured and secure tenancies, the landlord can use some other breach of the tenancy not involving rent arrears as a ground for possession. For example, if the tenancy contains a forfeiture clause on bankruptcy, the landlord could obtain a possession order on that ground.[97] Before the client petitions for bankruptcy, the tenancy agreement should be checked for such a clause and enquiries made about the landlord's policy on enforcing it.

If there is a suspended possession order already in force when the client goes bankrupt, the landlord could still apply for a warrant if the order was not complied with.

The safest course of action for a tenant with rent arrears or subject to a possession order who is considering bankruptcy is to make enquiries about the policies and practice of the landlord and the local district judge(s). If rent arrears have accrued after the date of the bankruptcy order, whether or not there are pre-bankruptcy rent arrears, there are no restrictions on the landlord taking proceedings.[98]

Transactions at an undervalue

A transaction is said to be made at an 'undervalue' if it involves an exchange of property for less than its market value. This may be quite innocent with everyone acting in good faith, but if a trustee considers that such a transaction has reduced the assets available to creditors, s/he can apply to the court, which can set the transaction aside.[99]

The trustee can apply to the court to have a transaction at an undervalue set aside if:[100]

- it was carried out in the five years before the date of the bankruptcy order; *and*
- the client was insolvent at the time or the transaction led to her/his insolvency; *or*
- the transaction was carried out within two years of the date of the bankruptcy order, regardless of whether or not the client was insolvent.

If the transaction was with an 'associate' (eg, partner, relative, partner's relative, business partner or employer), it is assumed that the client was insolvent at the time of the transaction. Such transactions could be:

- gifts (including money);
- working or selling goods for nothing or for an amount significantly less than the value of the labour or goods;
- giving security over assets for no benefit in return;
- transferring an interest in property to a former partner (but not under a court order on divorce unless there are exceptional circumstances, such as fraud[101]).

Preferences

If the client has done something before the bankruptcy which has put a creditor or a guarantor of one of her/his debts into a better position than it would have been in the event of the client's bankruptcy (eg, giving a voluntary charge or paying them in full), this may be a 'preference' if other creditors have not been similarly treated. In addition:

- the client must have intended putting them in a better position; *and*
- the client must have been insolvent at the time or the action must have led to her/his insolvency;[102] *and*

- the payment must have been made within six months before the date of the bankruptcy order (or within two years if the preference was to an 'associate' – eg, spouse, partner or other relative, business partner or employer/employee).[103]

If the preference was to an 'associate', it is assumed that the client intended putting her/him in a better position, unless it can be shown otherwise. An exception to this is if the person is only an associate because s/he is an employee.

Trustee's remedy

In the case of either transactions at an undervalue or preferences, the court can restore the position of the parties by, for example, requiring any property or money to be returned to the trustee, ordering the release of any security, or ordering payment to the trustee for goods or services. Protection is given to third parties who act in good faith without notice of the circumstances.[104] Generally, the trustee does not take court action for less than £5,000 but this does not mean s/he will not attempt other recovery action.

Enforcement action by creditors

Once a bankruptcy petition has been presented to the court or a bankruptcy order has been made, the court can order any existing court or enforcement action being taken by creditors to be discontinued in order to preserve the client's property for the benefit of all of her/his creditors. Once the bankruptcy order has been made, anyone who is a creditor of the client with a debt provable in the bankruptcy (see p450):[105]

- is prohibited from exercising any remedy against the property or person of the client in order to enforce payment of the debt; *and*
- is not allowed to start any new court action against the client before her/his discharge without the permission of the court – eg, for a post-bankruptcy debt.

A creditor who has attempted to enforce a judgment debt before the bankruptcy can benefit from this:

- in the case of execution against goods, if the goods have either been sold or money paid to the creditor to avoid execution before the date of the bankruptcy order;
- in the case of attachment of earnings orders, if the payment has actually been received by the creditor before the date of the bankruptcy order. Any existing attachment of earnings order should be revoked as the creditor will not be allowed to retain any future payments in any event;
- in the case of charging orders or third-party debt orders, if the order was made final before the date of the bankruptcy order.

If the client has a benefit overpayment, the Secretary of State cannot carry on making deductions from benefit to recover it. The Secretary of State must 'prove' for the debt in the usual way (see p450).[106] Whether or not an overpayment is a bankruptcy debt depends on when the overpayment occurred and when the decision to recover was made.

For the position on rent arrears, see p466, and on secured creditors, see below.

Discharge

Clients made bankrupt are discharged within a maximum period of 12 months, unless the Official Receiver or the trustee in bankruptcy applies to the court and the court is satisfied that the client is failing, or has failed, to comply with her/his obligations under the Insolvency Act 1986 – eg, she has not co-operated with the Official Receiver/trustee. In this case, the court may order the suspension of the 12-month period either for a set time or until a specified condition is fulfilled.[107] According to the Insolvency Service, about 40 per cent of clients get early discharge, the average period being after just over seven months.

If the Official Receiver files a notice at court within the 12-month period stating that no investigation of the client's conduct and affairs is necessary or that such an investigation has been concluded, the client will be discharged when the notice is filed.[108]

The effect of discharge

After discharge, the court issues a certificate to the client on request. There is a £70 fee. The client is automatically released from all her/his debts, except:[109]

- to secured creditors. If the home was sold, but insufficient equity raised to pay the secured lender, this debt is no longer secured, but the unsecured part remains unenforceable provided the mortgage or secured loan was taken out before the bankruptcy even if the home was not sold until after discharge. Any jointly liable person remains liable for the whole debt;
- benefit and tax credit overpayments if the decision to recover was not made until after the date of the bankruptcy order. If both the overpayment and the decision to recover were made before the bankruptcy, the client will be released from the overpayment on discharge unless the overpayment was incurred through fraud;[110]
- council tax for the remainder of the current year if the local authority has not obtained a liability order or served a final demand;[111]
- student loans (see p461);
- fines (but the client will be released from parking and other charges enforced through the Traffic Enforcement Centre);
- maintenance orders and other family court orders, child support and debts from personal injury claims (although the court does have the power to release liability for these in full or in part);
- debts incurred through fraud;

- social fund loans if the bankruptcy petition was presented on or after 19 March 2012;
- debt arising from certain other orders of the criminal court.

Occasionally, the trustee is still working on something (eg, the sale of a home) when discharge is granted. In this case, that asset can still be realised and distributed after discharge despite the fact that the recipients of funds could not otherwise pursue payment. The duties to co-operate with, and to provide information to, the Official Receiver and/or trustee continue after discharge for as long as it is reasonably required.[112] The Insolvency Service has set up regional trustee and liquidator units in order to deal with such long-term matters.

Credit reference agencies record bankruptcies, but it is not necessarily impossible to obtain credit again after discharge.

Annulment

A bankruptcy order can be annulled (cancelled) at any time by the court if the client has either repaid the debts and bankruptcy expenses in full,[113] or has provided full security for them, or if there were insufficient grounds for making the order in the first place.[114] The client then becomes liable once again for all the bankruptcy debts. A bankruptcy order can also be annulled if a creditors' meeting has approved an IVA proposal (see p427 and below).[115]

In cases involving petitions presented on or after 6 April 2010, where the bankruptcy is to be annulled on the grounds of full payment of the debts and expenses (including the trustee's remuneration and expenses), the client can apply to the court for a ruling that the trustee's remuneration charged and/or expenses incurred are excessive and should be disallowed.[116] Such an application must be made no later than five business days before the hearing of the application for annulment.

When deciding whether the debts have been paid or secured, the court can take into account a solicitor's undertaking to pay them out of funds due to be paid to the client.

The court has power to rescind a bankruptcy order if there has been a change of circumstances since the order was made and this will benefit the creditors.[117]

Post-bankruptcy individual voluntary arrangements

Before 1 April 2004 there were little-used provisions in the Insolvency Act 1986 for an undischarged bankrupt to enter into an IVA with her/his creditors. Very few were made, even though they could have resulted in the bankruptcy order being annulled. An insolvency practitioner was required to act as nominee and supervisor.

Fast-track voluntary arrangements

The Official Receiver can act as nominee and supervisor in fast-track, post-bankruptcy voluntary arrangements (FTVAs) in return for a fixed fee (£300 plus 15 per cent of all sums realised).[118] One-half (£857.50) of the Official Receiver's case administration fee in the bankruptcy (£1,715) will be recovered out of the money paid into the FTVA. This procedure is only likely to be relevant to clients who:

- were made bankrupt by a creditor, but do not want to be bankrupt;
- made themselves bankrupt without taking any advice and now realise that it was not the most appropriate option.

The client must complete a proposal form, supplied by the Insolvency Service. The form is submitted to the Official Receiver, together with the £300 fee plus a £15 registration fee. The only debts that can be included in an FTVA are those provable in the bankruptcy (see p450). The Official Receiver will not agree to a proposal unless the creditors will be better off under the FTVA than they would be under the bankruptcy. Any income payments should be offered over five years and the level of payments are subject to annual review. The Official Receiver can extend the FTVA for up to 12 months to enable any missed payments to be paid. Any other money received by the client during the period of the FTVA must be disclosed to the Official Receiver, who may require it to be paid into the arrangement.

Clients are likely to need assistance from an adviser, not only in completing the proposal form, but also about the FTVA in general.

If the Official Receiver does not agree the proposal and the £300 fee was paid by the client, it will be retained by the Official Receiver in the bankruptcy. If it was paid by a third party, it will be returned. There is no creditors' meeting. The Official Receiver sends out the proposal to creditors by post. It is not possible to modify it. If the proposal is accepted, the Official Receiver becomes the supervisor, notifies the Secretary of State and the court, which automatically annuls the bankruptcy order (which is likely to be the main objective of a client proposing an FTVA).

If the FTVA fails (eg, because the client does not maintain the agreed payments), the arrangement will terminate and:

- the Official Receiver can still realise any assets and distribute any funds in her/his possession in accordance with the arrangement;
- creditors are no longer bound by the arrangement and are free to pursue the client as they see fit.

There is no provision for the Official Receiver to apply for a bankruptcy order. FTVAs have not proved a success – to date, very few have been made.

6. **Debt relief orders**

Who can apply for a debt relief order

Debt relief orders (DROs) came into force on 6 April 2009.[119] From this date, clients who are unable to pay their debts and meet the eligibility conditions (see p474) can apply for an order in respect of their 'qualifying debts'.

Qualifying debts

Any secured debt is not a qualifying debt. Otherwise, any debt for an identifiable sum which is not an 'excluded debt' qualifies for a DRO. Excluded debts are:

- fines (including compensation and costs orders) and confiscation orders. According to the Official Receiver, this does not include costs of enforcement – eg, bailiffs' charges;
- child support assessments and maintenance orders;
- student loans;
- from 6 April 2010, damages for personal injury or death arising out of negligence, nuisance or breach of contractual, statutory or other duty
- from 19 March 2012, social fund loans.

Issues with particular types of debt

Business debts

Business debts are 'qualifying debts' for a DRO.

Foreign debts

Debts owed to overseas creditors should be included. Although the client is protected from enforcement action by the creditor in England and Wales, the DRO may not be recognised in other countries, including European Union member states and Scotland (which has its own legal system). The client may therefore face enforcement action in countries outside England and Wales, even after s/he has been released from liability for the debt in England and Wales.

Guarantors

If a client has a DRO, this does not release any guarantor (or any other person liable for the debt, such as a co-debtor) from her/his liability. Possible future liability under a guarantee is not a qualifying debt. There must be an actual liability to pay an amount either immediately or at some certain time in the future. This means that, until the client defaults, the guarantor has no liability. The adviser should check the terms of the guarantee to see at what point the guarantor becomes liable and whether s/he is liable for the outstanding balance owed to the creditor or just the client's missed payments.

Hire purchase agreements

If the agreement is in arrears, the amount due and unpaid must be included in the DRO. This includes the outstanding balance if this is due and payable under the terms of the agreement – eg, if it has been called in by the finance company.

If the agreement is in arrears but the outstanding balance is not due and payable, the arrears must be included in the DRO. The client can decide not to include the outstanding balance, which will not count towards the £15,000 total debt limit (see below). Advisers should look at the terms of the agreement and any notices the client has received from the finance company and check whether the agreement contains any terms under which it could be terminated if the client enters into any formal insolvency procedure.

If there are no arrears, the client can elect not to include the debt in the application and s/he will then remain liable for the remaining payments. The outstanding balance will not count towards the £15,000 total debt limit (see below).

Motor Insurers' Bureau claims

The Official Receiver says that any third-party claim which has either been settled by the Motor Insurers' Bureau or is the subject of a judgment against the client is a liquidated sum. Any compensation for personal injury or death included in the claim is an excluded debt (see p472). Any other types of claim (eg, for loss of earnings) are qualifying debts and should be included in the DRO (subject to the £15,000 total debt limit (see below).

Unenforceable debts

In principle, all unpaid qualifying debts should be included in a DRO application and, unless the client owes money to a 'loan shark' (see below), this is only an issue if the inclusion of the debt would take the client over the £15,000 total debt limit (see below).

The Official Receiver says that if an adviser has satisfied her/himself that a qualifying debt is unenforceable (eg, because it is 'statute-barred' – see p275) or is irredeemably unenforceable under the Consumer Credit Act 1974 (see p96) *and* there is evidence that the debt is unenforceable (eg, a court order or letter from the creditor acknowledging this), the client can choose not to include the debt in the DRO and the debt will not count towards the £15,000 total debt limit.

Note: if the Official Receiver subsequently finds out that a debt was not statute-barred or unenforceable and, as a result, the debts exceeded the £15,000 limit, the DRO will be revoked.

Debts owed to loan sharks (see p241) can be included in a DRO. However, the Official Receiver has said that if the client fears her/his safety, s/he can choose to leave the debt out.

Water charges

The client's water charges to the 31 March following the date of the DRO application are a qualifying debt and so must be included in the DRO. Most water companies have 'insolvency clauses' in their charges schemes whereby, in the event of the customer entering a formal insolvency procedure (such as bankruptcy or a DRO), her/his water charges are apportioned up to the date of the DRO/ bankruptcy order and the customer is then issued with a new bill for the remainder of the charging year to 31 March.

Although the client can choose to pay the new bill, the water companies' view can be challenged both as an attempt to exercise a remedy in respect of the debt and to contract out of the statutory insolvency scheme. Specialist advice should be sought in such cases.[120]

Qualifying conditions

In order to obtain a DRO, the client must be unable to pay her/his debts and must either be domiciled in England and Wales at the date of the application or have been ordinarily resident or carried out business in England and Wales during the previous three years. In addition, on the date the Official Receiver determines the application (the 'determination date') s/he must not:

- be an undischarged bankrupt, or subject to an individual voluntary arrangement (IVA), a bankruptcy restriction order (BRO), a bankruptcy restriction undertaking (BRU) or a debt relief restrictions order (DRRO) or debt relief restrictions undertaking (DRRU);
- have had a DRO made within the previous six years;
- have a bankruptcy petition pending against her/him (but see p443);
- have debts above the prescribed limit (currently £15,000);
- have surplus monthly income above the prescribed limit (currently £50);
- have property valued at above the prescribed limit (£999 for a single domestic motor vehicle and £300 for total other assets).

The Official Receiver can refuse to make a DRO if the client has entered into a transaction at an undervalue (see p467) or given a preference to anyone (see p467) at any time during the two years before the DRO application is made or during the period between the application date and the determination date. **Note:** these are different time limits to those for bankruptcy. **Note also:** the client need not have intended to prefer (although the Official Receiver will consider this when exercising discretion). Payments made to the client's creditors by third parties using their own funds are not considered to be preferences for the purpose of a DRO, neither are payments made by clients out of their surplus income to priority creditors.

The value of property and the amount of surplus income are calculated in accordance with regulations, which permit certain property to be disregarded. The following property is disregarded:

- tools, books and other items of equipment (but not motor vehicles) that are necessary for the client's personal use in her/his employment, business or vocation;
- clothing, bedding, furniture, household equipment and the necessary provisions for satisfying the client's basic domestic needs and those of her/his family;
- a single domestic motor vehicle belonging to the client and worth less than the prescribed amount (currently £1,000); *or*
- a single domestic motor vehicle belonging to the client which has been especially adapted for the client's use because of her/his disability.

Property is valued at its gross, rather than net, realisable (and not replacement) value and so clients who are homeowners do not qualify even if their property has negative equity.

When calculating the client's surplus (or available) income, the Official Receiver must take into account any contribution made by any member of the client's family to the amount necessary for the reasonable domestic needs of the client and her/his family. In practice, the client's financial statement must be completed using common financial statement principles (see p51). A DRO is an individual remedy and so, if the client is a member of a couple, the financial statement must show the client's available income and not that of the couple.[121]

Issues with particular types of expenditure

No payments can be included in the client's essential expenditure for any debt included in the DRO (except a debt subject to a walking possession agreement – see p399).

Rent arrears

Rent arrears are not an allowable expense even if they are payable under a suspended possession order or under an agreement made with the landlord.

Hire purchase payments

Ongoing hire purchase payments are only an allowable expense if:
- the client elects to omit the outstanding balance from the DRO (see p473); *and*
- the goods would be disregarded goods if they belonged to the client - ie, if they are:
  - a single domestic motor vehicle worth less than £1,000 or one that has been specially adapted because the client has a disability; *or*
  - necessary for her/his personal use in connection with her/his employment, business or vocation; *or*
  - necessary for satisfying the basic domestic needs of the client and her/his family.

Issues with particular types of property

Cash

Cash in hand or in a bank account can be disregarded to the extent that it is intended to be used to pay for the essential expenditure listed in the income/expenditure section of the application. Regardless of its original source, cash is property unless it represents arrears of benefits.

Money owed

If the client is owed money, it is regarded as property unless s/he has unsuccessfully attempted to recover the money and these attempts are documented. Arrears of child support are not property for this purpose.

Right to claim compensation

The client's right to claim compensation from another person or organisation is property, but not if that claim is purely personal to the client – eg, for personal injuries. However, if the claim includes a claim for a 'pecuniary loss' (eg, lost wages), the whole claim is regarded as property.[122] Claims for compensation to the Criminal Injuries Compensation Authority are not regarded as property even if pecuniary losses are included.

If the client is pursuing a claim, her/his solicitor should be contacted to confirm whether or not the other party has accepted liability for the claim and how much compensation the client is likely to receive and then specialist advice should be sought about whether the client's right will count as property for DRO purposes. **Note:** if a client becomes entitled to receive compensation during the 12-month DRO moratorium period (see p479) or even afterwards, this could lead to any DRO being revoked. This also applies to rights to action that are not regarded as property at the pre-DRO stage. It might be in client's best interests to resolve any potential or pending compensation claims before deciding whether or not a DRO is the most appropriate option.

This advice also applies to clients who have potential or pending claims for refunds of premiums for mis-sold payment protection insurance in connection with any credit agreements (see p102). The Official Receiver says:

- refunds are not property until the creditor or insurance company accepts the claim and the amount of any refund has been agreed;
- creditors can exercise any contractual right to set off the refund against any debt owed by the client. If this is done before the DRO application is made, it would not be regarded as a preference. If it is done during the 12-month DRO moratorium, it would not be regarded as a remedy in respect of the debt;
- any refund paid to the client during the moratorium period could result in the DRO being revoked.

Advisers should explore with clients whether they have (or have had) payment protection insurance with any credit debts and, if so, whether they think it was mis-sold. Clients should then decide whether or not to pursue a claim. Any funds received before the DRO application could be paid pro rata to qualifying creditors without involving any issue of preference. Clients should be warned that they could be contacted by claims management companies during the DRO moratorium and persuaded to pursue claims that could lead to their DRO being revoked.

Making the application

The application is made to the Official Receiver online through an approved intermediary. It must be made on a prescribed form and contain prescribed information. A fee is payable (currently £90), but there is no fee remission. The fee can be paid by instalments through Payzone or a post office over a six-month period, but clients who are close to the maximum debt ceiling will need to be aware that accruing interest and charges may take them over the limit if they take too long to pay the fee.

In order to reduce the costs and speed up the process, the Official Receiver makes certain assumptions when determining an application, unless s/he has reason to believe otherwise, that:
- the client is unable to pay her/his debts;
- the specified debts are qualifying debts; *and*
- the client satisfies the conditions for a DRO (see p474).

On receipt of an application and confirmation that the fee has been paid, the Official Receiver may:
- defer consideration of the application to enable her/him to make enquiries;
- refuse the application on the grounds that:
  – the client does not meet the criteria; *or*
  – the client has given false information in connection with the application; *or*
  – the application is not on the prescribed form or does not contain the prescribed information; *or*
  – the client has not answered the questions to the Official Receiver's satisfaction;
- make a DRO containing details of the client's qualifying debts.

The Official Receiver also carries out verification checks. The Individual Insolvency Register is checked to see if the client is currently an undischarged bankrupt, subject to an IVA, a bankruptcy restriction order or undertaking or a DRRO or DRRU, or has previously had a DRO. The Official Receiver also carries out a credit reference check through Experian to check the client's identity, residence and total debts. It is good practice for advisers to carry out these checks themselves and to address any issues disclosed before applying for a DRO – eg, if the credit report incorrectly shows that the client's total debts are over £15,000. If it is not possible to get the Experian report amended before submitting the DRO application, the evidence demonstrating the inaccuracy of the report should be submitted to the Official Receiver by email or fax before the application itself with a request that the evidence is taken into account when considering eligibility for the DRO. If this is not done, the DRO will be declined. The Official Receiver tends not to reconsider such decisions, but the client can resubmit the application provided either the report has been amended or the evidence is submitted. This will costs the client a further £90 fee.

After the application is made

Once the application is made, the client must co-operate with the Official Receiver. This includes providing any information that the Official Receiver may require.

If the Official Receiver declines to make the order, s/he must give her/his reasons to the client. The fee is not refunded. The client can apply to the court and ask it to overrule the decision to refuse the order. In practice, the Official Receiver is prepared to reconsider decisions and should be asked to do so before any court application is made.

If the DRO is made, details are registered in the Individual Insolvency Register (and on the client's credit reference file). If the client has reasonable grounds for believing that s/he or any member of her/his family who normally resides with her/him would be at risk of violence if her/his current address or whereabouts was disclosed, this can be flagged up on the application form. The Official Receiver then does not enter details of the client's current address on the Register, pending an application to the court for an order confirming that the client's details should not include her/his address. The application is made on Form 7.1A. The fee is £155 (remission can be applied for).

Any creditor listed in the order may object in writing to the DRO being made or to the inclusion of details of their debt(s) on the prescribed grounds (essentially, that the client is not eligible for the DRO; it is not a valid ground that the creditor does not want to be included) within the prescribed period (28 days after the creditor has been notified of the order). The Official Receiver must consider every objection and may conduct an investigation if s/he considers it appropriate. If the Official Receiver decides to revoke the DRO, s/he must give the client details of the objection and of the grounds and give the client 21 days in which to respond, stating why the DRO should not be revoked. If, nevertheless, the Official Receiver decides to revoke the DRO, s/he can either revoke it with immediate effect or at a future date no more than three months later in order to give the client time to make payment arrangements with her/his creditors. The client can apply to the court to overrule this decision.

Reporting changes in circumstances

Once a DRO is made, the client must inform the Official Receiver as soon as reasonably practicable of any increase in her/his income during the moratorium period, or of any property s/he acquires. The purpose of this is to ensure that the client remains eligible for the DRO and, if s/he is not, the DRO could be revoked. When reporting an increase in income, an up-to-date financial statement should also be provided.

Lump-sum payments of income (eg, arrears of benefits) are treated as income and apportioned over the period to which they relate to calculate the additional monthly income. The adviser should submit an up-to-date financial statement, amending any items of expenditure that have changed since the date of the DRO application and including (or increasing) any other items of essential expenditure that the client was previously unable to afford. If the client's surplus income is found to exceed £50 a month, the client's DRO could be revoked.

The annual uprating of benefits is not a change that needs to be reported. Receipt of winter fuel payments or a maternity grant need to be reported and will not lead to revocation of the DRO.

The effect of a debt relief order

Once the DRO is entered on the Insolvency Register, a moratorium takes effect in respect of the specified debts, and the creditors specified in the order have no remedy in respect of their debts. This means they cannot force the client to pay the debts included in the DRO. They are also prohibited from issuing proceedings to enforce their debts or from presenting a bankruptcy petition without the leave of the court. Any pending court proceedings may be stayed. The moratorium period is one year. During the moratorium, the client will be subject to the same restrictions as in bankruptcy – eg, on obtaining credit (see p452).

Unless the moratorium period is terminated early, at the end of the moratorium the client is discharged from her/his qualifying debts listed in the order (but not from any debts incurred through fraud[123]).

Payments to creditors

With a few exceptions, clients are not allowed to make payments to any creditor included in the DRO but, in appropriate cases, a third party can make the payments out of her/his own income on the client's behalf (see p480). The rights of secured creditors (including if a bailiff has a walking possession agreement) are unaffected and the client may continue to make payments in order to protect the goods.

The client can pay any rent arrears included in the DRO out of her/his surplus income if s/he is at risk of repossession.

Although the client could apply to vary an existing suspended possession order to pay current rent only or ask the court to suspend any post-DRO possession order on payment of current rent only, there is no guarantee that the court will make such an order and specialist housing advice should be sought before an application is made.

If a hire purchase debt is included in a DRO, to protect the goods from repossession by the creditor, a third party can either make the payments from her/his own income on the client's behalf or arrange to transfer the agreement into her/his own name with the consent of the creditor and the client.

Overpayments of benefits or tax credits cannot be recovered by deductions from ongoing benefits or tax credits either during or after the moratorium period (unless the debt was incurred through fraud when recovery by deductions can be resorted to after the end of the moratorium period).[124]

The role of intermediaries

In order to obtain a DRO, a client must apply through an approved intermediary. Intermediaries are authorised by competent authorities (such as Citizens Advice and the Institute of Money Advisers) and are not able to charge fees in connection with an application. The responsibilities of intermediaries include:
* assisting clients to make applications;
* checking that applications have been properly completed;
* sending applications to the Official Receiver.

Intermediaries are under a duty to:
* inform the client that the Official Receiver will carry out verification checks (see p477);
* assist the client to complete the online application if, after having the various debt options explained to her/him, s/he wishes to apply for a DRO. An intermediary must submit an application to the Official Receiver if instructed to do so by the client, even if s/he has been advised that there are other available options, that the application will be rejected and s/he will consequently lose the £90 application fee;
* draw the client's attention to all the qualifying conditions, the effects of a DRO (including the duties and restrictions on the client as well as the moratorium period and discharge from the scheduled debts); *and*
* explain the possible consequences of providing false information or omitting information from a DRO application – eg, the possibility that the DRO could be revoked and the consequences of that in relation to her/his creditors, plus possible criminal and/or civil penalties such as a DRRO (see p482).

An intermediary may also assist the client to:
* identify what information is required to complete an application;
* establish whether or not her/his total debts, income and assets exceed the prescribed amounts; *and*
* ensure the application is fully completed.

Intermediaries are advised to write 'confirmation of advice' letters covering these areas and, if the advice is that the client is not eligible for a DRO, to get the client to sign the letter if s/he insists on going ahead. The use of a standard post-DRO letter reminding clients of their responsibilities and what happens next is also recommended.

The Insolvency Service expects intermediaries to satisfy themselves that applications are accurate and, where possible, to verify the information supplied by clients. If the client insists on submitting the application against the intermediary's advice, the application can indicate this.

To assist intermediaries, the Insolvency Service has provided *Intermediary Guidance Notes* on completing the application, which are regularly updated, together with a regular newsletter. These are available from competent authorities. It is essential that intermediaries familiarise themselves with, and use, these documents when advising clients and preparing applications.

The role of the Official Receiver

The Official Receiver can amend the DRO during the moratorium period to correct errors or omissions. However, s/he is unable to add any debt(s) not specified in the application. This means that, unlike in bankruptcy (where provable debts are covered by the order even if they are not included in the statement of affairs), if any debt which would have been a qualifying debt for DRO purposes is omitted from the application, it cannot be added at a later date. Ultimately, it is the client's responsibility to inform the intermediary of all her/his debts. It is advisable for the client to obtain a copy of her/his credit reference reports (and essential to obtain a report from Experian) before an application is completed to ensure, as far as possible, that all qualifying debts are included.

In addition to being under a duty to report to the Official Receiver certain changes of circumstances and to co-operate with requests for information from the Official Receiver, if the client becomes aware after the DRO is made of any error or omission in the information supplied in support of the application, s/he must inform the Official Receiver as soon as possible.

The DRO notification letter sent to creditors also invites them to inform the Official Receiver of any of the client's conduct or behaviour that may be relevant.

The Official Receiver may revoke the order (but is not required to do so) if:
- information provided by the client is incomplete, inaccurate or misleading;
- the client has failed to co-operate with the Official Receiver or provide the required information;
- a bankruptcy order has been made against the client or s/he has proposed an IVA to her/his creditors;
- the Official Receiver should not have been satisfied that the client met the conditions for making a DRO (see p474);
- at any time after the client applies for the DRO, s/he no longer meets the conditions on the monthly surplus income and/or assets;
- the client dies (in which case, the DRO *must* be revoked).

The Official Receiver can revoke the DRO either with immediate effect or at a specified date no more than three months ahead. S/he must consider whether the client should be given the opportunity to make arrangements with her/his creditors for payment of her/his debts.

A creditor or client who is dissatisfied with the Official Receiver's decision can apply to the court to overrule this decision. In practice, the Official Receiver will reconsider any decision if invited to do so.

Offences and restrictions

As with bankruptcy, it is a criminal offence for the client to:
- make false representations or omissions in connection with a DRO application;
- fail intentionally to co-operate with the Official Receiver or knowingly or recklessly make false representations or omissions in relation to information supplied in connection with a DRO application or after a DRO is made;
- conceal or falsify documents;
- dispose of property fraudulently;
- deal fraudulently with property obtained on credit.

During the moratorium (or while a DRRO or DRRU is in force), the client cannot:
- obtain credit of £500 or more without revealing her/his status to the lender;
- trade in a name different to that in which the DRO was made without revealing the name in which the DRO was made to everyone with whom s/he has business dealings;
- be a director of a limited company without the permission of the court.

Breach of any of these requirements is a criminal offence.

If, during the course of any enquiries, the Official Receiver believes that the client has been dishonest or irresponsible (either before or during the period of the DRO), s/he can apply for a DRRO, or obtain a DRRU from the client, on the same grounds as a BRO/BRU can be applied for in bankruptcy and for the same two- to 15-year period (see p452). The effect of a DRRO/DRRU is to extend the restrictions that applied during the moratorium. Unless the court orders otherwise, the revocation of the DRO does not affect any DRRO/DRRU.[125]

Debt relief orders and bankruptcy

DROs have a lot in common with bankruptcy, but there are significant differences.
- Making a bankruptcy order is a judicial act; making a DRO is an administrative act.
- The cost to the client of applying for a DRO is considerably less than the cost of applying for a bankruptcy order.
- The client can apply for a bankruptcy order on her/his own, but needs the assistance of an intermediary in order to apply for a DRO.

- Creditors are able to object to a DRO being made but cannot object to a bankruptcy order being made on a debtor's petition.
- There is no maximum debt level for a bankruptcy order and no income or asset pre-conditions.
- If the client has entered into a transaction at an undervalue or given a preference within the prescribed period, this may be set aside by the trustee in bankruptcy, but could prevent the client even obtaining a DRO. On the other hand, there is no provision for the Official Receiver to set aside such a transaction if a DRO has been made.
- There is no provision for revoking a bankruptcy order on the grounds that the client's financial circumstances have improved prior to discharge.
- There is no provision for early discharge from a DRO.
- Assets do not vest in the Official Receiver, and so a DRO will not involve any realisation of assets or require clients to make any income payments to their creditors.
- A DRO only releases the client from the debts actually included in the application; bankruptcy releases the client from her/his 'bankruptcy debts' (see p469), whether or not they are listed in the statement of affairs.

Notes

2. **Administration orders**
1 s112 CCA 1984
2 *Preston Borough Council v Riley, The Times,* 19 April 1995, CA; see also *Various v Walker,* Walsall County Council, 3 January 1997 (*Legal Action,* May 1997); *Various v MM, HW & CE,* Birmingham County Council, 23 October 1997 (*Legal Action,* January 1998)
3 r5(6) and (8) CCR 39
4 *Various v MM, HW and CE,* Birmingham County Court, 23 October 1997 (*Legal Action,* January 1998); *A v Fenland District Council,* Kings Lynn County Court, August 1997 (*Adviser* 64 abstracts). The decision to the contrary in *Lane v Liverpool City Council,* Liverpool County Court, 19 May 1997 (*Adviser* 69 abstracts) appears wrongly decided in light of the decision in *Re Green* [1979] 1 All ER 832 that an attachment of earnings order is not an assignment of the debt. See also *Nolan v Stoke on Trent City Council* (*Adviser* 118 abstracts), in which the court held that continuing to receive money under an attachment of earnings order was a 'remedy' and ordered the local authority to refund the sums deducted since making the AO.
5 r14 CCR 39
6 s112(5) CCA 1984

3. **When to use bankruptcy and individual voluntary arrangements**
7   s360 IA 1986
8   s360 IA 1986
9   s1 Company Directors Disqualification Act 1986
10   s390 IA 1986

4. **Individual voluntary arrangements**
11   s262A IA 1986
12   Reg 8(b) Education (Student Loans) (Repayment) (Amendment) Regulations 2010, No.661
13   *CMEC v Beesley* [2010] EWCA Civ 1344 (CA) (*Adviser* 141 abstracts)
14   s256A IA 1986; r5.14A IR
15   s253 IA 1986
16   s252 IA 1986
17   s255 IA 1986
18   s258 IA 1986
19   *Rey v FNCB* [2006] EWHC 1386 (ChD) (*Adviser* 117 abstracts)
20   s260 IA 1986
21   r5.67 IR (as inserted by r298 Insolvency (Amendment) Rules 2010, No.686; see also M Gallagher, 'Bankruptcy etc: address withheld orders', *Adviser* 142
22   s262 IA 1986

5. **Bankruptcy**
23   s265 IA 1986; EU Reg 1346/2000
24   *Re Hancock* [1904] 1 KB 585, CA
25   r6.40A IR, as inserted by r319 Insolvency Amendment Rules 2010, No.686
26   See P Madge, 'Centre of Interest', *Adviser* 93
27   s287(2)b) IA 1986
28   s273 IA 1986
29   s274A IA 1986, as inserted by Sch 20 para 3 Tribunals, Courts and Enforcement Act 2007
30   s268 IA 1986
31   *Re a Debtor, The Times*, 6 March 1995, CA
32   *Skarzynski v Chalford Property Co.* [2001] BPIR 673 (ChD)
33   *Griffin v Wakefield Metropolitan Borough Council*, 24 March 2000, CA (*Adviser* 116 abstracts)
34   If the statutory demand is posted, it is deemed to be served on the second day after posting provided that day is a business day; if not, the next business day after that day (para 13.1.1 Insolvency PD CPR). If the 18-day time limit has passed, it can be extended by the court, provided the petition has not been issued (para 13.4.5 PD CPR).

35   *Bevin v Datum Finance* [2011] EWHC 3542 (ChD) (*Adviser* 151 abstracts)
36   paras 12.3 and 12.4 PD CPR
37   r6.5 IR
38   *Re Ridgeway Motors* [2005] EWCA Civ 92 (CA) (*Adviser* 109 abstracts)
39   For a more detailed discussion on dealing with creditors' petitions, see M Gallagher, 'Demands and Petitions', *Adviser* 111
40   *Lilley v American Express* [2000] BPIR 70 (ChD)
41   s271 IA 1986
42   *Ross and Holmes v HMRC* [2010] EWHC 13 (ChD)
43   r6.29 IR; see also *Harrison v Seggar* [2005] EWHC 411 (ChD)
44   s276 IA 1986
45   s291 IA 1986
46   s371 IA 1986
47   s358 IA 1986
48   s289 IA 1986
49   s293 IA 1986
50   r6.34 IR, which enables the court to suspend registration until further order.
51   s235B IA 1986 as inserted by r417 Insolvency (Amendment) Rules 2010, No.686. See also M Gallagher, 'Bankruptcy etc: address withheld orders', *Adviser* 142
52   s315 IA 1986
53   s307 IA 1986
54   r6.93 IR
55   s285 IA 1986
56   r12.3 IR
57   Sch 6 IA 1986
58   ss350-62 IA 1986 deal with bankruptcy offences.
59   Sch 4A para 4 IA 1986
60   Sch 21 EA 2002 and s389 IA 1986
61   Insolvency Service *Annual Report 2010/11*
62   Sch 4A para 2 IA 1986
63   Art 7 Enterprise Act 2002 (Commencement No.4 and Transitional Provisions and Savings) Order 2003, No.2093
64   rr6.241–6.244 I(A)R
65   Sch 4A paras 7–9 IA 1986
66   Sch 4A para 5 IA 1986
67   rr6.245–6.246 I(A)R
68   s283(2) IA 1986
69   ss308 and 309 IA 1986
70   s284 IA 1986
71   see M Gallagher, 'Bankruptcy: keeping the car', *Adviser* 122
72   s310 IA 1986
73   Chapter 37.1.82 TM

74 See L Charlton, 'Bankruptcy and Income Payments', *Adviser* 150
75 Sch 19 para 7 EA 2002
76 s310A IA 1986
77 *Re Landau (a bankrupt), The Times,* 1 January 1997
78 *Kilvert v Flackett, The Times,* 3 August 1998
79 s11 and Sch 2 Welfare Reform and Pensions Act 1999
80 *Raithatha v Williamson* [2012] EWHC 909 Ch (*Adviser* 151 abstracts)
81 s283A IA 1986
82 s313A IA 1986
83 Art 3 Insolvency Proceedings (Monetary Limits) (Amendment) Order 2004, No.547
84 s335A IA 1986, as inserted by TLATA 1996
85 Guidance states that 'sufficient equity' is £5,000. Exceptionally, where there is negative equity or in cases of disability (including requests based on caring responsibilities), the Official Receiver will consider transferring the client's share of the property back to her/him before the two-year, three-month review. For further information on dealing with the family home, see M Gallagher, 'Bankruptcy and the Family Home', *Adviser* 148
86 *Doodes v Gotham* [2006] EWCA Civ 1080
87 See para 31.35M Insolvency Service TM at http://tinyurl.com/987z25k
88 s335A IA 1986
89 *Ford v Alexander* [2012] EWHC 266 Ch (*Adviser* 151 abstracts)
90 See, for example, *Martin-Sklan v White* [2006] EWHC 3313 (ChD), *Nicholls v Lan* [2006] EWHC 1255 (ChD) (*Adviser* 122 abstracts) and *Brittain v Haghighat* [2009] EWHC 90 (ChD) (*Adviser* 132 abstracts)
91 If the non-bankrupt partner makes payments after the date of the bankruptcy order, any payments of capital will increase her/his share, but not any payments of interest or interest only: see *Byford v Butler* [2003] EWHC 1267 (Chd) (*Adviser* 104 abstracts)
92 *Stack v Dowden* [2007] UKHL 17 (*Adviser* 123 abstracts); *Jones v Kernott* [2011] UKSC 53, SC (*Adviser* 149 Housing abstracts)
93 *Stack v Dowden* [2007] UKHL 17 (*Adviser* 123 abstracts)
94 For a discussion on this issue, see M Allen, 'Whose House is it Anyway', *Quarterly Account* 8, IMA, Spring 2008
95 s285(3)(a) IA 1986
96 *Sharples v Places for People Homes; Godfrey v A2 Dominion Homes,* [2011] EWCA Civ 813, CA (*Adviser* 147 abstracts)
97 See for example, *Cadogan Estates v McMahon* [2001] 1 AC 378, HL
98 *Sharples v Places for People Homes; Godfrey v A2 Dominion Homes*
99 s342 IA 1986
100 ss339 and 341(1) IA 1986
101 *Hill v Haines* [2007] EWCA Civ 1284
102 s340 IA 1986
103 s341 IA 1986
104 s342 IA 1986
105 s285 IA 1986
106 *Secretary of State for Work and Pensions v Payne and Cooper* [2011] UKSC 60 (*Adviser* 149 abstracts)
107 s279 IA 1986
108 s279(2) IA 1986
109 s281 IA 1986
110 *R (Steele) v Birmingham City Council and Secretary of State for Work and Pensions* [2005] EWCA Civ 1824 (*Adviser* 115 abstracts); *Secretary of State for Work and Pensions v Balding* [2007] EWCA Civ 1327
111 *Re Nolton Business Centres Ltd* [1996] BCC 500, ChD (*Adviser* 109 abstracts). If the council has not served a final demand or obtained a liability order, only the arrears at the date of the bankruptcy order are a bankruptcy debt.
112 ss291(5) and 333(3) IA 1986
113 See D Pomeroy, 'Bankruptcy Annulment', *Adviser* 113 and *Halabi v Camden LBC* [2008] WLR(D) 46, in which the court held that the practice of annulling bankruptcy orders on the basis of a solicitor's undertaking to make the required payments was not legal and the annulment order should provide for it not to take effect until the trustee confirmed that all the required payments had actually been made.
114 s282 IA 1986
115 s261(1) IA 1986
116 r6.207A Insolvency (Amendment) Rules 2010, No.686
117 *Fitch v Official Receiver* [1996] 1 WLR 242, CA
118 s264 and Sch 22 Enterprise Act 2002

6. **Debt relief orders**

119 For an overview, see M Gallagher, 'Debt Relief Orders', *Adviser* 132 and, for details of resources available, see C Wilkinson, 'Debt Relief Orders and Resources', *Adviser* 148

120 See P Madge, 'Deep Water', *Adviser* 143

121 For guidance on drawing up financial statements in DROs, see P Madge, 'Consultancy Corner (1)', *Adviser* 137 and P Madge, 'A Single Statement', *Adviser* 147

122 See T Lett and G Skipwith, 'Consultancy Corner', *Adviser* 141

123 For the meaning of fraud in this context, see J Wilson, 'Consultancy Corner (2), *Adviser* 137

124 *Secretary of State for Work and Pensions v Payne and Cooper* [2011] UKSC 60 (*Adviser* 149 abstracts)

125 See C Butler, 'Debt Relief Restriction Orders', *Adviser* 151

Chapter 16

Business debts

This chapter covers:
1. Types of small business (below)
2. Stages of debt advice (p489)

This chapter covers certain types of debt that arise during or after running a business. It also looks at the ways in which the debts or strategies covered elsewhere in this *Handbook* need different consideration when advising a small businessperson.

This chapter must be used in conjunction with the rest of the *Handbook*. Provided the adviser is familiar with the processes of debt advice outlined throughout, this chapter will often be a starting point when dealing with someone who has recently run, or is running, a business.

This chapter is not a guide to business credit or business viability, which are both specialist areas in their own right.

Debt advisers often declare themselves unable to deal with a person's debts while s/he is still running a business, and it will usually be necessary to refer people to other professional specialists – eg, tax or business advisers. Business Debtline, a free telephone helpline for self-employed people and small businesses, can advise clients who are still trading (tel: 0800 197 6026). However, this chapter assumes that some limited involvement with the debts of a trading businessperson is possible. In addition, many ancillary debts (particularly after a person has ceased trading) can be handled by a debt adviser.

1. Types of small business

It is important to understand the type of business a client has because this determines her/his liability.

Sole trader

A person who is self-employed without business partners is described as a sole trader. Typical sole traders might include joiners, electricians and taxi drivers, and also sales people who work on a purely self-employed basis. Sole traders can work either in their own name or using a business name.

Sole traders are legally responsible for their business debts in exactly the same way as they are responsible for their personal debts.

Partnership

A partnership is the relationship that exists when two or more people carry out a business together in order to make a profit. A partnership can be informal – eg, if musicians perform together and share their expenses and payment. No formal written agreement is required for a partnership to exist, but this is useful if disputes or problems arise. Partnership agreements should cover how any profits are to be distributed (which will be equal unless stated otherwise) and how the partnership can be dissolved. In the absence of a partnership agreement, the Partnership Act 1890 will apply.

A partnership is considered a single legal entity. Unless the partnership rules state otherwise, contracts can be entered into by any one of the partners and will make all partners jointly and severally liable. There is one exception to this rule in that each partner always has sole liability for her/his own income tax. A partner is normally only responsible for debts accrued during the period in which s/he was a member of the partnership (although sometimes new partners agree to take responsibility for any partnership debts accrued by their predecessors). Partners continue to be responsible for debts accrued during their partnership, unless they all formally agree otherwise and their creditors agree to a transfer of their liability (perhaps to the remaining partners). However, it is rare for creditors to agree to this. Partners may even be held liable for debts incurred by the partnership after they have left, unless notice was given to the creditors. Outgoing partners should ideally seek legal advice when leaving a partnership to ensure they take all necessary action to avoid this happening.

Partnerships may trade under a particular business name or the names of the partners.

Limited companies

A limited company is a separate legal body that is established to trade and make a profit. It is distinctly separate to its directors, shareholders and managers. In most cases, losses will usually fall to the company rather than the individuals who have set it up, but there are exceptions and advisers should seek specialist advice. A limited company can be public (ie, where the shares can be bought or sold on the stock market) or private (where shares are owned and transferred among a limited number of people allowed by the company's rules). Companies are owned by their shareholders. They are run by their directors who may also be shareholders (in most small companies this tends to be the case), but they need not be. Directors are elected by shareholders and are employees of the company.

Companies are governed by legislation, much of which is administered by Companies House, where records of the company, its directors and accounts are kept. Company legislation is intended to encourage entrepreneurship by protecting unsuccessful business people from the individual consequences of corporate debts. Company law is complex and outside the scope of this *Handbook* – it is vital to advise clients to get specialist advice where appropriate.

Unlike in a partnership, the directors are not personally responsible for the debts of a company unless:

- they have agreed to act as guarantor for some, or all, of the company's debts. This is often the case with bank loans to small companies; *or*
- they have acted fraudulently and the company has been liquidated; *or*
- they have continued to trade while the company was insolvent and the company subsequently goes into insolvent liquidation.

The above list is not exhaustive and there are other reasons for a director's being held personally liable for a company debt. If liability is not clear, the adviser should always refer a client for specialist advice.

Credit arrangements made in the name of a limited company cannot be regulated under the Consumer Credit Act 1974.

Co-operatives and franchises

These are rare and specialist advice should be sought if liability is in doubt.

Limited liability partnerships

Limited liability partnerships were introduced in April 2000. They have some of the characteristics of a partnership and some of a company. The liability of the 'members' (not partners) to contribute to the debts of the partnership is limited to its assets. There is no recourse to personal assets unless a member has been personally negligent.

Queries about debts of a limited liability partnership should be referred to a legal specialist or an accountant with expertise in this area.

2. Stages of debt advice

This section highlights the factors to be taken into account in the debt advice process, as outlined in Chapter 3, when advising someone who either runs, or has run, her/his own business, whether as a sole trader, a partner or a company director.

Create trust

People who have run their own business may pose particular challenges to the debt adviser's trust-building skills. Being self-employed requires self-confidence and independence, which may make it difficult for a person to ask for help. If an employee becomes unable to pay her/his debts after being made redundant, at least s/he can see that the causes are beyond her/his control. However, someone whose indebtedness arises after the collapse of her/his own business may have to face feelings of personal failure in addition to the usual problems associated with serious debt. S/he may also have to consider the position of her/his employees. The client in debt may, therefore, need time to unburden her/himself of these feelings.

The debt adviser should also ensure that as much responsibility as possible for undertaking the tasks necessary to sort things out is carried by the businessperson. If s/he has already run a business (often for many years), s/he will feel both deskilled and disempowered if the debt adviser takes over simply because the business is no longer successful.

List creditors and minimise debts

Minimise debts by ceasing to trade

Note: lay advisers should not attempt to advise a company on ceasing to trade. This is an area that requires specialist advice.

If a client is still running a business but is seriously in debt, s/he should consider whether or not to continue trading. There is clearly no point in doing so if this is just increasing indebtedness and the situation is unlikely to change. In some cases, continuing to trade in this situation could become an offence at a later stage if the business is a limited company. This is a highly complex area and specialist help should be sought from a small business adviser, perhaps via Business Debtline or the business's own accountants. The process may be helped by drawing up a business financial statement for a reasonable period ahead. It is usually recommended that this should be for a period of no longer than three months, unless the business is a seasonal one.

Debt advisers should not attempt a business income and expenditure list for a limited company. In this case, the director of the limited company should obtain monthly drawings figures from its accountant that can be used as income on a personal financial statement.

The business financial statement is similar to the personal financial statement drawn up for the client, except that it deals with the income and outgoings of the business, in addition to the household income and expenditure.

- **All the business's assets.** This should include equipment or machinery with its approximate resale value (which will be different from amounts shown in professionally produced accounts, where the 'book value' is based on the original cost of an item and its theoretical life). The greatest asset of a business may be the work it has in hand and the debts owed to it. These are notoriously difficult to value. The likelihood of a debt owed to the business actually being paid must be assessed and the contractual status of work in hand measured. For instance, a painter and decorator may have agreed in the autumn to paint the exterior of an existing customer's house the following spring. If the customer loses her/his job during the winter, in the (usual) absence of any binding agreement the work may not materialise.

A realistic value for any premises or leases on premises that are owned should be estimated, perhaps by a local estate agent, although note that valuations of business premises are not usually free of charge (as they are for domestic premises). The client's estimate of value may, therefore, have to be sufficient. Business premises are particularly susceptible to a fall in value caused by developments elsewhere in the locality. For instance, the opening of a new supermarket could possibly cause a collapse in the business of a corner shop and potentially a fall in the value of its premises. In this way, a reduction in the market which causes a business to flounder can also reduce the value of its assets, which would otherwise have been its major protection from financial problems. The value of a lease is a complex matter that can only be accurately assessed by a professional. Leased business premises are not valued in the same way as domestic premises. The shorter the period that the lease has left to run, the less likely it is to be of any value. Note that if there is no one prepared to take over the lease, this might represent a liability rather than an asset (because the client/tenant otherwise remains liable for the rent until the lease expires).

Items like cars should always be valued at the price likely to be obtained at auction rather than a price an optimist might expect to get from a private sale. There are various used car price guides available from newsagents (and online) that give a trade price for reasonably modern cars, and these can be used as a guide.

- **Likely income to the business**. If the client is using a business financial statement to help forecast the future viability of the business, it may help to draw up a list of payments that the business might expect to receive based on a conservative, but realistic, assessment. Note the dates when payments can be expected.

- **Expenditure by the business**. A similar, dated list of payments that the business is required to make must be drawn up next. This must include, for example, bank interest and charges, lease or rental charges for both property and equipment, regular bills for fuel and other services (eg, telephones and waste disposal), payments required by suppliers, VAT payments, wages to any staff, and estimated tax and national insurance. Some expenditure can be split between business and personal use – eg, travel costs. Doing this would require the adviser to have some knowledge of how to complete a business financial statement. It may be appropriate to refer the client to a specialist adviser for this.

The excess income over expenditure will give a rough idea of how much is available for the businessperson to pay her/himself in 'drawings'. If there is no foreseeable likelihood of anything being available, this indicates that trading may need to come to an end. However, the client *must* seek expert assistance before taking such a major step, because items like liability for tax or payments due under a lease, which can be very complex, could make the difference between viability and insolvency. A lay adviser will not generally be qualified to make this decision.

If a client is trading as a partner, the decision to cease trading may not be hers/his alone. If one partner wants to cease trading but others do not, s/he should ensure that s/he has formally severed her/his partnership agreement in order to limit her/his liability to those debts that have accrued at that time. S/he should try to gain the agreement of creditors and ex-partners, preferably in writing, that s/he will not be liable for any debts which subsequently come to light, but which relate to the period of her/his membership of the partnership. If a partnership is informal and there is, therefore, no prescribed way of leaving it, legal advice should be sought so that an agreement can be drawn up to terminate it. If possible, this should include an agreement that those remaining in the business will 'indemnify' (ie, agree to pay instead of) those leaving against claims against them for past actions (or bills).

Sometimes, informal business partnerships exist between people who have personal relationships, such as married or cohabiting couples. It is often the custom that either party can enter into contracts on behalf of the partnership (for which both partners become jointly and severely liable). In such a case, it is important that suppliers are informed that the partnership no longer exists if this is desired. This is often the case when a personal relationship ends and thus a couple cease trading together.

Minimise other debts

Business borrowings are often secured by banks against a person's home. Sometimes such a security is not enforceable if the agreement was entered into as a result of undue influence or misrepresentation by the creditor or another client (see p89). This more commonly occurs where a person who is not the borrower is required to agree to a charge being made on a property in which s/he is either a joint owner or has another interest (perhaps because s/he lives with the owner). In one case, it was decided that a charge was not enforceable where a client's wife had signed it but had not been recommended to take separate legal advice and had been told that her husband's business would be closed down by the bank if she did not do so.[1]

If undue influence or other wrongdoing occurred at the time the security was signed, specialist or legal advice should be sought, as the law is complex in this area.

The debts owed by a person who has run a business may include tax debts. See below for ways in which these might be minimised.

List and maximise income

The scope for improving the income of a person running her/his own business is often greater than that of an employee. Specialist business advice can improve profitability, for instance, through better marketing, reducing production costs or overheads, or diversification. The debt adviser should, therefore, refer the client to someone who can help with this.

In addition, there are many grants and other facilities (eg, cheap loans) available to small businesses, which should be investigated. Business Link (tel: 0845 600 9006) can be a good place to start. The payment of tax may use up a substantial proportion of income and, therefore, the need to claim all the relevant individual tax allowances, reliefs and expenses that a business can offset against tax should be noted. Advisers should consider asking the client to consult with an accountant as this can be a complex area.

Self-employed people may be able to claim tax credits. The claim will be assessed on the previous year's net profit. If their profits are likely to be different over the coming period, they can include a projection. Council tax benefit, housing benefit, income-based jobseeker's allowance and income support may also be available, as well as disability benefits. If national insurance (NI) payments are up to date, it may be possible for a self-employed client to claim employment and support allowance if s/he is unable to work because of sickness.

List expenditure

In drawing up a financial statement for a businessperson, the debt adviser will need figures from the business financial statement as detailed above.

However, the personal financial statement is a different document and should be kept separate. The expenditure required by the business (even of a sole trader) should be listed separately from personal or household expenses. Sometimes this is not easy, particularly with a sole trader, where, for instance, a car might be needed for work and to provide family transport. The debt adviser should send the business financial statement along with a household financial statement to creditors.

The adviser should be careful not to double-count items shown as outgoings on the business account (and, therefore, reduce the available income), but which may also be paid as part of the household budget. For instance, if a car is used for both domestic and business purposes it should be apportioned partly to the business account before the drawings from the business are shown and then only the remaining (domestic) portion should be shown on the personal financial statement.

Deal with priority debts

Services

If a business has ceased trading and utility debts on commercial premises are outstanding, the gas and electricity bills may need to be treated as a priority. This is because gas and electricity suppliers have the power to disconnect home premises for non-payment of commercial bills if the supplies are in the same name and provided by the same supplier.[2] If someone traded from home, therefore, gas and electricity arrears will be priority debts. If s/he traded from part of the same building (eg, from a shop above which s/he lives), s/he should separate the suppliers to the two premises before arrears accrue to avoid the risk of disconnection of the domestic premises.

Water companies cannot disconnect a supply to any premises other than those to which the water was supplied and, since 30 June 1999, cannot disconnect the supply to residential premises.[3] It is not entirely clear how this affects mixed-use premises – eg, a flat above a shop. Ofwat has issued guidance stating it believes the disconnection of mixed-use premises could be illegal and reminds customers of their right to take court action if this happens. In practice, companies only disconnect mixed-use premises in rare circumstances.

Water companies have the right to disconnect separate non-domestic premises. The environmental risk of a business being without water could lead to the closure of the business.

Non-domestic rates

Non-domestic rates (business rates) may not be charged on empty premises, but this may vary between local authorities, so advisers may wish to check local discounts. If the ratepayer has a lease on the premises, s/he will be liable for the business rates for as long as her/his tenancy exists, even if the premises are empty. Non-domestic rates are collected and enforced in the same way as council tax, except that, for instance, tools of the trade are not exempt. Advisers should note this means that bailiffs can seize a ratepayer's property from anywhere (including her/his home address) once a liability order has been made. Another difference is that attachment of earnings orders and charging orders are not allowed for business rates, nor are deductions from benefits.

In practice local authorities may remit, or write off, large amounts of unpaid non-domestic rates. They have the power to remit unpaid business rates if there is 'severe hardship' and if it is reasonable to do so. Most local authorities will, in practice, use this power to write off unpaid rates if a business has ceased trading and those responsible for the rates depend on benefits, or if a business could close (with job losses) if rates were to be pursued. Local councillors should be approached to put pressure on officers if this is not done.[4]

Distress for rent

Distress (see p388) is a possibility as soon as any rent is overdue. No court order is necessary. If a client is continuing to trade, it is probably impossible to stop bailiffs from making a peaceful entry to her/his premises (since they are likely to be open to the public). Some landlords regard the seizure of the whole of a business's stock as the easiest way of recovering rent arrears, but this will usually force the client to cease trading. The fact that bailiffs could arrive unannounced, therefore, means that priority must be given to securing an arrangement with a business's landlord if the client wishes to continue trading. The landlord cannot use distress at the trader's home address (unless s/he has taken goods there to avoid them being seized).

Leased premises

Many businesses lease their work premises. Such arrangements are governed by the Landlord and Tenant Act 1954. In some cases, the unexpired part of a business lease can be a valuable asset that can be realised if the client decides to cease trading or trade from other premises. Professional advice should always be sought on the valuation of such leases. If a lease is to be 'assigned' to another person, legal advice should be sought. The permission of the landlord will be required. In certain circumstances, if the new tenant fails to pay her/his rent, the earlier tenant can still be held responsible. In order to protect against this future liability, it is sometimes better to agree with a landlord the surrender of a lease, even if the lease may be saleable for a premium.

A landlord may be prepared to accept the surrender of a lease (which ends the tenant's contractual obligations, such as rent and therefore business rates) if it is clear s/he is unlikely to get any more money from a particular tenant. If s/he wishes to sue for unpaid rent, a landlord must be able to show that s/he has mitigated the loss. If a client has ceased trading and is likely to remain unemployed for some time, and has responsibility for a lease, the debt adviser could approach the landlord directly. S/he should explain that the client is unlikely to meet her/his contractual obligations and, in some cases, landlords will agree to a surrender. It is important, however, for the adviser to ensure that s/he is not dealing with a lease which is of value (perhaps because it forms a small part of a redevelopment site or because the rent has been fixed at a low rate for many future years) before s/he gives it away. Specialist advice should be sought.

Other leases

Many businesses will have equipment like photocopiers, electronic scales or games machines which are held on a lease from owners. The debt adviser should first check whether or not the lease is a regulated agreement under the Consumer Credit Act (see p65). Many lease documents are complex and specialist help may be required.

A business lease will run for a number of years, during which time the owner of the goods (which may be a finance company) simply charges the rent to use them. At the end of the period there is no automatic transfer of the goods to the lessee but, in practice, items are often not taken back by lessors. A lease will usually contain provision for early settlement. However, in many cases, this figure will be almost as high (usually 95 per cent) as continuing to pay rent until the end of the lease period.

Once a lessee is in arrears with the rent, however, the courts can intervene under common law and alter any clause designed to penalise a lessee who is in arrears. Because the courts have this power only when arrears arise, it may be useful to allow business leases to fall into arrears if a client has decided to cease trading.

Business leases are complex and, as the sums of money involved can be substantial, expert advice should always be obtained before reaching any agreement with a lessor about early settlement (trading standards departments may be able to provide such advice).

In calculating the amount that should be paid by the client who is in arrears, the courts will ensure that the lessor receives only the actual amount of money that it has lost as a result of the termination. This should include either the goods or their full value at the time of termination. In addition, lessors should receive the amount that would have been paid in interest less an amount (usually 5 per cent a year) in recognition of the fact that they are receiving this money early. If a lease contains service charges for the leased equipment, the courts may reduce the future service charges that will not be required after the goods are returned.

VAT debts

Value added tax (VAT) is a tax on the increase in the value of most goods or services (some are exempt) between the time they are bought by a business and when they are sold. Businesses with a turnover of less than £77,000 a year (2012/13) do not have to register for VAT. All others have to submit returns at a frequency agreed with HM Revenue and Customs (HMRC) to show the difference between the VAT they pay to other suppliers (input tax) and the VAT they charge their customers (output tax). From April 2012 most businesses are legally required to submit their VAT returns online and pay electronically. If they have collected more VAT than they have paid, they must enclose this with their return and submit it by a due date (usually a month after the end of the relevant quarter). If a return is late, the amount due is increased by an automatic penalty. If a return is not made, HMRC can estimate the amount due and issue its own assessment, which becomes payable immediately.

Local HMRC officers who collect VAT vary greatly in their approach to struggling or failed businesses. In general, they consider themselves as collectors of a tax which has already been paid by a third party to the client and of which the client is only a custodian. While this may bear little relation to the realities of running a small business, it is an attitude that makes them assertive and swift in their recovery process.

Once payment is outstanding, the HMRC officer at a local office will usually use the threat of distress to force payment. This may initially consist of a visit, phone call or letter to state that distress will be used. A formal notice will then warn that immediate payment is required and bailiffs will be used in default.

A distress warrant is then signed by an HMRC officer (recourse to the courts is not necessary).[5]

The warrant will usually be executed by a firm of private bailiffs with an HMRC officer in attendance. HMRC can obtain a warrant to force initial entry, but this is very rare (see Chapter 14). However, most business premises are accessible to the public (including bailiffs) and therefore negotiation is essential. A client who is still trading should always try to give the bailiffs some money and treat this debt with utmost priority. Distress can provoke or escalate the collapse of a business, both by removing necessary stock or equipment and also by reducing confidence in the business.

The adviser who is faced with a client with unpaid VAT should:

- contact HMRC, explain the position and request a short time to organise the client's affairs;
- get an accountant to check the amount claimed (particularly if it is an assessed amount);
- explain the seriousness to the client. Use a small business adviser if necessary to look at the viability of the business – eg, its credit control procedures.

See Chapter 14 for details of how to deal with bailiffs. Advisers should note the detailed list of exempt goods.

Where distress is not appropriate, HMRC will often use bankruptcy as a means of collection (see Chapter 15).

Income tax debts

Self-employed people and businesses are responsible for making a return to HMRC, on which tax bills are based. Under the self-assessment system, taxpayers calculate their own tax and send a payment to accompany their return for a particular year. A small business should always get specialist help in claiming all the allowances against tax to which it may be entitled, and in treating its profits and losses in the most tax-efficient way. The tax bill is based on simple 'three-line accounts' for small businesses with a turnover of less than £30,000 a year. These are required to show:

- total turnover;
- total expenses and costs of purchases;
- net profit (gross profit less all the business expenses).

In addition to the tax due on its profits, a business may also owe tax (and NI contributions) on wages paid to employees.

The actual assessment process is outside the scope of this *Handbook* and the adviser should, where necessary, get specialist help to check the amount of tax demanded. TaxAid is a useful source of help (see Appendix 1).

If the client fails to file a tax return, HMRC will make its own 'determination' of how much tax is due and this is enforceable immediately. It can only be overturned by filing a return. HMRC can impose penalties for late filing of returns and/or non-payment of tax. If there is no tax to pay when the return is filed, the penalty will not be reduced and will therefore still be payable by the client. S/he can appeal the penalty on the grounds that s/he had a 'reasonable excuse' for the failure. It is still important to file returns, however late, as HMRC has a policy that time to pay arrangments will not be accepted until returns are up to date.

If a tax bill is unpaid, HMRC may:

- use a debt collection agency (see p29);
- use distress – ie, seize goods without a court order (see p392);
- use the magistrates' court (see p360);
- use the county court and follow the judgment with a third-party debt order, attachment of earnings order, information order, charging order or instalment order (see p298);
- seek a bankruptcy order (see p437).

As with VAT, HMRC is likely to be particularly strict if the money owed includes tax already collected by a business from employees and not passed on to HMRC. It should be noted that HMRC is not averse to starting bankruptcy proceedings, even if this is unlikely to lead to a payment being made.

A summons to the magistrates' court is usually used to collect unpaid tax of up to £2,000 if the debt is less than 12 months old. The client will be summonsed to appear at a hearing at which the magistrates will make an order that s/he pays the tax. The client should attend the hearing with a financial statement and ask to pay the tax by instalments. The courts are not able to consider arguments that the tax is not owed or the wrong amount is being claimed. If the client still does not pay, the magistrates may summons her/him to a committal hearing. At this, the client will need to show that s/he has not 'wilfully refused' or 'culpably neglected' to pay this tax (see p383). However, HMRC rarely uses this method of enforcement.

If the county court is used, the client can ask for an instalment order in the usual way.

HMRC is entitled to claim interest (3 per cent a year) on any unpaid tax until payment, and enforces this even after a county court judgment.[6] Once a judgment has been made, the possibility of an administration order exists if the debts are below £5,000 (see p419).

It is possible to negotiate with HMRC. Although it is generally easier to negotiate after the client has ceased trading, as with all negotiation, the outcome will depend on the circumstances of each individual case. If the taxpayer has been caused problems by maladministration, the Parliamentary and Health Service Ombudsman can be contacted via her/his local MP. There is also an adjudicator at HMRC, who may intervene in cases of particular hardship or unreasonableness, and appeals can be made to HMRC in cases where the wrong amount of tax is being charged.

Draw up a personal financial statement

Creating a personal financial statement for a client who is running her/his own business is no different from that of an employed person, except that expenses may need apportioning, as explained above, and the amount of her/his income may be less predictable. Both these things should be made clear on the personal financial statement. The figure for earnings ('drawings') net of tax and NI contributions should be taken from the business financial statement produced to help decide the viability of the business. It is important that the business budget is used to extract a figure for drawings, rather than asking a client how much s/he draws from the business. The client's drawings may well exceed profits. If this is the case, specialist advice should be sought. If the client is a director of a limited company, the accountant should be approached to obtain a monthly drawings figure, which can be used as income on the personal financial statement.

Choose a strategy for non-priority debts

Bankruptcy and individual voluntary arrangements are discussed in Chapter 15. Bankruptcy may often be the most satisfactory way out of the large debts that can arise after the failure of a business. Bankruptcy, in itself, does not necessarily mean the business must cease trading, particularly if there are no assets of significant value. However, it should be remembered that although discharge from bankruptcy may occur after one year, a person's credit rating will be affected for considerably longer and, if s/he wishes to run a business that will require credit in the future, bankruptcy can be an obstacle to this. Someone with an otherwise viable business but serious debts may be better advised to consider an individual voluntary arrangement.

Notes

2. Stages of debt advice
1 *Barclays Bank plc v O'Brien* [1993] 4 All ER 417, HL; see also *Royal Bank of Scotland v Etridge* (No.2) [2001] UKHL 44; [2002] HLR 4
2 Sch 6 para 1(6) EA 1989; Sch 2B para 7(1) and (3) GA 1986
3 s1 and Sch 1 Water Industry Act 1999
4 s49 LGFA 1988
5 Sch 11 para 5(4) Valued Added Tax Act 1994
6 TMA 1970

Chapter 17

Student debt

This chapter covers:
1. Financial support for students: introduction (below)
2. Stages of debt advice (p505)
3. Types of debt (p511)
4. Minimising debts (p522)
5. Maximising income (p522)
6. Dealing with priority debts (p542)

1. Financial support for students: introduction

Student finance for higher education has changed dramatically in the last 25 years. The availability and rates of student loans have steadily increased since their introduction in 1990 to help pay for the living costs of full-time undergraduates, and now include the substantial tuition fees of both full-time and part-time students. Consequently, the vast majority of students now graduate with some level of debt – the average student loan debt is likely exceed £40,000 by graduation.

The system has become increasingly complex, with four major revisions to the system since 1990. The last students funded under the 'mandatory grants' system available between 1962 and 1997 graduated in 2008, but advisers may still encounter a very small number of students funded under the system first introduced in 1998/99, as well as those funded under the two systems introduced in 2006/07 and 2012/13.

There are now three types of student loans: 'mortgage-style loans' available to mandatory grant recipients, and two income-contingent loan schemes, the most recent of which became available to new students in England and Wales from 2012/13.

There are different arrangements in England and Wales (and also in Scotland and Northern Ireland). Although both English and Welsh universities and colleges can, under certain conditions, charge new, full-time students up to £9,000 per year in 2012/13, Welsh-domiciled students receive an additional fee grant as well as different rates of student loans and grants

Students who meet the eligibility criteria can apply for a student loan for their fees of up to the rate charged. This is non-means tested. Welsh-domiciled students who started their course between 1 September 2006 and 31 August 2010 and who are studying in Wales (or who have started or will start their course from 1 September 2012 and who are studying anywhere in the UK) can also apply for a non-means-tested grant to cover part of their fees. This grant is not available to students who started their courses between 1 September 2010 and 31 August 2012.

Students in England and Wales can apply for a means-tested maintenance grant (or, if they are eligible to claim certain social security benefits, a special support grant). They can also apply for a student loan for living costs and may be eligible for a bursary from the institution and discretionary help from the Access to Learning Fund (England) or Financial Contingency Fund (Wales).

The few remaining students eligible for support under the pre-2006 system can also apply for a loan to cover any fee liability. No eligible undergraduate students, therefore, should now have to pay their fees before or during their course – although this option is still available.

Part-time undergraduate students have a separate system of funding. For those whose courses started before the 2012/13 academic year, fees are unregulated and vary widely. They can apply for grants to help with the cost of fees, but this may not cover the full amount. There is also a small course costs grant and, in Wales, extra allowances for students with children.

This system continues in Wales in 2012/13. In England, however, there have been major changes in 2012/13. Part-time fees will be fixed as a proportion of the full-time equivalent fees, and student loans are available to cover the cost of these. As the fee cap for full-time students will rise to £9,000, and universities see cuts to their teaching grants, this will nevertheless mean a significant increase in part-time fee levels. The small course costs grant will not be available to these students.

Students on certain healthcare-related courses such as nursing, midwifery, occupational therapy and the later years of medicine and dentistry courses are funded by the NHS under a separate scheme. They do not pay tuition fees.

With the exception of teacher training students on Postgraduate Certificate of Education courses and social work students on taught masters programmes, postgraduate students have very limited access to statutory government funds. Similarly, students who wish to study for a second (or subsequent) undergraduate course will find their access to funding severely restricted.

English-domiciled students applying for student finance must apply to a national body called Student Finance England (SFE), which is part of the Student Loans Company (SLC). Students in Wales apply to their local authority. Those on healthcare-related courses usually need to apply for support from the NHS in England or Wales and also to SFE.

Advising students

When advising students and ex-students about debt, the adviser may need to adopt some different strategies and should be aware that students expect to owe money prior to, and on completion of, their studies. Most creditors (banks and the SLC) have structured repayment programmes for 'normal' student debt once the student starts earning. Such indebtedness should not adversely affect the student's creditworthiness (eg, for obtaining a mortgage), although any repayments made (or due to be made) will be listed as outgoings in affordability calculations in future credit applications.

Most of this chapter follows the structure of the rest of this *Handbook*. Issues are discussed only if the position of the students differs from that of other clients. If an issue is not covered in this section, advisers should, therefore, refer to the main text.

Definitions

Home student. This chapter covers only home students in higher education living in England and Wales. A 'home student' is defined as:[1]

> a person settled in the UK within the meaning of the Immigration Act 1971 and the person is ordinarily resident in England or Wales on the first day of the first academic year of the course and has been ordinarily resident in the UK, the Channel Islands or the Isle of Man throughout the three-year period preceding the first day of the course. The residence must not have been wholly or mainly for the purpose of receiving full-time education.

'Ordinary residence' was defined in the case of *Shah and others v Barnet and others* in 1982 as: 'habitual and normal residence in the United Kingdom from choice or settled purpose throughout the prescribed period apart from temporary or occasional absences'.[2]

In addition, a student may be regarded as a home student if s/he, or a certain member of her/his family:

- has refugee status;
- is a European Union citizen with right of permanent residence, and who has been resident in the UK for three years or more;
- is a European Economic Area (EEA) or Swiss national who has taken up employment in the UK and was ordinarily resident in the EEA or Switzerland for three years immediately prior to starting the course;
- is the child of a Turkish national who has taken up employment in the UK and was ordinarily resident in the EEA, Switzerland or Turkey for three years immediately prior to starting the course;
- has been granted humanitarian protection or discretionary leave to remain in the UK.

All the above are still required to be ordinarily resident in England and Wales to be treated as a home student. Note that residency rules are complex, and a student may be eligible for home student fee rates but still be ineligible for student support. Local authorities or SFE determine whether a student is ordinarily resident in England or Wales, as this will affect what support is available. The financial position of international students is not discussed in this chapter. Advisers should contact UKCISA (see Appendix 1).

'Fixed-fee system' students Students referred to in this chapter as ''fixed-fee system' students are those who fall under the 1998–2005 funding system, as long as they began a designated course before 1 September 2006 and continued on that course after 31 August 2006. This includes students who moved directly on to an 'end-on' course after completing a different undergraduate course under the old regulations, and 'gap year' students – ie, those who were offered a place by 1 August 2005 and began their course before 1 September 2007.
It also includes those who transferred to a similar course at the same higher education (HE) institution before 1 July 2008.

'Old system' students Students referred to in this chapter as 'old system' students are those who fall under the 2006–2011 funding system who do not fall into one of the exceptions above, began a designated course between 1 September 2006 and 31 August 2012 and continue on that course after that latter date. This includes students who moved directly on to an 'end-on' course after completing a different undergraduate course under the old regulations, but *not* 'gap year' students as no provision was made to allow students to maintain entitlement to old system funding if they deferred entry from the 2011/12 academic year.

'New system' students are those students who start their course on or after 1 September 2012 and do not meet the 'end-on' course exception outlined above.

Full-time students. A student is eligible for support for a full-time course as long as the course is 'designated'. It must be a full-time course, a sandwich course or a part-time course for the initial training of teachers, at least one year in duration and be wholly provided by a publicly funded educational institution.

A **'designated course'** includes:[3]
– a first degree;
– an HE diploma;
– a BTEC higher national certificate or higher national diploma;
– initial teacher training;
– a course for the further training of teachers or youth and community workers;
– a course to prepare for certain professional examinations of a standard higher than 'A' levels or Scottish Highers, BTEC higher national certificate/higher national diploma, where a first degree is not required for entry;
– a course not higher than a first degree, but higher than those described in the above bullet point – eg, a foundation degree.

Part-time students. A student is a part-time student if the course has been designated as part time. There is no more precise definition, and usually a course is deemed part time if it does not meet the criteria to be classed as full time.

2. **Stages of debt advice**

The stages of debt advice described in Chapter 3 need to be applied when working with students, as with anyone else. There are, however, some additional issues to be considered at each stage. These are highlighted below.

Create trust

Most higher/further education institutions and students' unions/guilds/ associations offer money advice services. The majority of these are experienced in dealing with student debt and have student-specific information resources. Many students may, therefore, prefer to use this service. There can, however, be issues of impartiality, independence, confidentiality and trust arising when advisers work for the educational institution. This situation is further complicated when the institution is the creditor (see p518). It may not always be appropriate or ethical for an adviser employed by the institution to assist a student in this position. Even when the adviser works for the students' union/guild/association, the student may need reassurance that the service is confidential and/or impartial.

In order to create a position of trust with a student in need of debt advice, it is important for the adviser to be aware of the different causes of student debt and not to make a judgement about the position in which a client finds her/himself. Very often the client will not seek help for causes of problems, but their effects.

There are many reasons why a student may be in debt. In addition to the causes of indebtedness that apply to the general population, this can be as a result of:

- above-average course costs;
- local authority or Student Finance England (SFE) assessments not being a true reflection of parental disposable income;
- debts incurred before the client became a student;
- aggressive marketing towards the student group;
- tuition fees; *or*
- coping with an income paid in irregular instalments.

Some students can cope with increased levels of debt, accepting that a certain level of indebtedness is inevitable and part of the student experience. For others, it can have a more negative impact. The adviser could be faced with a student who may be extremely anxious, ashamed, desperate, worried or confused. The stage at which the student presents may also have an effect on her/his emotional state, as many wait until the situation can no longer be dealt with without external assistance before seeking help. The impact of all of this can be that the student may be experiencing poor health, mental ill health, relationship difficulties and difficulties with her/his course – eg, low marks, missed deadlines and exam failures. Some students may feel forced to withdraw from their course completely.

List creditors and minimise debts

When noting the status of the debt on the creditor list, it is important to consider the sanctions connected with non-payment in order to determine whether the debt should be recorded as a priority or non-priority. In addition to the criteria referred to in Chapter 8 (if non-payment would give the creditor the right to deprive the client of her/his home, liberty, essential goods and services or place in the community, that debt will have priority), the adviser needs to consider the sanctions available to and used by the institution if it is the creditor. Outstanding tuition fees can be listed as a priority debt. For some ex-students, outstanding tuition fees can remain a priority debt as the majority of institutions withhold the award until the debt is cleared. Students entering some professions (eg, teaching) need their degree conferring, or their degree certificate before they can take up employment. Prioritisation needs to be discussed with the client.

The adviser needs to be aware of the threats posed to the client by the recovery action, and whether they are appropriate – p520 details what sanctions should be imposed on the different types of debt s/he may have with the institution. Advisers need to be aware when negotiating with creditors that some types of student debt will become repayable in the future, and any offers of repayment need to reflect this.

List income

Student loans (for living costs) and some elements of grants are taken into account as income for benefit purposes. It is, therefore, important that loans are listed as such. Most creditors will otherwise suggest that they are used as a means of making repayments. Without them, the financial statement will show a hugely unrealistic deficit. However, advisers need to explain that this source of income is a loan used only for living expenses, that interest is accruing, and that repayment will be required at a future date.

Disabled students can receive non-means-tested additional allowances in their loan/grant. These are to help the student with the extra costs of being on a course of study; they are not to help with living expenses. It is not necessary to include them as income as they will have been already allocated.

Students with dependants may also be entitled to additional allowances. These should be included, but need to be balanced by the expenditure incurred – eg, childcare costs.

If a grant or any other additional allowance is paid, it must be listed as income.

Parental contributions, if paid regularly, should be listed as income. These are intended to make up for any shortfall in the grant/loan. Although financial statements from the SFE or the relevant local authority in Wales may refer to a 'family contribution' payment (or similar), this cannot be enforced and, in reality, many students do not receive any prescribed parental contribution.

Period to be used

Students, institutions and advisers tend to think of students' income within the framework of the instalment periods for which it is paid – ie, termly, quarterly or annually. Creditors are more likely to understand income expressed in weekly or monthly periods. Breaking down income into these periods is also a helpful exercise for students, as the irregular payment periods often reduce their budgeting ability or financial control.

If a grant is paid to a client, the adviser will need to establish the period for which it is meant to cover. If extra weeks' allowances are paid, the payment period should include the total number of weeks.

For final year students, this income will cease to be taken into account once the course has finished.

How income from a student loan is listed depends on the client's personal circumstances. It can be spread over 52 weeks if it is likely to be her/his main source of income over this period, or if s/he has an alternative income during the summer vacation, it can be listed as spread over the length of the course. The adviser must consider the financial benefit to the client when deciding how to show this income to creditors. The client should be made aware of the distinction between the income calculation for benefit purposes and that shown on a financial statement or part of a budget plan.

List expenditure

In addition to the items outlined in Chapter 3, students will have additional expenditure, which must be included and which may be required by the course. At this stage, the adviser can help the client identify areas where it may be possible to reduce expenditure – eg, by claiming help with health costs. This area is where the adviser can be of most use to a client, as many students will have little or no experience of budgeting and financial planning. This process should also highlight how debts have arisen and, therefore, help prevent further financial difficulty. The adviser should also help the client deal with irregular income, and both regular and irregular expenditure.

Cost	Period to be attributed	Ways of reducing cost
Tuition fees (full-time students)	For most students, these do not need listing here as repayment is deferred through a loan. The loan for tuition fees is only available to the student to pay the fees and not as general income.	Ensure that liability is correctly attributed. Ensure no (further) assistance is available. Students can apply for a loan to cover any fee liability. In Wales, eligible Welsh-domiciled students who started their courses before 1 September 2010 or after 1 September 2012 can apply for a non-means-tested grant to cover some of their fees and the adviser should ensure they have done so.
Tuition fees (part-time students)	For students in England who start a course on or after 1 September 2012, and whose intensity of study is at least 25 per cent (ie, the course takes no longer than four times the length of the equivalent full-time course), loans are available as for full-time students. Otherwise, if a source of income is paid directly to the institution and is available solely to pay tuition fees, it can be ignored in any financial statement (along with the corresponding tuition fee liability). If the income is paid to the student (and s/he then pays her/his own fees), apportion over the length of the course and include the corresponding amount of tuition fees.	Ensure the client has applied for fee support from the local authority or SFE. Check to see if any extra help can be provided from the Access to Learning Fund or from an employer.

Tuition fees (postgraduate/'second-degree' students)	If a source of income is paid directly to the institution and is available solely to pay tuition fees, it can be ignored in any financial statement (along with the corresponding tuition fee liability). If the income is paid to the student (and s/he then pays her/his own fees), apportion over the length of the course and include the corresponding amount of tuition fees.	Ensure that liability is correctly attributed. Ensure the client has been categorised correctly by the university or college and that no (further) assistance is available.
Books/reading packs	This needs to mirror the period of time over which the student loan/main source of income is attributed – over the length of the course (43 weeks). Advisers should, through experience, be able to attribute a realistic figure for particular courses within the institution. If this figure cannot be quantified, the adviser can use the annually set figure for books included in the student loan.	Suggest using the university library; sharing resources with students on the same course; second-hand book stalls or schemes; and local libraries. Students in the year above can advise on books that are absolutely necessary. Increasingly, core texts are available online.
Stationery	To be attributed over the length of the course.	Printing facilities should be provided by the institution. Cost needs to be measured against individual printing costs.
Materials – eg, fabrics, photographic equipment, costs related to field trips	As above.	As above. Bulk purchasing may reduce costs if possible.

Room insurance	Over the rental period, which can differ from the length of the course; *or* For the life of the policy/payment plan.	Advisers should check if this is necessary, as some policies held by parents can cover items temporarily removed from the family home. The amount of cover can be too little or too much depending on the student's personal effects.
Transport costs	Any transport costs the student may have may vary depending on time of year, personal circumstances and whether s/he has any dependants. If these costs cannot be attributed, use the annually set figure for travel in the loan, plus the cost of at least four journeys home per year. Some students on particular courses may have higher travel costs than others (eg, nursing students and those on teacher training courses), in which case this should be made clear.	Some students, usually those on professional courses related to health or social care, may be able to claim travel expenses related to placements, and advisers should check to ensure that they have done so. Season tickets are often available, as are discounted student travel cards.
Telephone/broadband	As above.	Almost all students own a mobile phone and will have broadband in their homes. Some creditors may need convincing that these are a necessity rather than a luxury, although most now do not question this. However, the student will need guidance on how to ensure costs are kept to a minimum – eg, on the type of contract, comparison of the different packages provided by providers, and alternatives such as using university-provided internet services.

Advisers will often have local knowledge (eg, shops and services that offer National Union of Students (NUS)-related discounts) that may help students who are new to the area reduce their expenditure. There is an NUS discount card called 'NUS extra', costing £12, which attracts nationally agreed discounts and can incorporate the International Student Identity Card for an additional £2.99 fee.

If the student and adviser decide to use a period of 43 weeks to list the main student income and expenditure, it is usually necessary to draw up a new financial statement showing revised figures for the remaining nine weeks, the long summer vacation. This statement does not need to include study-related costs and related funding.

3. **Types of debt**

This section lists some types of debt specific to students (and ex-students) and which are not included in Chapter 6.

Bank overdrafts

For a definition and the legal position, see Chapter 6.

Special features

Student overdrafts have certain features that are different to other clients. Most high street banks offer full-time undergraduate, and some postgraduate, students special interest-free overdrafts up to a set limit. This facility is only available on student accounts. Packages will, therefore, vary – eg, students in different academic years may have different overdraft limits. If the overdraft limit is exceeded, interest should be charged on the excess only. In these circumstances, the adviser should inform the bank that the student is seeking assistance with her/his finances. The adviser should try to negotiate an increase in the limit at least to reflect the new overdrawn figure. If the bank refuses, challenge the basis on which it is unauthorised – ie, if cheques have been honoured or funds have been released, this would have been authorised. Some banks have specialised student account managers.

Chapter 6 outlines the strategy for opening a new account in order to prevent an existing bank overdraft swallowing income. In the short term, advisers could also advise on the use of 'first right of appropriation'. This is when the client states how a deposit made into an overdrawn account should be used. The student should inform the bank, preferably in writing, what specific amounts are to be paid and to whom. The bank must carry out these directions from her/him. However, the bank may still charge for the use of the overdraft. This facility should only be used on a short-term basis and the adviser should discuss the overdraft with the client in terms of debt advice and maximising income.

Students may not be allowed an interest-free facility on a new account until they can show a closing balance on an existing account. If a student is unable to open an account (eg, because of low credit scoring) the adviser could contact the Money Advice Service (www.moneyadviceservice.org.uk) for information about basic bank accounts where basic facilities are available, even if overdrafts are not.

Most banks allow students terms that continue for a period after they have graduated. The length of time varies between banks and can often be extended by negotiation. This is preferable and advisers should negotiate this option rather than agreeing to overdrawn accounts being 'converted' into graduate loans, as it will be more beneficial to the student. Most banks offer preferential graduate terms – eg, free currency exchange and lower mortgage rates for limited periods.

Graduate loans

Personal loans are available to students after they graduate to cover costs related to graduation and starting work (eg, clothing, relocation costs) and to consolidate student debts. They are only usually authorised if the bank has evidence that the student has secured employment.

The legal position

Graduate loans are regulated by the Consumer Credit Act 1974 (see Chapter 4).

Special features

Graduate loans attract a preferential interest rate. Some banks offer a deferred period of repayment.

Professional studies loans

Professional studies loans are personal loans offered by certain high street banks to students undertaking certain professional qualifications, usually at a postgraduate level. As with all other personal loans, they are offered at a fixed or variable rate of interest. They have become extremely scarce in recent years as banks have tightened their lending policies.

The legal position

Like other personal loans, professional studies loans are regulated under the Consumer Credit Act 1974 (see Chapter 4).

Special features

The terms of these loans vary between the different banks and according to the type and duration of the student's course. The most significant common feature of these loans is deferred repayment. Interest usually accrues during this period. Some loans allow for repayment to be deferred until after the course has ended. In other cases, repayment begins part-way through the course.

Professional and career development loans

Professional and career development loans are similar to professional studies loans, with the added feature of having some government backing. For the legal position and definition, see the section on personal loans on p125.

Special features

Repayment is deferred during the course and for up to one month afterwards. During the deferment period, the Skills Funding Agency pays the interest on the loan. There may be circumstances in which the period of deferment can be extended when the loan becomes payable – eg, if the client is receiving an out-of-work benefit. The terms and conditions of the loan should be checked.

Mortgage-style or fixed-term student loans (pre-1998 students)

Full-time students who began their course between September 1990 and September 1998 (or who were treated as a continuing student when they began their course in the 1998/99 academic year) were eligible for mortgage-style or fixed-term loans which differ in several ways to the income-contingent loans, which have been available to new students since 1998 (see p514).

The Secretary of State for Business, Innovation and Skills (or the relevant devolved administration if the student was funded in Scotland, Wales or Northern Ireland) is the creditor; the Student Loans Company (SLC) acts as the agent. They are repaid over five or seven years, depending on how many loans were taken out.

Note: some mortgage-style loans were sold to private investors under the previous Labour government. This does not affect the terms and conditions of repayment, but it may mean some clients are repaying loans to a different agent (Honours Student Loans), which can be contacted at www.honoursstudentloans.co.uk.

Repayment can be deferred if the client's gross income is below 85 per cent of the national average earnings. Only income is taken into account in this calculation; no account is taken of the client's expenditure and financial commitments. An application for deferral should be made when repayment is due to start and applications for deferral must be made each year. Proof of income should be submitted with this – usually payslips for the preceding three months or a letter from an employer will be sufficient. Interest continues to be charged during any period of deferment.

Given this, it is important that the SLC is aware of any changes of address to prevent default action. Mortgage-style loans cannot be included in a bankruptcy petition or, as part of an individual voluntary arrangement (IVA).

The legal position

Agreements are regulated under the Consumer Credit Act 1974 (see p65).

Special features

Interest is at the rate of inflation. Repayment is not required until the April after the student has finished her/his course, either because s/he has completed or abandoned it. Repayments are monthly and are usually by direct debit from the client's bank account. The student will have signed an agreement to repay by direct debit at the time of borrowing.

Repayments are expected to be made over five years (seven years for those who borrowed for five years or more). If more than one loan is outstanding, they are repaid concurrently. The amount owed (including interest) is totalled and divided by the number of months (either 60 or 84) to arrive at monthly repayment. This is reviewed annually.

Provided repayments are not in arrears, any amount still due is cancelled after 25 years, or when the client reaches the age of 50 (whichever is earlier). If s/he last borrowed at the age of 40 or over, the outstanding amount is cancelled when s/he reaches the age of 60. They are also cancelled if the client dies, or is permanently incapacitated from work through disability.

As with other agreements regulated under the Consumer Credit Act, repayment of student loans is enforceable through the county court and the SLC has been quick to take court action against large numbers of borrowers. Problems may arise if a student has closed the bank account from which the SLC expects direct debit repayments and has not made alternative arrangements, or if the account is so overdrawn that the bank will not honour the direct debit arrangement.

Although information about student loan repayments is not passed to credit reference agencies, the government makes an exception for a small number of 'serial defaulters' of mortgage-style loans where other means of debt recovery have been unsuccessful. Details of arrears may, therefore, appear on a client's credit record.

Advisers should:
- check the client's gross income (and assist her/him to apply for deferment where appropriate);
- prioritise the debt accordingly.

Income-contingent student loans

Since 1998, income-contingent loans have been available to help higher education (HE) students meet their living costs. From September 2006, they are also available for tuition fees (see p519).

Scheme 1 loans are or were available to students who started their course between 1 September 1998 and 31 August 2012 (see p515). Scheme 2 loans have been available for new students since 1 September 2012 (see p516). There are different repayment and interest arrangements for each scheme.

Scheme 1 loans

The Department for Business, Innovation and Skills or, in Wales, the Welsh Assembly set the rates of loans for living costs. The amount depends on the year of study, type of course, where the student lives and household income. For students on courses which started after 1 September 2006, it may also depend on the amount of maintenance grant received. Subject to the maximum rate set, the student decides what level of loan is needed and applies to SFE or, in Wales, her/his local authority.

The tuition fee set by the institution for the student's course determines the maximum rate of a loan for fees. Under current arrangements this will not, in any case, exceed £3,465 in the 2012/13 academic year, and £3,465 plus inflation in later years. Again, within these limits, the student decides what level of loan is needed and applies to her/his local authority or SFE.

The legal position

The Secretary of State for Business, Innovation and Skills or, in Wales, the Welsh Assembly is the creditor; the SLC is the agent and repayments are made through HM Revenue and Customs (HMRC). The loan is exempt from the Consumer Credit Act,[4] although in practice it is treated as a 'low-cost loan' under the Act's provisions.

Special features

Interest is normally at the rate of inflation. However, as with low-cost loans, interest cannot be applied at a rate higher than 1 per cent above the highest base rate of any one of several nominated banks.

Repayment is made at 9 per cent of earnings over the threshold amount (currently £15,575 a year, and due to rise by the Retail Prices Index (RPI) each year until 2016/17). This may be different if the student lives overseas (see note on p516).

As with mortgage-style loans, repayment does not begin until the April after the student finishes or otherwise leaves the course. Clients paying tax through the Pay As You Earn (PAYE) system will have repayments deducted by their employer. As they are calculated over income payment periods, not on yearly income, some employees can overpay if their earnings are erratic. If at the end of the year this is the case, the client can obtain a refund. Self-employed clients will have their repayment calculated through the self-assessment system.

Clients living overseas must contact the SLC directly to arrange repayment. Living overseas for a certain period of time does not cancel liability for student loan repayment.

Tax credits do not count as income for SLC calculations. Extra repayments can be made, but it is unlikely that a client in debt will be able to consider this.

If a client started her/his course before September 2006, any outstanding income-contingent loan will be cancelled when s/he reaches 65. If s/he started the course on or after 1 September 2006, any outstanding loan will be 'written off' after 25 years (35 years for clients funded by the Student Awards Agency for Scotland). Like mortgage-style loans, they are also cancelled if the client dies or is permanently incapacitated from work through disability (see below).

Since 1 September 2004, it has not been possible to include income-contingent student loans in a bankruptcy petition and, since November 2009, they cannot be included in an IVA.

Failure to repay or update the SLC about changes can result in penalty charges being added to the outstanding loan amount. The interest rate can triple if the client goes overseas and fails to inform the SLC that s/he is no longer in the UK tax system, or fails to provide information about living overseas.

Note: clients living overseas may make payments at a different threshold amount, depending on the cost of living in that country. The SLC can advise on this.

Disabled clients

Any disability benefits received do not count towards the threshold income (even if they are taxable). The regulations state that if the Secretary of State is satisfied that, because of her/his disability, an ex-student is permanently unfit for work and s/he is receiving a disability-related benefit, liability for the loan is cancelled. There is no further guidance on how this is done and no definition of 'permanently unfit for work'. If the client complies with other benefit definitions of permanently unfit, advisers can use this when negotiating to have the debt cancelled. See CPAG's *Welfare Benefits and Tax Credits Handbook* for further information.

Checklist for action

- Check the client's income, taking into account the fact that repayments are being deducted by the employer or through self-assessment.
- Note on the financial statement that repayments will automatically be deducted and will, therefore, not be available income from the date repayments start.

Scheme 2 loans

There are a number of different rules on student loans for students who start their course on or after 1 September 2012.

The Department for Business, Innovation and Skills or, in Wales, the Welsh Assembly sets the rates of loans for living costs in the same way as for Scheme 1 loans, with different amounts depending on the year of study, type of course, and so on, as outlined above.

The tuition fee set by the institution for the student's course determines the maximum rate of a loan for fees. Under current arrangements, this will not, in any case, exceed £9,000 in the 2012/13 academic year. Within these limits, the student decides what level of loan is needed and applies to SFE or her/his local authority.

The legal position

The Secretary of State for Business, Innovation and Skills or, in Wales, the Welsh Assembly is the creditor; the SLC is the agent and repayments are made through HMRC. The loan is exempt from the Consumer Credit Act.[5]

Special features

Interest for Scheme 2 loans is variable. For full-time students, interest is charged at the rate of inflation (as measured by the RPI,) plus 3 per cent. From the April following graduation or the student otherwise leaving the course, the interest rate will vary depending on her/his income: below an annual income of £21,000 it is set at RPI; above £41,000 a year at RPI plus 3 per cent; and on a sliding scale between RPI and RPI plus 3 per cent on incomes between these two figures.

For part-time students, repayment starts either from the April following graduation, or from the date the student leaves the course, or after her/his fourth year of study, whichever comes first and regardless of how many years of study remain. Interest rates will then vary according to income, as for full-time students.

Repayment is made at 9 per cent of earnings over the threshold amount. However, no repayments will be taken before April 2016 at the earliest, even if the student completes or leaves her/his course before this date. If the student stops studying during this period, interest will reduce to RPI until April 2016. Voluntary repayments can be made during this time, but the adviser should consider whether this would financially benefit the client, particularly if s/he has other, more pressing, debts.

The thresholds may be different if the client lives overseas. The SLC can advise on this.

As with Scheme 1, clients paying tax through the PAYE system will have repayments deducted by their employers. As they are calculated over income payment periods, not on yearly income, some clients can overpay if their earnings are erratic. If, at the end of the year, this is the case, the client can obtain a refund. Self-employed clients have their repayment calculated through the self-assessment system.

Clients living overseas must contact the SLC directly to arrange repayment. Living overseas for a certain period of time does not cancel their liability to repay their student loan.

Tax credits do not count as income for SLC calculations. Extra repayments can be made, but it is unlikely that a client in debt will be able to consider this.

Outstanding income-contingent loans will be 'written off' after 30 years. Like mortgage-style loans, they are also cancelled if the client dies or is permanently incapacitated from work through disability (see p516).

Loans cannot be included in bankruptcy petitions or IVAs. Failure to repay or update the SLC about changes can result in penalty charges being added to the outstanding loan amount.

Checklist for action

- Check the client's income, taking into account the fact that repayments are being deducted by her/his employer or through self-assessment.
- Note on the financial statement that repayments will automatically be deducted and will, therefore, not be available income from the date repayments start.

Debts to the institution

Students are often in debt to their institutions for a wide variety of items – eg, library fines, hardship loans made by the institution, rent, tuition fees, accommodation and disciplinary fines. University regulations govern the circumstances in which fines may be imposed and fees are due. Liability should always be checked and appeal mechanisms used, where appropriate.

The main sources of students' indebtedness to their institutions are discussed below.

Accommodation charges

Most institutions provide accommodation for their students. Charges are made for the rent and services provided. Services usually include items such as fuel and cleaning. These charges may be called 'residence' or 'accommodation' fees.

The legal position

Rent is payable under the tenancy agreement or licence. The terms of these agreements may be in an individual's contract and/or in university regulations.

Special features

The accommodation provided directly by institutions to students varies. Some of this is in halls of residence, some in houses/flats in the locality owned by the university or leased to it by private landlords.

The length of tenancies may vary, but are rarely longer than 52 weeks, especially in halls of residence. Many tenancies will be for the academic year only – excluding the summer vacation. Some tenancies exclude all vacations. The usual practice is to charge three instalments. There may be a financial penalty for late payment. As in the case of tuition fees, students in financial difficulties may be able to negotiate delayed payments or a more flexible instalment arrangement.

The accommodation charge due for a student's current home is a priority debt. While institutions are often reluctant to evict or take court action against their own students, they do try and enforce repayment using other means – eg, by refusing to allow the student to return to university-managed accommodation in subsequent years. They may also refuse to allow the student to progress to the next year of study, or graduate from the course. This could be challenged (see p520).

Fines and other charges

Certain costs incurred by students arise from fines or charges. If an appeal procedure exists to resolve disputes about liability or amounts, a client should be encouraged to use it. Advisers may be able to assist by providing supporting information or representation. In some cases, institutions will take into account extenuating circumstances and may waive or reduce certain fines or charges.

The consequences of non-payment differ between institutions and according to the circumstances of each student. For instance, if a debt for tuition fees could legally prevent the student from graduating, it could also prevent her/him progressing to a course of further study or employment and, therefore, needs to be treated as a priority debt. However, if withholding qualifications would not impede the student's progress, the debt could be treated as non-priority. A student may consider any outstanding debts to an institution if s/he wishes to continue studying to be a priority. Advisers need to discuss this carefully with her/him, especially if the client has mistaken notions of the consequences of non-payment.

Tuition fees

Almost all students are liable for tuition fees, and student loans are available to pay these (see p525).

The maximum rate is equal to the fee rate for which they are liable. Students who begin their studies and then subsequently leave may be given a date by which they can do so without having to pay anything towards their fees. This date is fixed by the university.

For students who started courses before 1 September 2012 (or later than this date in Wales), the fee loan will match the full cost of the fee should the university or college wish to charge for a whole year, although there is some scope for negotiation to allow the fee to be divided over the academic year minus holidays, with the student only paying for the period s/he has actually attended. If a student has to pay fees after transferring from one university to another, the two institutions must negotiate with each other about the transfer of the payment. In theory, both could charge for a full year. However, guidance from Universities UK and GuildHE, the umbrella bodies for HE institutions in the UK, advises institutions not to charge these students fees outside their range of support. Although this is not binding, it is normally adhered to.

For full-time students who started their course on or after 1 September 2012 in England, the entitlement to fee loan support will be staggered over the year, in a pattern of 25:25:50. In other words, in term 1 the student can draw 25 per cent of her/his fee loan, a further 25 per cent in term two and the remaining 50 per cent in term three. Although universities and colleges can charge a full year's fees for only partial study, the Universities UK/GuildHE guidance is expected to remain in place and the Department for Business, Innovation and Skills strongly encourages the HE sector only to charge fees for which a student can access the requisite fee loan to cover.

There may still be scope to negotiate further if, for example, the client has completed only a few weeks of a term.

Recovery of debts to the institution

Methods of recovery vary between institutions. Many do not allow a student to continue into the next year of study if debts are outstanding. If the debt is for tuition fees, this procedure is probably legitimate. However, some institutions do not permit continuation where other charges are outstanding – eg, accommodation fees and library fines. This practice should be challenged. Similarly, if debts remain at the end of the student's course, most institutions refuse to give the student a certificate of qualification or allow her/him to collect her/his results. The Office of Fair Trading (OFT) has issued *Unfair Contract Terms Bulletins* (see www.oft.gov.uk) containing examples of institutions that have amended contractual terms. Its view is that institutions cannot threaten, or carry out, sanctions against students if they are able to withhold services provided in another, different contract. This means that universities cannot withhold academic services (eg, tuition, use of library facilities and publication of results) if debts remain outstanding for accommodation services, or if other breaches have occurred. Trading standards officers can, however, choose not to enforce the OFT guidance, in which case students will have to take action themselves.

Institutions now offer a wide range of financial incentives to students, including bursaries and scholarships. These will only be of significance as debts if it is claimed they have been awarded in error. If the client has provided incorrect information, it is possible the bursary may be recoverable and the adviser should prioritise accordingly. In all other cases, advisers should argue that the bursary awarded to the student informed her/his choice of institution, repayment could cause hardship and, if applicable, that repayment would not be possible for at least the remaining length of the course.

If a student is awarded a bursary and s/he has outstanding debts to the institution, the institution may choose to use the bursary to pay all or part of the debt rather than pay this money to the student. For clients who are 'old system' students there may be an element of mandatory bursary which must be paid directly to the student. Advisers should argue that other bursaries should be paid in such a way that the student can use them for their specified purpose, rather than simply paying off debts to the institution.

Institutions may make threats that are illegal in order to ensure payment. These practices put students under considerable pressure to pay outstanding charges and may constitute harassment (see p29). However, most students are anxious not to jeopardise their future and are reluctant to take any action other than to clear their debts in full.

Legislation, such as the Freedom of Information Act 2000 and the Data Protection Act 1998, may force institutions to re-evaluate these practices and give the adviser more options to explore when assisting clients who owe debts to the institutions. Likewise, rulings from the Office of the Independent Adjudicator may force institutions to reconsider such practices.

Advisers directly employed by the institution need to be aware of the potential conflict of interest when advising a student with debts to the same institution.

Overpaid grants for living costs

Students are required to repay some, or all, of their SFE/local authority grant for living costs if it has either been overpaid or if they leave their course (both temporarily or permanently) during a period for which a grant instalment has been paid in advance. In this latter case, the amount of grant for the weeks after the student has left her/his course will be calculated and repayment of only this amount is required.

The legal position

SFE and local authorities have a statutory duty to recover overpaid grants. The legislation requires them to do so during the period of the award where possible – ie, before the student completes her/his course. If a student receives more than one type of grant, an overpayment of one grant can be recovered from ongoing payments of any other grant. They have discretionary powers not to pursue recovery, but the circumstances in which they would do this are not defined.

Special features

Approaches may vary depending on individual circumstances but normally the relevant authority attempts to recover the amount in full by deducting it from the next instalment.

Advisers need to negotiate with SFE or the local authority in the usual way, arriving at an affordable level of repayment. However, if a student continues to receive a grant, SFE or the local authority is in a powerful position, as it holds the instrument of recovery in its own hands – the next instalment. Advisers should be aware that, while it is SFE or the local authority's statutory duty to recover during the period of the award, reductions of each future grant instalment are permissible within the legislation. If SFE or the local authority remains unwilling to extend the repayment period, evidence of hardship needs to be presented to higher levels of SFE management or perhaps to elected members of the authority concerned. Regulations state that the recovery action to be taken should be appropriate to the circumstances and so the adviser should ensure that SFE or the local authority is fully aware of the student's situation.

Overpaid income-contingent student loans

See p514 for definition and legal position.

Special features

This type of student loan is not regulated by the Consumer Credit Act. If the loan has been made properly (ie, the student is eligible but the amount is classed as an overpayment), it can be recovered from the amount of loan for which the student is eligible for the following academic year. If the student has completed her/his studies, recovery should be through the normal repayment process, although advisers may need to negotiate with the SLC for this to happen.

4. Minimising debts

See also Chapter 5.

Reducing council tax bills

Advisers must examine the client's liability for council tax. Any dwelling solely occupied by full-time students is exempt for council tax purposes.

A student is not jointly or severally liable to pay council tax if s/he lives in a house/dwelling in which s/he has an equal legal interest with others.

For non-students or part-time students who are liable, the bill may be reduced because full-time students attract a 'status discount'. Thus, if there is only one non-student or part-time student living in the property with one or more full-time students, a 25 per cent discount should be awarded.

Institutions may provide local authorities with lists of full-time students attending courses and, where requested, will issue a letter to a student establishing her/his status. Some institutions charge for this letter. Advisers should argue that this is not appropriate. Students should inform council tax offices of their status in order to obtain exemption from, or reduction of, council tax.

See CPAG's *Council Tax Handbook* for more information.

5. Maximising income

Information on student finance is now widely available online or in CPAG's *Student Support and Benefits Handbook*.

There have been a number of changes to student funding arrangements (see p501) and the information required to maximise income and check eligibility is complex. What follows is a guide to the likely sources of income for students in higher education (HE). Legislation for support and fees differs between England, Scotland, Wales and Northern Ireland.

Students seeking debt advice may be doing so as a result of not being able to manage irregular payments effectively when they have regular expenditure. Therefore, great care must be taken to establish future budgeting and financial management to prevent the situation worsening in future payment periods.

It may be appropriate for advisers to deal directly with some creditors and, in certain circumstances, to request that they overpay to assist the client with budgeting. Creditors need a detailed explanation of the student's funding situation to appreciate fully the request being made and to dispel some myths or misinformation they may have about money available to HE students.

Where the available help is means tested, the test will normally be carried out on the student's parental income, unless the student has independent status – ie:

- s/he is 25 or over at the start of the academic year for which s/he is applying; *or*
- s/he married or entered a civil partnership before the start of the academic year for which s/he is applying; *or*
- s/he has supported her/himself for at least three years before the start of the first year of the course; *or*
- s/he has no living parents; *or*
- s/he has care of at least one child on the first day of the academic year for which s/he is applying; *or*
- s/he is a part-time student.

If a student has independent status, her/his parents' (or step-parents') income will not be taken into account when Student Finance England (SFE) or the local authority or assesses her/his entitlement to means-tested support.

If none of the above applies, the student could still be treated as an independent student, if:

- her/his parents cannot be traced; *or*
- her/his parents live abroad and trying to trace them may put them in danger; *or*
- s/he is permanently estranged from her/his parents; *or*
- s/he is in the care of a local authority or voluntary organisation under a custodianship order on her/his 18th birthday, or immediately before the course, if s/he was not 18 when it began.

Income could be maximised by the client or adviser approaching SFE or the local authority and detailing her/his particular circumstances.

If a student is married or in a civil partnership, and is not separated, her/his spouse's or civil partner's income is included in the means test. Students aged 25 or over who started their course in September 2000 or later and who are living with a cohabiting partner of the opposite sex, and students aged 25 or over who started their course in September 2005 or later and live with a cohabiting partner of the same or opposite sex, also have their partner's income included.

In general, student support is available for the ordinary length of the course, plus a year, less any years of previously supported HE study. Additional years of support may be available if there were compelling personal reasons why the student did not complete a year or previous course. Applications are made to SFE or the local authority usually in a letter, and ideally written by the adviser. This would state the compelling personal reasons and their detrimental impact on the client's studies.

With the exception of supplementary grants (see p527), further support is not generally available for students who have used up their entitlement to funding. However, income-contingent loans for maintenance continue to be available to students who do not already have an honours degree and to graduate students on courses leading to a professional qualification such as medical doctor, veterinary doctor, dentist or architect. These rules should be highlighted to students thinking of withdrawing or transferring their course.

Bursaries

Students may be eligible for bursaries or scholarships from their university or college.

In England, 'old system' students must receive mandatory bursaries of 10 per cent of the maximum fee rate if the student is charged this and receives a full special support grant or maintenance grant (household income must be £18,360 or less for students who started in the 2006/07 or 2007/08 academic years; £25,000 for those who started in 2008/09 or later). Bursaries are paid separately from the standard student finance package.

Most institutions also offer other support to all students in addition to any mandatory bursaries.

There is no set upper limit and institutions can decide on the amounts they offer. Some are several thousand pounds or more, although high rates are very rare. Mandatory bursaries must be paid in cash, but other bursaries can be paid in cash or by other means – eg, by providing accommodation or course-related equipment. The criteria for these other bursaries vary: some bursaries and scholarships are awarded on the basis of income/geographical location only; others have an application process and some are awarded on the basis of, for example, academic or sporting achievement or potential. All institutions should publicise their bursaries or scholarships on their websites and the Universities and Colleges Admissions Service (UCAS) has a section on its website on each institution's funding opportunities (see Appendix 1).

Any HE institution bursary should not be treated as income for benefit purposes, provided the student is in receipt of the special support grant (see p530) and the bursary is not for living costs. The institution should provide the student with a letter confirming her/his bursary is for course-related costs.

In Wales, there is a separate national bursary scheme and details are available from Student Finance Wales.

Students on health-related courses may be eligible for separate bursaries from the NHS (see p532).

National scholarship programme

As part of the new system of student finance in England, the government is supporting a 'national scholarship programme' of additional support for some low-income students. In general, students will be aware of their entitlement before they start their course. In most cases, support will be in the form of 'fee waivers' that reduce fee liability as opposed to cash bursaries, but up to £1,000 can be given in cash.

Help with tuition fees

Fixed-fee system

The small number of remaining 'fixed-fee system' students can apply for non-repayable grants to meet the cost of their tuition fees. These are assessed on the student's income and that of her/his family (if s/he does not qualify for independent status). SFE or the local authority assess eligibility (full-time students and those on sandwich courses or a part-time courses of initial teacher training are eligible) and income. The client may be liable for all, part or none of the tuition fee. Advisers need to check the assessment has been done correctly. If a client has had a change of circumstances or the family income has decreased, s/he may be able to request that SFE or the local authority reassess the level of help given.

In 2012/13, full-time students who depend financially on their parents will not have to pay fees if their parents' residual income is less than £23,660 a year (£23,680 in Wales). If income is between £23,660 and £36,037 (£23,680 and £35,407 in Wales), they pay part of the fees. If it is £36,037 (£35,408 in Wales) or more they pay the full fee.

The maximum fee currently payable is £1,380. Since September 2006 no student has had to pay fees upfront; 'fixed-fee system' students who have to make a contribution can apply for a tuition fee loan.

Old/new system

Full-time students in England and Wales who started their courses on or after 1 September 2006 can apply for a tuition fee loan to cover the cost of their fees.

In addition, full-time 'old system' Welsh-domiciled students who started their course between 1 September 2006 and 31 August 2010 who are studying at Welsh institutions can apply for a grant to help pay their fees. This grant is not means tested, and is worth up to £2,085 a year. It is paid at whatever level will bring the fee charged to no more than £1,380. Students can apply for a loan to cover this remaining amount.

Full-time, 'new system' Welsh-domiciled students who start their course on or after 1 September 2012 can also apply for a fee grant, although in this case the grant is payable regardless of where in the UK the student chooses to study. Again, this is not means tested and can be worth up to £5,535 – reducing whatever fee is charged to no more than £3,465, with a loan being available to cover this remaining amount.

The Welsh fees grant is not available for Welsh-domiciled students starting their course between 1 September 2010 and 31 August 2012.

Part-time, English-domiciled students who started their courses before 1 September 2012 and Welsh-domiciled part-time students may be eligible for a means-tested grant to cover all or part of their fees.

Part-time, English-domiciled students who start their course on or after 1 September 2012 and who are studying at least 25 per cent intensity (ie, the course takes no longer than four times the length of the equivalent full-time course) can apply for a student loan to cover the cost of their fees in the same way as full-time students.

There are no age limits for help with tuition fees or for tuition fee loans. Payment is made directly to the institution by SFE or the local authority. If tuition fee help is received under the old system, it does not have to be repaid. Tuition fee loans, however, are repayable. The arrangements are the same as for income-contingent student loans (see below).

Income-contingent student loans

Students are required to meet the personal eligibility requirements – ie, where the student is living, previous attendance, funding and age.[6]

In order to support themselves, students are able to get support from loans, grants (for certain groups of students), bursaries and hardship funds.

Full-time, sandwich and part-time initial teacher training students who are aged up to 60 are eligible for a student loan for maintenance. Previous study affects their eligibility. Students who already hold an honours degree are not eligible for a maintenance loan unless their course carries an exemption. The Department for Business, Innovation, and Skills and the Welsh Assembly set the maximum loan available. The amount a student can borrow varies enormously and depends on the year of study, type of course, where the student is living and household income. Within these limits, the student decides what level of loan is needed and applies to SFE or her/his local authority. The amount can be changed later, up to the maximum set by SFE or the local authority – students apply for this on a loan adjustment form.

The loan is partially means tested on household income – ie, the student's income and that of her/his parents, spouse, civil partner or cohabiting partner, as appropriate. The amount a student can borrow can also be reduced if the student receives a maintenance grant, but not if s/he receives a special support grant.

Long courses loans

Students can apply for a set amount for each additional week they have to attend the course on top of the basic academic year. The amount of the long courses loan (previously, the extra weeks' allowance) depends on whether the student is living in the parental home, away from home or in London. The loans are made in addition to the student loan and may be means tested. They have to be repaid in the same way.

Studying abroad

Additional support is available to students who spend time studying abroad for at least eight weeks as part of a UK-based course (the period abroad does not have to be a compulsory part of the course). Students studying abroad for at least eight consecutive weeks who have to take out medical insurance also get help to cover these costs. Help is means tested and paid by SFE or the local authority. Insurance grants are equal to the policy. Travel costs are only paid if SFE or the local authority considers them reasonable. In any case, the first £303 of any claim will not be paid.

Change in circumstances

If a student has a change in circumstances during the year, s/he should inform SFE or the local authority in order to have the level of loan s/he can take out reassessed.

Supplementary grants

Certain 'supplementary' grants are available for full-time students with additional support requirements. Most are not available to part-time students in England, except the disabled students' allowance. All these grants are available to part-time Welsh-domiciled students, on a pro rata basis, assuming their course takes no longer than twice the time of the equivalent full-time course to complete.

Except for disabled students' allowance, supplementary grants are also means tested, both as part of the main means test for support and on the income of any dependants the student has.

Disabled students' allowance

Part-time students, full-time students, distance learners (including Open University students), postgraduate students and undergraduate students who have a disability which makes it more expensive for them to take their course may be entitled to a number of extra allowances for equipment, non-medical personal support, miscellaneous expenses and travel. Part-time students must complete the course in no more than twice the time it takes to complete the full-time equivalent course. Postgraduate students in receipt of awards from research councils (see p540) and those in receipt of NHS bursaries (see p532) are not eligible for a disabled students' allowance from SFE or the local authority, but receive very similar grants from those funders. The allowance is a non-repayable grant. It is not affected by the previous study rules and is not means tested. It is paid by SFE or the local authority, usually directly to any provider of approved specialist equipment or personal support.

Adult dependants' grant

Full-time students who have a spouse, partner or adult member of the family who is financially dependent on them may be eligible for a means-tested, non-repayable adult dependants' grant of up to £2,642 a year (£2,647 in Wales) in 2012/13, paid by SFE or the local authority in three instalments with the maintenance loan.

Childcare grant

Full-time students with independent status and with dependent children in registered, approved childcare can get a childcare grant. Payments are up to a maximum of 85 per cent of £175 a week for one child and £300 a week for two (£190 a week and £323 a week in Wales). This grant is non-repayable and is paid in three instalments by SFE or the local authority. It is not taken into account when calculating entitlement to means-tested benefits and tax credits.

Students cannot get this grant if they (or their partner) receive the childcare element of working tax credit.

Note that the grant is calculated using estimates of costs and this can often result in overpayments as the student may not inform SFE or the local authority that s/he is using less childcare than expected. Such overpayments are usually reclaimed in the same way as other overpaid grants (see p521). The student may need to negotiate with SFE or the local authority if the overpayment will cause hardship if taken in one lump sum from future payments.

Parents' learning allowance

Means-tested help with course-related costs can be paid to students with dependent children.

The maximum grant available is £1,508 a year. It is paid by SFE or the local authority in three instalments and is non-repayable. This grant is not taken into account when calculating entitlement to means-tested benefits and tax credits.

Other grants

Higher education grant

Full-time, 'fixed-fee system', sandwich, and part-time initial teacher training students who started their course in September 2004 or after may be entitled to this means-tested grant. The amount available is up to £1,000. Those with a family income of £16,750 (£16,765 in Wales) or less get the full amount. A student will get part of the amount if her/his income is between £16,750 and £22,735 (£16,765 and £22,750 in Wales), and none if income is above £22,735 (£22,750 in

Wales). The grant is paid in three instalments by SFE or the local authority. A student will not qualify for the grant in respect of an academic year unless s/he qualifies for fee support for that year (except if s/he is a student overseas on Erasmus or on a postgraduate flexible initial teacher training course).

Maintenance grant

The maintenance grant has been available for 'new system' full-time students in England since September 2006. It is means tested on the student's household income.

The means-test thresholds depend on the year in which the student started her/his course. In 2012/13, for those who started in 2006/07 or 2007/08, the full £2,984 grant is payable if household income is below £18,360. A partial grant is payable if income is between £18,361 and £39,333. If a student started in the 2008/09 academic year, the full amount is payable if household income is £25,000 or below, with a partial amount payable if income is up to £60,032. If a student started in the 2009/10, 2010/11 or 2011/12 academic year or later, these two thresholds are £25,000 and £50,020 respectively.

The maintenance grant for 'new system' students starting on or after 1 September 2012 is slightly higher at £3,250. The thresholds are £25,000 and £42,600.

If there is a change in the student's or family circumstances that affects income, SFE or the local authority should be notified so that the amount of the award can be recalculated. Students receiving the maintenance grant can also apply for the student loan for maintenance. However, loan entitlement will be reduced in lieu of the grant. The grants are paid in three instalments and are non-repayable.

Students in Wales apply for an Assembly learning grant (see below) and those able to receive means-tested benefits should apply for the special support grant (see p530).

Welsh Assembly learning grant

Students who normally live in Wales and who started their course in 2006/07 or later may be entitled to additional support from the Welsh Assembly. The Welsh Assembly learning grant provides financial support to help meet general living costs. There are two separate sets of arrangements depending on when the student started her/his course.

In 2010/11, those who started their course between 1 September 2006 and 31 August 2010, and whose household income is £18,370 or less, receive the maximum £2,906 grant. If their household income is between £18,371 and £39,329 they receive a partial grant. No grant is payable if household income is over £39,330.

Students who began their course in 2010/11 or in 2012/13 or later can receive up to £5,600. The maximum rate is available to students whose household income is £18,370 or less, with a partial grant for those with household incomes between

£18,371 and £50,020. Students who started in 2011/12 can receive a higher rate of £5,000 within the same income thresholds.

Under all arrangements, the student loan may be reduced in lieu of the grant. The grant is non-repayable and is paid in three instalments, one at the start of each term. Those able to receive means-tested benefits should apply for the special support grant (see below).

Note: 'fixed-fee system' students may also be entitled to extra help from the Welsh Assembly (also, confusingly, known as a Welsh Assembly learning grant). The maximum payable is £1,500 and it is means tested.

Special support grant

A means-tested special support grant is available for 'new system' students who started their course on or after 1 September 2006 and who are eligible for means-tested benefits (such as income support, housing benefit and council tax benefit).[7] The grant is intended to cover additional course costs such as books, equipment, travel and childcare. The amount of the grant, the income assessment arrangements and the payment arrangements are the same as the maintenance grant (see p529) or, for Welsh-domiciled students, the Welsh Assembly learning grant (see p529).

However, unlike the maintenance and Assembly learning grants, the amount of special support grant paid does not affect the amount of maintenance loan to which a student may be entitled. Students receiving the special support grant are not eligible for the maintenance grant. The special support grant is non-repayable. It is not taken into account when calculating entitlement to means-tested benefits and tax credits.

Travel allowances

Students who attend an institution outside the UK for at least eight weeks (whether obligatory or optional) and have taken out medical insurance, and those who must attend a placement in the UK away from their main college as part of a medical or dental course, are entitled to help with their travelling expenses, above the normal allowance paid in their loan. Students studying abroad can also claim help to cover the cost of medical insurance. The travel grant will not cover the first £303 of the expenses.

Disabled students may also qualify for help with travel in the disabled students' allowance (see p527).

Care leavers

Care leavers in England should be entitled to a one-off £2,000 bursary for entering higher education from their local authority.[8] Otherwise, local authorities remain responsible for providing support in all vacations to their care leavers. The adviser should therefore check to ensure all support is being provided.

In addition, most HE institutions now offer extra bursaries for care leavers as part of the Buttle UK quality mark for care leavers in higher education, and therefore should be approached to determine what funding is available.

Social work courses

Bursaries are available for students on social work degree or diploma courses in England, paid by the NHS Business Services Authority. Students are required to meet the residency eligibility criteria. To be eligible, students must be on an approved course, must not already hold an HE social work qualification and must not be receiving support from a social care employer. Undergraduates in England who are not subject to variable fees ('old system') will receive an allowance of £3,475 (in London) or £3,075 (elsewhere). Students' tuition fees are paid directly to the institution by 1 December. Students who are subject to variable fees ('new system' students) receive higher amounts (£4,975 in London; £4,575 elsewhere), as these include an element towards their tuition fees. These bursaries are non-means tested and paid in three instalments. Undergraduate students can also access the standard HE student support package from their local authority.

Undergraduate students who normally live in Wales and who are studying for a social work degree are entitled to the standard package of support for undergraduates. They are also eligible for assistance with their tuition fees and from the Care Council for Wales. Both new and existing students are eligible for this.

In addition, students receive a non-means-tested bursary of £2,500, and a further £500 towards travel costs for placements.

Full-time eligible postgraduates living in England receive a non-means-tested basic bursary from the NHS Business Services Authority, and can also apply for an additional mean-tested bursary. They also receive up to £3,440 for tuition fees, paid directly to the institution, and a contribution to practice learning (placement) opportunity expenses. A childcare grant, adult dependants' allowance and parents' learning allowance are also available, paid on the same basis as for undergraduates (see p528).

Eligible postgraduate students in Wales can apply to the Care Council for Wales for similar package of support.

Part-time fee grant and course grant

Part-time students on undergraduate courses in Wales, and in England whose courses started before 1 September 2012, and who are studying at least 50 per cent of an equivalent full-time course can apply for a means-tested grant for fees of between £820 and £1,230 (£690 and £1,025 in Wales). The amount depends on the intensity of the course. They can also get a course grant of up to £265 (£1,155 in Wales). This is to help with travel, book and other course-related costs. The student's income must be less than £16,845 for full support. Students will receive partial support if their income is between £16,845 and £28,066 (£16,865 and

£28,180 respectively in Wales). Applications are assessed by SFE or the local authority. Forms are available from these bodies.

Support is available for a maximum number of eight academic years.

Part-time students in England who started their course on or after 1 September 2012 can apply for fee loans in the same way as full-time students (see p525). They cannot apply for the course costs grant.

NHS bursaries

NHS bursaries are available for full-time or part-time pre-registration courses in England. For a current list of prescribed courses and up-to-date information, see www.nhsbsa.nhs.uk/students. Bursary applicants are subject to residence conditions. Bursaries are administered and paid by NHS Student Bursaries. NHS students are also eligible to apply to the Access to Learning Fund or the Financial Contingency Fund (see p540). Bursaries are awarded for each year of study. They are non-taxable and are paid in monthly instalments (the first instalment covers the first two months of training).

There are three types of NHS bursary. In all cases, the NHS pays the tuition fees.

A new bursary scheme for all NHS-funded degree and postgraduate diploma-level students starting on or after 1 September 2012 has been introduced. This provides students with a £1,000 non-means-tested bursary and an additional means-tested amount, depending on family income. Degree students can also apply for a reduced rate student loan. Postgraduate diploma NHS students are not eligible for student loans.

Additional allowances may also be payable for:
- disabled students;
- practice placement costs;
- students entering training from care;
- extra weeks' attendance;
- childcare (similar to the Department for Business, Innovation and Skills childcare grants, except that the allowance is up to 85 per cent of actual childcare costs to a maximum of £126.65 a week for one child and £187.85 a week for two or more children);
- adults and children who are financially dependent on the student; *and*
- a parents' learning allowance.

Students studying on a nursing, midwifery and operating department practitioner diploma course who started before 1 September 2012 are paid a non-means-tested bursary covering 45 weeks. This is a flat-rate basic maintenance grant. Diploma-level students are not eligible for student loans.

Students following a degree-level or postgraduate-level course who started before 2012/13 are eligible for a means-tested bursary. Additional allowances are available, as with the non-means-tested bursary (see p524). Undergraduate-level means-tested bursary holders can apply for a student loan and should consider doing so in order to maximise their income while training. They can also apply to the Access to Learning Fund or Financial Contingency Fund (see p540).

There are also maternity, paternity and adoption allowances. NHS Student Bursaries has details.

Arrangements for students in Wales are broadly the same. For information, contact the NHS Wales Student Awards Unit on 029 2019 6167.

Undergraduate medical and dental students living in England and Wales on standard five- or six-year courses in any UK country are eligible for NHS bursaries and help with their tuition fees in their fifth and sixth year of study. Those students in England and Wales on the four-year graduate-entry medical programmes are also eligible for NHS bursaries and help with tuition fees in years two to four of the course. Medical and dental students can also apply for NHS hardship funds through NHS Student Bursaries. Advisers should help clients to present their case, as there is no prescribed form or process. It is, therefore, advisable for the adviser to add a covering letter explaining the circumstances and the nature of the claim.

Teacher training incentives

These vary between England and Wales.

In England, there are training bursaries of up to £20,000. These depend both on the subject the student is studying to teach and the undergraduate degree mark they hold – the higher priority the subject and the higher the degree mark, the more money is available. Some students will not be entitled to any bursary.

The Teaching Agency lists which subjects qualify for the different amounts on its website at www.teaching.gov.uk.

The bursaries are generally paid monthly over nine months and are available for home students undertaking postgraduate courses that lead to qualified teacher status at colleges in England (Postgraduate Certificate in Education (PGCE) courses), but who are not currently employed as teachers. Some of the larger bursaries may have elements paid on the completion of certain stages of the course.

PGCE students in England can also apply for the full undergraduate package of support; teacher training students on graduate entry programmes funded via schools will receive a salary instead.

In Wales, home students on postgraduate courses leading to qualified teacher status at institutions in Wales (except those already qualified as teachers or employed as teachers) receive training grants of up to £15,000 on a similar banding structure to English students. Teacher Training and Education in Wales lists which subjects qualify for which levels of funding at www.teachertrainingcymru.org.

Some students studying in the Welsh language can apply for Welsh medium incentive supplements. Application is to the institution.

Bank overdrafts

Most of the major banks and some building societies offer interest-free overdraft facilities on students' current accounts, up to a set limit. These limits change each year and vary between banks. This special facility is essential to most students in maximising income, both to cover temporary periods of cash-flow shortage (eg, between payments of funding instalments) and for long-term financial management.

Clients who are prospective students with existing bank accounts should change to a student account with either their own or a different bank, in order to benefit from the facilities offered. When choosing a bank, students need to consider the following factors, rather than any 'free gifts' on offer:

- which bank offers the largest interest-free overdraft, and the period for which it is offered – generally these extend beyond the end of the course, but can vary;
- the proximity of the bank to where the student lives or studies;
- the availability of telephone and internet banking;
- the interest rates and charges imposed for exceeding the interest-free facility;
- the attitude of campus bank managers or student advisers in local banks – debt advisers in institutions or students' unions can be consulted on these matters.

Managers of campus banks are usually more familiar with student finance issues and, therefore, more sympathetic and realistic when difficulties arise.

A student's credit rating is checked when s/he opens a new account. S/he may be refused the usual student deal if there is a recorded history of credit problems. A student requires an account that will accept direct credits in order to receive her/his student loan. If a student has no bank account and is refused one because of her/his credit rating, the money adviser in the institution or students' union may be able to negotiate with the local or campus bank manager.

Bank loans

Banks will sometimes offer loans to students at competitive rates. A client should be advised, however, that the interest rates on loans from the SLC make them a cheaper form of long-term borrowing. A bank loan is usually offered towards the end of the student's course. If overdraft facilities appear no longer appropriate, the bank may offer to convert the overdraft to a loan. This offers the advantages of a lower interest rate than the excess overdraft and allows the student access to additional funds. However, unless the loan has a deferred repayment arrangement, the repayments are usually much greater than can be met from the student's income, and may create an overdraft in her/his current account that will result in her/him paying interest on two accounts. In this way, it can become a very expensive, usually unmanageable, option. Advisers should be aware that most banks will now allow student terms on their overdraft to extend to graduation and beyond (in some cases for a number of years) and this may, therefore, be a cheaper option.

Students often feel pressured into accepting loan arrangements, as the banks present them as a positive alternative and are reluctant to allow further borrowing on any other terms. A client will often be better off by ceasing to use the existing bank account and using an ordinary building society savings account. Advisers can then negotiate with the bank as with any other creditor. This strategy will, however, result in the loss of the interest-free overdraft facility.

See also p536 for information on professional studies loans.

Professional and career development loans

Professional and career development loans are deferred repayment personal loans available through a partnership between the Skills Funding Agency and two high street banks. Interest on the loan is paid by the Skills Funding Agency during the period of the course and for up to one month after. Repayment is deferred for the same period – longer periods of deferment are sometimes available in certain circumstances (see p513).

In practice, professional and career development loans are usually only available for certain types of postgraduate and professional courses (full time, part time or distance learning). This is because the course must last no longer than two years (although loans can be considered for up to two years of a longer course or a three-year course that includes work experience). Applicants must be 18 or over and must not have reasonable and adequate access to funds for their course or statutory funding. A student must intend to work in the European Union (EU) or Iceland, Norway or Liechtenstein after completing the course. Applicants must be ordinarily resident in the UK with an unlimited right to remain. Students will not qualify for a professional and career development loan if their right to remain in the UK is subject to restrictions. While non-EU nationals are eligible to apply for a loan, they must seek permission from the Home Office in order to study, train or work in the UK after their studies. Refer to UKCISA for advice (see Appendix 1).

Professional and career development loans are only available for vocational courses. Students can borrow between £300 and £10,000 to pay for up to 80 per cent of course fees, plus the full cost of travel, books, materials and other related expenses. If the client has been out of work for three months or longer, s/he can apply for 100 per cent of the course fees and, if the course is full time, living expenses. Banks will consider applications after the course has already started.

Further information can be obtained from the participating high street banks (Barclays or the Co-operative Bank) or from the information line on 0800 585 505. There is also a website at www.direct.gov.uk/pcdl.

Advisers can assist clients to make a realistic assessment of all non-course costs to ensure an adequate loan is requested. Also, clients should be advised to compare professional and career development loans with professional studies loans from banks (see below), as the interest rates and repayment terms of the latter can be more favourable. If a student receiving means-tested benefits obtains a professional and career development loan to fund her/his course, it is treated as income. If this reduces benefit entitlement, s/he should consider paying her/his tuition fees in full at the beginning of the course instead of by the more usual instalment methods.

Professional studies loans

These are now extremely rare, but some of the major banks make personal loans available to postgraduate (and sometimes also 'second-degree') students to cover their course fees and living costs. The loans usually offer deferred repayments, which begin only after the course has finished. Such loans are usually only available for specific courses, especially those leading to professional qualifications. The terms and amounts of loans vary between different banks, and a client needs to check which is most suitable for her/him and how the terms offered compare with those available from a professional and career development loan, if s/he is pursuing a course for which either might be payable. S/he also needs to consider whether s/he can afford the amount of indebtedness involved, which could exceed £5,000 a year.

Postgraduate bursaries

A variety of bodies make awards, but usually only one is appropriate to a particular area of study. It can be difficult to obtain an offer of grant aid to fund postgraduate study, especially in the arts and social sciences.

Postgraduate students can apply for studentships from research councils (see Appendix 1). Competition for these is usually very strong, and students normally need to have at least a degree classification of 2:1 at undergraduate level.

Disabled postgraduate students are eligible for a disabled students' allowance (see p527) from either a research council (see p540), SFE or their local authority if they have to pay extra costs in their postgraduate study as a result of their disability. Details of the levels and type of support available, and information on how to apply, are on each research council's website, or from SFE or the relevant local authority in Wales.

A client can obtain appropriate information and assistance from the department in which s/he intends to study and the university careers service. Clients should begin their enquiries well in advance of the start of their course – applications may need to be made at the start of the academic year before the year in which they intend to study. There are organisations which offer awards for vocational courses. A limited number of companies offer assistance to postgraduates. Sponsorship is usually linked to particular courses and institutions, rather than individual students. Clients should be advised to contact the appropriate careers/advice centres at the relevant institution.

Benefits

This section is intended as a general guide to eligibility. Advisers should refer to CPAG's *Welfare Benefits and Tax Credits Handbook* or *Student Support and Benefits Handbook* for full details. Most full-time students are not eligible to claim social security benefits. There are a few groups of full-time students who are not excluded from the means-tested benefits system. These are:

- lone parents, including lone foster parents (if the child is under 16 years old);
- disabled students who satisfy certain conditions;
- pensioners;
- students from abroad entitled to emergency payments because they are temporarily without funds for a period of up to six weeks (seek further advice on this from UKCISA – see Appendix 1);
- people who have refugee status and who are learning English;
- one of two full-time students with responsibility for a child under 16 years old (or under 20 and still in full-time non-advanced education, although only eligible for help during the summer vacation);
- students waiting to return to their course after taking time out because of illness or caring responsibilities.

Advisers need to highlight the rules on entitlement to benefit, and advise students not to accept automatically Department for Work and Pensions (DWP) or local authority statements that students cannot claim benefit.

Note: entitlement to income support (IS) has been reduced in the last few years and currently lone parents can only claim if their youngest or only child is under age five. However, those on full-time courses can continue to receive IS, even if a previous change to these rules would otherwise have made them ineligible, until the end of the course or until they stop receiving IS for another reason – eg, because their income increases. Lone-parent students who are affected by the changes can also claim jobseeker's allowance (JSA) in the summer vacation. See CPAG's *Welfare Benefits and Tax Credits Handbook* for more details.

The DWP and local authorities find the calculation of students' entitlement highly complex. In many offices, it is rare for the first decision to be correct. Clients must be advised to have their claims checked by an expert in the institution, students' union or local advice centre.

Advisers need to check that decision makers do not include the student loan as income for clients who are ineligible for loans. Advisers also need to inform clients who are entitled to benefits, but reluctant to take out a loan or a full loan, that the full loan will be taken into account whether or not it is taken out.

Professional and career development loans are also taken into account as income. However, most of this income is ignored. Only that part of the loan paid and used for certain living costs is taken into account. For full details, see CPAG's *Welfare Benefits and Tax Credits Handbook*.

In general, grants or loans paid specifically for tuition fees or course costs are disregarded. If a student receives allowances towards extra expenses because of a disability (see p527), these are disregarded in full when calculating her/his benefit entitlement. The childcare grant and parents' learning grant are also disregarded.

Council tax benefit

Full-time students are not liable for council tax if they live in accommodation occupied solely by students on a full-time course (or other people who are exempt).

Those who are liable for council tax are entitled to council tax benefit (CTB) during their period of study if they fall into one of a small number of categories. Advisers need to check whether the client falls into one of these categories, or if s/he has a partner who is eligible to claim CTB on her/his behalf. The period of study applicable in each case should also be checked as, in most cases (and unlike for IS), this excludes the summer vacation and, therefore, the student may be able to claim during this period.

For further details, see CPAG's *Welfare Benefits and Tax Credits Handbook*.

Child tax credit

Students are eligible to apply for child tax credit. Those getting the maximum amount (and no working tax credit) are entitled to free school lunches for their child(ren). Help is means tested and paid by direct debit by HM Revenue and Customs, which has a calculator facility on its website to help work out eligibility and the amount available (http://taxcredits.hmrc.gov.uk).

Health benefits

See also Chapter 7.

Students under 19 and those on IS, income-based JSA and some tax credit claimants, qualify for health benefits. Otherwise, students must apply for assistance on the grounds of low income using Form HC1. These forms are often held by student services departments in institutions, students' unions/guilds/associations or health centres.

For further details, see CPAG's *Welfare Benefits and Tax Credits Handbook*.

Housing benefit

Advisers need to check whether their client is exempt from the rule that full-time students are not entitled to housing benefit (HB), or whether they have a partner who is eligible to claim on their behalf.

The period of study applicable should be checked as, in most cases (and unlike for IS), this excludes the summer vacation and, therefore, the student may be eligible to claim during this period.

Some students who need to maintain two homes may be eligible for payment of housing costs on both.

For further details, see CPAG's *Welfare Benefits and Tax Credits Handbook*.

Income support

Advisers should check whether their client is exempt from the rule that full-time students are not entitled to IS, or whether s/he has a partner who is eligible to claim on her/his behalf.

If a student works during the vacations and her/his IS includes an amount for her/his housing costs, the adviser needs to check that the hours and/or level of earnings do not result in a loss of entitlement to IS for housing costs.

Under certain circumstances, a student or her/his partner may be entitled to housing costs for two homes.

For further details, see CPAG's *Welfare Benefits and Tax Credits Handbook*.

Income-based jobseeker's allowance

If the student has a partner who is able to claim income-based JSA, s/he should be aware that working in the vacations may result in a loss of benefit.

For further details, see CPAG's *Welfare Benefits and Tax Credits Handbook*.

Students taking time out (intercalating students)

Some students need to leave their course temporarily – eg, because of ill health, exam failure, or family or personal problems. Benefit regulations state that full-time students are excluded from IS, HB and CTB for the whole duration of their period of study. For precise definitions of this period for each benefit, see CPAG's *Welfare Benefits and Tax Credits Handbook*. Students who are exempt from the full-time student rule are entitled to those benefits during a period of temporary absence from their course.

Students cannot get IS or JSA while they are ill (unless they are classed as a 'disabled student'), but they can claim JSA, HB, and CTB once the illness or caring responsibilities have come to an end. They can claim from this point until they restart the course or up to the day before they start the new academic year. They can only qualify if they are not eligible for student support during this period.

For other students, the definition of student in the regulations results in 'intercalating students' still being treated as though they were on a full-time course and therefore not entitled to IS, HB and CTB. Students in this situation should obtain advice from their students' union or institution on alternative means of support.

Charities

See also p189.

There are many charities which provide assistance to students. However, support is usually in the form of small grants and it is highly unusual for a student to be able to access full funding through charitable routes. Many charities also experience high demand for their funds.

Applications are more likely to succeed if the student is close to completing her/his course, and/or where funding arrangements have broken down. There are a number of fund-finding vehicles specialising in helping students access money from trusts and charities, such as the Educational Grants Advisory Service.

Research councils

There are seven research councils that fund postgraduate study:
- Biotechnology and Biological Sciences Research Council (www.bbsrc.ac.uk);
- Engineering and Physical Sciences Research Council (www.epsrc.ac.uk);
- Economic and Social Research Council (www.esrc.ac.uk);
- Medical Research Council (www.mrc.ac.uk);
- Natural Environment Research Council (www.nerc.ac.uk);
- Science and Technology Facilities Council (www.stfc.ac.uk);
- Arts and Humanities Research Council (www.ahrc.ac.uk).

Access to Learning and Financial Contingency Funds

The Access to Learning Fund is an annual allocation from central government to higher education institutions (via the funding councils) to be disbursed to students in financial difficulty.

In Wales, the fund is called the Financial Contingency Fund and the rules are broadly similar. Students' eligibility is based on the satisfaction of residency and immigration conditions, as for statutory support.

The Access to Learning Fund can be used by institutions to help students who are surviving on a low income who may need additional financial help to continue their higher education. Funds can be allocated when the student needs to meet a particular cost not being funded from elsewhere, to ease financial hardship, when emergency help is needed and when a payment would prevent a student from discontinuing her/his course of study. It can only be used to help home students on a full-time course of higher education, or part-time students who are studying at least one-quarter of an equivalent full-time course in England, or one-half in Wales.

Priority groups for funding are:
- students with children, especially lone parents;
- mature students, particularly those with existing financial commitments;
- students from low-income families;
- disabled students;
- students entering higher education from care;
- students in their final year of study.

Funds cannot be used to help pay tuition fees for full-time students, but part-time students may be able to receive help for their fees.

Institutions are encouraged to set aside money to assist with financial difficulties arising during the summer vacation, and students who have temporarily suspended their studies are still eligible to apply for hardship funds.

If a student is entitled to a student loan, s/he must usually have taken out the full amount to which s/he was entitled in the current academic year before being eligible for help from the Access to Learning Fund (or, at least, any payment will be calculated as if s/he had). Institutions decide eligibility and how much to allocate.

Payments are usually grants, although loans can be issued in certain circumstances. Loans should be interest-free, but if they remain unpaid, they can be classed as a debt to the institution (see p518). Advisers can help students to make successful applications by identifying the criteria and priorities of a particular institution's funds, and providing evidence or a supporting letter to show how the particular student meets the criteria.

Hardship funds may be used for emergency payments/loans to help students who have not yet received their loan payment at the start of the year.

Universities are required to have a Fund allocation appeals procedure. Thus, if a student has been refused a payment, or paid too little, the adviser should assist her/him to use this. Even successful applicants should be advised to reapply if their circumstances change during the year, as further assistance could be forthcoming.

Many Fund administrators have a great deal of discretion in deciding or recommending grants, and have to process vast numbers of applications. Intervention by an adviser on behalf of a student could be most effective in improving her/his prospects.

Fund administrators have the power to make third-party payments, including payments direct to creditors. Creditors who are pressing for payment are often willing to allow more time if a payment is to be made directly by an institution.

For the purpose of means-tested benefits, payments from the discretionary hardship funds (such as the Access to Learning Fund and the Financial Contingency Fund) are treated as voluntary and charitable payments. See CPAG's *Welfare Benefits and Tax Credits Handbook* for more information.

Access to Leaning Fund allocations to institutions have reduced this year and it is likely they will continue to reduce in the future.

Additional funds to assist students

Many institutions and some students' unions/guilds/associations and religious groups have a number of small funds available to meet specific circumstances, as well as general hardship funds. Some funds will make grants, others will make interest-free loans available. Students should consult the student services department or students' union/guild/association at their own institution for advice.

Employment

See also the section on benefits (p537) for the impact on benefits of working and below for information on tax refunds.

Traditionally, undergraduate students have worked during their vacation periods; many now also work part time through the term time. Income from part-time or casual work is disregarded for the purposes of assessing student support. Advisers need to warn clients of the uncertainties of relying on vacation work to supplement their mainstream income. Annual budgeting based on the expectation of an income from vacation work will falter if a job fails to materialise or is offered for fewer hours or weeks than anticipated.

Increasingly, institutions and students' unions provide information on jobs available to students. The institution may have regulations restricting the number of hours students are allowed to work. Aside from these, advisers need to help clients to balance their time between employment and study, and to check that the student is profiting financially from the work after travel and other expenses are taken into account.

Tax refunds

A student who has been working before starting her/his course, or for part of the year, should be advised to claim a refund of income tax when the employment ceases by completing Form P50 (usually available from students' unions/guilds or tax offices). The form should be submitted to the tax office of her/his last employer, along with the student's P45.

6. **Dealing with priority debts**

See Chapter 8.

Deciding on priority debts to the institution

Certain debts to the institution may need to be treated as priorities because of the consequences of non-payment. Wherever non-payment carries a legitimate threat of loss of accommodation, the debt should be treated as a priority (as outlined in Chapter 8). However, in addition, there are some cases where the legitimate threat of not being able to continue with study or not being allowed to graduate will lead to prioritisation. See p520 for those debts that could lead to this. 'New system' student loans should be prioritised, given that repayments are taken directly from wages when they become due.

Notes

1. **Financial support for students:
   introduction**
   1 Sch 1 E(SS) Regs
   2 For the extract of the judgment, see
     notes for guidance in Sch 1 E(SS) Regs
   3 Sch 2 E(SS) Regs

3. **Types of debt**
   4 s8 SSLA 2008
   5 s8 SSLA 2008

5. **Maximising income**
   6 E(SS) Regs
   7 ss124(1)(e) and 130(2) SSCBA 1992
   8 The Children Act 1989 (Higher
     Education Bursary) (England)
     Regulations 2009

Appendices

Appendix 1

Useful organisations

Trade bodies

Association of British Insurers

51 Gresham Street
London EC2V 7HQ
Tel: 020 7600 3333
www.abi.org.uk

Association of Chartered Certified Accountants

29 Lincoln's Inn Fields
London WC2A 3EE
Tel: 020 7059 5000
www.accaglobal.com

British Bankers' Association

Pinners Hall
105-108 Old Broad Street
London EC2N 1EX
Tel: 020 7216 8800
www.bba.org.uk

British Cheque and Credit Association (BCCA)

Portal Business Centre
Dallam Court, Dallam Lane
Warrington WA2 7LT
Tel: 01925 426 090
www.bcca.co.uk

British Insurance Brokers' Association

8th Floor
John Stow House
18 Bevis Marks
London EC3A 7JB
Tel (members): 0844 770 0266
Consumer helpline: 0870 950 1790
www.biba.org.uk

Civil Enforcement Assocation

513 Bradford Road
Batley WF17 8LL
Tel: 0844 893 3922
www.civea.co.uk

Consumer Credit Association

Queens House
Queens Road
Chester CH1 3BQ
Tel: 01244 312 044
www.ccauk.org

Consumer Credit Trade Association

Suite 4 The Wave
1 View Croft Road
Shipley BD17 7DU
Tel: 01274 714 959
www.ccta.co.uk

Council of Mortgage Lenders

Bush House
North West Wing
London WC2B 4PJ
Tel: 0845 373 6771
www.cml.org.uk

Credit Services Association

2 Esh Plaza
Sir Bobby Robson Way
Newcastle upon Tyne NE13 9BA
Tel: 0191 217 0775
www.csa-uk.com

Finance and Leasing Association

2nd Floor
Imperial House
15-19 Kingsway
London WC2B 6UN
Tel: 020 7836 6511
www.fla.org.uk

High Court Enforcement Officers Association

50 Broadway
London SW1H 0RG
Tel: 020 7152 4017
www.hceoa.org.uk

Insolvency Practitioners Association

Valiant House
4-10 Heneage Lane
London EC3A 5DQ
Tel: 020 7623 5108
www.insolvency-practition-ers.org.uk

Institute of Chartered Accountants in England and Wales

Chartered Accountants' Hall
Moorgate Place
London EC2R 6EA
Tel: 020 7920 8100
Level 1
Metropolitan House
421 Avebury Boulevard
Milton Keynes MK9 2FZ
Tel: 01908 248 250
www.icaew.co.uk

UK Payments Administration

2 Thomas More Square
London E1W 1YN
Tel: 020 3217 8200
www.ukpayments.org.uk

Ombudsmen and regulatory bodies

Parliamentary and Health Service Ombudsman (England)

Millbank Tower
Millbank
London SW1P 4QP
Tel: 0345 015 4033
www.ombudsman.org.uk

Local Government Ombudsman

PO Box 4771
Coventry CV4 0EH
Tel: 0845 602 1983/0300 061 0614
www.lgo.org.uk

Public Services Ombudsman for Wales

1 Ffordd yr Hen Gae
Pencoed CF35 5LJ
Tel 0845 601 0987
www.ombudsman-wales.org.uk

Financial Ombudsman Service

South Quay Plaza
183 Marsh Wall
London E14 9SR
Tel: 0800 023 4567/0300 123 9123
www.financial-ombudsman.org.uk

Legal Ombudsman (England and Wales)

PO Box 6806
Wolverhampton WV1 9WJ
Tel: 0300 555 0333
www.legalombudsman.org.uk

Pensions Ombudsman

11 Belgrave Road
London SW1V 1RB
Tel: 020 7630 2200
www.pensions-ombudsman.org.uk

Ombudsman Services: Energy

PO Box 966
Warrington WA4 9DF
Tel: 0330 440 1624
www.ombudsman-services.org/
energy.html

Financial Services Authority

25 The North Colonnade
Canary Wharf
London E14 5HS
Tel: 0845 606 1234
Helpline: 0845 606 1234
www.fsa.gov.uk

The Insolvency Service

4 Abbey Orchard Street
London SW1P 2HT
Tel: 0845 602 9848
www.insolvency.gov.uk

Office of Fair Trading

Fleetbank House
2-6 Salisbury Square
London EC4Y 8JX
Tel: 020 7211 8000
Helpline: 0845 404 0506
www.oft.gov.uk

Information Commissioner's Office

Wycliffe House
Water Lane
Wilmslow SK9 5AF
Tel: 0303 123 1113/01625 545 745
www.ico.gov.uk
(for complaints concerning out-of-date or inaccurate personal information)

The Law Society (England and Wales)

113 Chancery Lane
London WC2A 1PL
Tel: 020 7242 1222
www.lawsociety.org.uk

The Adjudicator's Office

8th Floor
Euston Tower
286 Euston Road
London NW1 3US
Tel: 0300 057 1111/020 7667 1832
www.adjudicatorsoffice.gov.uk

Office of Gas and Electricity Markets (Ofgem)

9 Millbank
London SW1P 3GE
Tel: 020 7901 7000
www.ofgem.gov.uk

Ofcom (Communications Regulator)

Riverside House
2a Southwark Bridge Road
London SE1 9HA
Tel: 020 7981 3000
Advice/complaints: 0300 123 3000/
020 7981 3040
www.ofcom.org.uk

Ofwat (Water Services Regulation Authority)

Centre City Tower
7 Hill Street
Birmingham B5 4UA
Tel: 0121 644 7500
www.ofwat.gov.uk

Department for Business Innovation and Skills

1 Victoria Street
London SW1H 0ET
Tel: 020 7215 5000
www.bis.gov.uk

Department for Communities and Local Government

Eland House
Bressenden Place
London SW1E 5DU
Tel: 0303 444 0000
www.communities.gov.uk

Department for Education

Castle View House
East Lane
Runcorn
Cheshire WA7 2GJ
Tel: 0370 000 2288
www.education.gov.uk

Welsh Assembly Government

Cathays Park
Cardiff CF10 3NQ
Tel: 0845 010 3300/0300 060 3300
http://wales.gov.uk

Organisations giving advice or representing advice networks

AdviceUK

WB1
PO Box 70716
London EC1P 1GQ
Tel: 0300 777 0107
www.adviceuk.org.uk

Association of British Credit Unions Ltd

Holyoake House
Hanover Street
Manchester M60 0AS
Tel: 0161 832 3694
www.abcul.org

Business Debtline

Tel: 0800 197 6026
www.bdl.org.uk

Citizens Advice

Myddelton House
115-123 Pentonville Road
London N1 9LZ
Tel: 020 7833 2181
Advice: 0844 411 1444 (England)
0844 477 2020 (Wales)
www.citizensadvice.org.uk

Consumer Focus

Fleetbank House
Salisbury Square
London EC4Y 8JX
Tel: 020 7799 7900
www.consumerfocus.org.uk

Education and Skills Wales

Tel: 0845 010 3300
http://wales.gov.uk/topics/
educationandskills

Institute of Money Advisers

4 Park Court
Park Cross Street
Leeds LS1 2QH
Tel: 0113 242 0048
www.i-m-a.org.uk

Law Centres Federation

PO Box 65836
London EC4P 4FX
Tel: 020 7842 0720
www.lawcentres.org.uk

Money Advice Service

Holborn Centre
120 Holborn
London EC1N 2TD
Tel: 0300 500 5000
or 0300 500 5555 (Welsh)
www.moneyadviceservices.org.uk

Money Advice Trust

21 Garlick Hill
London EC4V 2AU
Tel: 020 7489 7796
www.moneyadvicetrust.org

National Debtline

Tel: 0808 808 4000
www.nationaldebtline.co.uk

National Union of Students

4th Floor
184-192 Drummond Street
London NW1 3HP
Tel: 0845 521 0262
www.nus.org.uk

TaxAid

304 Linton House
164-180 Union Street
London SE1 0LH
Tel (advisers only, 9am-5pm):
020 7803 4950
Helpline (clients, 10am-12pm Mon-
Thurs): 0345 120 3779
www.taxaid.org.uk

UCAS (Universities and Colleges Admission Service)

Rosehill
New Barn Lane
Cheltenham GL52 3LZ
Tel: 01242 222444
Customer contact: 0871 468 0468
www.ucas.ac.uk

UKCISA: UK Council for International Student Affairs

9-17 St Albans Place
London N1 0NX
Tel (advice line, 1pm-4pm Mon-Fri):
020 3131 3576
www.ukcisa.org.uk

Appendix 2

Useful publications

A debt adviser should have access to the latest edition of most of the following books.

Debt

Cheshire, Fifoot and Furmston's Law of Contract, M Furmston and others, Oxford University Press

Consumer Credit Act 2006: a guide to the new law, J Smith and S McCalla, The Law Society

Woodroffe and Lowe's Consumer Law and Practice, G Woodroffe and R Lowe, Sweet and Maxwell

Consumer Credit Law and Practice, D Rosenthal, Bloomsbury Professional

Debt Relief Order Toolkit Citizens Advice Specialist Support, available online at www.cabadvisernet.org.uk to subscribers to Advisernet or at www.wiseradviser.org to registered users

Fisher and Lightwood's Law of Mortgage, P Morgan and others (author), W Clarke (ed), LexisNexis

Tolleys Tax Guide, C Hayes, R Newman (authors) and F Lagerberg (ed), LexisNexis

* *Council Tax Handbook,* A Murdie, CPAG, £17 (9th edition, December 2011)

* *Fuel Rights Handbook,* C Torsney and others, CPAG, £21 (16th edition, December 2012)

Manual of Housing Law, A Arden and A Dymond, Sweet and Maxwell

* *Guide to Housing Benefit and Council Tax Benefit,* M Ward and S Lister, Shelter/CIH £30 (2012/13 edition)

Personal Finance Handbook, J Lowe, CPAG, £16.50 (3rd edition, November 2009)

Personal Insolvency: law and practice, G Davis, M Haywood, M Crystal and M Phillips, Lexis Nexis

Increasing resources

* *Welfare Benefits and Tax Credits Handbook*, CPAG, £42 or £10 for claimants (2012/13, April 2012).

* *Child Support Handbook*, CPAG, £28 (20th edition, August 2012)

* *Social Security Legislation Volume I: non-means-tested benefits and employment and support allowance*, Bonner, Hooker and Poynter, Sweet and Maxwell. £98 for the main volume (2012/13 edition, September 2012)

* *Social Security Legislation Volume II: income support, jobseeker's allowance, state pension credit and the social fund*, Wood, Poynter, Wikeley and Bonner, Sweet and Maxwell. £98 for the main volume (2012/13 edition, September 2012)

* *Social Security Legislation Volume III: administration, adjudication and the European dimension*, Bonner, Rowland and White, Sweet and Maxwell. £98 for the main volume (2012/13 edition, September 2012)

* *Social Security Legislation Volume IV: tax credits, and HMRC-administered social security benefits*, Wikeley and Williams, Sweet and Maxwell. £98 for the main volume (2012/13 edition, September 2012)

* *Social Security Legislation – updating supplement to Volumes I, II, III & IV*, Sweet and Maxwell. £60 for the updating supplement (2012/13 edition, due March 2013

* *CPAG's Housing Benefit and Council Tax Benefit Legislation*, Findlay, Poynter, Wright, George and Williams, CPAG. £105 for the main volume plus updating supplement (2012/13 edition, main volume December 2012)

* *Child Support: the legislation*, Jacobs, CPAG. £87 for the main volume (10th edition, Summer 2011)

* *Disability Rights Handbook*, Disability Alliance. £29.50 (2012/13 edition, May 2012)

A Guide to Grants for Individuals in Need, C Chronnell, £75, Directory of Social Change

Voluntary Agencies Directory, NCVO, £75 (£40 members)

Charities Digest, £39, Waterlow Legal and Regulatory

Tolley's Employment Handbook, E Slade, LexisNexis

Butterworth's Employment Law Handbook, P Wallington, LexisNexis

Courts and the law

Anthony and Berryman's Magistrates' Court Guide, F G Davies (ed) LexisNexis

The Civil Court Practice, LexisNexis

Black's Law Dictionary, West Publishing

Defending Possession Proceedings, J Luba, D McConnell, J Gallagher and N Madge, Legal Action Group

Insolvency Legislation: annotations and commentary, L Doyle and A Keay, Jordans

Muir Hunter on Personal Insolvency, J Briggs and C Brougham (eds), Sweet and Maxwell

Practical Banking and Building Society Law, A Arora, Oxford University Press

Charging Orders Against Land: law, procedure and precedents, P Walker and M Buckley, Barry Rose Law Publishers

Enforcement of Local Taxation, A Murdie and I Wise, Legal Action Group

A Law of Seizure of Goods: debtors' rights and remedies, J Kruse, Hammicks Legal Publishing

Bailiffs: the law and your rights, J Kruse, PP Publishing, 2011, £14.99

Sources of Bailiff Law, J Kruse, PP Publishing, 2012, £36

Skills

Client Care for Lawyers, Avrom Sherr, Sweet and Maxwell

Periodicals

Adviser
The Development Centre
Coxwell Avenue
Wolverhampton Science Park
Wolverhampton WV10 9RT
www.advisermagazine.org.uk

Arian
Citizens Advice Specialist Support
Quebec House
Castlebridge
5-19 Cowbridge Road East
Cardiff CF11 9AB
email: arian@citizensadvice.org.uk

Quarterly Account
Institute of Money Advisers
First Floor
4 Park Court
Park Cross Street
Leeds LS1 2QH
www.i-m-a.org.uk

* Indicates that books are available from CPAG. For a full publications list and order form see www.cpag.org.uk/bookshop; write to CPAG, 94 White Lion Street, London N1 9PF; or call 020 7837 7979.

Appendix 3

Abbreviations used in the notes

AC	Appeal Cases
All ER	All England Reports
Art(s)	Article(s)
BCC	Bailii court cases
BPIR	Bankruptcy and Personal Insolvency Reports
CA	Court of Appeal
CC	County court
CCR	County Court Rules
CCLR	Consumer Credit Law Reports
CPR	Civil Procedure Rules
ChD	Chancery Division
Cr App R	Criminal Appeal Reports
EG	Estates Gazette
EU CCD	European Union Consumer Credit Directive
EWCA	England and Wales Court of Appeal
EWHC	England and Wales High Court
FLR	Family Law Reports
HC	High Court
HL	House of Lords
HLR	Housing Law Reports
JP	Justice of the Peace
JPR	Justice of the Peace Reports
KB	King's Bench Reports
para(s)	Paragraph(s)
PD	Practice Direction
QB	Queen's Bench Reports
QBD	Queen's Bench Division
r(s)	Rule(s)
reg(s)	Regulation(s)
s(s)	Section(s)
Sch(s)	Schedule(s)
SI	Statutory instrument
UKHL	United Kingdom House of Lords
UKSC	United Kingdom Supreme Court
WLR	Weekly Law Reports
WLR(D)	Weekly Law Reports Daily

Acts of Parliament

AEA 1971	Attachment of Earnings Act 1971
AJA 1970	Administration of Justice Act 1970
AJA 1973	Administration of Justice Act 1973
CA 2003	Courts Act 2003
CAA 1995	Criminal Appeal Act 1995
CCA 1974	Consumer Credit Act 1974
CCA 2006	Consumer Credit Act 2006
CCA 1984	County Courts Act 1984
CJA 1982	Criminal Justice Act 1982
CLSA 1990	Courts and Legal Services Act 1990
COA 1979	Charging Orders Act 1979
EA 1989	Electricity Act 1989
EA 2002	Enterprise Act 2002
FSMA 2000	Financial Services and Markets Act 2000
GA 1986	Gas Act 1986
IA 1986	Insolvency Act 1986
JA 1838	Judgments Act 1838
LA 1980	Limitation Act 1980
LGA 2003	Local Government Act 2003
LGFA 1988	Local Government Finance Act 1988
LPA 1925	Law of Property Act 1925
MCA 1980	Magistrates' Courts Act 1980
MCA 2005	Mental Capacity Act 2005
MOA 1958	Maintenance Orders Act 1958
PCCA 1973	Powers of Criminal Courts Act 1973
RA 1977	Rent Act 1977
SCA 1981	Senior Courts Act 1981
SGA 1979	Sale of Goods Act 1979
SGSA 1982	Supply of Goods and Services Act 1982
SSAA 1992	Social Security Administration Act 1992
SSCBA 1992	Social Security Contributions and Benefits Act 1992
SSLA 2008	Sale of Student Loans Act 2008
TCA 2002	Tax Credits Act 2002
TC&EA 2007	Tribunals, Courts and Enforcement Act 2007
TLATA 1996	Trusts of Land and Appointment of Trustees Act 1996
TMA 1970	Taxes Management Act 1970
WRA 2012	Welfare Reform Act 2012

Regulations and other statutory instruments

Each set of Regulations or Order has a statutory instrument (SI) number and a date. Ask for them by giving that date and number.

CC(AE) Regs	The Community Charges (Administration and Enforcement) Regulations 1989 No.438
CC(IJD)O	The County Courts (Interest on Judgment Debts) Order 1991 No.1184
CC(IR) Regs	The Consumer Credit (Information Requirements and Duration of Licences and Charges) Regulations 2007 No.1167
CT(AE) Regs	The Council Tax (Administration and Enforcement) Regulations 1992 No.613
CT(AE)(A) Regs	The Council Tax (Administration and Enforcement) (Amendment) Regulations 1992 No.3008
E(SS) Regs	The Education (Student Support) Regulations 2008 No.529
HB Regs	The Housing Benefit (General) Regulations 1987 No.1971
HCCCJO 1991	The High Court and County Courts Jurisdiction Order 1991 No.724
I(A)R	The Insolvency (Amendment) Rules
IR	The Insolvency Rules 1986 No.1925
PSR Regs	The Payment Services Regulations 2009 No.209
SS(C&P) Regs	The Social Security (Claims and Payments) Regulations 1987 No.1968
TC(PC) Regs	The Tax Credits (Payments by the Board) Regulations 2002 No.2173
UTCC Regs	The Unfair Terms in Consumer Contracts Regulations 1999 No.2083

Other information

CPR	Civil Procedure Rules
DCG	Debt Collection Guidance
DMG	Debt Management Guidance
PD	Practice Direction
TM	Technical Manual

Index